Regional Patterns and the Cultural Implications of Late Bronze Age and Iron Age Burial Practices in Britain

Nicole Roth

BAR British Series 627

2016

Published in 2016 by
BAR Publishing, Oxford

BAR British Series 627

Regional Patterns and the Cultural Implications of Late Bronze Age and Iron Age Burial Practices in Britain

ISBN 978 1 4073 1530 0

Printed in England

PUBLISHING

BAR titles are available from:

        BAR Publishing
        122 Banbury Rd, Oxford, OX2 7BP, UK
EMAIL   info@barpublishing.com
PHONE   +44 (0)1865 310431
FAX   +44 (0)1865 316916
        www.barpublishing.com

The following work is dedicated to Jenna L. Higgins

Acknowledgements

The following study is the result of my doctorial study at the University of Sheffield (2008-2011). To begin, I must express my deepest gratitude to Mike Parker Pearson (supervisor), Andrew Chamberlain (supervisor), and John Barrett (advisor). I am grateful to you all for your endless support and guidance through this research. I am especially thankful to Mike for the insightful conversations on the Iron Age, being supportive during the difficult times, having extraordinary patience when it comes to my grammar, and I am extremely fortunate to have worked with him. My thanks to Andrew for providing invaluable help with the methodology and statistics, without his guidance I may still be staring blankly at a computer. I am very thankful for the support and insight from John, whose conversations was always enlightening and helped me to think outside the box.

My thanks go to all the wonderful people who have facilitated archival material and providing helpful answers to general enquiries about sites. A special thanks to Alan Jacobs and David Allen, both of the Hampshire County Museum Services, for their assistance with the Danebury, Danebury Environs Programme, Easton Lane and Winnall Down archives. Dr. Rebecca Redfern who kindly answered questions related to the Maiden Castle skeletal material and provided her recent articles on the topic. Thanks to Dr. Christine Hamlin of the University of Wisconsin for offering her insightful dissertation concerning mortuary practices, gender, and material in Iron Age Dorset. My gratitude goes to Ms. Sally Thompson and Ms. Sarah Poppy at Cambridge Archaeological Unit for facilitating the archival material for Hinxton Quarry. Thanks to Sir Barry Cunliffe for graciously answering my questions about the Danebury material. Thanks to Christopher Evans for providing further insight into the Hutchinson site. My thanks go to Jacqueline McKinley who graciously contributed a copy of the Potterne osteological report. My deepest thanks go to Karen Walker at Wessex Archaeology who provided invaluable assistance for the Maiden Castle archives. I would especially like to thank Andy Crockett, Helen Glass, Stuart Foreman, and Stephen Haynes who kindly allowed early access to the Channel Tunnel Rail Link reports prior to their publications on ADS. In addition, special thanks to Colin Merrony and Lauren McIntyre, both of the University of Sheffield, for sharing their information on the recent excavations and the inhumation from Gwilliam of Bilham.

My gratitude also goes to the many people and institutions that graciously granted permission for the reproductions of site plans depicted in this manuscript. Many thanks to Stuart Foreman and the Oxford Wessex Archaeology Joint Venture and HS 1LID (White Horse Farm, Beechbrook Woods, and Stone Farm Bridleway), Terence Lawson and the Kent Archaeological Society (Jubliee Corner), the relatives of Kathleen M. Kenyon and the Royal Archaeological Institute (Sutton Walls), Anooshka Rawden and the Society of Antiquaries of London (Maiden Castle), Luke Barber and the Sussex Archaeological Society (Norton), Edward Biddulph and Oxford Archaeology (Gravelly Guy), Pippa Bradley and Wessex Archaeology (Potterne, A27 Westhampnett, Maiden Castle, and Battlesbury Bowl), Julia Sandison and the Hampshire Field Club (Winnall Down and Micheldever Wood), Paul Johnson and the National Archive Image Library (Gussage All Saints), Sir Barry Cunliffe (Danebury and Suddern Farm), Steve Minnitt and John Coles (Glastonbury Lake Village), and special thanks to Keith Parfitt for allowing the use of a Mill Hill's site plan from his personal collection. I would also like to thank the students at Northern Kentucky University who aided in redrawing site plans; namely Adelle Bricking, Amanda Moss, Cassandra Penley, and Pamela Thomas (all image reproductions were done by these students and the author).

I would also like to give special recognition to many of my fellow colleagues and friends at the University of Sheffield. In particular, thanks to Toby Martin, Jessie Slater, Sarah Viner, Ryan Eldridge, Jose Lopez, Grace Corbett, Gareth Perry, Annie Bethell, Rose Brady, Rhys Bethell, Rachel Symonds, Kate O'Neill, Maureen England (University of Durham), and Las Swift (University of Durham). In addition, my thanks go to Toby Pillatt and Derek Pitman, both of the University of Sheffield, for being extremely 'patient' as they showed me the 'complicated' workings of ArcGIS. Also, special thanks to Josh Dorenkamp for his guidance on Adobe Photoshop. I am eternally grateful to Alison Bestwick (University of Sheffield) for her invaluable help and always offering a friendly ear to listen to my rants. Special thanks to Kirsty Squires who has been there every step of the way and whose conversations about funerary archaeology have been most fundamental to this research. I would also like to thank Jonathan Haws and Phil DiBlasi, both of the University of Louisville, who both provided the foundation for where I am today.

I would like to thank my family and Graham Thompson for their love and support. Lastly, I would like to offer my sincerest gratitude to Jenna Higgins. We both share a love and deep curiosity for prehistoric burial practices, which sprung numerous long talks on the subject at our local pub. Jenna was always there to offer support and insight and, without her, this research may have never come about. Therefore, I would like to send a special thank you to her for being an amazing friend and archaeologist.

Table of contents

List of figures... vi

List of tables xi

Abstract xiii

Chapter One Introduction and background 1

Chapter Two Theoretical context and framework 13

Chapter Three Methodology... 20

Chapter Four General overview and the statistical and quantitative analyses of the archaeological features and contexts... 31

Chapter Five Statistical and quantitative analyses of the manners of disposal 41

Chapter Six Statistical and quantitative analyses of the inhumations, articulated bones, disarticulated bones, and cremations.. 65

Chapter Seven Statistical and quantitative results from sites with 20 or more occurrences.............................. 84

Chapter Eight Regional patterning and burial trends.. 171

Chapter Nine Discussion.. 204

Chapter Ten Regionality and burial practices 223

Chapter Eleven Conclusion and recommendations for future research 228

Bibliography.. 232

Guide to the appendix... 255

Appendix Available as a download... www.barpublishing.com/additional-downloads.html

List of figures

1.	1	County map of Britain indicating the geographical boundaries of the study highlighted in grey	1
3.	1	County map of Britain indicating the geographical boundaries of the study highlighted in red (also see Figure 1.1)	20
3.	2	Map indicating the 100 sites studied	21
3.	3	Diagram illustrating the placement of a deposit	27
3.	4	Diagram depicting the cardinal areas of a structure	28
3.	5	Diagram depicting the quadrants of a structure	28
3.	6	Diagram depicting the division between front and back of a structure	28
3.	7	Diagram depicting the division between the right and left side of a structure	29
4.	1	Distribution of studied sites (see also Figure 3.2)	31
4.	2	Frequency of archaeological features' orientation, including larger sites	34
4.	3	Frequency of archaeological features' orientation, excluding larger sites	34
4.	4	Frequency of archaeological features' date and context, including larger sites	35
4.	5	Frequency of archaeological features' date and context, excluding larger sites	35
4.	6	Frequency of context type and date, including larger sites	37
4.	7	Frequency of context type and date, excluding larger sites	37
4.	8	Frequency of contexts' manner of disposal and date, including larger sites	37
4.	9	Frequency of contexts' manner of disposal and date, excluding larger sites	38
4.	10	Frequency of contexts' location and date within site and archaeological feature, including larger sites	38
4.	11	Frequency of context's location within a site and date, including larger sites	39
4.	12	Frequency of contexts' location and date within site and archaeological feature, excluding larger sites	39
4.	13	Frequency of contexts' location within a site and date, excluding larger sites	40
5.	1	Frequency of occurrences with archaeological features' orientation, including larger sites	44
5.	2	Frequency of occurrences with structures' orientation, including larger sites	45
5.	3	Frequency of occurrences within structures' quadrants, including larger sites	46
5.	4	Frequency of age with structures, including larger sites	46
5.	5	Frequency of occurrences with round structures' orientation, including larger sites	47
5.	6	Frequency of occurrences within round structures' quadrants, including larger sites	48
5.	7	Frequency of occurrences with structures' orientation, excluding larger sites	50
5.	8	Frequency of occurrences with structures' quadrants, excluding larger sites	50
5.	9	Frequency of occurrences with round structures' orientation, excluding larger sites	51
5.	10	Frequency of occurrences with round structures' quadrants, excluding larger sites	52
5.	11	Manner of disposal and date, including larger sites	54
5.	12	Manner of disposal and date, excluding larger sites	54
5.	13	Age of occurrences and date, including larger sites	54
5.	14	Age of occurrences and date, including larger sites	55
5.	15	Age of occurrences and date, excluding larger sites	55
5.	16	Age of occurrences and date, excluding larger sites	55
5.	17	Sex of occurrences and date including larger sites, including larger sites	56
5.	18	Sex of occurrences and date, excluding larger sites	56
5.	19	Age of occurrences and manner of disposal, including larger sites	57
5.	20	Age of occurrences and manner of disposal, including larger sites	57
5.	21	LBA: age of occurrences and manner of disposal, including larger sites	57
5.	22	EIA: age of occurrences and manner of disposal, including larger sites	58
5.	23	MIA: age of occurrences and manner of disposal, including larger sites	58
5.	24	LIA: age of occurrences and manner of disposal, including larger sites	58
5.	25	Age of occurrences and manner of disposal, excluding larger sites	59
5.	26	Age of occurrences and manner of disposal, excluding larger sites	59
5.	27	LBA: Age of occurrences and manner of disposal, excluding larger sites	60
5.	28	EIA: Age of occurrences and manner of disposal, excluding larger sites	60
5.	29	MIA: Age of occurrences and manner of disposal, excluding larger sites	60
5.	30	LIA: Age of occurrences and manner of disposal, excluding larger sites	61
5.	31	Sex of occurrences and manner of disposal, including larger sites	61
5.	32	Sex of occurrences and manner of disposal, excluding larger sites	61
5.	33	Frequency of occurrences' placements within structures quadrants, including larger sites	62
5.	34	Frequency of occurrences and their location within structures, including larger sites	62
5.	35	Frequency of occurrences and their location within structures, excluding larger sites	63
5.	36	Frequency of occurrences and their location with round structures, including larger sites	63
5.	37	Frequency of occurrences and their location with round structures, excluding larger sites	63
6.	1	Dates of inhumations	66
6.	2	Frequency of inhumation orientation, including larger sites	66
6.	3	Frequency of inhumation orientation, excluding larger sites	68
6.	4	Frequencies of inhumations' age	68
6.	5	Date of inhumations and condition, including larger sites	69
6.	6	Date of inhumations and condition, excluding larger site	69

6.	7	Age of inhumations and date, including larger sites	69
6.	8	Age of inhumations and date, including larger sites	69
6.	9	Age of inhumations by date, excluding larger sites	70
6.	10	Age of inhumations by date, excluding larger sites	70
6.	11	Age of inhumations and context, including larger sites	70
6.	12	Age of inhumations and context, excluding larger sites	71
6.	13	Frequency of inhumation locations within a structure, including larger sites	71
6.	14	Frequency of inhumation locations within round structures, including larger sites	71
6.	15	Frequencies of portions of limb present according to side	72
6.	16	Frequencies of elements, including larger sites	75
6.	17	Frequency of elements, excluding larger sites	75
6.	18	Frequency of elements and side of body, including larger sites	75
6.	19	Frequency of elements and side of body, excluding larger sites	76
6.	20	Frequencies of disarticulated bones with archaeological features' orientation, including larger sites	76
6.	21	of disarticulated bones with archaeological features' orientation, excluding larger sites	76
6.	22	Date and element, including larger sites	77
6.	23	Date and element, excluding larger sites	78
6.	24	Date and element, including larger sites	78
6.	25	Date and element, excluding larger sites	78
6.	26	Element and side of the body, excluding larger sites	79
6.	27	Element and side of the body, including larger sites	79
6.	28	Frequency of disarticulated bones and placements with structures' quadrants, including larger sites	79
6.	29	Location of disarticulated bone within structures, including larger sites	80
6.	30	Location of disarticulated bone within round structures, including larger sites	80
6.	31	Location of disarticulated bone within structures, excluding larger sites	80
6.	32	Date and urn, excluding larger sites	82
6.	33	Date and urn, excluding larger sites	83
7.	1	Distribution of all sites with 20 or more human remains occurrences	84
7.	2	Site plan of Potterne illustrating the area of excavation	85
7.	3	Frequency of disarticulated bone elements	86
7.	4	Frequency of disarticulated bones' elements and sides	86
7.	5	Frequency of pathologies	87
7.	6	Frequency of trauma	87
7.	7	Site plan of Battlesbury Bowl depicting feature groups	88
7.	8	Plan of Feature Group 1, depicting boundary features, from Battlesbury Bowl	88
7.	9	Plan of Feature Group 2 from Battlesbury Bowl	88
7.	10	Plan of Feature Group 4, showing Roundhouse 6159 and Structure 5643, from Battlesbury	88
7.	11	Frequency of context types	89
7.	12	Frequency of inhumations' pathologies	90
7.	13	Frequency of inhumations' associated materials	90
7.	14	Frequency of disarticulated bones according to context types	91
7.	15	Frequency of disarticulated bone elements	91
7.	16	Frequency of disarticulated bone elements (2)	91
7.	17	Frequency of disarticulated bones' trauma	92
7.	18	Frequency of disarticulated bones' associated materials	92
7.	19	Site plan of Danebury showing where known human deposits are	93
7.	20	Frequency of contexts by date and type	94
7.	21	Frequency of human remains according to manner of disposal and date	95
7.	22	Frequency of occurrences by context types	95
7.	23	Frequency of occurrences by manner of disposal and age	96
7.	24	Frequency of occurrences by manner of disposal and sex	96
7.	25	Frequency of pathologies	96
7.	26	Frequency of trauma	97
7.	27	Frequency of associated materials	97
7.	28	Frequency of animal species	97
7.	29	Frequency of occurrences associated with archaeological features	98
7.	30	Frequency of occurrences according to round structures' quadrants	98
7.	31	Frequency of inhumations according to date	99
7.	32	Frequency of inhumations according to context types	99
7.	33	Frequency of inhumations according to layouts	99
7.	34	Frequency of inhumations according to positions	100
7.	35	Frequency of inhumations according to orientations	100
7.	36	Frequency of inhumations according to facial directions	100
7.	37	Frequency of inhumations according to age	101
7.	38	Frequency of inhumations according to pathologies	101
7.	39	Frequency of inhumations according to trauma	101
7.	40	Frequency of inhumations' associated materials	102
7.	41	Frequency of inhumations' associated animal species	102
7.	42	Frequency of articulated bones' associated materials	102
7.	43	Frequency of disarticulated bones according to date	103
7.	44	Frequency of disarticulated bones according to context types	103
7.	45	Frequency of disarticulated bones' elements	104

7.	46	Frequency of disarticulated bones' elements and sides	104
7.	47	Frequency of disarticulated bones' age	104
7.	48	Frequency of disarticulated bones' pathologies	105
7.	49	Frequency of disarticulated bones' trauma	105
7.	50	Frequency of disarticulated bones' associated materials	105
7.	51	Frequency of disarticulated bones' associated animal species	106
7.	52	Frequency of disarticulated bones associated with archaeological features	106
7.	53	Frequency of disarticulated bones according to age and element (cranium and post-cranium)	107
7.	54	Frequency of disarticulated bones according to age and element (2)	107
7.	55	Site plan of Gravelly Guy indicating places of human remains deposits	108
7.	56	Frequency of archaeological features with associated human remains	109
7.	57	Frequency of archaeological features' orientations	109
7.	58	Frequency of contexts according to date	109
7.	59	Frequency of context types with human remains deposits	110
7.	60	Frequency of contexts according to manner of disposal and single/multiple deposits	110
7.	61	Frequency of human remains according to structures' quadrants	111
7.	62	Frequency of occurrences according to structures' quadrants and locations	111
7.	63	Frequency of occurrences according to placement within and right/left of structures	111
7.	64	Frequency of occurrences according to manner of disposal and depths	112
7.	65	Frequency of occurrences according to manner of disposal and single/multiple deposits	112
7.	66	Frequency of inhumations according to date	113
7.	67	Frequency of inhumations' context types	113
7.	68	Frequency of inhumations' layouts	113
7.	69	Frequency of inhumations' orientations	114
7.	70	Frequency of inhumations' age	114
7.	71	Frequency of inhumations' associated materials	114
7.	72	Frequency of disarticulated bones' date	115
7.	73	Frequency of disarticulated bones according to context types	115
7.	74	Frequency of disarticulated bones' elements	116
7.	75	Frequency of disarticulated bones' associated materials	116
7.	76	Frequency of disarticulated bones according to single/multiple deposits and elements (3)	116
7.	77	Frequency of disarticulated bones according to age and single/multiple deposits	117
7.	78	Frequency of disarticulated bones according age and elements (3)	117
7.	79	Site plan of Gussage All Saints in the Early Iron Age	118
7.	80	Site plan of Gussage All Saints in the Middle Iron Age indicating human remains deposits	118
7.	81	Site plan of Gussage All Saints in the Late Iron Age indicating human remains deposits	119
7.	82	Site plan of Gussage All Saints in the Late Iron Age showing the cardinal areas for the archaeological features	119
7.	83	Frequency of context types with human remains	120
7.	84	Frequency of contexts according to manner of disposal	120
7.	85	Frequency of contexts according to date and manner of disposal	120
7.	86	Frequency of occurrences according to manner of disposal and date	121
7.	87	Frequency of inhumations' contexts	121
7.	88	Frequency of inhumations' layouts	122
7.	89	Frequency of inhumations' positions	122
7.	90	Frequency of inhumations' orientations	122
7.	91	Frequency of inhumations' age	123
7.	92	Frequency inhumations' pathologies	123
7.	93	Frequency of disarticulated bones' elements	124
7.	94	Frequency of disarticulated bones' elements and sides	124
7.	95	Site plan of Winnall Down in the Early Iron Age indicating human remains deposits	125
7.	96	Site plan of Winnall Down during the Middle Iron Age indicating human remains deposits	125
7.	97	Frequency of context types	126
7.	98	Frequency of contexts according to manner of disposal	126
7.	99	Frequency of contexts according to manner of disposal and date	127
7.	100	Frequency of inhumations' context types	127
7.	101	Frequency of inhumations' layouts	128
7.	102	Frequency of inhumations' date and age	128
7.	103	Frequency of disarticulated bones' context types	129
7.	104	Frequency of disarticulated bones' elements	129
7.	105	Frequency of disarticulated bones' age	130
7.	106	Frequency of disarticulated bones' elements and age	130
7.	107	Frequency of disarticulated bones according to date and context types	131
7.	108	Frequency of disarticulated bones according to date and age	131
7.	109	Site plan of Glastonbury Lake Village indicating areas of human remains	132
7.	110	Frequency of archaeological features' functions	133
7.	111	Frequency of occurrences according to manner of disposal and age	133
7.	112	Frequency of occurrences according to manner of disposal and age	133
7.	113	Frequency of inhumations'' associated materials	134
7.	114	Frequency of disarticulated bones' elements	134
7.	115	Frequency of disarticulated bones' trauma	135
7.	116	Frequency of disarticulated bones' associated materials	135

7.	117	Frequency of disarticulated bones' cardinal directions	135
7.	118	Site plan of Micheldever Wood indicating human remains deposits	136
7.	119	Frequency of context types	137
7.	120	Frequency of contexts according to manner of disposal	137
7.	121	Frequency of inhumations' context types	138
7.	122	Site plan of White Horse, Pilgrim's Way, West and East of Boarley Farm showing area of excavation	139
7.	123	Site plan of White Horse, Pilgrim's Way, West and East of Boarley Farm showing only LBA features and human remains deposits	140
7.	124	Site plan of White Horse, Pilgrim's Way, West and East of Boarley Farm showing only LBA features and human remains deposits	140
7.	125	Plan of Structure 2584 illustrating human remains deposits	141
7.	126	Frequency of disarticulated bones' elements	142
7.	127	Frequency of disarticulated bones' associated materials	142
7.	128	General site plan of Beechbrook Wood showing all archaeological	143
7.	129	Plan of Ditch 1164/6011 with Late Bronze Age human remains	144
7.	130	Plan of Middle Iron Age Enclosure 3072 with associated human remains deposits	144
7.	131	Plan of Enclosure 1020 and 1022 indicating human remains deposits	145
7.	132	Plan of archaeological features north of Enclosure 1020 indicating human remains deposits	145
7.	133	Frequency of contexts' date	146
7.	134	Frequency of context types	147
7.	135	Frequency of cremations' associated materials	147
7.	136	Site plan of Suddern farm indicating human remains deposits	148
7.	137	Plan showing the cemetery, indicating human remains deposits	148
7.	138	Frequency of contexts according to manner of disposal	149
7.	139	Frequency of occurrences according to age and manner of disposal	150
7.	140	Frequency of occurrences according to age and manner of disposal	150
7.	141	Frequency of inhumations' layouts	150
7.	142	Frequency of inhumations' orientations	151
7.	143	Frequency of inhumations' age	151
7.	144	Frequency of inhumations' trauma	151
7.	145	Frequency of inhumations according to conditions and single/multiple deposits	152
7.	146	Frequency of disarticulated bones' elements	153
7.	147	Frequency of disarticulated bones' elements and sides	153
7.	148	Site plan of Maiden Castle indicating areas of human remains deposits	154
7.	149	Plan of the war cemetery	154
7.	150	Frequency of contexts according to date	155
7.	151	Frequency of context types	156
7.	152	Frequency of inhumations' date	156
7.	153	Frequency of inhumations' context types	156
7.	154	Frequency of inhumations' layouts	157
7.	155	Frequency of inhumations' positions	157
7.	156	Frequency of inhumations' orientations	157
7.	157	Frequency of inhumations' trauma	158
7.	158	Frequency of inhumations' associated materials	158
7.	159	Frequency of disarticulated bones' context types	159
7.	160	Frequency of disarticulated bones' elements	159
7.	161	Frequency of disarticulated bones' associated materials	159
7.	162	Site plan of Sutton Walls	160
7.	163	Plan of west entrance of Sutton Walls indicating human remains deposits	161
7.	164	Frequency of inhumations' trauma	162
7.	165	Frequency of disarticulated bones' elements	162
7.	166	Site plan of Mill Hill indicating human remains deposits	166
7.	167	Frequency of inhumations' layouts	165
7.	168	Frequency of inhumations' orientations	165
7.	169	Frequency of inhumations' facial directions	165
7.	170	Frequency of inhumations' pathologies	166
7.	171	Frequency of inhumations' associated materials	166
7.	172	Frequency of inhumations according to facial directions and sex	166
7.	173	Site plan of Westhampnett indicating human remains deposits	167
7.	174	Frequency of context types	168
7.	175	Frequency of cremations' pathologies	169
7.	176	Frequency of cremations' associated materials	169
8.	1	Distribution of Late Bronze Age sites according to manner of disposal	172
8.	2	Distribution of Early Iron Age sites according to manner of disposal	173
8.	3	Distribution of Middle Iron Age sites according to manner of disposal	174
8.	4	Distribution of Late Iron Age sites according to manner of disposal	175
8.	5	Distribution of Late Bronze Age sites according to context type	176
8.	6	Distribution of Early Iron Age sites according to context type	177
8.	7	Distribution of Middle Iron Age sites according to context type	178
8.	8	Distribution of Late Iron Age sites according to context type	179
8.	9	Distribution of Late Bronze Age sites according to age	180
8.	10	Distribution of Early Iron Age sites according to age	181

8.	11	Distribution of Middle Iron Age sites according to age	182
8.	12	Distribution of Late Iron Age sites according to age	183
8.	13	Distribution of Late Bronze Age sites according to sex	184
8.	14	Distribution of Early Iron Age sites according to sex	185
8.	15	Distribution of Middle Iron Age sites according to sex	186
8.	16	Distribution of Late Iron Age sites according to sex	187
8.	17	Distribution of Late Bronze Age cremation sites according to sex	188
8.	18	Distribution of Middle Iron Age cremation site according to sex	189
8.	19	Distribution of Late Iron Age cremation sites according to sex	190
8.	20	Distribution of sites according to structure type	191
8.	21	Distribution of sites according to front/back placement	192
8.	22	Distribution of sites according to right/interior and left/perimeter placement	193
8.	23	Distribution of sites that have monument reuse	194
8.	24	Site plan of Stone Farm Bridleway	195
8.	25	Distribution of sites that have human remains in areas of economic significance	196
8.	26	Site plan of Jubilee Corner	197
8.	27	Distribution of sites that have human remains as liminal markers	198
8.	28	Site plan of Norton	199
8.	29	Distribution of sites with cranial elements	200
8.	30	Distribution of sites that have evidence of post-mortem handling of skulls	201
8.	31	Distribution of sites that have evidence of complex treatment to the human remains	202
9.	1	Frequency of the location of contexts according to date	212
9.	2	Frequency of the location of contexts according to date, excluding Danebury	212
9.	3	Frequency of the location of contexts according to date	212
9.	4	Distribution of sites with human remains associated with architectural features	213
9.	5	Figure illustrating the frequency of human remains in and around structures	214
9.	6	Diagram illustrating the frequency of human remains in and around structures	215
9.	7	Diagram illustrating the frequency of human remains in and around structures	216

List of tables

1.	1	Iron Age chronological sequence	4
1.	2	Earliest Iron Age Style Groups	6
1.	3	Early Iron Age Style Groups	7
1.	4	Middle Iron Age-Late Iron Age Style Groups	7
1.	5	Style Divisions of the Middle Iron Age-Late Iron Age ceramic groups	7
1.	6	Late Iron Age Style Groups	7
3.	1	List of studied sites	22
3.	2	Associated materials	24
3.	3	Age group 1 and 2	24
3.	4	Disease classifications with accompanying pathological definitions	24
3.	5	Traumatic indicators	24
3.	6	Position of skeleton variables	25
3.	7	List of elements	26
3.	8	Variables for portion of element	56
3.	9	Variables of the archaeological feature type trait	27
3.	10	Variables of the function of an archaeological feature trait	27
4.	1	Sites with numbers of human remains occurrences	32
4.	2	Quantity of occurrences sites	33
4.	3	Number of sites with manner of disposal	33
4.	4	Period of deposition with sites	33
4.	5	Frequency of archaeological features containing human remains by date	33
4.	6	Frequency of archaeological features' type	33
4.	7	Frequency of archaeological features' function	33
4.	8	Frequency of contexts' date	36
4.	9	Frequency of context type	36
4.	10	Frequency of contexts with manner of disposal	36
5.	1	Frequency of occurrences and date	41
5.	2	Frequency of manners of disposal	41
5.	3	Frequency of occurrences with context type	41
5.	4	Frequency of sex	42
5.	5	Frequency of pathological indicators	42
5.	6	Frequency of traumatic indicators	42
5.	7	Frequency of associated material	42
5.	8	Frequency of animal species	42
5.	9	Percentage of human remains to animal bones	43
5.	10	Date of occurrences with archaeological features, including	44
5.	11	Frequency of manner of disposal with archaeological features, including larger sites	44
5.	12	Frequency of occurrences with archaeological features' type, including larger sites	44
5.	13	Frequency of manner of disposal with archaeological features' functions, including larger sites	44
5.	14	Frequency of occurrences with structure type, including larger sites	45
5.	15	Frequency of occurrences with structures' function, including larger sites	45
5.	16	Frequency of occurrences within structures, including larger sites	45
5.	17	Frequency of occurrences near architectural features, including larger sites	45
5.	18	Date of occurrences with structures, including larger sites	46
5.	19	Manner of disposal with structures, including larger sites	46
5.	20	Frequency of occurrences with round structures, including larger sites	47
5.	21	Manners of disposal with round structures, including larger sites	47
5.	22	Frequency of occurrences within round structures, including	47
5.	23	Age with round structures, including larger sites	47
5.	24	Frequency of occurrences with 'other' archaeological features' function, including larger sites	48
5.	25	Date of occurrences with 'other' archaeological features, including larger sites	48
5.	26	Manner of disposal with 'other' archaeological features, including larger sites	48
5.	27	Frequency of occurrences within 'other' archaeological features, including larger sites	48
5.	28	Date of occurrences with post-built structures, including larger sites	49
5.	29	Manner of disposal with post-built structures, including larger sites	49
5.	30	Frequency of occurrences with post-built structures' function	49
5.	31	Date of occurrences with archaeological features, excluding larger sites	49
5.	32	Manner of disposal with archaeological features, excluding larger sites	49
5.	33	Frequency of occurrences with archaeological features' type, excluding larger sites	49
5.	34	Frequency of occurrences with archaeological features' function, excluding larger sites	49
5.	35	Frequency of occurrences within archaeological features excluding larger sites	49
5.	36	Date of occurrences with structures, excluding larger sites	50
5.	37	Frequency of occurrences with structures' function, excluding larger sites	50
5.	38	Manner of disposal in structures, excluding larger sites	51
5.	39	Date of occurrences with round structures, excluding larger site	51
5.	40	Frequency of occurrences with structures' functions, excluding larger sites	51
5.	41	Frequency of occurrences within round structures, excluding larger sites	51

5.	42	Manner of disposal with round structures excluding larger sites	51
5.	43	Date of occurrences with 'other' structures, excluding larger sites	52
5.	44	Frequency of occurrences with structures' function, excluding larger sites	52
5.	45	Frequency of occurrences within 'other' structures, excluding larger sites	52
5.	46	Manner of disposal with 'other' structures, excluding larger sites	52
6.	1	Frequencies of inhumations' contexts	67
6.	2	Frequencies of inhumations' layouts	67
6.	3	Frequencies of inhumations' positions	67
6.	4	Frequencies of inhumations' pathologies	67
6.	5	Frequencies of inhumations' traumatic indicators	67
6.	6	Frequencies of inhumations' associated materials	67
6.	7	Frequencies of animal species associated with inhumations	67
6.	8	Frequencies of inhumations with archaeological feature types	67
6.	9	Date of inhumations with archaeological features	67
6.	10	Frequencies of inhumations within archaeological features	67
6.	11	Frequencies of inhumations with archaeological features' function	68
6.	12	Date of articulated bones	72
6.	13	Frequencies of articulated bones' context types	72
6.	14	Frequency of body portions present	72
6.	15	Frequencies of associated materials with articulated bones	72
6.	16	Date of disarticulated bones	72
6.	17	Frequencies of disarticulated bones by context	73
6.	18	Frequencies of disarticulated bones by depth	73
6.	19	Age of disarticulated bones	73
6.	20	Frequencies of disarticulated bones' pathologies	73
6.	21	Frequencies of disarticulated bones' traumatic indicators	74
6.	22	Frequencies of associated materials with disarticulated bones	74
6.	23	Frequencies of animal species with disarticulated bones	74
6.	24	Frequency of disarticulated bone with archaeological features	74
6.	25	Frequencies of disarticulated bones with archaeological features' function	74
6.	26	Date of disarticulated bones with archaeological features	75
6.	27	Frequencies of disarticulated bones within archaeological features	75
6.	28	Date of cremations	81
6.	29	Frequencies of cremations' contexts	81
6.	30	Frequencies of cremations and urns	81
6.	31	Frequencies of cremations' pathologies, including larger sites	81
6.	32	Frequencies of associated materials with cremations	81
6.	33	Frequency of animal species with cremations, including larger sites	82
6.	34	Date of cremations with archaeological features	82
6.	35	Frequencies of cremations with archaeological features	82
6.	36	Frequencies of cremations with archaeological features' function	82
6.	37	Locations of cremations within archaeological features	82
7.	1	List of sites, numbered to correspond with Figure 7.1	85
7.	2	List of midden site	85
7.	3	List of settlement sites	85
7.	4	List of settlement/cemetery sites	85
7.	5	List of cemetery sites	85
7.	6	Danebury's ceramic phases and corresponding time periods	94
7.	7	Frequency of inhumations' orientations	128
7.	8	Frequency of disarticulated bones' elements and sides	129
7.	9	Frequency of inhumations' orientations	138
7.	10	Frequency of disarticulated bones' elements and sides	141
7.	11	Frequency of inhumations' positions	152
7.	12	Frequency of disarticulated bones' pathologies	152
7.	13	List of areas and numbers of human remains deposits	154
7.	14	Frequency of disarticulated bones elements and sides	158
7.	15	Frequency of contexts' cardinal directions	164
7.	16	Frequency of inhumations' positions	164
7.	17	Frequency of cremations' associated materials	164
9.	1	Percent of cremation weights under 100g	210

Abstract

The following study investigates potential regional patterns of Iron Age burial practices and the cultural implications thereof. It is a literary-based assessment of 100 sites that date between the Late Bronze Age and the Late Iron Age that all contain human remains. The analysis consists of a systematic methodology that allows one to assess objectively relationships between burial characteristics, both on the site level and regional scale. This approach indicated a temporal relationship with the manner of disposal (inhumations, disarticulated bones and cremations), which is also regionally distinct. Furthermore, this study highlights other common and repeated Iron Age burial themes, such as differential treatment to infants, incorporating earlier monuments in their burial traditions, using remains to mark places of liminal qualities and economic significance, and bone deposition adhering to a specific spatial pattern with buildings, particularly roundhouses. In essence, the study demonstrates that the processing of the corpse and the spatial context of the human remains deposit are central for understanding the community's perception of the bones and, thus, the meaning of the deposition. The core concept is that Iron Age communities practised various ritual processes, each with a different purpose, but using the same medium - human remains.

Chapter One

Introduction and background

Introduction

The death of an individual is an inevitable event that necessitates a basic reaction from society to dispose of the body in some fashion. Disposal can range from an elaborate series of rituals to a simple act of discarding the corpse. These different methods are thought in some way to reflect perceptions of death, and this is the premise that underlies archaeologists' attempts to understand past mortuary practices. The distinctive reaction to death in the British Iron Age has left little evidence in the way of a burial record. The small quantity of skeletal material uncovered is nowhere near representative of the assumed total population (Carr and Knüsel 1997, 168). Iron Age human remains have been uncovered from settlement sites within pits, boundary areas, and other domestic contexts, associated with domestic material. In essence, the British Iron Age lacks a typical 'formal' area for disposing of the dead. That is to state, the methods by which the majority of the dead population were processed and disposed of are not evident within the archaeological record, and this is geographically widespread throughout most of Iron Age Britain. In the past twenty years, research into Iron Age burial practices has focused on how human remains have tended to be deposited in reoccurring contextual configurations, with lengthy time gaps between depositions, suggesting a degree of ritualistic activity (Cunliffe 1992; Hill 1994, 1995b, 1996).

The purpose of this study is to identify and interpret the intent driving Iron Age burial practices. Similar burial rites are present across most of Britain, and it may be indicative of a common set of practices. There are, however, variations within these practices. Investigating burial traditions, therefore, on the wider geographical scale may reveal regional patterns. Such patterns may signify different groups' interpretation and renegotiation of a similar set of burial customs. Thus, this study's objective is to investigate potential regional patterning of British Iron Age burial customs. It will focus on the archaeological evidence from the Late Bronze Age up to the Late Iron Age. Skeletal evidence from the Late Bronze Age is included in this investigation due to its similarities (both in the archaeological and burial record) to the Early Iron Age (Brück 1995, 246; Haselgrove 1999, 113).Evidence for the study comes from sites located within central and southern Britain (**Figure 1.1**). In approaching this study, all the basic elements of Late Bronze Age and Iron Age burial practices will be assessed. These refer to a range of characteristics developed at various stages of disposal, from the

processing of the body immediately after death to the actual deposition in the ground. They include examinations of how human remains were disposed of (e.g. inhumation, disarticulated bone, or cremation), how the body was processed and manipulated prior to deposition, the demographic profile, and potential significance attributed to particular areas and contexts chosen for the deposition. Ultimately, the study will work through a series of core research questions:

How were individuals processed and disposed of, and why?
Which individuals were chosen for deposition, and why?
I s there a preference in the spatial setting for human remains and why?
How did these burial practices change over time and how can we explain this?

The study will ascertain whether variations in burial rites across a geographical area take the form of a series of practices distinctive to individual sites, cluster in certain areas, show blurred distinctions across a large geographical area, or reveal no discernible pattern. The variations in these burial characteristics may reveal regional patterns, from which intentions can be inferred and interpreted. For this research, it is not enough to describe the nature of the archaeological record; but instead, to present an interpretation of burial traditions during the first millennium BC that mobilises socially-embedded explanations of action.

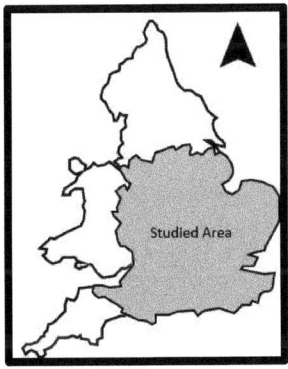

Figure 1.1 Map of Britain indicating the geographical boundaries of the study highlighted in grey

Background to the Late Bronze Age and the Iron Age

The following sections introduce the British Late Bronze Age and the Iron Age, defining the archaeological characteristics of the period and thereby presenting the historical context within which to explore the periods' burial practices. While a detailed discussion of every aspect of the period is beyond the scope of this research, discussion will focus on several key themes relating to aspects of daily life of Late Bronze Age and Iron Age communities. These include discussions on chronology, environment, subsistence and economic systems, habitation and material residues, and treatment of the dead. Pottery and burial rites have often been used to ascribe regional groupings to the archaeological record, and, for each of these cases, the discussion will describe the basis for such regional divisions and address the validity of their interpretations. The chapter closes with a summary of the presented information and a brief discussion of the approaches to regional studies in the Late Bronze Age and the Iron Age.

Developing a chronology

In order to set a temporal scheme for this study, it is beneficial to visit the history of past scholars' work in this area. This will allow a clear picture into the progression of the study into its current, academic environment. Particularly, the discussion starts with notable works in the early 1900s, their attempts in defining the Iron Age and its chronology from the archaeological record, while remarking on the impacts of these scholars' interpretations on the social narratives of Iron Age communities.

An early account for dating the beginning of the Iron Age is from O.G.S. Crawford's (1922) article titled 'A Prehistoric Invasion of England'. In this publication, Crawford (1922, 27) places the close of the Bronze Age and the beginning of the Iron Age between 800-700 BC, which is the time marked by a large-scale invasion of people from the Continent. Crawford (1922, 30) draws on similarities of metal objects (e.g. bronze razors), ceramics (fingertip decorated style in southern England and the Deverill-Rimbury type in Wessex) and square camps as indicators of a continental population penetrating Britain. Such material and evidence uncovered in Britain showed a close resemblance of that from the Continent, specifically in France and Switzerland, which meant, according to Crawford (1922, 33), a similar people. Thus, Crawford and contemporaries, such as Abercromby (1912), view the Late Bronze Age-Early Iron Age transition as a period where invaders arrived and brought a specific 'cultural package' into Britain from the Continent. This idea of invasion, or an external influence, as a mechanism for social change and development dominated in Iron Age studies throughout the next forty years.

One of the most influential scholars in the early part of Iron Age studies is Christopher Hawkes. In his 1931 work

on hillforts, Hawkes first proposes the *cultural entities* of Iron Age Britain deemed 'Iron Age A, B and C'. Hawkes sets (1931, 60, 62) the beginning of the Iron Age in the sixth century BC where immigrants from the Continent, specifically the Lower Rhine (Hallstatt), entered into Britain, which coincided with the introduction of iron. He refers to these people as Iron Age A, the following wave of migrating people as Iron Age B, and those after Iron Age C (Hawkes 1931, 64). The Iron Age B, beginning in the fourth century, is characterised by continental migrants represented archaeologically by hillforts, brooches and decorated pottery, which is similar to the La Tène I-III period for the Continent (Hawkes 1931, 76-77, 88). Invasions of the Belgic tribes from northern Gaul in 75 BC are the proposed onset for the Iron Age C, represented by the Aylesford-Swarling-Welwyn type of pedestal urns and other material. The first invasion of the Belgic people specifically penetrated Britain through the southeast in Kent and spreads northwards past the Thames, and a second wave of immigrants infiltrating Hampshire (Hawkes 1931, 88-89). Hawkes' scheme was adopted quickly amongst scholars and the 'Iron Age A, B and C' became common terminology in relating archaeological material to the cultural package defined by these groupings.

Although many generally accepted the 'ABC' system, it was not without its critics. For example, Maud Cunnington (1932, 27) questioned Hawkes' proposal of a second Belgic invasion, characterised by the appearance of bead-rimmed pottery in Wiltshire, Dorset and Hampshire. Cunnington (1932, 29) focused on the ceramic evidence of the second invasion and asserts that the style changes of the bead-rimmed pottery does not necessarily denote an invasion, but may be the result of a developing technology. She further elaborates that the distribution of this ceramic type is wide and not constrained to a particular area (Cunnington 1932, 30). In addition to Cunnington's critiques, other problems were beginning to be recognised with Hawkes' ABC system. Those implementing the scheme needed to modify its classifications in order to accommodate excavated material, for example Mortimer Wheeler's (1943) work at Maiden Castle and Kathleen Kenyon's (1953) at Sutton Walls.

Thus, in 1959, Hawkes' elaborated on his scheme in his publication, 'The ABC of the British Iron Age'. In this work, Hawkes' (1959, 172) divides Britain into a series of provinces and regions based on the archaeological evidence and the physical characteristics of the terrain. He then sets up a fixed chronological scheme coined Iron Age 1 (550-350 BC), Iron Age 2 (350-150 BC), and Iron Age 3 (150 BC to the Roman period) which was '...taken from the Continent, where they stem from Mediterranean historical chronology' (Hawkes 1959, 174). Hawkes (1959, 172) again asserts the 'ABC' denote cultural entities defined from the archaeological material. Ultimately, Hawkes devised a systematic method to distinguish geographical areas, with the appropriate culture group, within the entire chronological scheme.

Hawkes' sequence relies on relative dating techniques and the assumption that cultural and material change in Britain only occurred through the immigration of continental populations, which then diffused throughout the island. Continental migration was not a new concept (see above); Caesar provides the first account of immigrant populations in Britain during his conquest of Gaul, describing the natives of southern Britain as Belgic immigrants from the Continent (Caesar *Commentarii de Bello Gallico*, 110). This account is of great importance, for it provides the foundation for later scholars' interpretations of archaeological material through their relation with the Continent. Unfortunately, Hawkes' (1959) method failed to interpret adequately Britain's internal development. The view of the British Iron Age, in essence, became one of a stagnant population with the only impetus for cultural change coming from continental influences that penetrated the isle. It is not the purpose of this study to assert that there was absolutely no contact, influence or exchange between the Continent and Britain, only that it did not *dictate* all the developments of British communities.

The end of the 'ABC' system came shortly after Hawkes' 1959 paper. In 1960, Hodson (1960; 1962; 1964) outlined critical philosophical problems with Hawkes' system. He argues firstly that the 'ABC' limits the degree of interpretation by requiring academics to 'fit' material into preconceived groupings (Hodson 1960, 138). Furthermore, the strict geographical boundaries prevent the possibility of groups moving beyond these regions (Hodson 1960, 138). Hodson (1960, 138) also critiques the fixed chronological system, arguing that the continental dates are not absolute and it is unsound to rely so heavily on them for dating the British material. Instead, archaeology needs to be more objective, Hodson (1960, 140; 1962, 153) asserts, and rely on type-sites and type-fossils in creating groupings. Hodson (1964) proposed, alternatively, a new chronological scheme that divides the Iron Age into two periods. The first period is the early pre-Roman Iron Age from 750/700 BC (based on Hallstatt C metalwork) to 100/50 BC (La Tène D metalwork) and, secondly, the late pre-Roman Iron Age from 100/50 BC to the Roman Period (based on material culture such as currency bars and decorated saucepans). Grahame Clarke's paper in 1966 solidified the end of the 'ABC' system. Clarke (1966, 172) criticised British prehistorians for attributing any change or development seen in the archaeological record as evidence of foreign invaders or influence. Specifically for the Iron Age, Clarke (1966, 186) proposes that prestigious material may be local traditions with continental inspirations, and that hillforts may have been more of a form of expression for a society as opposed to solely a product of invading forces.

Another major contribution to defining an Iron Age chronology comes from the excavations at Danebury

(Hampshire) led by Barry Cunliffe (1984a). This chronological sequence relies heavily on ceramic styles, largely pertains to Wessex, and has been continuously refined as new evidence has emerged (Cunliffe 1984a; 2005, 32). Due to their sensitivity to changing styles, ceramic assemblages are a reasonably dependable chronological indicator (Cunliffe 2005, 87). This scheme divides the period into the Earliest Iron Age (800-600 BC), the Early Iron Age (600-400/300 BC), the Middle Iron Age (400/300-100 BC) and Late Iron Age (100 BC-AD 43). This temporal setting, and terminology, is generally used for most archaeologists; although, the dates are by no means fixed and vary throughout different areas in Britain (details of the ceramic sequence, style and regional groupings shall be discussed later in this chapter). The abundance of ceramics from Iron Age sites allows archaeologists to track varying style sequences and arrange them chronologically, but this method is not without its problems. The usage of particular ceramic styles was not widespread across the island nor was their adoption uniform. Therefore, it is not a universal chronological indicator, and it is regionally sensitive (see Brundell 2008 and Collis 1977e).

Recently, the Earliest Iron Age (based on ceramic styles) has been identified as the transitional time between the Late Bronze Age and Early Iron Age, situating the beginning of the Iron Age at around 800 BC (Collis 1977a, 6; Cunliffe 2005, 32; Hill 1995a, 75). It is thought that a definitive characteristic of the Bronze Age-Iron Age transition is the change in the society's emphasis from bronze to iron goods (Needham 2007, 49). How the change in metal use came about is debatable, but there are three possibilities explaining the most probable cause. The first, a steady transition to iron replacing bronze; second, bronze was quickly abandoned for tools and iron became the more socially accepted metal to use; and lastly, there may have been a severe lack of bronze resources which iron then replaced (Needham 2007, 49). Defining the divide between the Late Bronze Age (1150-800 BC) and the Early Iron Age (800-470 BC) by metal use may be putting too much emphasis on the material (Brück 2007, 24; Needham 2007, 40). This may be true for the archaeological record because the Late Bronze Age consists primarily of settlement and field system evidence, similar to the Iron Age (Brück 1995, 245). This point, in conjunction with similarities in settlement evidence and depositional practices, highlights a degree of continuity between the Late Bronze Age and the Early Iron Age (Brück 1995, 246; Haselgrove 1999, 113). Furthermore, the divide between the Late Bronze Age and the Early Iron Age may be more of the emergence of a new social system that emphasises labour, agriculture, and salt production than a switch from bronze to iron (Needham 2007, 58).

In closing, this section has reviewed the historical development of Iron Age studies in regards to the main works in establishing a chronological system. There continues to be debates and uncertainties in the chronology, and a single dating scheme cannot adequately characterise all of Britain during the Iron Age. Instead, the work thus far can allow one to offer a general and broad temporal scheme for most of Britain. **Table 1.1** illustrates the broad chronological divisions this study will employ.

Table 1.1 Iron Age chronological sequence (Brück 2007, 24; Cunliffe 2005, 32; Needham 2007, 40)

Late Bronze Age (LBA)	1150-800 BC
Earliest/Early Iron Age (EIA)	800-470 BC
Middle Iron Age (MIA)	470-100 BC
Late Iron Age (LIA)	100 BC-AD 43

Environment

Britain possesses a truly variable landscape, a product of the last Ice Age (Reed 1990, 18-20). About 12,000 years ago, the glaciers began to retreat and the receding glaciers consequently shaped much of the landscape (Reed 1990, 18). Overall, prehistoric Britain had a temperate climate, much like today, although the climatic conditions of the island began to change during the transition between the Late Bronze Age and Early Iron Age. The early first millennium BC saw a deterioration of the climate, with a general increase in levels of rainfall and a temperature drop of about 2°C (Bell 1982, 118; 1996, 5; Darvill 2010, 244; Robinson 1984, 7). Around 600 BC, the climatic conditions began changing much to the state present today (Darvill 2010, 244). Across the landscape, the deciduous woodland, which once covered the majority of Britain, saw significant tree clearance during the Bronze Age to make way for farming and this open landscape expanded into the Iron Age (Reed 1990, 31). The natural environment and terrain of the island is suitable for varying agricultural regimes and animal husbandry.

Subsistence and economic systems

The natural environment of an area influences the location and subsistence practices of a community, and, thus, affects the activities of daily life (Rapp and Hill 1998, 53). The majority of Iron Age communities subsisted on a regime comprising of crop cultivation and animal husbandry (Haselgrove 1999, 115). Direct evidence for mixed farming regimes includes charred crop grains and faunal remains of domestic animals found in settlement sites. Typically, Iron Age populations exploited plants such as spelt wheat, emmer wheat, bread/club wheat, six-row barley, oats, and rye (Jones 1996, 31). In respect to animals, sheep, cattle, pig, horse, and dog are the most represented animal species in excavations (Maltby 1996, 20). The exploitation of sheep and cattle for milk and meat is prevalent in the majority of sites (Maltby 1996, 20).

Although mixed farming practices are evident in Iron Age sites, there is also a small degree of regional variation among them. The subsistence systems in southern central England largely consisted of a diverse crop-intensification regime with animal husbandry (Cunliffe 2005, 429). There are high occurrences of sheep and cattle, with sheep more frequent in the assemblage (Hambleton 1999, 87). In addition, the presence of sheep bones in proportion to cattle increases from the Early Iron Age into the Late Iron Age (Hambleton 1999, 87). The cause for the increase in sheep may tie in with the intensification of arable production (Hambleton 1999, 87). The Upper Thames area also practised a mixed farming regime (Darvill 2010, 262), although cattle bones are more frequent in faunal assemblages when compared to Wessex (Hambleton 1999, 88). The dominant subsistence system in eastern England and East Anglia was also a mixture of agriculture and animal husbandry (Hill 2007, 21). Interestingly, pig bones have a higher representation though not to the same degree as sheep or cattle in the faunal assemblages from the Upper Thames and Wessex (Albarella 2007, 395; Hambleton 1999, 90). There is a high percentage of cattle, however, compared to sheep (it should be noted that sheep were still present in high quantities), which suggests that cattle were more vital resource for eastern England and East Anglia (Hambleton 1999, 89).

Evidence for subsistence systems in the northern areas of England is less abundant than for the south. The available evidence from the Peak District suggests the Iron Age populations were practicing agriculture and stock rearing with the possibility that Bronze Age field systems continue to be in use (Edmonds and Seaborne 2001, 184, 194). The subsistence systems in northeast England appear to have been a mix of arable production and animal husbandry, with variations in the scale of farming between communities (van der Veen 1992, 159). Evidence from northern England and southern Scotland implies that the Iron Age communities were also engaged in arable production with a diverse range of animal husbandry strategies (Hambleton 1999, 90).

In addition to the archaeological evidence for subsistence systems, recent analysis has offered insights into the diet of Iron Age populations. Stable isotope analysis of bone collagen from ten sites across East Yorkshire, East Lothian, Cornwall and Hampshire has revealed that the inhabitants consumed remarkably high levels of animal protein (Jay and Richards 2007, 180). Additionally, a high frequency of caries in the skeletal assemblage suggests consumption of cereal grains in high quantities (Jay and Richards 2007, 187). There is, however, little evidence suggesting fish consumption, even in the coastal areas (Jay and Richards 2007, 182; see also Jay 2008). This evidence may suggest there was a type of social prohibition preventing people from exploiting aquatic resources (Dobney and Ervynck 2007, 409).

Habitation and material residues

The discussion turns now to how Late Bronze Age and Iron Age populations organised their daily lives. This is of particular importance, since the archaeological record of these periods comprises primarily of settlement sites. The abundance of domestic material remains is a distinguishing trait for the Middle to Late Bronze Age and Iron Age, and contrasts starkly with the Neolithic and much of the earlier Bronze Age, which are instead marked by the many ceremonial monuments which make up a large segment of the landscape (Brück 1995, 245). The Late Bronze Age and Iron Age display various settlement forms scattered across the British landscape, with the dominant settlement type being the small-enclosed farmstead, probably reflecting a single-family unit (Haselgrove 1999, 117). The majority of domestic sites yield evidence showing continuous and permanent occupation; although, there are some instances of settlements being seasonally used (Hill 1995a, 61). Additionally, there are community-based domestic settlements, such as Gravelly Guy in Oxfordshire (Lambrick and Allen 2004) and Great Barford Site 2 (High Barns Road) in Bedfordshire (Webley 2007b; 2007c). The main community-scale settlement forms, found throughout Britain, are open settlements, single- and multi-ditched enclosed settlements, and hillforts (Cunliffe 2005, 253). Although each settlement type is found throughout the island, they do display general regional trends.

Open settlements, as the name implies, are domestic sites lacking an enclosing bank or ditch. This settlement type is frequent in East Anglia and eastern England (Darvill 2010, 261). During the Early Iron Age in East Anglia, settlements were located along river valleys and the Fen edge (Bryant 1997, 23). However, by the Late Iron Age there was an increase in settlement expansion and intensification in the area (Bryant 1997, 127). Open settlements in eastern England vary in size and it has been suggested that the settlement pattern may hint at communally 'owned' land (Hill 2007, 19-21).

Single- and multi-ditch enclosed sites are comprised of single or multiple encircling ditches around a habitation area. These settlement forms are especially prevalent in parts of Wessex, the Cotswolds, and areas of the West Midlands (Cunliffe 2005, 248; 253). In the Lower Severn and Cotswolds, enclosed settlements were widespread and, during the Late Iron Age, many are clustered together (Moore 2007, 43). Enclosed settlements are also frequently found in north and northeast England, from 600 BC to 100 BC, although the majority of the settlement evidence from this region consists of enclosed homesteads (Darvill 2010, 267). Sites such as Winnall Down (Hampshire), Barton Court Farm (Oxfordshire) and Bromfield (Shropshire) offer a few examples of single enclosed settlements, while Suddern Farm (Hampshire) is a prime model for a multi-enclosed domestic site.

Hillforts, a very recognisable settlement form, have the same characteristics as a single/multi-enclosed site but lie on or near the summits of hills (Cunliffe 2005, 347). Some hillforts, such as Danebury (Hampshire) and Maiden Castle (Dorset), have intricate and complex series of ramparts and ditches, with elaborate entrances (see Cunliffe 2005, 347-402 for a detailed discussion of the development and construction of hillforts). Hillforts are primarily located in Wessex and the Welsh Marches, with a few in northern England and areas of eastern Scotland (Haselgrove 1999, 113; Darvill 2010, 267).

The morphology of hillforts suggests a defensive function for these sites. This idea is especially evident with the presence of 'war' cemeteries near the entrances of the hillforts of Maiden Castle (Wheeler 1943) and Sutton Walls (Kenyon 1953). However, John Collis (1996, 90) stresses that enclosures or boundaries may have been a means to demonstrate the status of a settlement through the architecture. Similarly, investigations at Scratchbury hillfort (Wiltshire) concluded that the architectural layout of the hillfort was not intended for defensive purposes (Bowden and McOmish 1989, 13). Scratchbury is highly visible from the surrounding landscape and neighbouring hilltops overlook the interior of the site, highlighting that, from a military point of view, this placement would not be ideal for defence. Instead, the intent behind the design of Scratchbury's enclosures was to be highly visible from the outside; its enclosures acted as a mechanism to prevent those on the outside from participating in what took place within (Bowden and McOmish 1989, 12). Recently, the general trend of scholars to shy away from discussion of warfare and violence has come under criticism (Armit 2007; James 2007). Evidence such as skeletal trauma, weapon finds and hillforts strongly suggests that violence was a part of Iron Age life and to ignore this would be misleading (James 2007, 170-171). Thus, it is conceivable that hillforts had multiple purposes and acknowledgment of their military role in no way negates their other more symbolic functions (James 2007, 164; Armit 2007, 36).

Banjo enclosures and middens represent other types of activity and site classification. Banjo enclosures are not as typical as other habitation sites, and their defining characteristic is a long single entrance leading into a circular enclosure resembling a banjo. The banjo enclosures at Nettlebank Copse and Micheldever Wood, both in Hampshire, are prime examples of this site type. The banjo enclosures most likely relate to animal husbandry, though not solely; some banjo sites produce habitation evidence and grain storage pits within the enclosures, such as Micheldever Wood (Fasham 1987, 63). Midden sites appear sporadically across Britain. These site types are typically large accumulations of the by-products of everyday living, which can sometimes be found on a substantial scale. For example, an excavated midden at East Chisenbury (Wiltshire) measured about 200m in diameter, covering close to 3.5-4.0ha (McOmish 1996, 69). These refuse sites provide a plethora of discarded material culture, such as ceramics, animal bones and metal artefacts. The Late Bronze Age to Early Iron Age midden sites in the Vale of Pewsey (Wiltshire), close to All Cannings Cross and Stanton St. Bernard, yielded structural evidence in the form of pits, postholes and platforms, suggesting this particular site may have been the arena of other activity rather than solely a refuse area (Tullet 2008, 15).

Field systems and land divisions are examples of other features found distributed through the landscape. Many of field systems throughout the countryside date to the early to mid-second millennium BC (Fleming 1987, 192; Darvill 2010, 215; Edmonds and Seaborne 2001, 177). In some areas, such as Wessex and the Thames Valley, during the transition from the second to first millennium BC many of these Bronze Age field systems were abandoned (Yates 1999, 158; Field 2008, 216; Hey 2007, 166). In the Upper Thames Valley, substantial land boundaries were constructed in the Early Iron Age and, in some instances, cut through the former field system (Hey 2007, 170). However, the reuse of Bronze Age field systems in the Iron Age may have been widespread across the country (Field 2008, 208).

Settlement morphology may relate to and reflect social organization, leading archaeologists to theorise the social structure of past populations through the remains of their settlement spaces. For example, the excavations at Danebury, led by Barry Cunliffe, suggested that hillforts functioned as the central place of dominance and redistribution, presumably with a hierarchical system of chiefly control. Cunliffe (1983, 44) theorises that the emergence of developed hillforts came about as a product of population pressure, which in turn placed stress on the land, resulting in the need to define territories. He postulates that the abandonment of some hillforts in the Middle Iron Age was in response to the consolidation of power among a handful of highly developed hillforts (Cunliffe 2005, 590). In this sense, these hillforts were production centres: importing material, producing goods, and redistributing materials back to the surrounding sites. The position and placement of the hillforts in the landscape represent a controlling role within their geographical areas (Cunliffe 2005, 390). Large stretches of territories would thus have been under the control of these hilltop fortresses and so would the vast range of resources within the area. It is likely that the surrounding farmsteads would have produced and supplied all the food consumed at the commanding hillfort (Cunliffe 1983, 118).

The central place and redistribution theory has come under fair criticism. Hill (1996) argues that hillforts functioned on a symbolic level - as discussed with settlement enclosures- while Sharples (1991a) asserts that excavation materials derived from other hillforts, such as Maiden Castle, fail to support the central place explanation. In other words, similar settlement forms do not mean similar functions (Toase 2008, 27-28). Twenty years after the proposal of the central place, it is still an often-accepted theory in Iron Age studies, even though the archaeological evidence does not fully support it (Toase 2008, 26). Some areas have few hillforts therefore central place theory may not apply and '...different models which recognize regional variation in the social development of

Iron Age Britain are required' (Morris 1994, 371). It is quite apparent that there can never be a single over-arching explanation for the social dynamics of Iron Age communities, but instead, each new excavation and study simply adds to the complexity of the pre-existing theories for the field.

Settlement sites are formed from a series of archaeological features and structures. The roundhouse is the structure most commonly associate with the Iron Age. In southern Britain, they were constructed from organic materials, most probably wood and turf, whereas in the north, they tended to be stone built (Darvill 2010, 269). Typically, the only surviving evidence of this building type in the ploughed landscape of southern Britain is in the form of drainage gullies that once encircled the structures, a series of postholes aligned in a circular pattern, and, in some instances, only a pair of postholes signifying the entrance (Haselgrove 1999, 117). Other building types, not as common as roundhouses, were rectangular structures represented by postholes and related belowground features. Groups of postholes, numbering between four and six, are also a common occurrence within habitation sites, possibly representing granaries (Gent 1983, 359). Other features that presumably have been employed for grain storage are pits (Reynolds 1974, 129-130). Some pits are massive in size, with a large storage capacity, and are prevalent on certain sites.

Iron Age sites and archaeological features have yielded a wealth of material culture, primarily from pits, ditches/gullies and postholes. The abundance of material remains implies a significant level of production. Hypothetically, there were three levels of production: first, the site level that provided for the household or community; second, production for wider exchange networks; and lastly, the production of goods primarily for the elite or wealthy members of society (Haselgrove 1999, 125; Hill 1995a, 62). Pottery was produced on a massive scale, (Collis 1977e, 29) and this is the most abundant material recovered. By using the quantity and prevalence of ceramic material on sites, one may construct style zones each consisting of '...a defined geographical region within which, in a particular time frame, a distinct range of pottery is commonly in use' (Cunliffe 2005, 83). The regional and material groupings are based on fineware assemblages and the following tables (information derived from Cunliffe 2005, 87-120) provide a synopsis of the ceramic material from most of southern Britain.

Table 1.2 Earliest Iron Age Style Groups (c. 800-600 BC)

Ceramic Groups	Areas
Early All Cannings Cross group	Wessex Chalklands
Later All Cannings Cross group	Wessex Chalklands
Kinneridge-Caburn group	Southern Coast
Highstead group	Kent, Surrey, and north side of the Thames

West Harling-Fegate group	East Anglia
Staple Howe group	Yorkshire
Ivinghoe-Sandy group	West Midlands

Table 1.3 Early Iron Age Style Groups (c. 600-400/300 BC)

Ceramic Group	Area
All Cannings Cross-Meon Hill group	Central Wessex
Park Brow-Caesar's Camp group	South east Britain
Long Wittenham-Allen's Pit group	Upper Thames Valley and Cotswolds
Chinnon-Wandlebury group	Chilterns, north to the Fens and south to the Thames Valley
Damsden-Linton group	Eastern England
Highstead-Dollard Moor group	Kent

Southwest Britain contains too little evidence to create a group

Table 1.4 Middle Iron Age-Late Iron Age Style Groups (c. 400/300-50 BC), each ceramic group contains further divisions based on differing styles (Cunliffe 2005, 103)

Ceramic Group	Area
Saucepan Form	Central south
Highly Decorative Necked Jar Wares	South west
Decorated Bowl	South and East Midlands
Decorated Bulbous Jar	Eastern England

Table 1.5 Style Divisions of the Middle Iron Age-Late Iron Age ceramic groups (Cunliffe 2005, 103-116)[1]

Saucepan Pot Form

Caburn-Cissbury Style	Southcote-Blewburton Hill
St. Catharine's Hill-Worthy Down	Croft Ambrey-Bredon Hill
Yarnbury-Highfield	Lydney-Llanmelin
Hawk's Hill-West Clandon	Glastonbury-Blaise Castle Hill

Decorated Bowl

Satanton Harcourt-Cassington	Hunsbury-Draughton
Miscellaneous decorated bowls	Plain bowls

Decorated Bulbous Jar

Sleaford Dragonby	Mucking-Crawford
Late Caburn-Saltdean	Miscellaneous decorated jars

Other Ceramic Style
Maiden Castle-Marnhull Style

Table 1.6 Late Iron Age Style Groups

Ceramic Group	Area
Aylesford-Swarling group	Eastern Britain and Midlands
Atrebatic group	Southern Britain
Durotrigian group	Dorset
South-Western Cordoned Wares	South west

[1] The table outlines the style groups that are within this research's study area.

Furthermore, Cunliffe (1982; 2005, 103, 588) argues that the stylised pottery groups of the Middle and Late Iron Age, mainly in central and southern Britain, represent ethnic groups. He draws particular reference to the style zones within the hillfort-dominant zone (central and southern coast of Britain extending northwards along the Welch border) (Cunliffe 1982, 168). By the second century BC, the distribution of these ceramic styles appears to respect the tribal boundaries that are known in the first century AD and, thus, may be reflective of these respective ethnic identities (Cunliffe 1982, 168), and this is further backed by coin distributions in the later Iron Age (see Allen 1961). For example, the regional spread of the saucepan pot style closely mimics the area occupied by the Atrebates (Cunliffe 1982, 168).

Collis (1977a; 1977e) highlights some flaws in Cunliffe's claim that later Iron Age ceramic styles could be indicative of tribal groups and ethnic identity. He argues that creating such 'culture' groupings may work for material classification, but that such schemas are related too quickly with tribal affiliations (Collis 1977a, 3). Ceramic styles are found outside their primary distribution area, such as Durotrigian wares within the Dumnonii territory, and this possibly could reflect economic links not political affiliations (Collis 1977a, 4; 1977e, 29). Lastly, our evidence for tribal boundaries is based on sources that post-date the Roman invasion; therefore, there is a question as to how accurately they portray pre-conquest political geography (Collis 1977e, 29). Ceramic styles might have been a forum for expressions of identity; however, how much meaning these items held to the community and their affiliation within a larger tribe cannot be soundly determined. Consequently, attempts to use ceramic styles to determine wider social structure as political affiliation are fraught with difficulty. The material distribution, in essence, may correlate with tribal boundaries but one cannot assert the strength of this connection had on the local and individual level for Iron Age populations.

Relying on pottery as a chronological indicator can be misleading. Particular styles may not be present in some areas (e.g. eastern England), which can lead scholars to assume little or no activity there. Matthew Brundell (2008, 196) elaborates on this subject by arguing that '...profusely decorated assemblages may have existed *alongside* plainware pottery groups in the Early Iron Age, the two types possibly being deposited in different ways and/or places' [Brundell's emphasis]. This highlights how reliance on ceramics as chronological indicators can potentially have a negative impact on tracing site and societal development. In a similar vein, petrological analysis has been crucial in determining the origin of pottery fabric and distinguishing between local and non-local wares (Peacock 1970). The importance of this type of analysis has been demonstrated in studies that have traced the movement of pottery fabrics, such as the ceramic movement between the Herefordshire-Cotswolds and Malvern areas (Peacock 1968), as well as the fact that some of the East Midlands' pottery originally derived from sources in central Leicestershire (Knight *et al.* 2003).

Metal artefacts, iron in particular, are frequently found on Iron Age sites, which indicate a level of industrial activity. Most communities were able to source iron ore within the local region (DeRoche 1997, 20; Darvill 2010, 20; Tylecote 1986, 126-127), whether from mines or from post-ploughing surface collection. The Devon-Cornwall area, for example, may have been the main source of iron ore for communities in Wessex (Hingley 1997, 10, 13). Alternatively, iron, either in the form of scrap or finished goods, may have filtered into the southern area of Britain from continental sources (Northover 1984, 126). Other areas around the country with iron ore sources include the Lower Thames Valley, the Hampshire basin, and the Jurassic cores of the Midlands (Salton and Ehrenrich 1984, 147-149). Areas in Northamptonshire and the Forest of Dean (Gloucestershire) have produced evidence of iron ore exploitation (Haselgrove 1999, 125). The most frequent finished iron goods include brooches, jewellery, tools, weapons and currency bars (Hingley 1990a; 1997, 13; 2006). Moreover, coins begin to become particularly common during the later Iron Age (Allen 1961). Iron objects, however, generally appear most frequently in deposits from the third and second centuries BC (Hingley 1997, 14). This is evident in eastern England where there is a high concentration of fine metalwork and particularly true of Norfolk, where numerous hoards containing a variety of metal objects dating to the later Iron Age have been uncovered (Hill 2007, 21; Hutcheson 2007).

Domestic debris, such as loom weights, spindle whorls and quernstones, is commonly found in pits and enclosure ditches (Haselgrove 1999, 126). Areas in east and southeast England have produced evidence of possible trade of quernstones alongside iron and salt (Hill 2007, 21). Salt production and trade, in particular, is apparent through ceramic salt containers and briquetage assemblages (ceramic debris related to salt production) (Morris 1994, 2007). Salt was probably a much sought-after commodity for its use as a preservative. Evidence implies that salt production was occurring before the Iron Age (Morris 1994, 384), although its production intensified in the Middle Iron Age (Morris 1994, 386). Production sites were along the coast as well as in inland areas near brine spring sources (Morris 2007, 440). For example, evidence of salt production and potential trade is apparent in the Red Hills (Essex) and in the Lincolnshire fenlands (Bryant 1997, 29; Morris 2007).

Much of the excavated material relates to craft production, exchange, and movement of goods throughout Britain. The extent and scale of craft production is suggestive of a hierarchical command system, possibly headed by centralized production and redistribution centres (Cunliffe 2005, 505). Goods no doubt have an economic purpose, but may also have a social one too. Gift exchange, for example, could plausibly explain many instances of craft

movement as an effort to build social and political relationships between communities and individuals (Sharples 2007, 178-179). However goods moved throughout the island, the point to emphasise is that both materials and ideas were in circulation, indicating the inter-connection of communities.

Human remains

The preceding sections have briefly outlined the nature of the Iron Age archaeological record and illustrate the physical world in which Iron Age burial practices operated. The main bulk of published excavation reports are dedicated to describing excavated material, which is important in interpreting the workings of past groups but, in many instances, this amount of attention is not given to burial evidence. Human burials or deposits are typically afforded only a brief description within the body of reports, while the full osteological assessment is relegated to the report's microfiche or to a box deep within the archives. One could argue this being counterproductive since a central goal in archaeology is to investigate past societies and one could argue that it is a bit counterproductive to give little attention to the remains of actual past people.

The focus of the following section is to outline the locations and contexts that contain human remains. It will also address regional groupings within the study area, in terms of the burial rite and their implications. By doing so, it will construct the basis on which to interpret the depositional process of the human remains. A peculiar aspect of the British Iron Age is the near absence of an archaeologically recognisable burial tradition. The archaeological record is overwhelmingly comprised of settlement evidence, thus these 'informal' contexts have produced a limited range of skeletal remains. The estimated population for the entire British Iron Age stands at roughly between two and five million inhabitants (Hill 1995a, 61), and the amount of skeletal material found represents about 6.0 per cent or less of the assumed population (Wait 1985a, 116).

For the Late Bronze Age and Iron Age, the vast majority of recovered skeletal remains are from settlements. In Late Bronze Age contexts, skeletal remains are found typically in states of disarticulation and their deposition favours areas around roundhouses and ramparts/boundaries (Brück 1995, 257). Similarly, for the Iron Age, site boundaries and entrances appear to be favoured locations for the deposition of human remains (Wait 1985a, 98). For example, the western entrance ditches of Sutton Walls, an Iron Age hillfort, contained multiple inhumations (Kenyon 1953, 8). In addition, cremation deposits were found within the main enclosure at Barton Court Farm, a Late Iron Age farmstead, with a further cremation deposit discovered near the entrance of a rectangular enclosure (Miles 1986, 3:B14; 4:C5 [microfiche]). Boundaries between blocks of land or structures were also common places for depositing human remains. A skull and mandible, for example, were set within separate ditches that led into the northwest entrance of Sidbury Hillfort (Wiltshire) (Bradley *et al.* 1994, 41-46). During excavations of a series of linear ditch systems at Windy Dido in Hampshire (as part of the wider Danebury Environs Programme), six teeth and a phalanx were uncovered within the ditch system – although whether this was an intentional or accidental deposit is unclear (Cunliffe and Poole 2000f, 20).

The presence of formal cemetery evidence is extremely uncommon for the period, but a number have been identified in Britain. Most notable are the 'Arras' culture cemeteries of East Yorkshire, famous for the discovery of chariot burials (Stead 1991). An inhumation cemetery (also containing a few cremation burials) was discovered at Mill Hill, in east Kent, with the bodies placed around (and in respect to) a Bronze Age burial mound (Parfitt 1995). The site of Hinxton Quarry, in south Cambridgeshire, yielded a small cremation cemetery, with ring-ditches encircling a few of the cremation deposits (Hill *et al.* 1999). A Middle Iron Age site at Yarnton (Oxfordshire) revealed two separate burial grounds on the periphery of the open settlement (Hey *et al.* 1999, 557). Additionally, the enclosed settlement of Suddern Farm possessed a small cemetery, within an old quarry complex, located on the outskirts of the site (Cunliffe and Poole 2000e). Frequently, contexts such as ditches/gullies, ramparts, occupation assemblages, postholes, and – especially - pits accumulate the highest occurrences of human remains (Wait 1985a, 88). Characteristically, skeletal remains within a deposit are commonly at the basal layer of a context, or intermixed within the fill (Wait 1985a, 83). Remains are not generally found in isolation, many often being associated with animal bones, ceramic material, quernstones, and other domestic debris (Cunliffe 1992, 73). A trend sporadically seen in the burial record, though not to the level of a regional grouping, is burials with swords (Collis 1973). Collis (1973, 131) suggests that burials with weapons represent individuals from a high-economic standing in the community. In addition, such burials often date to the mid-first century BC and are mainly present in Wessex and, particularly, in Yorkshire (Collis 1973, 131). The patterns in the disposal of the dead and its associated material suggest a structured and ritualised deposition practice (Hill 1995b), though the implications of this assertion will be evaluated in the following chapter.

Iron Age human remains are typically found in the following states: as inhumations (both complete and partial), cremations, disarticulated elements or partially articulated bones (Cunliffe 2005, 552). Currently, as a whole, there is not a visible relationship between the sex, age of the deceased, and the condition of the body (Wilson 1981, 145). The most frequently occurring skeletal state is disarticulated elements (notably during both the Late Bronze Age and Early Iron Age) followed by inhumations. In earlier excavation reports, disarticulated remains were seen as either casual or accidental inclusions within the

archaeological record (Wilson 1981, 127). Through further analysis, however, it has become apparent that depositions of disarticulated bones reflect a selective process by which some parts of the skeleton were preferred over others. Indeed, skulls were the most favoured bone for deposition followed by long bones, in particular the femur (Brück 1995, 247; Parker Pearson 1996, 123).

Towards the end of the Early Iron Age and throughout the Middle Iron Age, inhumations begin to become more prevalent in the archaeological record (Wait 1985a, 254). During the Early Iron Age, the site exterior was the principal locality for skeletal deposition, though deposits within the settlement's interior became more frequent during the Middle Iron Age (Wait 1985a, 254). The positioning of inhumed individuals ranges from very loosely flexed to tightly contracted, with placement on either the left or right side (Whimster 1981a, 136); the corpse is seldom extended without any flexion. The orientation of the deceased's head would commonly, but not solely, align to the east and north (Whimster 1981a, 14, 21, 28, 48).

Cremation deposits were typically rare during the Iron Age until the later part of the period, when the Aylesford-Swarling rite emerged during the Late Iron Age in southeast Britain (later in this section, there will be a more detailed discussion of this rite). The Aylesford-Swarling rite is a burial tradition characterised by '...urned cremation burials in small graves with accompanying grave goods and are often found as isolated burials or in flat cemeteries' (Fitzpatrick 1997a, 208). The burial characteristics of the Aylesford-Swarling rite are similar to those of northern France and it is believed that the appearance of Late Iron Age cremation burials in Britain is the result of cross-Channel contact (Fitzpatrick 1997a, 208-209). There are instances of cremation rites, however, prior to the Late Iron Age. For example, at the site of Stone Farm Bridleway (Kent), the grave fills of four inhumations contained a re-deposition of cremated remains dating to the Early/Middle Iron Age (McKinley 2006b). The small amount of burnt bone from Stone Farm Bridleway ranges from 0.7 to 7.7 grams and signifies a distinct secondary burial rite (Riddler *et al.* 2006, 6-7). Lastly, partially articulated remains are characteristic of the Iron Age, but not to the same degree as disarticulated remains and inhumations (Wilson 1981, 133). One example of a partially articulated deposit comes from excavations at New Buildings (Hampshire), part of the Danebury Environs Programme, where a complete human foot, separated at the ankle, was discovered within a disused quarry pit (Cunliffe and Poole 2000d, 79).

Consideration of the nature of skeletal remains implies a strong argument for exposure (excarnation) of the deceased preceding deposition (Carr and Knüsel 1997, 167). Exposure, over varying lengths of time, sufficiently explains the high number of disarticulated bones, as well as the tightly contracted inhumations and the occurrences of partially articulated remains. It is possible that the four-post structures often found on sites may have served as scaffolds for exposure (Carr and Knüsel 1997, 168). However, small bones, such as phalanges, metacarpals, and metatarsals, are rarely found near these structures or within depositions, possibly indicating that this exposure took place at remote locations away from the settlement sites (Wait 1985a, 248). A re-evaluation of osteological material from Gussage All Saints (Dorset) and Maiden Castle revealed that the bones possessed the osteological indicators (gnawing, cut marks, and dry bone fractures) that conform to excarnation and secondary burial practices (Redfern 2008a, 283, 293). Niall Sharples (2010, 289) suggests, alternatively, another means by which disarticulated and articulated remains enter the archaeological record. Burial evidence from Suddern Farm and Cockey Down, both within west Wessex, indicates that '....the reuse of old burials may provide a source for the isolated and partially articulated remains found in pits in enclosures and hillforts' (Sharples 2010, 277). Sharples (2010, 289) elaborates '...that old bones were deliberately sought out to provide bones that could be removed, taken to settlements and subsequently deposited in grain storage pits'.

It may not be an issue on whether decomposition took place above or below ground. Disarticulated bones can derive from both open air and underground means of excarnation; thus, one may argue these are different methods of allowing the corpse to decompose to the state of manageable pieces, as Gillian Carr points out (2007, 447). The variation in skeletal evidence leaves one to think that it is perfectly logical to accept that Iron Age communities implemented various techniques of defleshing a corpse, as opposed to employing only one method of excarnation.

There are three main burial rites that are regionally distinct and fall within the study area of this research (refer back to **Figure 1.1**). The first, outlined by Rowan Whimster (1981a), are the inhumations within central and southern Britain prior to the La Tène III period. This tradition largely concentrates in Wessex and spreads northeast towards East Anglia (Whimster 1981a, 4-30). Within the inhumation tradition, Whimster (1981a) outlines four subgroups based on the contexts containing the burials. These subgroups are as follows: inhumations in pits ('pit-burials'), ramparts and banks, graves, and ditches. The inhumation tradition is a very broad and geographically widespread group and, due to the absence of reliable dates (Whimster 1981a, 5), there lacks a comprehensive understanding in the chronological development. Whimster (1981a; 1981b) provided one of the first extensive studies of Iron Age burial practices (see chapter two), and attempts to understand the funerary rite prior to the later Iron Age. The inhumation tradition of central and southern Britain created a basis for other scholars in the field. A disadvantage, however, in this grouping is that disarticulated bones were not considered in this regional tradition. Human remains are frequently

recovered in the state of disarticulation prior to the later Iron Age and, consequently, their significance is not recognised within this geographical and temporal setting.

The second regional burial rite appears in the Iron Age around the first century BC, clusters along the southern coast of Dorset and is known as the Durotrigian inhumations. The name derives from the tribe, the Durotriges, thought to inhabit the area during this period (Whimster 1981a, 37). Durotrigian inhumations are characterised by formal burial grounds consisting of '...simple earth graves or, more rarely, stone-lined cists' (Whimster 1981a, 37). Pottery vessels (largely pre- and post- Durotrigian ceramic wares) and animal bones typically accompany the inhumation (Whimster 1981a, 40; Collis 1977c, 9), and sites such as Maiden Castle (Wheeler 1943), Owslebury (Collis 1968; 1970; 1977d) and Whitcombe (Whimster 1981a, 40) contain a number of Durotrigian-type burials. Geographically, this burial tradition is restricted to the southern coast of Dorset and is virtually absent in the northern area of this county, as Whimster (1981a, 42) highlights. This regional bias implies that the cohesion amongst the Durotriges may not be as strong as has been traditionally thought, and that there may have existed social differences between its communities (Whimster 1981a, 42).

The last regional burial tradition within the study area is the Aylesford-Swarling cremation rite. This funerary tradition consists of cremation burials in flat graves (either isolated or within a cemetery), with the ashes typically set in cinerary urns, associated with distinctive pottery (typically wheel-made pedestal urns) and other material, such as brooches and coins (Whimster 1981a, 155; Birchall 1964, 22; Stead 1969, 49). The Aylesford-Swarling rite appears in the first century BC and concentrates largely in southeast Britain in Kent and Essex, and expands towards the east into Dorset and Somerset as well as to the north, past the Thames, into Cambridgeshire (Birchall 1964, 21-23; Whimster 1981a, 147). Sites such as Westhampnett (Fitzpatrick 1997a), King Harry Lane (Stead 1969), Aylesford (Evans 1890), and Swarling (Bushe-Fox 1925) are prime examples of the Aylesford-Swarling burial tradition. The emergence of the Aylesford-Swarling cremation rite is thought to be the result of Belgic tribe's colonisation of these areas, and Ian Stead (1976) highlights this continental connection, specifically with Gaul and Italy, from similarities in pottery and brooch types. The prime aspect of this funerary tradition is its sudden appearance in southeast Britain, which is supposedly clear evidence of an incoming continental influence on the manner of disposal (cremation) and associated material culture. With particular reference to the act of cremating a corpse, there is a question of how much this rite can be equated with continental migration. There is evidence of Iron Age communities practising cremation in the southeast prior to the induction of the Aylesford-Swarling tradition (see above). In addition, Carr (2007, 445) suggests that Middle Iron Age customs, such as a period of decomposition prior to burning, may be part of the burial custom. Thus, there is an issue as to what extent the Aylesford-Swarling tradition comprises a purely foreign import, and to what degree local customs filter into this practice.

Each of these three regional traditions highlights key elements in the burial record. Firstly, the inhumation tradition in central and southern Britain shows there remains little understanding of the burial practice prior to the Late Iron Age on a large regional scale. This grouping, furthermore, may be flawed since not all of the burial evidence, in terms of the disarticulated bones, was included in this assessment. Secondly, the Durotrigian inhumation rite signifies there are differences in burial practices between neighbouring communities even though they are considered part of a cohesive group, which leaves a question as to why this may be. Lastly, the Aylesford-Swarling cremation tradition is seen as an indication of external influence and population infiltrating Britain in the Late Iron Age. The discussion, however, raised the issue of a potential native influence in this rite with a local reinterpretation of a continental practice.

There is still an issue of the negative evidence, in respect to the absence of most of the population in the burial record. The 'missing' Iron Age population may be a product of the processing techniques afforded to the deceased. When conducted properly, exposure of the dead, by whatever means, would have resulted in the complete destruction of a skeleton, unless the remains of the body were collected and deposited soon after (Madgwick 2008, 107). However, cremation is also a viable alternative explanation for the lack of skeletal material. In Caesar's account of Gaulish funerary procedures, he states that '[f]unerals are on a large expensive scale...everything which they believe the dead man loved in life is given to the flames' (Caesar quoted in Tierney 1960, 273). Richard Madgwick (2008) suggests that Iron Age populations were practising cremation in an area away from the domestic settlement, and then possibly later giving the burnt leftover remains a watery deposition, which is difficult to prove. Watery contexts produce human remains along with a high frequency of metalwork (Bradley and Gordon 1988; Darvill 2010, 290). Votive deposits of both metalwork and human remains occur in the earlier half of the Iron Age, but display a significant increase in the later part of the Iron Age (Bradley 1998, 161). Unfortunately, votive deposits of human remains are relatively less well understood since the focus has been on the metal artefacts recovered (Bradley 1998, 108; Bradley and Gordon 1988, 503).

The burial evidence - and lack thereof - denotes the complexity of Iron Age burial practices and the community's manipulation of multiple techniques of disposing of the corpse in fulfilment of a cultural rite. To account for the missing burial population, the answer may be as simple as that the burial tradition has yet to be uncovered. In other words, archaeologists might be looking in the wrong areas. The burial areas identified at Suddern Farm and Yarnton imply that it is plausible that there are socially defined places for depositing the dead, though excavations have not discovered them.

Taphonomy, defined as the '...study of processes that operate on organic remains after death to generate archaeological skeletal deposits' (Micozzi 1991, 3), plays a vital role in determining the survival of skeletal remains. Taphonomic processes, either natural or by human intervention, may account for the lack of burial material in the Iron Age, especially if no other bone material (either animal or human bones from other periods) survives. The duration of time needed for a body to skeletonise completely is dependent on the environmental and depositional context (Micozzi 1991, 49). Human bone comprises of protein fibres and mineral crystals; once the soft tissue decomposes, the chemical composition of the surrounding soil affects the remaining skeleton (Trueman and Martill 2002, 371; Micozzi 1991, 53). Therefore, bone survival is dependent on the burial environment (Child 1995, 20). The more acidic the soil (a lower pH), the faster the bone will degrade, as opposed to alkaline soils (with a higher pH) which are better suited for bone survival (Child 1995, 21). Climatic conditions, such as freezing and thawing, or wetting and drying of bone, rapidly increase the speed of breakdown of bone (Child 1995, 21). Consequently, it is important to consider taphonomic processes as a possible reason for the limited amount of skeletal material in the Iron Age.

Summary

The preceding sections have briefly explored the relationship between the environment, subsistence and economic systems, habitation types, and material residues that create the Iron Age archaeological record. The manner and contexts in which skeletal materials have been found indicate complex funerary and depositional processes, of which only a small fraction of the population is represented. To account for the missing population, disposal techniques, missing burial locations, and taphonomic issues have been discussed, but there can only be speculation on this topic. Instead, renewed investigation of the existing skeletal evidence will allow new considerations to emerge concerning Iron Age burial practices.

In addition, this chapter discussed past approaches to regional studies for the Iron Age, largely in terms of material culture (specifically ceramic styles) and burial traditions. An early attempt in a collective, regional study is Hawkes' (1931; 1959) 'ABC' classifications, which relied on a defined material package to indicate migrating populations from the continent and their spread through Britain. Although such an approach to Iron Age studies has been mostly abandoned since the 1960s, the underlying principles to this method persist. One example of this is Cunliffe's (1982; 2005, 103, 588) assertion that later Iron Age ceramic styles represent ethnic groups. The flaws in Cunliffe's argument have been highlighted (see

Collis 1977a; 1977e), but the key element is Cunliffe's attempt to use a particular material to signify a unified people, which echoes back to Hawkes' argument. Furthermore, there is a question in the degree of cohesion amongst larger tribal entities, which has been highlighted by the distribution of the Durotrigian inhumations. On the issue of regional burial groups, the established school of thought for the Aylesford-Swarling rite is that it is a continental tradition implanted into Britain during the first century BC. This idea, however, lacks consideration of the possible native influences and development for this burial practice. For the Late Bronze Age and the earlier Iron Age burial record, there is a lack of a collective understanding for the funerary rites on a regional scale, particularly focusing on the internal development that incorporates all manners of disposal.

Human remains from Iron Age contexts are the product of a series of cultural processes guided by social rules. From this perspective, it is possible to begin to identify the social mechanisms that motivated the processes, and, ideally, discern elements of the cultural make-up of Iron Age communities. Theoretically, this can be accomplished through assessing patterns in the processing and manipulation of the body, identifying areas of deposition, and hypothesising which members of the community the remains represent. Ultimately, this approach will give the technical aspects of Iron Age burial a context, enabling identification of the social processes that created the Iron Age burial record.

Chapter Two

Theoretical context and framework

Introduction

'The archaeological world is a cultural world'
- J.E. Robb (1998, 331), *The Archaeology of Symbols*

The preceding quote embodies the tone of the following discussion. For archaeologists, understanding past cultures is central to every investigation. However, the social meaning behind excavated material is often lost when too much focus is placed on the technical aspects of the physical object, such as explaining the techniques of *how* a pot is decorated as opposed to *why* a pot is decorated in that fashion (Robb 1998, 331). Objects do not define people - people define the objects. The entire archaeological record provides the material residues and contextual setting of the activities of past cultures. For burial practices, the human remains and depositional contexts are central to inferring the ideological and cultural mechanisms of past societies.

The following chapter discusses previous interpretations of the Iron Age burial record. It begins by reviewing past studies of Iron Age burial practices; specifically, it centres on the cornerstone studies that are the foundation for more recent theories on this topic. Lastly, the chapter ends by outlining the theoretical focus of this study.

Previous research in Late Bronze Age and Iron Age burial practices

The following section discusses previous research and interpretations in Late Bronze Age and Iron Age burial practices. It begins by explaining early works that were a major contribution to this area of study. Chief among these early works are Catherine E. Wilson's and Rowan Whimster's publications in the early 1980s. Additionally, the discussion will also include details of Gerald Wait and J. D. Hill's studies that are also strong influences on current research into Iron Age burial practices. Subsequently, the section continues to outline other works on Iron Age burial practices that illustrate main themes important to our interpretation of the burial record.

To begin, in the early 1980s Catherine E. Wilson's (1981) *Burials within Settlements in Southern Britain during the Pre-Roman Iron Age* compiles a comprehensive overview of the burial evidence in southern Britain. The study investigates the burial evidence from fifty-three sites, which include both settlements and hillforts. The main objective for Wilson's (1981, 161) research was to provide a relatively extensive study of the evidence in order to define the treatment of the dead and its related practices. The research set down a series of dominant disposal trends that make up the burial record (see chapter one for details on the burial record). Additionally, Wilson focuses on the varying means of disposal in order to identify a native burial tradition and explain the reasons for the differential treatment of the corpse. According to her survey, crouched inhumations are the most frequent burial type in the archaeological record (Wilson 1981, 162). In addition, the sex of an individual did not appear to influence the disposal methods for the complete burial group (Wilson 1981, 145). Wilson's evidence suggests that there was an attempt to keep the body whole and, thus, segments of articulated remains represent a type of insult to the deceased (Wilson 1981, 133). As for disarticulated bone, there are a small number of instances of this disposal method in Wilson's sample (Wilson 1981, 131). Wilson further explains that if one leaves aside infant burial, massacre, Roman and other 'doubtful' sites, the number of instances of disarticulated bone is considerably lower (Wilson 1981, 133). She reasons, thus, that disarticulated bones are not a main characteristic of the Iron Age burial record (Wilson 1981, 133).

In the same year as Wilson's study, Rowan Whimster (1981a; 1981b) published his *Burial Practice in Iron Age Britain: a discussion and gazetteer of the evidence c. 700 B.C. - A.D. 43*. From this work came an exhaustive catalogue of all 'formal' deposits of human remains from mainland Britain (Whimster 1981a, 2). The study incorporates all the archaeological evidence from reports published up to 1976. In his investigation, Whimster (1981a, 2-3) collects and records information pertaining to the treatment, posture and orientation of the remains, the shape and size of graves, and the size and locale of burial grounds. Whimster's (1981a) study also includes site details, such as the site type, and contextual materials, such as artefacts associated with human remains. Furthermore, Whimster's (1981a) investigation describes a series of geographical areas relating to types of burial practice (see chapter one). Another example of these geographical areas, not outlined previously in chapter one, is the La Tène burial tradition in East Yorkshire. The East Yorkshire burials date to the middle and later part of the Iron Age, and are characterised by inhumations cemeteries with many burials under barrows (Whimster 1981a, 75-128).

Both Wilson and Whimster's works provide the foundations for future studies in British Iron Age burial practices. In reference to Whimster's work, no other study rivals its comprehensive nature and it remains one of the most frequently cited sources for Iron Age burial practices. However, both studies follow the academic practice of the time by outlining and defining burial traditions, and lack an in-depth investigation into the social mechanisms motivating these burial practices. These studies, consequently, use the burial evidence to draw comparisons between depositional traditions in order to produce arbitrary and static 'culture' group categories. In addition, the studies lack full exploration into the chronological context for human remains deposits. This academic approach does not adequately investigate the complexity of burial practices in the social sense. Hence, the changing social context of Iron Age societies does not appear to be a strong factor in their conclusions.

After Wilson and Whimster's early works, Gerald Wait (1985a; 1985b) published *Ritual and Religion in Iron Age Britain*, which serves as the next major contribution to our knowledge of Iron Age burial customs. Wait's (1985a; 1985b) study centres on an assessment of human remains deposited within settlement sites. The study evaluates twenty-eight domestic sites - ten hillforts and eighteen settlements - in southern Britain, of which twenty-two contained skeletal materials (Wait 1985a, 88). As with most of the Iron Age, Wait's (1985a, 116) sample produced a small amount of human remains. Given the low frequency of bones, excarnation or cremation is theorised to be the preferred burial rite for the majority of the population, both of which would leave little to no archaeological trace (Wait 1985a, 116). Furthermore, the processing of the corpse likely occurred away from domestic sites, accounting for the lack of skeletal material in the archaeological record. In chronological terms, Wait (1985a, 116) identifies a correlation between the disposal treatment of human remains and locations of their deposition. The amount of the corpse present in the record increases through time whiles the location of the deposits move towards the interior of the site (Wait 1985a, 116). The archaeological evidence from the studied sites points to a change in the burial custom around the Middle Iron Age, indicated by the increase in inhumation burials. The rise in numbers of inhumations may be due to a decrease in the amount of time allotted for decomposition during exposure, possibly suggesting a reduction in time of the transitional period for the dead (Wait 1985a, 255).

Wait (1985a, 118-119) proposes three possibilities for the identity of the human remains. The first is that the skeletal material represents political elite, which he believes to be an unlikely possibility (Wait 1985a, 118). He argues against Iron Age human remains being elites because there is a lack of elaborate rites and their burials are not set in 'special' places (Wait 1985a, 118). Furthermore, Wait (1985a, 118) asserts that all elite individuals usually receive the same burial rite, which the variability of the Iron Age burial record does not support. The flaw in this reasoning is that Wait assumes *all* elites will have elaborate and special burial areas and fails to consider that

Iron Age communities may not have expressed their status in this fashion (Ucko 1969, 266, 268). Additionally, he asserts that if these were elites, then there would not be such variability in the burial practices, but this assertion assumes a universal and singular culture for all of Iron Age Britain and does not consider individual groups' reinterpreting and changing their burial tradition.

The second possibility for the identity of human remains is that they were the victims of sacrifice, which Wait also finds unlikely, except for a few possible examples from hillforts (Wait 1985a, 119). He reasons that their explanation as sacrificial victims may account for complete inhumations in hillfort boundaries and foundation burials, but does not account for the high number of infant inhumations (Wait 1985a, 119). Wait (1985a, 119) explains that infants '...appear to be uncommon victims' for sacrifice. Additionally, the possibility of sacrifice does not adequately explain complete inhumations uncovered on rural farmsteads where the social context, Wait (1985a, 119) reasons, does not seem an appropriate scenario for ritualised violence. Lastly, the human material may be from '...those whose lifestyle and death was in some manner abnormal', which appears to be the most likely possibility (Wait 1985a, 119). He figures that the human remains are of those who were social outcasts (criminals, witches, religious heretics, and so on) because this segment of the population typically does not receive the normal burial rite (Wait 1985a, 119). Social outcasts, furthermore, typically receive a variety of different burial treatments and their remains are generally associated with a community's refuse, which Wait (1985a, 119-120) asserts explains adequately the Iron Age burial record. Although Wait's study did not intend to be a comprehensive investigation, it marks a change in the interpretative approach to burial practices. The study signals the emergence of a contextual assessment of Iron Age burial evidence, as well as the theorising the cultural implications and ideological views from the method of processing the corpse. In addition, Wait's study addresses the chronological change in the burial practice. However, Wait's study includes only sites from Wessex and, therefore, his findings may not relate to areas outside Wessex during the Iron Age.

Another influential study is J.D. Hill's (1995b) work, *Ritual and Rubbish in the Iron Age of Wessex: a study on the formation of a specific archaeological record*. Hill's study differs from the previous three studies in that the assessment focuses on the contextual nature of deposition as opposed to focusing on the burial practices. It consists of a critical examination of the accumulation of depositional fills in order to interpret the archaeological record and, in essence, moves away from asserting hypothetical assumptions about the formation of the archaeological record (Hill 1995b, 2).

Hill's (1995b, 101) main argument is that the deposits are ritualistic because of the structured nature of, and lengthy time gaps between, deposits. Additionally, Hill (1995b,

79) describes the symbolic nature of ritual deposits because of their location within the site and, from these, outlines four variables that dictate their placement:

A concern with the direction of the rising sun, east, and other cardinal points of the compass.
A distinction between the inside and outside of the enclosure
A distinction between the front and back of the enclosure
Emphasis on the threshold.

Furthermore, he illustrates how settlement enclosures function as symbolically defining boundaries. The interpretation largely rests on the patterning in settlements' orientation. In his assessment, there was a distinct preference for structure orientations to the east, southeast and west (Hill 1996, 103). The placement of ritual deposits at the threshold and in spatially divided areas reinforces the symbolic separation between the known and unknown, or liminal areas (Hill 1995b, 6). Hill (1996, 109) argues that the elaboration of entranceways into hillfort sites best illustrates the symbolic emphasis placed on thresholds.

Hill (1995b, 105) asserts that the treatment of human remains within ritual deposits parallels that of animal remains. He argues that the assessments of the skeletal material cannot be independent from the other associated material, or the human bone given special recognition (Hill 1995b, 100). Overall, Hill's (1995b) investigation presents a strong argument for the ritualistic nature of deposits based on the long periods between depositions, and highlights the need to take into account the social meanings of these contexts. However, similar to Wait, Hill's study sample includes just a handful of sites, mainly from Hampshire, restricting the study to a small area and the same findings may not be universal for all of Britain. Furthermore, Hill (1995b, 105) argues that human remains should not be assessed separately from their associated material. It is apparent, however, that there is differential treatment of human remains in the Iron Age and it is essential to investigate why certain human bones are found within structured deposits and what differentiates them from other burial contexts. Without losing the contextual setting, it is necessary to explore what the human material contributed to this ritual practice and to define its meaning.

The approaches to Iron Age burial practices since Wilson (1981), Whimster (1981a-b), Wait (1981a-b), and Hill (1995b) rely upon the social interpretation of ritual deposits. Current studies into Iron Age burial practices focus on aspects of the creation of human remains deposits and offer various explanations. For example, the skeletal material from the midden site at Potterne (Wiltshire) shows that human bones went through a lengthy process of manipulation by the living prior to deposition (Waddington 2008, 154). The osteological assessment reveals indicators of weathering and polishing of the skeletal material (Waddington 2008, 154). Evidence from Potterne, for both human remains and other associated material, hints at the site functioning as more than an area for refuse: it was also a place for social reproduction for the community (Waddington 2008, 162). The vertical stratigraphy of the midden, as well as the accumulated material, signals the changing significance of the site. The complex, repeated, and lengthy processes that human remains and associated material underwent indicates that Potterne was a place of communal activities that relate to the identity of the society as a whole.

In addition, recent studies have focused on the reassessment of skeletal material from past excavations. For example, Rebecca Redfern (2008a) has conducted an osteological re-examination of the human remains from Maiden Castle and Gussage All Saints, both in Dorset, in order to identify indicators for excarnation and secondary burial treatment. The findings from the study reveal that skull and long bone elements meet the osteological criteria, such as animal gnawing, for excarnation and secondary burial (Redfern 2008a, 293). Redfern's study indicates the need for reassessment of the skeletal material, especially from older excavations, to take account of recent advances in osteological techniques. These reassessments of skeletal material allow a more concrete history of the processes that affected the osteological remains before deposition.

The processing of the corpse may connect to how the individual was viewed by society, thus theoretically explaining the variety of burial practices seen in a community (Madgwick 2008, 111). In his study of the skeletal material from Winnall Down (Hampshire) and Danebury (Hampshire), Richard Madgwick (2008) argues that the length of time allowed for the body to decompose relates to the social standing of that person. Madgwick (2008, 111) reasons that the time allotted for decomposition reflects the length of the liminal transitional period given to the deceased. He suggests that the articulated remains from Winnall Down and Danebury are those of social outcasts, since these individuals were not given the same length of time for decomposition as those represented by disarticulated bones (Madgwick 2008, 111). His study denotes that animal remains were exposed more than the human material, thereby implying that the human material was processed differently from animal remains (Madgwick 2008, 107). Madgwick's (2008, 108) study also theorises that exposure occurred in a very controlled environment, probably subterranean, given the lack of excarnation indicators on the human remains. Since the skeletal material only represents a fraction of the estimated living population, Madgwick (2008, 108) suggests the remainder of the population were either exposed or cremated, and then received an aquatic deposition, a process which would have left no trace in the archaeological record. Though Madgwick's conclusions are highly speculative and require further investigation, the study offers an insightful look into how the processing of the deceased may hint at the culture's perception of the deceased's personal identity. However, to re-establish a personal identity can be very problematic in archaeology. A person's identity within a society is highly contextual and relates to specific social interaction and events (Fowler 2004, 3). The cultural system guides a person's actions and sets the social environment within which the individual operates.

In a similar vein, the individual's participation within a ritual process, like burial, is important for continuously recreating a sense of communal and personal identity. 'The role of rituals in the creation of belonging is suggested by the fact that social integration and a sense of unity are among the most noted outcomes and functions of ritual' (Marshall 2002, 360). The 'identity' of individuals is constantly developing and evolving within the social environment that communicates through the ritual process (Pred 1986, 7). Thus, one may assert that the material remains of an action combined with the continuity of human action within a space, aids in reconstructing the development of both communal and individual identity.

Moving away from the concept of identity, violence and warfare in Iron Age societies is another possible explanation for human remains deposits in the Iron Age archaeological record. Historical accounts (Caesar, Diodorus, and Strabo; in Tierney 1960) describe the violent behaviour of Iron Age people. A study by Craig, Knüsel and Carr (2005) re-examines the skeletal material from Danebury in an attempt to argue that some skeletal deposits may be the result of violent deaths, mutilation, and exhibition of the deceased. The data, however, in the reassessment did not conclusively support their hypothesis. The percentage (7.9 per cent) of the remains possessing evidence of violence is inadequate to fully support their interpretation, and further study may benefit from larger samples gathered from more sites (Craig *et al.* 2005, 170-174). Similarly, Redfern (2008b) investigates the extent to which warfare was a part of Iron Age life, as well as evidence for violence on female skeletons. In this study, the skeletal evidence from Maiden Castle reveals traumatic indicators on female skeletons, suggesting that Iron Age women were active participants in episodes of violence (Redfern 2008b, 149). Though interpretations concerning violence and warfare only relate to a small segment of the skeletal material, it does offer an alternative explanation.

From the extensive excavations at Danebury, Barry Cunliffe (1992; 1995; 2005) suggests that 'special deposits' (those containing human and animal remains) within pits represent a type of offering. Cunliffe (1995, 78) further explains that the variability in the state of the human remains signifies whether the individuals are internal or external members of the society. Those from the external world, he reasons, are represented by skulls, which are enemy trophies, and complete inhumations (excluding infants) are sacrifice victims (Cunliffe 1995, 75, 77). He argues that complete inhumations are victims of sacrifice because of the lack of depositional difference between Danebury's inhumations and Lindow man, an Iron Age sacrifice victim found in a bog (Cunliffe 1995, 75; see Stead *et al.* 1986). Partial bodies, infant inhumations, and isolated bones (other than skulls) represent individuals from the internal world of the community (Cunliffe 1995, 78). The contextual evidence for isolated bones, Cunliffe (1995, 77) suggests, indicated that these are casual losses. Infant burials within the settlement are separate from the normal burial rite because they were not viewed as human yet by the society (Cunliffe 1995, 78). In turn, partial bodies represent the ancestors of the community brought in from the excarnation fields (Cunliffe 1995, 76). All of the skeletal deposits, both the remains from the internal and external world, were propitiatory offerings (Cunliffe 1995, 78). He reasons that the majority of pits at Danebury functioned as storage facilities for grain, and human remains within pits were offerings to ensure fertility (Cunliffe 1992, 82). This interpretation illustrates how the purpose of an archaeological feature, with related ritual deposits, can contribute to defining the meaning of a depositional act. For Cunliffe's (1992; 1995; 2005) assessment, the interpretation is well reasoned. However, it is also too simplistic of an argument to explain fully the social workings of depositional practice. The fertility explanation as the motivation behind a particular action tends to become too generic and offers few avenues towards further understanding of Iron Age society.

Another concept, the 'agriculture metaphor', rests on the organisation and placement of granaries and storage pits, which contain ritualistic deposits (Williams 2003). The metaphor draws parallels between the life/death dualistic divide of space within roundhouses and settlements and the unending cyclicity of an agriculture year (Williams 2003). The agriculture metaphor, in conjunction with the fertility approach, illustrates how burial deposits are a marriage between contents, context, and function, and how these components work to define one another. Through the transformation process, all three are ascribed new meanings within the ritualistic process. Though insightful, the concept of the agriculture metaphor is susceptible to the same critiques as the fertility interpretation, insofar as it is too generic and fails to account adequately for the observed variation in burial and depositional patterns. The agriculture metaphor explanation does not encompass all contexts of disposal (i.e. ditches and postholes), and may not be suitable for such contexts.

Adam Gwilt (1997) suggested a similar concept to the fertility argument based on his research on the site Wakerley in Northamptonshire. One aspect of Gwilt's study (1997) focused on the enclosures and their associated depositional processes with certain materials. One type of material in particular is bead-rimmed carinated bowls, which are associated often with Aylesford-Swarling cremation burials (Gwilt 1997, 160). At Wakerley, in a former enclosure ditch (Enclosure B), which may have been a stock enclosure (Jackson and

Ambrose 1978, 122), are high concentrations of broken carinated bowls as well as infant burials (Gwilt 1997, 160; Jackson and Ambrose 1978). Gwilt (1997, 160) suggests a relationship between the carinated bowls and death, emphasised by the infant burials, and its insurance for communal success through the productivity of the herd.

Alternatively Niall Sharples (2010, 277) argues that, in some areas of Wessex, disarticulated bones on settlements may be the result of the deliberate re-excavation of older graves. Using Suddern Farm and Cockey Down as examples, he elaborates that the reuse of burials for the selected retrieval of bones signifies access to the ancestors of the community (Sharples 2010, 289). These actions, therefore, reflect the communities' perception of personhood, and signify that the individual was not highly valued (Sharples 2010, 289). In other words, '[t]he individual was no more than a fragment of that community' (Sharples 2010, 290). Complete burial, in contrast, represents individuals excluded from the group of ancestors, possibly because they violated social rules (Sharples 2010, 290-291, 300).

The contextual nature of a deposit is central for interpreting ritual depositions. The location of ritual deposits within the settlement, or structure, can potentially inform us about other aspects of the society's cultural mentality. For example, in an investigation of the deposition of Iron Age currency bars, Richard Hingley (1990a, 95) argues that past scholars viewed currency bars as functional objects without any regard to their social or symbolic significance. The predominant location for currency bar deposits was close to boundary earthworks. Hingley (1990a, 98) suggests the placement of currency bars in these locations may work to define liminal spaces. What Hingley's study highlights is the risk of applying personal or modern definitions to objects, and the danger of ascribing a single function to objects when that may not have been the case. In essence, the intentional placement of an object into a new context may redefine the object's meaning for that society. In such cases, the repetition of the depositional action is necessary for its recognition.

Two studies by Joanna Brück (1995; 1999) illustrate how the locations of human remains influence the meaning of the depositional act. Brück's (1995; 1999) studies discuss evidence from the British Middle to Late Bronze Age, yet show the progression of the theoretical framework in Iron Age depositional practices. The later Bronze Age archaeological record, similar to that of the Iron Age, consists largely of settlement evidence and replaces one that used to consist mainly of henges and barrows (Brück 1995, 245). Bronze Age skeletal remains are found in similar contexts to those of the Iron Age: the majority are within boundary and entrance contexts (Brück 1995, 261; 1999, 153). The placements of these deposits in such spaces indicate the marking of liminal places, and the skeletal remains are reasoned to be symbols signifying areas of transition from the unknown to the known (Brück 1999, 154, 158). In the broader sense, this also shows how

a space influences meaning ascribed to the human bones deposited in these areas.

Human remains may function to symbolise core aspects of a social belief system (Chapman 1994, 48). The meaning of a place in correlation with symbolic activity reflects the social constructs of place and activity. Additionally, the temporal context in which an activity occurred is of great importance (Chapman 1994, 54). Ian Armit and Victoria Ginn (2007) illustrate such a concept in their assessment of human remains from Iron Age domestic contexts in Scotland. Their investigation of thirty-seven sites reveals that roundhouse structures were often associated with deposits of human remains, and treatment of the skeletal material is similar to that found in southern Britain (Armit and Ginn 2007, 115, 126). In the contextual and locational analysis, they suggest that the depositions did not merely define liminal areas within a structure or site, but mark liminal moments (Armit and Ginn 2007, 125). The liminal moments refer to the construction, renovation, or abandonment of a structure; thus, the transition between fixed states. The concept of liminality in conjunction with temporal and spatial framing of an action provides a different avenue for consideration - it offers one further variable needed to reconstruct accurately the social conditions that provoked the depositional act.

The material residues of an action within a structure communicate the ordering of a society's routine (Barrett 1989, 305). The organisation of activities within Middle Bronze Age settlements, and the consequential material residues, suggests that the lifecycles of the inhabitants and the settlement were interrelated (Brück 1999, 158). The roundhouse, in this instance, symbolically represents the manner in which the community perceived the world and universe, and could hypothetically dictate the organisation of activities within these spaces (Brück 1999, 158). Habitation structures reflect society's view of the world and the functioning social system. The structure organises the activities that take place within it and, in turn, these repetitive actions define the form and components of the structure (Hingley 1990b, 125).

Past research (Fitzpatrick 1994; 1997; Parker Pearson 1999a; Parker Pearson and Richards 1994b) suggests that Iron Age society was symbolically structured and ordered with reference to solar movements and cosmological referents. The basis for this idea is that the onset of roundhouse construction in the Bronze Age coincides with the cessation of monument building, and implies that roundhouses adopted the symbolic and ideological significance that circular monuments (such as henges and stone and wood circles) once represented (Fitzpatrick 1997, 77). Furthermore, Iron Age societies on the Continent were constructing rectangular structures, yet Britain held on to the tradition of curvilinear architecture. This action could signify a deeper connection to this roundhouse style, and the possible social values it represented (Hingley 1990b, 133). Roundhouses may have been a continuation of the circular monuments, with the ritualistic meanings transferred to the domestic sphere.

The excavations carried out at the Early Iron Age roundhouse at Dunston Park, Thatcham (Berkshire) reveal how activities within a space adhered to the cosmological referents (Fitzpatrick 1994). They revealed the orderliness of the material distribution within the roundhouse. The right, or 'clean', side of the structure (as one enters) yielded few remains, while the left, or 'dirty', side produced a variety of material debris associated with different categories of domestic activity (Fitzpatrick 1994, 68). The easterly orientation of the roundhouse and the distribution of material illustrate how architecture, and the organisation of activities within the space, incorporates cosmological referents in ordering domestic life (Fitzpatrick 1994, 69).

Entrance orientation data from both settlement enclosures and roundhouses hint at a symbolic relationship with cosmological referents. The entrance orientations may possibly define the movement and organisation of activities within these structures and, thus, the central focal point for movement within the structure (Fitzpatrick 1997, 77). The predominance and uniformity of roundhouse doorways being oriented to the east and southeast signify that social orderings were mimicking the movements of the sun (Parker Pearson 1999a; Parker Pearson and Richards 1994b, 47). The homogeneity of these structures' orientations has been investigated to offer a possible environmental explanation to the pattern (McOmish 1996). However, the study shows that the entrances' orientation did not rely on favourable environmental conditions within the location, and that a more socially related explanation for this pattern is needed to understand this practice (McOmish 1996, 92).

Segregation of activities in domestic structures and the patterning they produced relate to how daily human actions define and manipulate the space and its meaning (Parker Pearson and Richards 1994a, 5). Meanings attributed to a space are not static, but change through time. The recurrences and variations of material deposits in these spaces highlight the development of and redefine the meanings given to this context (Parker Pearson and Richards 1994a, 6). Many structures in this period followed this binary separation, suggesting that the threshold was central to the organisation of space, especially considering the frequencies of foundation deposits and burials, associated with entrances (Hill 1996, 103). Doorways dictated the movement into the dwelling, and were the start and end of the cyclicity of the actions performed within which defined the space.

Alternatively, Rachel Pope (2007) argues that the cosmological argument with the right/left divide is over-used. She further asserts that this concept rests on just a handful of site evidence, yet is applied universally (Pope 2007, 206, 210). Instead, Pope (2007, 221) proposes there is variation in roundhouse spatial organisation, but with

two main trends. The first trend is the use of the front, for daily activities, and of the back for sleeping and storage (Pope 2007, 221). The second trend is the difference between the centre, which is the focus of activity, and the periphery, which is the area for livestock, farming and craftwork (Pope 2007, 221).

Similarly, Leo Webley (2007d) investigated the validity of the right/left organisation argument. In his study, Webley (2007d, 132) focused on the life history and depositional patterns of artefacts from nine, Late Bronze Age/Early Iron Age roundhouses from southern England. His findings indicate that while the building was in use, the food preparation area was on the right side of the structure (upon entering) based on the location of clay-lined pits, which is a contradiction to the original right/left argument (Webley 2007d, 141-142). Moreover, the accumulation of artefacts on the left-half of a roundhouse (as one enters) occurred after the structure went out of use; thus, were the product of structured depositional practices that are part of a post-abandonment rite, not daily life (Webley 2007d, 141).

In summary, this synopsis of past research illustrates the variations in the interpretation of the burial and archaeological record for the British Iron Age. Approaches to Iron Age burial patterns incorporate a number of themes to explain and understand the variability of mortuary practice. These themes include fertility offerings, signification of liminal moments and areas, victims of violence, and representation of different forms of identity. The theoretical themes are important elements and provide a general basis for understanding social processes in Iron Age culture. In essence, current approaches show that deposits of human remains represent more to the community than the physical remains of the deceased individual. However, the current explanations of Iron Age burial practices run the risk of becoming overarching and potentially restrictive for further interpretation of the burial practices. Armit (2007, 127) stresses that no overarching theme would be sufficient to categorise and explain all the cultural implications of the various manners in which the dead were treated. Additionally, most Iron Age research has been too site-specific, and has failed to place site studies within their wider geographical context (Haselgrove *et al.* 2001, 17).

Thus, investigation is needed into the variations of Iron Age burial practices in order to illustrate the individuality of the community and the characteristics thereof. It has been nearly thirty years since the works of Wilson (1981), Whimster (1981a-b) and Wait (1985a-b), and Iron Age studies are in need of a reassessment of the burial evidence across a large geographical area. What is necessary is to expand on the current understanding of Iron Age burial practice by incorporating a more in-depth focus into the study of the social mechanisms that motivated the living to dispose of their dead in particular ways.

Theoretical focus

Burial ritual is a social process that is the culture's response to death (Metcalf and Huntington 1991, 62). Death triggers particular actions that the living performs collectively on the deceased. The living are the major actors in the burial process (Parker Pearson 1999b, 3). They perform the burial rite to satisfy a particular social need brought on by death and, thus, the act is reflective of the living society (Goldhahn 2008, 63; Parker Pearson 1993). Therefore, the archaeological remains of this process '...link the treatment of the dead to other aspects of social life' (Parker Pearson 1999, 145). The burial record from the British Iron Age depicts a variety of actions performed on the dead. Through the processing of the corpse, the living manipulated the deceased's body, which in turn became an object with socially specific meaning. In other words, the transformation rite led to '...the removal of one identity and emergence of another' (Fowler 2004, 80). Potentially, the subsequent human remains symbolise something beyond their material composition. Whether this be a reflection of the living's view of the deceased, or its meaning could transcend the individual's identity and represent a more abstract concept. To determine this, it is key to uncover the social motivation behind the act. The variation in the Iron Age burial record, however, precludes any one universal explanation. Human bones, thus, may have different meanings and significance to different societies, and even within the same group (Goldstein 1981, 54). In addition to this, culture in itself is always changing and developing along different avenues and it follows that this change impacts the burial rites.

On the basic level, there are three components in the treatment of the dead central to this study: the processing of the corpse (action), human remains (physical product of the action), and spatial setting. These three elements, and associated characteristics, are the cornerstone in identifying geographic and temporal patterns. All of which relate to the social context that the living acted within to produce said burial record. Thus, the following study seeks to achieve more than describing and outlining the actions the living performed on the dead, but to also explore the impact this process had on the living. From an archaeological perspective, it is often very difficult to reconstruct the social context of burial rites and to determine their underlying motivation. Only the skeletal material and spatial context remain in the archaeological record as indicators of the past action. These two components, therefore, are central in reconstructing the act of deposition. The bones and spatial setting, furthermore, are also instrumental in identifying the changing nature of burial rites through their repetition.

In sum, centring the focus of the study on these three elements allows for a macro and micro - comparison of the burial record. The archaeological evidence suggests a common burial tradition shared by Iron Age societies influenced by local traditions; thus, the investigation will be able to address the inter-relationship between communities and their perception of the burial rite on a geographical scale. This approach will serve to demonstrate *why* burial practices were conducted in a particular fashion on the site level, as well as illustrating how the practice develops in relation to other communities on the regional scale.

Chapter Three

Methodology

Introduction

Central to archaeology is the material unearthed from excavations, but archaeology is not as simple as just recording what evidence is present and what it not. The archaeologist's challenge lies in the various processes by which we turn material remains into accurate narratives of past societies. The critical and quantified analysis of the data is the foundation for all interpretation. This study's conclusions rely on the burial evidence from a sample of sites within the studied geographical area. The data for this investigation comprise of particular burial traits from excavated sites. The following chapter details the specific burial traits used for data, the methods of data collection, statistical analyses employed, and outlines the approach used to identify regional patterns from the gathered information. Additionally, it briefly outlines the approach for interpreting the results from the statistical and quantitative analyses as well as the reasons for employing ethnographic studies.

Site selection

The investigation began by composing a list of Iron Age sites meeting particular requirements. The first requirement is that the sites included in the study must date between the Late Bronze Age (1150 BC) and the Late Iron Age (100 BC-AD 43). Within this time span, sites may be either single or multi-period. In addition, it is required that excavations must be complete with an accompanying report (whether published or unpublished). There is no preference for site form; all types such as domestic settlements, cemeteries, and field systems were included in the study. Furthermore, sites must also lie within the geographical boundary that stretches from the south of England up to South Yorkshire (see **Figure 3.1**). Finally, the main stipulation is that the included sites *must* contain human remains. The amount of skeletal evidence from the excavations is not a determining factor for site selection; the quantity of skeletal material may range from one disarticulated bone to an entire cemetery.

Three main search avenues identified sites possessing the preceding requirements. The first line of enquiry is through academic publications that reference specific sites containing human remains (for example Wait 1985a). In addition, within the burial discussion of many site reports, authors make special note of skeletal evidence from other neighbouring sites, all of which are included in this study's site list (for example see Timby *et al.* 2007 and Evans 2008). The second search avenue is the Archaeology Data Service (http://ads.ahds.ac.uk/). By searching into individual archaeological agencies on the

Archaeology Data Service (ADS), the study was able to obtain unpublished, salvage excavation reports (also known as 'grey literature'). The last search engine is Heritage Gateway, which consists of a county-by-county search. In Heritage Gateway, the search was restricted to show only Late Bronze Age and Iron Age sites that contain 'Religious Ritual and Funerary' evidence. Ultimately, these search procedures produced the final site list that consists of 404 sites (as of 2009) within the studied area.

The study's objective is to interpret the cultural intent behind Late Bronze Age and Iron Age mortuary practice and discern potential regional patterns. This was done by investigating who the dead were and how they were processed, as well as where they were deposited within the site. Therefore, a large sample of Iron Age sites containing human remains was needed for the analysis. Initially (and ideally) all 404 were to be analysed, but it quickly became apparent that owing to time constraints this would be unrealistic. Therefore, from the site list, the analysis includes a sample selection of one hundred sites (roughly 25 per cent, see **Figure 3.2**). These sites had to adequately represent the geographical area and time periods under investigations. Additionally, it was necessary to include a respectable number of thoroughly investigated sites (which have formed the base of prevailing Iron Age burial interpretations) along with less well-known or 'new' sites. Furthermore, factors of source availability and the quality of information within reports

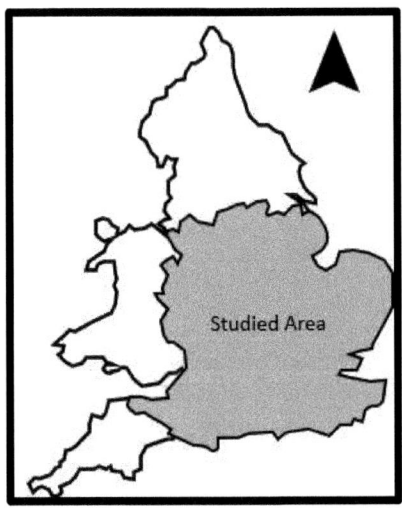

Figure 3.1 Map of Britain indicating the geographical boundaries of the study highlighted in grey (also see Figure 1.1)

were crucial in the site selection process. Thus, purposive selection ('judgement') sampling was employed to select sites for analysis. This type of sampling allows one to '...define obvious criteria of relevance, and use these criteria as a basis for picking a manageable number of intrinsically important observations' (Mueller 1975 quoted in Baxter 2003, 43), which produces a representative sample of sites that is adequate for the research objective.

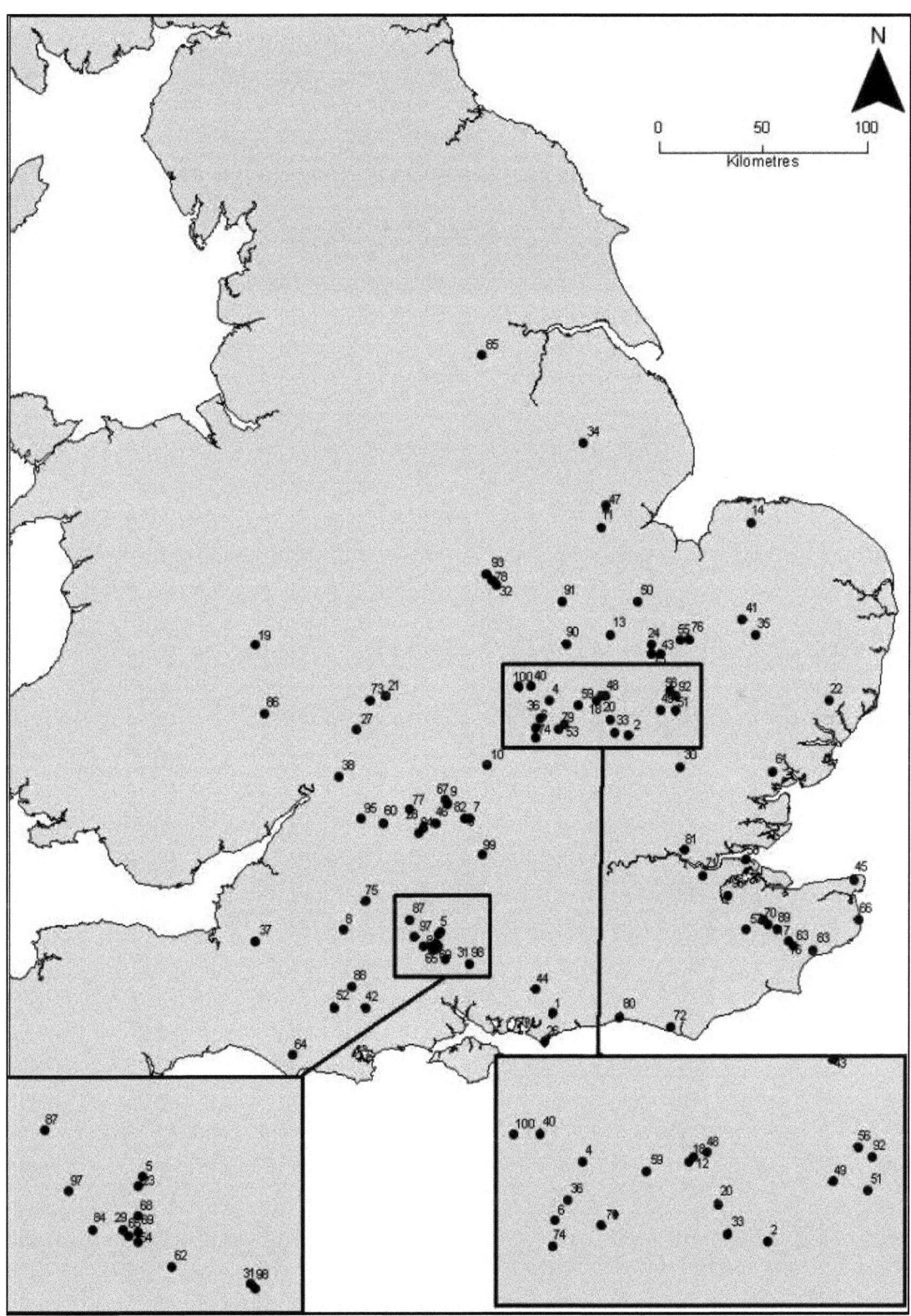

Figure 3.2 Map indicating the 100 sites studied (with Table 3.1)

Table 3. 1 List of sites studied

1	A27 Westhampnett	51	Hinxton Quarry (IA Cemetery)
2	A505 Baldock Bypass	52	Hod Hill
3	Ashville	53	Home Farm
4	Aspreys, Olney	54	Houghton Down
5	Balksbury Camp	55	Hurst Lane Reservoir
6	Bancroft	56	Hutchinson
7	Barton Court Farm	57	Jubilee Corner
8	Battlesbury Bowl	58	Kingsmead Park
9	Beard Mill, Stanton Harcourt	59	Land off Bromham Road
10	Bicester Fields Farm	60	Latton Lands
11	Billingborough	61	Layer-de-la-Haye
12	Birchfield Road	62	Little Somborne
13	Black Horse Farm, Old Great North Road	63	Little Stock Farm
14	Bloodgate Hill	64	Maiden Castle
15	Bluntisham (6 Rectory Road)	65	Micheldever Wood
16	Boys Hall Balancing Pond	66	Mill Hill
17	Beechbrook Wood	67	Mingies Ditch
18	Brewer's Hall Farm North	68	Nettlebank Copse
19	Bromfield	69	New Buildings
20	Broom	70	North Shoebury
21	Broom (Area E)	71	Northumberland Bottom
22	Burgh	72	Norton
23	Bury Hill	73	Old Yew Hill Wood
24	Camp Ground	74	Oxley Park West
25	Chapel Mill	75	Potterne
26	Chichester Road	76	Prickwillow Road
27	Conderton Camp	77	Roughground Farm
28	Coxwell Road	78	Rushey Mead
29	Danebury	79	Salford
30	Duckend Car Park (Stansted Airport)	80	Slonk Hill
31	Easton Lane	81	South Hornchurch
32	Elms Farm	82	Spring Road Municipal Cemetery
33	Etonbury Farm Bund	83	Stone Farm Bridleway
34	Fiskerton Causeway	84	Suddern Farm
35	Ford Place Nursing Home	85	Sutton Common
36	Gayhurst Quarry	86	Sutton Walls
37	Glastonbury Lake Village	87	The Sidbury Double Linear Ditch
38	Gloucester Business Park Link Road	88	Tollard Royal
39	Gravelly Guy	89	Tutt Hill
40	Great Houghton	90	Twywell
41	Grimes Graves	91	Wakerley
42	Gussage All Saints	92	Wandlebury Ringwork
43	Haddenham Site V	93	Wanlip
44	Harting Beacon	94	Watchfield
45	Hartsdown Technology College	95	West Hay Field
46	Hatford Quarry	96	White Horse Stone/Pilgrims Way/ West and East of Boarley Farm
47	Helpringham Fen	97	Windy Dido
48	High Barns Road	98	Winnall Down
49	High Street	99	Woodcote Road
50	Highfields Farm	100	Wootton Hill Farm

The collected data from the selected sites derive predominately from published and unpublished reports, supplemented by archival material when needed. Data collection began with consulting the published and unpublished reports, and, in most instances, these sources included all the information required for this study. However, in some cases, not all the necessary information was present in the reports, thus requiring consultation of the archival material. Given time and monetary constraints, it was impractical to visit all the sites' archives. Thus, only for sites where key information was absent from the reports, or lacking in particular details, was a visit to the archives necessary. During archive visits, the consulted material consisted of the original osteological reports and inventory, context sheets, field notes, and site plans. In some cases, unfortunately, there was conflicting information between the archival material and the published reports. In such events, the archival information was used in this study's analysis over the published reports, though the discrepancies are noted within the appendix to avoid any confusion. All information, including the skeletal data, derives from these sources, and this study's author did not perform any osteological analysis.

Terminology

Before explaining the details of the data collection, it is necessary to define the terminology utilised in the following discussion. Although, it may appear basic, it is essential to avoid unnecessary confusion.

Archaeological feature defines a human-built structure such as a roundhouse, field system, or Bronze Age mound.

Context defines the physical deposit that the artefact and skeletal evidence derives from, such as a pit, ditch, posthole, or grave.

Layer refers to the stratigraphical level within a context.

Human remains occurrence (or occurrence) refers to the deposit of an *individual* skeletal unit within a layer/context. A layer or context may contain multiple occurrences.

For example, excavations at Site *X* reveal evidence of an Iron Age roundhouse with a single pit within the interior of the structure. The basal layer of the pit contains a single adult inhumation accompanied by a juvenile left femur and a mature adult cranium. In this case, the roundhouse is the archaeological feature; the pit is the context, the basal layer of which contains three human remains occurrences (one inhumation and two disarticulated bone occurrences).

Data collection

The study analysed each site individually. Basic information collected for each site includes details on the site type, description of the terrain, duration of occupation, and geology. The reason for recording the geological information is to ascertain whether the soil conditions of the site might have affected bone preservation, which in turn would result in a smaller number of occurrences. Information regarding each human remains occurrence falls under three broad categories. The first category consists of the demographic status and disposal characteristics of the skeletal material. Second includes the contextual traits, and the third category is the location of the deposit. Each of the categories includes a number of variables with descriptive states that details the nature of the deposit. To clarify, if an inhumation lay with its head oriented to the north, the orientation is the variable described by the state, which is north.

A database, designed in Microsoft Excel 2007, stores each site's datasets. The database for a site consists of each human remains occurrence and its variables and states. The variables' states are numerically coded, which *inter alia* facilitates subsequent statistical analysis. Each variable contains an 'Unknown/None' state which

signifies there is no information on the specific trait or it was absent from the deposit.

Data collection began with recording basic information for each human remains occurrence, regarding the skeletal number, context number, and source reference. In addition, all occurrences include the date of deposition (Late Bronze Age, Early Iron Age, etc.). The data recording includes the associated material culture with the human remains. The material culture divides into seventeen categories (**Table 3.2**), a modification of the twenty-seven artefact categories defined by Wait (1985a, 52-53). The 'other' category for associated material includes items not found frequently enough on Iron Age sites to receive their own grouping, such as glass and beads. Furthermore, if animal bones were present in the deposit, the data records specify the species and the depositional nature of the animal remains (as in inhumation or disarticulated bone). The total number of excavated animal bones from the site was noted to compare with the total number of human remains occurrences, ultimately to address potential taphonomic issues, which may have affected the preservation of the deposit.

Demographic profile

The demographic traits for each occurrence comprise age groups, sex, pathological, and traumatic indicators.

Age groups

Age of skeletal material divides into a series of age groups (**Table 3.3**), which is a modification of Buikstra and Ubelaker (1994, 9). For statistical purposes, the five age categories simplify into a second age division, which includes sub-adult (0-20 years old) and adults (21+ years old).

Sex

The classification of biological sex for the skeletal material consists of four categories: male, male?, female and female?. Once again, for ease in statistical testing, a simplified sex group consisting of only male and female was created.

Pathological indicators

Pathological indicators define the marks left on bone by disease. For this investigation, eight states relate to the disease groups that are recognisable from the pathological trait (**Table 3.5**).

Traumatic indicators

Traumatic indicators refer to traces on the bone that are the result of violent or traumatic incidents. Twelve states characterise the traumatic variable (**Table 3.6**). Furthermore, the 'other' category describes evidence of some type of trauma, for which the cause is unknown. In addition, a description of the trauma includes whether the trauma occurred ante-, peri- or post-mortem, to establish possible cause of death and life history. The trauma category includes post-mortem indicators on bone in order to establish a sequence of handling or manipulation of the skeletal material prior to deposition.

Table 3. 2 Associated material

Natural Material/Layer
Worked Bone
Complete Ceramic Vessel
Ceramic Vessel (intentionally broken)
Pottery Sherds
Quern Stone
Jewellery
Military Material
Domestic Debris
Plant Remains
Metal Tools/Artefacts
Ash/Charcoal
Worked Stone
Animal Bone
Sling Stones
Other

Table 3. 3 Age groups

Age Group 1	Age Group 2
Infant (0-3)	
Child (4-12)	Sub-adult
Adolescent (13-20)	(0-20)
Adult (21-35)	Adult
Mature Adult (35+)	(21+)

Table 3. 5 Traumatic indicators

Fracture	Bone modification
Cut Mark	Gnawing
Blunt force trauma	Scarring
Dismemberment	Striae
Burning	Weathering
Polishing	Other

Table 3.4 Disease classifications with accompanying pathological definitions

Pathological Indicators	Definitions
Congenital Disease	'...Pathological changes in the normal development during intrauterine life' (Aufdereide and Rodríguez-Martin 1998, 51) Examples: spina bifida and microcephaly
Dental Disease	Pathology affects the teeth and gum of an individual (Roberts and Cox 2003, 31) Examples: caries and ante-mortem tooth loss
Joint Disease	'...Pathological condition characterized by the loss of joint cartilage and subsequent lesions resulting from direct interosseous contact within diarthrodial joints' (Aufdereide and Rodríguez-Martin 1998, 93) Examples: osteoarthritis and osteophytes
Infectious Disease	Presence of a pathogenic agent resulting illness (Roberts and Cox 2003, 32-33) Examples: tuberculosis and leprosy
Metabolic Disease	A disease affecting the normal metabolism, and often are '...indicators of stress' (Roberts and Cox 2003, 33) Examples: anaemia and rickets
Neoplastic Disease	Neoplastic disease is '...a mass of localized tissue growth whose cellular proliferation is no longer subject to the effects of normal growth-regulating mechanisms' (Aufdereide and Rodríguez-Martin 1998, 371) Example: tumours
Haematological Disease	Pathology affecting the blood (Roberts and Cox 2003, 33) Example: osteochondroses dissecans
Other	Describes an occurrence that possess pathological indicators but of unknown cause

Manner of disposal

Each human remains occurrence is grouped into four disposal categories: inhumation, articulated bones, disarticulated bone, and cremation. The division between categories rests on the *intentional* placement of the skeletal remains. A series of variables and descriptive states corresponds with each of the four disposal categories.

Inhumation

An inhumation represents the interment of a complete (or partially complete) skeleton either shortly after death or after a period of decomposition. The descriptive variables for inhumations consist of the completeness, layout, orientation, position and facial direction of the skeleton.

Completeness of skeleton

The completeness of a skeleton includes two states: complete or incomplete. A 'complete' inhumation means that over sixty percent (60 per cent) of the skeleton was present at the time of excavation, while 'incomplete' indicates less than sixty percent was present.

Layout of skeleton

Layout of a skeleton denotes the position of the corpse within the deposit. To determine the layout, plans and pictures were consulted first, and, if none were available, the database entry is derived from the description in the relevant report. The layout defines an inhumation as either extended, flexed, crouched, or contracted. An extended inhumation means a skeleton with legs lying straight with unbent knees. A flexed inhumation describes a skeleton with the knees bent, with both pulled towards the torso, but where the angle at which the femora articulate with the acetabulum exceeds 90° from the spinal column. Crouched inhumation defines a skeleton with both knees bent, pulled towards the torso, where the angle at which the femora articulate with the acetabulum does *not* exceed 90° from the spinal column. A contracted inhumation defines a skeleton with the knees tightly bent and the legs firmly against the torso. The contracted position suggests that a degree of decomposition, or removal of the flesh, has taken place prior to the skeleton's interment, and possibly implies that the individual was bound.

Orientation of skeleton

The orientation of an inhumation defines the compass direction on which the axis of the spine is aligned (north, northeast, etc.).

Position of skeleton

The position of an inhumation defines the anatomical side on which the skeleton lays within the deposit. The skeleton's position falls within one of ten states (**Table 3.6**). For statistical purposes, a second division simplifies the ten variables into five: left side, right side, supine, prone, and other.

Table 3. 6 Position of skeleton variables

Left side	Left side-supine
Right side	Right side-supine
Prone	Upright
Upside down	Supine
Right side-prone	Left side-prone

Facial direction of skeleton

The facial direction of an inhumation describes the cardinal direction in which the skull faces and consists of the same states as the orientation.

Articulated bones

Articulated bones describe the intentional deposition of a selected segment of the corpse, which is still articulated. The articulated bones include parts of a corpse that may have separated during decomposition or been intentionally severed from the rest of the skeleton. Descriptive variables of articulated bones include the side and portion present of the skeleton.

Portion present

The portion of the skeleton trait describes the segment of the corpse present within the deposit. This variable divides into five states: upper limb, lower limb, torso, phalanges (when unable to distinguish whether the elements derive from the hand or foot), and cranium (including skull with *at least* one cervical vertebra still articulated).

Side of skeleton

The side of the skeleton defines the anatomical side the articulated bone derives from. The variables for the side trait include: right, right?, left, left?, and none (this variable is only relevant to the torso and cranium). For statistical purposes, a second division simplifies the five variables into three: right, left, and none.

Disarticulated bone

Disarticulated bone refers to the deposition of an individual bone (also referred to as an element) from a skeleton. Traits relating to disarticulated bone include the element, portion of the element, and side.

Element

The element variable defines the bone present in the deposit (**Table 3.7**). However, the data collection did not distinguish between the individual carpals, metacarpals, tarsals, metatarsals, vertebrae, parts of the pelvis, teeth, and phalanges. Instead, the specific bone went under the bone group's heading, and was then noted in the observations on the recording sheet. For example, if a deposit contains a scaphoid and lunate, each would be marked individually as a carpal and then distinguished in the observations. For statistical purposes, a second and third division was created to reduce the element variables. The second division condenses the elements into five groups: cranium, upper limb, lower limb, torso, and phalanges. The third division includes two categories: cranium or post-cranial.

Table 3. 7 List of elements

Skull	Metacarpal
Mandible	Phalanx
Vertebra	Pelvis
Clavicle	Femur
Scapula	Patella
Rib	Tibia
Sternum	Fibula
Humerus	Tarsal
Ulna	Metatarsal
Radius	Tooth
Carpal	

Portion of element

The portion of the element trait defines the segment and state of the bone present in the deposit (**Table 3.8**).

Table 3. 8 Variables for portion of element

Proximal
Shaft
Distal
Complete
Fragmentary
Incomplete

Side

The side of a bone describes the anatomical side of the skeleton the element derives from. The side of the disarticulated bone follows in the same manner as the articulated limb side trait, which also includes the second side division for statistical purposes.

Cremation

A cremation deposit describes the deliberate burning of a corpse, followed by, in most cases, the collection of the remains for deposition. The descriptive traits of a cremation deposit include the weight, evidence of fragmentation, and presence or absence of an urn.

Weight

The weight of a cremation trait contains no variables; instead it is a numeric entry with the weight recorded in grams to one decimal point.

Evidence of fragmentation

Fragmentation of cremated bone defines the intentional breaking of the bone after the burning of the corpse has ceased. The recorded information includes whether the cremated bone possesses evidence of fragmentation or not.

Presence of an urn

An urned cremation implies that the cremated remains were placed *within* an urn, or some type of container, while an unurned cremation implies the opposite. In some instances, the cremated bone was scattered around a vessel, not placed directly within it. In such instances the cremation has been be marked as unurned.

Context data

Data on the occurrence's context is designed to record the contextual setting for the deposition. The context traits for each occurrence include context type, depth of context and occurrence, type of deposit, multiple or single deposit and context fill.

Context type

The context type trait defines the archaeological context the occurrence is recovered from. This variable's states include a pit, ditch/gully, rampart/bank, posthole, grave (intentionally dug to contain human remains), or other. The 'other' group describes contexts that are not found frequently on Iron Age sites, such as scoops and mining shafts.

Depth

The depth of a context includes the numeric measurement, in metres to two decimal places, of both the context and the occurrence. In addition, the depth of the occurrence accompanies a brief description of the soil layer from which the skeletal material was recovered. For statistical purposes this study follows the method employed by Hill (1995b, 34) where the context depth is divided into thirds (top, middle and bottom), and the occurrence's depth then assigned according to these depth divisions. In many instances, the site reports do not provide the context and occurrence's depth. In such cases, the occurrence's depth data derives from context section plans or written descriptions.

Type of deposit

The type of deposit trait includes three variables: primary, primary intrusive, and natural. A primary deposit refers to an occurrence that is intentionally set within a context, while a primary intrusive deposit defines an occurrence also intentionally placed in a context, yet disturbing a pre-existing skeletal deposit. A natural deposit implies an occurrence entering into the context by natural conditions, such as erosion, and lacks the human intent behind the placement.

Multiple or single deposit

The multiple or single trait denotes whether a human remains occurrence is present within the same layer as other occurrences, or is isolated.

Context fill

The context fill trait defines the nature of the soil accumulation over the occurrence. Determination of the fill type allows one to identify the post-depositional nature of the context after the occurrence's placement. For example, the context fill describes whether a context was left open to naturally silt up or immediately backfilled. The variable's state divides into either silting, backfill, or building (which implies the occurrence is set within the construction of a feature like a wall or rampart).

Location data

The final data category is information describing the location of an occurrence's deposition. The location data focus on where skeletal deposition occurred in order to determine whether particular areas favoured specific funerary practices. To accomplish this objective, the location data falls into two categories. The first category is the occurrence's location in relation to the site, and the other, when applicable, is its association with an archaeological feature.

Site

When an occurrence is not set in relation to an archaeological feature, then its location consists of data relevant to its placement in respect to the site. The location data consists of two core variables: placement in or out of the site and its association with an architectural feature.

Placement with respect to the site

The placement with respect to the site, a revised version of Cunliffe and Poole (2000a-f), describes whether an occurrence is set inside, outside, or on the boundary of a site (**Figure 3.3**). The placement variable comprises of three states: interior, perimeter, and exterior. Much of the placement variable depends on the site's physical arrangement. For example, the occurrence's placement data can be accurately assigned in enclosed settlements or hillforts. However, the placement data for open settlements and cemeteries cannot be determined, unless the full extent of activity is defined through excavations.

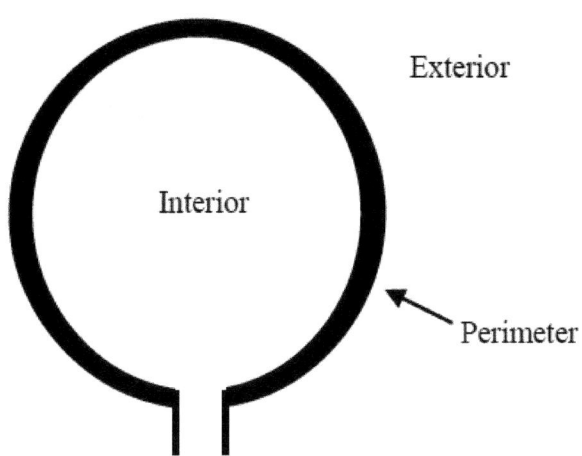

Figure 3.3 Diagram illustrating the placement of a deposit

Architectural feature

The architectural feature variable defines whether an occurrence is associated with a site and/or building's structural components and the type thereof. The states for the architectural feature trait include entrance, wall, posthole-entrance, posthole-wall, and boundary. For statistical purposes, the architectural feature group condenses into two groups: entrances (includes entrance and posthole-entrance) and boundary (includes boundary, wall and posthole-wall).

Archaeological feature

In instances where an occurrence is associated with an archaeological feature, the location data includes information on its placement relative to the structure. The location data for archaeological features comprises the structure's type, function, and entrance orientation. In addition, recording includes data regarding the placement, cardinal areas, and architectural feature traits for both the occurrence's placement in the archaeological feature, and the feature's placement within the site.

The type of archaeological feature trait defines the structure type the occurrence is associated with (**Table 3.9**). The construction date of the archaeological feature is also recorded following the same date divisions as the human remains occurrences. The 'other' category denotes a structure not defined by this variable's grouping, such as a Bronze Age mound, pit alignment, and iron bloomery.

Function of the archaeological feature

The function of the archaeological feature trait describes the primary (or multiple) activity or use of the structure (**Table 3.10**). The 'other' category describes a function of a structure undefined by the variable's groupings, such as an animal paddock.

Table 3. 9 Variables of the archaeological feature type trait

Round Structure
Rectangular Structure
Irregular Structure
2-Post Structure
Multi-Post Structure
Settlement Enclosure
Field System Boundary
Other

Table 3 10 Variables of the function of an archaeological feature trait

Domestic/Occupation
Processing
Storage
Midden/Refuse
Enclosure/Boundary
Funerary/Ritual
Other

Orientation of the archaeological feature

The orientation trait defines the cardinal direction (north, northeast, east, southeast, south, southwest, west, and northwest) that the structure's entrance (if present) faces. For structures that possess more than one entrance, the data collection includes those orientations as well. In the case of field boundaries, the orientation refers to the alignment of the feature.

Location data for occurrences

Location data for human remains occurrences associated with archaeological features consist of the placement, cardinal area, and architectural feature traits. Most of the traits follow the same principles previously outlined in the location data for *Sites*. The differences are that the placement trait relates to the occurrence's setting relative to the structure. The cardinal area, a modified version of Cunliffe and Poole (2000a-f), defines the occurrence's location around the structure in respect to the compass directions. The cardinal area data allow accurate identification of any favoured areas for skeletal deposition. To appraise the cardinal areas, a compass-based diagram centres on the feature's plan, and the section the occurrence's deposit sits within determines the variable's state (**Figure 3.4**). Occurrences near post structures or 'other' features (such as Bronze Age barrows or pit alignments) are examined with reference to the cardinal direction in which they lie in relation to the feature. However, when human remains are associated with round, rectangular or irregular structures (also referred to simply as structures), the cardinal directions are grouped into three different categories, each dependent on the structure's entrance orientation (as one enters). The first category examines the human remains' placement at the right/front, right/back, left/back and left/front of a

structure ('quadrants' see **Figure 3.5**). The second category investigates placement of skeletal remains at either the front or the back of the structure (see **Figure 3.6**), and the third category establishes whether bones were interred on the right or left side of the entrance, as one enters the structure (see **Figure 3.7**). These divisions then can be used to explore potential trends of deposition within specific structures.

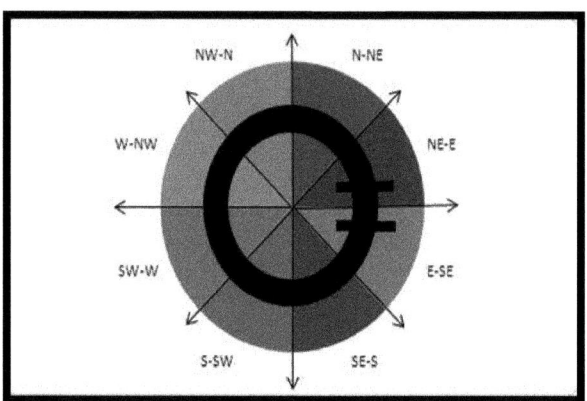

Figure 3. 4 Diagram depicting the cardinal areas of a structure

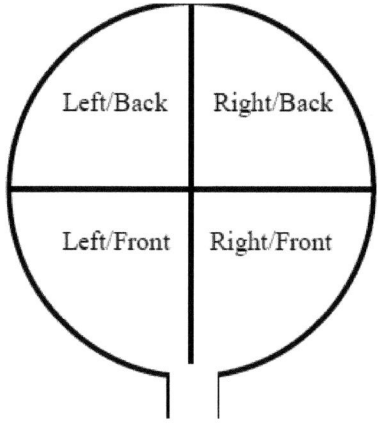

Figure 3.5 Diagram depicting the quadrants of a structure

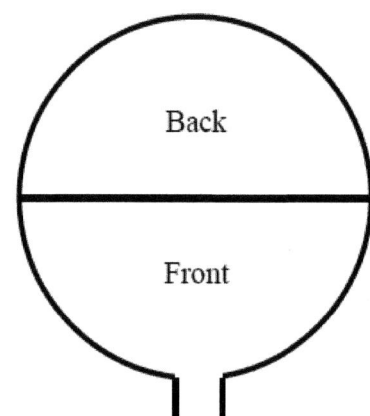

Figure 3.6 Diagram depicting the division between the front and back of a structure

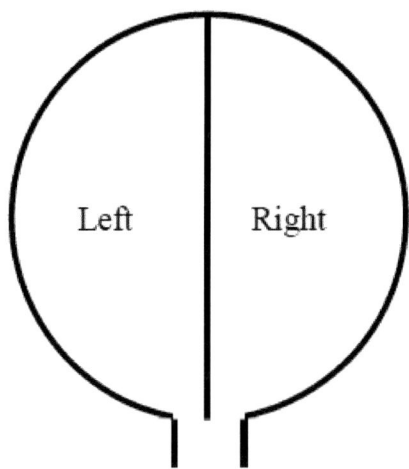

Figure 3.7 Diagram depicting the division between the right and left side of a structure

Data Summary

In sum, the designed methodology of this investigation offers a detailed and systematic approach for analysing the burial material for individual sites and on the regional scale. The assessment of cultural practices relies predominantly on subjective material, yet the study's system provides a method of taking the subjective material and objectively analysing the evidence. In order to assess burial practices, numerous variables need to be taken into account; this, in turn, creates a large quantity of data. Unfortunately, when working with large datasets, mistakes are unavoidable. One problem is the simple mismarking of information during recording for the database, as well as misprints within site reports. Such minor human errors filter into studies and are unavoidable. In addition, discrepancies between this author's database and the site reports will occur. The discrepancies are due to various modes of defining particular burial attributes and categories. For instance, an excavator may describe an inhumation in the flexed position, though in this study's database it may be defined as crouched if it fits within the outlined definition of a 'crouched' inhumation. Lastly, as previously stated, all the osteological information derives solely from the site reports, and the author conducted no skeletal assessment. This becomes a concern when working with older excavations (typically those prior to the 1980s). The osteological methods used to assign demographic traits, such as sex and age, were not as accurate or developed as they are today. However, some skeletal material from older excavations has undergone reassessment (for example, Rebecca Redfern's [2008a] work on Maiden Castle and Gussage All Saints) and, when possible, the

more recent analysis was used in conjunction with the earlier osteological reports.

Statistical and quantitative testing, regional patterning and interpretation

The purpose of the statistical analysis is to reveal potential relationships and patterns between the multiple variables and states of the skeletal, context, and location data, as well as their developments over time. For example, the data can be used to investigate how the manner of disposal may have influenced the occurrence's location through time. To achieve the study's objective requires the employment of a series of statistical and quantitative analysis. To begin, the coded data was inputted into a designed database in Microsoft Excel 2007. In Excel 2007, quantitative analysis began with the frequencies of all traits' variables on the site level and regional scale. For the pathological, traumatic, and associated material traits, the frequency results are the limit of the examination. The reason for this is because the study's objective centres on the behaviour directed towards the corpse. Although much information can come from investigating the pathological, traumatic, and associated material in more depth, it is not part of this investigation's primary focus and therefore it was decided that these variables would have a limited analysis. Additionally, in Excel 2007, the mean averages were calculated of variables containing numerical data (cremation weights, context depth, and occurrence depth).

After basic, quantitative analyses in Excel 2007, all the coded data were imported into SPSS 18.0 for statistical testing. Prior to importing the data into SPSS 18.0, all the 'Unknown/None' variables were excluded in Excel 2007 to prevent skewing of the statistical tests. In SPSS 18.0, the data underwent standard statistical analysis to determine the strength of relationships between the variables' states. The primary statistical test for demonstrating the strength of a relationship between two variables is the chi-square test for independence. With the chi-square test, there is an assumption that there is an expected count of five or more in each cell (Pallant 2007, 214). When testing the relationship between two variables, if the chi-square test violates this assumption, then Fisher's Exact Probability Test was used.[2] A probability of 5 per cent (0.05) or less signifies a 'significant' relationship between tested variables to advocate the rejection of the null hypothesis (Rowntree 1981, 118). Considering the nature of the data, only traits with more than twenty occurrences were deemed to have a sufficient sample size for relationship statistical testing on the site and regional level (Rowntree 1981, 92).

In order to ascertain regional patterns, significant relationships between the data were mapped according to the sites that possess those specific burial traits. ArcGIS

---

[2] The Fisher's Exact Probability Test may only be employed if the tested variables are in a two-by-two table (Pallant 2007, 214).

ArcView 9.3 is the programme used in creating the regional distribution maps. The distribution maps were assessed subjectively to identify regional patterns. The reason for this subjective approach is because the burial traits already demonstrated a significant relationship prior to mapping and the regional patterns identified in this process were visually apparent and did not require further analysis (see chapter eight). The interpretation of the statistical results and regional patterns relies upon a cultural approach while expanding on current theories in Iron Age burial practices previously outlined in chapter two.

In closing, this chapter has outlined the type of burial data collected for this investigation. Furthermore, it details the statistical and quantitative tests employed to discern relationships between burial characteristics and the approach taken to interpret the relationships. The following chapters will relay the quantitative and statistical results from the individual sites, and highlight geographical and regional patterns identified from the analysis

Chapter Four

General overview and the statistical and quantitative analyses of the archaeological features and contexts

Introduction

The following chapters (chapters four, five, six, and seven) detail the results from the quantitative and statistical analysis of all the studied sites within this investigation's sample. The present chapter begins with a brief description of the nature of the studied sample. This follows by a discussion of the archaeological features that have associated human remains deposits and their respective variables and states (see chapter three). After this, the discussion turns to the quantitative and statistical results of contexts that contain human remains and its variables and states. The chapter closes with a brief summary of the reported results in an effort to begin constructing a narrative of the nature of Late Bronze Age and Iron Age burial practices. The following two chapters (chapters five and six) discuss in detail the attributes of the human remains. Each of the subsequent results chapters only address the relevant results that contribute to our understanding of Iron Age burial practices. The objective for these chapters is to create a general overview of the different elements of Iron Age burial practices, which will ultimately provide the foundation for investigating potential regional patterning (chapter eight).

In addition, most of the studied sites (n=85) had fewer than 20 human remains occurrences. Fifteen sites had 20 or more occurrences, and of these, a few had over a hundred. Chapter seven details the individual results of each of the sites with 20 or more occurrences. Therefore, in an effort to prevent the sites with over 20 occurrences from overshadowing the data from sites with under 20, the statistical and quantitative analyses follow two methods (**Table 4.1** outlines the total number of human remains occurrences from each studied site, see also **Figure 4.1**). The first method is an analysis of the entire occurrences from all the studied sites (referred to as the 'larger sample'), including the sites with more than 20 occurrences. The second method excludes the larger sites, and analysis is limited to the sites with fewer than 20 occurrences (referred to as the 'smaller sample'). After which, there is a comparison of the results from the two methods.

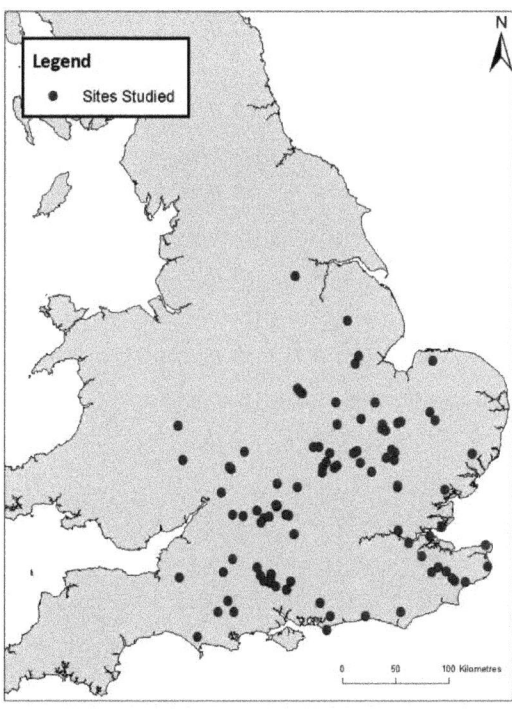

Figure 4. 1 Distribution of studied sites (see also Figure 3.2)

Table 4. 1 Sites with numbers of human remains occurrences

Site	Occurrences	Site	Occurrences
A27 Westhampnett	192	Hinxton Quarry (IA Cemetery)	11
A505 Baldock Bypass	2	Hod Hill	8
Ashville	7	Home Farm	2
Aspreys, Olney	1	Houghton Down	4
Balksbury Camp	2	Hurst Lane Reservoir	4
Bancroft	6	Hutchinson	1
Barton Court Farm	8	Jubilee Corner	6
Battlesbury Bowl	34	Kingsmead Park	3
Beard Mill, Stanton Harcourt	1	Land off Bromham Road	6
Beechbrook Wood	20	Latton Lands	5
Bicester Fields Farm	1	Layer-de-la-Haye	3
Billingborough	6	Little Somborne	6
Birchfield Road	2	Little Stock Farm	6
Black Horse Farm, Old Great North Road	5	Maiden Castle	100
Bloodgate Hill	1	Micheldever Wood	20
Bluntisham (6 Rectory Road)	1	Mill Hill	46
Boys Hall Balancing Pond	2	Mingies Ditch	3
Brewer's Hall Farm North	2	Nettlebank Copse	5
Bromfield	1	New Buildings	17
Broom	16	North Shoebury	6
Broom (Area E)	2	Northumberland Bottom	7
Burgh	1	Norton	2
Bury Hill	3	Old Yew Hill Wood	1
Camp Ground	2	Oxley Park West	4
Chapel Mill	7	Potterne	103
Chichester Road	2	Prickwillow Road	3
Conderton Camp	4	Roughground Farm	3
Coxwell Road	12	Rushey Mead	1
Danebury	401	Salford	4
Duckend Car Park (Stansted Airport)	6	Slonk Hill	2
Easton Lane	13	South Hornchurch	15
Elms Farm	6	Spring Road Municipal Cemetery	5
Etonbury Farm Bund	1	Stone Farm Bridleway	14
Fiskerton Causeway	3	Suddern Farm	186
Ford Place Nursing Home	1	Sutton Common	6
Gayhurst Quarry	2	Sutton Walls	40
Glastonbury Lake Village	49	The Sidbury Double Linear Ditch	3
Gloucester Business Park Link Road	1	Tollard Royal	1
Gravelly Guy	107	Tutt Hill	3
Great Houghton	2	Twywell	3
Grimes Graves	2	Wakerley	10
Gussage All Saints	67	Wandlebury Ringwork	5
Haddenham Site V	2	Wanlip	1
Harting Beacon	4	Watchfield	8
Hartsdown Technology College	1	West Hay Field	4
Hatford Quarry	1	White Horse Stone etc.	21
Helpringham Fen	1	Windy Dido	2
High Barns Road	8	Winnall Down	121
High Street	2	Woodcote Road	6
Highfields Farm	4	Wootton Hill Farm	1

Overview of the studied sites

The following section provides a brief overview and introduction of the data breadth from the sites chosen for the study sample. Studied sites in the sample yielded a wide quantity of human remains, which **Table 4.2** shows, but most contain fewer than ten occurrences. In all, the one hundred studied sites produced 1,874 human remains occurrences within 1,118 contexts. Most of the sites had human remains in various states of disposal, as **Table 4.3** outlines. In addition, many of the studied sites have human remains deposits from multiple phases of the Iron Age (**Table 4.4**). Thus, the studied sites cover multiple chronological phases and disposal types, and varying degrees of quantity of human remains, which ultimately provides an adequate and heterogeneous sample for analysis.

Table 4. 2 Quantity of occurrences on sites

Human Remains Occurrences	Number of Sites
20 or more	15
11-19	9
1-10	76

Table 4. 3 Number of sites with manner of disposal

Manner of disposal	Number of sites
Inhumation	21
Articulated bones	1
Disarticulated bone	16
Cremation	19
Multiple manners	43

Table 4. 4 Period of deposition with sites

Period of deposition	Number of sites
LBA	3
EIA	13
MIA	18
LIA	20
Un-phased IA	8
Multiple periods	38

Archaeological feature analysis

Quantitative results

From all the sites studied, 204 archaeological features have associated human remains, of which 52 per cent are from the 15 sites with 20 or more occurrences. Archaeological features of Middle Iron Age date are the most well represented (**Table 4.5**), and round structures (roundhouses) are the most frequently occurring feature type (**Table 4.6**). The 'other' archaeological feature category denotes a structure that is not defined by this variable's groupings, such as Bronze Age barrows, pit

alignments, and an iron bloomery. Of the total number of archaeological feature, 152 have a known function and, from the smaller sample, 79 have a known purpose (**Table 4.7**). For both samples, archaeological features with a domestic function occur most frequently (37 per cent for the larger sample and 34 per cent for the smaller). Additionally, as with feature type, the 'other' function represents a purpose undefined by the variable's grouping, such as a mining shaft. Furthermore, the 'multiple functions' category signifies that they have more than one purpose, such as a building that was both a domestic and a processing area. Just under half (46 per cent) of the archaeological features from the larger sample have only disarticulated bones placed within the building's vicinity (31 per cent for the smaller sample). In addition, pits are the most frequent context for human remains when associated with an archaeological feature (44 per cent for the larger sample and 39 per cent for the smaller). Lastly, an eastern orientation of entrances for these features is most common for both samples (37 per cent for the larger sample and 27 per cent for the smaller sample, see **Figures 4.2-3**). The 'manner of disposal' section (below) provides information on the location of human remains in and around archaeological features

Table 4. 5 Frequency of archaeological features containing human remains by date

Dates	Larger sample	Smaller sample
LBA	19	17
EIA	31	14
MIA	68	35
LIA	47	20
IA	34	8

Table 4.6 Frequency of archaeological features' type

Type	Larger sample	Smaller sample
Round Structure	75	33
Rectangular Structure	16	10
Irregular Structure	6	3
2-Post Structure	2	0
Multi-Post Structure	17	5
Settlement Enclosure	22	11
Boundary	19	14
Other	37	22

Table 4. 7 Frequency of archaeological features' function

Function	Larger sample	Smaller sample
Domestic	57	27
Processing	5	2
Storage	3	1
Midden	1	0
Enclosure	36	21
Funerary/Ritual	21	17
Other	11	5
Multiple Functions	18	6

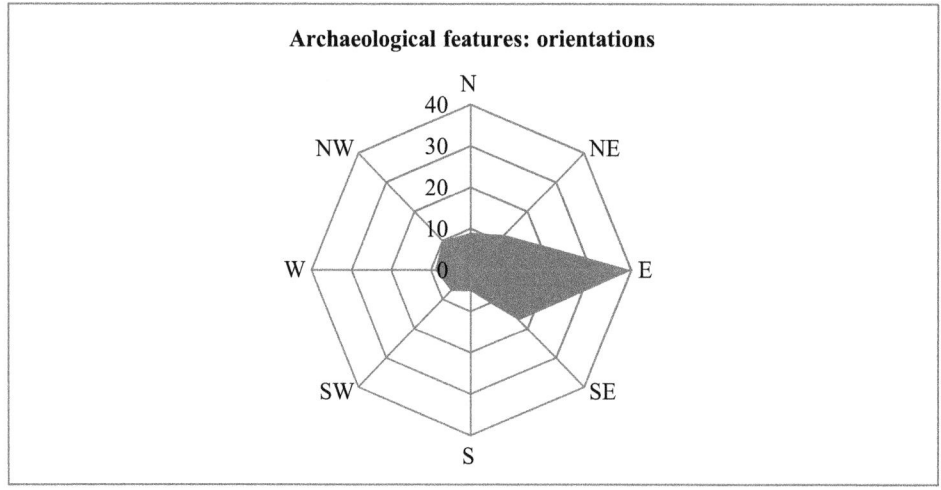

Figure 4. 2 Frequency of archaeological features' orientation, including larger sites

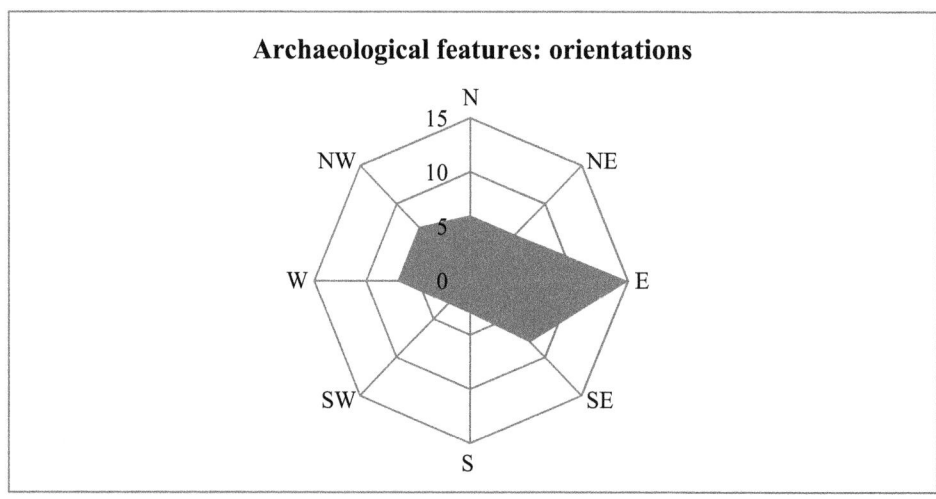

Figure 4. 3 Frequency of archaeological features' orientation, excluding larger sites

Statistical results

The statistical analysis of the archaeological features returned limited results. For the sample that excludes larger sites, most of statistical tests could not be carried out because of the small sample size. For the few statistical tests, none returned a significant relationship between variables. Nonetheless, for the larger sample there is a significant relationship between the date of a feature and the associated context type in which human remains were placed (χ^2=8.423, p=0.015). For statistical purposes, the context groups were divided between 'pits' and 'non-pits' (which includes postholes, graves, ditches and so forth) and, as **Figure 4.4** illustrates, pits are the most common context with archaeological features in the Early and Middle Iron Age. In the Late Iron Age, non-pit contexts become much more frequent, potentially signifying a change. These non-pit contexts consist largely of graves, ditches and the 'other' group of contexts, such as house layers, pyre-related features and scoops. However, the non-pit contexts from the Late Iron Age derive from only a handful of sites; in particular, a

greater proportion are from Glastonbury Lake Village (n=15), which leads us to question whether this relationship is significant. In comparison, the smaller sample demonstrates no significant relationship between the date of an archaeological feature and the context (χ^2=2.467, p=0.481). For the smaller sample, the analysis only tested the relationship between pit and ditch contexts since these variables were the most frequent in this category. **Figure 4.5** illustrates that pits continued to be the most frequent context for human remains that were associated with archaeological features throughout the Iron Age. However, this test has a low count of cases; it illustrates that choice of context between pits and ditches was comparatively unchanged throughout the Iron Age.

In sum, the archaeological feature analysis returned limited information. However, it appears that these varying types of buildings were associated with the deposition of human remains. The statistical analysis may hint at a chronological change in the contexts chosen for human remains, though this may be due to a few sites with higher volumes of occurrences skewing the overall data. The analysis of the 'manner of disposal' (below) will investigate this connection in more depth, along with the spatial relationships within these archaeological features.

Context analysis

Quantitative results

Over a quarter (26 per cent) of the contexts that contained human remains are from sites with fewer than 20 occurrences. From all the studied sites, including those with 20 of more occurrences, a greater proportion of the contexts (39 per cent) date to the Late Iron Age; however, when the larger sites are excluded, the Middle Iron Age is the most common period (28 per cent) (see **Table 4.8**). Pits are the most frequent contexts for human remains (43 per cent larger sample; 49 per cent smaller sample, see **Table 4.9**). The sample that includes all the sites shows

that all manners of disposal (except contexts with articulated bone and multiple manners) are comparably equal in their representation, with disarticulated bone being the most frequent (37 per cent, **Table 4.10**). When excluding those sites with over 20 occurrences, there is a similar trend, although cremations have a slightly higher count than other forms of disposal (34 per cent, **Table 4.10**). For contexts from all sites studied, the mean average of known depths is 0.82m (n=664), while the mean average for depth of disposal of human remains is 0.36m (n=272). When excluding the larger sites, the mean average is 0.60m (n=178) and the disposal depth is 0.40m (n=86). As for the context's spatial position in the interior, perimeter, or exterior of a structure or site, for all sites interiors are the most common (41 per cent), while perimeters are more frequent in the smaller sample (42 per cent). If a context is near an architectural feature, the greater proportions are placed near boundary areas, such as a wall or alongside an enclosure (66 per cent larger sample; 76 per cent smaller sample).

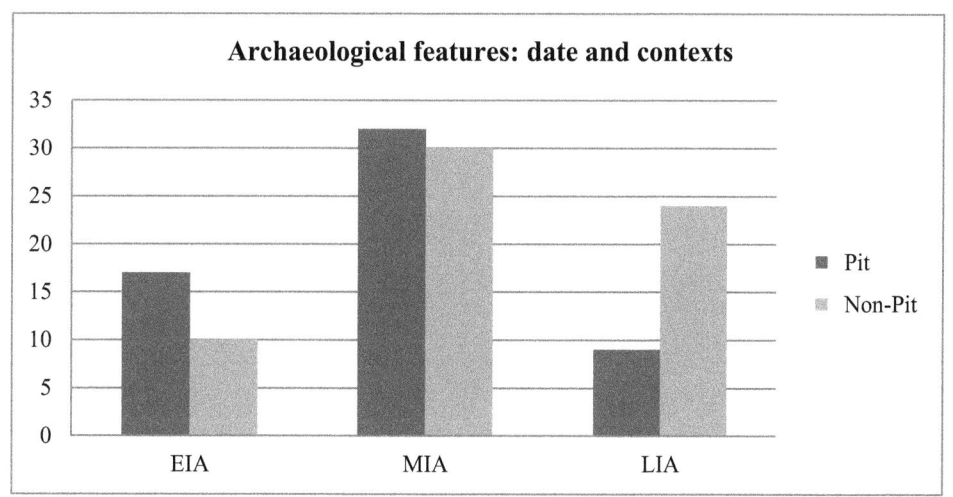

Figure 4. 4 Frequency of archaeological features' date and context, including larger sites

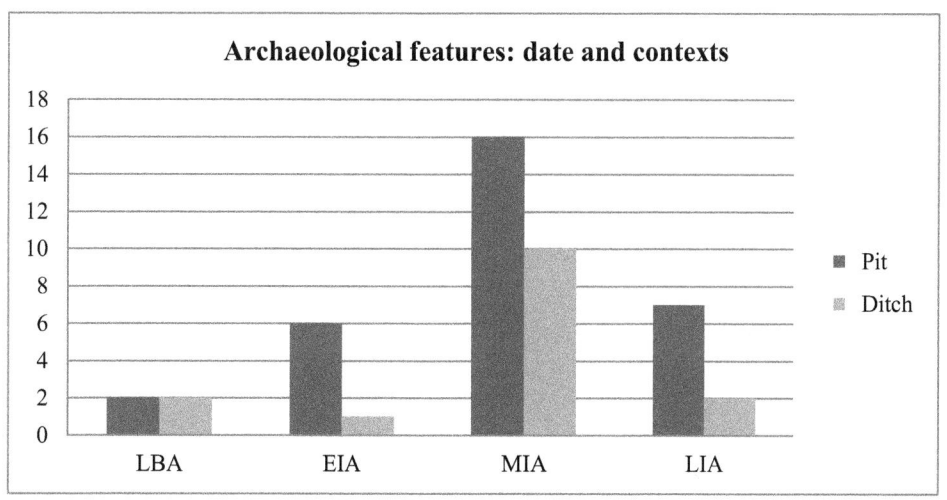

Figure 4. 5 Frequency of archaeological features' date and context, excluding larger sites

Table 4. 8 Frequency of contexts' date

Date	Larger sample	Smaller sample
LBA	49	43
EIA	201	57
MIA	362	81
LIA	438	75
IA	68	31

Table 4. 9 Frequency of context type

Types	Larger sample	Smaller sample
Pit	469	133
Ditch	102	45
Rampart	6	2
Posthole	43	16
Grave	302	55
Other	165	18

Table 4. 10 Frequency of contexts with manner of disposal

Manner of disposal	Larger sample	Smaller sample
Inhumations	335	91
Disarticulated bones	418	92
Cremations	310	97
Articulated bones	2	2
Multiple manners	53	5

Statistical results

The analysis of the context variables returned a number of results, some statistically significant, relating to the dates of contexts. From the larger sample, there is a significant relationship between context and date (χ^2=264.439, p=0.000), and **Figure 4.6** illustrates this relationship. It is apparent that, before grave contexts replaced pits, the latter dominated throughout the Early and Middle Iron Age. In addition, the frequency of context types in the Early and Middle Iron Age is proportionally similar and may hint at continuity between the two periods. It should be noted that the 'other' category for context type denotes contexts such as ditches, postholes, scoops, and so forth, which are combined together for statistical purposes. However, it must be taken into account that 48 per cent of the total pits from the Early and Middle Iron Age are from a single site, Danebury (Hampshire), which has undoubtedly influenced the overall picture. The increase in the number of grave contexts in the Late Iron Age is probably the result of the larger sample consisting of cemetery sites, namely Westhampnett (Sussex) and Mill Hill (Kent), which heavily influence the statistical result. On the other hand, when comparing the larger sample with the smaller, a different picture seems to emerge. There is a significant relationship between context type and date in the smaller sample (χ^2=6.710, p=0.035). For statistical purposes, context type has been divided into two broad categories: pit and non-pit. The non-pit group represents context types such as ditches, graves, and postholes, whose low numbers individually would prevent any statistical testing.

In this sample, **Figure 4.7** illustrates a relatively even number of pits with associated human remains during the Early, Middle, and Late periods. The non-pit contexts' frequency increases, practically doubling, between the Early and Middle Iron Age and becomes more frequent than pits. In addition, during the Middle Iron Age, 50 per cent of the non-pit features consist of ditch contexts from a number of sites. This does not correlate with the results from the larger sample. In other words, the larger sample hints at a possible continuity in context choice between the Early and Middle Iron Age, with a change occurring in the Late Iron Age. The smaller sample, on the other hand, shows a major change between the Early and Middle Iron Age, and then again between the Middle and Late Iron Age.

There appears to be another temporal relationship within the context category. For both the larger and smaller samples, a statistically significant pattern emerges between the date and manner of disposal within each context (larger sample: χ^2=409.482, p=0.000; smaller sample: χ^2=42.511, p=0.000). Both samples appear to show a distinct change in burial practice between the Middle and Late Iron Age, with cremations occurring more frequently than either inhumations or disarticulated bone in the Late Iron Age (**Figure 4.8**). The results also portray contexts with disarticulated bone occurring more frequently in the Early and Middle Iron Age, followed by their distinct decline in the Late Iron Age. The sharp increase of contexts with cremation explains the highly significant result for each test, corresponding with the emergence of the Aylesford-Swarling cremation rite. Prior to the Late Iron Age, cremations are present, but in very low numbers, especially in the Middle Iron Age. An exception is notable in the smaller sample for the Early Iron Age (**Figure 4.9**), when contexts with cremations are not entirely dominated by contexts with inhumations and disarticulated bones, as is seen in the larger sample. Interestingly, with the smaller sample, cremation contexts make up a large proportion of contexts from the Late Bronze Age before decreasing in the Early and Middle Iron Age (the sample size is too small for statistical testing). This trend is also visible within the larger sample and, for each sample, this does not necessarily imply that the cremation rite was abandoned, only that it is not always archaeologically visible. Furthermore, contexts containing inhumations appear to increase steadily from the Early into the Late Iron Age for the larger sample. In contrast, the smaller sample shows inhumation contexts peaking during the Middle Iron Age and then slightly decreasing in the Late Iron Age.

This final section will explore the relationship between the dates of deposits and the spatial locations of contexts within sites or their structures (interior, perimeter, and exterior). For the larger sample, a chi-square test for independence indicated a significant relationship between location and date (χ^2=29.966, p=0.000, **Figure 4.10**). This sample shows that contexts with human remains occurred more frequently in site's interiors during the Early and Middle Iron Age whereas, by the Late Iron Age, the

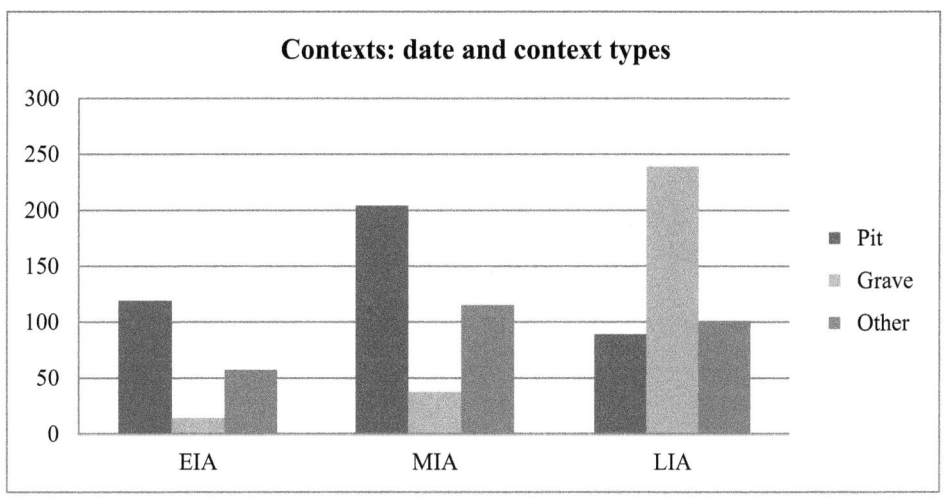

Figure 4. 6 Frequency of context type and date, including larger sites

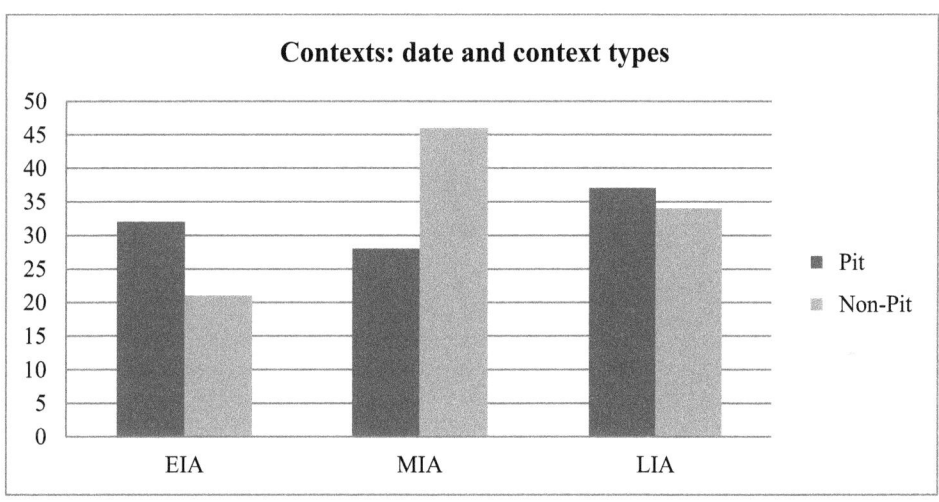

Figure 4. 7 Frequency of context type and date, excluding larger sites

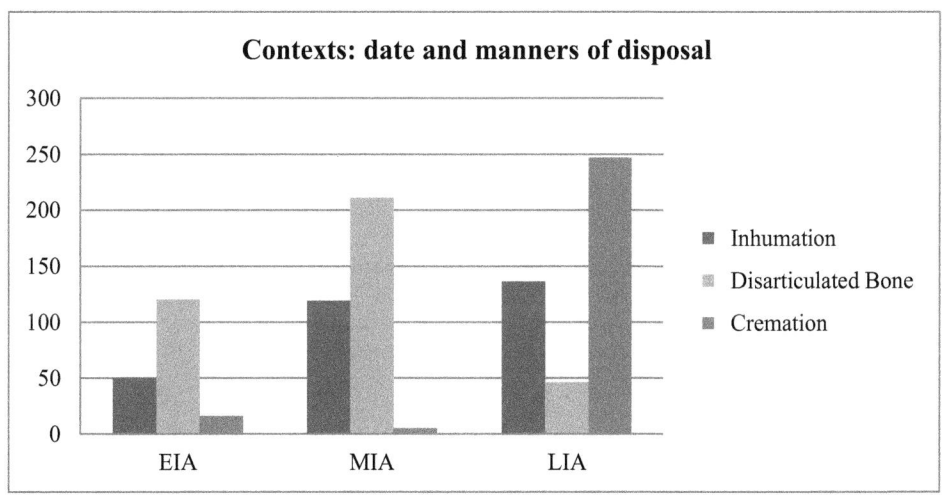

Figure 4. 8 Frequency of contexts' manner of disposal and date, including larger sites

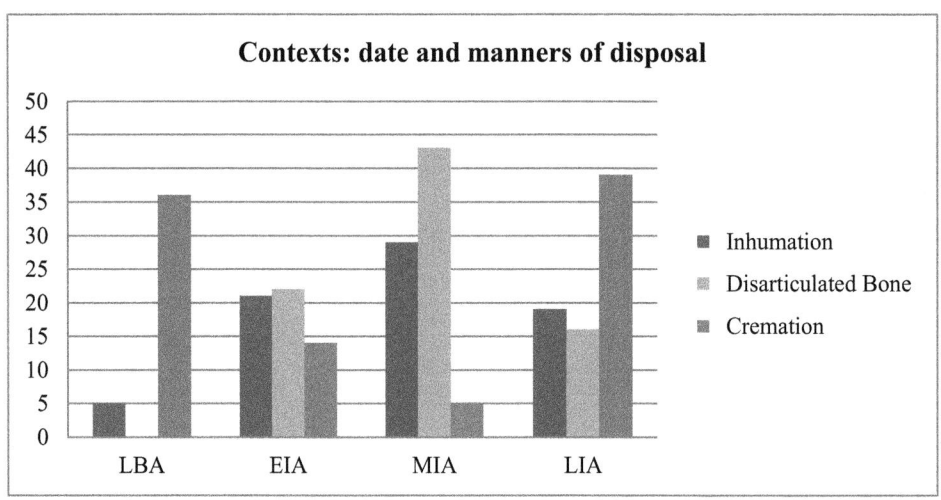

Figure 4. 9 Frequency of contexts' manner of disposal and date, excluding larger sites

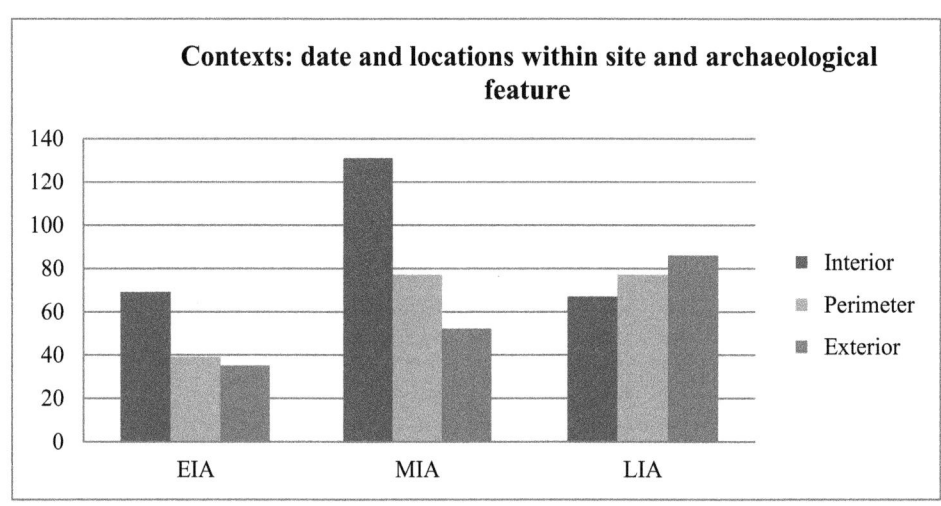

Figure 4. 10 Frequency of contexts' location and date within site and archaeological feature, including larger sites

interior, perimeter, and exterior were utilised in relatively even proportions. The level of significance is probably due to the high frequency of contexts within the interior during the Middle Iron Age, drastically reducing in the Late Iron Age. However, 56.5 per cent of the contexts from the Early and Middle Iron Age are from a single site, namely Danebury, where the most of the excavated area is within the interior of this hillfort, which heavily influences the test results. In the large sample, there appears to be a steady increase through time into the Late Iron Age of contexts occurring around the perimeter. This pattern is also evident when focusing on contexts' placements within the site (**Figure 4.11**).

In contrast, the smaller sample potentially shows a different picture. Again, there is a significant relationship between date and the location of contexts within sites and archaeological features (χ^2=13.279, p=0.010, **Figure 4.12**). However, during the Early and Late Iron Age, the frequency of contexts with human remains in interiors, perimeters, and exteriors is comparably even, yet in the Middle Iron Age there is an increase of contexts within perimeters as well as a slight decrease of contexts in exteriors. The result from the smaller sample corresponds with the statistical result of context type by date, discussed above. In the Middle Iron Age, there is a high frequency of ditches containing human remains and, typically, ditches define the boundaries (perimeters) of a site or structure, which would explain why a high number of human remains were found within contexts along the perimeter. Once again, by focusing just on contexts' spatial placement within the site, a similar pattern emerges (no statistical test due to sample size). As **Figure 4.13** illustrates, there is a high frequency of contexts along site perimeters in the Middle Iron Age, which relates to the frequency of ditch contexts. However, in the Early Iron

Age, there are few contexts along site perimeters. Nonetheless, the smaller sample shows more variety and a possible change in placement of human remains throughout the Iron Age.

The analyses of the contexts suggest a variation of burial practice with respect to chronology. In particular, there seems to be differing preferences for context types for occurrences from the Early to the Late Iron Age. Moreover, the disposal state for human remains changes distinctly throughout the Iron Age. The statistical results appear to show a decrease in contexts with disarticulated bone, coinciding with an increase in deposits containing cremations by the Late Iron Age. Lastly, the locations (interior, perimeter, and exterior) of contexts that contain human remains within a site or structure appear to differ from one period to another.

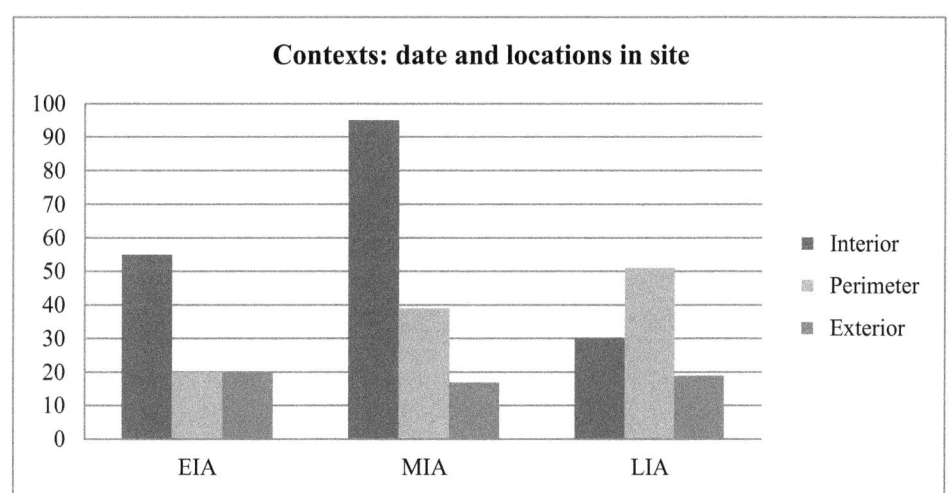

Figure 4. 11 Frequency of context's location within a site and date, including larger sites

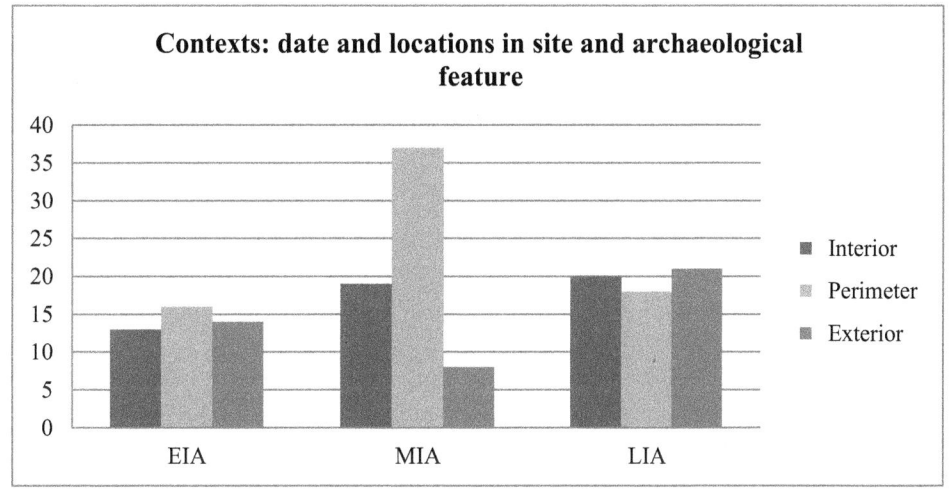

Figure 4. 12 Frequency of contexts' location and date within site and archaeological feature, excluding larger sites

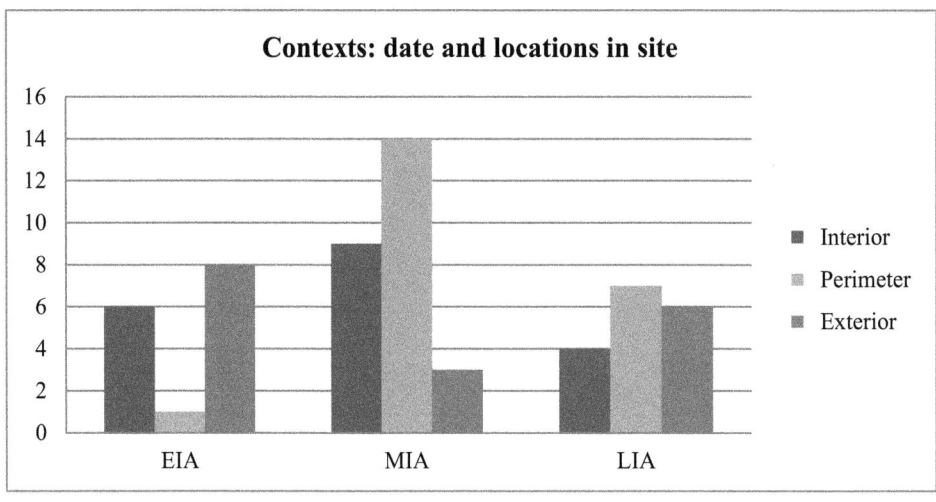

Figure 4. 13 Frequency of contexts' location within a site and date, excluding larger sites

Summary

To stress again, the current archaeological evidence shows that the deposition of human remains during the Late Bronze Age and the Iron Age was a minority rite. The studied sample for this investigation represents a quarter of known sites that contain skeletal material; therefore, the studied data is a sample of a minority rite. As with the nature of samples, not all possible cases can be included within the study. For example, sites such as King Harry Lane (Stead 1969) and Owslebury (Collis 1968; 1970; 1977d) contain a large amount of skeletal evidence, are well-researched and provided crucial information in Iron Age burial studies and its formation, although they were not included in the studied sample. There are varying reasons for exclusion of these sites and others, such as source availability and the commitment to incorporate lesser researched sites. However, the findings from this study can be comparable to excluded sites and allow one to add to the overall burial narrative. Sites within the sample contain varying quantities of human remains, differing methods of processing, and depositing the dead as well as dating throughout the Late Bronze Age and the Iron Age. In essence, it provides a suitable selection of this minority rite and is sufficient for the research objectives of this study.

The statistical analysis of the archaeological features with associated human remains did not return any meaningful results. However, as we can see from the quantitative analysis, archaeological features, particularly roundhouses, were components in the burial practice. In some instances of the burial rite, Iron Age communities deemed certain archaeological features, such as Bronze Age mounds, suitable places for depositing the dead in some fashion. Thus, one can argue there is a spatial relationship between the features and the human remains, which the extent of this connection will require further investigation. In turn, the statistical analysis of the contexts that housed human remains indicated a change in the manner of disposal, context type, and the spatial location. Thus, it suggests the depositional practice for human remains is not fixed, but varies throughout the Late Bronze Age and the Iron Age. The results imply that the handling of the skeletal material, their use and, possibly, meaning differed. The implications of such results may be clearer later when the solely focuses solely on the nature of human remains and how they are found.

Chapter Five

Statistical and quantitative analyses of the manners of disposal

Introduction

The second results chapter addresses the quantitative and statistical results of all the human remains. In doing so, the discussion centres on the chronological change of deposits, associated materials, contextual placement, and spatial location for all the manners of disposal (inhumation, articulated bones, disarticulated bone, and cremation) together. In addition, there is particular emphasis on the spatial relationship of human remains and their associated archaeological features. As with the format of chapter four, only the relevant statistical results will be under discussion and the presentation of the data will follow the same, comparative format of the 'larger' and 'smaller' sample method. The intent of this chapter is to provide a wide and comprehensive overview of the entire burial record within this thesis' sample. The following chapter (chapter six) will discuss in detail the individual manners of disposal (inhumation, articulated bones, disarticulated bone, and cremation) and their respective variables and states independently to provide greater insight into the forthcoming patterns in the burial record.

Manner of disposal analysis

Quantitative analysis

As previously stated, the one hundred studied sites produced 1,874 human remains occurrences, with the most frequently occurring dating to the Middle Iron Age (n=682, **Table 5.1**). However, the sites that contain over 20 occurrences constitute over 80 per cent of the total sample. The remaining eighty-five sites produced 367 human remains occurrences, with a greater proportion dating to the Late Iron Age (n=109, **Table 5.1**). For both the larger and smaller samples, disarticulated bone is the most frequent manner within the archaeological record (54 per cent of the larger sample and 35 per cent of the smaller, **Table 5.2**). Over 40 per cent of occurrences are within pits, the most frequent context type for each sample (**Table 5.3**).

Table 5. 1 Frequency of occurrences and date

Dates	Larger sample	Smaller sample
LBA	110	53
EIA	426	67
MIA	682	101
LIA	573	109
Unphased IA	83	37

Table 5. 2 Frequency of manners of disposal

Manners	Larger sample	Smaller sample
Inhumations	514	122
Disarticulated bones	1007	129
Cremations	336	113
Articulated bones	17	3

Table 5. 3 Frequency of occurrences with context type

Types	Larger sample	Smaller sample
Pit	787	161
Ditch	201	79
Rampart	6	2
Posthole	56	17
Grave	410	65
Other	367	23

The adult age group has the highest representation in both the larger and smaller samples, which is 59 per cent and 71 per cent respectively. Males are also the most frequent sex within the archaeological record for both samples (**Table 5.4**). Furthermore, from all the sites, 275 occurrences possess pathological indicators: 171 occurrences had a single pathological indicator while 104 had multiple afflictions. The smaller sample includes 71 occurrences with pathological indicators (n=37 single; n=34 multiple). For the larger sample, joint disease is the most common pathology (n=137), while in the smaller sample, dental disease is the most frequent (n=44, **Table 5.5**). The 'other' pathology group represents occurrences that possess pathological indicators, but of unknown cause. From the total number of human remains occurrences, 241 have evidence of trauma, of which 203 have a single indicator while 38 have multiple. From the larger sample, the most common type of trauma are cut marks (n=47, **Table 5.6**), and most of these appear to have happened post-mortem. For the smaller sample, 53 occurrences have evidence of some sort of traumatic episode, most with a single indicator (n=40; multiple: n=13). The most frequently occurring trauma for the smaller sample is bone fractures (n=13, **Table 5.6**), commonly occurring post-mortem. As with the pathology, the 'other' trauma category represents evidence of some type of trauma, but the cause is unknown.

The smaller sample of sites has 238 occurrences associated with various items of material culture. Most of these occurrences have multiple types of material deposited with the human remains (n=98 occurrences with a single type of material; n=140 occurrences with multiple). Pottery sherds are the most frequent type of artefact found, being present with 113 occurrences, and animal bone the second most frequent (n=102, **Table 5.7**). In addition, the 'other' category for the associated material, such as glass and beads, includes items found not frequently enough on Iron Age sites to receive their own grouping. Human remains associated with animal bones are most frequently with multiple species. For the smaller sample, cow is the most frequent animal species associated with human remains of animal species while sheep are the next most common species (**Table 5.8**). From the larger sample of sites[3], 903 occurrences have associated material, of which 355 have a single type of material and 548 have multiple. The most commonly occurring item associated with human remains is animal bone (385 occurrences, mostly disarticulated, **Table 5.7**). The most common species found with human remains is sheep (106 occurrences) although many are with multiple species (n=99, **Table 5.8**).

As previously stated in chapter three, the data collection recorded the total count of animal bones by period from each site to compare with the amount of human remains occurrences. The objective for this line of analysis is to offer a general, comparative model of whether the quantity of human remains is the result of taphonomic processes (e.g. bone survival dependent on soil conditions) or intentional selection by Iron Age communities. From the sample of 100 sites, only 70 have accurate counts of the total animal bones by period. **Table 5.9** illustrates these sites' human remains to animal bones ratios. The analysis shows human remains represent 0.22 per cent of the animal bone assemblage from this particular sample. The implications of this result is that bone survival and other taphonomic issues may not be a strong influence in the under representation of human remains for the Iron Age. Instead, the low count compared to animal bones may be a product of social reasons, which the implications of such will be, discussed later (chapter nine).

Table 5. 4 Frequency of sex

Sex	Larger sample	Smaller sample
Males	234	53
Females	180	40

Table 5. 5 Frequency of pathological indicators

Pathologies	Larger sample	Smaller sample
Congenital Disease	28	10
Dental Disease	133	44
Joint Disease	137	40
Infectious Disease	20	9
Metabolic Disease	18	7
Neoplastic Condition	11	0
Haematological Disease	37	4
Other	36	5

Table 5. 6 Frequency of traumatic indicators

Trauma	Larger sample	Smaller sample
Fracture	46	13
Cut mark	47	10
Blunt force	9	4
Dismemberment	13	4
Burning	22	1
Bone modification	10	3
Gnawing	33	3
Scarring	27	0
Striae	2	0
Weathering	29	10
Polishing	14	10
Other	32	11

Table 5. 7 Frequency of associated material

Materials	Larger sample	Smaller sample
Natural Material	94	31
Worked Bone	89	4
Ceramic Vessel	202	35
Sherd	263	113
Quern Stone	67	5
Jewellery	95	25
Military Material	12	1
Domestic Debris	125	16
Plant Remains	69	13
Metal Artefacts	185	41
Ash/Charcoal	257	67
Worked Stone	53	8
Animal Bone	385	102
Sling Stones	45	2
Other	76	24

Table 5. 8 Frequency of animal species

Species	Larger sample	Smaller sample
Cow	97	22
Sheep	106	20
Pig	72	15
Dog	16	2
Horse	59	12
Deer	13	10
Bird	12	7
Other	54	9

---

[3] This does not include the data from Potterne, which is a midden site.

Table 5. 9 Percentage of human remains to animal bones

Site	Occurrence	Animal	Occurrence/ Animal	Site	Occurrence	Animal	Occurrence/ Animal
Ashville	7	2487	0.28 per cent	Hurst Lane Reservoir	4	6179	0.06 per cent
Aspreys, Olney	1	79	1.27 per cent	Hutchinson	1	12500	0.01 per cent
Balksbury Camp	2	1005	0.20 per cent	Latton Lands	5	2835	0.18 per cent
Bancroft	6	3340	0.18 per cent	Little Somborne	6	1666	0.36 per cent
Barton Court Farm	8	2300	0.35 per cent	Little Stock Farm	6	462	1.30 per cent
Battlesbury Bowl	34	27813	0.12 per cent	Maiden Castle	100	11681	0.86 per cent
Bicester Fields Farm	1	3893	0.03 per cent	Micheldever Wood	20	8357	0.24 per cent
Billingborough	6	10360	0.06 per cent	Mingies Ditch	3	6143	0.05 per cent
Birchfield Road	2	1247	0.16 per cent	Nettlebank Copse	5	14059	0.04 per cent
Black Horse Farm	5	3505	0.14 per cent	New Buildings	17	3697	0.46 per cent
Boys Hall Balancing Pond	2	2	100.00 per cent	Northumberland Bottom	7	5834	0.12 per cent
Burgh	1	3117	0.03 per cent	Norton	2	340	0.59 per cent
Bury Hill	3	5626	0.05 per cent	Old Yew Hill Wood	1	2	50.00 per cent
Chapel Mill	7	54	12.96 per cent	Oxley Park West	4	1507	0.27 per cent
Coxwell Road	12	5477	0.22 per cent	Potterne	103	134000	0.08 per cent
Danebury	401	241530	0.17 per cent	Prickwillow Road	3	1339	0.22 per cent
Duckend Car Park	6	39	15.38 per cent	Roughground Farm	3	367	0.82 per cent
Easton Lane	13	3297	0.39 per cent	Salford	4	4960	0.08 per cent
Etonbury Farm Bund	1	10	10.00 per cent	Slonk Hill	2	1294	0.15 per cent
Fiskerton Causeway	3	166	1.81 per cent	Spring Road Municipal Cemetery	5	96	5.21 per cent
Ford Place Nursing Home	1	252	0.40 per cent	Stone Farm Bridleway	14	1897	0.74 per cent
Gloucester Business Park Link Road	1	198	0.51 per cent	Suddern Farm	186	18188	1.02 per cent
Gravelly Guy	107	44156	0.24 per cent	Sutton Common	6	418	1.44 per cent
Great Houghton	2	1180	0.17 per cent	Sutton Walls	40	2147	1.86 per cent
Gussage All Saints	67	15500	0.43 per cent	The Sidbury Double Linear Ditch	3	54	5.56 per cent
Haddenham Site V	2	1608	0.12 per cent	Tollard Royal	1	315	0.32 per cent
Harting Beacon	4	99	4.04 per cent	Tutt Hill	3	4	75.00 per cent
Hartsdown Technology College	1	217	0.46 per cent	Twywell	3	750	0.40 per cent
Hatford Quarry	1	577	0.17 per cent	Wakerley	10	468	2.14 per cent
Helpringham Fen	1	90	1.11 per cent	Wandlebury Ringwork	5	1809	0.28 per cent
High Barns Road	8	3851	0.21 per cent	Watchfield	8	611	1.31 per cent
High Street	2	2	100.00 per cent	West Hay Field	4	2	200.00 per cent
Highfields Farm	4	264	1.52 per cent	White Horse Stone	21	5231	0.40 per cent
Home Farm	2	241	0.83 per cent	Winnall Down	121	10193	1.19 per cent
Houghton Down	4	6000	0.07 per cent	Woodcote Road	6	594	1.01 per cent
				Total	1460	649581	0.22 per cent

Manners of disposal: occurrences associated with archaeological features

To begin, the locational and statistical analyses in comparing occurrences between sites will focus on those human remains associated with archaeological features. From all the studied sites, over four hundred human remains occurrences were near structures (n=456). By excluding the larger sites from this figure, the total number of occurrences decreases to just under two hundred (n=194). The following sections discuss occurrences associated with archaeological features by each feature type and begins with the larger sample followed then by the smaller.

Larger sample: occurrences with archaeological features

For the larger sample, a greater proportion of occurrences with structures date to the Middle Iron Age (n=165, **Table**

5.10) and almost half are disarticulated bone (**Table 5.11**). Occurrences were most often found in association with round structures (roundhouses) (**Table 5.12**) as well as with features that typically have a domestic function (n=120, **Table 5.13**). The 'other' function for structures signifies buildings with purposes not defined by the variables' traits, such as drainage ditches. Just over one hundred occurrences are associated with structures oriented to the east (n=109, **Figure 5.1**). Demographically, most occurrences associated with structures are adults (n=192, sub-adults n=161), and only 81 occurrences have a known sex, of which most are males (n=44, females n=37).

Table 5. 10 Date of occurrences with archaeological features, including larger sites

LBA	35
EIA	57
MIA	165
LIA	161

Table 5. 12 Frequency of occurrences with archaeological features' type, including larger sites

Round structure	160
Rectangular structure	47
Irregular structure	22
2-post structure	3
Multi-post structure	29
Settlement enclosure	42
Boundary	40
Other	113

Table 5. 11 Frequency of manner of disposal with archaeological features, including larger sites

Inhumation	150
Disarticulated bone	214
Cremation	90
Articulated bones	2

Table 5. 13 Frequency of manner of disposal with archaeological features' functions, including larger sites

Domestic	120
Processing	18
Storage	3
Midden	1
Boundary	59
Funerary/ritual	77
Other	18
Multiple functions	57

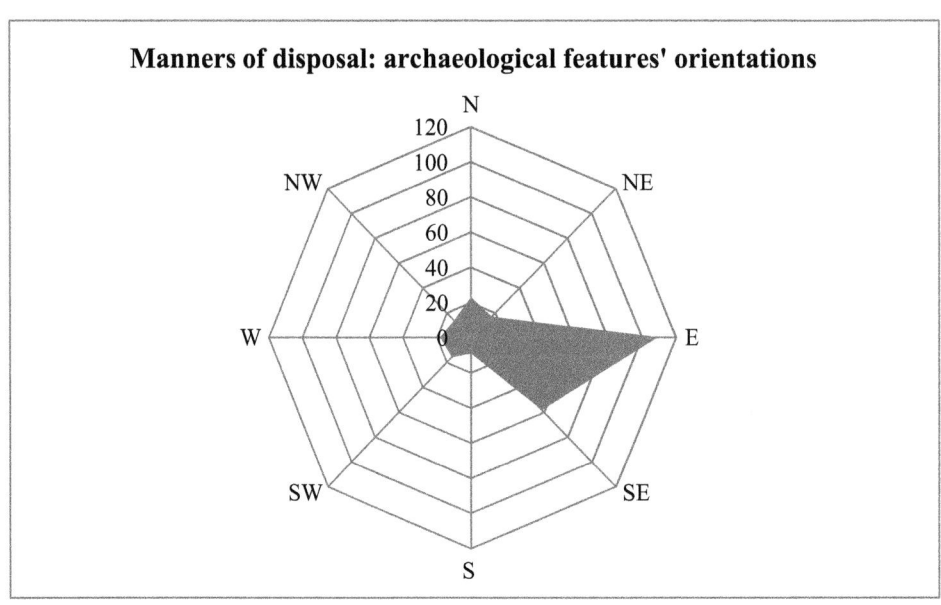

Figure 5. 1 Frequency of occurrences with archaeological features' orientation, including larger sites

Larger sample: occurrences with round, rectangular and irregular structures

Human remains were most frequently associated with round structures (n=160, **Table 5.14**). Many of these were roundhouses that are identified as structures with a domestic function (n=104, **Table 5.15**). There is a low count of human remains with western facing structures, which follows the quantitative analysis from archaeological features, and there is no discernible difference in the depositional characteristics between eastern and non-eastern orientated buildings. Human remains occur more frequently with structures oriented to the east (n=79, **Figure 5.2**). Furthermore, skeletal material

is relatively evenly placed within interiors, perimeters and exteriors of these buildings, although interiors have the highest frequency of human remains (n=85, **Table 5.16**). In terms of a building's quadrants, the each segment is represented and the left/front is the most frequent (n=43, **Figure 5.3**). Occurrences are relatively evenly distributed between the front (n=78) and back (n=65) of a structure, and this distribution is the same for the right (n=74) and left (n=69) sides of a building. Human remains associated with architectural features of these building types were frequently found near the boundary areas of these buildings (65 per cent), followed by placement near or within their entrances (35 per cent, **Table 5.17**).

Table 5. 14 Frequency of occurrences with structure type, including larger sites (see also Figure 5.12)

Round structure	160
Rectangular structure	47
Irregular structure	22

Table 5. 16 Frequency of occurrences within structures, including larger sites

Interior	85
Perimeter	74
Exterior	62

Table 5. 15 Frequency of occurrences with structures' function, including larger sites

Domestic	104
Processing	3
Storage	1
Funerary	10
Other	2
Multiple functions	37

Table 5. 17 Frequency of occurrences near architectural features, including larger sites

Entrance	36
Boundary	66

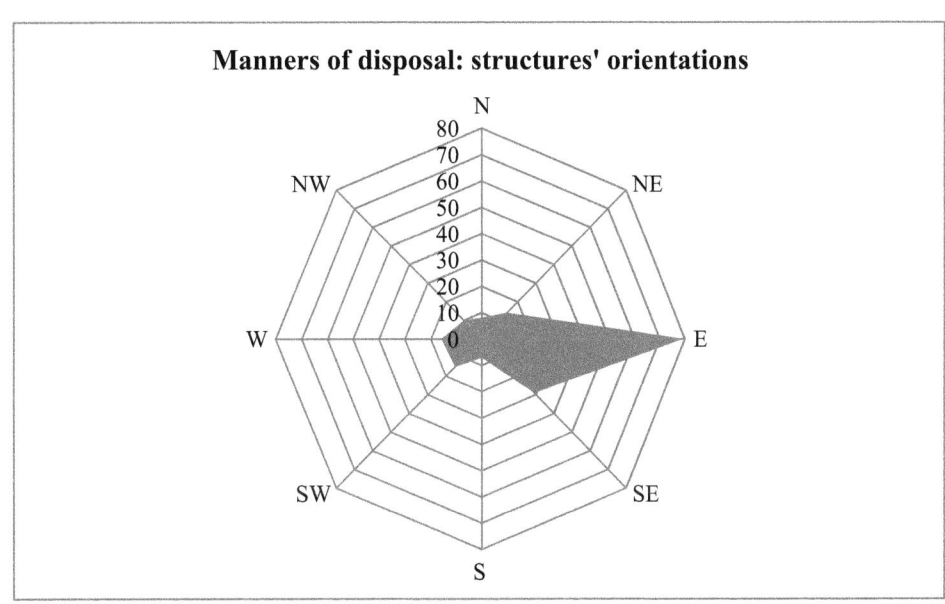

Figure 5. 2 Frequency of occurrences with structures' orientation, including larger sites

In the larger sample, occurrences with round, rectangular, or irregular structures most often date to the Middle Iron Age (n=113, **Table 5.18**). Disarticulated bone (n=126, **Table 5.19**) is the most common form of disposal associated with these structures. Thirty-three occurrences were assigned a biological sex, of which males (n=16) and females (n=17) are comparably even in representation. The sub-adult age category (n=111; adults: n=83),

particularly the infants (n=93), contains the highest number of individuals of the age group associated with these structures (see **Figure 5.4**). Interestingly, 76 per cent of such occurrences with infants are from three of the sites with 20 or more occurrences, namely Gravelly Guy (Oxfordshire), Gussage All Saints (Dorset), and Winnall Down (Hampshire).

Table 5. 18 Date of occurrences with structures, including larger sites

LBA	9
EIA	25
MIA	113
LIA	64

Table 5. 19 Manner of disposal with structures, including larger sites

Inhumation	79
Disarticulated bone	126
Cremation	23
Articulated bones	1

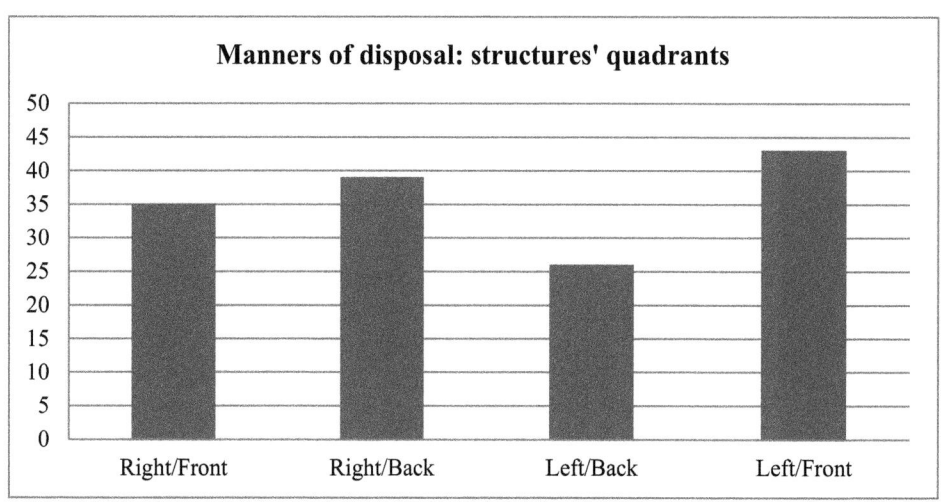

Figure 5. 3 Frequency of occurrences within structures' quadrants, including larger sites

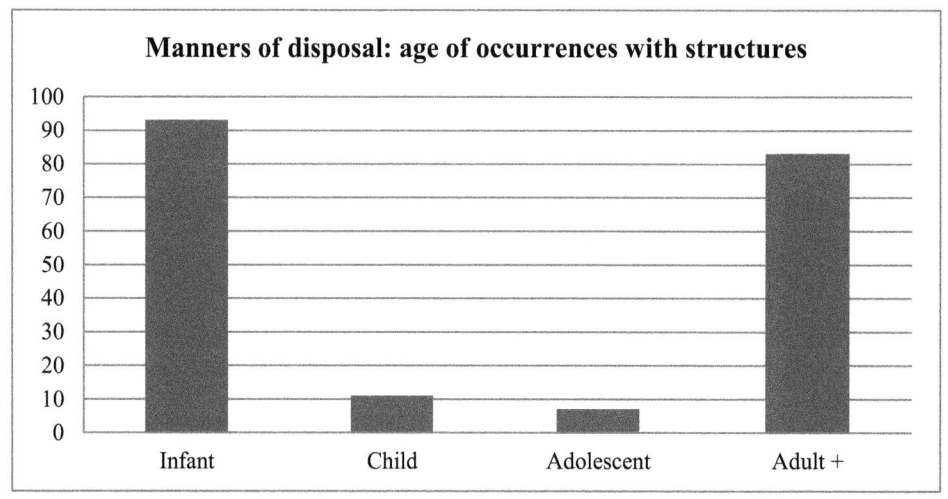

Figure 5. 4 Frequency of age with structures, including larger sites

Larger sample: occurrences within roundhouses and other round structures

Just over half (51 per cent) of the occurrences associated with round structures come from three of the sites with over 20 occurrences: Danebury, Glastonbury Lake Village, and Gravelly Guy. Overall, a greater proportion of occurrences with round structures date to the Middle Iron Age (67 per cent, **Table 5.20**), and are largely disarticulated bone (64 per cent, **Figure Table 5.21**). As above, many of the occurrences are associated with roundhouses (round structures that have a domestic function), and very few are associated with structures used for other functions such as storage or processing. Human remains are often associated with buildings that have an eastern orientation (n=51) or a southeastern orientation (n=29) (**Figure 5.5**). Just over half (52 per cent) of round structures with a southeast orientation are from a single site, Gravelly Guy. All quadrants of a round structure are well represented with the left/front being more frequent (n=32, **Figure 5.6**). The majority of the human bones

found in round structures were within the interior areas of the building (n=66, **Table 5.22**). These favour the front halves (n=59) over the back areas (n=35). In addition, occurrences are slightly more frequent on the left half (n=49) than the right hand side of these round structures (n=44). As for the architectural features, occurrences are relatively evenly distributed near either the boundaries or entrances of round structures, although boundary features (n=31) occur slightly more frequently than entrances (n=27). There are only 19 occurrences that have known biological sex and males and females are almost equally represented (females n=10; males n=9). Sub-adults, again, have the highest representation (n=73; adults: n=57) and, specifically, infants are most frequent (n=60, **Table 5.23**). Interestingly, 38 per cent of infant occurrences are from one site, namely Gravelly Guy. As with above, the depositional and burial characteristics between the eastern and non-eastern orientated buildings are similar.

Table 5. 20 Frequency of occurrences with round structures, including larger sites

LBA	9
EIA	16
MIA	96
LIA	22

Table 5. 22 Frequency of occurrences within round structures, including

Interior	66
Perimeter	36
Exterior	50

Table 5. 21 Manners of disposal with round structures, including larger sites

Inhumation	46
Disarticulated bone	102
Cremation	11
Articulated bones	1

Table 5. 23 Age with round structures, including larger sites

Infants	60
Child	8
Adolescent	5
Adult +	57

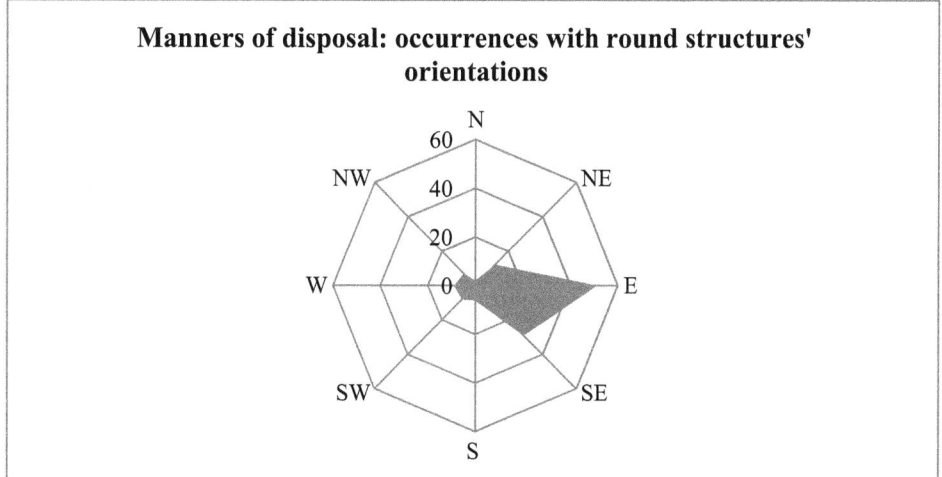

Figure 5. 5 Frequency of occurrences with round structures' orientation, including larger sites

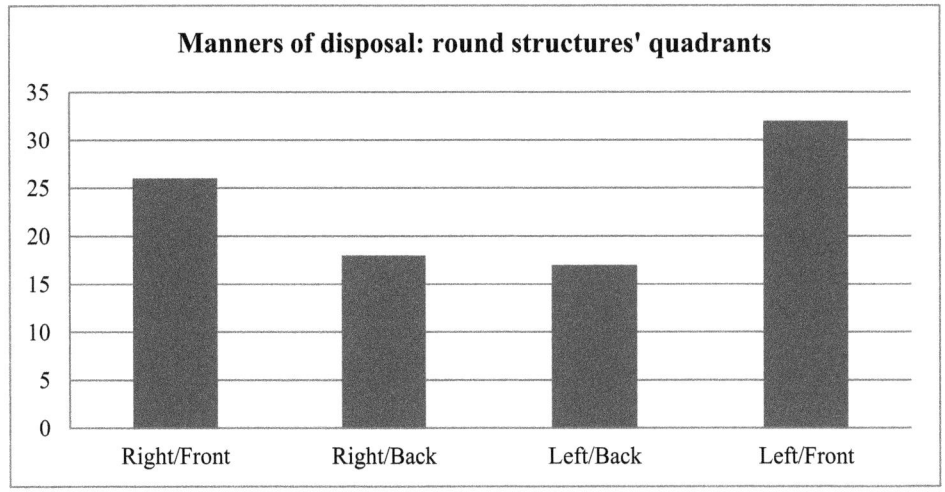

Figure 5. 6 Frequency of occurrences within round structures' quadrants, including larger sites

Larger sample: occurrences with 'other' archaeological features

Of the entire human remains occurrences, over half are associated with 'other' archaeological features that have a funerary purpose (57 per cent, **Table 5.24**) and, of this total, many are Bronze Age barrows. Most occurrences with 'other' features date to the Late Iron Age (n=64, **Table 5.25**), and are commonly inhumations (n=48, **Table 5.26**). Occurrences with 'other' features were frequently placed outside the feature (n=59), as opposed to within interiors or along its perimeters (**Table 5.27**). Of the 113 occurrences with 'other' features, only 28 have a known biological sex, of which females have a slightly higher representation than males (females n=17; males n=11). Finally, occurrences falling within the adult age group are more frequently associated with 'other' archaeological (n=57; sub-adult: n=29).

Table 5. 24 Frequency of occurrences with 'other' archaeological features' function, including larger sites

Domestic	16
Processing	13
Midden	1
Enclosure	1
Funerary/ritual	60
Other	12
Multiple functions	2

Table 5. 25 Date of occurrences with 'other' archaeological features, including larger sites

LBA	16
EIA	16
MIA	14
LIA	64

Table 5. 26 Manner of disposal with 'other' archaeological features, including larger sites

Inhumation	48
Disarticulated bone	26
Cremation	38
Articulated bones	1

Table 5. 27 Frequency of occurrences within 'other' archaeological features, including larger sites

Interior	29
Perimeter	25
Exterior	59

Larger sample: occurrences with post-built structures

Post-built structures include both two- and multi-post buildings. It should be noted that a greater proportion of occurrences associated with post-structures derive from a single site, Danebury (56 per cent). Occurrences associated with these types of structures frequently date to the Middle Iron Age (n=17) and, interestingly, no human remains in this sample are found with post-built structures in the Late Iron Age (**Table 5.28**). Furthermore, most of the human remains are disarticulated bone (n=22, **Table 5.29**). Only a small fraction (n=9) of occurrences are near the post-built structures with a known function (**Table 5.30**). Three of the occurrences are near a post-structure at South Hornchurch believed to have another purpose ('other' function) rather than being used for as a storage facility or drying rack (Guttman and Last 2000, 334). The other occurrence associated with a post-structure with an 'other' function is a disarticulated bone from Danebury where the structure may serve at a type of watchtower (Cunliffe 1984a, 94, 99). Human remains occurrences are more frequent outside post-built structures (n=15), followed by placement along their perimeters (n=11); a small number are found within the interiors (n=3). Demographically, only 22 occurrences have known ages, of which both sub-adult (n=10) and adult groups (n=11) are equally represented. As for biological sex, only four are known, all of which all are males.

Smaller sample: occurrences associated with archaeological features

The 85 sites that make up the smaller sample represent 43 per cent of the original total of human remains associated with archaeological features. Most of the occurrences date to the Middle and Late Iron Age (**Table 5.31**), and, as with the larger sample, most occurrences are of disarticulated bone (n=68, **Table 5.32**). Occurrences are more frequently associated with 'other' (n=55) and round (n=52) structures (**Table 5.33**). One hundred and sixty-two occurrences are associated with archaeological features that have a known function, and a domestic purpose has the highest frequency (n=58, **Table 5.34**). Skeletal remains (within, along or outside the features) are found mostly along the perimeters of the buildings (n=91) than within the interiors or exteriors (**Table 5.35**). Furthermore, human remains are more frequent in boundaries (n=92) than entrances (n=28), which directly relates to the frequency of occurrences along the perimeters of buildings. A greater proportion of occurrences that were assigned to a biological age category fell within the adult group (n=107; sub-adult: n=37). The biological sex of 44 occurrences were known, of which they were more frequently males (n=27; females n=17).

Table 5. 28 Date of occurrences with post-built structures, including larger sites

LBA	4
EIA	7
MIA	17

Table 5. 29 Manner of disposal with post-built structures, including larger sites

Inhumation	5
Disarticulated bone	22
Cremation	5

Table 5. 30 Frequency of occurrences with post-built structures' function

Storage	4
Funerary	1
Other	4

Table 5. 31 Date of occurrences with archaeological features, excluding larger sites

LBA	31
EIA	30
MIA	57
LIA	58

Table 5. 32 Manner of disposal with archaeological features, excluding larger sites

Inhumation	60
Disarticulated bone	68
Cremation	64
Articulated bones	2

Table 5. 33 Frequency of occurrences with archaeological features' type, excluding larger sites

Round structure	52
Rectangular structure	25
Irregular structure	6
Multi-post structure	8
Settlement enclosure	21
Boundary	27
Other	55

Table 5. 34 Frequency of occurrences with archaeological features' function, excluding larger sites

Domestic	58
Processing	7
Storage	1
Enclosure	35
Funerary/ritual	40
Other	7
Multiple functions	14

Table 5. 35 Frequency of occurrences within archaeological features excluding larger sites

Interior	59
Perimeter	91
Exterior	39

Smaller sample: occurrences with round, rectangular, and irregular structures

For the smaller sample, occurrences associated with round, rectangular, or irregular structures commonly date to the Middle Iron Age (n=36, **Table 5.36**), and are far more frequently associated with round structures (n=52, see **Table 5.33**). Additionally, occurrences are overwhelmingly more common with roundhouses (structures that have a domestic purpose (n=42), **Table 5.37**). The single occurrence associated with a structure with an 'other' function is a disarticulated bone placed along the perimeter of a rectangular, ditched enclosure that may have been an animal paddock. In addition, the occurrences associated with buildings with multiple functions all have domestic correlates as well as serving as areas for funerary activities. Buildings with their entrances opening to the east commonly have a higher number of human remains associated with them (n=23, **Figure 5.7**). Interestingly, all the compass directions for orientations are well represented, except for the southwest (n=0). The interior (n=20) and exterior (n=18) of these buildings are similarly represented, but they occur less frequently than occurrences along the perimeters of structures (n=40). The left/front quadrants of structures contain the highest amount of human remains (n=23) and the other three quadrants are well represented (**Figure 5.8**). Occurrences are frequently in front halves (n=36) than back (n=23) and favour left segments (n=34) than right (n=25).

Table 5. 36 Date of occurrences with structures, excluding larger sites

LBA	9
EIA	11
MIA	36
LIA	15

Table 5. 37 Frequency of occurrences with structures' function, excluding larger sites

Domestic	42
Funerary	8
Other	1
Multiple functions	5

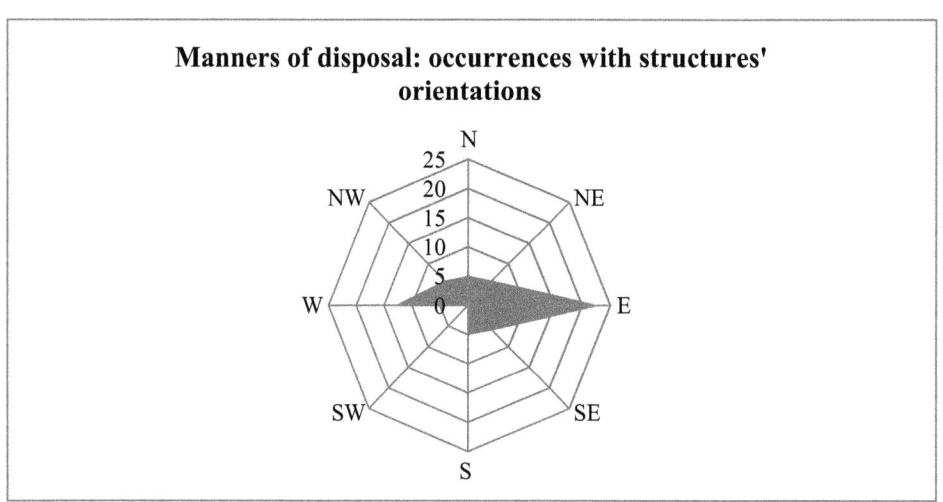

Figure 5.7 Frequency of occurrences with structures' orientation, excluding larger sites

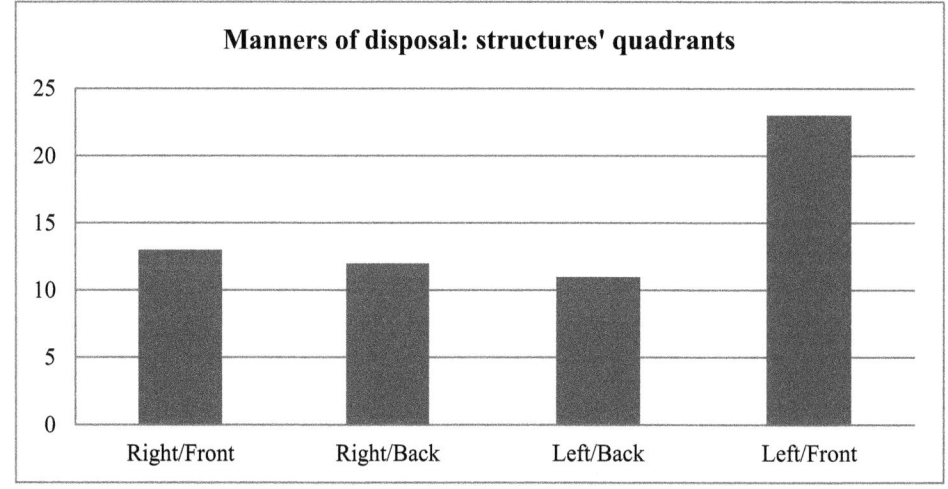

Figure 5. 8 Frequency of occurrences with structures' quadrants, excluding larger sites

Disarticulated bones are the most common occurrences of human remains found with round, rectangular, and irregular structures (n=33, **Table 5.38**). Adults have the highest representation of the age groups (n=47, sub-adults n=18); while only 19 occurrences have a known biological sex, the greater proportion are males (n=11).

Smaller sample: occurrences within roundhouses and other round structures

Overall, 52 occurrences are associated with round structures from the smaller sample, with nearly half these human remains with a known date belong to the Middle Iron Age (n=24, **Table 5.39**). Where functions of buildings are known, a higher frequency of occurrences are with roundhouses (buildings that have a domestic purpose (n=32, **Table 5.40**). The only funerary/ritual function is from a roundhouse at Black Horse Farm (Cambridgeshire) that contained a single infant inhumation (Newton 2008, 14-15). The archaeological evidence from the building (Roundhouse 3) at Black Horse Farm suggests a high-status structure used as a shrine (Newton 2008, 14-15, 39). The infant inhumation is an unphased Iron Age deposit but its proximity to Roundhouse 3 implies that they were contemporary, and the associated infant burial may have reinforced the symbolic quality of the building (Newton 2008, 15, 38-39). The remaining occurrences are with buildings that served both domestic and funerary purposes. Most occurrences are with round buildings that opened to the east (n=20, **Figure 5.9**). Similar to the larger sample, there is no discernable difference in the depositional nature of human remains between eastern and western facing buildings. Additionally, many of the occurrences are found along the perimeters of these buildings (n=26), with a relatively even number of occurrences within the interiors and exteriors of structures (**Table 5.41**). There also appears to have been a preference for the boundary areas of round structures (n=19), although entrances are also well represented within this sample (n=16). Each quadrant of round structures is represented but there are high numbers of occurrences in the left/front of round buildings (n=20, **Figure 5.10**). Furthermore, a large portion of the human remains are placed in the front halves (n=29) of round structures as opposed to the back (n=13), and they strongly favour the left half (n=30) of the building over the right (n=12).

Table 5. 38 Manner of disposal in structures, excluding larger sites

Inhumation	27
Disarticulated bone	33
Cremation	21
Articulated bones	1

Table 5. 39 Date of occurrences with round structures, excluding larger site

LBA	9
EIA	2
MIA	24
LIA	6

Table 5. 40 Frequency of occurrences with structures' functions, excluding larger sites

Domestic	32
Funerary	1
Multiple functions	5

Table 5. 41 Frequency of occurrences within round structures, excluding larger sites

Interior	11
Perimeter	26
Exterior	11

Table 5. 42 Manner of disposal with round structures excluding larger sites

Inhumation	15
Disarticulated bone	25
Cremation	11
Articulated bones	1

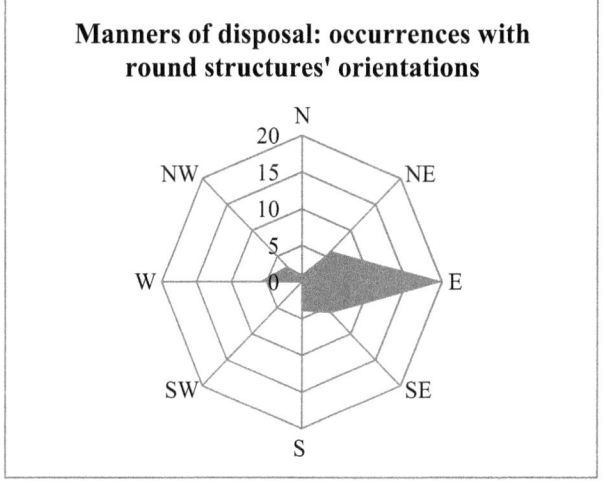

Manners of disposal: occurrences with round structures' orientations

Figure 5. 9 Frequency of occurrences with round structures' orientation, excluding larger sites

Smaller sample: occurrences with 'other' structures

Many of the occurrences from the smaller sample are associated with structures referred to as 'other'. Most date to the Late Iron Age (n=20), although there are reasonable numbers of human remains dating to the Late Bronze Age (n=14) and Early Iron Age (n=13) (**Table 5.43**). However, a decrease in these numbers is apparent during the Middle Iron Age. These structures with associated remains usually have a funerary purpose, such as funerary ring ditches or Bronze Age barrows (**Table 5.44**). The 'other' purpose category (n=2) for these structures includes functions undefined by the variables' traits, such as an animal paddock. The human remains are equally divided in terms of placement either within interiors, along perimeters or exteriors of 'other' structures, although the perimeter areas are slightly more frequent (n=20, **Table 5.45**). Inhumations and disarticulated bones have an almost equal count within 'other' structures, but cremated remains are the most frequent form of disposal associated with these types of structures (n=26, **Table 5.46**). Adults are the most common age group associated with 'other' structures (n=33; sub-adults: n=9), and only eleven occurrences could be sexed: seven individuals were females and only four males.

Smaller sample: occurrences with post-built structures

A few occurrences from the smaller sample are associated with post-built structures, and all derive from just five sites. Most date to the Late Bronze Age (n=4), a single one to the Early Iron Age and the remaining to the Middle Iron Age (n=3). These occurrences are most frequently cremations (n=5), while the rest of the human remains are disarticulated bones (n=3). Only five of them occurrences have an assigned age, of which most are sub-adults (n=3), and none were given a sex.

Table 5. 43 Date of occurrences with 'other' structures, excluding larger sites

LBA	14
EIA	13
MIA	5
LIA	20

Table 5. 44 Frequency of occurrences with structures' function, excluding larger sites

Domestic	16
Processing	7
Enclosure	1
Funerary/ritual	25
Other	2

Table 5. 45 Frequency of occurrences within 'other' structures, excluding larger sites

Interior	19
Perimeter	20
Exterior	16

Table 5. 46 Manner of disposal with 'other' structures, excluding larger sites

Inhumation	14
Disarticulated bone	14
Cremation	26
Articulated bones	1

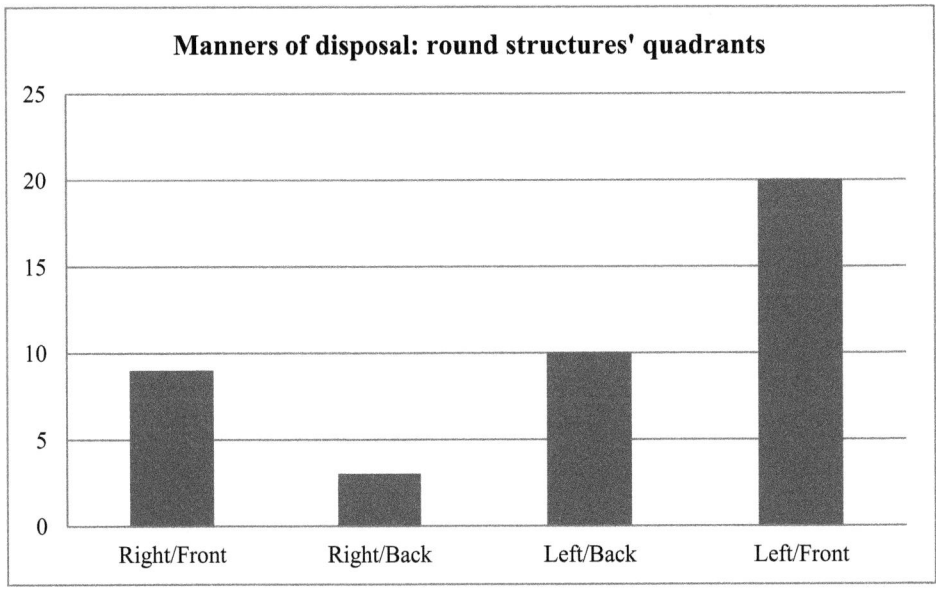

Figure 5. 10 Frequency of occurrences with round structures' quadrants, excluding larger sites

Statistical analysis

To begin with, the statistical analysis of the manner of disposal excludes the articulated bone category due to their low numbers. The statistical analysis of both the larger and smaller sample returned a variety of results. Both the larger and smaller samples returned a significant relationship between the date[4] and form of disposal (larger sample: χ^2=697.895, p=0.000; smaller sample: χ^2=112.013, p=0.000). For the larger sample, as **Figure 5.11** illustrates, there is an overwhelmingly high quantity of disarticulated bones from the Early (n=324) and Middle Iron Age (n=485), followed by a sharp decrease in the Late Iron Age (n=89). This high number of disarticulated material, when compared to inhumations and cremations from the same time periods, may be a strong influence on the high probability result (p=0.000). However, it should be noted that 87 per cent of the disarticulated bones from the Middle Iron Age derive from ten of the sites that have over 20 occurrences. Specifically, Danebury provides 38 per cent of the total sample of disarticulated bone from the Middle Iron Age. In contrast, there is a steady increase in inhumations from the Early into the Late Iron Age. Interestingly, cremations occur in relatively low numbers compared with inhumations and disarticulated bones. In the Late Iron Age, the numbers of cremation deposits significantly increase. The apparent rise in popularity of cremation correlates with the emergence of the Aylesford-Swarling cremation rite in southeast England. For the 23 sites with cremation occurrences in the Late Iron Age, most lie within the southeast, extending northwards towards the East Midlands. The sites are within the counties of Kent (eight sites), West Sussex (one site), Bedfordshire (three sites), Essex (three sites), Cambridgeshire (three sites), Oxfordshire (two sites), Buckinghamshire (one site), Leicestershire (one site), and Wiltshire (one site). The most westerly Late Iron Age cremation occurrence that has been recorded within the studied sample is the site of Latton Lands in Wiltshire. Two Late Iron Age cremation occurrences were recorded from Latton Lands, the first a small quantity of redeposited cremated bone mixed within the fill of an inhumation, and the second a small cremation burial placed within an enclosure's entrance (Powell *et al.* 2008, 44-45).

The smaller sample provides a similar pattern to that of the larger sample with regard to the fluctuating counts for forms of disposal during the Iron Age. This is especially evident in the steady increase of inhumations from the Early to the Late Iron Age, as well as in the dramatic increase of disarticulated bone into the Middle Iron Age followed by a decline in the Late Iron Age (**Figure 5.12**). With regard to deposits of cremated bones, there is a high count of these occurrences in the Late Bronze Age compared to inhumations and disarticulated bones. As

with the larger sample, however, cremation occurrences decreased in the Early and Middle Iron Age, only to resurge in the Late Iron Age. When considering the smaller sample, there appear to be two transitional periods since there is a change in the preferred form of disposal between the Late Bronze Age and the Early Iron Age, and then again between the Middle and Late Iron Age. There is a significant relationship between manner of disposal and dates in the Late Bronze Age and Early Iron Age (χ^2=38.261, p=0.000). In the Early Iron Age, inhumations and disarticulated bone are comparably even and are more frequent than cremations whereas, as we have discussed, cremations dominate in the Late Bronze Age. Additionally, there is a significant relationship between manner of disposal and dates in the Middle and Late Iron Age (χ^2=59.842, p=0.000). Between these two periods, the dissimilarity lies in the significant decrease in disarticulated bone in the Late Iron Age coinciding with an increase of cremations in the same period. Thus, the larger and smaller sample both show that varying forms of disposal vary significantly according to date and indicate periods of notable change with regard to burial practice.

There is a significant relationship, for the larger sample, between age at death and chronological date (χ^2=23.935, p=0.000, **Figure 5.13**). In this sample, the number of occurrences assigned to the adult age group steadily increases from the Early to Late Iron Age, while the sub-adult group increases from the Early to the Middle Iron Age, becoming almost evenly matched with the adult group by the Middle Iron Age, before decreasing in the Late Iron Age. If the age groups are broken down into more specific categories (infant, child, adolescent and adult), it is evident that infants comprise a greater proportion of the sub-adult group (**Figure 5.14**). In addition, there is an increase in infants present in the archaeological record during the Middle Iron Age (n=173). However, 93 per cent of infant occurrences from the Middle Iron Age belong to only eight of the sites with over 20 occurrences. In particular, Winnall Down provides 37 per cent of the total of Middle Iron Age infants in the sample and Gravelly Guy 23 per cent. The smaller sample shows a statistically insignificant relationship between the age at death and date (χ^2=5.307, p=0.151). As **Figure 5.15** illustrates, the adult age group typically has a much higher frequency than the sub-adult category during all periods from the Late Bronze Age to the Late Iron Age. When the age groups are broken down into more narrow categories, there is a steady increase in infants from the Early to the Late Iron Age (**Figure 5.16**). The results from both the larger and smaller samples may reflect those age categories with a high fatality rate, either elderly adults or infants. Alternatively, this pattern in both the larger and smaller samples may signify that the main age categories for this minority burial rite were the adult and infant groups, the latter mainly in the Late Iron Age. This may be more evident on these sites with higher numbers of occurrences.

---

[4] For the larger sample, occurrences from the Late Bronze Age were not included in any of the statistical tests concerning date since the count (Late Bronze Age n=110) is considerably lower than that of the Early, Middle and Late Iron Age.

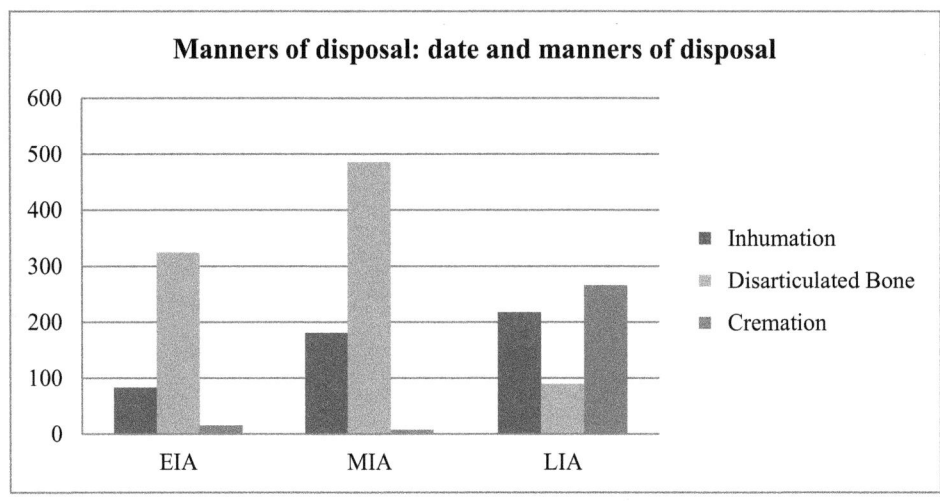

Figure 5. 11 Manner of disposal and date, including larger sites

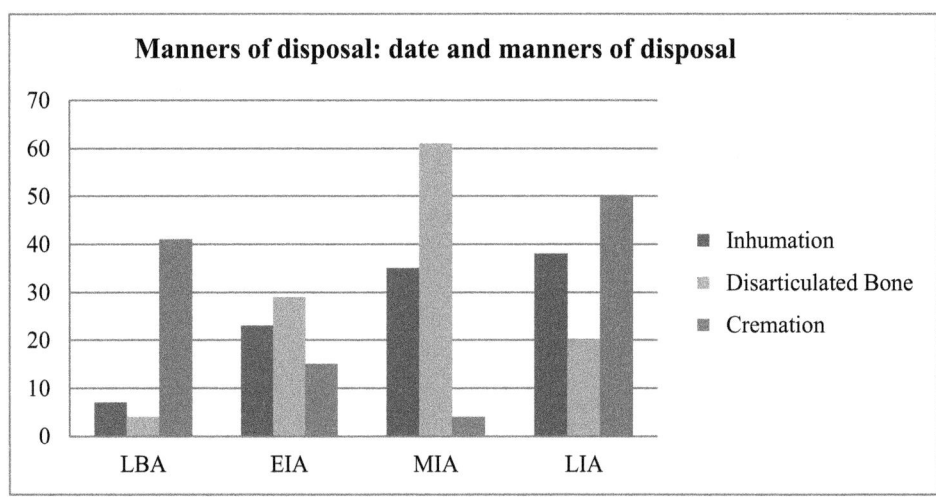

Figure 5. 12 Manner of disposal and date, excluding larger sites

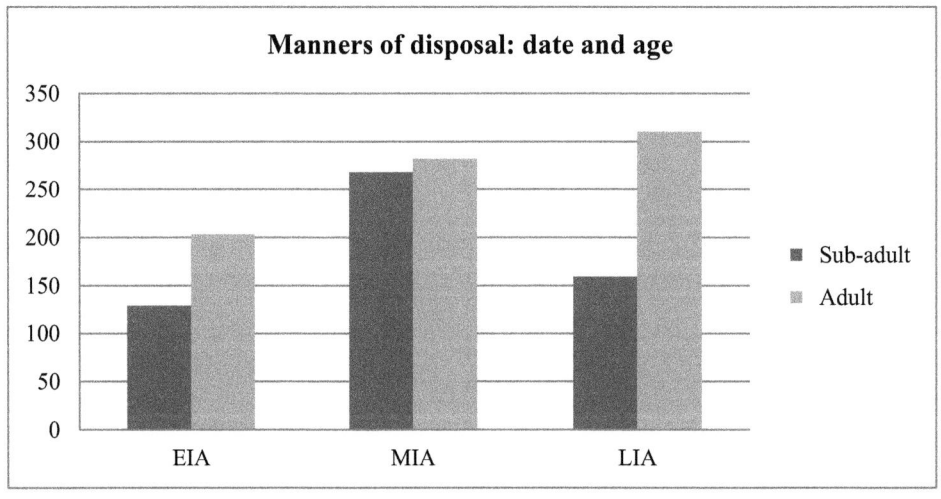

Figure 5. 13 Age of occurrences and date, including larger sites

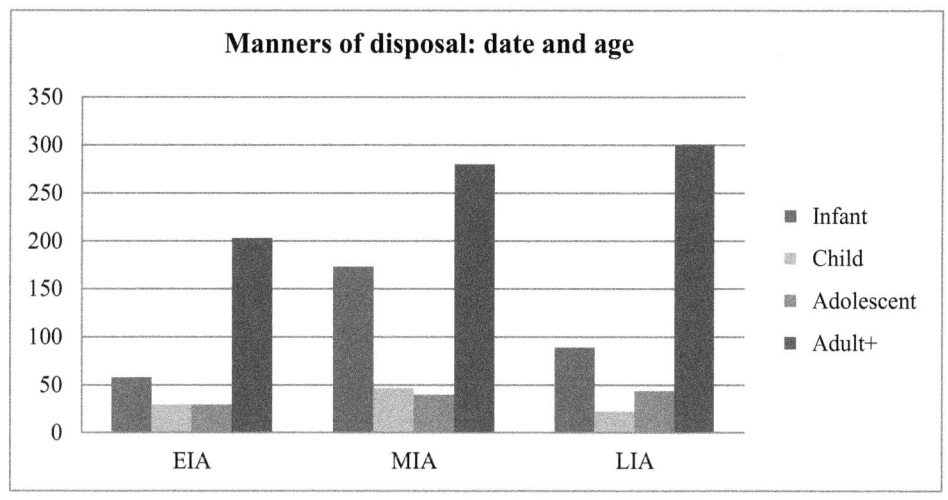

Figure 5. 14 Age of occurrences and date, including larger sites

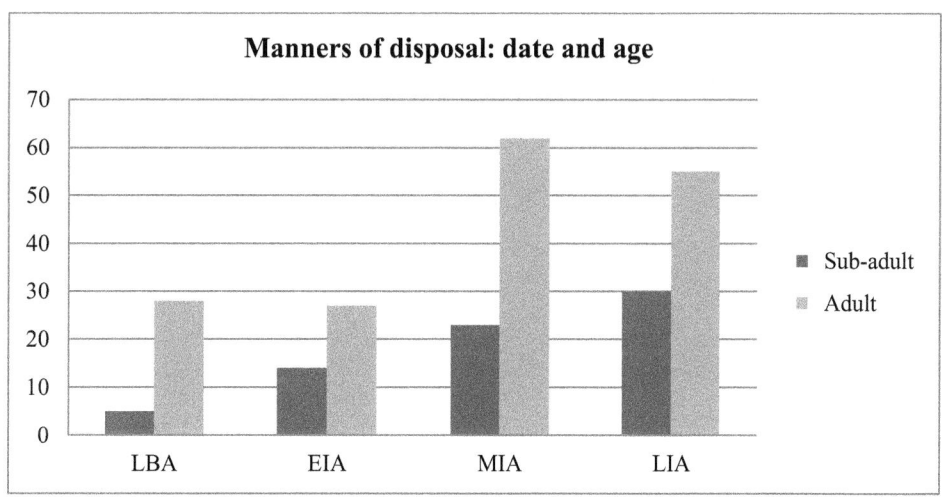

Figure 5. 15 Age of occurrences and date, excluding larger sites

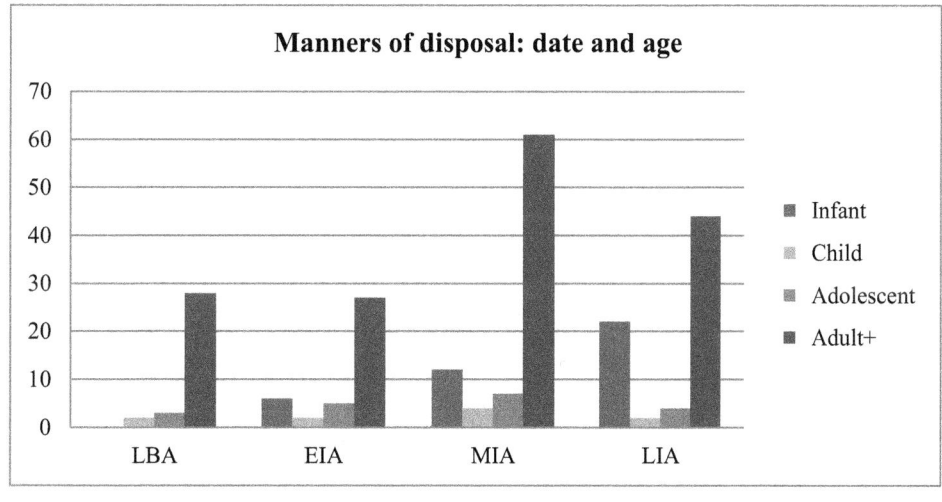

Figure 5. 16 Age of occurrences and date, excluding larger sites

There was no significant relationship between biological sex and chronological date for the larger sample (χ^2=5.283, p=0.071, **Figure 5.17**). The smaller sample was too small for a statistical test. In addition, there appears to be no preference in terms of biological sex when depositing human remains throughout the Iron Age (see **Figure 5.18**). The smaller sample illustrates that the Late Bronze Age is the only period when females outnumbered males, although the numbers are very small from this period (males n=3; females n=6).

The larger sample has a significant relationship between the age (sub-adult and adult) of occurrences and their form of disposal (χ^2=59.082, p=0.000, **Figure 5.19**). Likewise, by running the same chi-square test with narrower age categories, biological age and form of disposal continue to show a significant relationship (χ^2=108.297, p=0.000). As **Figure 5.20** illustrates, the child and adolescent groups are present but infrequent in all forms of disposal. Adults tend to be most frequent in all manners of disposal, and infants occur more frequent in inhumations but almost entirely absent in cremations. Sites with over 20 occurrences represent 83 per cent of total infant inhumations. Chronologically, infant inhumations become more frequent in the Middle and Late Iron Age; especially in the latter period (see **Figures 5.21-24**). Besides inhumations, infants are well represented in disarticulated bones. The extent to which infant disarticulated bones are the result of disturbed burials is unclear. For example, Gravelly Guy has high numbers of infant loose bone but the contextual evidence cannot clearly state whether the disarticulated remains are the result of human or natural disturbance or they were deposited in that manner (Lambrick and Allen 2004, 462). The disarticulated infant bones at Coxwell Road (Oxfordshire) share similar contextual characteristics as Gravelly Guy (Smith 2004, 256). However, there are instances of loose infant bone intentionally deposited such as Oxley Park West where an infant cranial and vertebra fragments were placed in the southwest posthole of a four-post structure (Brown *et al.* 2009, 51). The adult category illustrates fluctuations in forms of disposal; this is especially notable when considering the increase of adult inhumations from the Late Bronze Age into the Late Iron Age, as well as the high count of cremations in the Late Bronze Age.

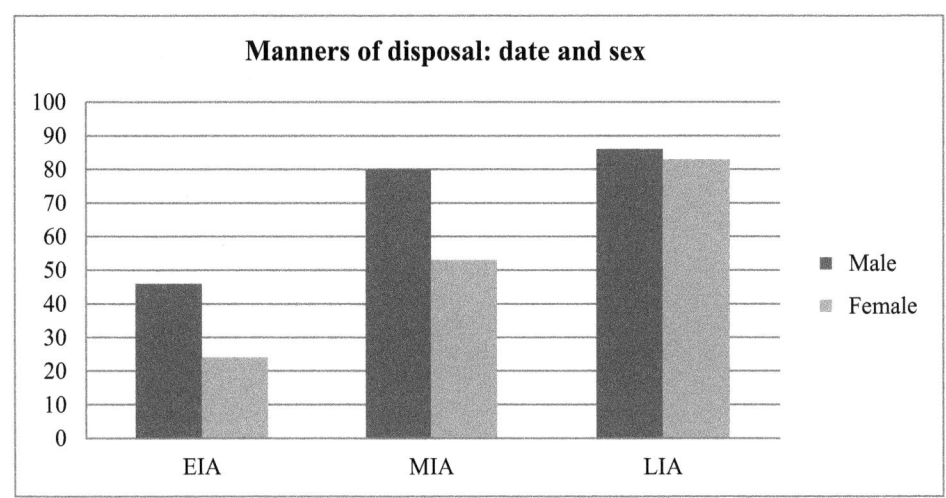

Figure 5. 17 Sex of occurrences and date including larger sites, including larger sites

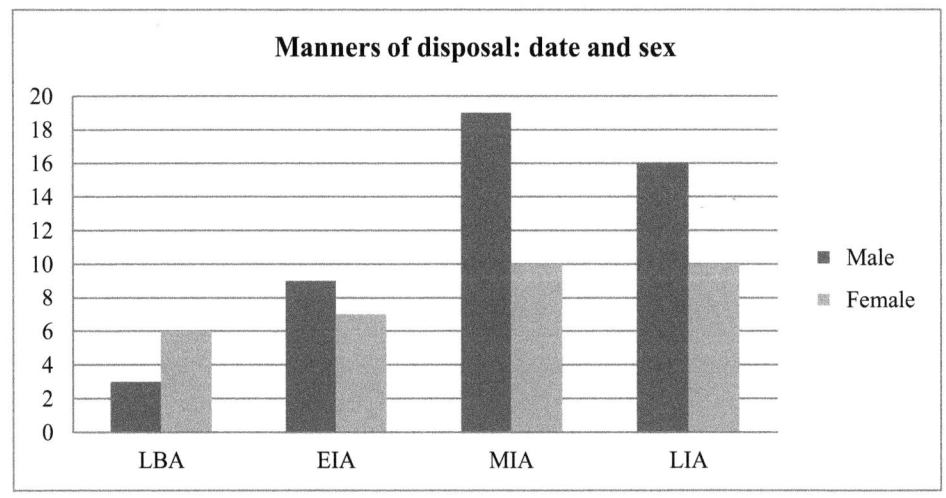

Figure 5. 18 Sex of occurrences and date, excluding larger sites

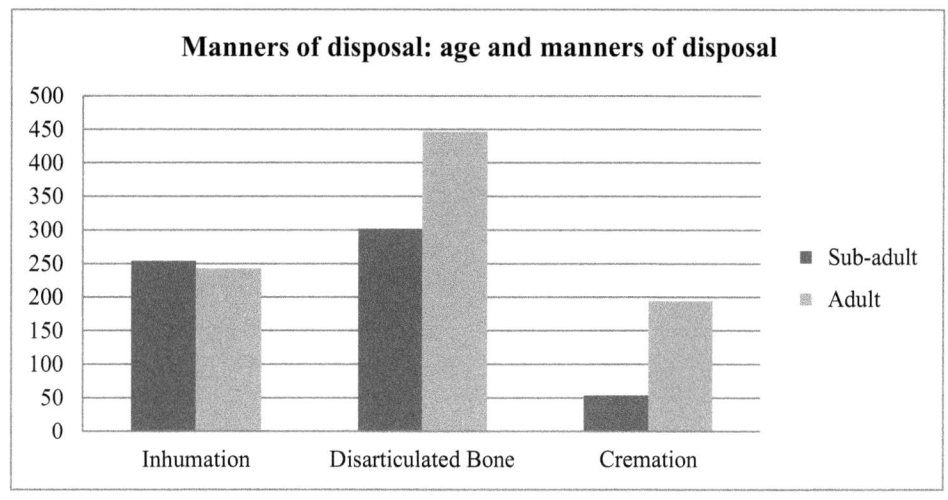

Figure 5. 19 Age of occurrences and manner of disposal, including larger sites

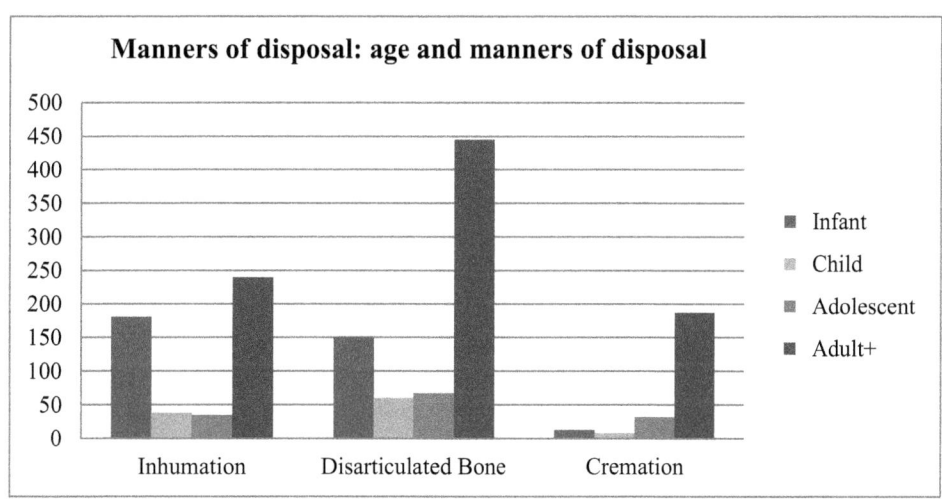

Figure 5. 20 Age of occurrences and manner of disposal, including larger sites

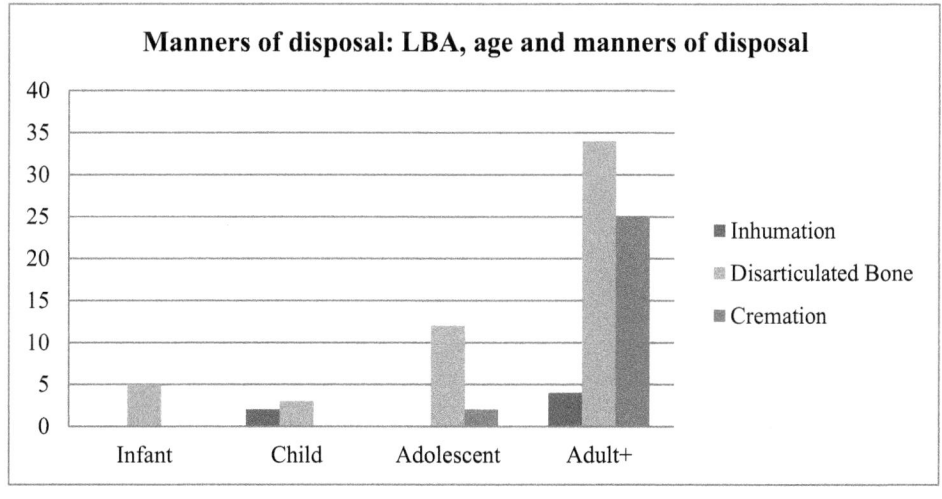

Figure 5. 21 LBA: age of occurrences and manner of disposal, including larger sites

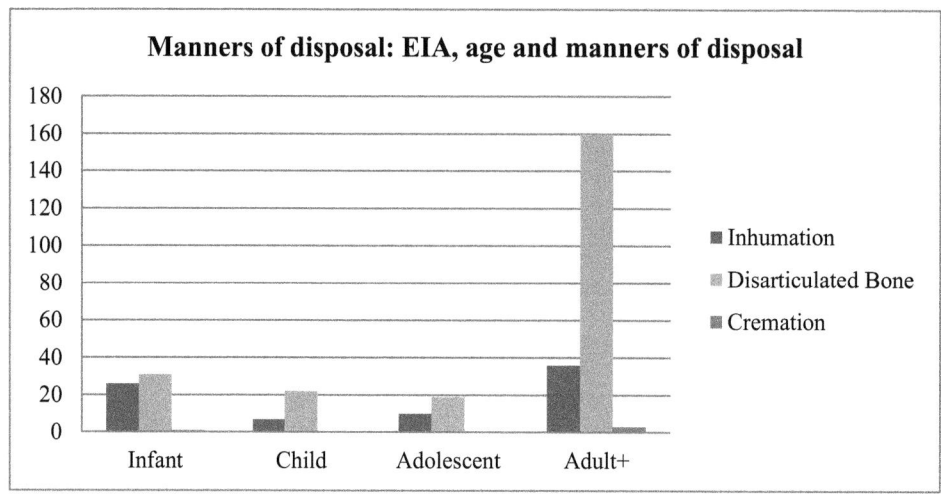

Figure 5. 22 EIA: age of occurrences and manner of disposal, including larger sites

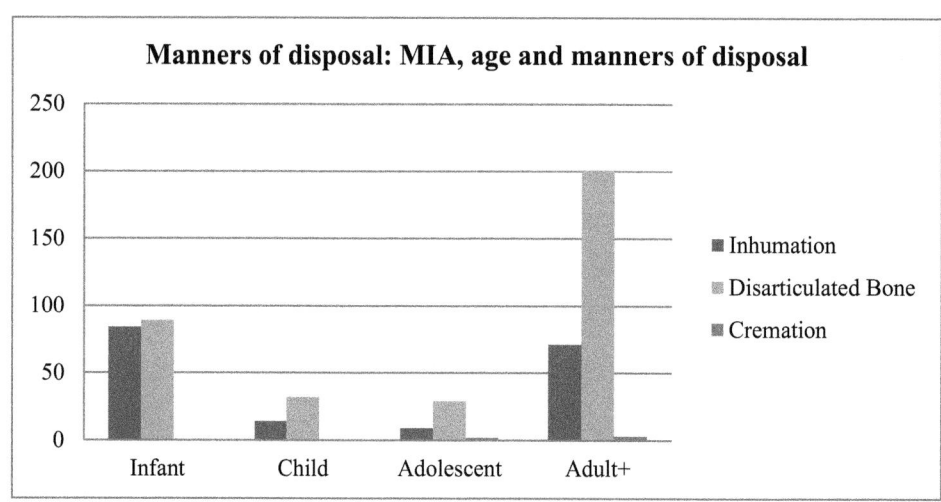

Figure 5. 23 MIA: age of occurrences and manner of disposal, including larger sites

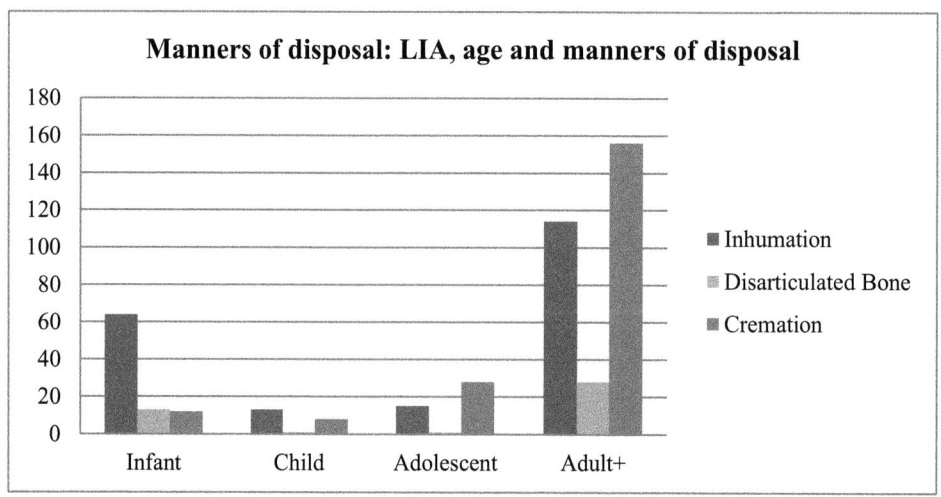

Figure 5. 24 LIA: age of occurrences and manner of disposal, including larger sites

For the smaller sample, there is also a significant relationship between age (sub-adult and adult) and form of disposal (χ^2=11.185, p=0.004, **Figure 5.25**). In this sample, the adult age group is still the most frequent, and evenly distributed across all manners of disposal. On the other hand, sub-adults are more frequent as inhumations than as disarticulated bones or cremations. When broken into more specific age categories, the trend is similar to the larger sample; adults are well represented for each form of disposal, and infants are common as inhumations and rare among cremations (**Figure 5.26**). Chronologically, the smaller sample is similar to the larger. A few differences were observed: in the Late Bronze Age adults were more often cremated than inhumed or disarticulated, while infant inhumations in the Late Iron Age are slightly more numerous than adult inhumations in the same period (see **Figures 5.27 -30**).

For both the larger and smaller sample, there is a significant relationship between sex and manner of disposal (larger sample: χ^2=26.603, p=0.000; smaller sample: χ^2=7.652, p=0.022). **Figures 5.31-32** show that males are more frequent than females in inhumations and among disarticulated bones, and their proportions are similar for both samples. However, females have a higher count than males in cremations in both the larger and smaller sample. It must, however, be taken into consideration that there is a low count of sexed occurrences for cremations in comparison to inhumations and disarticulated bones. The low count of sexed cremations is potentially due to the survival and recovery of sexually diagnostic bones. Nonetheless, this relationship may possibly indicate a differentiation between forms of disposal based on the biological sex of the individual.

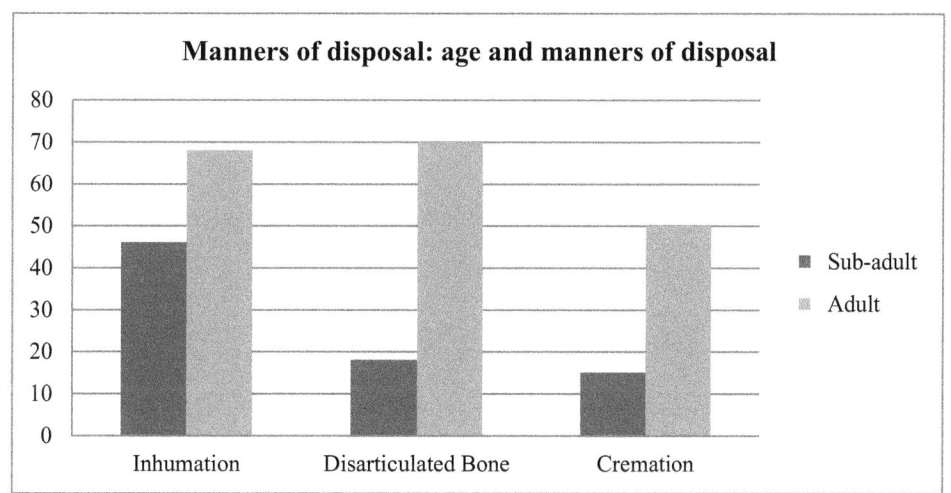

Figure 5. 25 Age of occurrences and manner of disposal, excluding larger sites

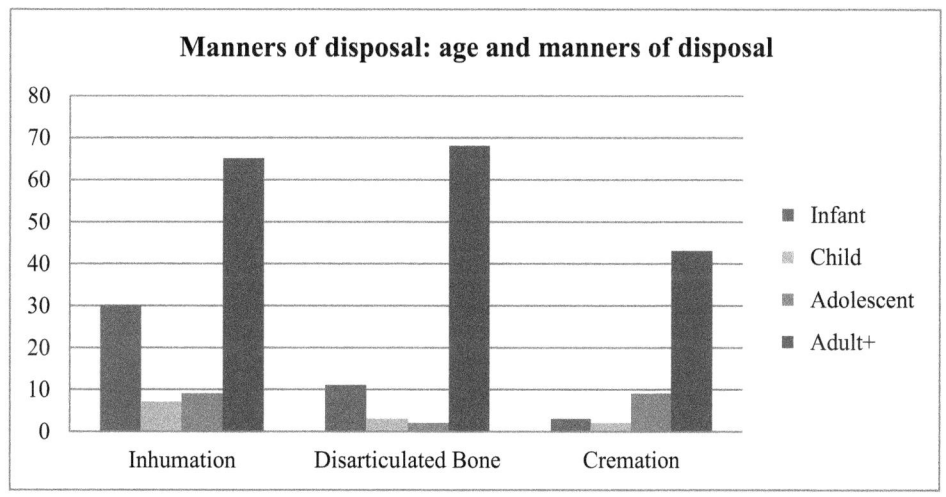

Figure 5. 26 Age of occurrences and manner of disposal, excluding larger sites

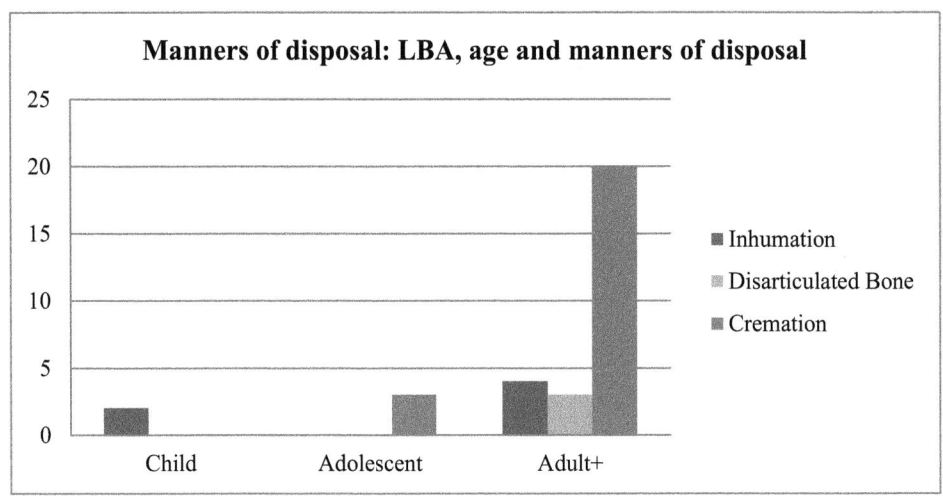

Figure 5. 27 LBA: Age of occurrences and manner of disposal, excluding larger sites

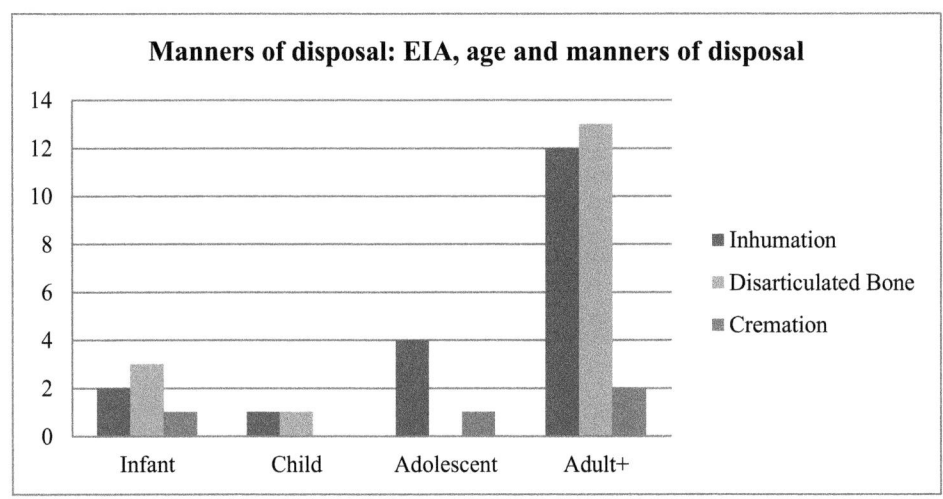

Figure 5. 28 EIA: Age of occurrences and manner of disposal, excluding larger sites

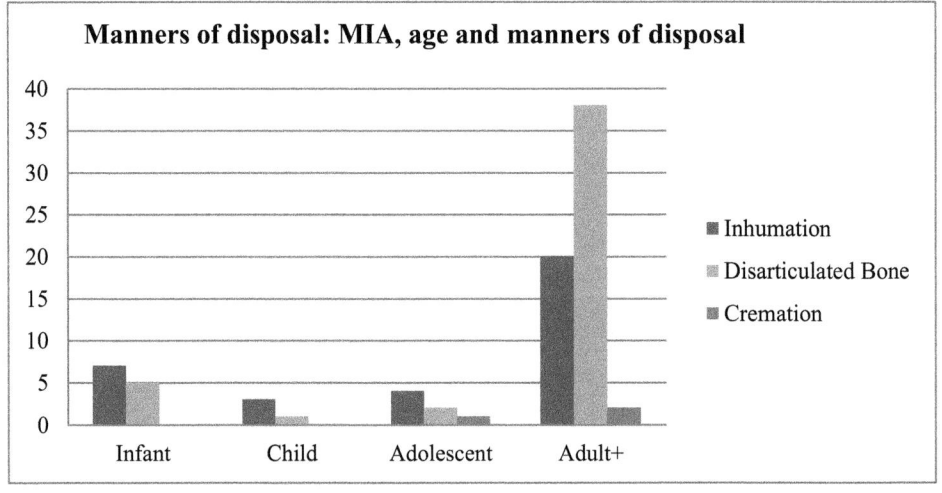

Figure 5. 29 MIA: Age of occurrences and manner of disposal, excluding larger sites

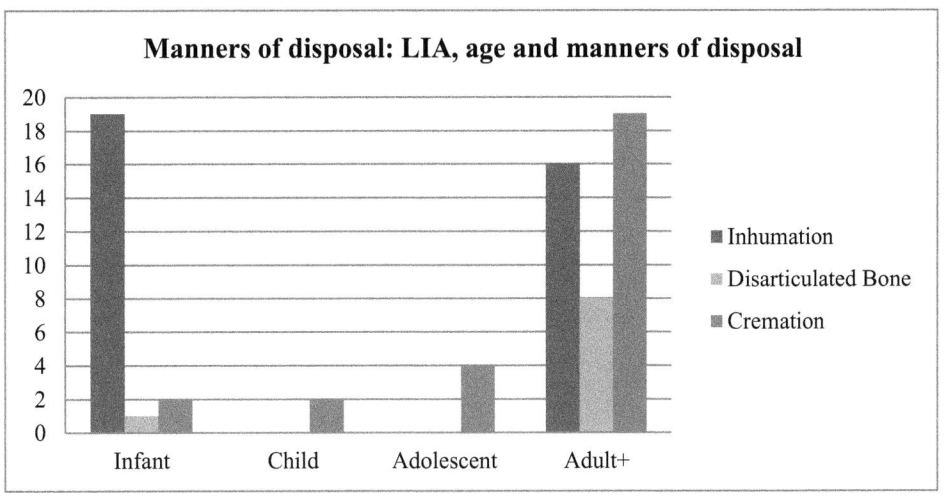

Figure 5. 30 LIA: Age of occurrences and manner of disposal, excluding larger sites

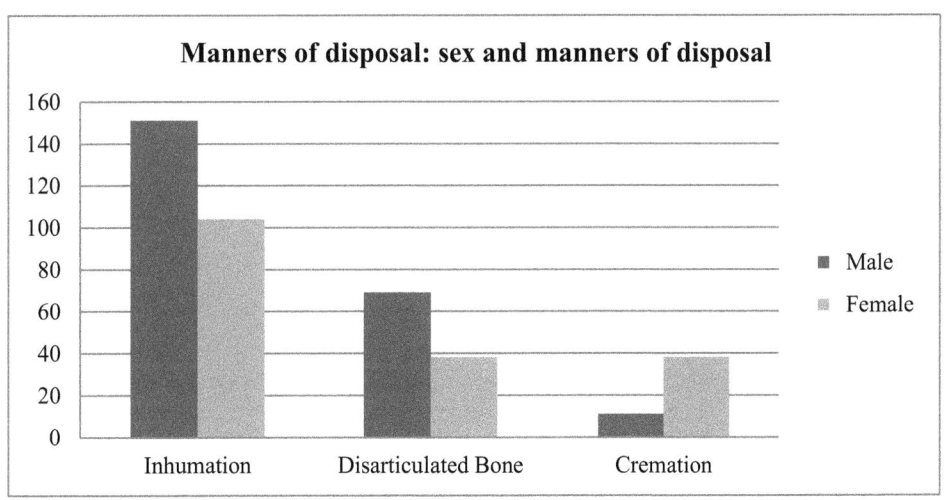

Figure 5. 31 Sex of occurrences and manner of disposal, including larger sites

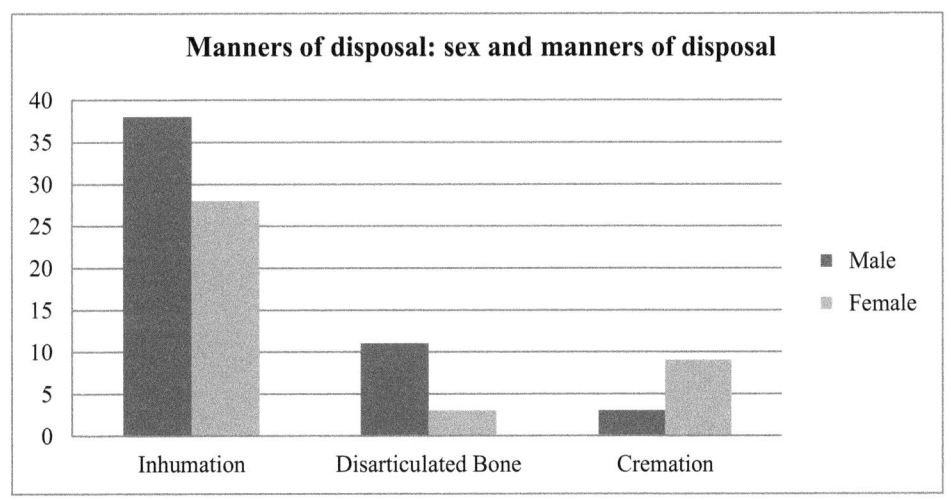

Figure 5. 32 Sex of occurrences and manner of disposal, excluding larger sites

There is a significant relationship between the placement of occurrences (interior, perimeter and exterior) and their location in round, rectangular and irregular structures' quadrants for the larger sample (from looking in, χ^2=34.309, p=0.000). **Figure 5.33** illustrates there is a high number of human remains occurring the left/front perimeter of structures. A chi-square test indicates a significant relationship, for both samples, between placement of occurrences and their location within structures (round, rectangular, and irregular) on either the right or left side (larger sample: χ^2=20.316, p=0.000; smaller sample: χ^2=11.486, p=0.003). The larger sample, **Figure 5.34**, illustrates occurrences on the right sides of structures almost equal to those in interiors, perimeters, and exteriors of structures. However, placement on the left side is common along the perimeters of structures, but is rare within interiors. The same trend is true of the smaller sample: a high count of occurrences is recorded along perimeters on the left sides of structures, but the left side within the interior has few examples (**Figure 5.35**). In addition, for both samples, over half of these structures are roundhouses with a domestic function (larger sample: 50 per cent; smaller sample: 58 per cent).

When considering the placement of occurrences in and around round structures only, this trend appears again. The sample size was too small for both samples to test the relationship between placements and round structures' quadrants. However, for the larger sample, there is a statistically significant relationship between human remains placement in the interior, perimeter, or exterior and whether they lie on the left or right side of the round structure (χ^2=21.098, p=0.000, **Figure 5.36**). As for the smaller sample, a chi-square test could not be carried out because of sample size. Yet, as **Figure 5.37** depicts, a similar pattern appears. However, there is not a strong presence of occurrences in the interior of round structures on their right side, although those placed along the perimeter on the left side are represented strongly. Overall, these statistical results suggest a probable set of depositional practices that guided the placement of human remains within structures, concerning the spatial difference and setting along the structures' boundaries.

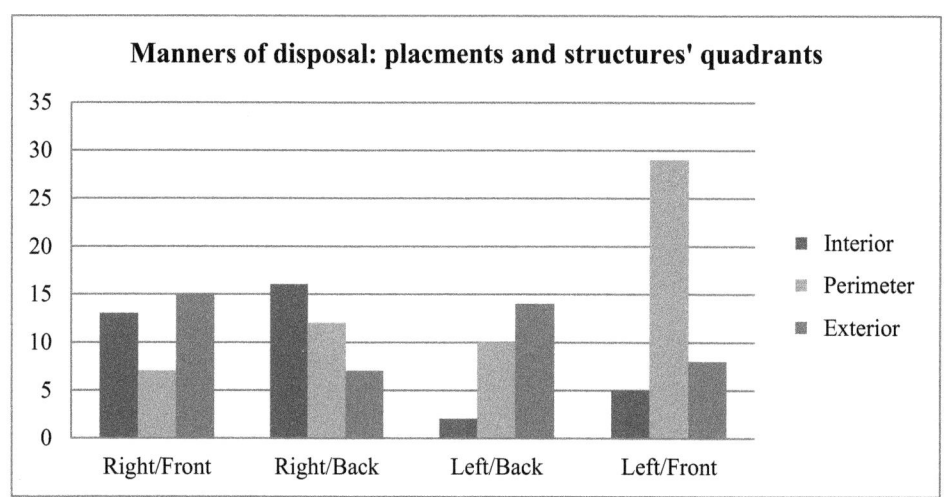

Figure 5. 33 Frequency of occurrences' placements within structures quadrants, including larger sites

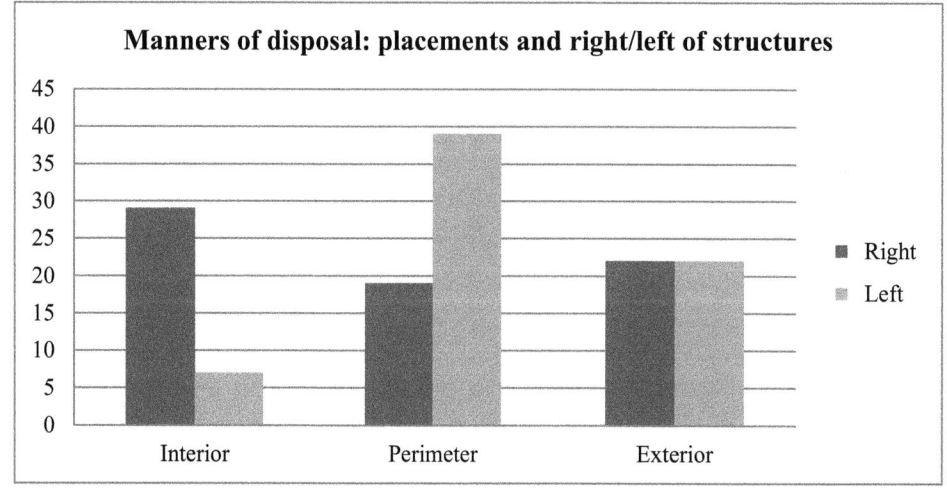

Figure 5. 34 Frequency of occurrences and their location within structures, including larger sites

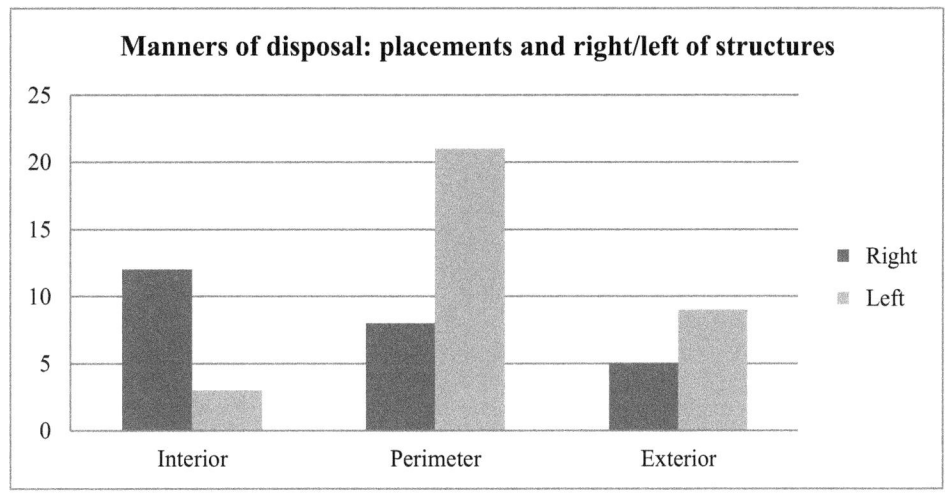

Figure 5. 35 Frequency of occurrences and their location within structures, excluding larger sites

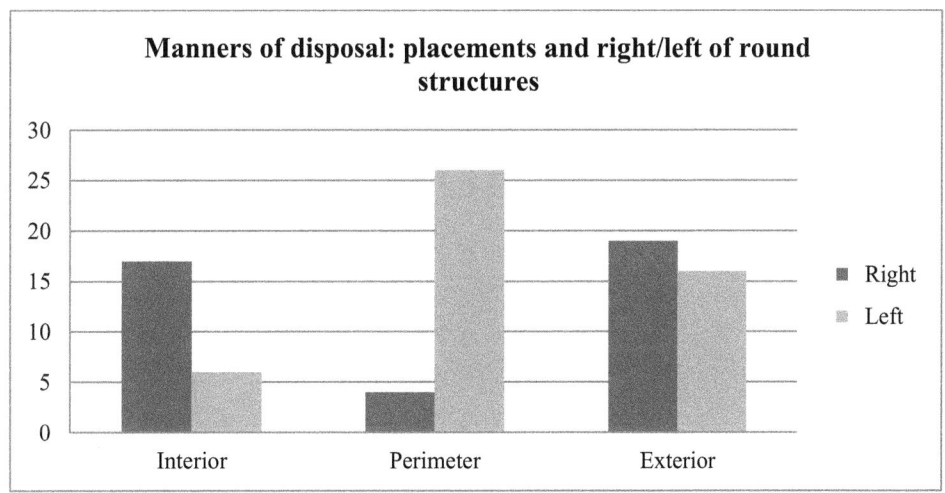

Figure 5. 36 Frequency of occurrences and their location with round structures, including larger sites

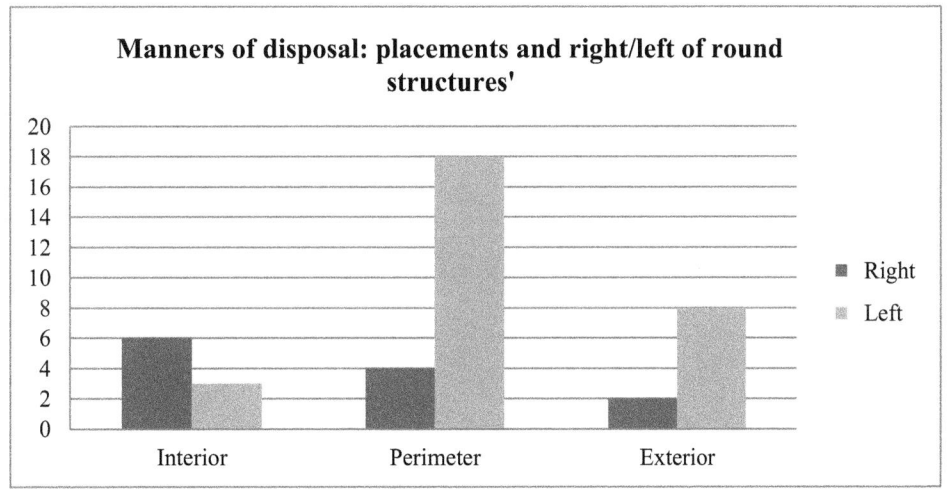

Figure 5. 37 Frequency of occurrences and their location with round structures, excluding larger sites

Summary

Overall, the statistical and quantitative analyses of the manner of disposal reveals many trends in Iron Age burial practice. The comparative analysis between human and animal bones indicates that the human skeletal material is a fraction of the animal bone assemblage, suggesting social reasons, not solely taphonomic, for the low amount. The result also conforms to the idea that the deposition of human remains is a minority rite. There appears to be a general change from the Late Bronze Age to the Late Iron Age. In particular, two transitional periods in burial practice can be identified: the first between the Late Bronze Age and the Early Iron Age, and the second between the Middle Iron Age and the Late Iron Age. The transitions are marked by changes in cremation and disarticulation, products of different methods for the near complete breakdown of the corpse. This result compliments the findings from the context analysis, which also indicated a chronological change in the processing of the dead. Additionally, infant burials become increasingly more frequent by the Late Iron Age. Adults have more variation in manner of disposal, while infants do not appear much in cremation deposits. This may suggest age preferences, or distinctions, for different forms of disposal. On the same point, the sex of an individual does not appear to have influenced deposition during the Iron Age. There may be a sex preference in manner of disposal, as females are identified more frequently than males in cremations burials. Lastly, the analysis suggests that the spatial organisation of human remains within structures (round, rectangular, and irregular) was dependent on their placement within the interior and perimeter. This result implies that particular archaeological features were focal points in this minority rite, and that the placement of skeletal material may follow some sort of social guidelines.

Chapter Six

Statistical and quantitative analyses of the inhumations, articulated bones, disarticulated bones, and cremations

Introduction

The following chapter presents the results from the quantitative and statistical analysis of the human remains from all of the studied sites. Each of the manners of disposal will be under discussion independently in order to create a clear depiction of the burial patterns that have emerged in the previous two chapters. This chapter begins by presenting the analytical results of the inhumations, followed then by the articulated bones, the disarticulated bones, and the cremations, before ending on a summarisation of the overall findings. Similar, to the previous two chapters, the discussion will only address the relevant results that contribute to our understanding of Iron Age burial practices, and it will follow the same 'smaller' and 'larger' sample format.

Inhumation analysis

Quantitative analysis

Of the 514 inhumations from the 100 studied sites, 76 per cent are from sites with over 20 occurrences. A greater proportion of inhumations, from both samples, date to the Late Iron Age (larger sample n=222; smaller sample n=41) (**Figure 6.1**). For the larger sample, inhumations are more commonly found in pits, as opposed to the smaller sample where graves are the most frequent (**Table 6.1**). Each sample has a high frequency of both pits and graves, but the sites with over 20 occurrences (which belong in the larger sample) have a high number of inhumations in pits. For example, Danebury provides 28 per cent of the total of inhumations in pits. The 'other' context group for each sample denotes context types such as scoops, floor layers, and so forth.

Complete inhumations are slightly more frequent than incomplete ones for both samples (larger sample n=241, incomplete: n=222; smaller sample n=52, incomplete: n=51). Furthermore, most inhumations are in crouched positions for both samples (**Table 6.2**), as well as oriented towards the north (**Figures 6.2-3**). For the larger sample, inhumations are more frequently found on their right sides (n=89, **Table 6.3**) while, for the smaller sample, left sides are more frequent (n=24, **Table 6.3**). The difference between the larger and smaller sample for body position is that sites with over 20 occurrences account for 81 per cent of the total number of inhumations resting on their right sides.

In the larger sample, most inhumations belong to the sub-adult age group (n=257, adult: n=240). However, when broken down into narrower age groups, adults are most frequent (n=236, **Figure 6.4**). For the smaller sample, adults are most frequent in inhumations (n=68, sub-adult: n=47), and, for the narrower age groups, there are twice as many adults as infants in inhumations, the second most frequent age group (**Figure 6.4**). Additionally, male inhumations are more frequent than females in both samples (larger sample n=151, female: n=104; smaller sample n=38, female: n=28).

In all, 168 inhumations have pathological indicators; 80 of these inhumations had single afflictions and 88 had multiple pathological indicators. The most common pathology is dental disease, which was present in 103 inhumations (closely followed by joint disease, present in 102) (**Table 6.4**). For the smaller sample, 55 inhumations have pathological indicators, 25 have single indicators and 35 have multiple afflictions. Similar to the larger sample, dental disease is the most frequent pathology in the smaller sample (present in 41 inhumations) (**Table 6.4**). For both the larger and smaller samples, the 'other' category of pathology represents types of disease of unknown cause. The larger sample contains 104 inhumations with evidence of a traumatic episode, 87 with a single and 17 with multiple indicators. The most common trauma observed in inhumations in this sample is bone fracture, present in 35 inhumations (**Table 6.5**). Additionally, most of the trauma in inhumations in the larger sample occurred ante-mortem (n=52). For the smaller sample, only 22 inhumations had evidence of trauma, of which 20 have single indicators and only two have multiple traumas. In the smaller sample, the most common traumatic indicator is bone fracture again; these were noted in 11 inhumations (**Table 6.5**) and, like the larger sample, the most frequent trauma occurred pre-mortem (n=12).

Within the larger sample, 230 inhumations have associated material. Of these, 100 inhumations had a single item and the remaining 130 had multiple artefacts in their deposit. The most commonly associated material is animal bone, which was present in 110 inhumations (**Table 6.6**). Commonly, for the larger sample, inhumations with animal bone included more than one species. Cow is the most frequently occurring species in inhumations, being present in 33 instances (**Table 6.7**). For the smaller sample, 68 inhumations have associated material (25 with a single item and 43 with multiple) and animal bone is, once again, the most frequent, being present with 40 occurrences (**Table 6.6**). In addition, from this sample of animal bone within inhumations, only 17 have a known species, of which cow is the most frequent, being present in nine inhumations (**Table 6.7**). Furthermore, for both the larger and smaller sample, the associated material in the 'other' group pertains to material such as glass or beads; the natural materials refer to limestone slabs, chalk or similar natural occurring material, deliberately placed with or over the human remains.

Overall, 150 inhumations are associated with archaeological features, and 60 per cent are from the sites with over 20 occurrences. For the larger sample, the occurrences are most frequent within 'other' features (n=47) closely followed by round structures (n=46) (**Table 6.8**). The 'other' archaeological features category largely consists of occurrences around Bronze Age barrows, in particular the site of Mill Hill, Kent, where a

Late Iron Age inhumation cemetery is set around a barrow. On the other hand, the smaller sample shows occurrences in round structures (n=15) closely followed by 'other' features (**Table 6.8**). From the larger sample, many of the occurrences associated with archaeological features date to the Late Iron Age (n=70, **Table 6.9**). However, the smaller sample has occurrences typically dating to the Middle Iron Age (n=18, **Table 6.9**). For the larger sample, most occurrences are within the exterior of their associated archaeological features (n=65, **Table 6.10**), as opposed to the smaller sample where most inhumations are positioned along perimeters (n=29, **Table 6.10**). Finally, inhumations from the larger sample are commonly associated with archaeological features that have a funerary purpose (n=36, **Table 6.11**), which undoubtedly relates to many of the occurrences being associated with barrows. For the smaller sample, features with a domestic function have the most occurrences of any type of function (n=17, **Table 6.11**).

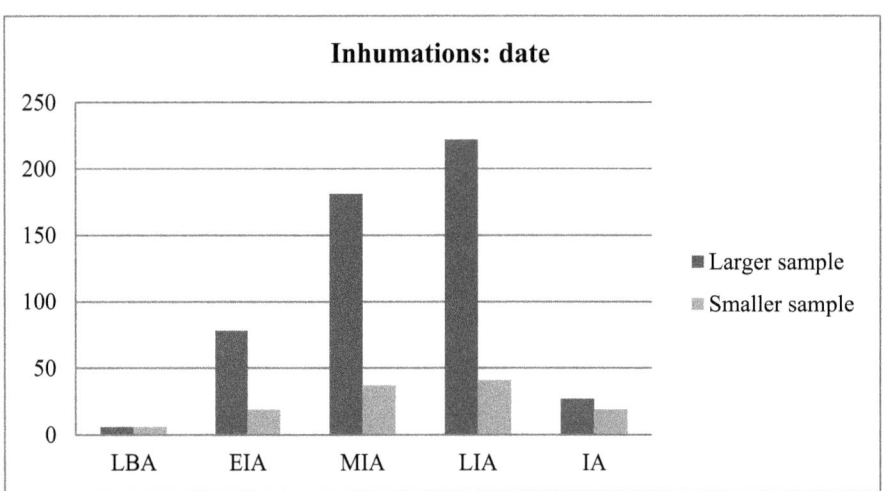

Figure 6. 1 Dates of inhumations

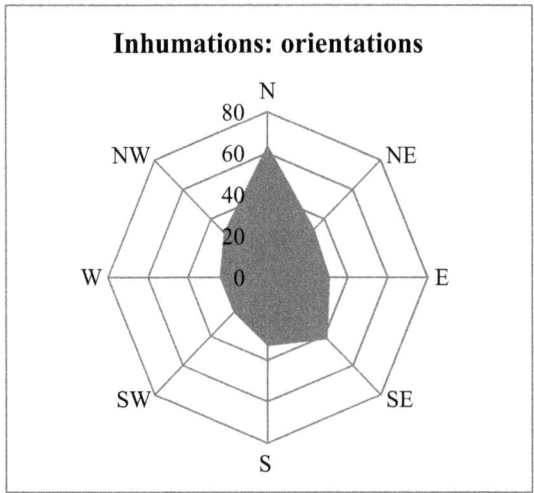

Figure 6. 2 Frequency of inhumation orientation, including larger sites

Table 6.1 frequencies of inhumations' contexts

Types	Larger sample	Smaller sample
Pit	210	39
Ditch	58	22
Rampart	5	2
Posthole	5	0
Grave	183	48
Other	34	6

Table 6.2 Frequencies of inhumations' layouts

Layouts	Larger sample	Smaller sample
Extended	68	12
Flexed	73	9
Crouched	117	37
Contracted	25	11

Table 6.3 Frequencies of inhumations' positions

Positions	Larger sample	Smaller sample
Left side	79	24
Right side	89	18
Supine	82	13
Prone	13	5

Table 6.4 Frequencies of inhumations' pathologies

Pathologies	Larger sample	Smaller sample
Congenital Disease	22	10
Dental Disease	103	41
Joint Disease	102	33
Infectious Disease	16	7
Metabolic Disease	14	6
Neoplastic Condition	5	0
Haematological Disease	23	2
Other	11	1

Table 6.5 Frequencies of inhumations' traumatic indicators

Trauma	Larger sample	Smaller sample
Fracture	35	11
Cut Mark	23	2
Blunt Force	5	1
Dismemberment	10	4
Burning	3	1
Bone Modification	4	0
Gnawing	7	0
Scarring	17	0
Striae	1	0
Other	19	7

Table 6.6 Frequencies of inhumations' associated materials

Materials	Larger sample	Smaller sample
Natural Material	45	15
Worked Bone	27	2
Ceramic Vessel	26	6
Sherd	62	37
Quern Stone	5	2
Jewellery	32	9
Military Material	7	1
Domestic Debris	25	7
Plant Remains	11	2
Metal Artefacts	44	15
Ash/Charcoal	36	9
Worked Stone	17	1
Animal Bone	110	40
Sling Stones	11	0
Other	19	7

Table 6.7 Frequencies of animal species associated with inhumations

Species	Larger sample	Smaller sample
Cow	33	9
Sheep	32	3
Pig	17	2
Dog	7	0
Horse	19	5
Deer	6	6
Other	7	1

Table 6.8 Frequencies of inhumations with archaeological feature types

Type	Larger sample	Smaller sample
Round structure	46	15
Rectangular structure	21	12
Irregular structure	12	1
Multi-post	5	0
Settlement enclosure	7	7
Boundary	11	11
Other	47	14

Tables 6.9 Date of inhumations with archaeological features

Date	Larger sample	Smaller sample
LBA	4	4
EIA	17	9
MIA	45	18
LIA	70	16
IA	14	13

Table 6.10 Frequencies of inhumations within archaeological features

Locations	Larger sample	Smaller sample
Interior	42	19
Perimeter	41	29
Exterior	65	11

Table 6.11 Frequencies of inhumations with archaeological features' function

Functions	Larger sample	Smaller sample
Domestic	34	17
Processing	2	0
Storage	1	0
Enclosure	15	15
Funerary	36	8
Other	3	1
Multiple functions	31	8

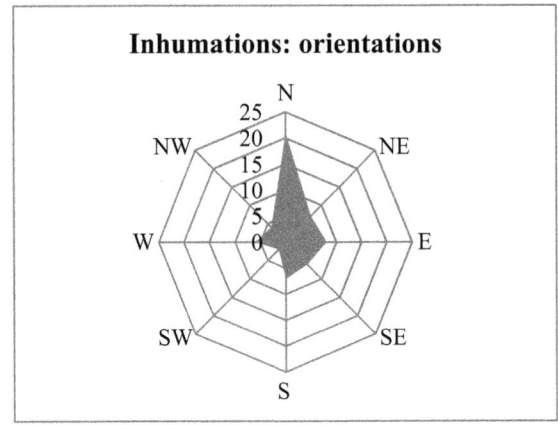

Figure 6. 3 Frequency of inhumation orientation, excluding larger sites

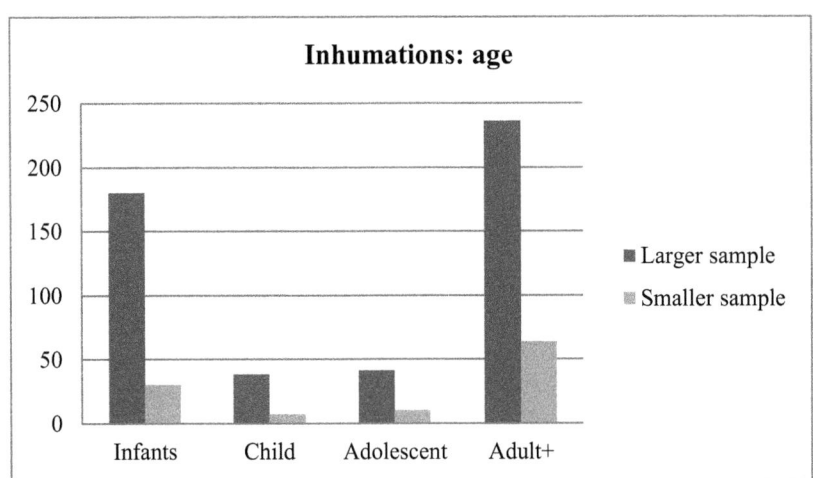

Figure 6. 4 Frequencies of inhumations' age

Statistical analysis

Chronologically, there is a significant relationship between period and completeness of an inhumation for the larger sample (χ^2=7.852, p=0.020). As **Figure 6.5** illustrates, incomplete and complete inhumations are comparatively equally represented during the Early and Late Iron Age. However, during the Middle Iron Age there is an increase in complete inhumations. For the smaller sample, there was no significant relationship (χ^2=2.228, p=0.368, **Figure 6.6**), although the frequencies of complete and incomplete inhumations by period are very similar to those of the larger sample.

For the larger sample, there is a significant relationship between the age (sub-adult and adult) of inhumations and their date (χ^2=8.613, p=0.013, **Figure 6.7**). This correlates with the results, on the same variables, in the 'manner of disposal' section (see chapter five). Sub-adult inhumations outnumber the adults in the Early and, especially, Middle Iron Age. However, adult inhumations steadily increase in frequency from the Early Iron Age to the Late Iron Age, when this age group has a higher representation than sub-adults do. When separating out the age categories (infant,

child, adolescent, and adult), there is a spike of infant inhumations during the Middle Iron Age and these are more frequent than the adult age group (**Figure 6.8**). Eight of the sites that have over 20 occurrences provide 92 per cent of infant inhumations in the Middle Iron Age. In contrast, the smaller sample did not return a significant result between age (sub-adult and adult) of inhumations and date (χ^2=3.068, p=0.216). **Figure 6.9** illustrates that adult inhumations are more frequent than sub-adults in the Early and Middle Iron Age, before decreasing slightly in the Late Iron Age. The sub-adults gradually increase size from the Early to the Late Iron Age when they slightly outnumber the adults. By focusing on the more specific age categories for the smaller sample, there is a notable increase of infant inhumations in the Late Iron Age (**Figure 6.10**). For the smaller sample, the Late Iron Age infant inhumations derive from seven sites; one of these, Wakerley (Northamptonshire), makes up half of the total. Thus, if there is a relationship between biological age and chronology, it may exist at the individual site level as opposed to the regional scale.

The larger and smaller samples both have a significant relationship between an inhumation's age and its context type (larger sample: χ^2=27.634, p=0.000, **Figure 6.11**; smaller sample: χ^2=12.551, p=0.002, **Figure 6.12**). The main difference between the larger and smaller samples' results is that the larger sample has a notably higher count of sub-adults in pits, although nine of the 20 larger sites make up 91 per cent of the total of sub-adult inhumation burials in pits. Nonetheless, the frequencies are comparatively the same between the two samples with respect to age groups in ditch and grave contexts. The low number of adult inhumations in ditch contexts must be noted, and it appears to show that only two types of contexts (pits and graves) are favoured for this age group. This is in contrast to the sub-adult group where, besides their high numbers in pits within the larger sample, the distribution is almost even across the context types.

The statistical analysis relating to the placement of inhumations in and around structures has been performed solely on the larger sample,[5] since the smaller sample's variables contained less than 20 cases. Nonetheless, for inhumations associated with round, rectangular, and irregular structures, there is a significant relationship between their placement and whether they are on the right or left side of the structure (χ^2=14.098, p=0.001). **Figure 6.13** depicts this bias of inhumations to be set on the right side of the interior of a structure (round, rectangle, or irregular), as was seen in the 'manner of disposal' analysis, and this pattern is the same for inhumations associated with round structures (**Figure 6.14**).

In summary, the inhumation analysis offers further insight into similar age group distinctions shown by the 'manner of disposal' analysis. Although infant inhumations increased into the Late Iron Age, the relationship between age categories and period seems to vary on particular sites and is not a general trend during the Iron Age. The analysis suggests a difference for inhumations and their contexts of deposition according to age. Sub-adults are buried more likely in ditch contexts, while adults are typically inhumed in pits or graves. The analysis shows the deposition of inhumations associated with structures follow the same spatial pattern as was seen in the 'manner of disposal' section.

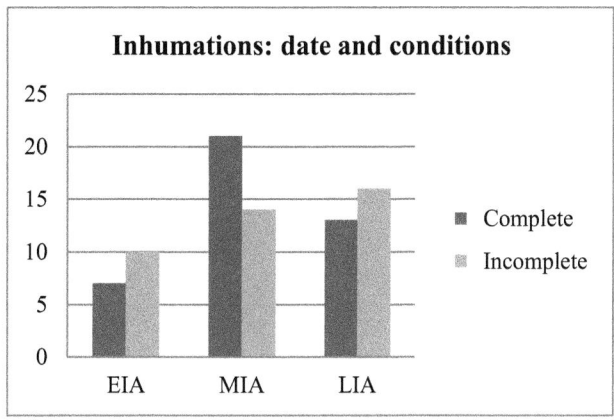

Figure 6. 6 Date of inhumations and condition, excluding larger site

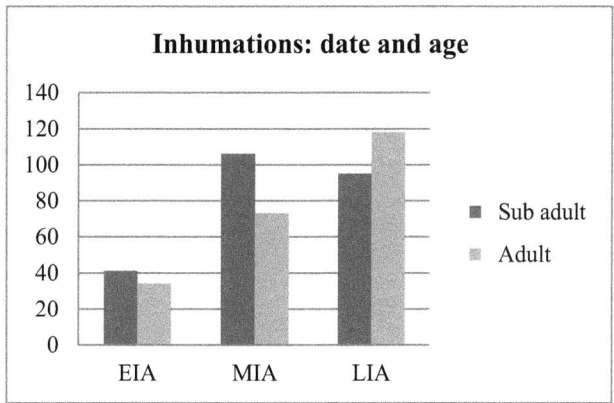

Figure 6.7 Age of inhumations and date, including larger sites

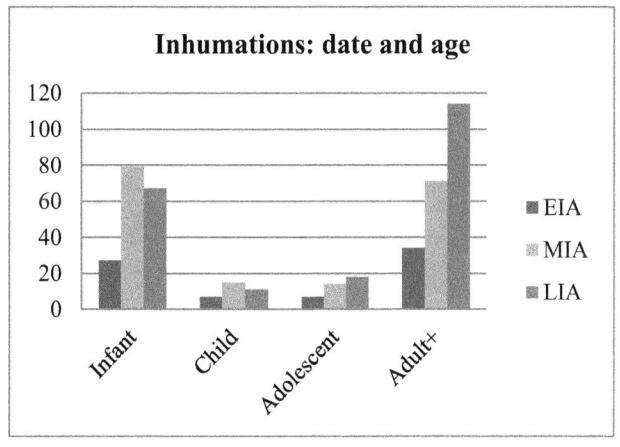

Figure 6. 8 Age of inhumations and date, including larger sites

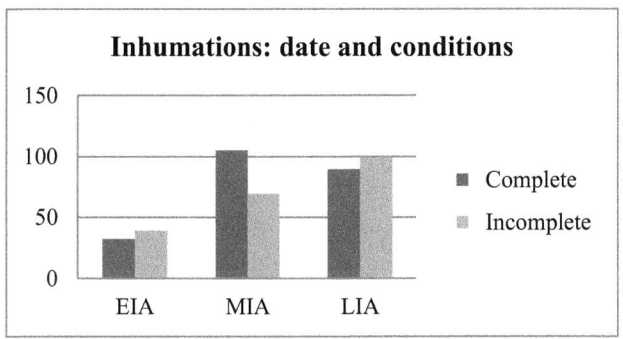

Figure 6. 5 Date of inhumations and condition, including larger sites

---

[5] Statistical testing for the placement of inhumations in relation to the structures' quadrants was in violation of the chi-square assumption.

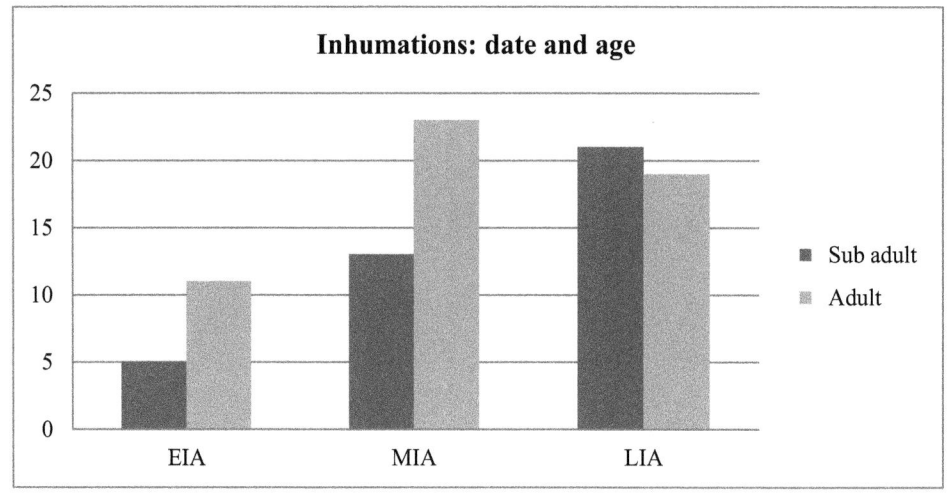

Figure 6. 9 Age of inhumations by date, excluding larger sites

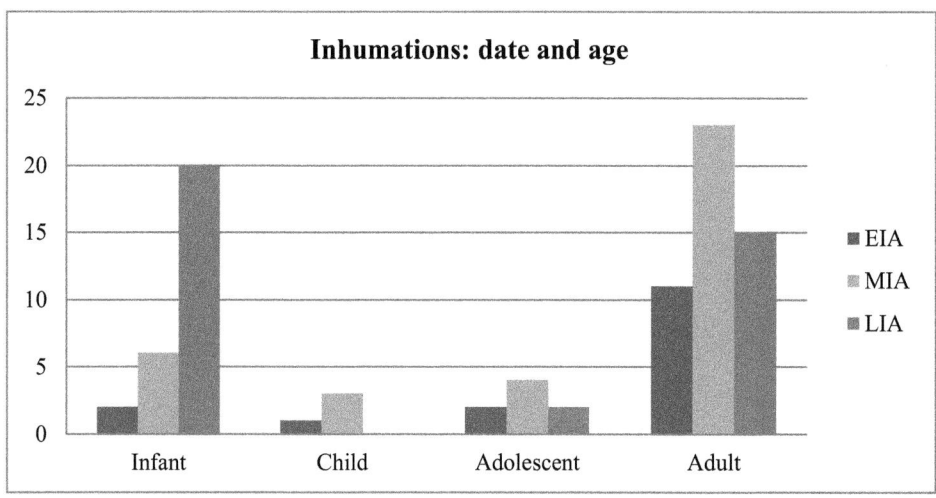

Figure 6. 10 Age of inhumations by date, excluding larger sites

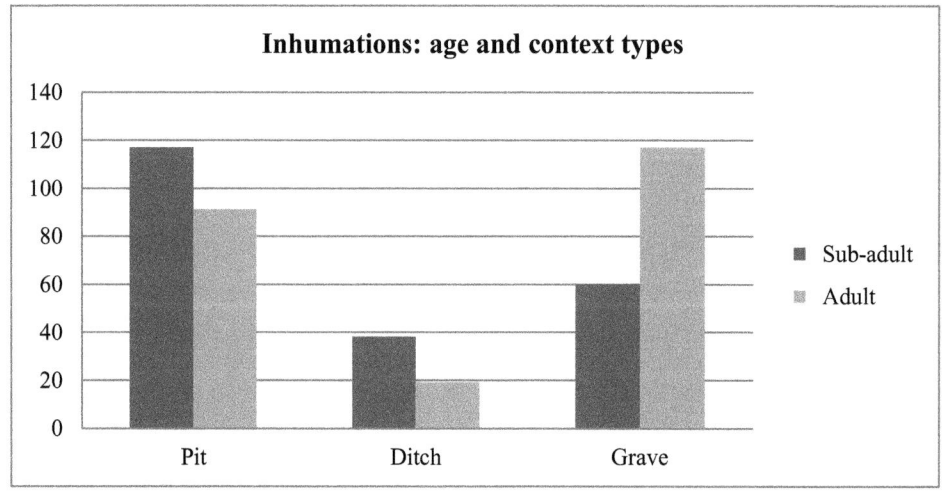

Figure 6. 11 Age of inhumations and context, excluding larger sites

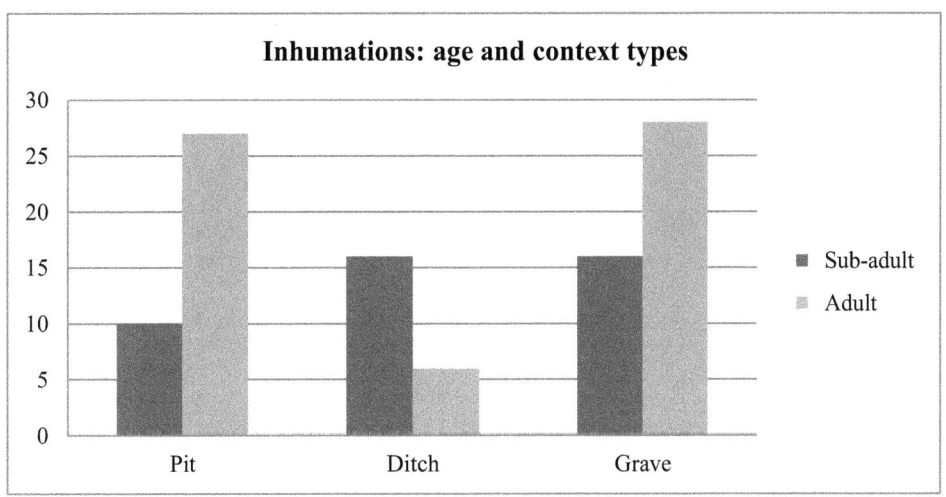

Figure 6. 12 Age of inhumations and context, excluding larger sites

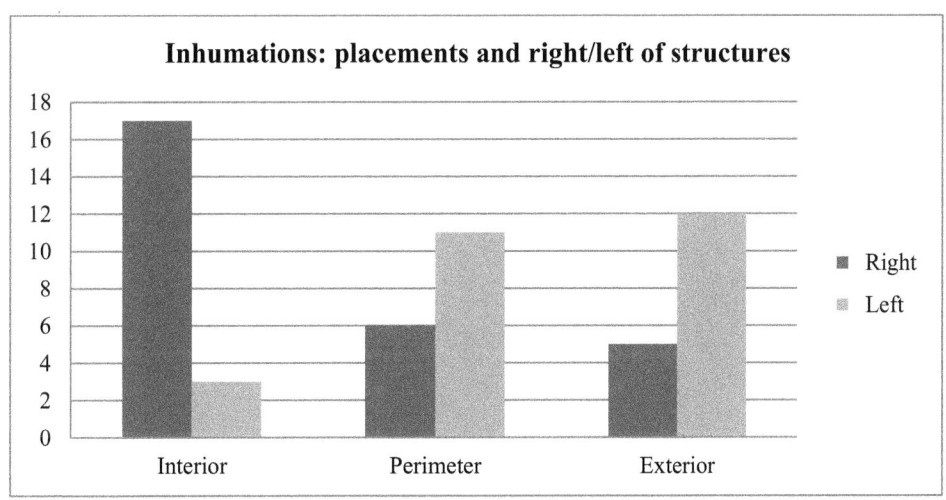

Figure 6. 13 Frequency of inhumation locations within a structure, including larger sites

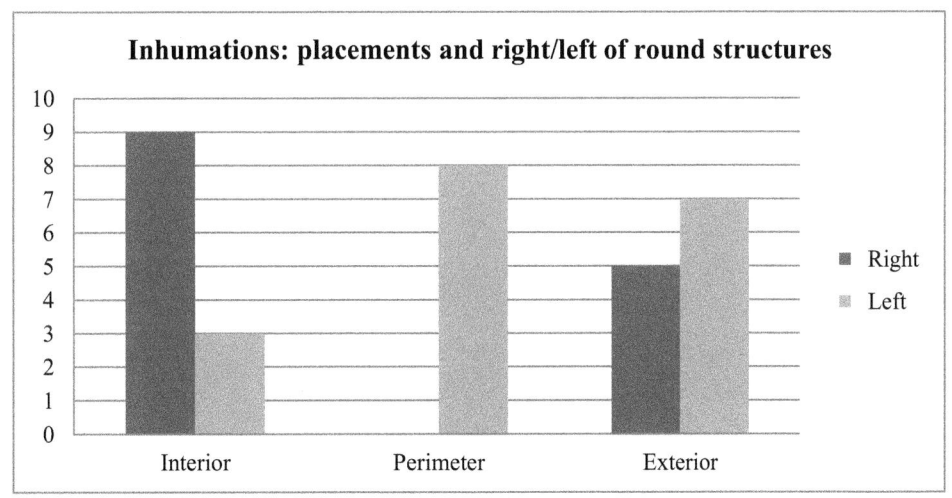

Figure 6. 14 Frequency of inhumation locations within round structures, including larger sites

Articulated bones analysis

Quantitative analysis

Seventeen articulated bones came from seven sites within the entire studied sample and they most frequently date to the Middle Iron Age (n=11, **Table 6.12**). In addition, articulated bones were commonly found within pit contexts (n=7, **Table 6.13**), with the lower limbs the most frequently occurring body portions (n=8, **Table 6.14**). Only six occurrences have a known side, the right side being more frequent (n=4, **Figure 6.15**). Demographically, there are more adults (n=11) than sub-adults (n=2). Moreover, only three of the occurrences are sexed; all males. Two of the articulated bones have pathological indicators (one single and one with multiple afflictions), and both have signs of joint disease. Besides having joint disease, one has signs of pathology of an unknown cause. In addition, two occurrences have a single traumatic indicator, evidence in both cases of peri-mortem dismemberment. As for associated material, seven occurrences have multiple items associated with them. The most common material is animal bone, present in all seven of these cases (**Table 6.15**). Sheep is the most common species, occurring in five of these deposits. There is no statistical analysis of the articulated bone because of its small sample size.

Table 6. 12 Date of articulated bones

LBA	1
EIA	4
MIA	11
LIA	1

Table 6.13 Frequencies of articulated bones' context types

Pit	7
Ditch	3
Grave	1
Other	3

Table 6. 14 Frequency of body portions present

Upper Limb	3
Lower Limb	8
Torso	5
Crania	1

Table 6. 15 Frequencies of associated materials with articulated bones

Sherd	1
Quern Stone	1
Domestic Debris	5
Plant Remains	1
Ash/Charcoal	5
Worked Stone	1
Animal Bone	7
Other	1

Table 6. 16 Date of disarticulated bones

Date	Larger sample	Smaller sample
LBA	58	6
EIA	321	26
MIA	484	60
LIA	91	22
IA	53	15

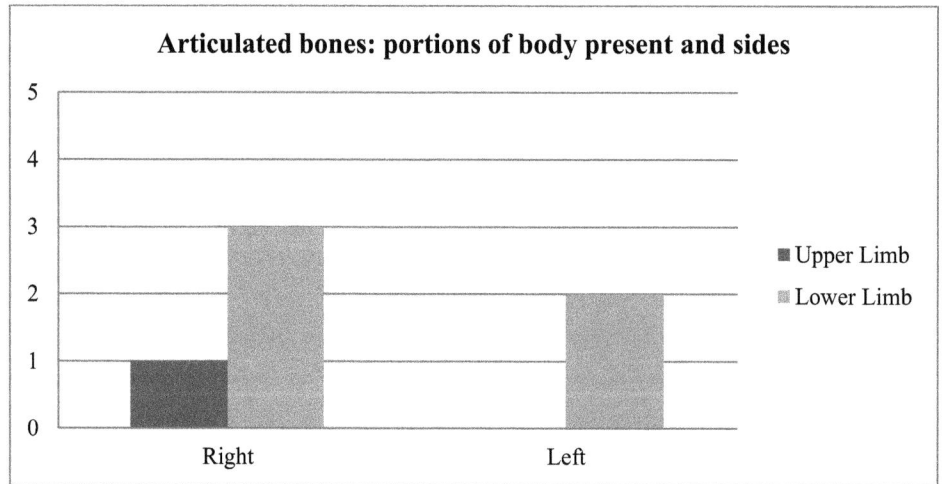

Figure 6. 15 Frequencies of portions of limb present according to side

Disarticulated bone analysis

Quantitative analysis

Overall, 1007 pieces of disarticulated human bone came from the entire sample of studied sites. The smaller sample, which consists of 38 sites, represents only a small fraction (13 per cent) of the total. It is evident that the sites with over 20 occurrences dominate the entire sample. For example, the remains from Danebury constitute 33 per cent of the larger sample, having nearly three times the amount of disarticulated bone than all 38 sites from the smaller sample combined. Nonetheless, from both the larger and smaller samples, disarticulated bone most commonly dates to the Middle Iron Age (**Table 6.16**). For both samples, pits are the most frequent context type for deposition (**Table 6.17**). For the smaller sample, there are a high proportion of ditch contexts in relation to pits, which is not evident in the larger sample. As for the depth at which remains are buried, for both samples the top, middle and bottom levels are almost evenly represented, although the top segment is slightly more frequent (**Table 6.18**).

Table 6.17 Frequencies of disarticulated bones by context

Types	Larger sample	Smaller sample
Pit	486	53
Ditch	124	48
Rampart	1	0
Posthole	39	7
Grave	64	0
Other	278	11

Table 6.18 Frequencies of disarticulated bones by depth

Depth	Larger sample	Smaller sample
Top	198	21
Middle	109	17
Bottom	161	20

Table 6.19 Age of disarticulated bones

Age	Larger sample	Smaller sample
Sub-adult	299	20
Adult	450	68

The skull is the most frequent element found on Iron Age sites (**Figures 6.16-17**). Furthermore, elements from the right side of the body are more frequent than the left. Interestingly, for the larger sample, both the right and left sides of the body are relatively equally represented for most elements (**Figure 6.18**). However, for the smaller sample, as **Figure 6.19** illustrates, side varies with individual element. All the femora and fibulae from the smaller sample are from the right side. The only lower limb bone from the left side is a single tibia. In comparison, the elements from the upper limbs are from both sides of the body.

Demographically, the adult age group is the most frequent for both the larger and smaller sample (**Table 6.19**). Additionally, a small percentage of the disarticulated bones from both samples can be assigned a biological sex: males (larger sample: n=69; smaller sample: n=11) are more frequent than females (larger sample: n=38; smaller sample: n=3). For the larger sample, 73 disarticulated bones possess pathological indicators: 63 have just single indicators and 10 have multiple, of which dental disease is the most frequent pathology (**Table 6.20**). As for the smaller sample, only nine occurrences have pathological indicators (6 with single and 3 with multiple), of which 'other' pathologies of an unknown cause are the most frequent (**Table 6.20**). From the larger sample, 133 disarticulated bones[6] have traumatic indicators (112 with single and 21 with multiple). Weathering is the most frequent, being present in 28 occurrences (**Table 6.21**). In addition, most of the trauma on disarticulated bones has occurred post-mortem (n=64). As for the smaller sample, 30 disarticulated bones possess some sign of trauma (20 single and 10 multiple). Polishing of the bone is the most frequent trauma (**Table 6.21**), most of which (as with the larger sample) occurred post-mortem (n=13).

Table 6.20 Frequencies of disarticulated bones' pathologies

Pathologies	Larger sample	Smaller sample
Congenital Disease	6	1
Dental Disease	25	2
Joint Disease	14	1
Infectious Disease	4	2
Metabolic Disease	3	1
Neoplastic Condition	5	0
Haematological Disease	14	2
Other	12	3

---

[6] Rebecca Redfern (2008a; 2008b; 2009) has carried out a reassessment of the disarticulated bones from Gussage All Saints and Maiden Castle and has found traumatic indicators indicative of secondary burial practices not identified in the original osteological reports. Unfortunately, this present analysis does not include Redfern's findings since it was uncertain what particular occurrences possess these indicators. However, the following chapter explains Redfern's conclusions in better detail for these two sites.

From the larger sample, 378 occurrences have associated material, 136 with single and 242 with multiple items. Animal bones are the most frequent item, being present with 204 occurrences (**Table 6.22**). Typically, disarticulated bones are found with multiple animal species, of which 55 occurrences are with cow (**Table 6.23**). For the smaller sample, 82 occurrences have associated material (35 with single and 47 with multiple items). Pottery sherds are the most frequent, being present with 54 occurrences (**Table 6.22**). Animal bone is the second most frequent (present with 43 occurrences), usually with multiple species. Sheep is the most common species, being present with 11 occurrences (**Table 6.23**).

There are 214 disarticulated bone occurrences associated with archaeological features in the larger sample, and 32 per cent of those derive from the smaller sample. For both samples, most of this disarticulated bone is found in association with round structures (**Table 6.24**). Disarticulated bones from the larger sample are more commonly associated with features orientated to the east (**Figure 6.20**), while the smaller sample contains occurrences that are typically associated with structures opening to the southeast (**Figure 6.21**). There are small numbers of disarticulated bones associated with features opening towards non-eastern directions yet the low count is insufficient to discern in any difference in their deposition to those associated with eastern orientated buildings. Additionally, occurrences commonly favour archaeological features with a domestic function (**Table 6.25**). For both samples, most of the disarticulated bone occurrences associated with archaeological features dating to the Middle Iron Age (**Table 6.26**), and many are of adults (larger sample: n= 83, sub-adult: n=70; smaller sample: n=34, sub-adult: n=11). For the larger sample, only 15 of the occurrences have been assigned biological sex and, of these, males (n=8) are slightly more numerous than females (n=7). As for the smaller sample, only four have a known sex, most of them males (n=3). Moreover, for both samples, most occurrences are found along the perimeters of archaeological features (**Table 6.27**), and, in terms of their associations with architectural features, they are more commonly associated with boundaries (larger sample: n=89; smaller sample: n=39) than with entrances (larger sample: n=26; smaller sample: n=10).

Table 6. 21 Frequencies of disarticulated bones' traumatic indicators

Trauma	Larger sample	Smaller sample
Fracture	10	2
Cut Mark	24	8
Blunt Force	4	3
Dismemberment	1	0
Burning	19	0
Bone Modification	6	3
Gnawing	26	3
Scarring	10	0
Striae	1	0
Weathering	28	3
Polishing	14	10
Other	13	4

Table 6. 22 Frequencies of associated materials with disarticulated bones

Materials	Larger sample	Smaller sample
Natural Material	41	9
Worked Bone	58	2
Ceramic Vessel	7	1
Sherd	147	54
Quern Stone	61	5
Jewellery	12	6
Military Material	2	0
Domestic Debris	94	9
Plant Remains	45	5
Metal Artefacts	69	7
Ash/Charcoal	127	12
Worked Stone	13	1
Animal Bone	204	43
Sling Stone	34	2
Other	38	10

Table 6. 23 Frequencies of animal species with disarticulated bones

Species	Larger sample	Smaller sample
Cow	55	9
Sheep	49	11
Pig	29	8
Dog	9	1
Horse	40	7
Deer	7	3
Bird	3	2
Other	11	4

Table 6. 24 Frequency of disarticulated bone with archaeological features

Types	Larger sample	Smaller sample
Round structure	102	25
Rectangular structure	14	3
Irregular structure	10	5
2-post structure	3	0
Multi-post structure	19	3
Settlement enclosure	23	10
Boundary	17	8
Other	26	14

Table 6. 25 Frequencies of disarticulated bones with archaeological features' function

Function	Larger sample	Smaller sample
Domestic	74	29
Processing	2	1
Storage	2	1
Midden	1	
Enclosure	35	13
Funerary/ritual	8	8
Other	11	2
Multiple functions	14	2

Table 6. 26 Date of disarticulated bones with archaeological features

Date	Larger sample	Smaller sample
LBA	4	4
EIA	30	12
MIA	116	36
LIA	41	12

Table 6. 27 Frequencies of disarticulated bones within archaeological features

Location	Larger sample	Smaller sample
Interior	69	15
Perimeter	81	40
Exterior	54	9

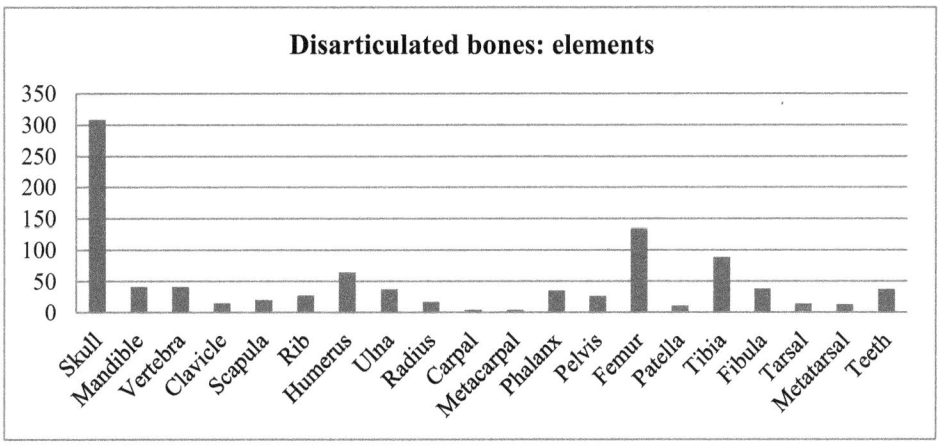

Figure 6. 16 Frequencies of elements, including larger sites

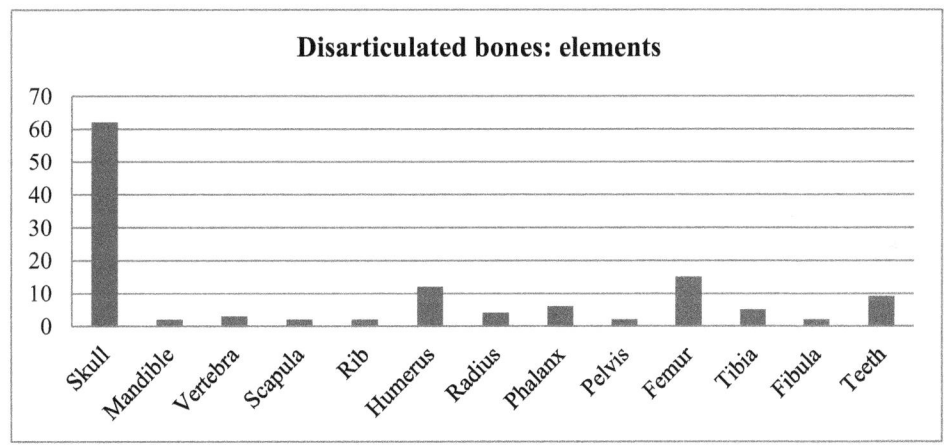

Figure 6. 17 Frequency of elements, excluding larger sites

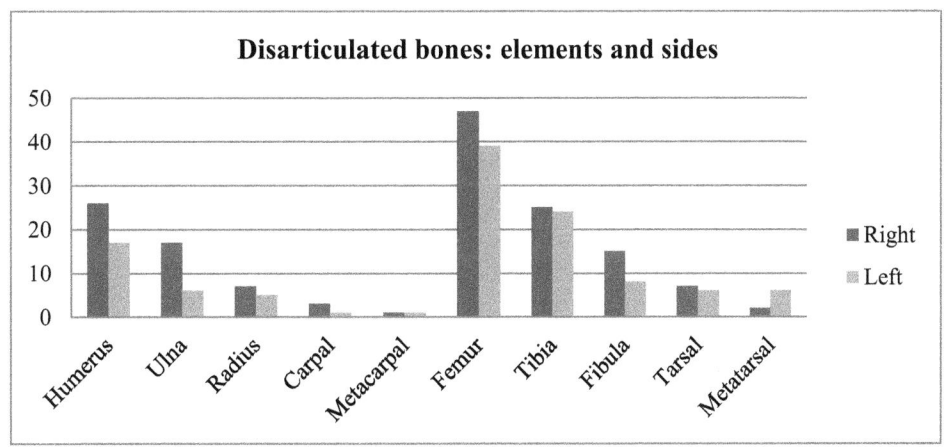

Figure 6. 18 Frequency of elements and side of body, including larger sites

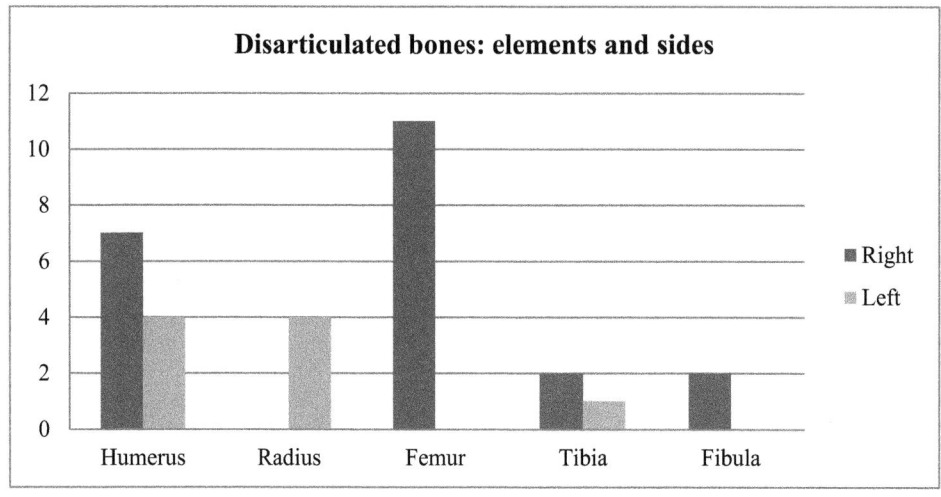

Figure 6. 19 Frequency of elements and side of body, excluding larger sites

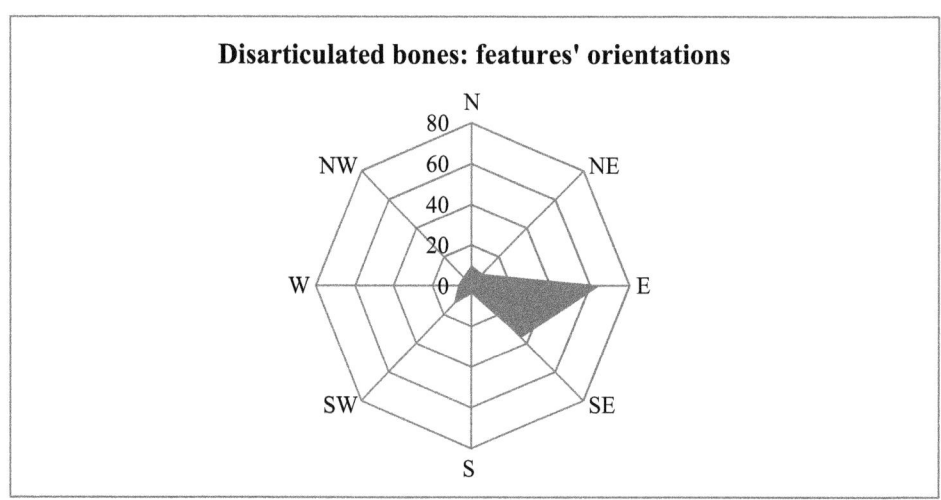

Figure 6.20 Frequencies of disarticulated bones with archaeological features' orientation, including larger sites

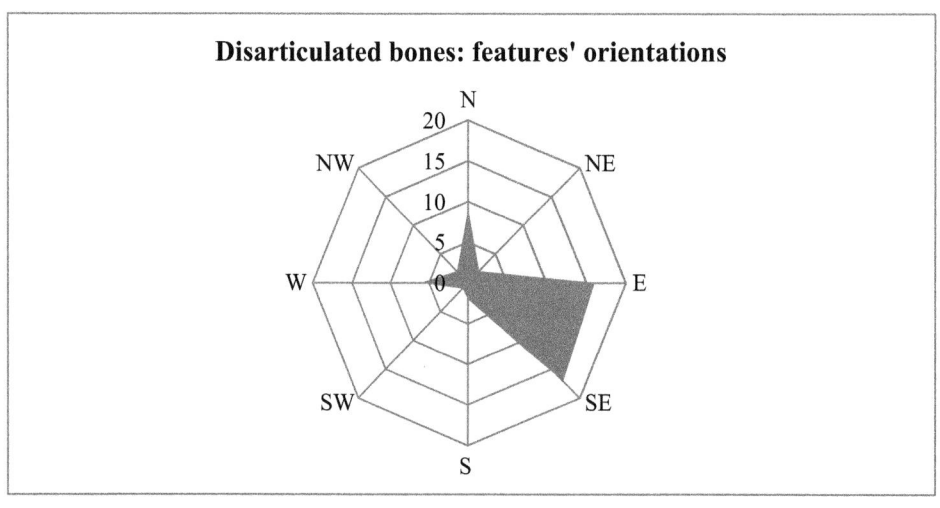

Figure 6. 21 Frequencies of disarticulated bones with archaeological features' orientation, excluding larger sites

Statistical results

The statistical analysis, interestingly, indicates there is *no* significant relationship, for both samples, between anatomical element selection and date (larger sample: $\chi^2=1.262$, p=0.532, **Figure 6.22**; smaller sample: $\chi^2=1.099$, p=0.577, **Figure 6.23**). The larger sample has a high count of crania but, even so, post-cranial elements outnumber them. In contrast, in the smaller sample, crania occur more frequently than post-cranial elements throughout the Iron Age. Beyond this dissimilarity, the statistical test may signify that, with each sample, there was not a change in the selection of elements for deposition during the Iron Age. This pattern is supported by the fact that the element proportions of crania, upper and lower limbs, torsos, and phalanges frequency remain relatively consistent during the Early, Middle, and Late Iron Age for each sample (see **Figures 6.24-25**).

Additionally, there is a significant relationship between upper and lower limbs and sidedness in the smaller sample (Fisher's Exact Probability Test, p=0.26, n=33). **Figure 6.26** illustrates that lower limb elements are predominantly from the right side of the body while, for the upper limbs, both the left and right side are even. This result coincides with the frequencies of the smaller sample, previously discussed above. The larger sample shows that there is no significant relationship between sidedness and selected element ($\chi^2=2.881$, p=0.110, **Figure 6.27**). In the larger sample, the frequency of upper and lower elements and their anatomical side are similar. In respect to the smaller sample, this result may signify that there is an anatomical side preference depending on the element. More specifically, elements from the lower limbs are typically from the right side in the smaller sample. This relationship may not be evident in the larger sample, since the high count of disarticulated bones from the sites with 20 or more occurrences may suggest that no such dedication was made on these larger sites. Alternatively, the right-side pattern on the smaller sites could be due to chance.

The placement of human remains in relation to structures' quadrants could not be done for both samples due to small numbers but, as **Figure 6.28** shows, there is visually a preference for disarticulated bones placed in left/front perimeters of structures. Additionally, the larger sample produces a significant relationship between the placement of human bones on the right or left side of structures (round, rectangular, and irregular) and in their locations (interior, perimeter, and exterior) ($\chi^2=11.686$, p=0.003, **Figure 6.29**). Occurrences on the right side are relatively even in interiors, perimeters and exteriors. However, there is a high number of disarticulated bones for the left-side perimeters of structures, and a considerably low number on the left sides of interiors. In the larger sample, a similar trait is observable for the location of disarticulated bone in and around round structures only. Occurrences within roundhouse interiors are more frequent on the right side, while those placed along the perimeter of the building are found more often on the left side. Furthermore, the larger sample has a significant relationship between these right/left and placement variables for roundhouses ($\chi^2=14.458$, p=0.001, **Figure 6.30**). No statistical test could be performed on the smaller sample due to small sample size. Nonetheless, the frequency of these variables in the smaller sample shows a similar pattern to the larger sample (**Figure 6.31**). These results correlate with those from the inhumations and manner of disposal, and further support the possibility of deliberate placing when depositing human remains in buildings.

In general, the disarticulated bone analyses show some interesting aspects. First, it appears to show no change in bone selection during the Iron Age, and potentially implies continuity in this aspect of the practice. Second, the statistical results appear to show that lower limb bones (from the smaller sample) were intentionally chosen from the right side of the body. Finally, the placement of disarticulated bones in structures (round, rectangular, and irregular) also follows the same spatial organisation previously noted in the analyses of inhumations and the manner of disposal.

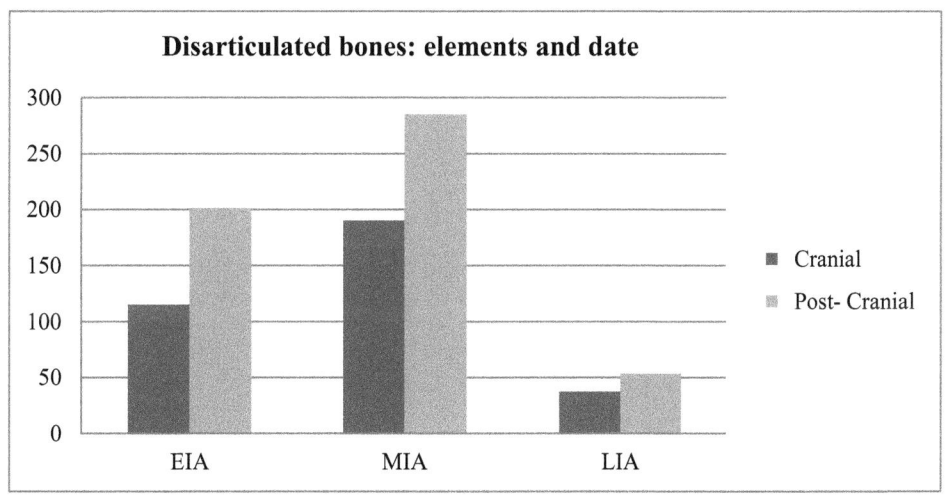

Figure 6. 22 Date and element, including larger sites

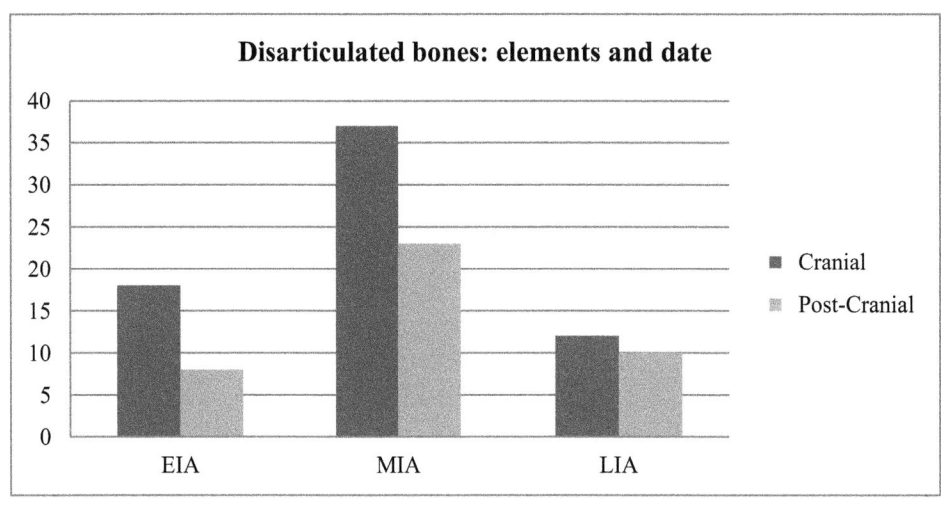

Figure 6. 23 Date and element, excluding larger sites

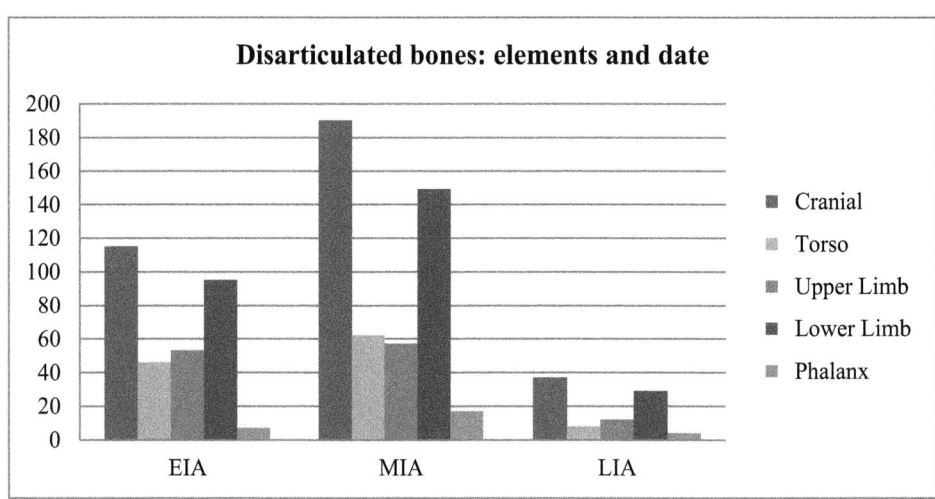

Figure 6. 24 Date and element, including larger sites

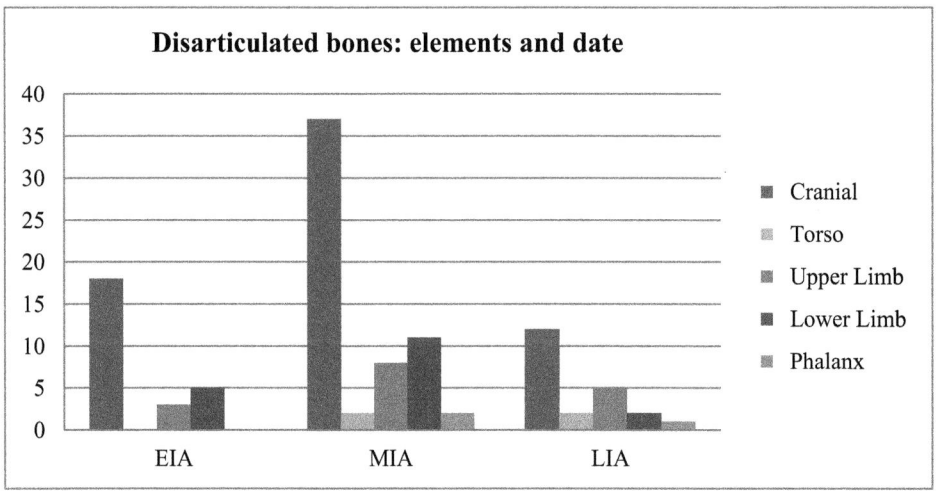

Figure 6. 25 Date and element, excluding larger sites

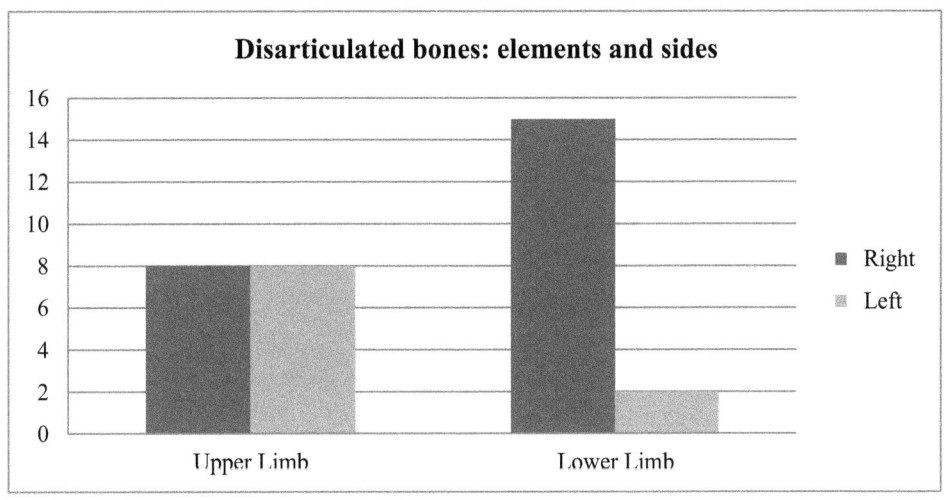

Figure 6. 26 Element and side of the body, excluding larger sites

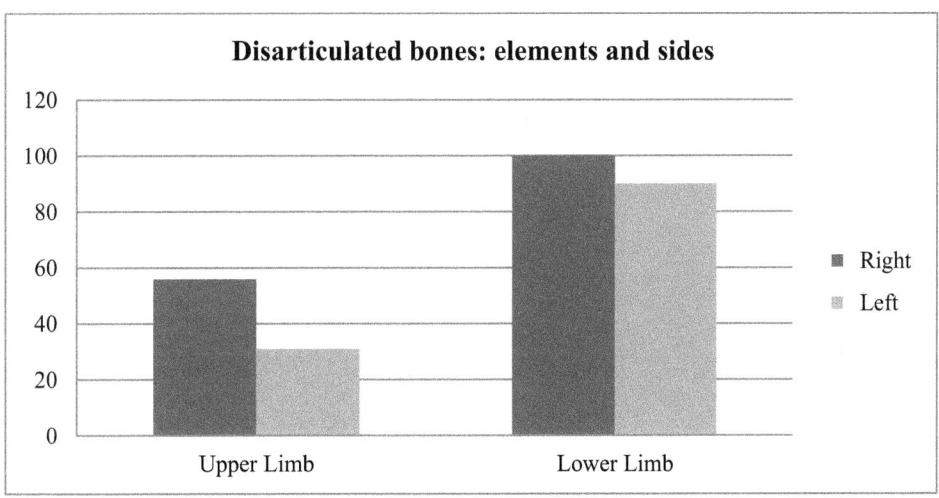

Figure 6.27 Element and side of the body, including larger sites

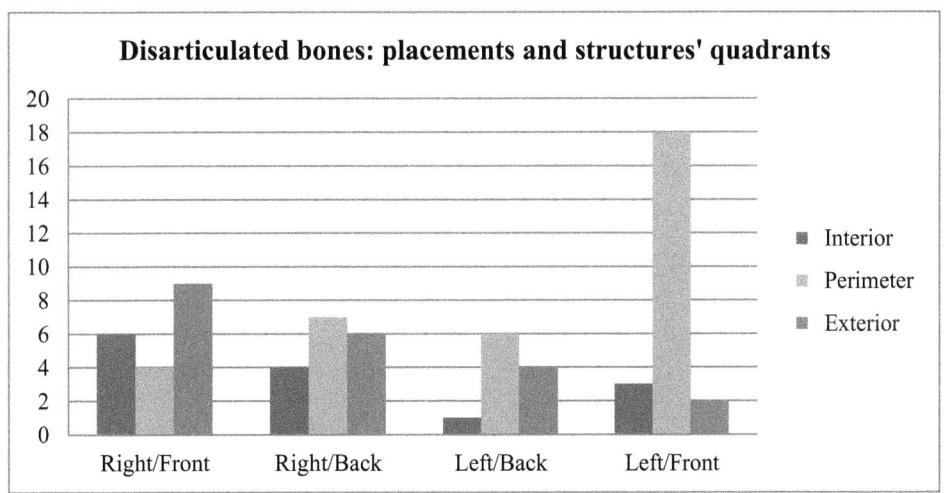

Figure 6. 28 Frequency of disarticulated bones and placements with structures' quadrants, including larger sites

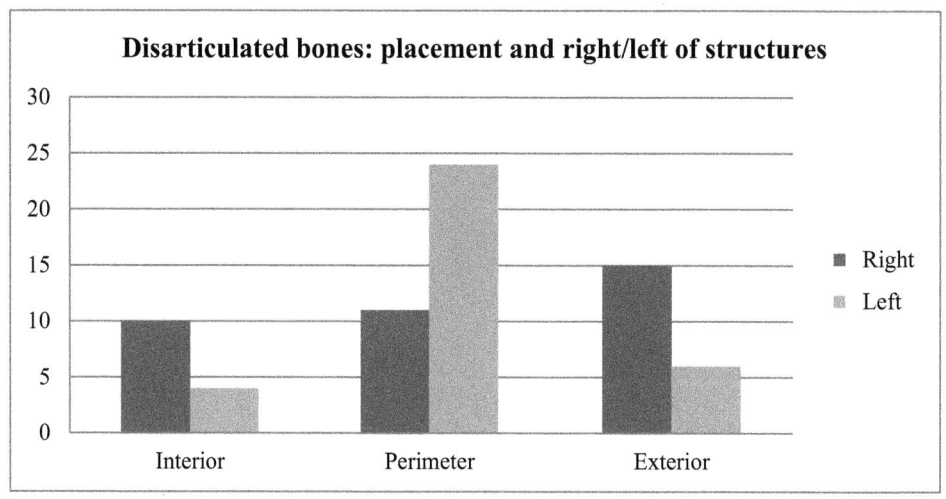

Figure 6. 29 Location of disarticulated bone within structures, including larger sites

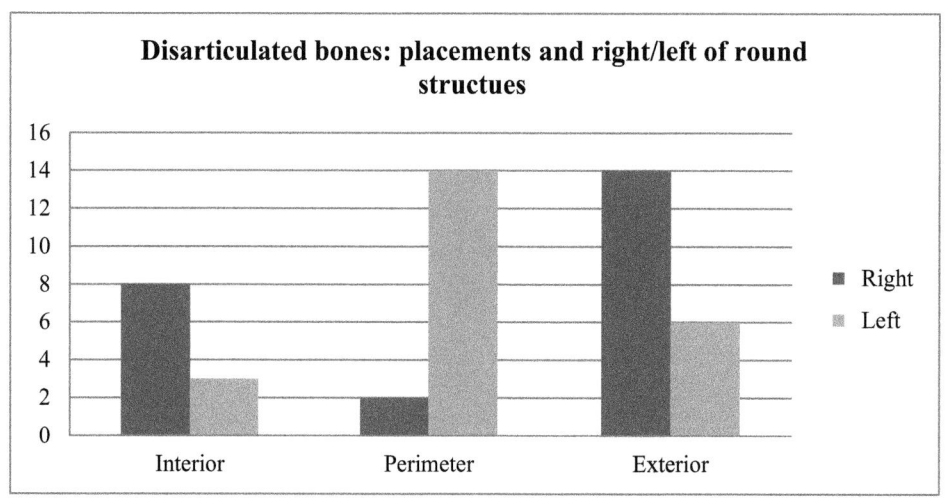

Figure 6. 30 Location of disarticulated bone within round structures, including larger sites

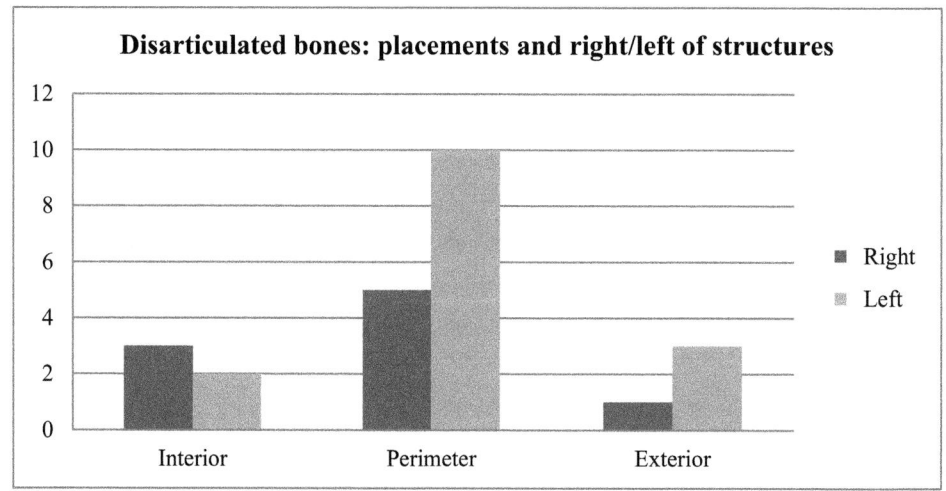

Figure 6. 31 Location of disarticulated bone within structures, excluding larger sites

Cremation analysis

Quantitative analysis

There are 336 cremation occurrences from all the studied sites, of which the smaller sample constitutes 34 per cent of the total. For both samples, most occurrences date to the Late Iron Age (**Table 6.28**). However, in the smaller sample there is a higher count of cremations in the Late Bronze Age in relation to the Late Iron Age while, in the larger sample there are nearly four times as many occurrences in the Late Iron Age. This is because the large sample contains data from Westhampnett, a Late Iron Age cremation cemetery constituting nearly 57 per cent of the cremation sample. Cremation deposits are most often set in grave contexts (intentionally dug to hold cremated bones) among the larger sample (**Table 6.29**). In contrast, pits are the most common context type in the smaller sample, while there is a relatively low number from graves (**Table 6.29**). Additionally, the 'other' context group for both samples denotes undefined contexts, such as pyre-related features and natural hollows. Furthermore, for the larger sample, 311 cremations have a known weight, averaging 185.8g. For the smaller sample, 98 cremations have a known weight, averaging 243.2g. Cremation occurrences within each sample are typically not deposited in urns (**Table 6.30**).

Table 6. 28 Date of cremations

Date	Larger sample	Smaller sample
LBA	46	41
EIA	16	15
MIA	7	4
LIA	264	50
IA	3	3

Table 6. 29 Frequencies of cremations' contexts

Types	Larger sample	Smaller sample
Pit	84	69
Ditch	16	7
Postholes	12	10
Grave	162	17
Other	52	5

Table 6. 30 Frequencies of cremations and urns

	Larger sample	Smaller sample
Urn	36	25
Unurned	260	85

Table 6. 31 Frequencies of cremations' pathologies, including larger sites

Dental Disease	5
Joint Disease	19
Metabolic Disease	1
Neoplastic Condition	1
Other	12

The adult age group has the highest representation amongst cremation occurrences for both samples (larger sample: n=210, sub-adult: n=8; smaller sample: n=54, sub-adult: n=11). For the large sample, 49 cremations have a known sex, of which females are most common (n=38; males n=11). The smaller sample has 12 cremations of known biological sex, of which females (n=9) are again more frequent (males, n=3). Furthermore, 32 occurrences from the larger sample possess pathological indicators, 27 with single and 5 with multiple indicators, of which joint disease is the most common affliction, being present on 19 occurrences (**Table 6.31**). For the smaller sample, six cremations have evidence of pathology (five single and one multiple), of which joint disease is again the most frequent, being present in four occurrences. From all of the cremation occurrences, only two within the larger sample have evidence of trauma (one has a fracture and the other has indicators of weathering).

Additionally, for the larger sample, 288 cremation occurrences have associated material, 119 with a single item and 169 with multiple materials. For this sample, ceramic vessels were the most frequent item, being present in 169 cremation occurrences (**Table 6.32**). Animal bone is present in 64 occurrences. A greater proportion of the animal bone was cremated and, due to the survival of diagnostic elements, most of the species could not be determined ('other' species group). However, of the known species, pig is the most frequent, being present in 24 cremation occurrences (**Table 6.33**). As for the smaller sample, 87 occurrences have associated material (38 with single and 49 with multiple items), of which ash/charcoal, undoubtedly from pyre debris, is the most frequent (**Table 6.32**). However, animal bone is present in 18 occurrences: for these, the majority of the animal bones were cremated and the species is not known ('other' species). Of the bones that could be assigned to a species, sheep is the most frequent, being present in five cremation occurrences (**Table 6.33**).

Table 6. 32 Frequencies of associated materials with cremations

Material	Larger sample	Smaller sample
Natural Material	8	7
Worked Bone	4	0
Ceramic Vessel	169	28
Sherd	53	20
Jewellery	51	10
Military Material	3	0
Domestic Debris	1	0
Plant Remains	12	6
Metal Artefacts	72	19
Ash/Charcoal	89	47
Worked Stone	22	5
Animal Bone	64	18
Other	18	4

For the larger sample there are 90 cremation occurrences associated with structures and, for the smaller sample, there are 68 occurrences. In addition, frequencies are similar between these samples, with minor differences for some variables. For both samples, most of the occurrences associated with structures date to the Late Iron Age (**Table 6.34**). Additionally, many of the occurrences are associated with 'other' structures (**Table 6.35**). Most of the cremations associated with archaeological features have a funerary purpose and comprise mainly of Bronze Age barrows and funerary ring ditches (**Table 6.36**). The adult age group is the most frequent age category (larger sample: n=47, sub-adult: n=7; smaller sample: n=38, sub-adult: n=7). For each sample, occurrences were interred comparatively evenly within the interiors, perimeters, or exteriors of structures, though the interiors were slightly more favoured (**Table 6.37**).

Table 6. 33 Frequency of animal species with cremations, including larger sites

Species	Larger sample	Smaller sample
Cow	4	1
Sheep	23	5
Pig	24	4
Dog	1	1
Unidentifiable	42	8

Table 6. 34 Date of cremations with archaeological features

Date	Larger sample	Smaller sample
LBA	26	24
EIA	9	9
MIA	5	4
LIA	49	30
IA	1	1

Table 6. 35 Frequencies of cremations with archaeological features

Features	Larger sample	Smaller sample
Round structure	11	11
Rectangular structure	12	10
Multi-post structure	5	5
Settlement enclosure	12	4
Boundary	12	8
Other	38	30

Table 6. 36 Frequencies of cremations with archaeological features' function

Functions	Larger sample	Smaller sample
Domestic	11	11
Processing	14	6
Enclosure	9	7
Funerary/ritual	32	28
Other	4	4
Multiple Functions	12	4

Statistical results

The statistical analysis of the cremation occurrences returned limited results for both samples. As previously stated, the cremation cemetery at Westhampnett constitutes over half of the total cremation sample and, thus distorts the results for the larger sample.[7] Furthermore, the smaller sample also returned limited meaningful results, there being a significant relationship between the date of an occurrence and the presence of an urn (χ^2=23.439, p=0.000, **Figure 6.32**). For this particular test, the four date variables were combined into two: Earlier Iron Age (Late Bronze Age and Early Iron Age) and Later Iron Age (Middle and Late Iron Age). Cremations set in an urn during the Earlier Iron Age are virtually absent from this sample. There are two exceptions, both Late Bronze Age cremations from Kent, and these burials were either the only feature, or one of a few features from this period, on their sites. In addition, in the larger sample there was also a single Late Bronze Age cremation deposited within an urn, also from a site in Kent. During the Late Iron Age, for the smaller sample, nearly 48 per cent of cremations are found within urns. By looking at this same data by period (Late Bronze Age, Early, Middle, and Late Iron Age), it is apparent that urned cremations are, not surprisingly, predominantly Late Iron Age feature (**Figure 6.33**).

Finally, as previously stated, there is little information that can be taken from the cremation analysis. The increase of cremations in urns may signify variation in urns during the Late Iron Age but this is a well-known phenomenon in southern Britain.

Table 6. 37 Locations of cremations within archaeological features

Locations	Larger sample	Smaller sample
Interior	32	25
Perimeter	27	24
Exterior	31	19

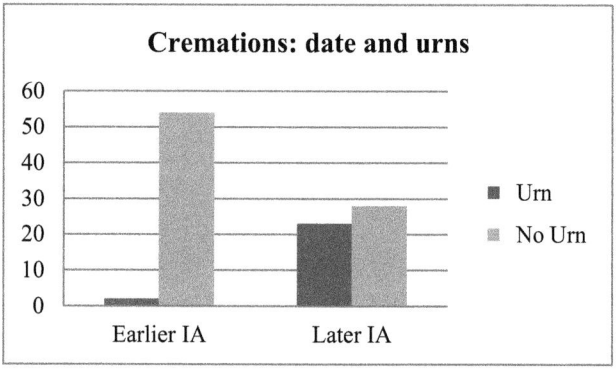

Figure 6. 32 Date and urn, excluding larger sites

---

[7] The following chapter discusses the statistical analysis of Westhampnett in detail.

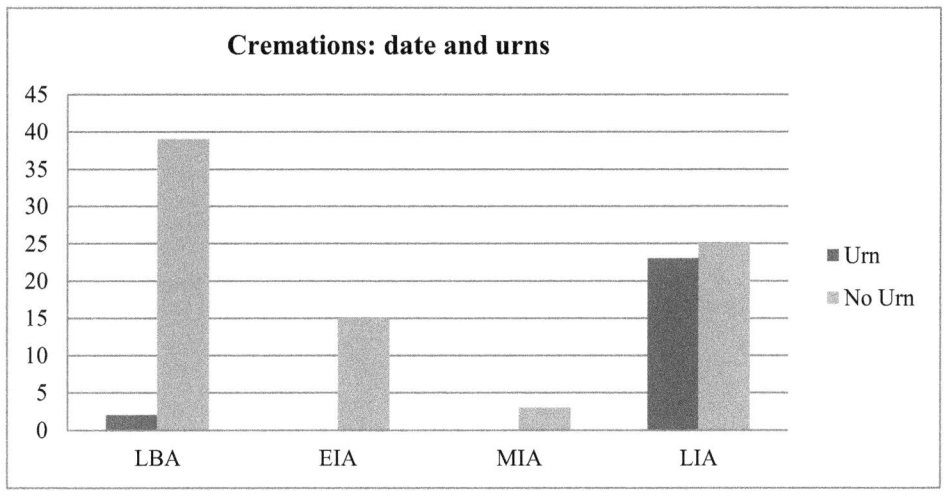

Figure 6. 33 Date and urn, excluding larger sites

Summary

In conclusion, the individual quantitative and statistical analyses for the methods of disposal yielded results that provide insights into various aspects of Iron Age burial practices. Generally, disarticulated bones show continuity in selection throughout the Iron Age, with a possible preference for lower limb elements from the right side of the body. The inhumation analysis suggests a relationship between the date and biological age of the deceased on certain sites. Additionally, the cremation analyses show a higher frequency of female cremations. In all, the results reveal different processes of the burial practice. There is evidence for distinct spatial organisation of human remains within structures with respect to divisions between right and left, as well as the interior and perimeter, which is particularly evident with the inhumations and disarticulated bones. Overall, the results show a fluctuating pattern through time in the manner of disposal, especially for disarticulated bones and cremations. The social implications of the findings from the past three chapters will be further explored in the following chapters.

Chapter Seven

Statistical and quantitative results from sites with 20 or more occurrences

Introduction

This is the final chapter that addresses the results from the statistical and quantitative analysis for this investigation. It focuses solely on the individual sites with 20 or more human remains occurrences and **Figure 7.1** and **Table 7.1** illustrate their distribution. Fifteen sites contain over 20 occurrences, ranging from 20 to over 400. Each site is categorised by site type, which will also be their presentation order in the discussion (see **Table 7.2-5**). The examination begins with midden sites, of which there is only one such site, Potterne (Wiltshire), that has over 20 human remains. Next, the discussion turns to settlement sites that contain high quantities of skeletal material. Then the chapter examines settlement sites with accompanying cemeteries, before ending with cemetery sites. Within each of the site type categories (middens, settlements, settlements/cemeteries, and cemeteries), the individual site are arranged chronologically starting from the earliest

to the latest. The reason for this arrangement is to demonstrate the temporal development in the burial rite in the context of similar site organisation.

The discussion focuses on each site individually with a brief site history being given, as well as a description of the archaeological features, contexts and 'manner of disposal' variables, following the similar structure adopted in chapters four, five, and six. Furthermore, there are accompanying site plans illustrating known locations of human remains deposits[8] and, as with the previous result chapters, the discussion centres solely on statistically significant results.[9] Statistical results that do not contribute to our understanding of Iron Age burial practices are excluded from the discussion.

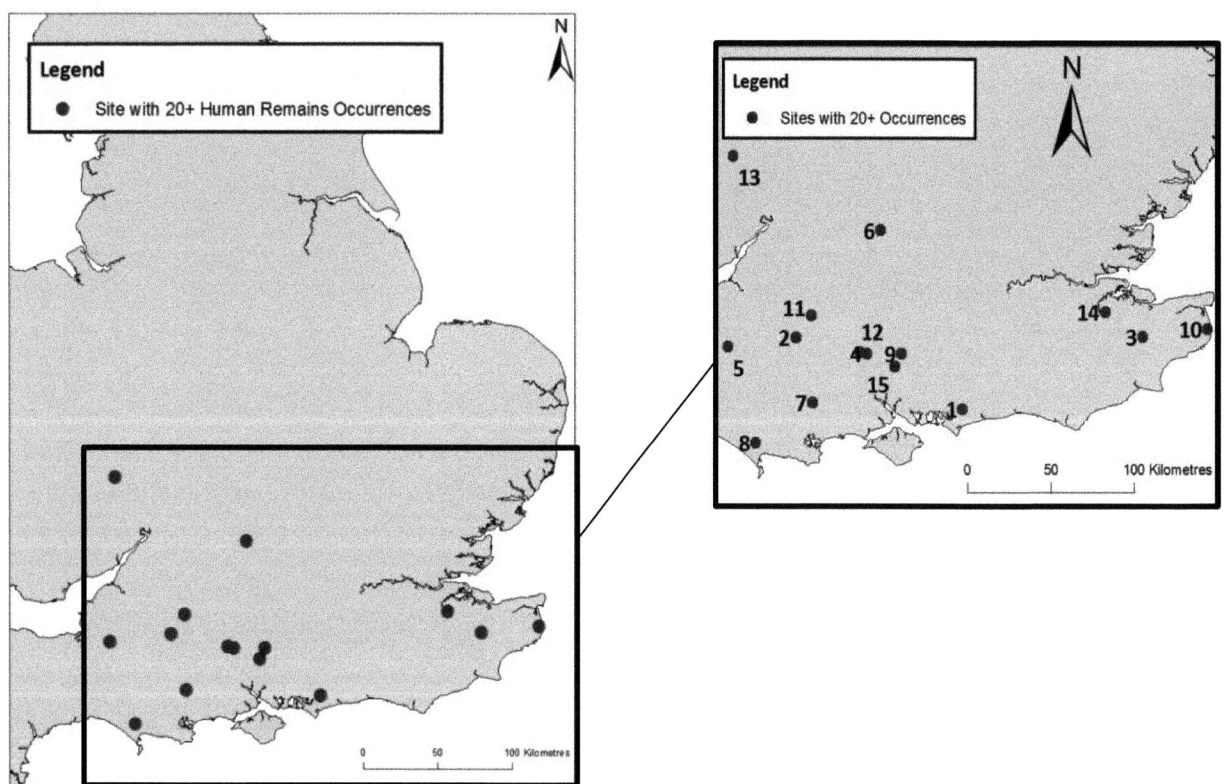

Figure 7. 1 Distribution of all sites with 20 or more human remains occurrences

---

[8] All distribution plots of human remains deposits indicate the presence of bones not their quantity.
[9] All the 'unknown' variables were removed before the quantitative and statistical analyses.

Table 7. 1 List of sites, numbered to correspond with Figure 7.1

1	A27 Westhampnett	8	Maiden Castle
2	Battlesbury Bowl	9	Micheldever Wood
3	Beechbrook Wood	10	Mill Hill
4	Danebury	11	Potterne
5	Glastonbury Lake Village	12	Suddern Farm
6	Gravelly Guy	13	Sutton Walls
7	Gussage All Saints	14	White Horse Stone
	15	Winnall Down	

Table 7. 2 List of midden site

Site	Date (human remains)
Potterne	LBA/EIA

Table 7. 3 List of settlement sites

Site	Date (human remains)
Battlesbury Bowl	LBA, EIA, MIA and LIA
Danebury	EIA, MIA and LIA
Gravelly Guy	EIA, MIA and LIA
Gussage All Saints	EIA, MIA and LIA
Winnall Down	EIA and MIA
Glastonbury Lake Village	MIA and LIA
Micheldever Wood	MIA and LIA

Table 7. 4 List of settlement/cemetery sites

Site	Date (human remains)
White Horse	LBA, EIA, MIA and LIA
Beechbrook Wood	LBA, EIA, MIA and LIA
Suddern Farm	EIA, MIA and LIA
Maiden Castle	EIA, MIA and LIA
Sutton Walls	LIA

Table 7. 5 List of cemetery sites

Site	Date (human remains)
Mill Hill	EIA, MIA and LIA
A27 Westhampnett	LIA

Midden

Potterne (ST 996 591)

The archaeological site of Potterne, in northwest Wiltshire, lies upon the Upper Greensand overlain by Argillic Brown Earths (Lawson 2000, 4). A village cemetery occupies the area and, consequently, the site was discovered in the course of grave-digging (Lawson 2000, 1). Originally, Potterne (also known as Blackferry) was believed to be a settlement yet the excavations by Wessex Archaeology, between 1982 and 1985, revealed '... a vast rubbish heap with an apparently unbroken sequence of Late Bronze Age and Early Iron Age deposits of unprecedented richness' (Lawson 2000, 1). The Potterne

midden covers at least 3.5 ha, of which only 0.75 per cent was unearthed in the excavations, and the deepest point of the midden measures 1.3m thick (Lawson 2000, 13). In addition, the bottom of the midden deposit contains evidence of structures and occupation activity possibly as early as the Middle Bronze Age (Lawson 2000, 25, 33). As for the skeletal material uncovered at Potterne, 139 fragments of disarticulated bones (MNI=15) were collected from 97 'spits' (McKinley 2000, 96). None of the human remains possesses marks of butchery or gnawing, though many show evidence of wear (McKinley 2000, 98). 'Variations in condition of the bone suggest the bone fragments were probably subject to different depositional and redepositional procedures at different stages' (McKinley 2000, 99). For this study, information relating to the individual contexts of the human remains for Potterne was not recorded. This is due to the complex nature of the midden in that any attempt to separate out contexts would result in arbitrary divisions. As previously stated there are 139 bone fragments uncovered from Potterne, and a portion of these bone fragments were conjoining pieces or multiple fragments of the same element (McKinley 2000, 96; Archives). Jacqueline McKinley, who performed the osteological analysis for Potterne, kindly provided access to the copies of the original osteological report. From these osteological reports, in conjunction with the published material, 103[10] human remains occurrences are recorded from Potterne. The difference in the two numbers (139 and 103) is the result of three occurrences being conjoins (2526 (Zone 9), 3400 (Zone 13), and 3413/3416 or 2413/3416) and two occurrences being multiple fragments (2799 (Zone 10) and 2811 (Zone 10)). Exact quantification of these fragments and joining breaks is unknown, although it is believed, but cannot be securely stated, that they make up the remaining difference in numbers.

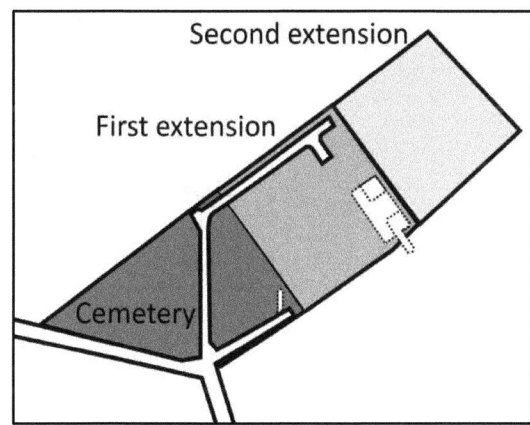

Figure 7. 2 Site plan of Potterne illustrating the area of excavation (after Lawson 2000, 6); ©Wessex Archaeology, with permission

[10] An undated infant burial was uncovered towards the bottom of the midden (McKinley 2000, 99-100) but was not included in this study's analysis due to the uncertainty of its date.

Disarticulated bones (n=103)

All of the disarticulated bones are Late Bronze Age/Early Iron Age in date, and are from secondary deposits. The occurrences are more frequent in the main midden context (n=97), except for six occurrences deriving from posthole contexts within the midden. Multiple deposits (n=91) within the same spit are more frequent than single deposits (n=2). The skull is the most commonly occurring element (n=39; **Figure 7.3**). For elements given a side, the right side is the most frequently represented (n=27, left n=18; **Figure 7.4**).

Demographically, adults are the most common (n=70, sub-adult n=32) and, of the disarticulated bones which could be sexed, males were more frequent than females (n=14, females n=6). Thirteen occurrences had pathological indicators, two of them multiple, the most frequent of which is dental disease (n=7; **Figure 7.5**). Twenty-seven occurrences had traumatic indicators, two of them multiple, and the most common form of trauma was weathering (n=18; **Figure 7.6**).

The statistical analysis for disarticulated bones did not return any meaningful results. No information relating to the occurrences' location around the site was taken because the excavations covered only on a small portion of the midden, and the enormous size of this feature prevents any meaningful analysis of spatial location.

Summary

Although the statistical analysis of the disarticulated bones from Potterne did not return any meaningful results, it does provide an ideal example of post-mortem handling of human remains in the Late Bronze Age/Early Iron Age. Potterne's disarticulated bones show signs of the community's continuous handling and using of human remains as a complex social activity (Waddington 2008). In addition, human bones from Potterne provide an example of a site with high numbers of cranial elements compared to other bones. This supports the claim that crania were preferred parts of the human skeleton employed in these activities carried out at Potterne and other sites.

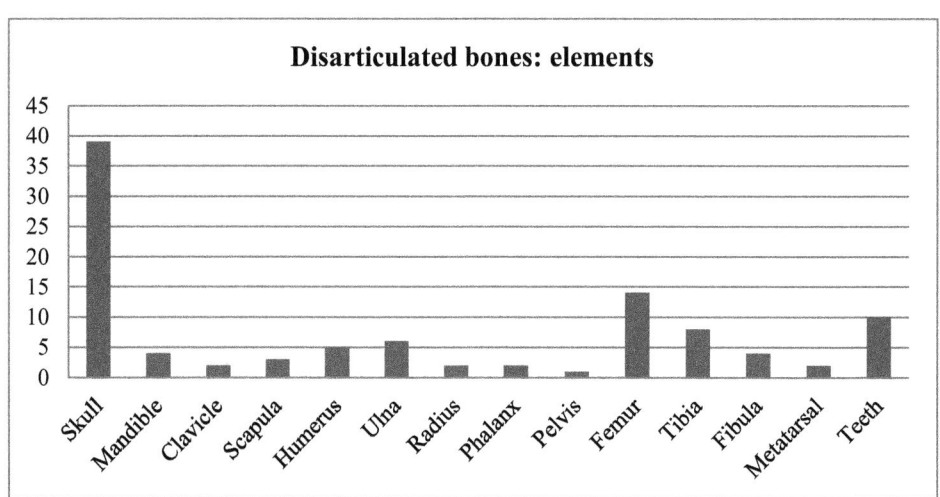

Figure 7. 3 Frequency of disarticulated bone elements

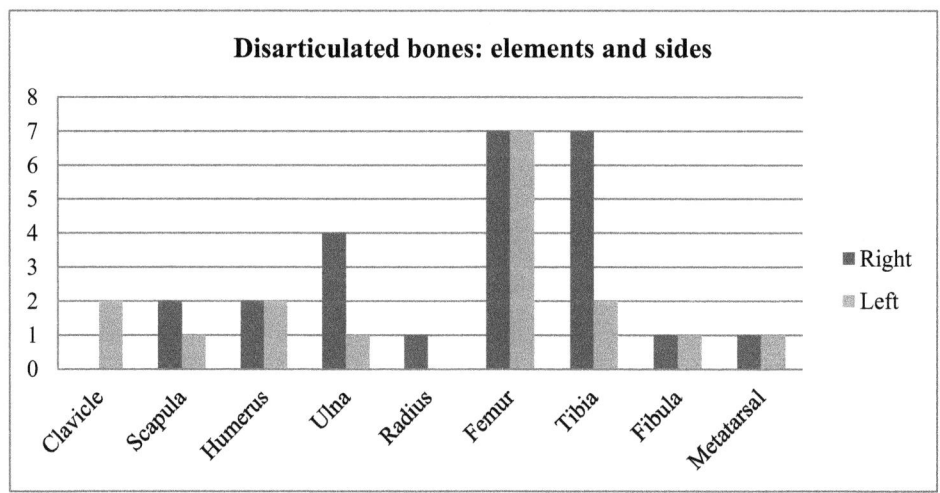

Figure 7. 4 Frequency of disarticulated bones' elements and sides

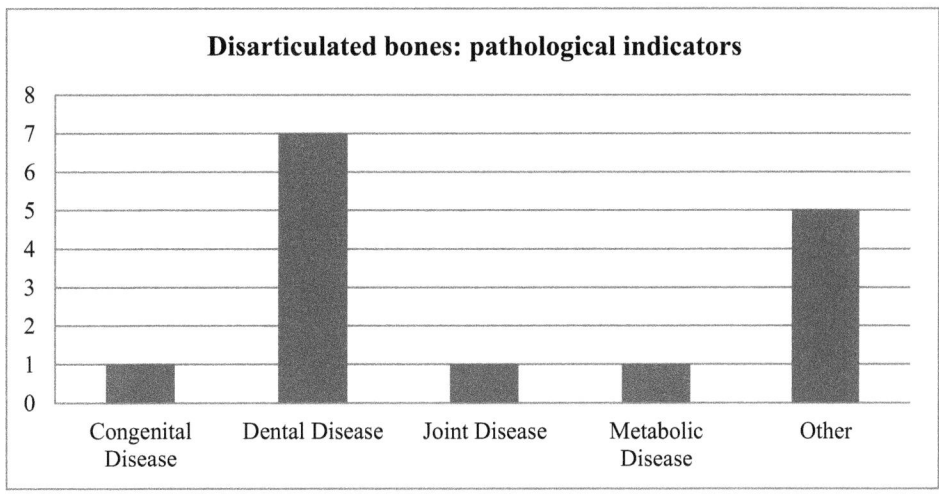

Figure 7. 5 Frequency of pathologies

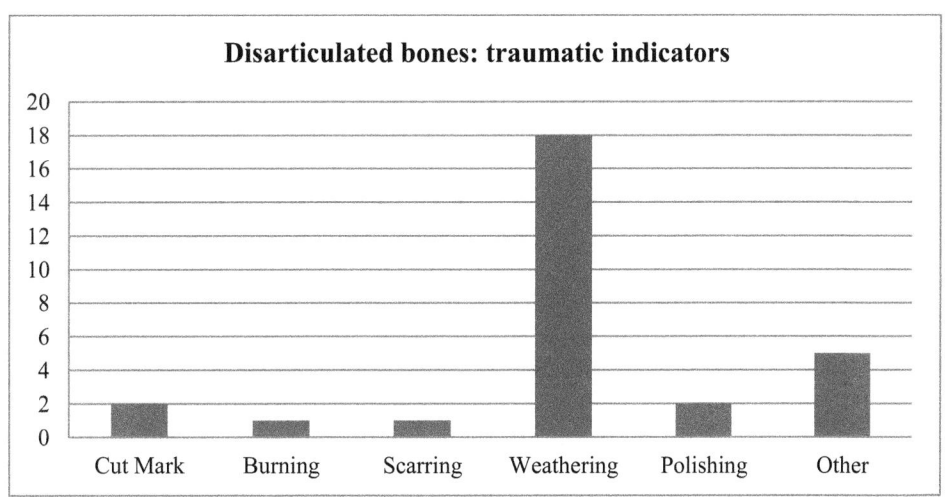

Figure 7. 6 Frequency of trauma

Settlements

Battlesbury Bowl (ST 8990 4600)

The archaeological site of Battlesbury Bowl lies on Salisbury Plain, in Wiltshire, on a chalk outcrop overlooking the Wylye Valley (Ellis and Powell 2008, 1). Excavations by Wessex Archaeology took place in 1999 in advance of and during the building of the Southern Range Road (Ellis and Powell 2008, 1). Battlesbury Bowl is a hillfort and the excavations, totalling 0.6 ha, were carried out just below the hillfort's northern ramparts (Ellis and Powell 2008, 9). Settlement activity at Battlesbury Bowl began in the Late Bronze Age, and lasted into the Late Iron Age (Ellis and Powell 2008, 15). Twenty-one contexts contain human remains, totalling 34 human remains occurrences consisting of 27 disarticulated bones,

six inhumations, and one articulated limb (McKinley 2008). Human remains were present in all major Iron Age phases of the site. The osteological analysis, conducted by Jacqueline McKinley, reveals that the Late Bronze Age-Early Iron Age disarticulated bones possess marks '...indicative of some level of exposure linked to deliberate human manipulation involving excarnation and possible "curation"' (McKinley 2008, 81-82). In addition, the later Middle Iron Age and Late Iron Age skeletal material provides secure indicators of dismemberment (McKinley 2008, 82).

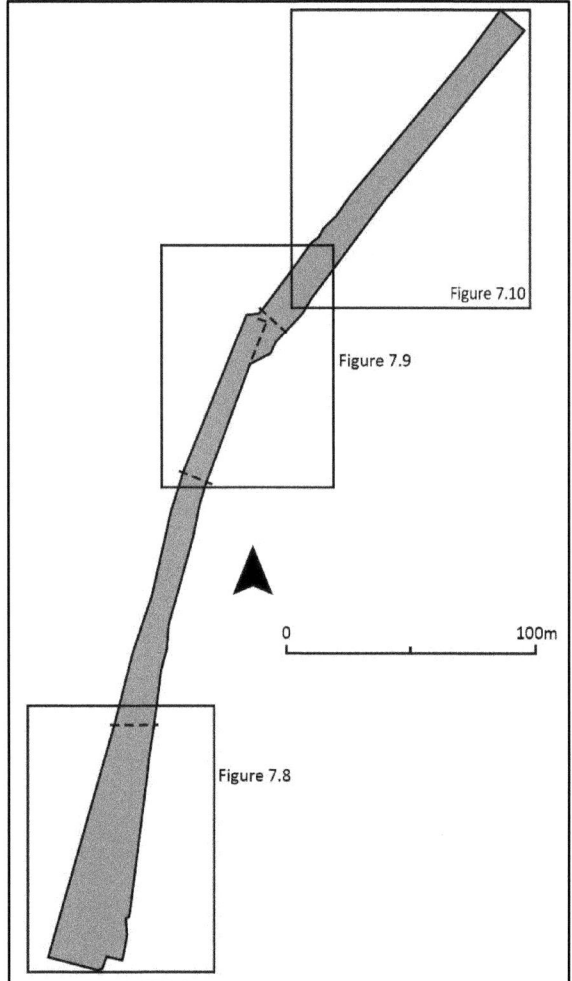

Figure 7. 5 Site plan of Battlesbury Bowl (after Ellis and Powell 2008, 16); ©Wessex Archaeology, with permission

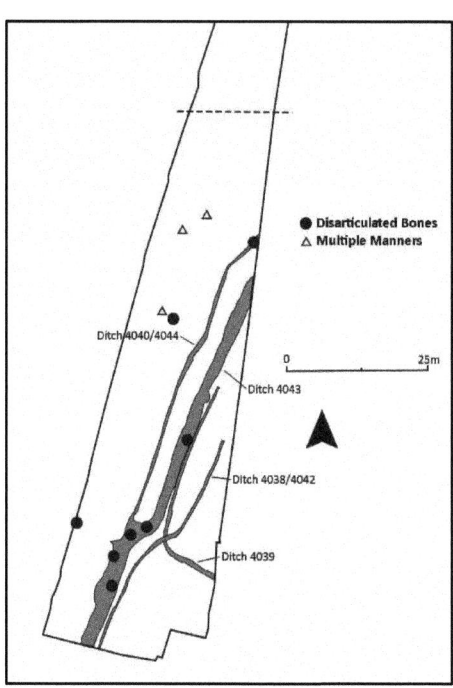

Figure 7. 6 Battlesbury Bowl, depicting only boundary features and human remains deposits (after Ellis and Powell 2008, 18); ©Wessex Archaeology, with permission

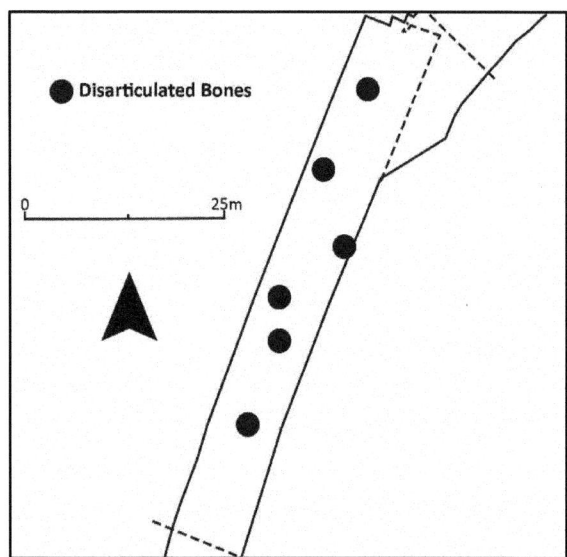

Figure 7. 9 Battlesbury Bowl, depicting only human remains deposits (after Ellis and Powell 2008, 20); ©Wessex Archaeology, with permission

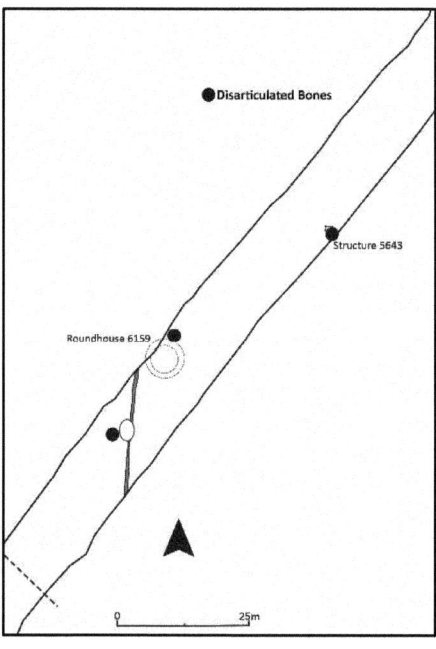

Figure 7. 10 Battlesbury Bowl, showing Roundhouse 6159, Structure 5643, boundary features, and human remains deposits (after Ellis and Powell 2008, 21); ©Wessex Archaeology, with permission

Analysis of archaeological feature (n=5)

There are five archaeological features with associated human remains from Battlesbury Bowl. Three are boundary features dating to the Late Bronze Age and Early Iron Age that contain disarticulated bones within the ditches (Ellis and Powell 2008, 20-24; **Figure 7.8**). Additionally, a Middle Iron Age roundhouse (Roundhouse 6159) has three disarticulated bones within a single pit just outside and to the north-to-northeast of the structure (Ellis and Powell 2008, 25-29; **Figure 7.10**). Lastly, there is a four-post structure (Structure 5643), possibly a granary, with a single disarticulated bone in its southeastern posthole (Ellis and Powell 2008, 29; **Figure 7.10**).

Analyses of contexts (n=21)

Of the 21 contexts containing human remains occurrences, most date to the Early Iron Age (n=14, Middle Iron Age n=3, Late Iron Age n=2, and unphased Iron Age n=2). Human remains occur predominantly in pit contexts (n=11; **Figure 7.11**)[11], and are single deposits (n=14, multiple deposits n=7). Most of the contexts were placed along the perimeters of the ditch features discussed above (n=8, exterior n=1). Statistical testing of context variables did not yield any significant results.

Analysis of manner of disposal

Inhumations (n=6)

All the inhumations date to the Middle (n=3) or Late Iron Age (n=3) and were found in pits (n=6), either within the middle (n=2) or bottom (n=2) segments of the context (two have unknown depths). Many are primary deposits (n=3, secondary n=2), and all are associated with other human remains occurrences such as disarticulated bones. In addition, all the inhumations[12] are complete, and are crouched (n=2), flexed (n=1), and contracted (n=1), resting on their left sides (n=3) or right side (n=1). The inhumations' orientations did not reveal any consistency in cardinal direction (northwest n=2, east n=1, and southeast n=1). Inhumations are predominately adult (n=5, sub-adult n=1) and male (n=4, female n=2), and all have multiple pathological indicators. The most common inflictions is a disease of an unknown cause ('other' n=7; **Figure 7.12**)[13], and there are two cases of trauma; both are of an unknown cause. All the inhumations have associated material, four with multiple items; the most common type is natural material (such as sandstone) and animal bone (n=4; **Figure 7.13**). Two inhumations are associated with horse remains and one with a sheep bone.

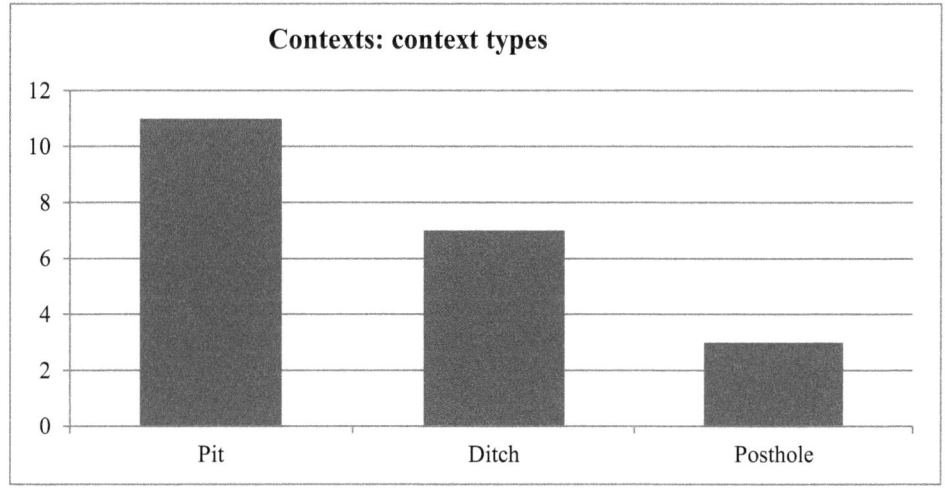

Figure 7. 11 Frequency of context types

---

[11] There is a difference in numbers for context types because context 4012 is misidentified as a pit in the osteological report (McKinley 2008, 72); however, it is a ditch context (Ellis and Powell 2008, 12).

[12] Only four of the inhumations have known burial characteristics; the other two are unknown.
[13] 'Other' pathologies signify disease on a bone but of an unknown cause.

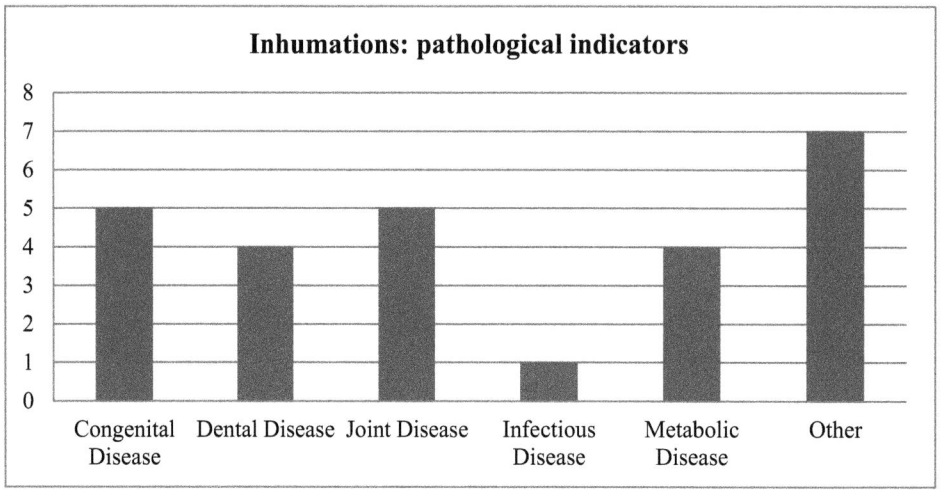

Figure 7. 12 Frequency of inhumations' pathologies

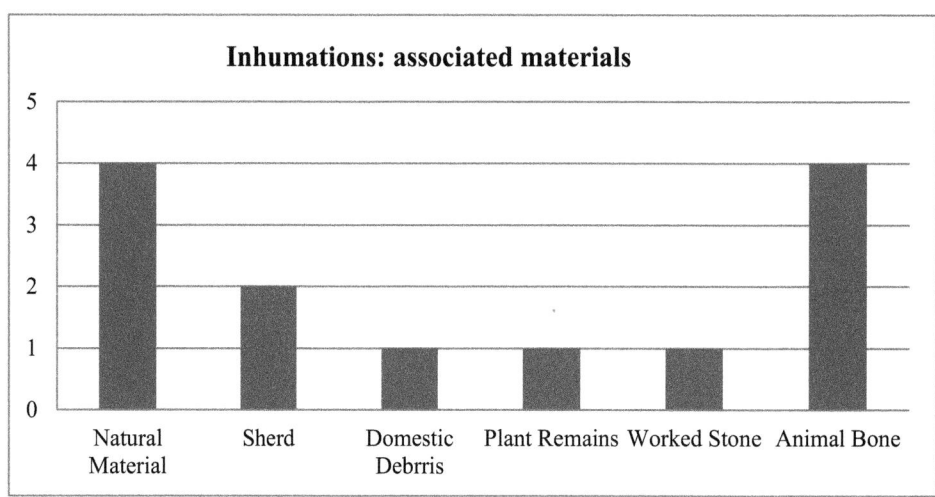

Figure 7. 13 Frequency of inhumations' associated materials

Articulated bone (n=1)

There is one articulated limb from Battlesbury Bowl, dating to the Middle Iron Age and found at the bottom of a pit associated with an inhumation. It is a secondary deposit of a lower right limb from an adult male.

Disarticulated bones (n=27)

Over half of the disarticulated bones date to the Late Bronze Age/Early Iron Age (n=15, Middle Iron Age n=6, Late Iron Age n=3) and were recovered from pits (n=15; **Figure 7.14**). Some of the disarticulated bones were within the top segment of their contexts (n=4, middle n=1, bottom n=3). A greater proportion are single (n=20, multiple n=7), redeposited bones. Skulls are the most frequently occurring element (n=8; **Figure 7.15**), although lower limbs are the most commonly represented portion

of the body (n=11; **Figure 7.16**). Unfortunately, the sidedness of elements was not available in the osteological report. Disarticulated bones are mostly from adults (n=18, sub-adults n=9), and only five could be sexed, with females representing just over half (n=3, males n=2). Only four occurrences have a single pathological indicator, commonly being congenital disease (n=2) and 'other' pathologies (n=2) of unknown origin. Many of the disarticulated bones have traumatic indicators (four with multiple) typically occurring post-mortem (n=10), with the most common being animal gnawing (n=7; **Figure 7.17**). Over half of the occurrences have multiple associated materials and are frequently associated with pottery sherds (n=14; **Figure 7.18**). Twelve disarticulated bones were associated with archaeological features as discussed above. Eight bones are from the ditch systems, three from the roundhouse and one from the four-post structure. The statistical testing of the disarticulated bone associations did not yield any significant results.

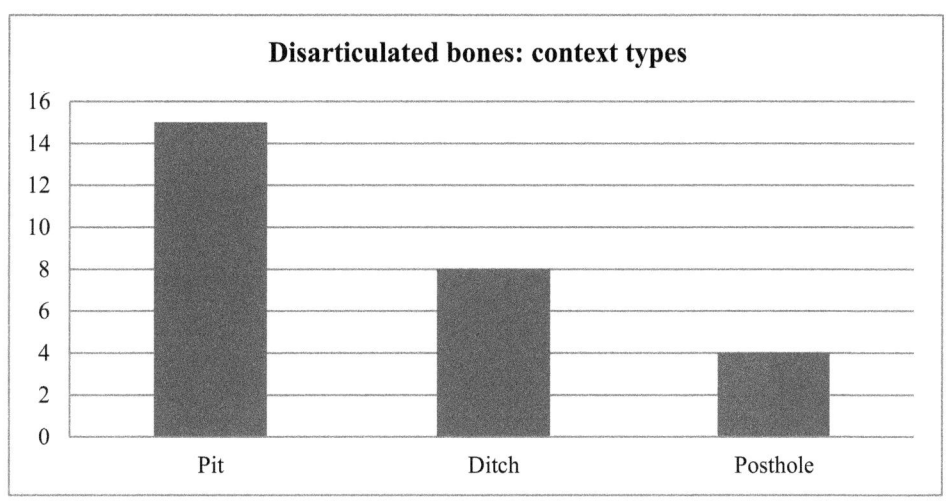

Figure 7. 14 Frequency of disarticulated bones according to context types

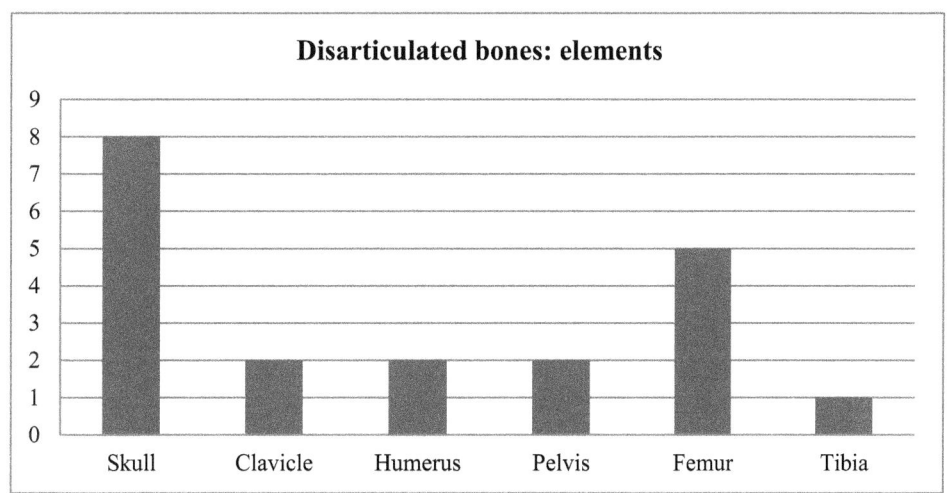

Figure 7. 15 Frequency of disarticulated bone elements

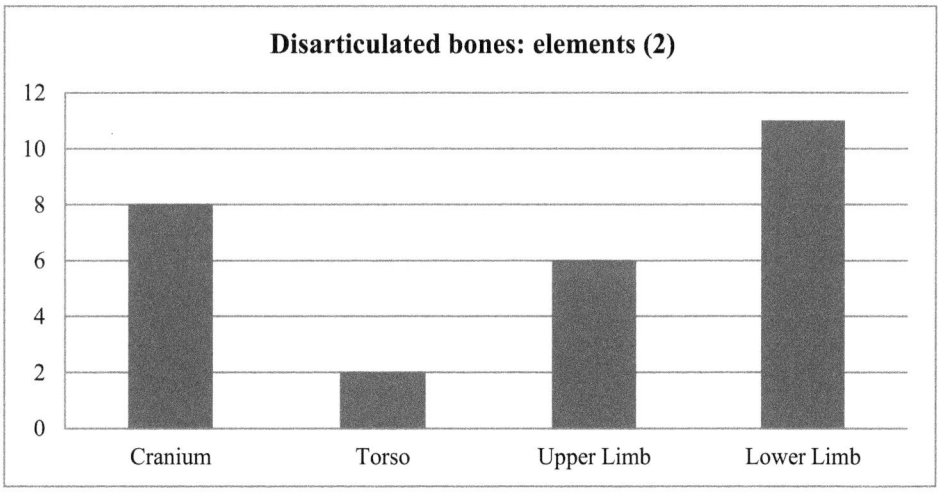

Figure 7. 16 Frequency of disarticulated bone elements (2)

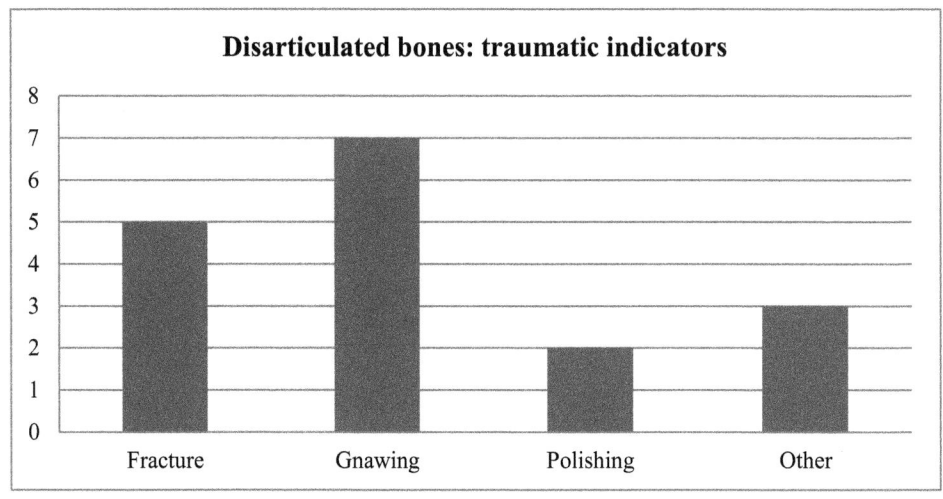

Figure 7. 17 Frequency of disarticulated bones' trauma

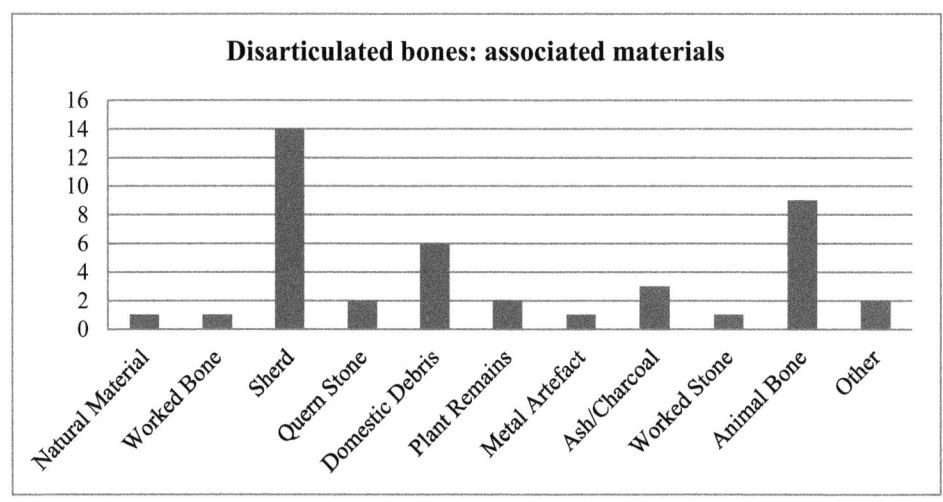

Figure 7. 18 Frequency of disarticulated bones' associated materials

Summary

The statistical analysis of Battlesbury Bowl showed little insight into burial characteristics. In turn, the human remains from Battlesbury Bowl show depositional and handling characteristics that correlate with general interpretations of Iron Age burial practices. For example, it is suggested that four-post structures may function as excarnation racks although there is little evidence to support that claim (Carr and Knüsel 1997, 168). Battlesbury Bowl has a four-post structure with an associated disarticulated bone within one of the postholes. The disarticulated bone is a redeposited cranial fragment and the contextual evidence suggests that it was placed intentionally into the posthole and had not fallen in from platform above the post structure. Additionally, many of the human remains show evidence of post-mortem handling and curation, such as weathering and animal gnawing, and this may suggest that the bones represented the remains of the group's ancestors (McKinley 2008). Post-mortem handling is a common trait in Iron Age burial practices and the remains from Battlesbury Bowl and Potterne conform to this notion.

Danebury (SU 32 37)

Danebury is an Iron Age multivallate hillfort on the Wessex chalklands with three distinct enclosures; the inner earthwork encloses 5.3 hectares with the outer encircling 16.2 hectares (Hampshire) (Cunliffe 1995, 5). Excavations were carried out at Danebury over twenty consecutive years (1969-1988) under the supervision of Barry Cunliffe. By the end, roughly 57 per cent of the site had been fully excavated, predominately within the interior (Cunliffe 1995, 5). The first enclosure, the outer, was constructed sometime during the eighth and seventh century BC (cp 1-2, Early Iron Age) (Cunliffe 1995, 19). Occupation evidence from Danebury suggests that dense habitation at the hillfort spanned about 500 years throughout most of the Iron Age (Cunliffe 1995, 13). There are two entrances into the hillfort, one to the east and the other towards the southwest with a main road that connecting the two (Cunliffe 1995, 20). By 270 BC, the southwest entrance was intentionally blocked and most of the ramparts refurbished (Cunliffe 1995, 17). Interestingly, the spatial organisation of the site shows a bilateral division between the left/right areas along the main road. In the early period of occupation, the left side of the site (with respect to the east entrance) contained high numbers of habitation features, while the right side has mainly storage pits for grain. When the southwest entrance was later blocked there was a switch in spatial organisation, with occupation evidence now favouring the right side of the site (with respect to the east entrance) and storage units on the left half (Cunliffe 1995, 25). The change in spatial organisation indicates a significant connection between the two entrances and their influence on activity within the site (Cunliffe 1995, 42).

The size and scale of the excavation produced an extraordinary amount of information. Many structures were uncovered such as curvilinear, two-post, and multi-post structures. Additionally, excavations identified 2,308 pits (1,707 fully excavated) and about 10,000 postholes (Cunliffe 1995, 5). A large quantity of pottery (roughly 158,000 sherds) was recovered, helping to establish a chronological sequence for the site (Brown 1995, 53, 61; Cunliffe 1995, 17-18). The chronological sequence is defined by ceramic phases in conjunction with radiocarbon dates (see **Table 7.6**) (Cunliffe 1995, 17-18). In total, 401 human remains occurrences, consisting of 63 inhumations, 332 disarticulated bones, and six articulated limbs from 224 contexts, were recovered from Danebury. Bari Hooper (1991) conducted the osteological analysis and Lucy Walker (1984a-b) compiled the skeletal report for Volume 2.[14]

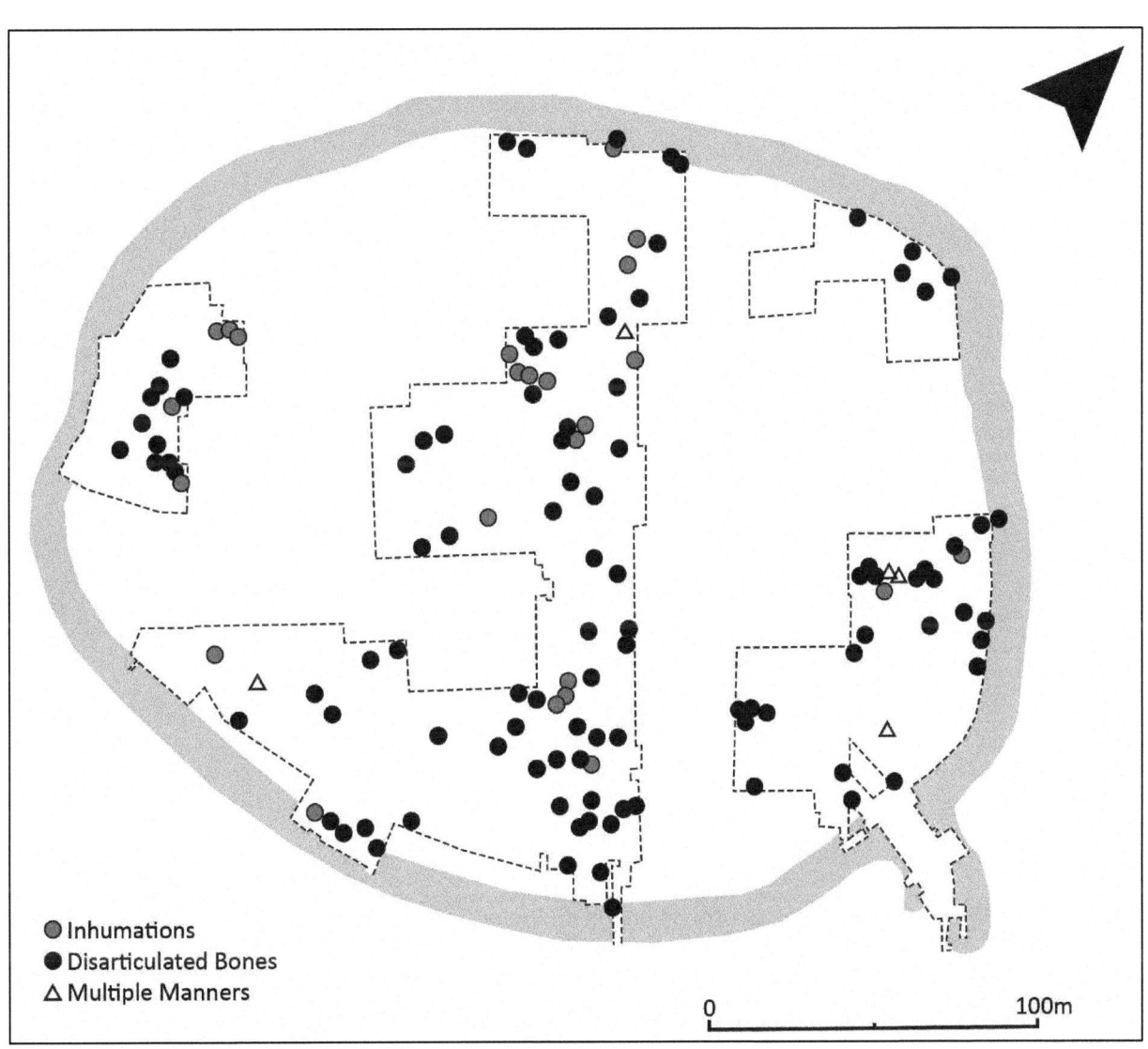

Inhumations
Disarticulated Bones
Multiple Manners

0   100m

Figure 7. 17 Site plan of Danebury showing where known human deposits are (after Cunliffe 1995, 3); with permission

---

[14] All the cardinal directions are based on true north, not grid north.

Analysis of archaeological features (n=38)

Thirty-eight archaeological features have associated human remains occurrences, most of which are roundhouses (n=12, round structures with a domestic function), followed by various areas around the settlement enclosure (ten different areas of the enclosure, multi-post structures n=9, two-post structures n=2 and five of an unknown type[15]). Furthermore, many of the archaeological features date to multiple Iron Age phases (n=22, Early Iron Age n=10, Middle Iron Age n=6). Only eight of the roundhouses have a known orientation, mostly opening towards the eastern half of the compass (northeast n=2, east n=1, southeast n=2, south n=1, southwest n=1 and northwest n=1). None of the statistical tests returned any meaningful results but the 'manner of disposal' section addresses these human remains associated with specifically round structures in more detail.

Table 7. 6 Danebury's ceramic phases and corresponding time periods

Cp 1 and 2	EIA
Cp 3, 4 and 5	EIA/MIA
Cp6	MIA
Cp 7	MIA/LIA
Cp 8 and 9	LIA

Analysis of contexts (n=224)

There are 224 contexts with human remains and over half of the contexts with human remains date to the Middle Iron Age (n=115; **Figure 7.20**). Most of the contexts with human remains are pits (n=164) followed by 'other' contexts (n=43), such as scoops and layers. Predominantly, these contexts have only disarticulated bones within the deposit (n=177, inhumations n=34, multiple manners n=13). A greater proportion of the contexts contain single deposits (n=160, multiple deposits n=53, both single and multiple deposits n=6). In addition, when associated with an architectural feature human remains contexts typically favour the boundary of the site or structure (n=19, entrance n=9). The statistical analysis of contexts did not return any meaningful results.

Analysis of manner of disposal (n=401)

Many of the human remains date to the Middle Iron Age (n=224, Early Iron Age n=151, Late Iron Age n=12, and unphased Iron Age n=14; **Figure 7.21**) and an overwhelming number of human remains are within pits (n=324; **Figure 7.22**)[16]. Furthermore, most of the occurrences with a known depth are in the bottom segments of contexts (n=85, top n=56, middle n=56) and human remains are almost evenly distributed between single (n=203) and multiple (n=198) deposits.

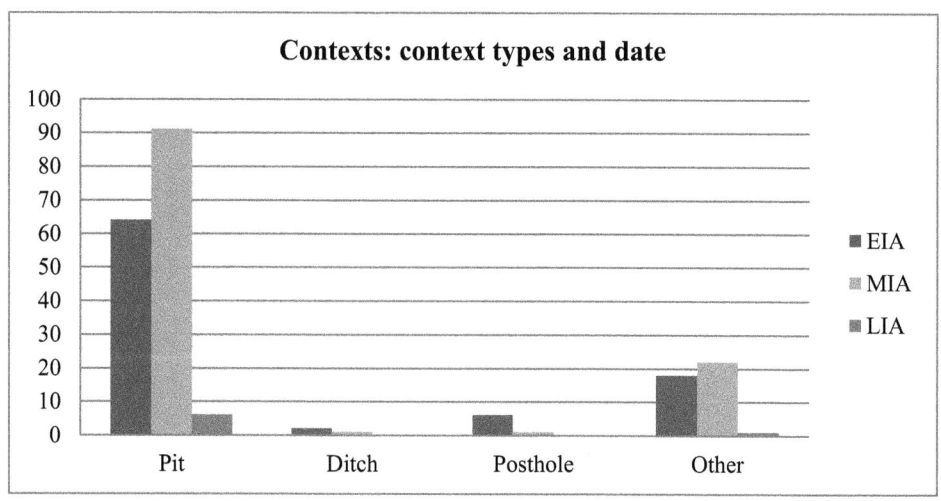

Figure 7. 20 Frequency of contexts by date and type

---

[15] For these five features there is not enough structural evidence to specify the feature type.

[16] The 'other' context category refers to contexts not defined by this study's groupings, such as layers and scoops.

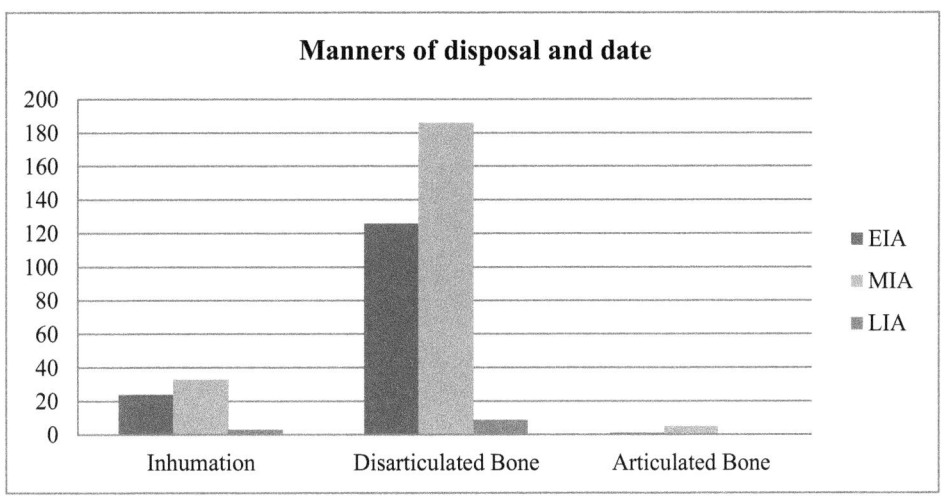

Figure 7. 21 Frequency of human remains according to manner of disposal and date

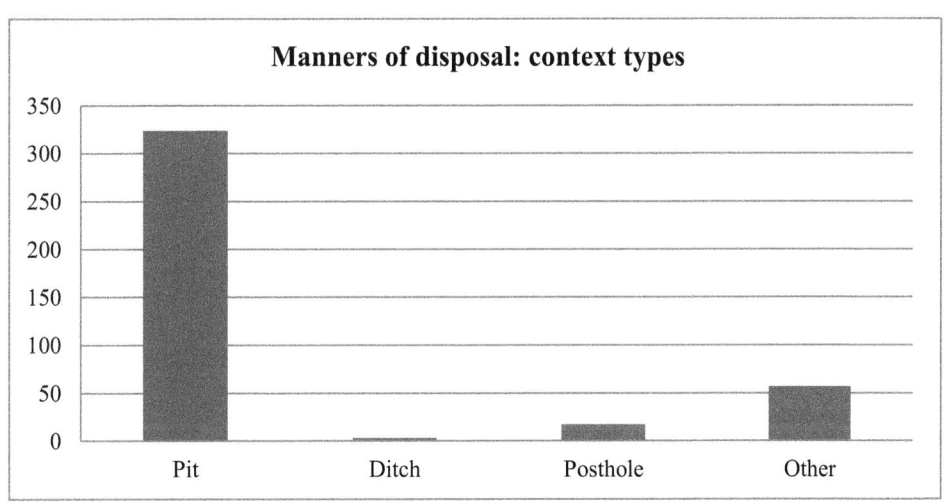

Figure 7. 22 Frequency of occurrences by context types

Demographically, adults are the most represented age group (n=147) followed by children (n=55; **Figure 7.23**). Only 82 human remains occurrences are sexed; males (n=51) are more frequent than females (n=31; **Figure 7.24**). Fifty-eight human remains occurrences have pathological indicators, 42 with single and 16 with multiple indicators, of which haematological disease is the most common (n=26; **Figure 7.25**). There are 64 human remains with traumatic indicators (56 with single), of which scarring of the bone is the most common (n=23; **Figure 7.26**). Additionally, 246 human remains have associated material (83 with a single material type) of which animal bone is the most common (n=137; **Figure 7.27**) and typically of cow (n=58; **Figure 7.28**).

There are 54 human remains occurrences associated with the 33 archaeological features (excluding the unknown features) and, of these, most commonly bones are found in association with roundhouses (n=23, **Figure 7.29**). Fifteen of the human remains associated with round structures have a known placement.[17] Most are in right/back segments of these buildings (n=9; **Figure 7.30**). Furthermore, more are on right halves (n=13) than left (n=2), in back segments (n=9) than front (n=6). Eleven occurrences have a known location in round structures; the interior (n=10, perimeter n=1) is the most frequent. The only meaningful statistical relationship for 'manner of disposal' is discussed above; none of the other variables returned any insightful results.

---

[17] Locational information for this analysis includes round structures' orientation and bone placement in this respect.

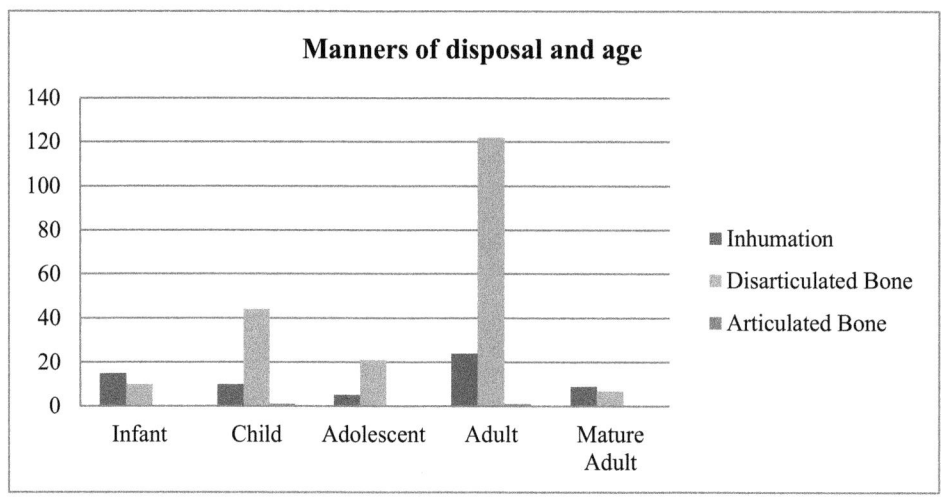

Figure 7. 23 Frequency of occurrences by manner of disposal and age

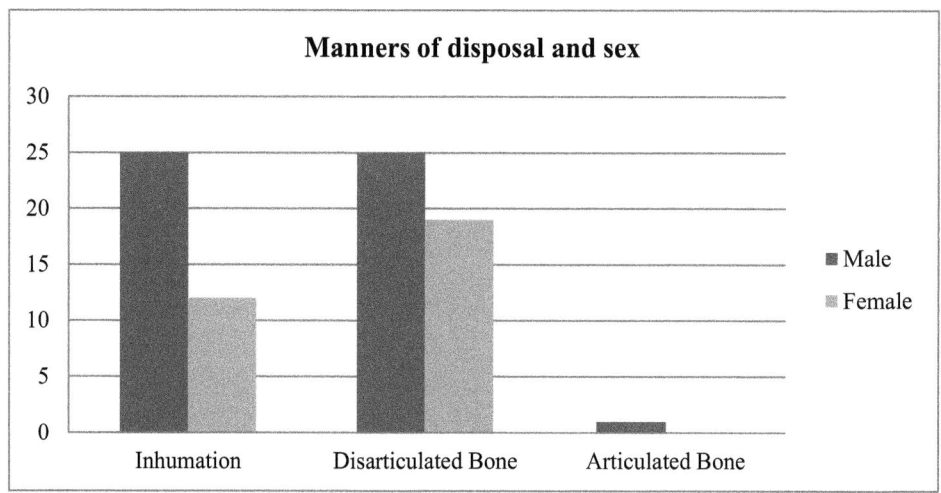

Figure 7. 24 Frequency of occurrences by manner of disposal and sex

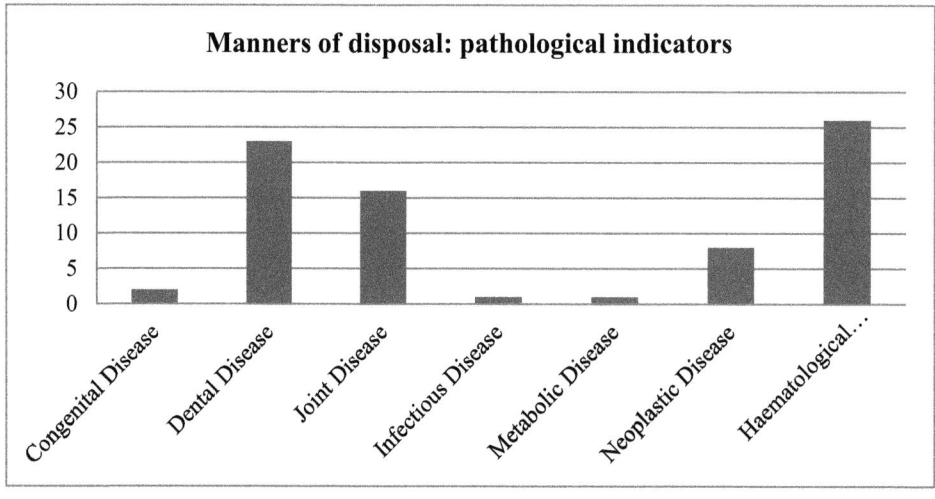

Figure 7. 25 Frequency of pathologies

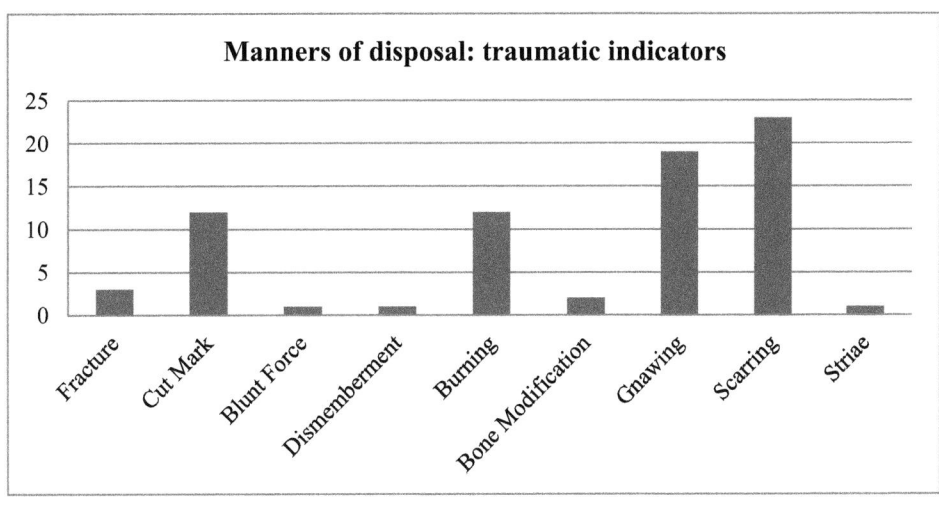

Figure 7. 26 Frequency of trauma

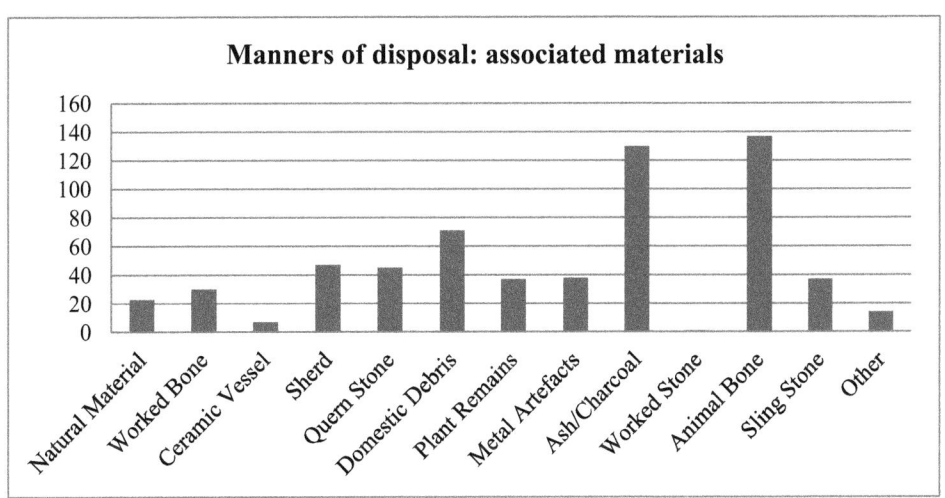

Figure 7. 27 Frequency of associated materials

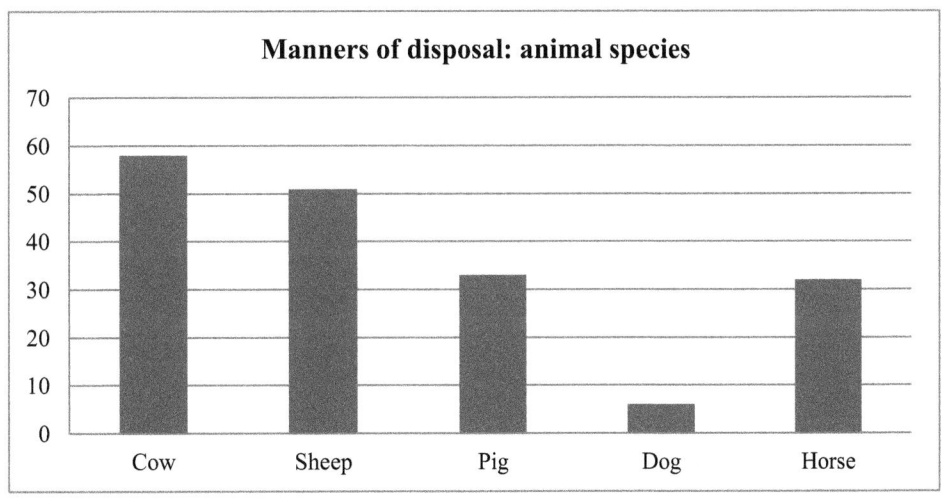

Figure 7. 28 Frequency of animal species

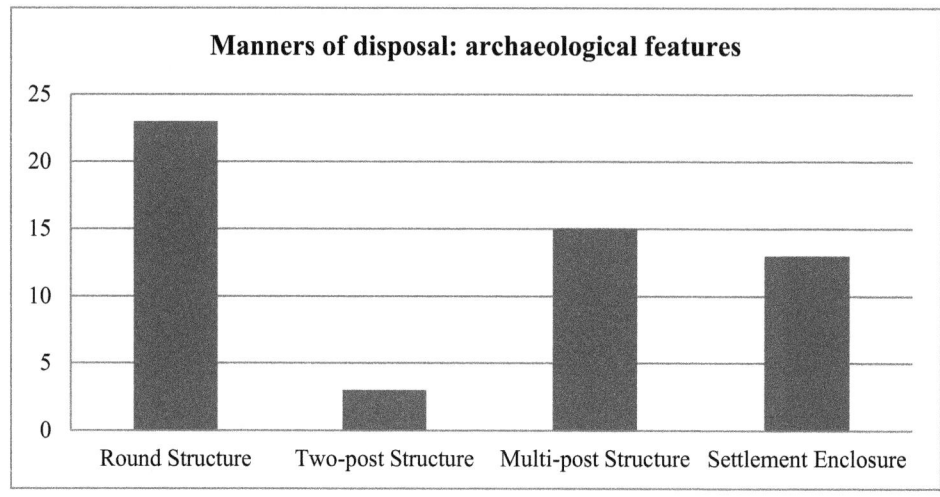

Figure 7. 29 Frequency of occurrences associated with archaeological features

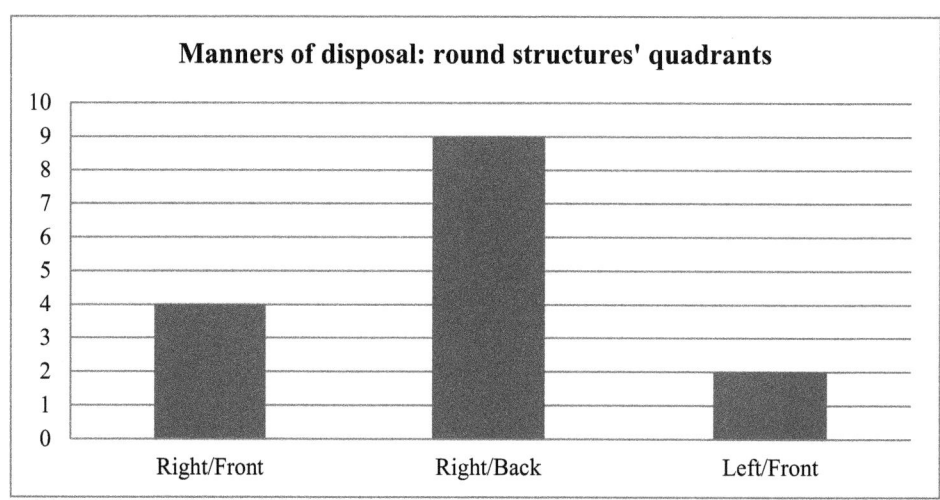

Figure 7. 30 Frequency of occurrences according to round structures' quadrants

Inhumations (n=63)

Most of the inhumations from Danebury date to the Middle Iron Age (n=33; **Figure 7.31**), and are overwhelmingly from pits (n=53; **Figure 7.32**). Typically, the inhumations are within the bottom portion of the context (n=22, top n=8, middle n=5) and are frequently single deposits (n=38, multiple deposit n=25). The inhumations are typically complete (n=36, incomplete n=25), often lying flexed (**Figure 7.33**). Many lie on their right sides[18] (**Figure 7.34**) and are mostly oriented towards the north (n=11; **Figure 7.35**). Facial directions are more frequently to the east (n=8; **Figure 7.36**) and, interestingly, none face towards the northeast. Just over half of the inhumations are adults (n=33; **Figure 7.37**) and the next most frequent age group are infants (n=15) and,

for those inhumations that can be sexed, most are males (n=25, females n=12). Thirty-one of the inhumations have pathological indicators (13 with multiple indicators) the most common being haematological disease (n=15; **Figure 7.38**). Twenty-one inhumations possess traumatic indicators (five with multiple) the most common of which is 'scarring' on the bone deriving from an unknown cause (n=14; **Figure 7.39**). In all, 47 inhumations have associated material present in their deposit (31 with multiple materials), most frequently animal bone (n=30; **Figure 7.40**) of which sheep and cow are the most represented species (both n=16; **Figure 7.41**). Only 11 inhumations are associated with archaeological features of which seven are roundhouses and four are multi-post structures. The statistical analysis did not return meaningful, significant results.

---

[18] The single inhumation in the 'other' position refers to the individual placed in the sitting position.

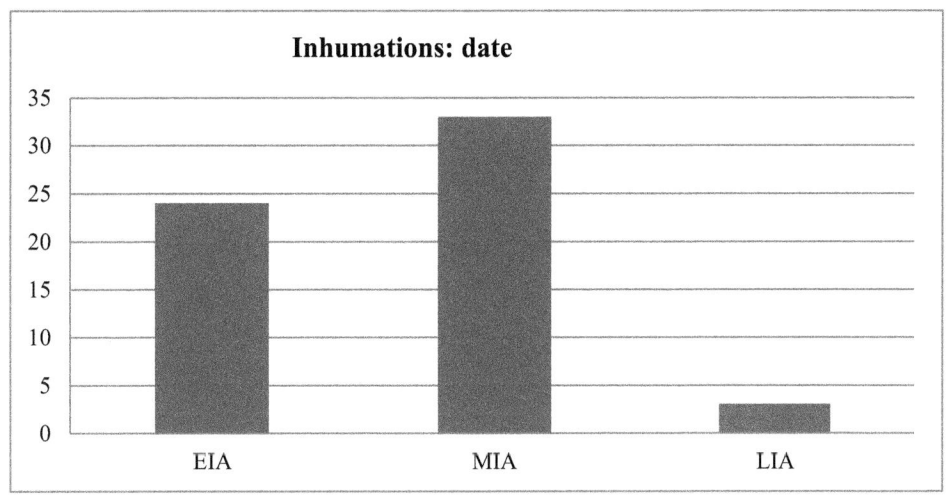

Figure 7. 31 Frequency of inhumations according to date

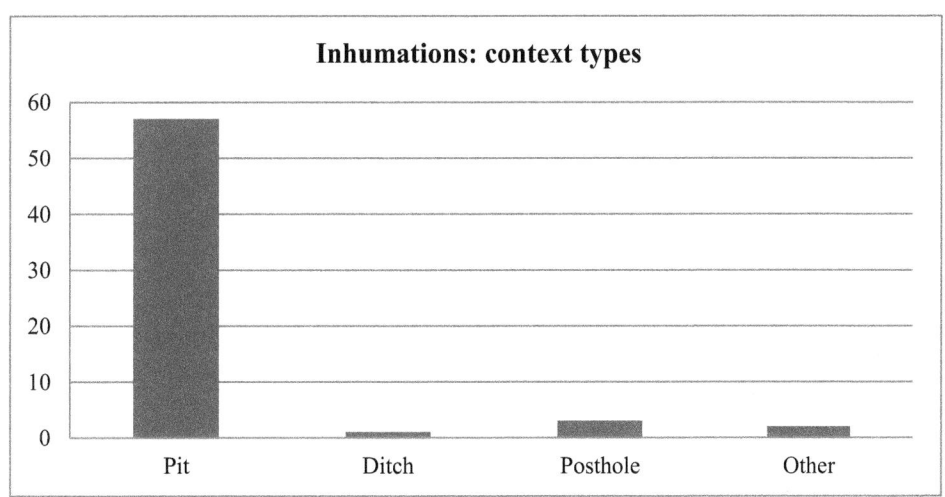

Figure 7. 32 Frequency of inhumations according to context types

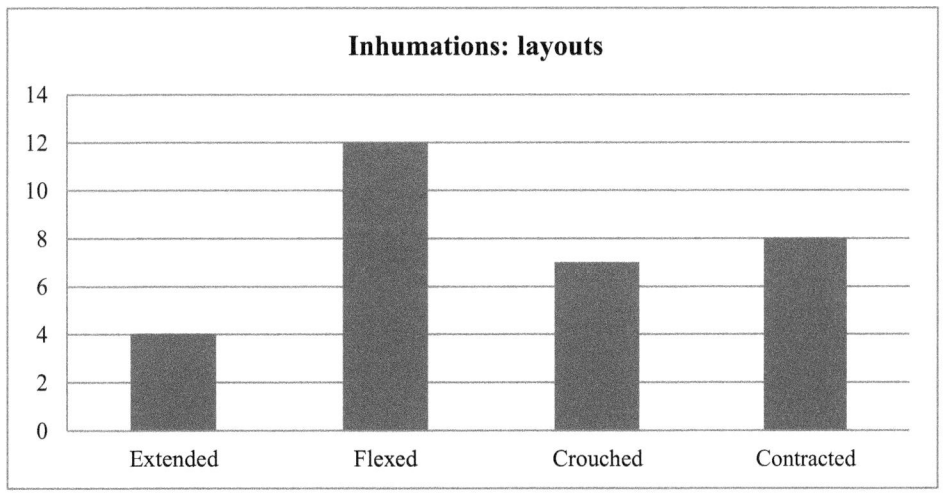

Figure 7. 33 Frequency of inhumations according to layouts

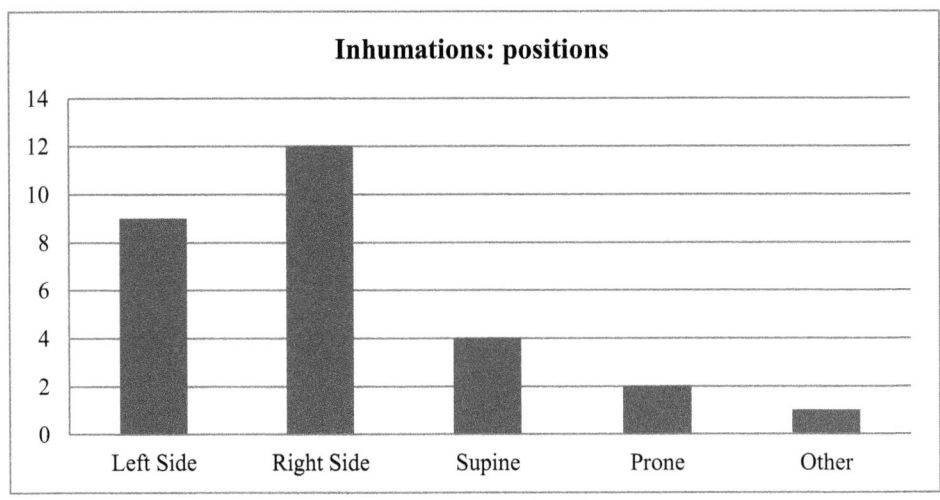

Figure 7. 34 Frequency of inhumations according to positions

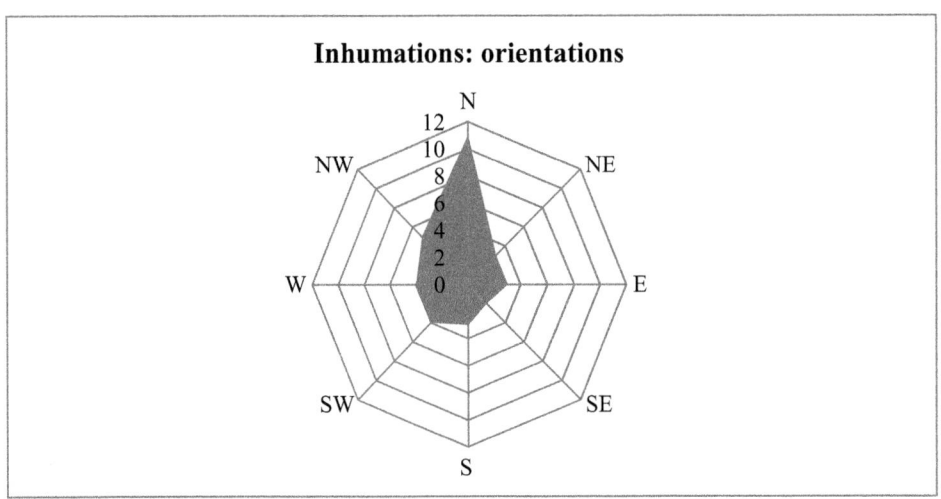

Figure 7. 35 Frequency of inhumations according to orientations

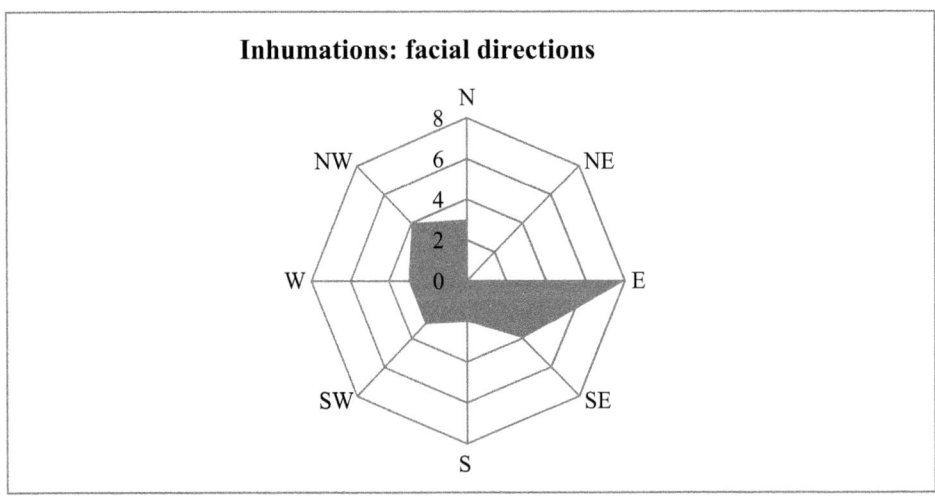

Figure 7. 36 Frequency of inhumations according to facial directions

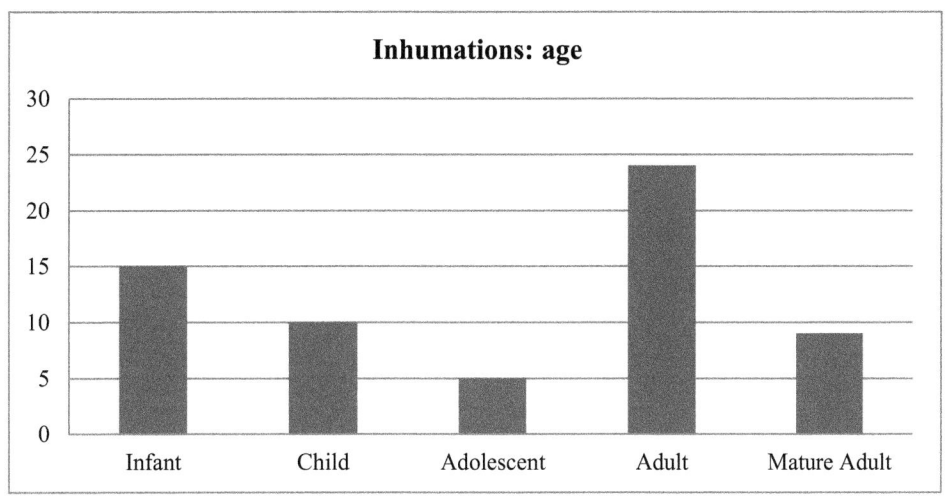

Figure 7. 37 Frequency of inhumations according to age

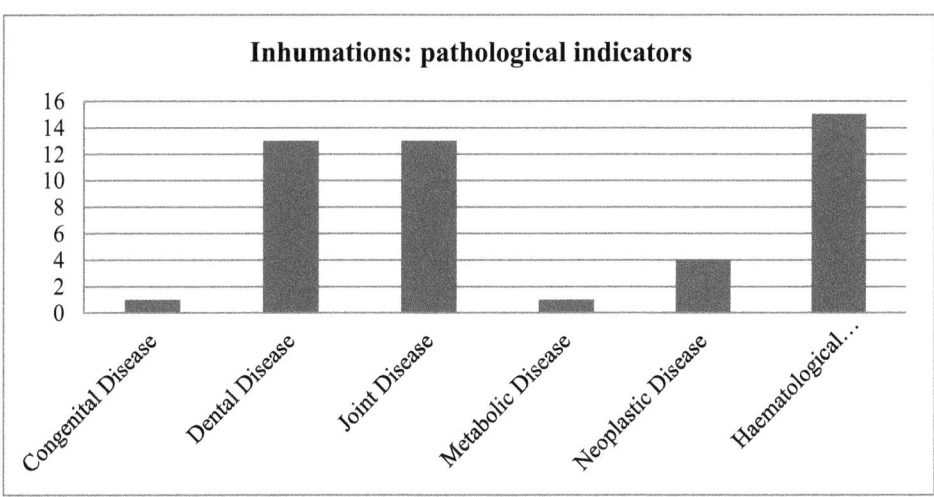

Figure 7. 38 Frequency of inhumations according to pathologies

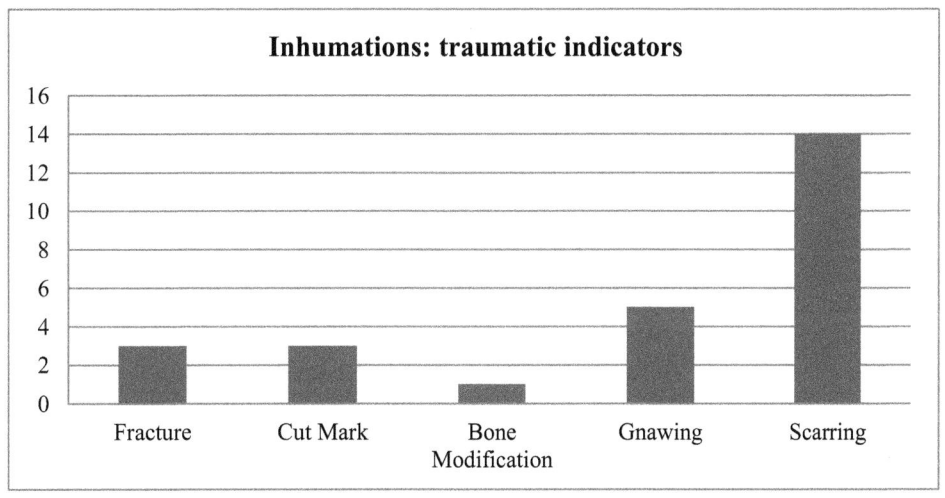

Figure 7. 39 Frequency of inhumations according to trauma

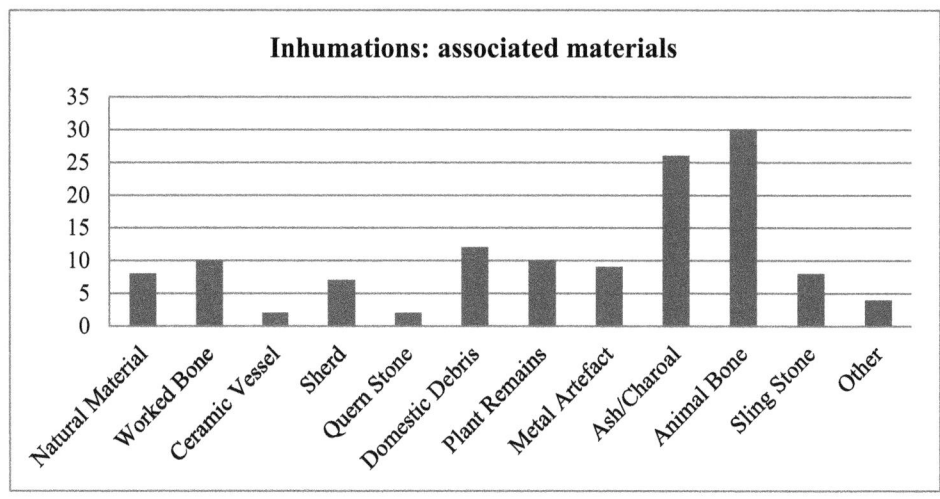

Figure 7. 40 Frequency of inhumations' associated materials

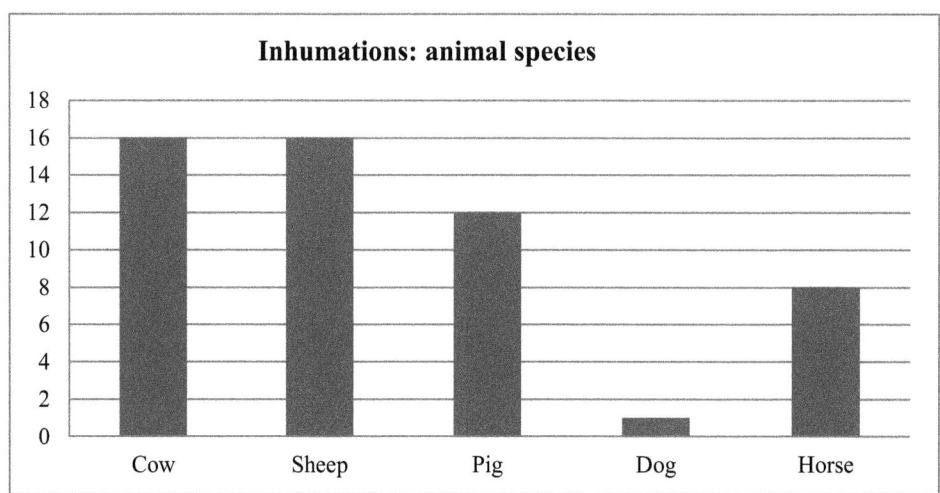

Figure 7. 41 Frequency of inhumations' associated animal species

Articulated bones (n=6)

There are only six articulated bones from Danebury, all of which are from pit contexts, and most date to the Middle Iron Age (n=5, Early Iron Age n=1). Many articulated bones are primary deposits (n=4, two unknowns), often in the bottom segments of the context (n=4, two unknowns), and associated with other human remains (n=5, single deposit n=1). Most of the articulated bones are from the torso (n=4, upper limb n=1, lower limb n=1, both with an unknown side). For example, one occurrence is a pelvis with the femora still articulated with the acetabulum, but severed just a few inches from the femora heads (Hooper 1991, 14:G7 [microfiche]). Two of the articulated bone occurrences are aged, one is an adolescent and the other is an adult. Furthermore, only one occurrence is sexed: a male. Five of the six articulated bones are associated with multiple types of material and animal bone and ash/charcoal are the most frequent occurring items (both n=5; **Figure 7.42**). Of the animal bone, cow is represented with four occurrences and pig with one.

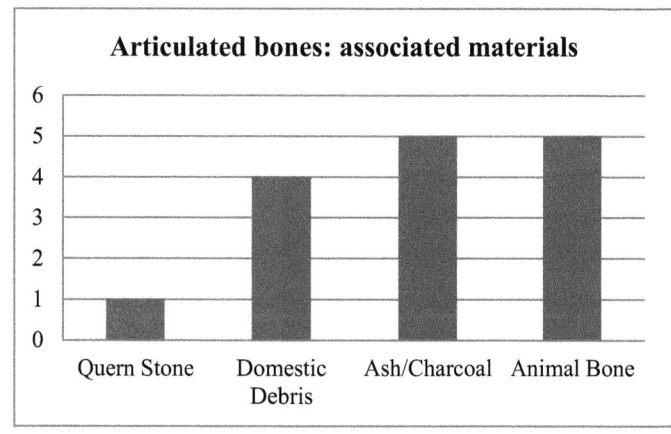

Figure 7. 42 Frequency of articulated bones' associated materials

Disarticulated bones (n=332)

Disarticulated bones make up a large proportion (82.8 per cent) of all the human remains occurrences. Most disarticulated bones date to the Middle Iron Age (n=186; **Figure 7.43**), and are from pit contexts (n=261; **Figure 7.44**). A small proportion of the disarticulated material could be assigned depth, of which each segment has roughly equal numbers of occurrences, but the bottom segment occurs slightly more frequently (n=59, top n=48, middle n=54). By far the highest occurring element is the skull (n=106; **Figure 7.45**) followed by the femur (n=42). Both sides of the body are relatively evenly represented for each element but, overall, right sides predominate (n=67, left sides n=54; **Figure 7.46**).

Demographically, adult bones are the most common in the sample (n=122; **Figure 7.47**) followed by those of children (n=44). A small fraction of disarticulated bone could be sexed of which males are the most commonly represented (n=25, female n=19). Twenty-seven

occurrences have pathological indicators (three with multiple pathologies) and the most common affliction is haematological disease (**Figure 7.48**). As for trauma, 42 have traumatic indicators, four of them multiple; most frequent is animal gnawing whilst most trauma occurred post-mortem (**Figure 7.49**). One hundred and ninety-four occurrences have associated material, 127 with multiple materials. Most frequent of these is animal bone (n=102; **Figure 7.50**), of which the most commonly represented species is cow (n=38; **Figure 7.51**).

Forty-three disarticulated bone occurrences are associated with archaeological features (excluding unknown feature types), most commonly round structures (n=16; **Figure 7.52**) followed by the settlement enclosure (n=13). Disarticulated bones associated with round structures are found mostly in back halves (n=7) of the building as opposed to fronts (n=4) as well as on right sides (n=10) rather than left (n=1).

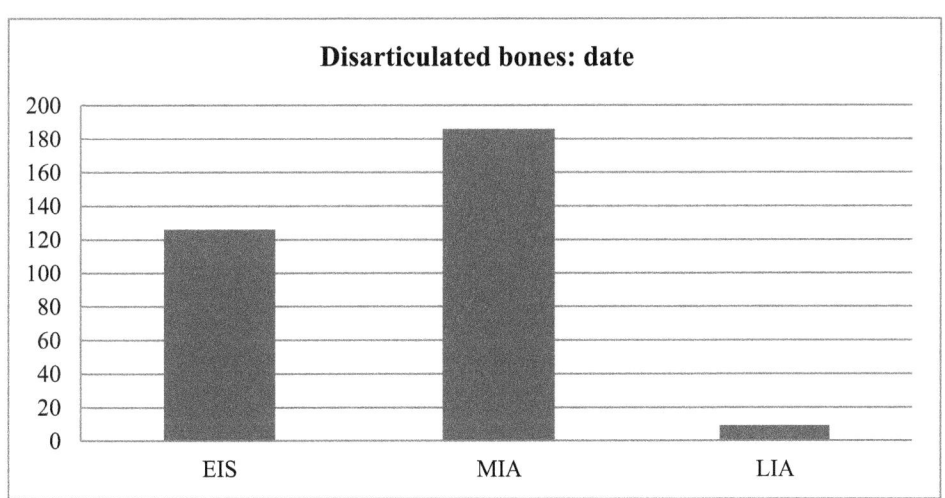

Figure 7. 43 Frequency of disarticulated bones according to date

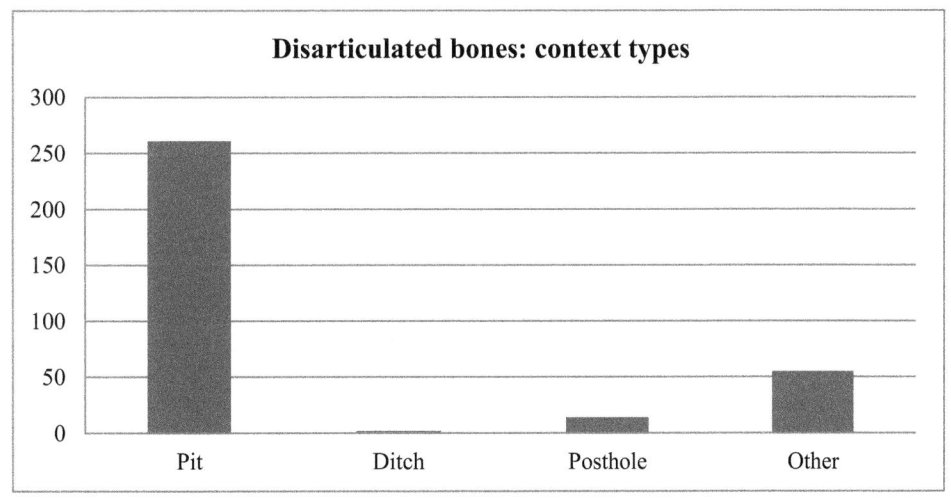

Figure 7. 44 Frequency of disarticulated bones according to context types

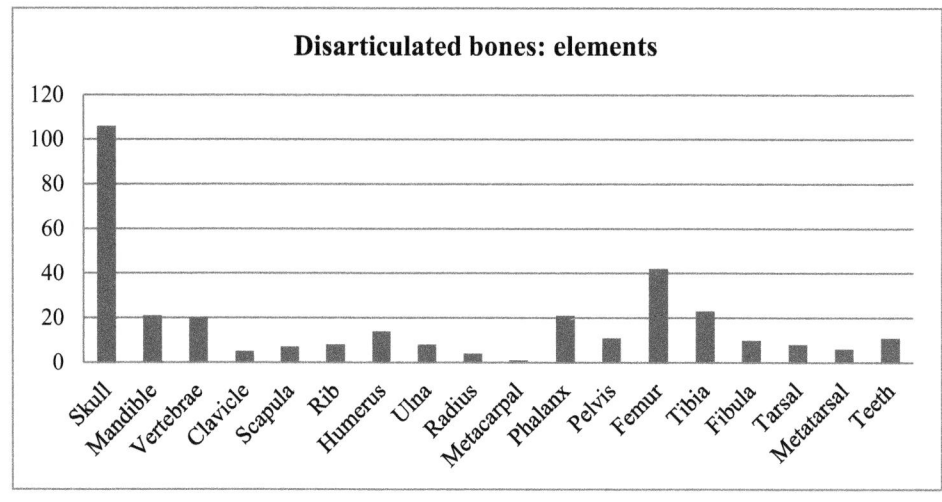

Figure 7. 45 Frequency of disarticulated bones' elements

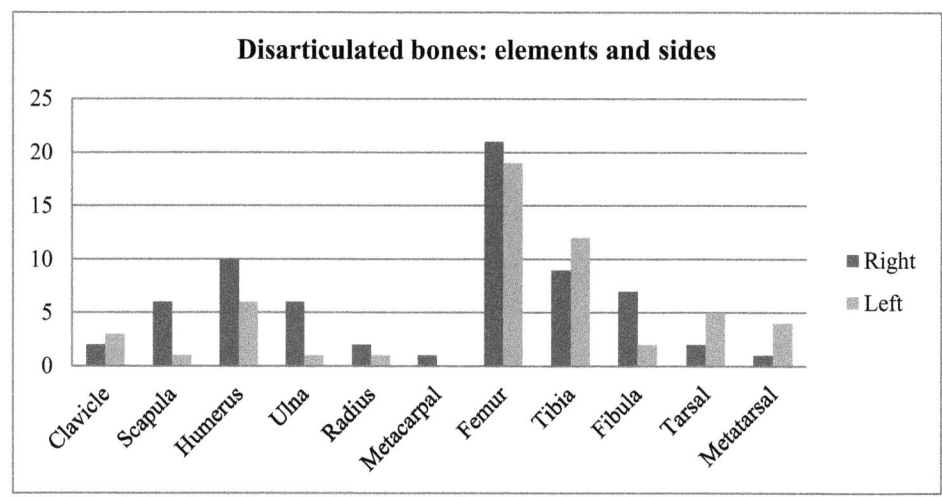

Figure 7. 46 Frequency of disarticulated bones' elements and sides

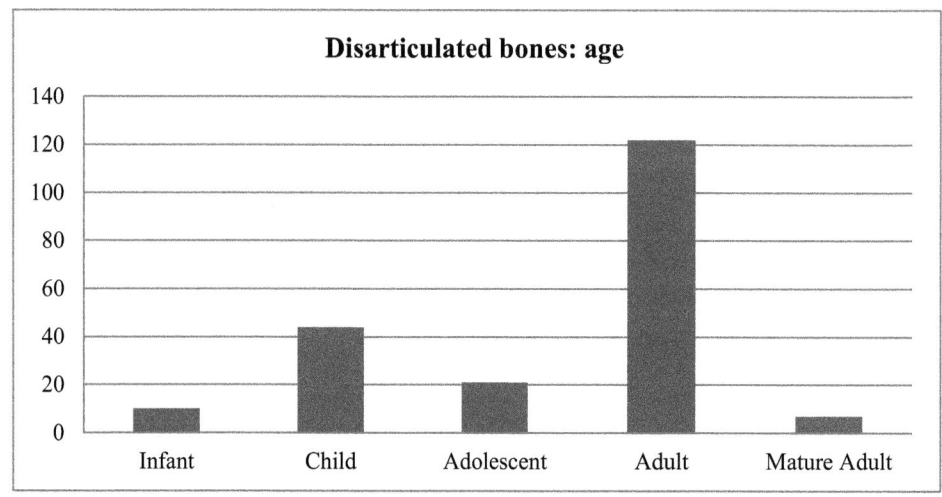

Figure 7. 47 Frequency of disarticulated bones' age

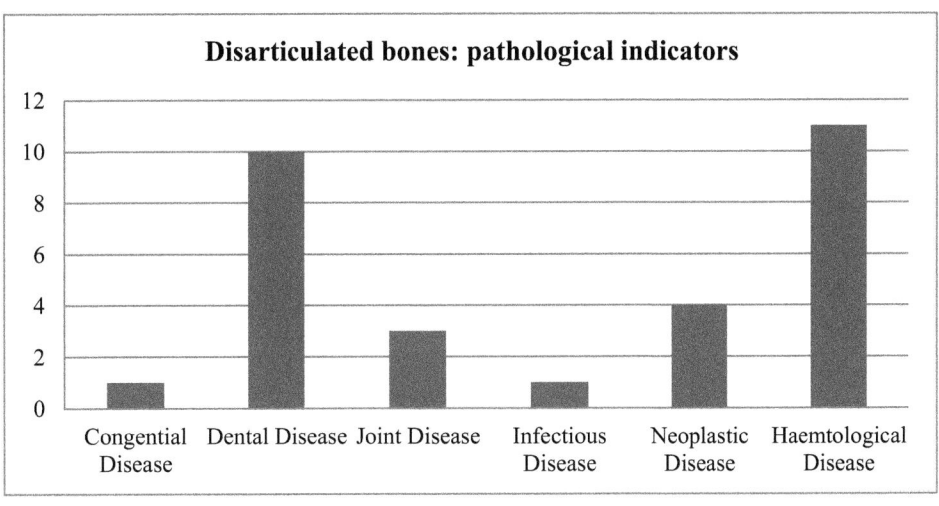

Figure 7. 48 Frequency of disarticulated bones' pathologies

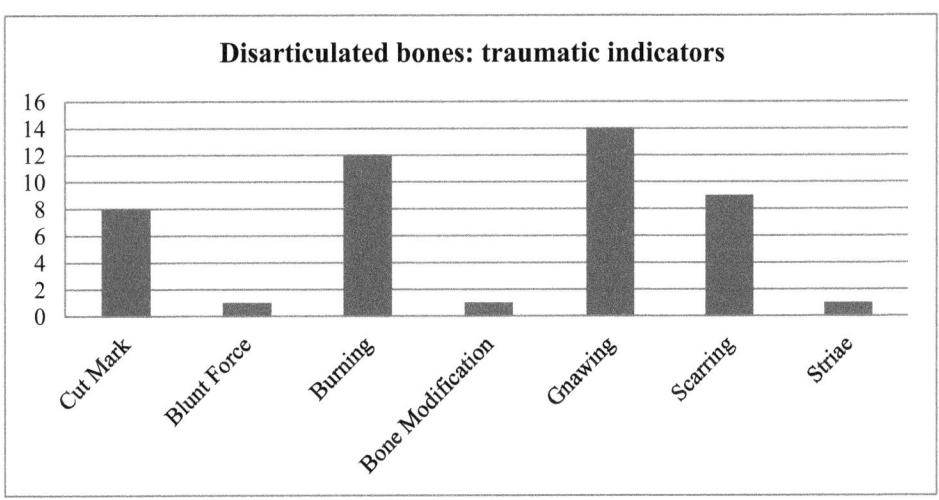

Figure 7. 49 Frequency of disarticulated bones' trauma

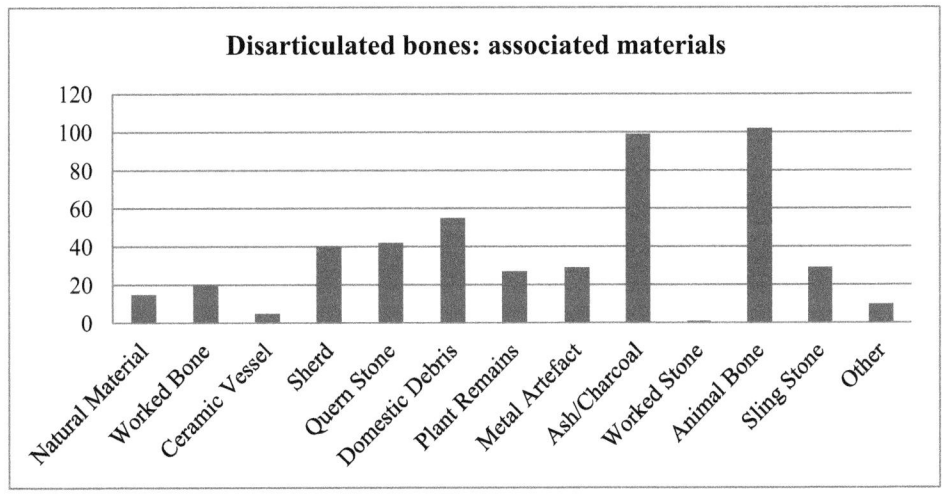

Figure 7. 50 Frequency of disarticulated bones' associated materials

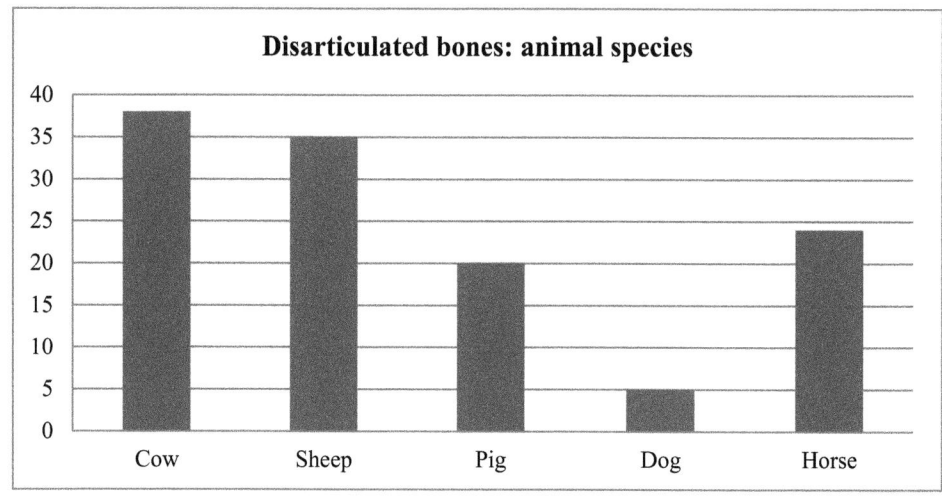

Figure 7. 51 Frequency of disarticulated bones' associated animal species

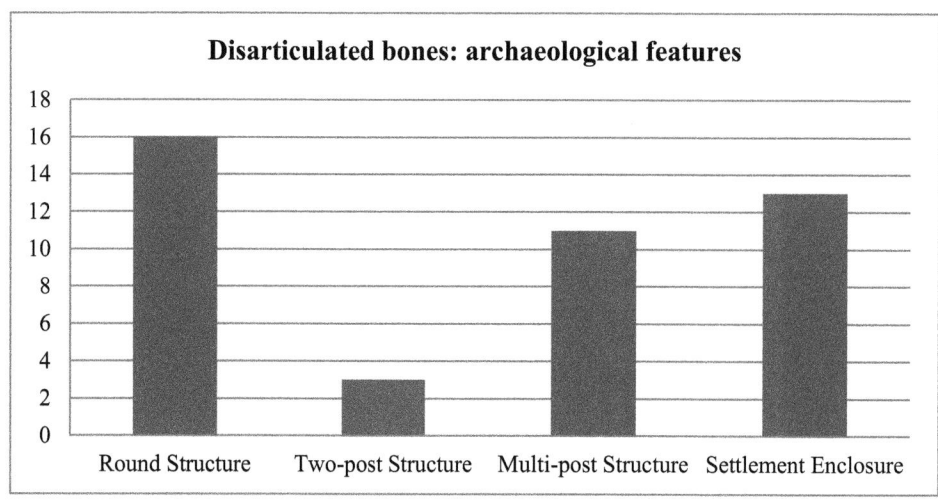

Figure 7. 52 Frequency of disarticulated bones associated with archaeological features

Many of the statistical tests returned a number of significant relationships between the disarticulated bone variables. However, the large sample size of the disarticulated bone undoubtedly affects the statistical results, and thus calls into question the relevance of this relationship. This is the case for the following results:

- context type and date (χ^2=11.916, p=0.001)
- element (2)[19] and single/multiple deposit (χ^2=9.236, p=0.026)
- element (3)[20] and single/multiple deposit (χ^2=6.965, p=0.001)

These tests' results are not insightful for Danebury's burial patterns. The quantitative analysis indicates that disarticulated bones are commonly those of adults, found in pits, and consisting of crania. Thus, the high numbers of these variables in statistical tests consistently return

significant results yet offer nothing new or insightful in terms of burial trends.

However, one significant relationship warrants further discussion. A chi-square test for independence indicates a significant relationship between element (3) and age variables (χ^2=5.759, p=0.016; **Figure 7.53**). Although the sample size probably affects the result of the statistical test, it does indicate a potential preference for the crania of adults. This point is better illustrated when looking at element (2) and age (no statistical test could be done on these two variables since it is in violation of the assumption of each cell having an expected count of five or more). **Figure 7.54** show that adult disarticulated bones have a high proportion of cranial elements, while sub-adults are relatively represented evenly in the element (2) categories. This may indicate that the community actively sought out older individuals' skulls whereas other elements and the crania of sub-adults did not receive similar attention.

---

[19] Cranium, torso, upper limb and lower limb
[20] Cranium and post-cranium

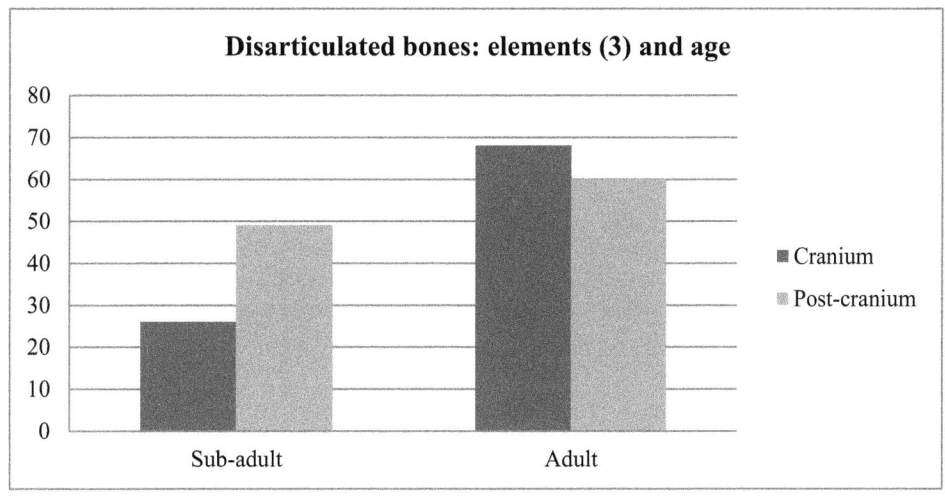

Figure 7. 53 Frequency of disarticulated bones according to age and element (cranium and post-cranium)

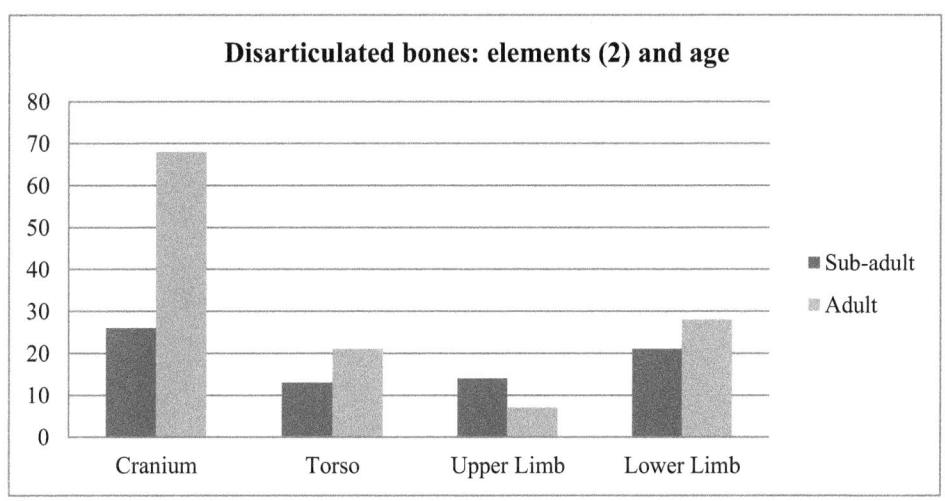

Figure 7. 54 Frequency of disarticulated bones according to age and element (2)

Summary

In sum, the quantitative and statistical analyses for Danebury did not reveal anything unknown about the site. The burial patterns correlate with the findings in chapter four. In particular, a preference for cranial elements in disarticulated bone deposits is clearly apparent at Danebury. Furthermore, most human remains were deposited in pits; their high number of is the key element for Cunliffe's interpretation that these deposits symbolise propitiatory offerings to ensure agricultural fertility (Cunliffe 1992; 1995, 78; see chapter two for details).

Gravelly Guy (SP 403 053)

Gravelly Guy lies on a marshy floodplain area near the Thames and Windrush rivers at Stanton Harcourt (Oxfordshire), and sits upon Calcareous limestone of the second terrace of the Thames Valley (Lambrick and Allen 2004, 32, **Figure 7.55**). Due to advancing gravel extraction, excavations were carried out from 1981 to 1986 under the direction of both George Lambrick and

Tim Allen (Lambrick and Allen 2004, 1). The excavations revealed a complex history of occupation and activity at the site, yielding evidence spanning from the Neolithic to Roman times. The Early and Middle Iron Age saw the construction of a complicated linear settlement on the edge of the second gravel terrace (Lambrick 2004, 103). The settlement is unenclosed, although it is evident that occupation activity was spatially confined (Lambrick 2004, 149). In addition, occupation favoured the northwestern end of the settlement during the Early Iron Age, and then the settlement focus moved to the southeastern area in the Middle Iron Age (Lambrick 2004, 153). During the Late Iron Age, occupation shifted again to the northern area of the site (Allen 2004, 161). The residents of Gravelly Guy practiced surplus producing, mixed farming regime, and horse-rearing (Lambrick 2004, 487). In addition, 107 human remains occurrences, consisting of 34 inhumations, 72 disarticulated bones, and one cremation from 78 contexts, were recovered from Gravelly Guy (Wait 2004). The skeletal assemblage represents a possible 70 individuals with roughly 25 infants (Wait 2004, 223). A number of human remains are associated with archaeological features and all the locational information relates to these structures. Mary Harman conducted the osteological analysis.

Analysis of archaeological features (n=19)

Nineteen archaeological features have associated human remains occurrences, with most features dating to the Early Iron Age (n=8) and Middle Iron Age (n=7, Late Iron Age n=2). The most common feature type is the roundhouse (n=11; **Figure 7.56**), and typically the features have a domestic function (n=10, processing n=1 and boundary marker n=1). Most features have associated pit contexts containing the human remains occurrences (n=12, ditches n=4 and multiple context types n=3), and features typically have disarticulated bones (n=8) or multiple manners of disposal (n=7) associated with them (features with only inhumations n=2). Fifteen of the

features have a known orientation, of which the most frequent opens to the east (n=6; **Figure 7.57**).

Analysis of contexts (n=77)

Most of the contexts with human remains occurrences date to the Middle Iron Age (n=40; **Figure 7.58**), and are pits (n=60, the 'other' category refers to scoops; **Figure 7.59**). Many of the contexts have only disarticulated bone (n=43, inhumations n=33, and multiple manners n=1). Many contexts contain only single deposits of human bone (n=60, multiple deposits n=15). Of the known context fills the most frequent are backfilled (n=59, silting n=2). Many of the contexts occur on the perimeter of an archaeological feature (n=18, interior n=11 and exterior n=13) and a small proportion of contexts are associated with architectural features, of which boundary areas are the most frequent (n=22, entrances n=4).

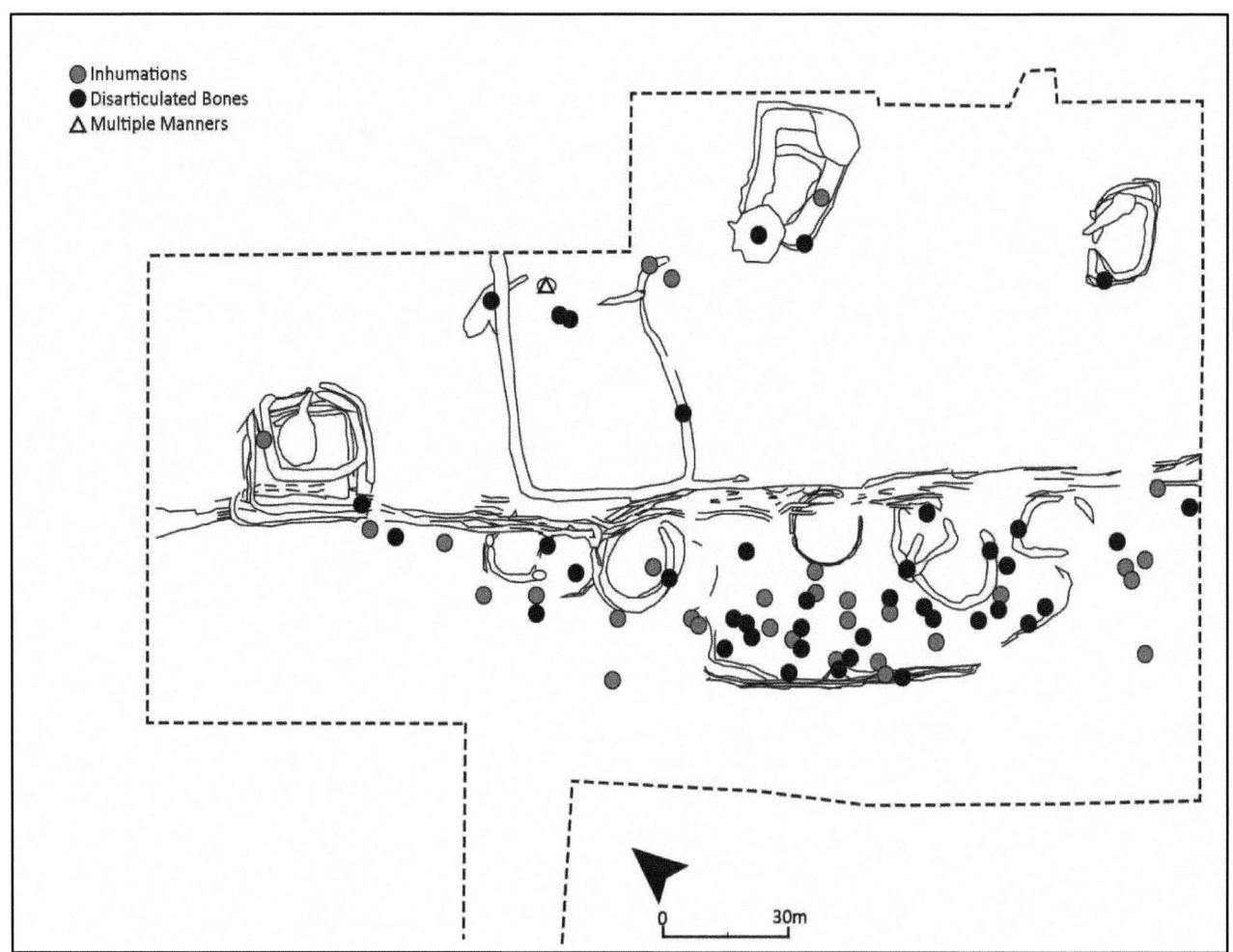

Figure 7. 55 Site plan of Gravelly Guy only depicting human remains deposits and associated features (after Lambrick and Allen 2004, fig. 1.4); ©Oxford Archaeology, with permission

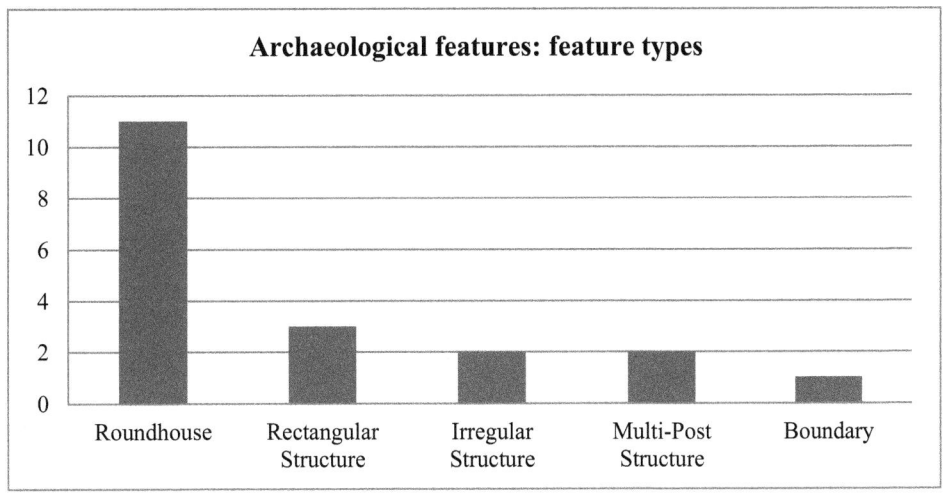

Figure 7. 56 Frequency of archaeological features with associated human remains

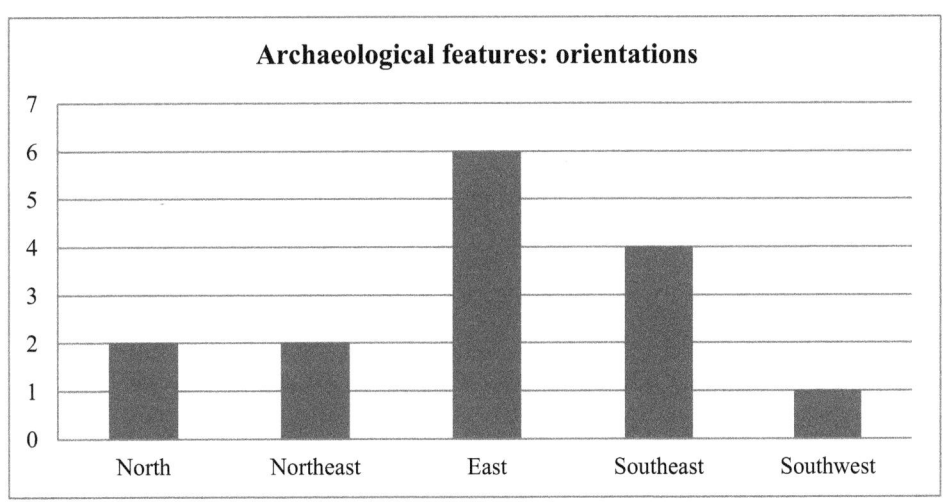

Figure 7. 57 Frequency of archaeological features' orientations

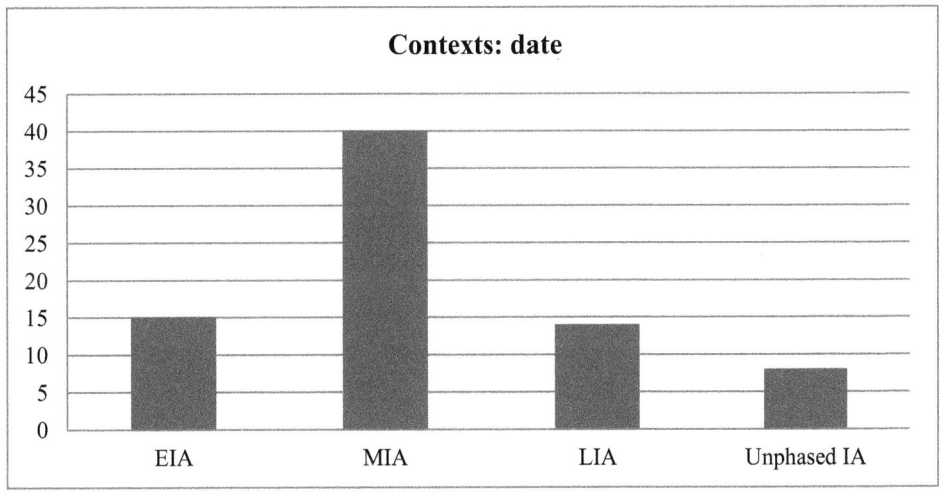

Figure 7. 58 Frequency of contexts according to date

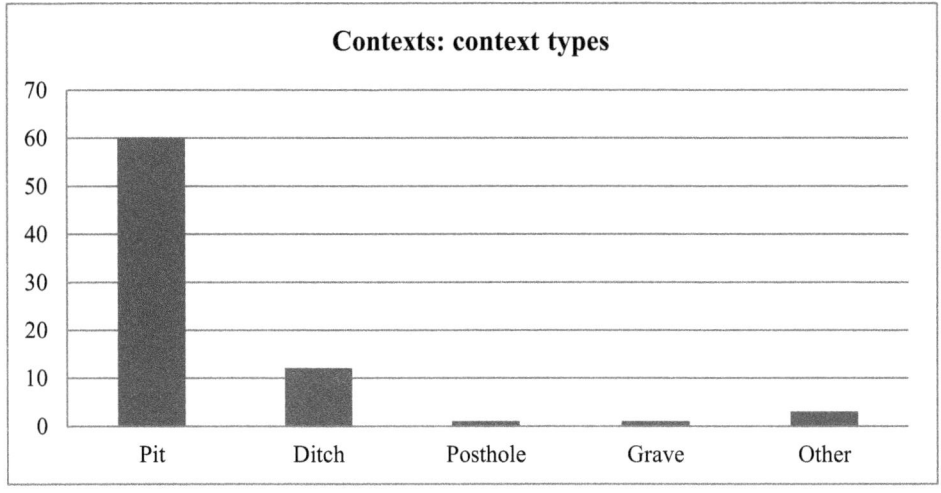

Figure 7. 59 Frequency of context types with human remains deposits

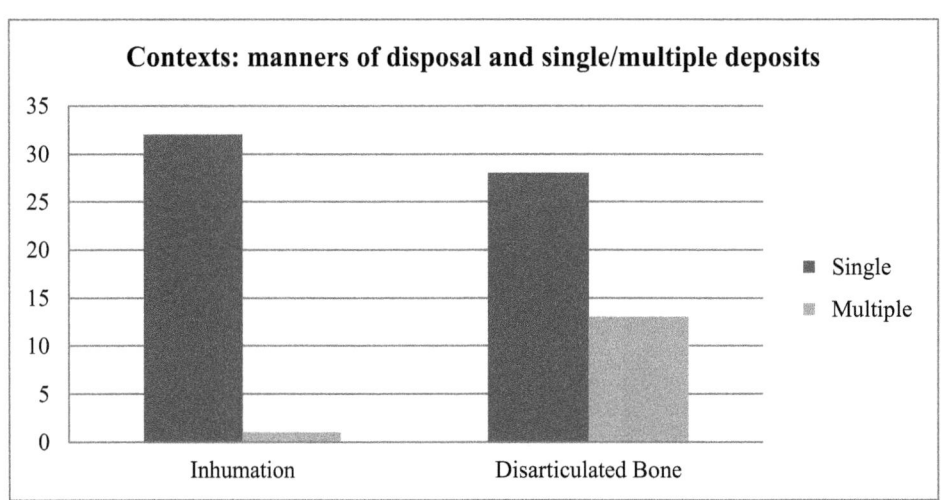

Figure 7. 60 Frequency of contexts according to manner of disposal and single/multiple deposits

Context statistical analysis

Most of the statistical tests on the context variables did not yield significant results. However, a chi-square test for independence indicates a significant relationship between the manner of disposal and single/multiple deposits (χ^2=8.002, p=0.005; **Figure 7.60**). The result may be influenced by sample size but the test indicates that contexts with inhumations rarely have other skeletal material associated with them. Disarticulated bone contexts have a number of cases with other skeletal material, although they are most frequently single deposits.

Analysis of manner of disposal (n=107)

There are 16 round, rectangular, and irregular structures that have human remains occurrences associated with

them. The buildings that have fully recordable locational information[21] have 39 associated human bone deposits. Most human remains are distributed in the left/front area of a structure (n=14); they are more frequent in left halves (n=21) than right (n=18) as well as towards the fronts (n=25) of buildings than their backs (n=14). Although the sample size was too small to return any statistical results, it is evident that the placement of human remains in and around buildings corresponds with the findings in chapter four. **Figure 7.61-3** illustrate that there is a preference for bones to be deposited in perimeters of left/front areas of buildings as well as right-sided interiors and left perimeters. The spatial organisation of human remains within buildings seen on the regional scale is also evident at Gravelly Guy.

---

[21] Buildings' orientation and occurrences' cardinal directions (see chapter three for details).

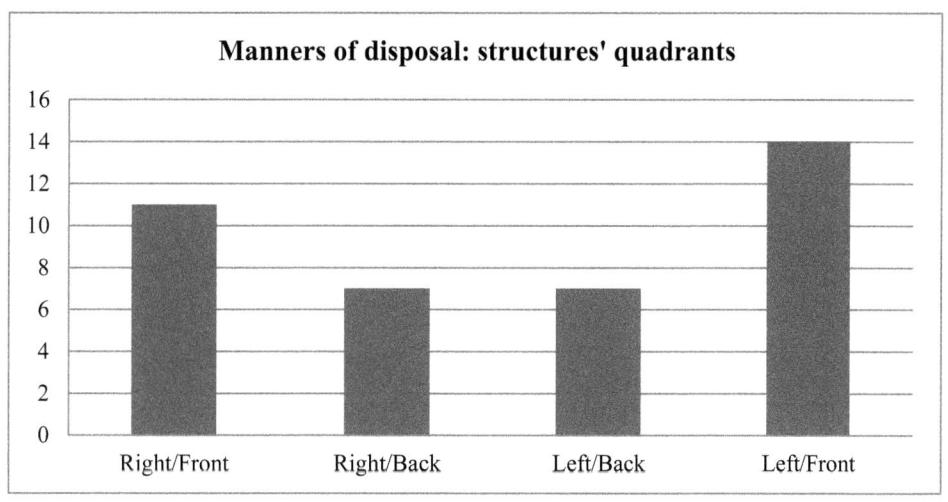

Figure 7. 61 Frequency of human remains according to structures' quadrants

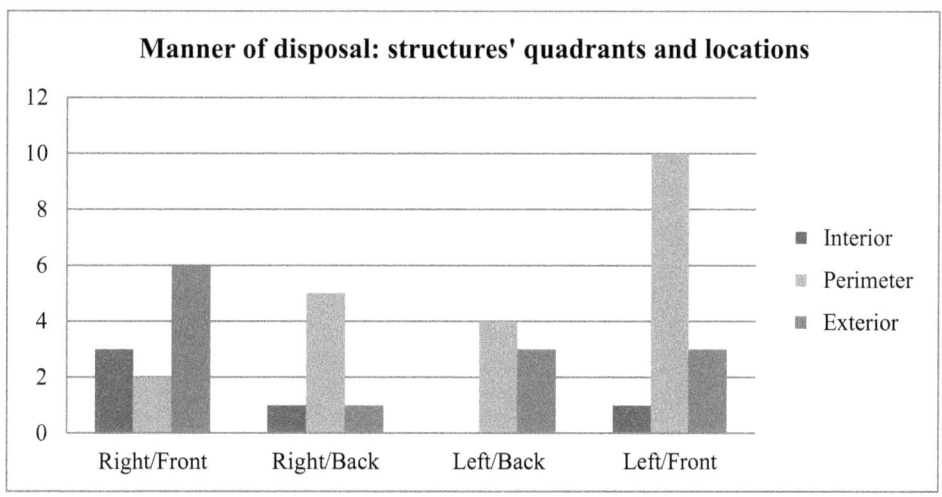

Figure 7. 62 Frequency of occurrences according to structures' quadrants and locations

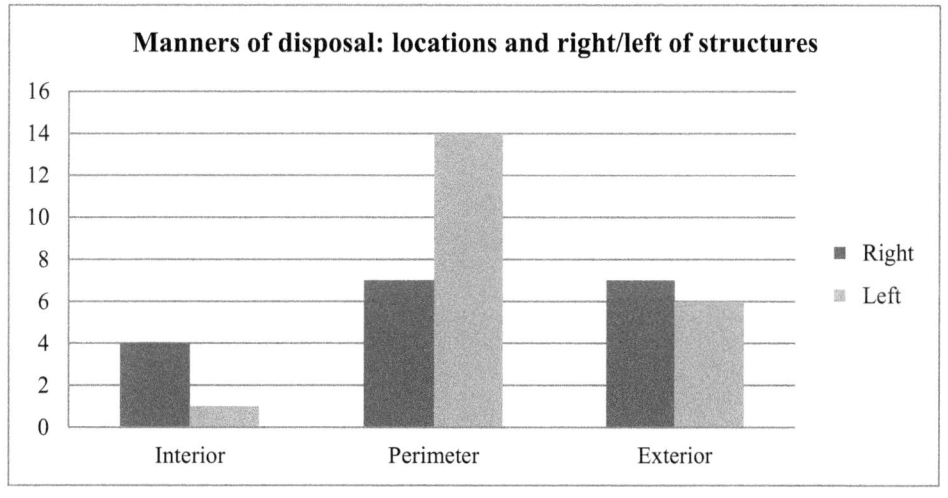

Figure 7. 63 Frequency of occurrences according to placement within and right/left of structures

Furthermore, two statistical tests returned significant results for the manner of disposal. The first is a significant relationship between the manner of disposal and depth (χ^2=14.214, p=0.000). **Figure 7.64** illustrates that inhumations are distributed almost evenly between the top, middle and bottom segments of contexts. Disarticulated bones, on the other hand, are far more frequent in the top segments of their contexts. The second statistical test revealed a significant relationship between the manner of disposal and single/multiple deposit variables (χ^2=24.689, p=0.000; **Figure 7.65**). This test correlates with the context analysis and follows the same implications discussed above.

Inhumations (n=34)

Many of the inhumations from Gravelly Guy date to the Middle Iron Age (n=20; **Figure 7.66**), and are most often in pit contexts (n=28; **Figure 7.67**). The inhumations are typically not associated with other human remains

occurrences (n= 32, multiple deposits n=2). The inhumations are mostly complete (n=23, incomplete n=11), mainly crouched (n=13; **Figure 7.68**), laid on their right sides (n=10, left side n=5 and supine n=2), and frequently oriented to the northeast (n=4; **Figure 7.69**). Demographically, sub-adults (n=29) are more frequent than adults (n=5). **Figure 7.70** illustrates inhumations' age categories and it is evident that there are considerable numbers of infants. Few inhumations could be assigned to sex but most are females (n=4, males n=1). Six inhumations have pathological indicators (five with multiple indicators) of which the most common is dental disease (n=5, joint disease n=3 and metabolic disease n=3). One individual has a traumatic indicator that is a pre-mortem fracture. Thirteen have associated materials (seven with multiple materials) of which the most frequent is animal bone (**Figure 7.71**). The statistical analysis did not yield any meaningful results for inhumations.

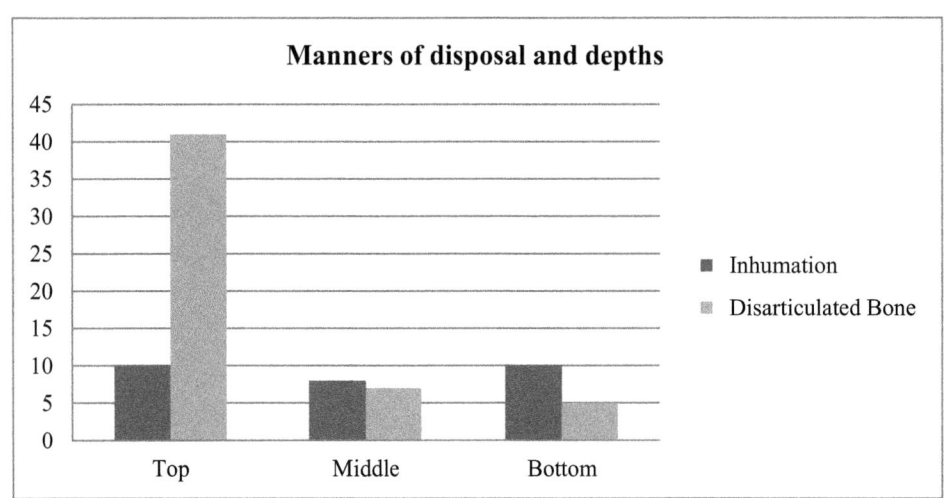

Figure 7. 64 Frequency of occurrences according to manner of disposal and depths

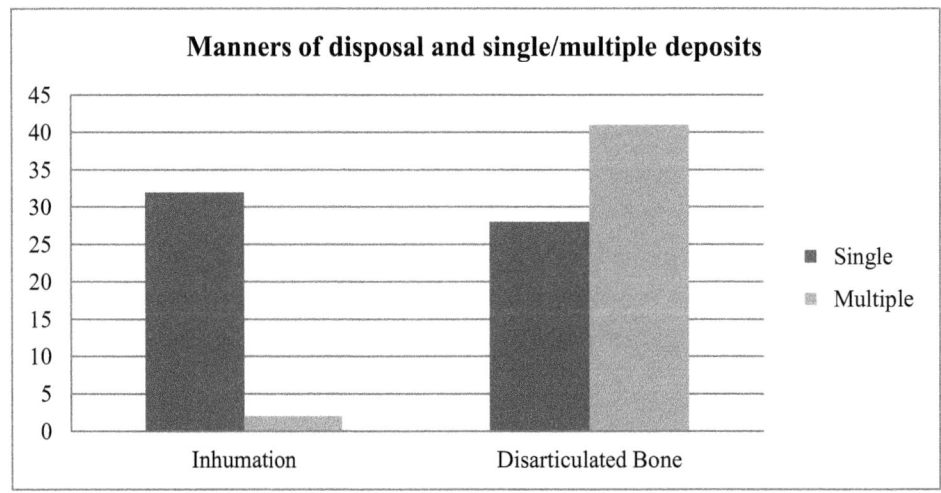

Figure 7. 65 Frequency of occurrences according to manner of disposal and single/multiple deposits

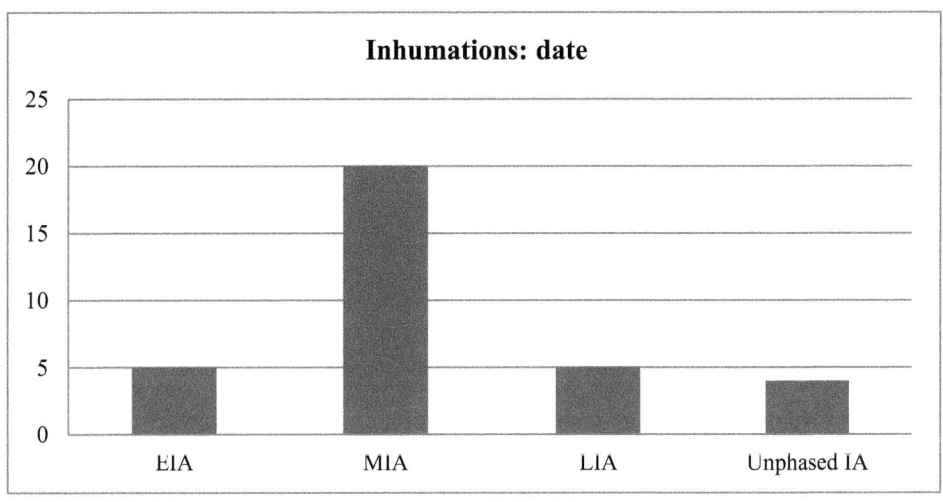

Figure 7. 66 Frequency of inhumations according to date

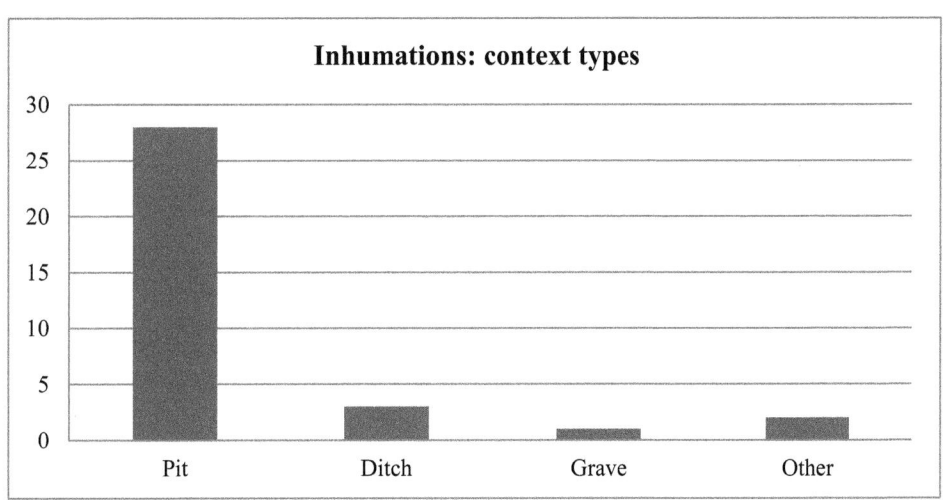

Figure 7. 67 Frequency of inhumations' context types

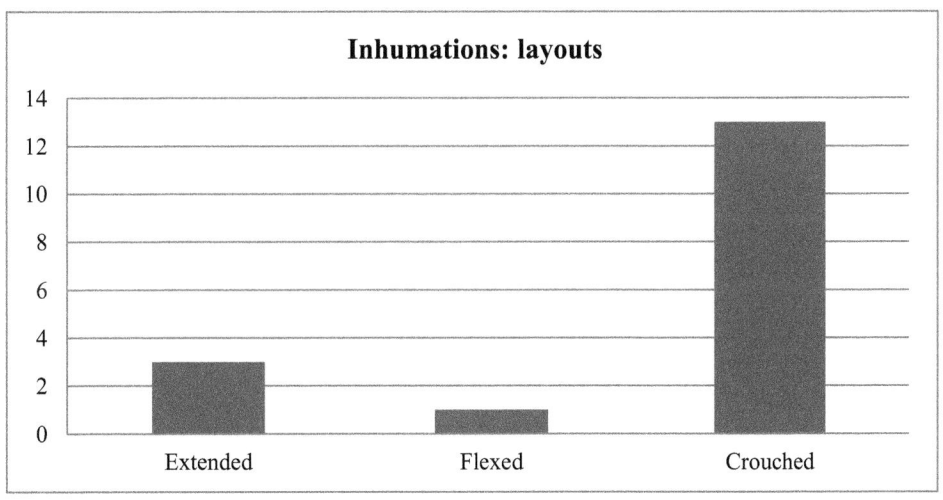

Figure 7. 68 Frequency of inhumations' layouts

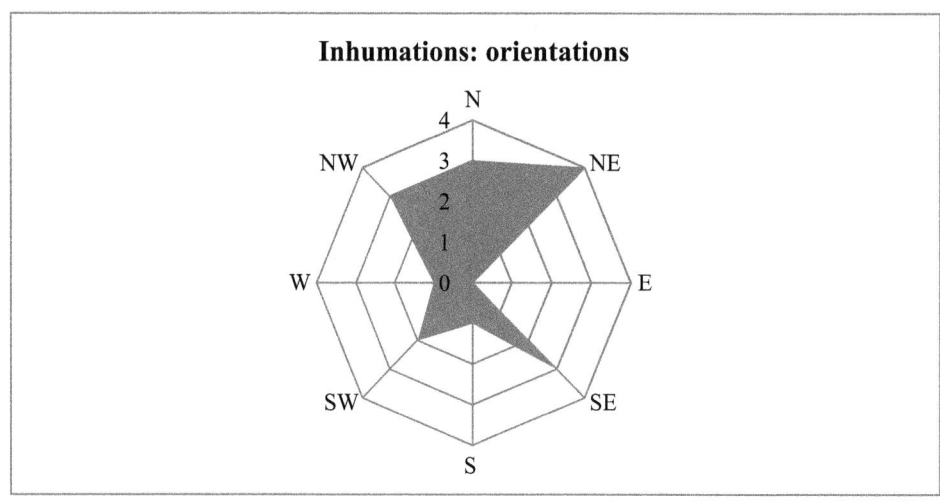

Figure 7. 69 Frequency of inhumations' orientations

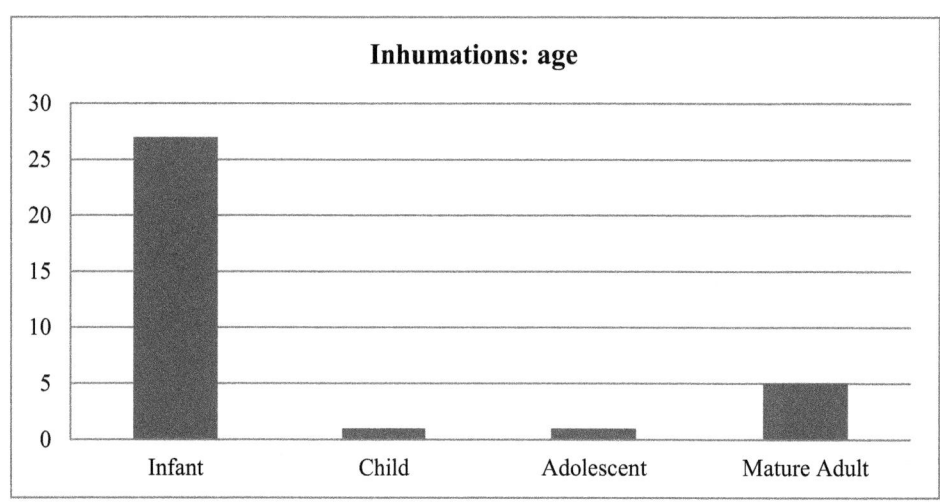

Figure 7. 70 Frequency of inhumations' age

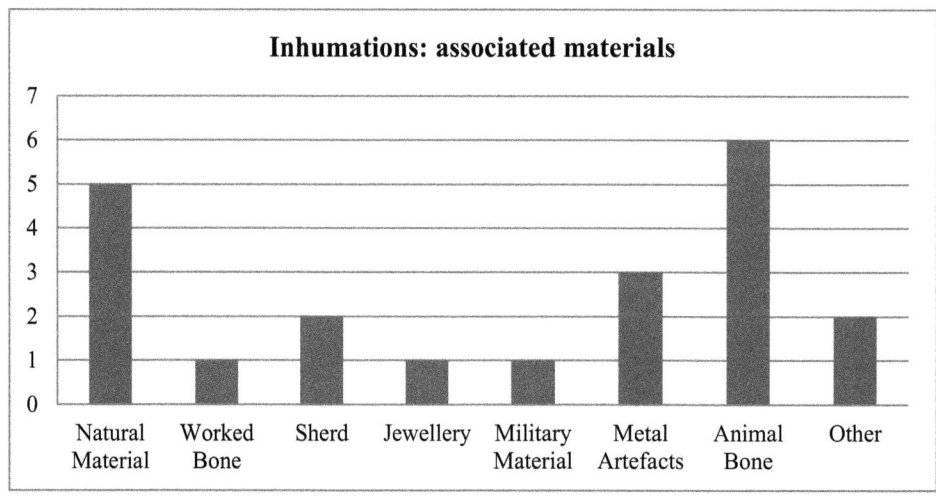

Figure 7. 71 Frequency of inhumations' associated materials

Disarticulated bones (n=71)

Most of the disarticulated bone date to the Middle Iron Age (n=30; **Figure 7.72**), with over half of the occurrences from pit contexts (n=51; **Figure 7.73**). Many were associated with other occurrences (n=41, single deposit n=28), and the most frequent element is both the femur and tibia (n=16; **Figure 7.74**). Unfortunately, anatomical sides of the elements were not given in the report. Sixty-eight disarticulated bones have an assigned age, of which 53 are of infants and the remaining are of adults (n=15). Similar to inhumations, a high proportion of the disarticulated bones are those of infants. One disarticulated bone has a pathological indicator, which is dental disease, and only one other has trauma: bone modification and weathering, both post-mortem. Nineteen disarticulated bones have associated materials, ten with multiple materials; the most common is animal bone (n=6; **Figure 5.75**).

A limited number of statistical tests returned significant results for the disarticulated bone variables. The following variables yielded significant relationships: element (3) and single/multiple deposit (χ^2=6.854, p=0.009; **Figure 7.76**), single/multiple deposit and age (χ^2=14.877, p=0.000; **Figure 7.77**) and element (3) and age (Fisher's Exact Probability Test, n=69, p=0.001; **Figure 7.78**). It is apparent that the results include the same three variables tested against each other, and these significant relationships are probably due to the sample size and the large count of post-crania and sub-adult elements (primarily infants) within deposits associated with other human remains. There is a possibility that the infant bones derive from disturbed burials. However, the extent of disturbance and its overall effect on the state of the infant remains cannot be securely determined from the contextual evidence (Harman 2004, 462).

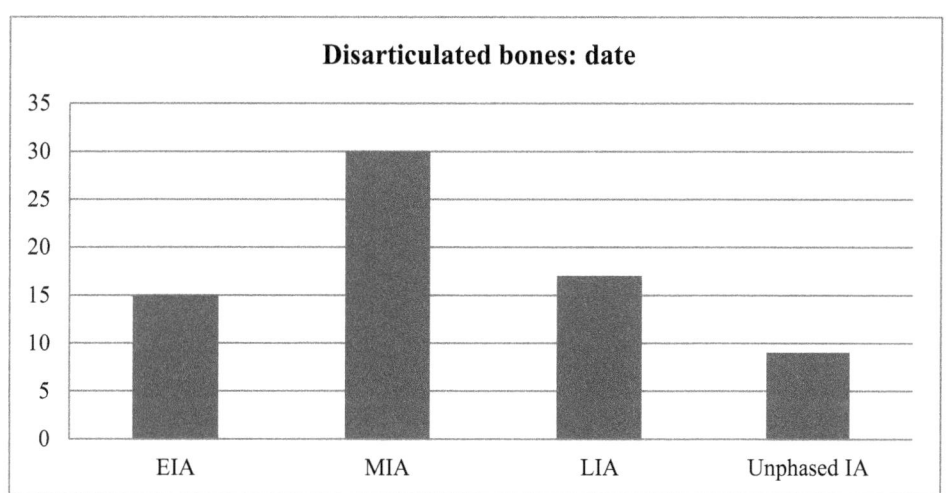

Figure 7. 72 Frequency of disarticulated bones' date

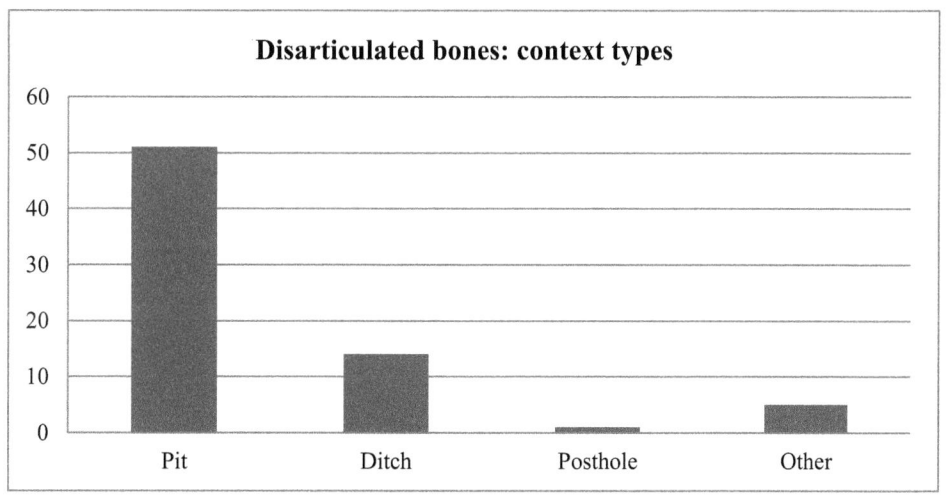

Figure 7. 73 Frequency of disarticulated bones according to context types

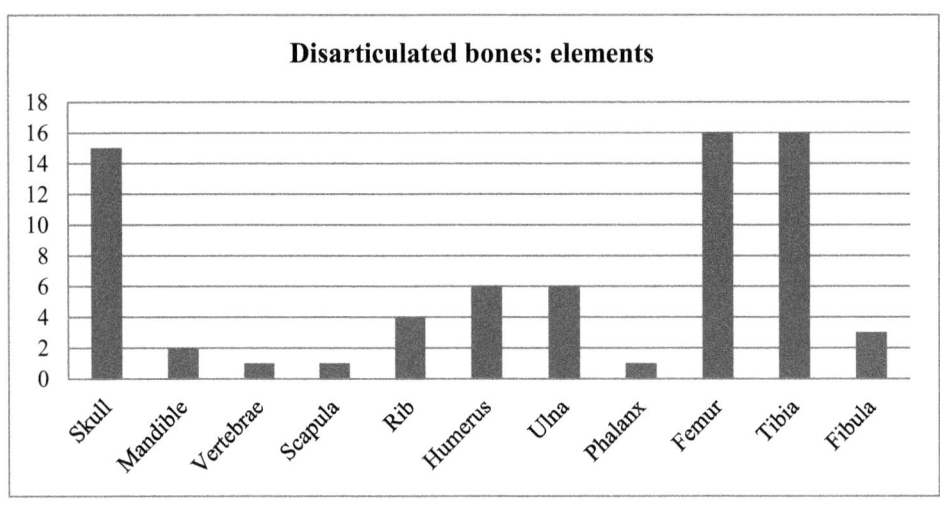

Figure 7. 74 Frequency of disarticulated bones' elements

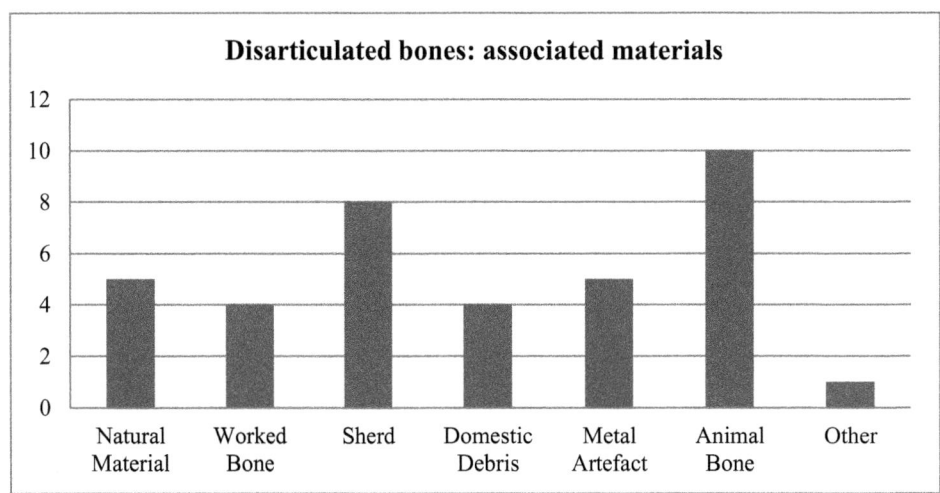

Figure 7. 75 Frequency of disarticulated bones' associated materials

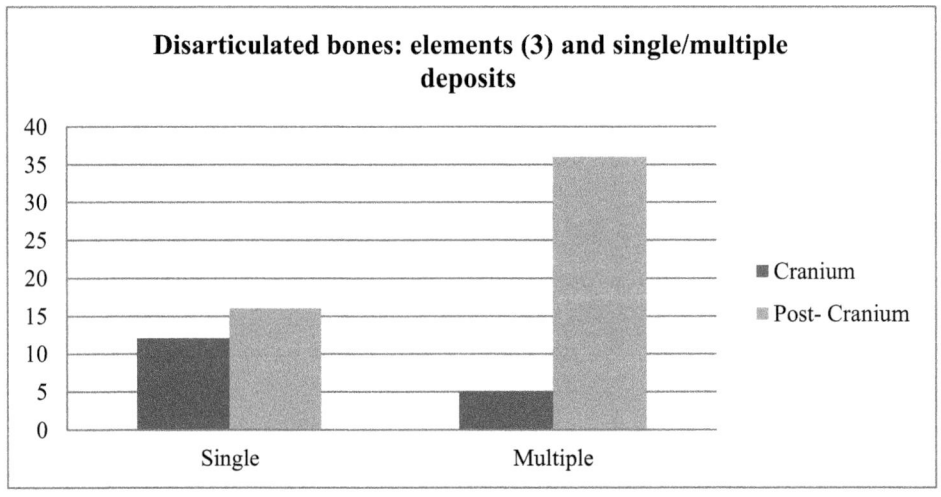

Figure 7. 76 Frequency of disarticulated bones according to single/multiple deposits and elements (3)

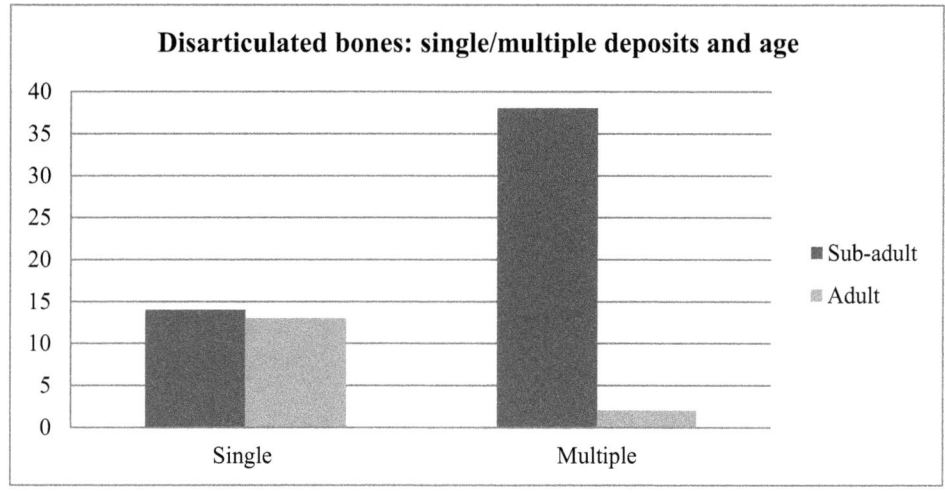

Figure 7. 77 Frequency of disarticulated bones according to age and single/multiple deposits

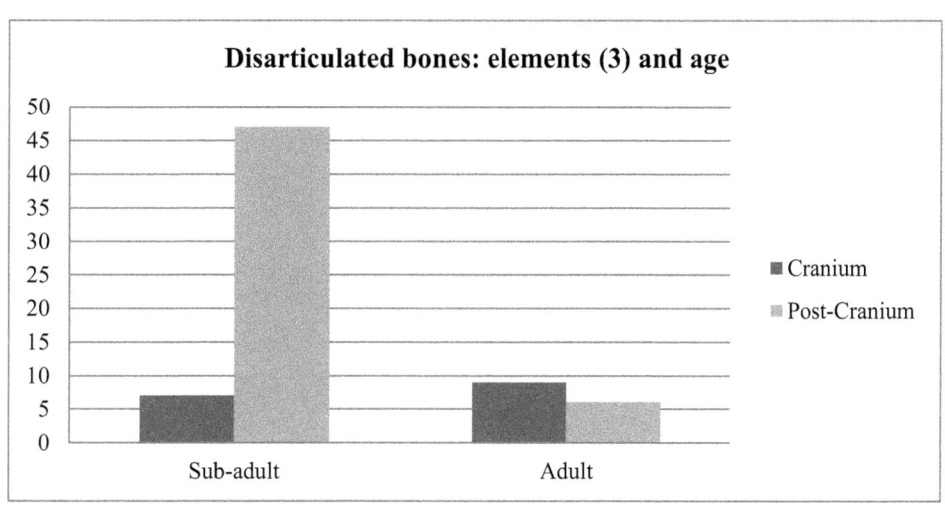

Figure 7. 78 Frequency of disarticulated bones according age and elements (3)

Cremation (n=1)

Gravelly Guy contains a single cremation of Late Iron Age date, found within the top segment of a pit. The cremation, weighing 810g, is a primary deposit associated with two other disarticulated bone occurrences. It is not within an urn and is an adult of unknown sex. The cremation is associated with animal bone, a pottery sherd, a metal artefact and ash/charcoal.

Summary

The burial evidence from Gravely Guy has some interesting aspects that correlate with the overall findings for Iron Age burial practices. It is one of the few sites with a long burial history and loosely reflects the changes in manner of disposal. For example, the Early/Middle Iron Age burial evidence from Gravelly Guy consists of inhumations and disarticulated bones and then a cremation in the Late Iron Age. This corresponds to the overall change in Iron Age burial practices, with disarticulated bones and inhumations favoured in the Early and Middle Iron Age and then cremations in the Late Iron Age. Additionally, human remains associated with structures (round, rectangular, and irregular) at Gravelly Guy follow similar spatial patterning seen elsewhere in southern Britain during the Iron Age. The spatial patterning relates to the right/left divide within a building, and human remains are particularly common in the left/front of a structure. Lastly, Gravelly Guy has an unusual high proportion of infant remains among both inhumations and disarticulated bones; this is not characteristic of most Iron Age settlement sites where typically skeletal material is from adults.

Gussage All Saints (ST 998 101)

Gussage All Saints is an Iron Age enclosure on Dorset chalklands (Wainwright 1979, viii, **Figure 7. 79 -82**). The single enclosed settlement encircles three acres in area and was excavated in its entirety in 1972 (Wainwright 1979, viii). The enclosure opens towards the southeast with two antennae ditches stemming from the entrance (Wainwright 1979, 3). Gussage All Saints has two major phases of activity in the Iron Age: the first in the Early Iron Age and the second in the Middle Iron Age, with

limited activity in the later part of the Iron Age (Wainwright 1979, 3). Settlement activity continued between the two major phases. The site's inhabitants practiced a mixed arable economy with metalworking and trade activity (Wainwright 1979, 187-190). Human remains derived from 44 contexts that yielded 67 occurrences, consisting of 48 inhumations and 19 disarticulated bones. Carol A. Keepax (1979) conducted the initial osteological analysis, and Rebecca Redfern (2008a; 2008b; 2009) reassessed of the skeletal material more recently.

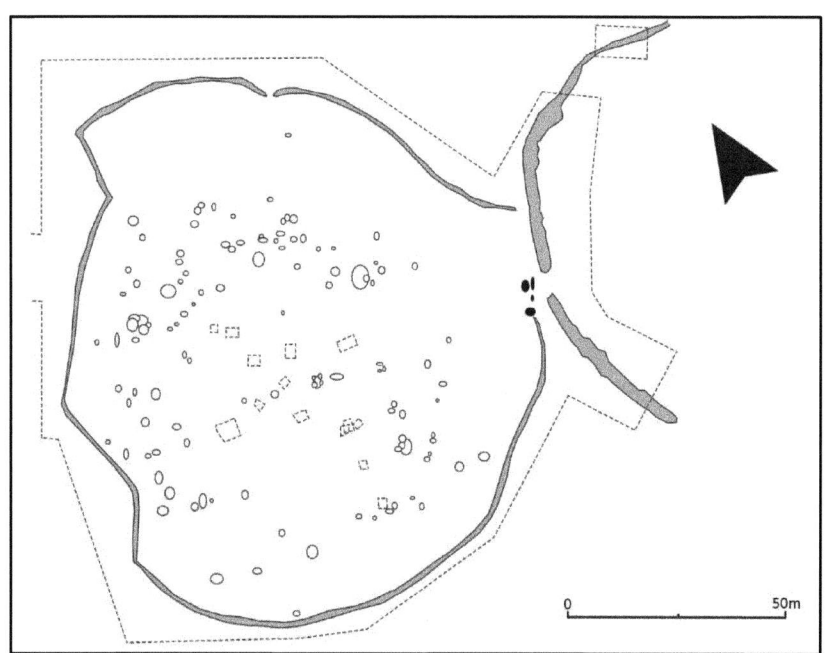

Figure 7. 79 Site plan of Gussage All Saints in the Early Iron Age (locations of human remains are unknown in this phase) (after Wainwright 1979, 17); with permission by the National Archive Image Library

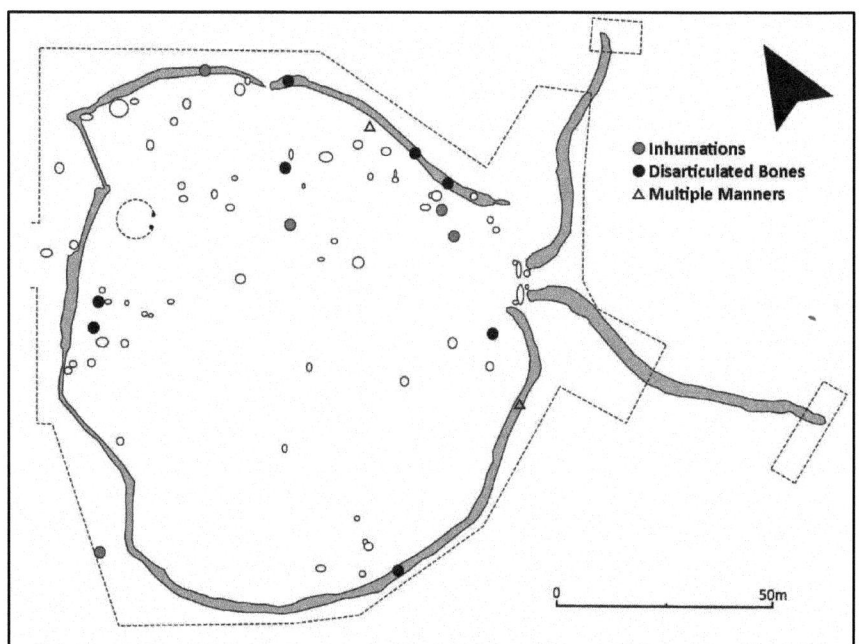

Figure 7. 80 Site plan of Gussage All Saints in the Middle Iron Age indicating human remains deposits (after Wainwright 1979, 22); with permission by the National Archive Image Library

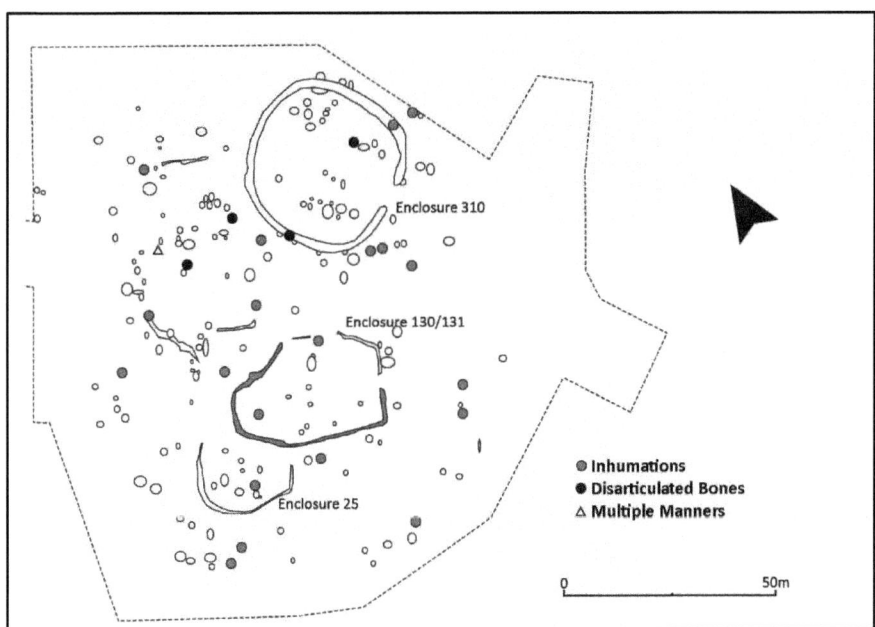

Figure 7.81 Site plan of Gussage All Saints in the Late Iron Age indicating human remains deposits (after Wainwright 1979, 6-7); with permission by the National Archive Image Library

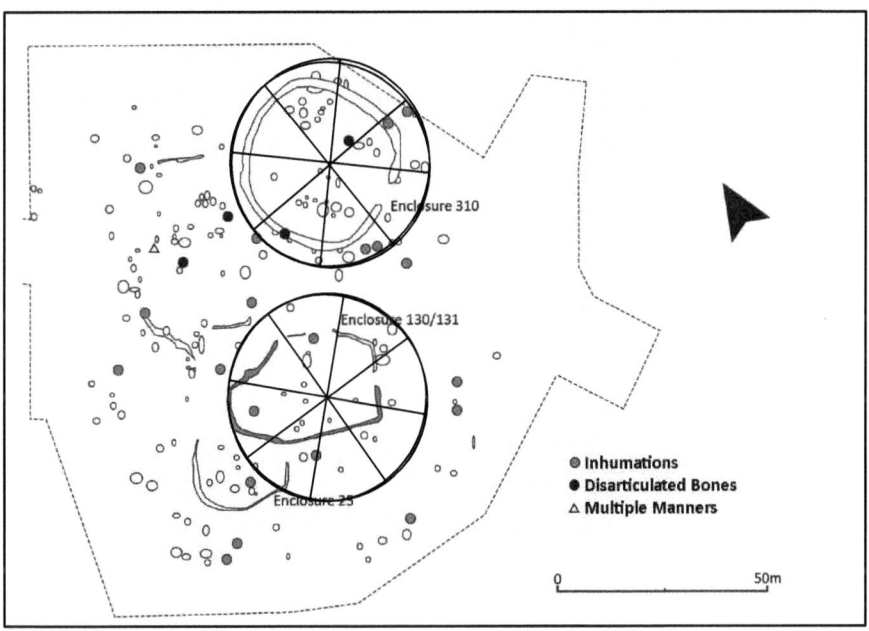

Figure 7. 82 Site plan of Gussage All Saints in the Late Iron Age showing the cardinal areas for the archaeological features (after Wainwright 1979, 6-7); with permission by the National Archive Image Library

Analysis of archaeological features (n=3)

Three archaeological features from Gussage All Saints have 21 associated human remains. All three of the structures date to the Late Iron Age and consist of two irregular and one round structure (**Figure 7.81-82**)[22]. The first irregular structure (Enclosure 25) is crescent moon-shaped; it may have been a boundary feature but the

limited evidence makes this unknown (Wainwright 1969, 29-30). Inside Enclosure 25 is a pit containing a single infant inhumation. The other irregular structure (Enclosure 130/131) is roughly trapezoidal and has 11 associated inhumations within its ditches and few pits (Wainwright 1969, 29). The third archaeological feature is a roundhouse (Enclosure 310, round structure with a domestic function) whose entrance opens to the southeast (Wainwright 1969, 27-29). Enclosure 310 has eight associated human remains (seven inhumations and one disarticulated bone) placed throughout the structure within its pits and enclosing ditches.

---

[22] Ditches 130 and 131 (part of Enclosure 130/131 highlighted in grey) contained two inhumations but their exact placement cannot be determined.

Analysis of contexts (n=44)

Forty-four contexts have human remains, 30 of them single and 14 multiple deposits. Most date to the Late Iron Age (n=28, Middle Iron Age n=15 and Early Iron Age n=1) and are pits (n=33; **Figure 7.83**); most contain only inhumations (**Figure 7.84**). Many contexts lie within the interior of the site (n=24) followed by the perimeter (n=6), with two outside. The statistical analysis of the context data returned limited results. A Fisher's Exact Probability Test established a significant relationship between the manner of disposal and date (n=40, p=0.002). This increase in inhumations during the Late Iron Age may have influenced the significance test, although visually there was a clear change in preference for the manner of disposal between the two periods (see **Figure 7.85**).

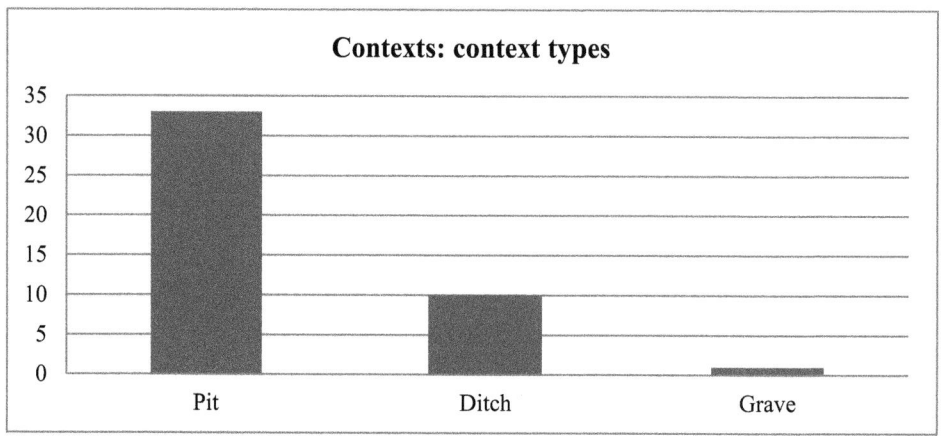

Figure 7. 83 Frequency of context types with human remains

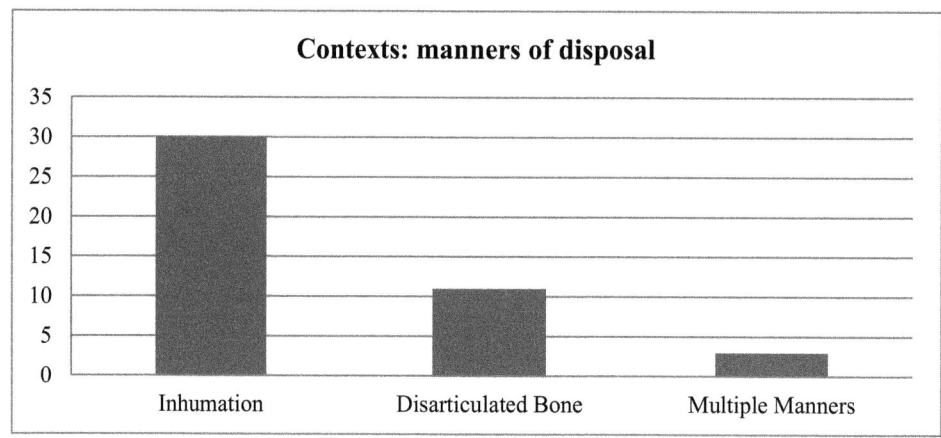

Figure 7. 84 Frequency of contexts according to manner of disposal

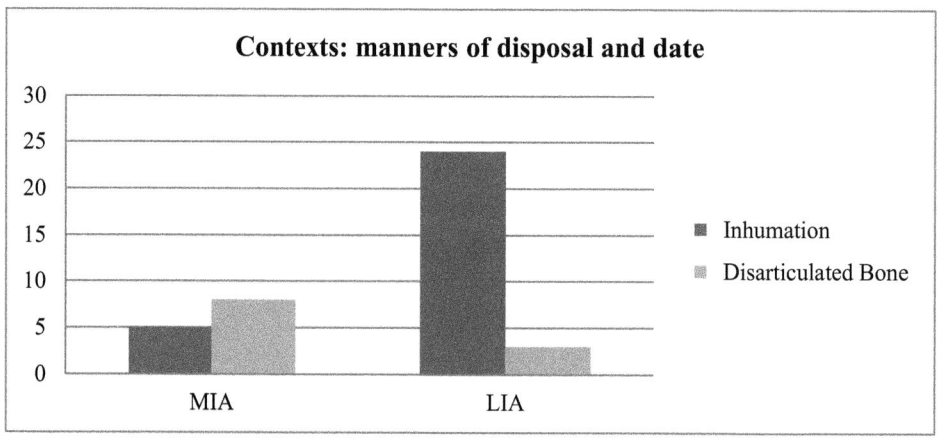

Figure 7. 85 Frequency of contexts according to date and manner of disposal

Analysis of manner of disposal (n=67)

The statistical analysis for the manner of disposal yielded a similar result to the context analysis. A chi-square test for independence indicated a significant relationship between the manner of disposal and date[23] (χ^2=19.433, p=0.000; **Figure 7.86**). This further shows a change in the manner of disposal between the Middle and Late Iron Age. Furthermore, it correlates with the burial trends outlined in chapter four, illustrating a change in processing between the Middle and Late Iron Age with corpses typically staying more complete.

Inhumations (n=48)

Most inhumations date to the Late Iron Age (n=40, Middle Iron Age n=7 and Early Iron Age n=1), are in pits (n=40; **Figure 7.87**) as single interments (n=29, multiple deposits n=17). Most of the inhumations are incomplete (n=32, complete n=10), typically crouched (n=15; **Figure 7.88**) lying on their right sides (n=9; **Figure 7.89**) and oriented to the north (n=9; **Figure 7.90**). Demographically, there is an unusually high numbers of infants (n=38; **Figure 7.91**) in comparison to adults (n=8 includes adults and mature adults). Only ten inhumations have a known sex, of which many are females (n=7, male n=3). Eleven inhumations have pathological indicators (nine with multiple) and the most common being dental disease (n=8; **Figure 7.92**). Five inhumations have traumatic indicators; two individuals exhibit damage to their elbows (from an unknown cause) and another two have ante-mortem fractures. The fifth inhumation has an ante-mortem fracture and a peri-mortem cut-mark.

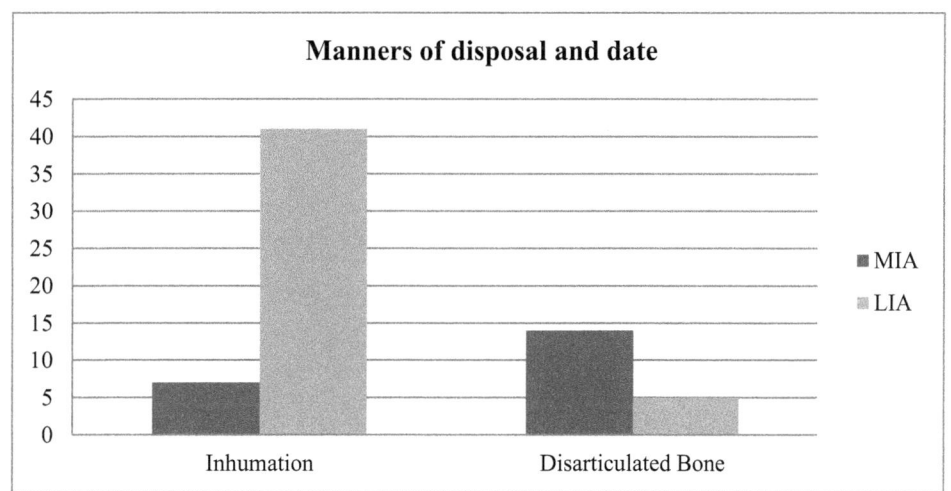

Figure 7. 86 Frequency of occurrences according to manner of disposal and date

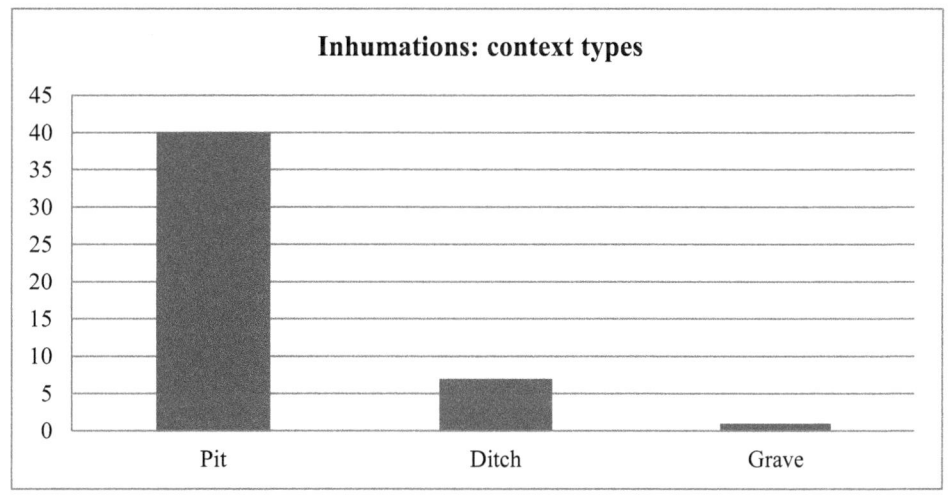

Figure 7. 87 Frequency of inhumations' date

---

[23] For statistical purposes, the test excluded the single, Early Iron Age inhumation.

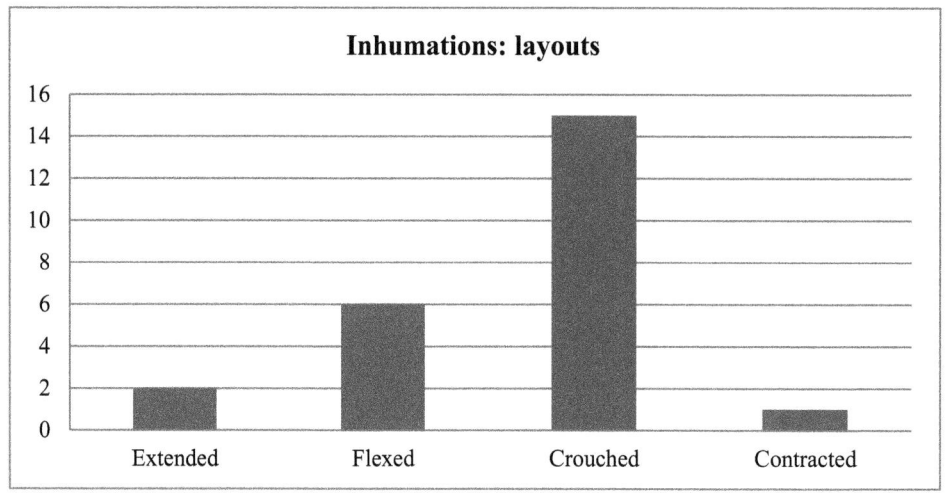

Figure 7. 88 Frequency of inhumations' layouts

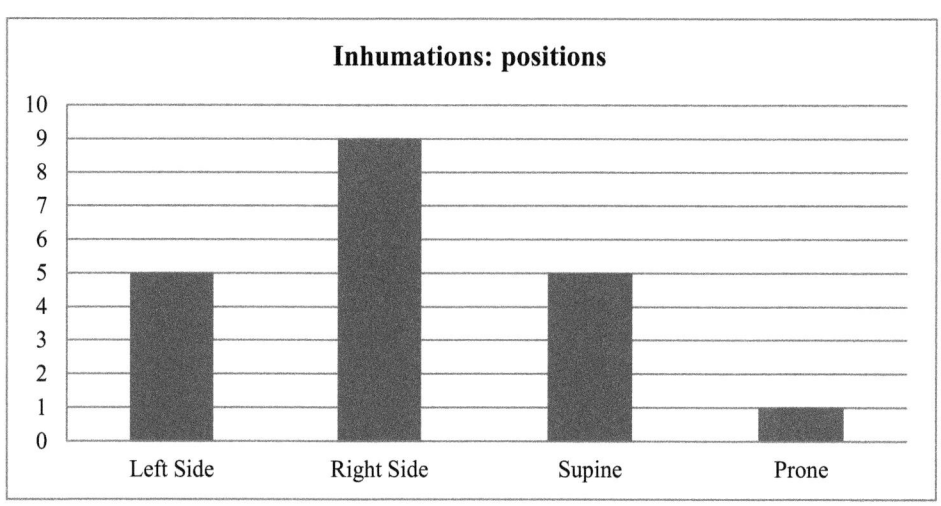

Figure 7. 89 Frequency of inhumations' positions

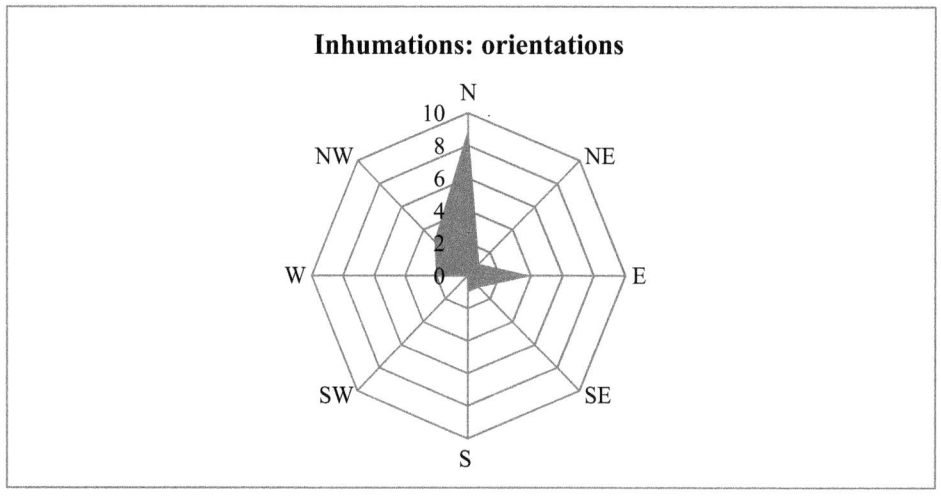

Figure 7. 90 Frequency of inhumations' orientations

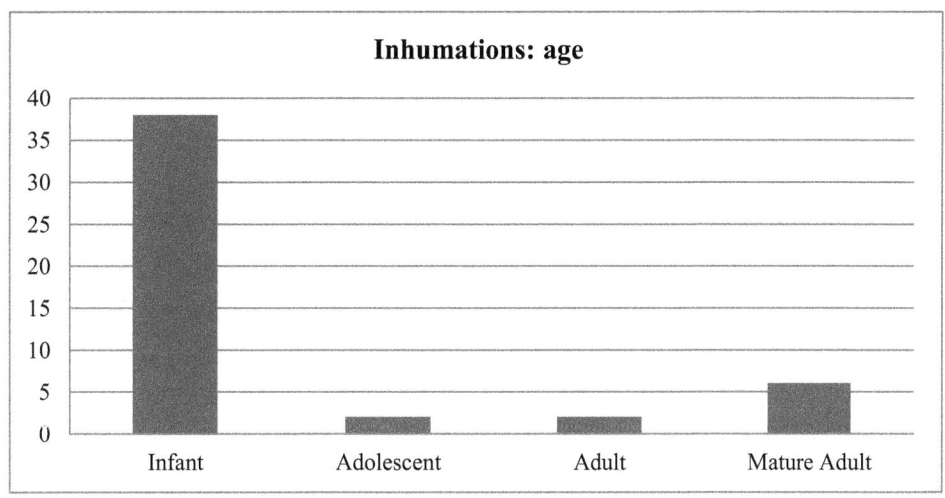

Figure 7. 91 Frequency of inhumations' age

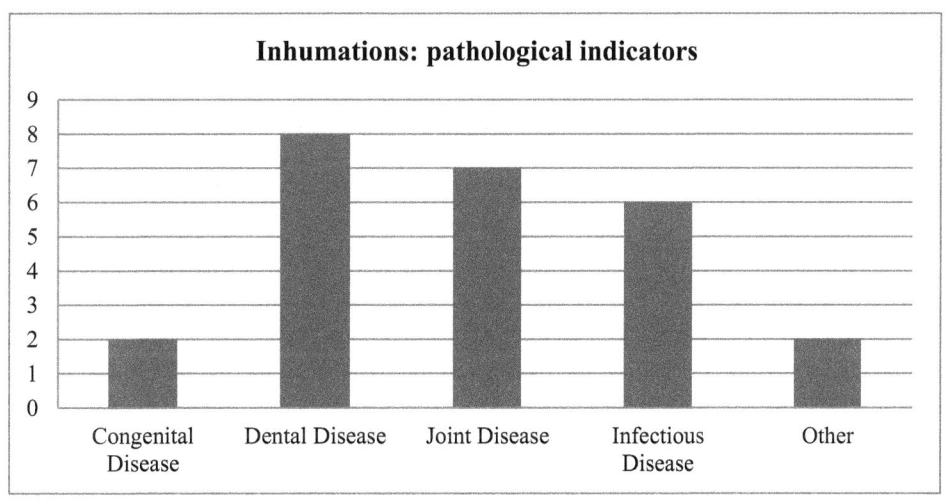

Figure 7. 92 Frequency inhumations' pathologies

Disarticulated bones (n=19)

Over half of the disarticulated bones date to the Middle Iron Age (n=14, Late Iron Age n=5), and are most often in ditches (n=10, pits n=9). The disarticulated bones are evenly spread between the middle and bottom segments of contexts (both n=3, 13 unknown depths), and are typically single deposits (n=7, multiple n=3). The most common element found is the skull (n=10; **Figure 7.93**). Six elements are sided and both the left and right are equally represented (both n=3; **Figure 7.94**). Two disarticulated bones are aged, with one from an adolescent and the other from an older adult, but none of the elements is sexed. Only one disarticulated bone has associated material, which is a pottery sherd. Another disarticulated bone has signs of osteoporosis. The original osteological report did not report any traumatic indicators among the disarticulated material. However, a reassessment of the

skeletal material identified '... evidence for soft-tissue removal, peri-mortem and dry fractures' on long bones and cranial fragments' (Redfern 2008a, 291), which could correlate with secondary burial practices.

Summary

An interesting characteristic of the human remains at Gussage All Saints is the remarkably high proportion of infant inhumations in the burial record. A similar pattern is also seen at Gravelly Guy yet this is an uncommon feature of Iron Age burial practices. Furthermore, Redfern's (2008a) reassessment strongly suggests that many of the bones underwent a series of secondary burial rites and a degree of post-mortem handling, which is similar to the evidence from Battlesbury Bowl. Gussage All Saints' skeletal evidence shows a switch in the burial rite between the Middle and Late Iron Age, with inhumations becoming more frequent (especially infants). This result correlates with the findings from all the other studied sites, that there was a significant decrease in disarticulated bones in the Late Iron Age and a corresponding increase in inhumations.

Winnall Down (SU 498 303)

From 1976 to 1977, the M3 Archaeological Rescue Committee carried out excavations at Winnall Down in advance of the M3's construction (Fasham 1985, 1). Winnall Down lies on the Upper Chalk at the boundary of Winchester and Chilcomb in Hampshire (Fasham 1985, 3). A total of 1.26 ha was examined, revealing an Iron Age domestic site (Fasham 1985, 7). The excavations show

that occupation began in the Late Bronze Age and lasted into the Roman period (Fasham 1985, 7). In the Early Iron Age, Winnall Down was an enclosed settlement that, in the Middle Iron Age, became an open settlement, after the enclosure ditch had been allowed to silt up naturally (Fasham 1985, 127). Although the Early Iron Age ditch had silted over by the Middle Iron Age, it was still visible during this period (Fasham 1985, 130). From Winnall Down, 121 Early and Middle Iron Age human remains occurrences were noted, consisting of 25 inhumations and 96 disarticulated bones, within 43 contexts (Bayley *et al.* 1985; Archives). Justine Bayley (1985) performed the osteological analysis of the skeletal material from Winnall Down.

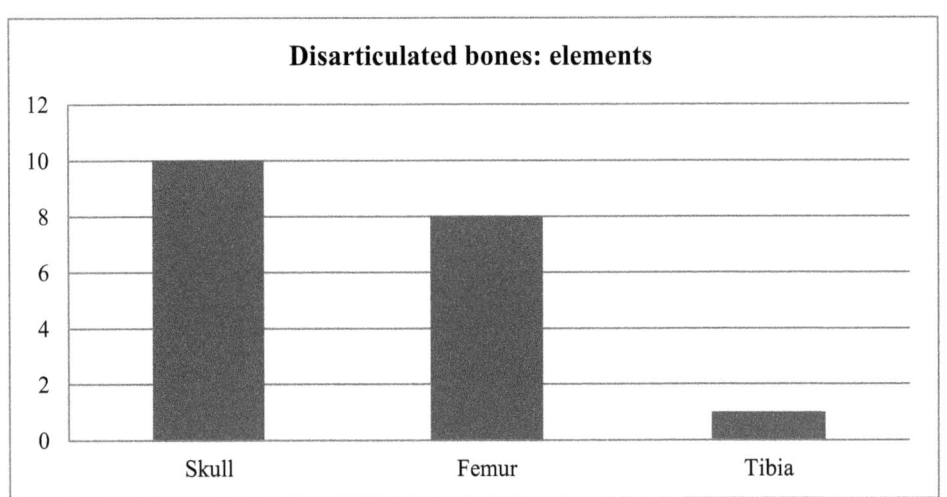

Figure 7. 93 Frequency of disarticulated bones' elements

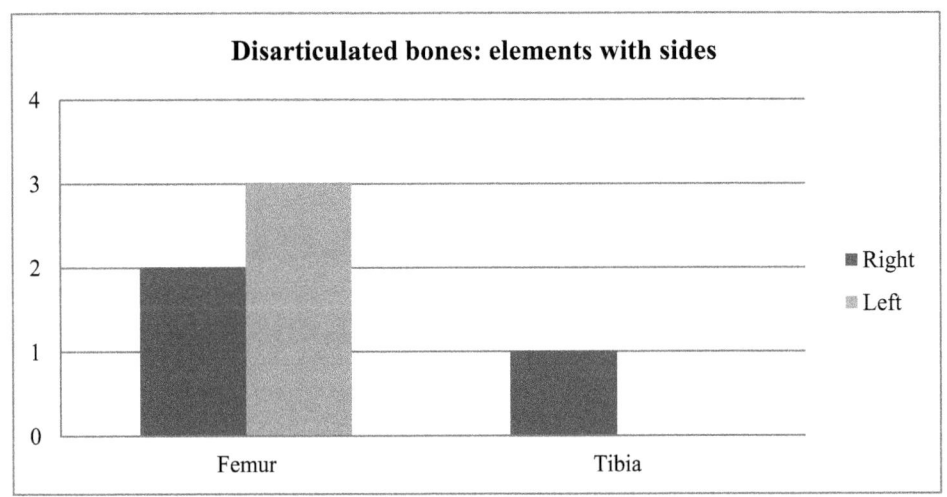

Figure 7. 94 Frequency of disarticulated bones' elements and sides

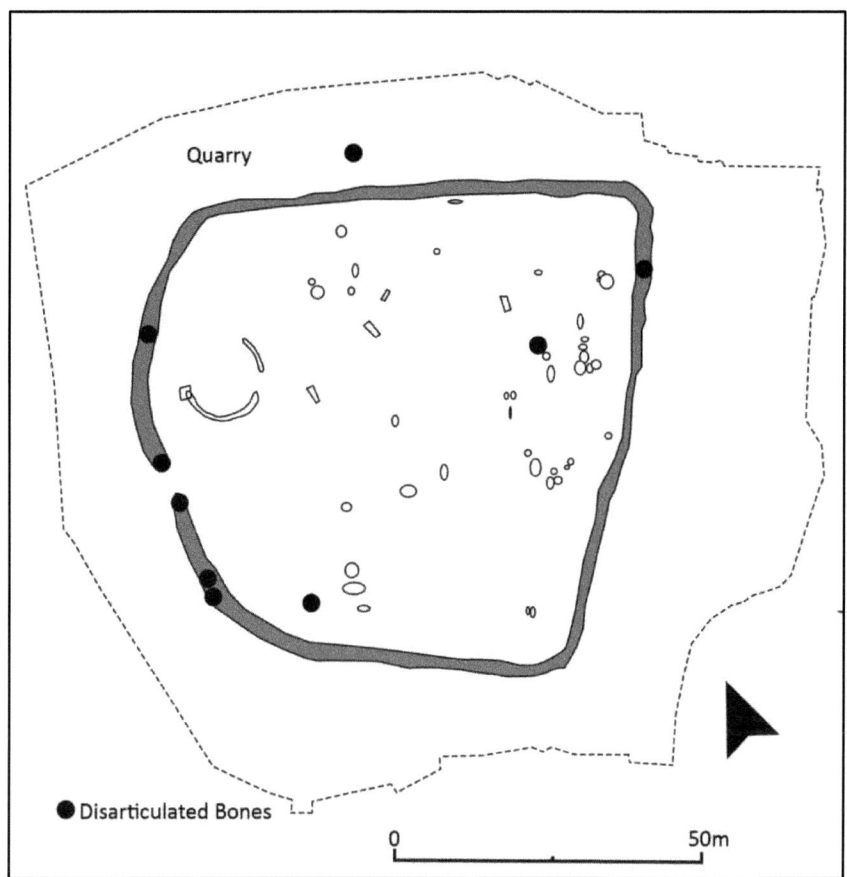

Figure 7. 95 Site plan of Winnall Down in the Early Iron Age indicating human remains deposits (after Fasham 1985, 12); with permission by the Hampshire Field Club

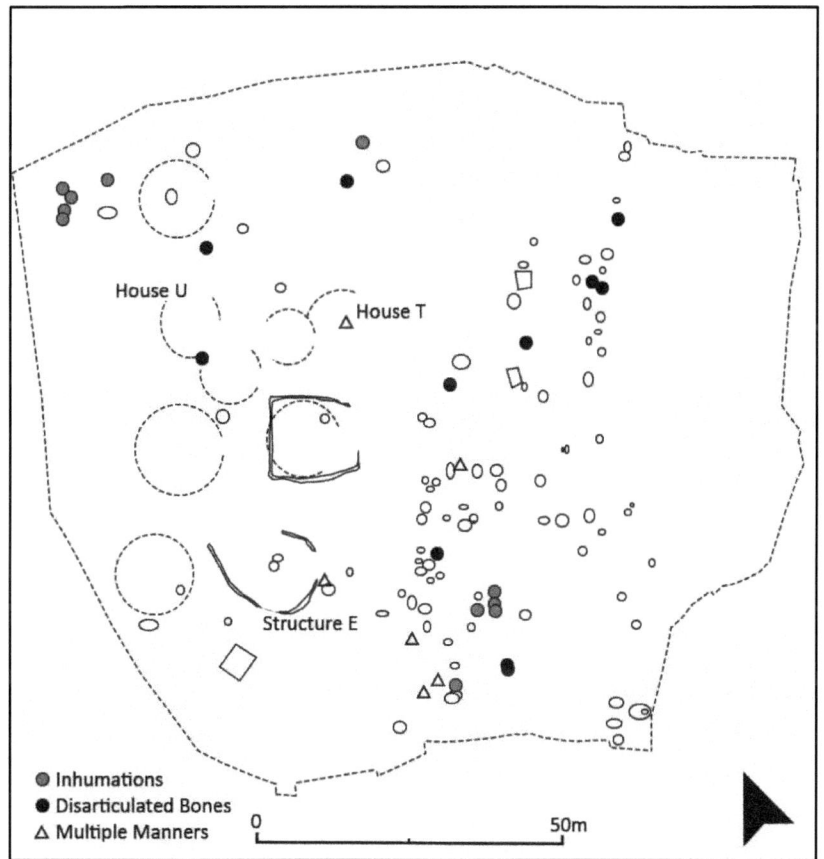

Figure 7. 96 Site plan of Winnall Down during the Middle Iron Age indicating human remains deposits (after Fasham 1985, 19); with permission by the Hampshire Field Club

Analysis of archaeological features (n=3)

Three archaeological features, all of Middle Iron Age date, have associated human remains occurrences (**Figure 7.96**). Two of these are round structures (House T and U) and the other an irregular structure (Structure E); all have an unknown function. The two round structures lie to the northwest-to-north area of the site and the irregular structure is to the southwest-to-west. All three of these structures have associated human remains (both inhumations and disarticulated bones) in pits.

Analysis of contexts (n=43)

Many of the contexts with human remains occurrences date to the Middle Iron Age (n=31, Early Iron Age n=12) and are pits (n=22; **Figure 7.97**). Most of the contexts have only disarticulated bones present (n=22; **Figure 7.98**). The contexts have mainly single occurrences (n=22,

multiple deposits n=12 and both single and multiple deposits n=5). Thirty-one contexts have depth measurements averaging 1.03m, and only 12 occurrences have a known depth that averages 0.38m.

A Fisher's Exact Probability test revealed a significant relationship between the manner of disposal and date (n=36, p=0.025; **Figure 7.99**). It seems evident that the cause of the significant relationship of these two variables is the high number of inhumations in the Middle Iron Age period. Even so, this result shows a change in the manner of disposal between the Early and Middle Iron Age at Winnall Down. The burial evidence from the Middle Iron Age shows an almost even number of inhumations and disarticulated bones, whereas the Early Iron Age burial remains consist of a small number of inhumations but a large quantity of disarticulated bones. It suggests that the Middle Iron Age community was interring complete bodies more often than their predecessors were.

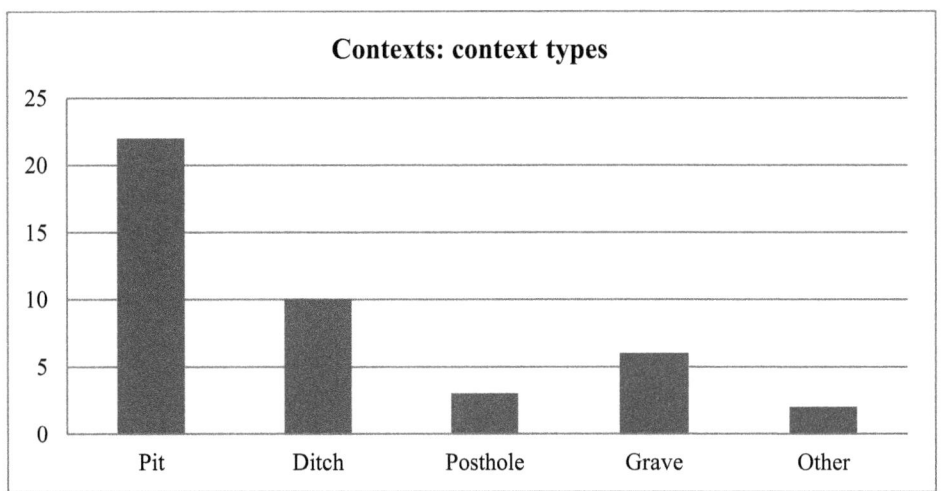

Figure 7. 97 Frequency of context types

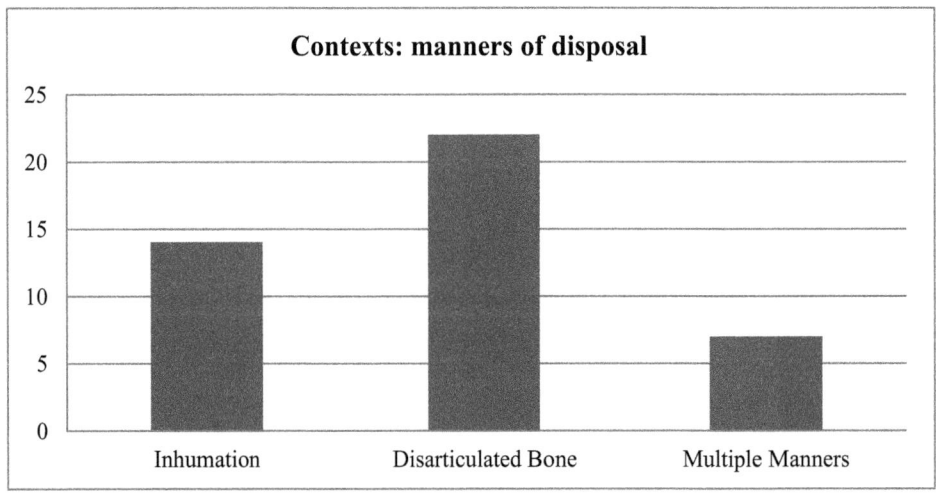

Figure 7. 98 Frequency of contexts according to manner of disposal

Analysis of manner of disposal analysis (n=121)

Inhumations (n=25)

A greater proportion of the inhumations date to the Middle Iron Age (n=23, Early Iron Age n=2), and are commonly within pits (n=14; **Figure 7.100**). Many of the inhumations are not associated with other human remains (n=13, multiple deposits n=5). Commonly, the inhumations are complete (n=16, incomplete n=9), and tend to be crouched (n=8; **Figure 7.101**), resting on either their left or right sides (both n=5). A fraction of the inhumations have a known orientation, of which they are most frequently towards the northwest (n=3; **Table 7.7**).

Demographically, sub-adults have the highest representation (n=20, adults n=5) and are primarily infants (n=16; **Figure 7.102**). Seven inhumations have an assigned sex, many being females (n=5, males n=2). Six inhumations have pathological indicators (three with multiple) and the most common of which is joint disease (n=4, dental disease n=3 and 'other' n=2). One inhumation has a traumatic indicator that is a pre-mortem fracture. In addition, one inhumation has associated material consisting of a chalk block with bones of a sheep and unidentified species. The statistical analysis of inhumations did not return any meaningful results.

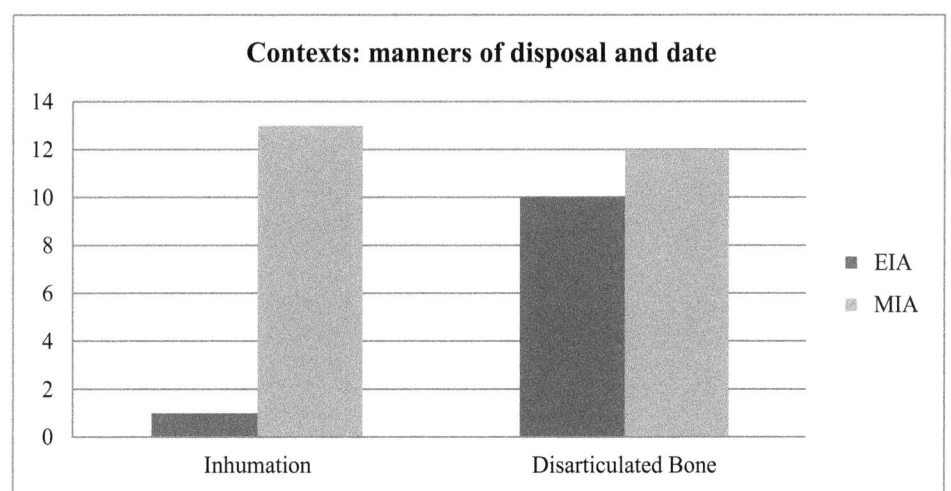

Figure 7. 99 Frequency of contexts according to manner of disposal and date

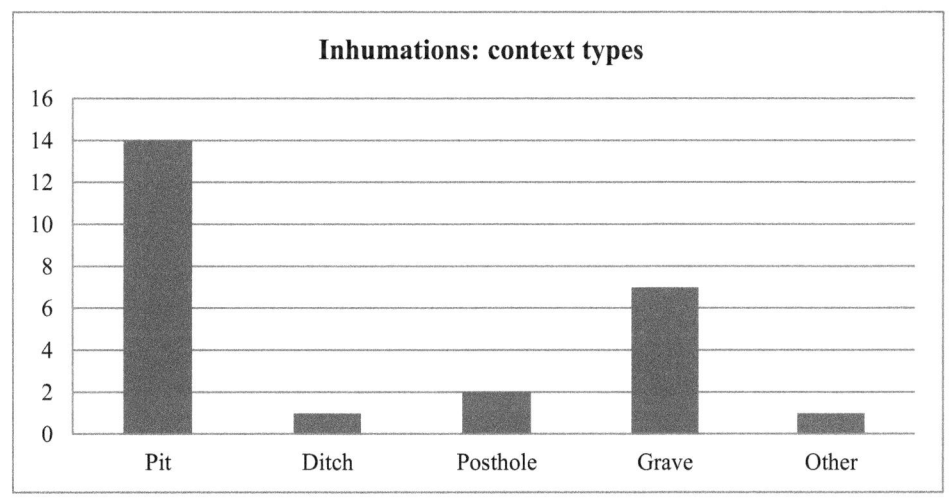

Figure 7. 100 Frequency of inhumations' context types

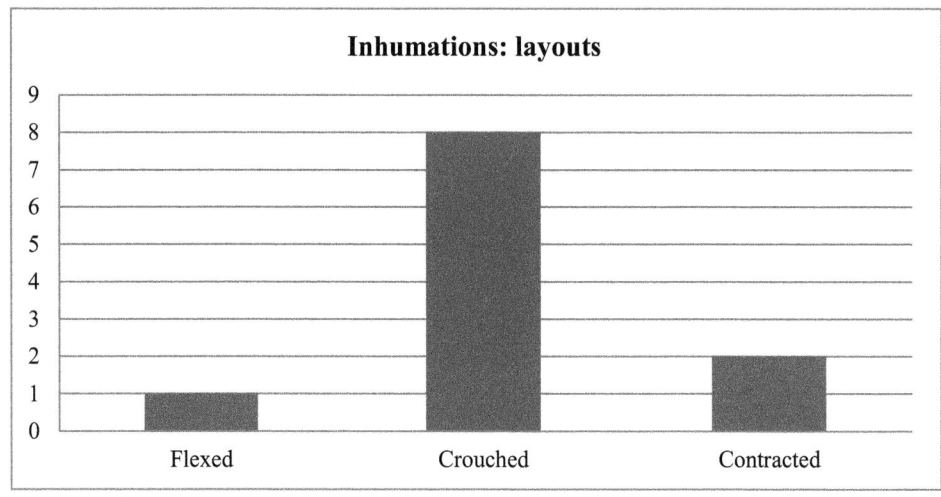

Figure 7. 101 Frequency of inhumations' layouts

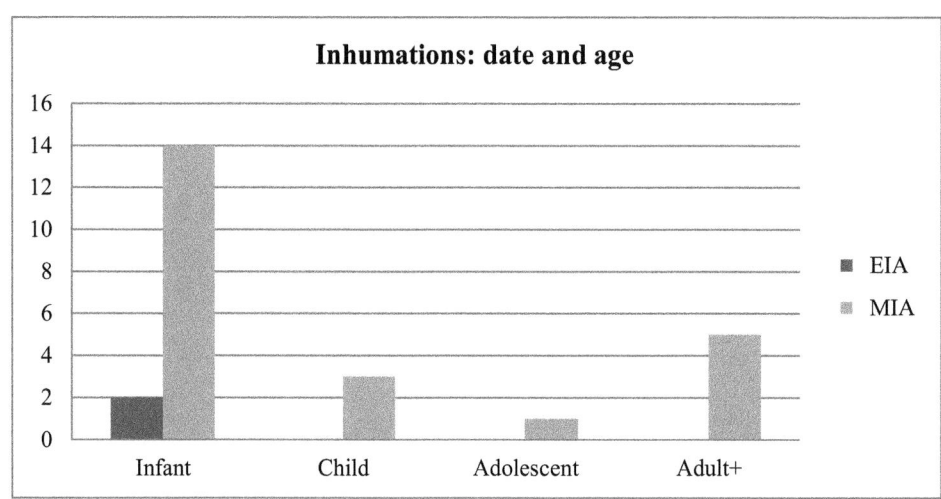

Figure 7. 102 Frequency of inhumations' date and age

Table 7. 7 Frequency of inhumations' orientations

North	1
Northeast	1
East	1
Southeast	2
South	0
Southwest	1
West	2
Northwest	3

Disarticulated bones (n=96)

Over half of the disarticulated bones date to the Middle Iron Age (n=70, Early Iron Age n=26), and lie within pit contexts (n=65; **Figure 7.103**). Most disarticulated bones are associated with other human remains such as inhumations and other disarticulated bones (n=71, single deposits n=18). The skull and femur are the most common elements occurring within the disarticulated bone sample (both n=15; **Figure 7.104**). A limited number of elements have a known side of the body, of which the left is the most frequent (n=5, right n=2; **Table 7.8**). A greater proportion of the disarticulated bones are from sub-adults (n=60, adult n=32) with many from infants (similar to inhumations; **Figures 7.105-6**) and all of an unknown sex.

Four possess single pathological indicators, of which joint disease is the most frequent (n=3, dental disease n=1). One disarticulated bone has evidence of possible burning. In addition, only one has associated material that consists of an animal bone of an unidentified species. Most of the disarticulated bones lie on the perimeter of the Early Iron Age site (n=21, interior n=2 and exterior n=3).

Table 7. 8 Frequency of disarticulated bones' elements and sides

Element	Right	Left
Humerus	0	1
Ulna	1	0
Femur	0	3
Patella	1	1

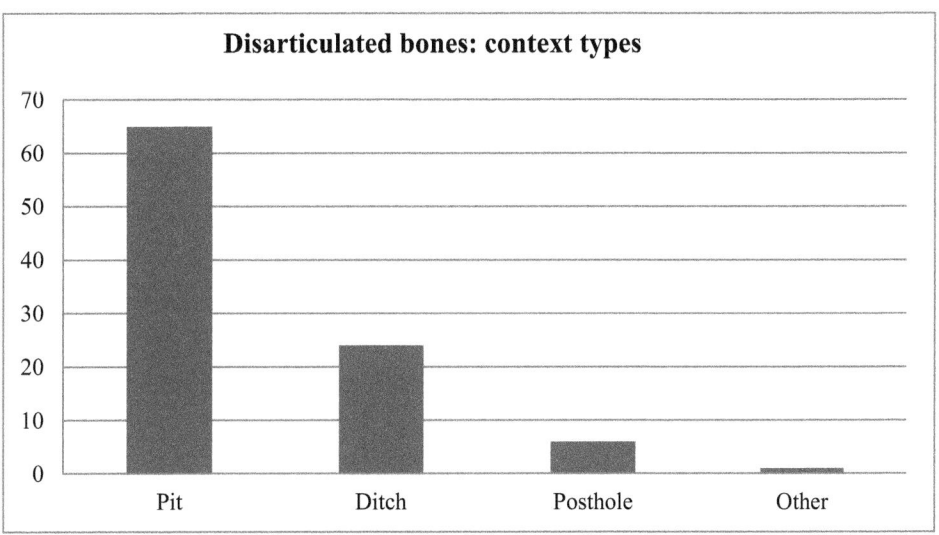

Figure 7. 103 Frequency of disarticulated bones' context types

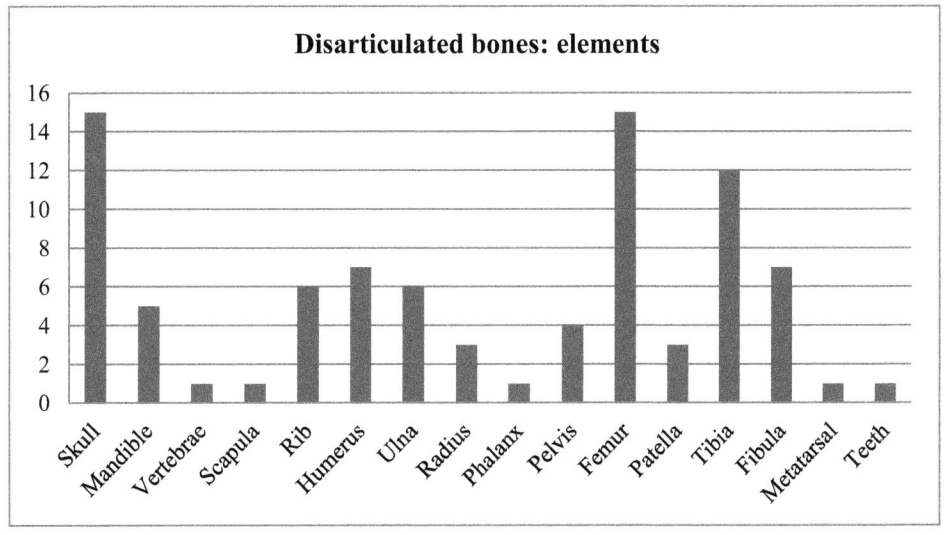

Figure 7. 104 Frequency of disarticulated bones' elements

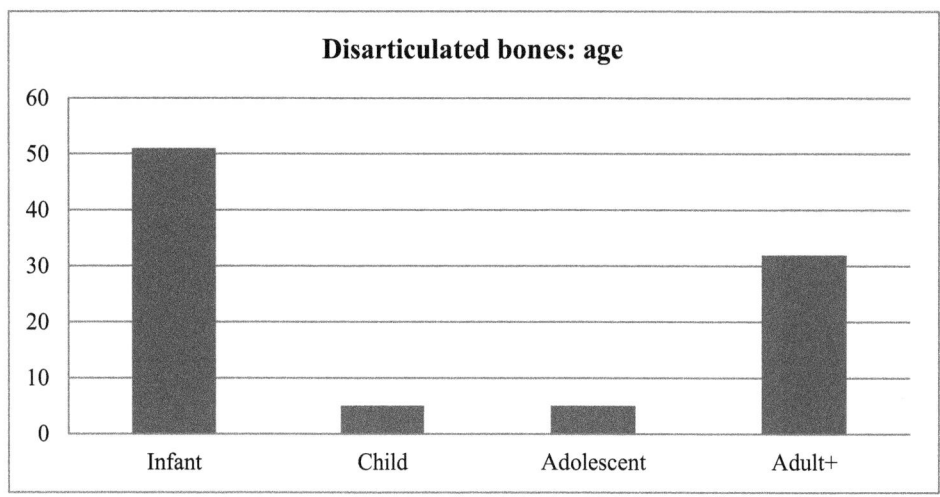

Figure 7. 105 Frequency of disarticulated bones' age

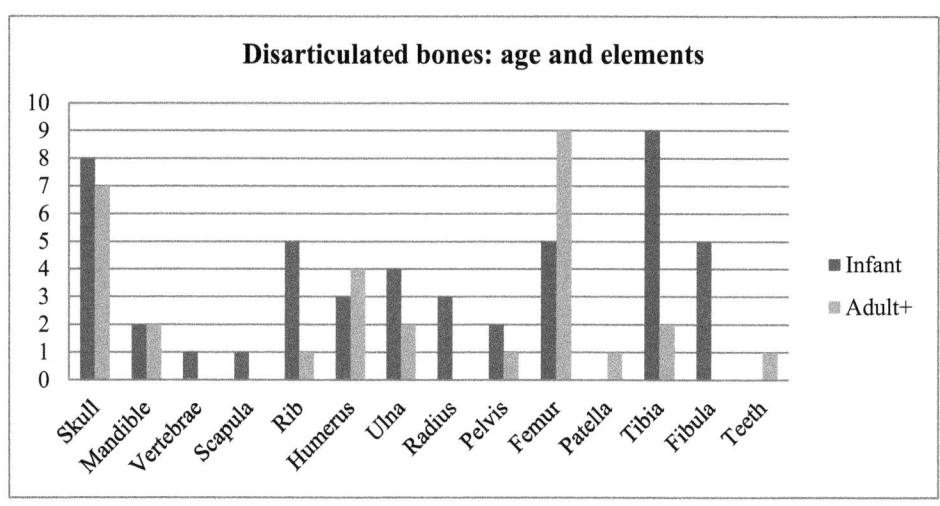

Figure 7. 106 Frequency of disarticulated bones' elements and age

Statistical testing of the disarticulated bone variables produced a number of significant results. However, all the significant results are probably the result of the high numbers of certain variables. For example, there is significant relationship between context types and date (χ^2=43.030, p=0.000). The high number of pits in the Middle Iron Age influenced this significant outcome; however, as **Figure 7.107** illustrates that in the Early Iron Age ditches were the favoured context for deposition then switches to pits. Additionally, there is a significant relationship between age (infants and adults) and date (χ^2=40.515, p=0.000). **Figure 7.108** clearly shows that adult remains were frequently deposited in the Early Iron Age while, in the Middle Iron Age, infant bones overwhelmingly made up most of the disarticulated material.

Summary

The burial evidence from Winnall Down has an uncommonly high proportion of infant remains, similar to Gravelly Guy and Gussage All Saints. This is unusual since most of the skeletal material from Iron Age sites is typically that of adults. Furthermore, the burial evidence shows a change in the occurrences deposited between the Early and Middle Iron Age from mostly adult disarticulated bones in the Early Iron Age to infant remains in the Middle Iron Age.

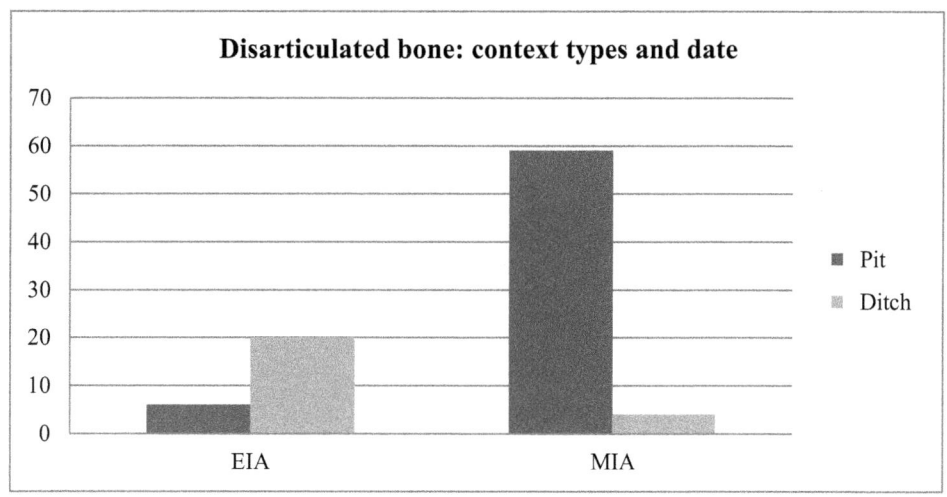

Figure 7. 107 Frequency of disarticulated bones according to date and context types

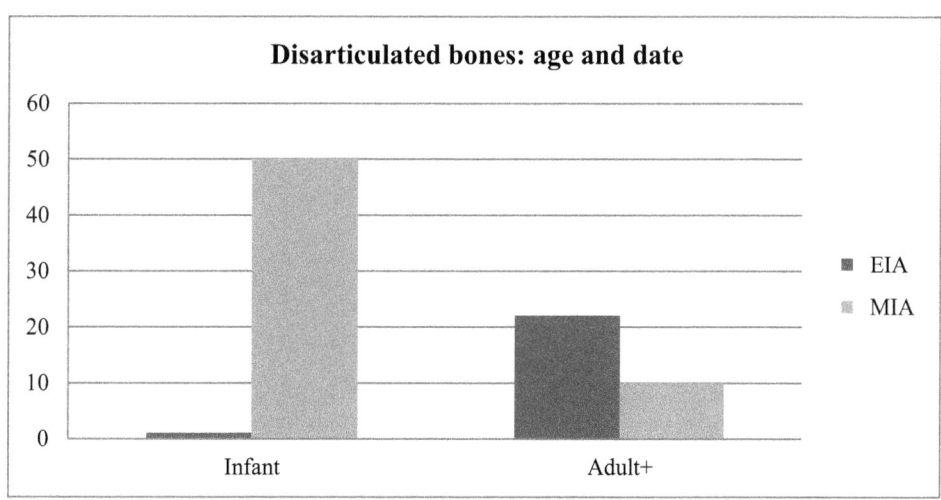

Figure 7. 108 Frequency of disarticulated bones according to date and age

Glastonbury Lake Village (ST 493 408)

Glastonbury Lake Village, in the Brue Valley (Somerset), is an Iron Age wetland settlement site discovered by Arthur Bulleid in 1892 (Coles and Minnit 1995, 1; **Figure 7. 109**). Shortly after the site's discovery, excavations began in 1882 until 1898, recommencing in 1904 to 1907 under the direction of Arthur Bulleid and Harold St. George Gray (Coles and Minnit 1995, 1, 21). Within the eleven years of fieldwork, the entirety of the settlement was excavated, equating to about one hectare (Coles and Minnit 1995, 7). In 1993, Coles and Minnit (1995) began a re-appraisal of Bulleid and Gray's work. The re-appraisal of the excavation consists of a re-examination of Bulleid and Gray's publications and notes, as well as a reassessment of the environment, structure and contextual characteristics of Glastonbury Lake Village (Coles and Minnit 1995, 19). During the Iron Age, Glastonbury Lake Village was a small settlement site residing in a tree-swamp environment (Coles and Minnit 1995, 135). This setting has waterlogged conditions that are excellent for

preserving organic material such as wood. The site contains 90 mounds, of which many represent former enclosed and open structures that had to be continuously 'renovated' due to the site's unstable environment (Coles and Minnit 1995, 99). Habitation at Glastonbury Lake Village began around 250 BC and lasted until roughly 50 BC (Coles and Minnit 1995, 178). A number of mounds produced human remains either within their floor contexts or around their exteriors. In total, 49 human remains occurrences, consisting of 13 inhumations and 36 disarticulated bones, were recovered from 38 contexts.

Analysis of archaeological features (n=30)

Thirty archaeological features (mounds) have associated human remains occurrences, all of the features date to the Middle/Late Iron Age. Most of the features are roundhouses (n=16, 'other'[24] n=9 and unknown n=5; **Figure 7.109**), and domestic use is their most frequently

---

[24] 'Other' refers to a structure type undefined by the 'variables' traits, in this case such as a landing stage for the site.

attributed function (n=13; **Figure 7.110**)[25]. Most of the features have only disarticulated bones associated with them (n=21, inhumations n=7, and multiple manners n=2). All the features are within the interior of the site except one that is outside the settlement area and may have been the community's midden area (Coles and Minnit 1995, 73-74). None the features' variables returned any valid, significant results.

Analysis of contexts (n=38)

All of the contexts with human remains occurrences date to the Middle/Late Iron Age, and are 'other' contexts (described as floor/house layers). Most of the contexts contain only disarticulated bones (n=28, inhumations n=7, and multiple manners n=3), and typically have single deposits (n=31, multiple deposits n=7). A small portion of context fills are known, of which all are fills from building episodes (n=10). Most contexts occur outside the archaeological features (n=25, interior n=13), and are typically found in boundary areas (n=8, entrance n=1). None of the context variables returned any significant results.

Analysis of manner of disposal (n=49)

Most of the statistical tests did not return any significant results for manner of disposal. However, a chi-square test for independence indicates a significant relationship between the manner of disposal and age (χ^2=13.398, p=0.000; **Figure 7.111**). This high level of significance may be due to the sample size in each category. However, the test implies that sub-adults were frequently deposited as inhumations and adults as disarticulated bones. Furthermore, this result may suggest that processing differed according to the age of the individual. The age categories (**Figure 7.112**) exhibit a high number of infant inhumations. This finding correlates with the results from chapter four that show an increase of infants and inhumations in the burial record during the Middle/Late Iron Age. High counts of infants at Glastonbury Lake Village are similar to the burial evidence from Gravelly Guy, Gussage All Saints, and Winnall Down.

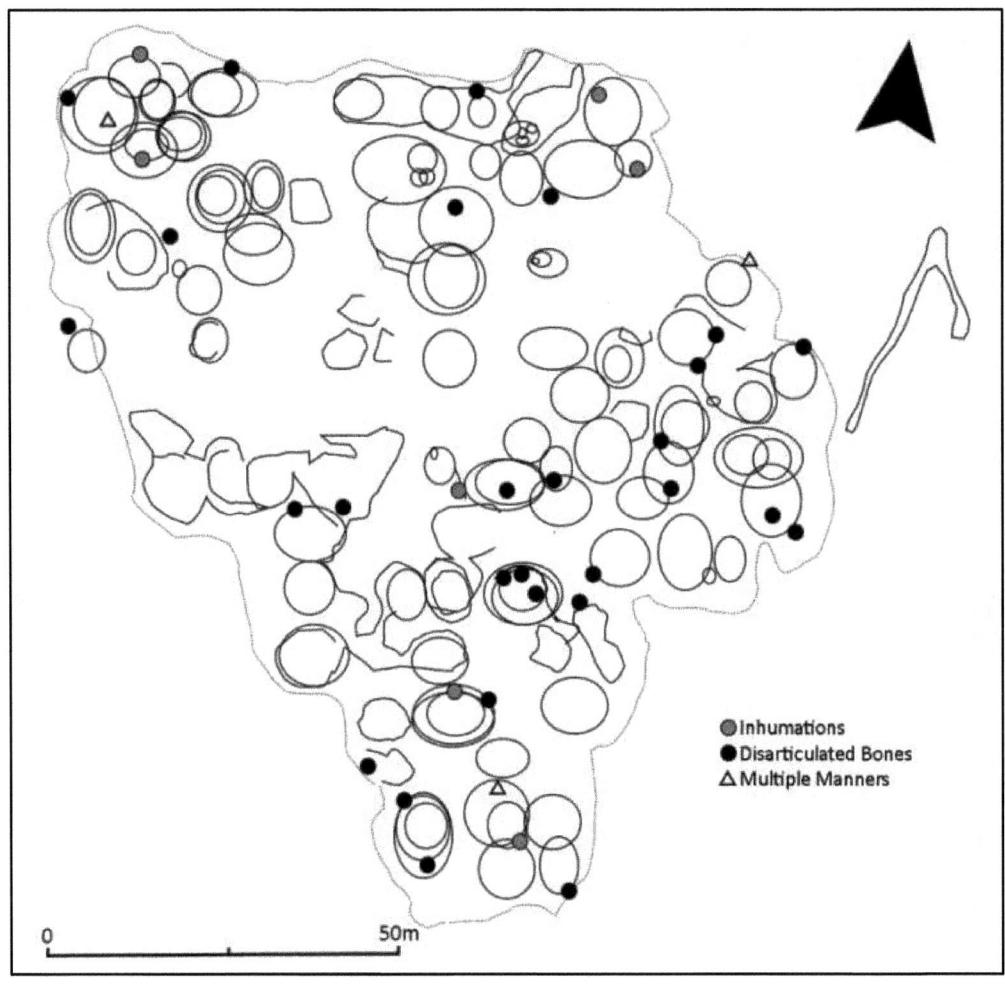

Figure 7. 109 Site plan of Glastonbury Lake Village indicating areas of human remains deposits (after Coles and Minnit 1995, Figure 8.14); with permission

---

[25] 'Other' refers to the structures' function as a landing.

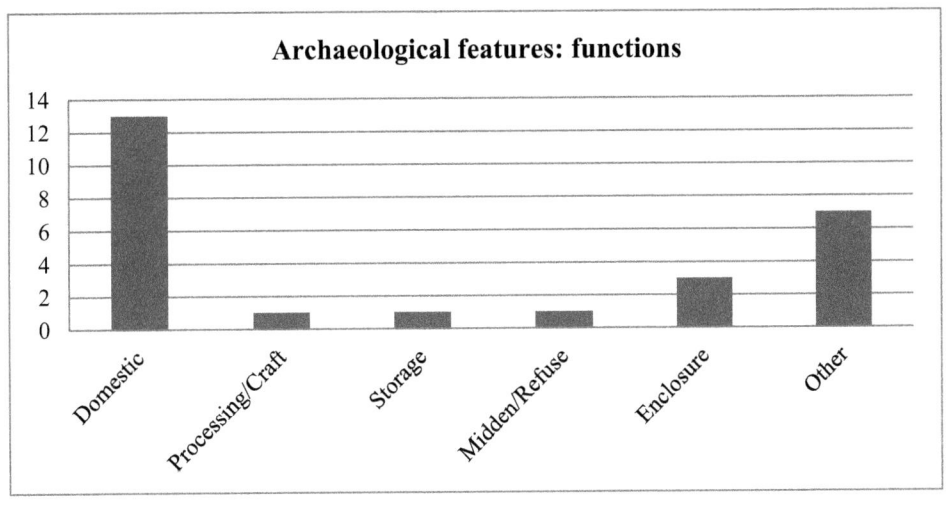

Figure 7. 110 Frequency of archaeological features' functions

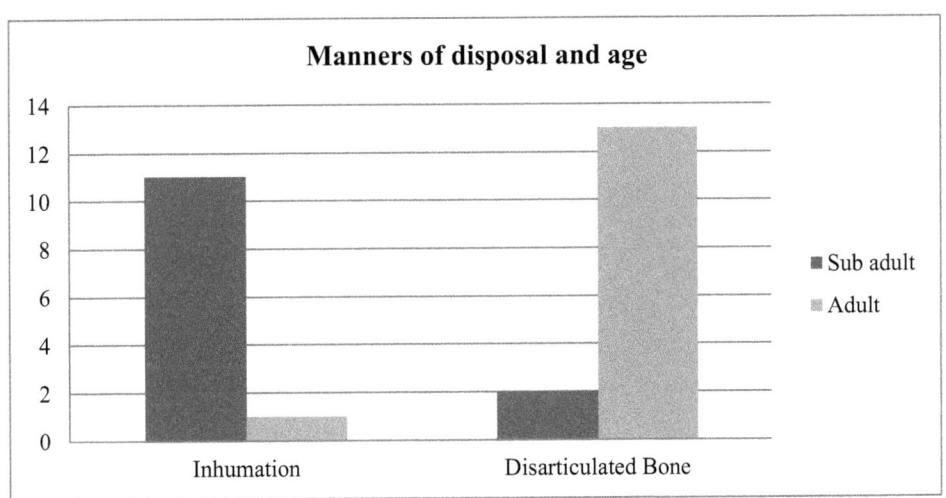

Figure 7. 111 Frequency of occurrences according to manner of disposal and age

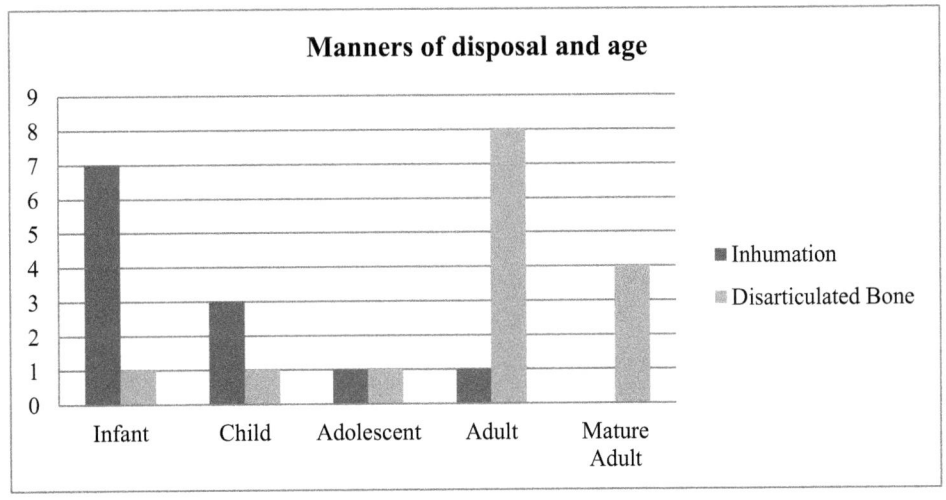

Figure 7. 112 Frequency of occurrences according to manner of disposal and age

Inhumations (n=13)

All of the inhumations date to the Middle/Late Iron Age, and are typically single deposits (n=7, multiple deposits n=6). Most are in an incomplete state (n=7, complete n=6) and, as discussed above, are predominantly sub-adults (n=11, adult n=1). All of the inhumations have associated material, twelve with multiple materials, and the most common of these is worked bone (n=9; **Figure 7.113**). Inhumations occur frequently in the exterior area of a feature (n=8, interior n=5). There is no consistency in the cardinal directions in which inhumations are deposited but they typically occur in northern areas of archaeological features (n=7, southern areas n=3) with only a small fraction (n=2) near architectural features, both of which are boundaries.

Disarticulated bones (n=36)

All of the disarticulated bones date to the Middle/Late Iron Age, and most are single deposits (n=24, multiple deposits n=12). The highest occurring element is the skull (n=21; **Figure 7.114**), Three elements have a given side of which left is more frequent (two left tibiae and one right humerus). Adults are the most common (n=13, sub-adults n=2), and a small fraction of the disarticulated bones could be sexed, with males (n=3) and females (n=3) being equally represented. Seven of the disarticulated bones have traumatic indicators, three with multiple traumas. The most common form of trauma is cut marks, and a greater proportion of the trauma occurred peri–mortem (n=3, peri/post-mortem n=2, post-mortem n=2; **Figure 7.115**). Thirty-four disarticulated bones have associated materials with 28 having multiple items; worked bone is the most common material (n=25; **Figure 7.116**). A greater frequency of the disarticulated bone is from the exterior area of the archaeological features (n=23, interior n=13), particularly in northwest-to-north areas (n=6; **Figure 7.117**). A small proportion of the disarticulated bones are near architectural features, of which boundary areas are the most common (n=8, entrance n=1). None of the statistical tests for disarticulated bones returned any meaningful results.

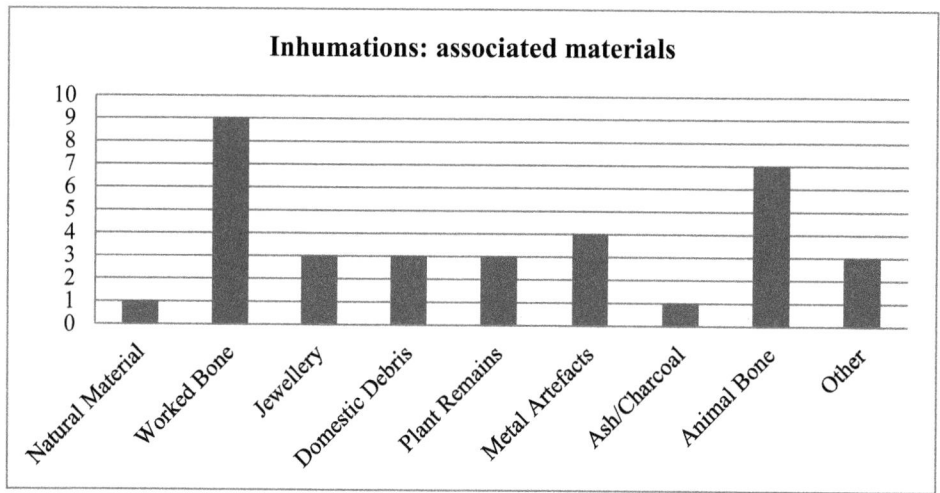

Figure 7. 113 Frequency of inhumations'' associated materials

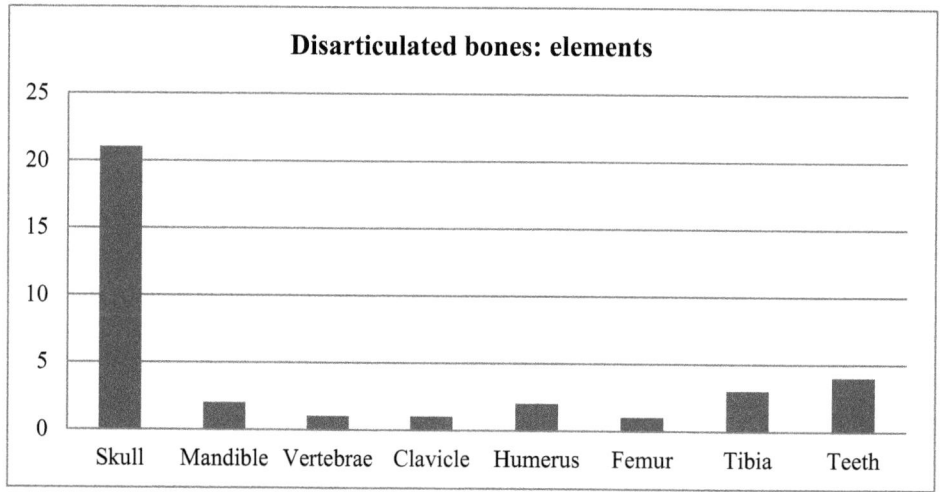

Figure 7. 114 Frequency of disarticulated bones' elements

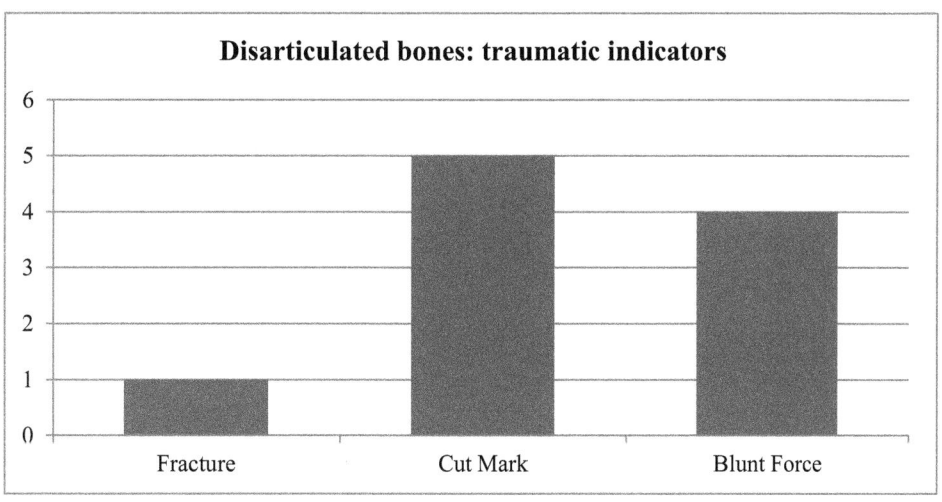

Figure 7. 115 Frequency of disarticulated bones' trauma

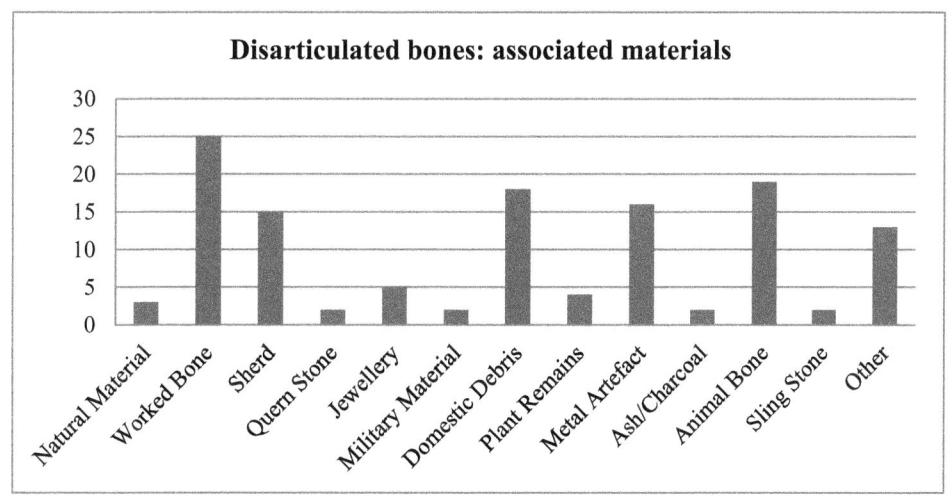

Figure 7. 116 Frequency of disarticulated bones' associated materials

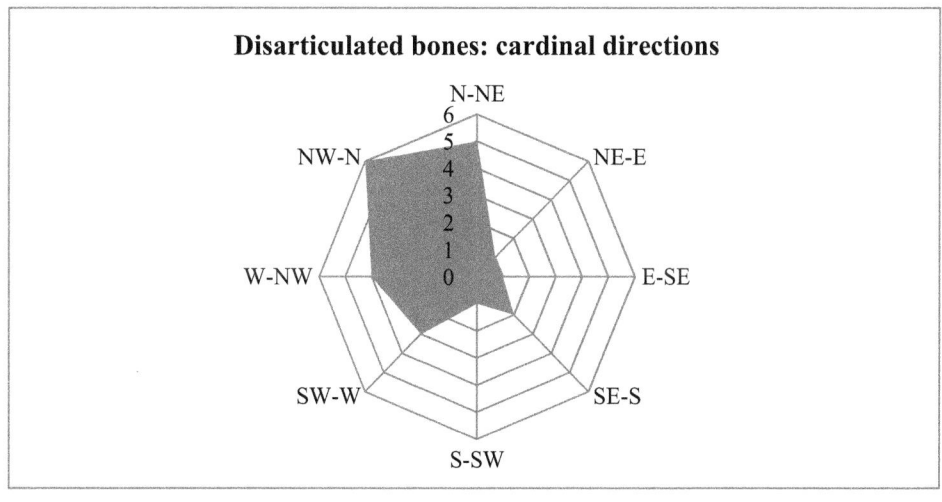

Figure 7. 117 Frequency of disarticulated bones' cardinal directions

Summary

In sum, the human remains from Glastonbury Lake Village depict intriguing burial characteristics that correspond loosely with burial trends occurring generally during the Middle/Late Iron Age. For one, the skull is the most frequent element by a large margin than the other bones that suggests a degree of selection. In addition, there are high numbers of infant inhumations and adult disarticulated bones. This pattern may suggest that the community strived to break the deceased's body down into manageable parts with particular attention paid to the skull. In turn, sub-adults may not have been viewed as full members of society or important enough to receive the treatment that resulted in disarticulation. Furthermore, the high number of infants at Glastonbury Lake Village is analogous to Gravelly Guy, Winnall Down, and Gussage All Saints.

Micheldever Wood (SU 527 370)

Due to the building of the M3 motorway, between 1975 and 1978 the M3 Archaeological Rescue Committee carried out excavations on the banjo enclosure at Micheldever Wood, near Micheldever (Hampshire) (Fasham 1987, 1). Micheldever Wood lies on a clay-with-flint spur on top of the Upper Chalk (Fasham 1987, 1). There are three main phases of activity at the site beginning in the Early Iron Age and lasting into the Roman period (Fasham 1987, 6-15). The banjo enclosure ditch and bank was constructed in the Middle Iron Age (Phase 2). It enclosed an area of 0.2 ha and opened from the west by a long entranceway (Fasham 1987, 8). The excavation recovered a handful of inhumations and disarticulated bones from pit and ditch contexts, with a high representation of sub-adults (primarily infants). Twenty human remains occurrences, consisting of 15 inhumations and five disarticulated bones, were recovered from 12 contexts. F.V.H. Powell (1987) conducted the osteological analysis of the human remains.

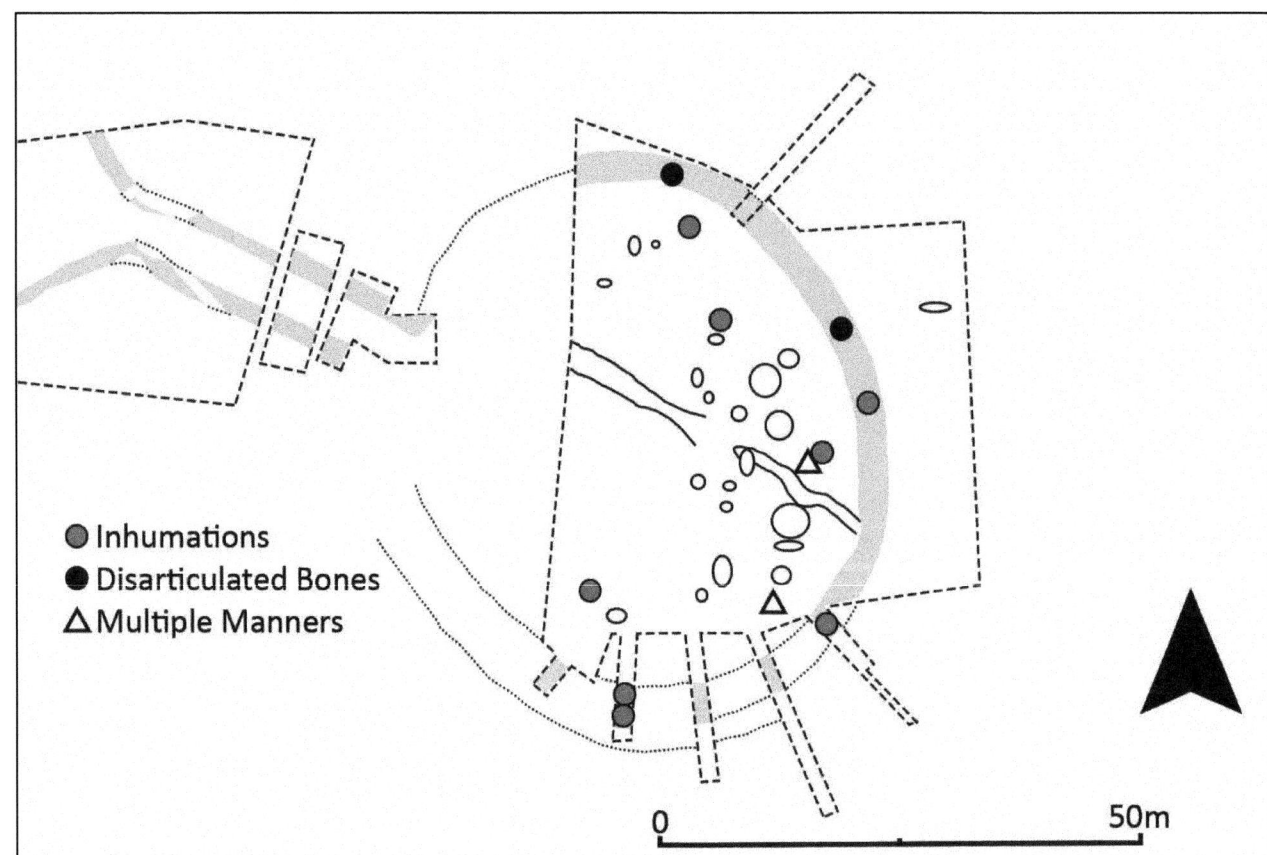

Figure 7. 118 Site plan of Micheldever Wood indicating human remains deposits (after Fasham 1987, 3); with permission by the Hampshire Field Club

Analysis of contexts (n=12)

Of the 12 contexts that contained human remains occurrences, most date to the Middle Iron Age (n=11, Late Iron Age n=1). The most frequent type of context is the pit (n=6; **Figure 7.119**), and many contain only inhumations (n=8; **Figure 7.120**). Human remains' contexts were found only in the interior (n=6) and perimeter (n=6) of the site.

Analysis of manner of disposal (n=20)

Inhumations (n=15)

Many of the inhumations date to the Middle Iron Age (n=14, Late Iron Age n=1) and were found in pit contexts (n=10; **Figure 7.121**). Most inhumations were incomplete (n=9, complete n=6), and only two could have their layout determined, both being extended. Orientation did not show any consistency in direction (**Table 7.9**) and only two body positions could be determined, both supine. Demographically, all the inhumations are sub-adults, including 13 infants. Only one inhumation is sexed and is a male. No inhumations possess traumatic indicators, and two have the presence of a single pathological indicator, one being a neoplastic condition and the other a haematological disease. None of the inhumations had associated material. There is no statistical testing for inhumation variables since the total count falls below the limit of 20.

Disarticulated bones (n=5)

All of the disarticulated bones date to the Middle Iron Age, with most placed in ditch contexts (n=3, pits n=2). The disarticulated bone assemblage consists of two cranial fragments from adults, a left and right tibia from an infant (presumably from the same individual) and an incomplete atlas vertebra. None of the occurrences could be sexed. The disarticulated remains did not have any pathological or traumatic indicators, and there was no associated material.

Summary

The statistical analysis of Micheldever Wood for manner of disposal did not return any significant results. The small sample size for human remains from this site prevented statistical testing. Despite the limited evidence, the majority (about 75 per cent) of the human remains from Micheldever Wood were infants. This pattern is similar to the burial record at Gravelly Guy, Glastonbury Lake Village, and Gussage All Saints where each of these sites had high numbers of infants, suggesting a common practice shared between these sites.

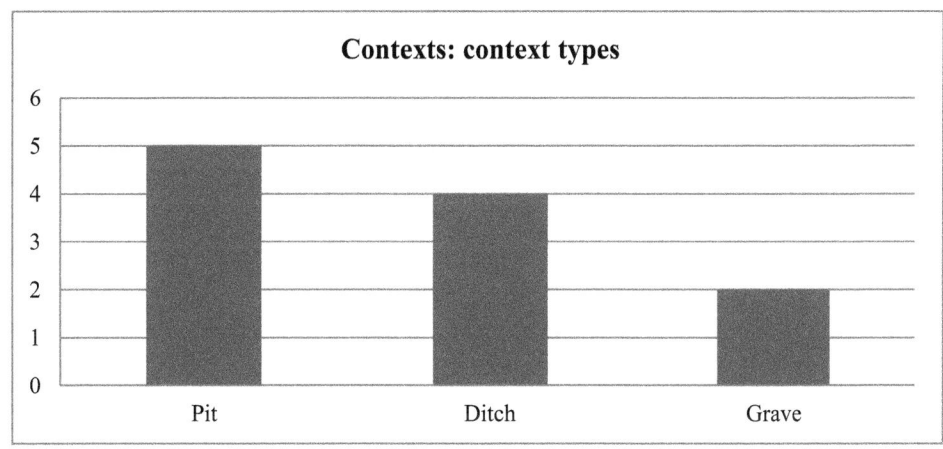

Figure 7. 119 Frequency of context types

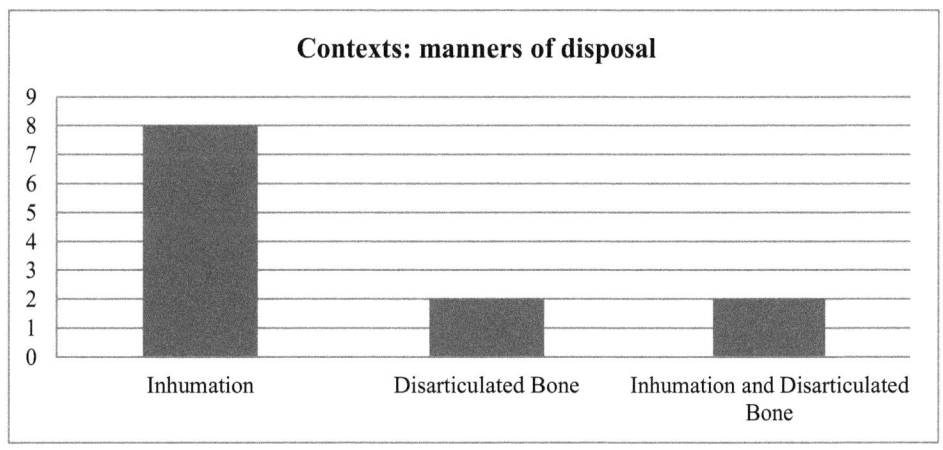

Figure 7. 120 Frequency of contexts according to manner of disposal

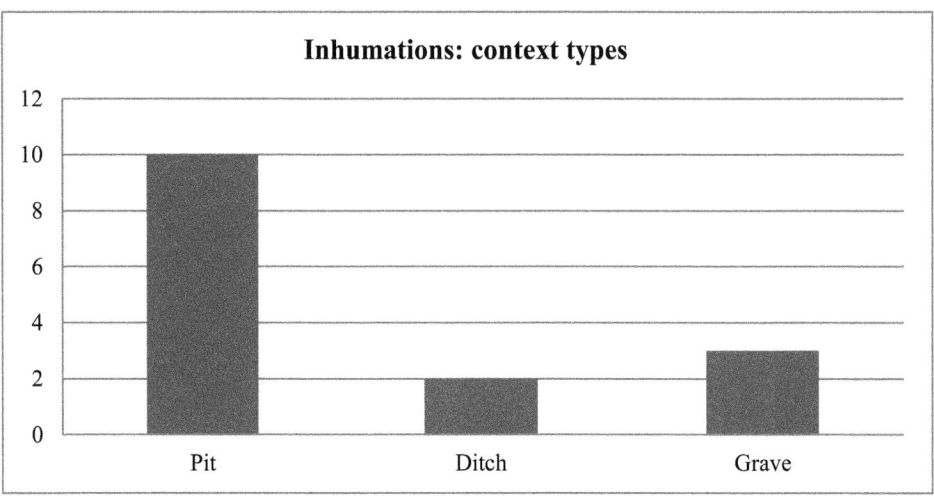

Figure 7. 121 Frequency of inhumations' context types

Table 7. 9 Frequency of inhumations' orientations

Northeast	2
South	1
Southwest	1
West	1
Northwest	1

Settlement/cemeteries

White Horse, Pilgrim's Way, West and East of Boarley Farm (TQ 7530, 6220)[26]

The conjoining sites of White Horse, Pilgrim's Way, West and East of Boarley Farm are near Aylesford, Kent, on top of the Cretaceous Middle Chalk (Hayden *et al.* 2006, 2, **Figure 7. 122- 24**). The sites sit at the foot of the North Downs escarpments on the eastern side of the Medway Gap (Hayden *et al.* 2006, 2). In all, Oxford Archaeological Unit excavated 4.4 ha between 1998 and 1999, in advance of the construction of the Channel Tunnel Rail Link (Hayden *et al.* 2006, 1). Human activity is present from the Mesolithic period to Roman times. There is limited evidence of Late Bronze Age activity apart from a couple of pits containing cremated bones (Hayden *et al.* 2006, 10). However, a mixed farming settlement began in the Early Iron Age and lasted into the Middle Iron Age (Hayden *et al.* 2006, 10). During this time, a number of inhumations, disarticulated bones, and cremations were placed around the occupation areas. Spatial analysis of the site shows that cremation deposits were concentrated in the southern areas, while inhumations and disarticulated bones were mostly found to the west (Hayden *et al.* 2006, 135). In addition, metalworking activity concentrated in

the eastern portion of the sites, with a large number of post structures to the north (Hayden *et al.* 2006, 136). The inhumations and cremations have later radiocarbon dates than the disarticulated bones, and arguably '...were made at or near the time that settlement was abandoned' (Hayden *et al.* 2006, 170). The sites were abandoned towards the end of the Middle Iron Age, and limited activity recommenced in the Late Iron Age (Hayden *et al.* 2006, 10). A total of 21 human remains occurrences, consisting of two inhumations, 14 disarticulated bones and five cremations, came from 12 contexts dating from the Late Bronze Age, Early/Middle Iron Age and Late Iron Age[27]. Annesofie Witkin (2006c) conducted the osteological analysis of the skeletal material.

Analysis of the archaeological feature (n=1)

One archaeological feature (Structure 2584; **Figure 7.125**) has associated human remains occurrences. The feature is a round structure of Early/Middle Iron Age date, and possibly a roundhouse. An inhumation and two disarticulated bones were found in two pits associated with this feature, which lies in the south-to-southwest.

---

[26] Special thanks to Stephen Haynes (Cultural Heritage) for allowing access to these site reports prior to publication.

[27] Location of the Late Iron Age cremation deposit is unknown

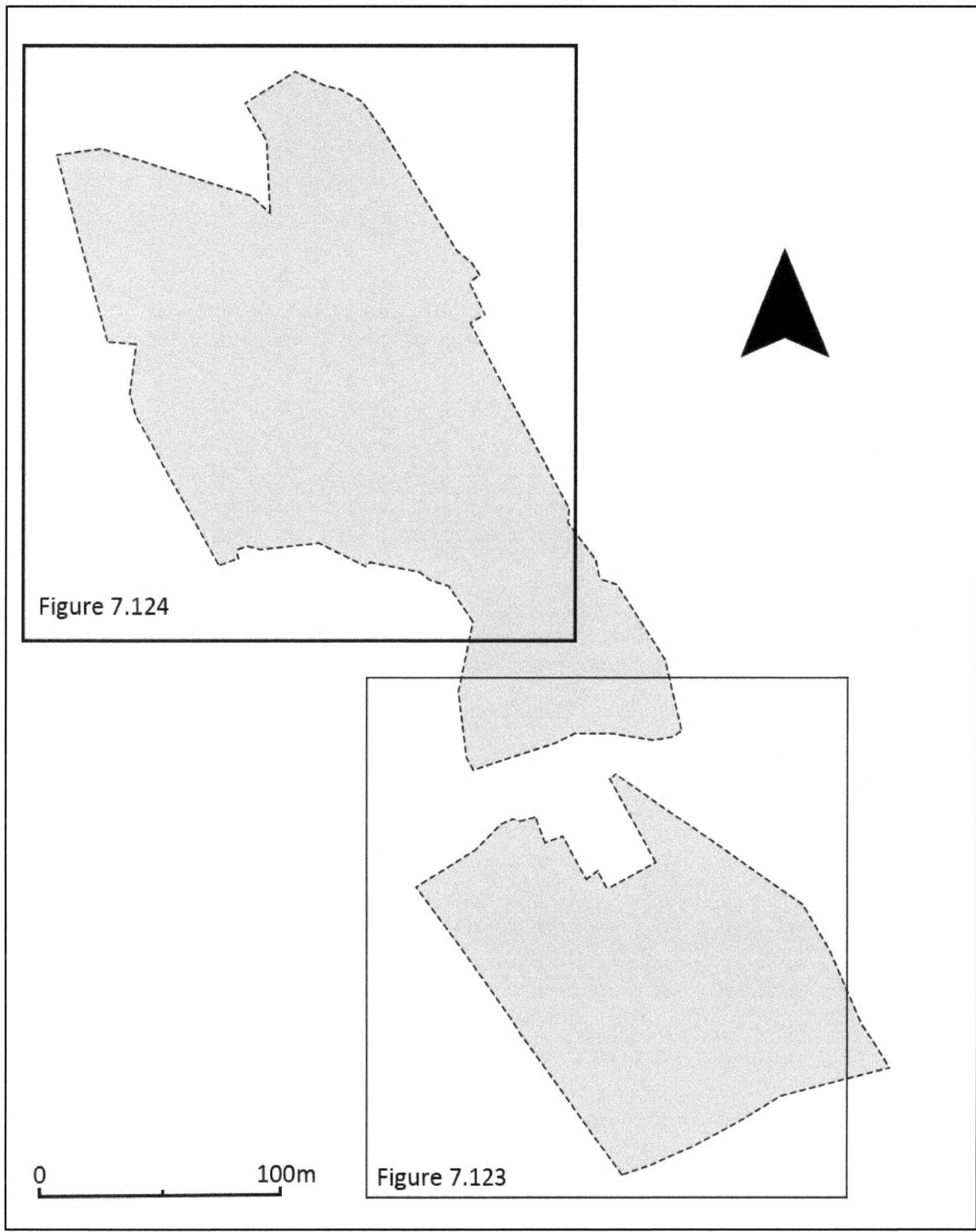

Figure 7. 122 Site plan of White Horse, Pilgrim's Way, West and East of Boarley Farm showing area of excavation (after: Oxford Wessex Archaeology Joint Venture and HS 1 LTD, fig. 3; with permission)

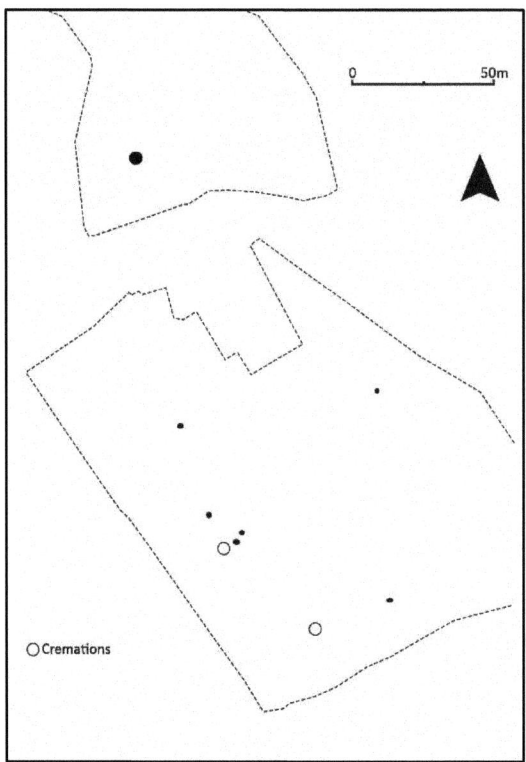

Figure 7. 123 Site plan of White Horse, Pilgrim's Way, West and East of Boarley Farm showing only LBA features and human remains deposits (after: Oxford Wessex Archaeology Joint Venture and HS 1 LTD, fig. 64; with permission)

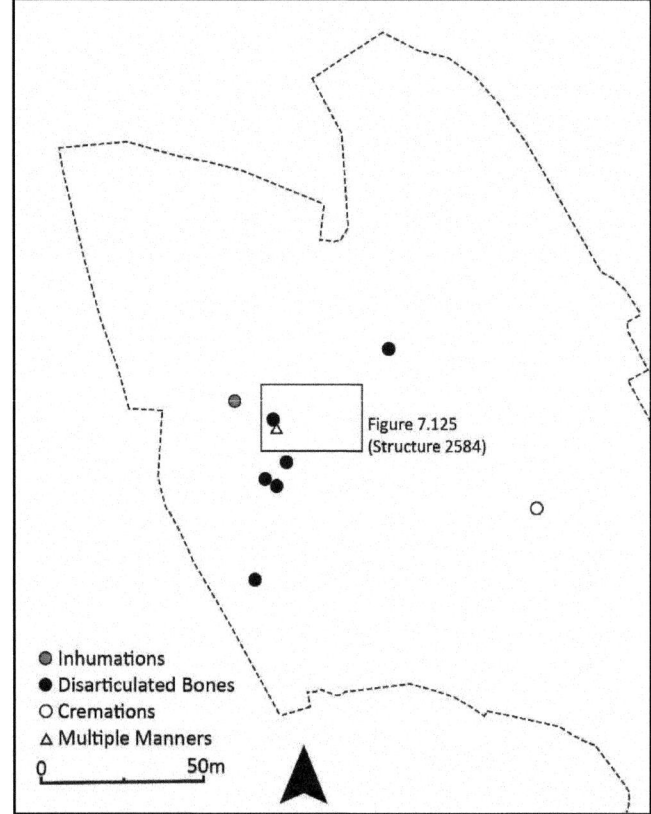

Figure 7.124 Site plan of White Horse, Pilgrim's Way, West and East of Boarley Farm showing only EIA/MIA human remains deposits (after: Oxford Wessex Archaeology Joint Venture and HS 1 LTD, fig. 103; with permission)

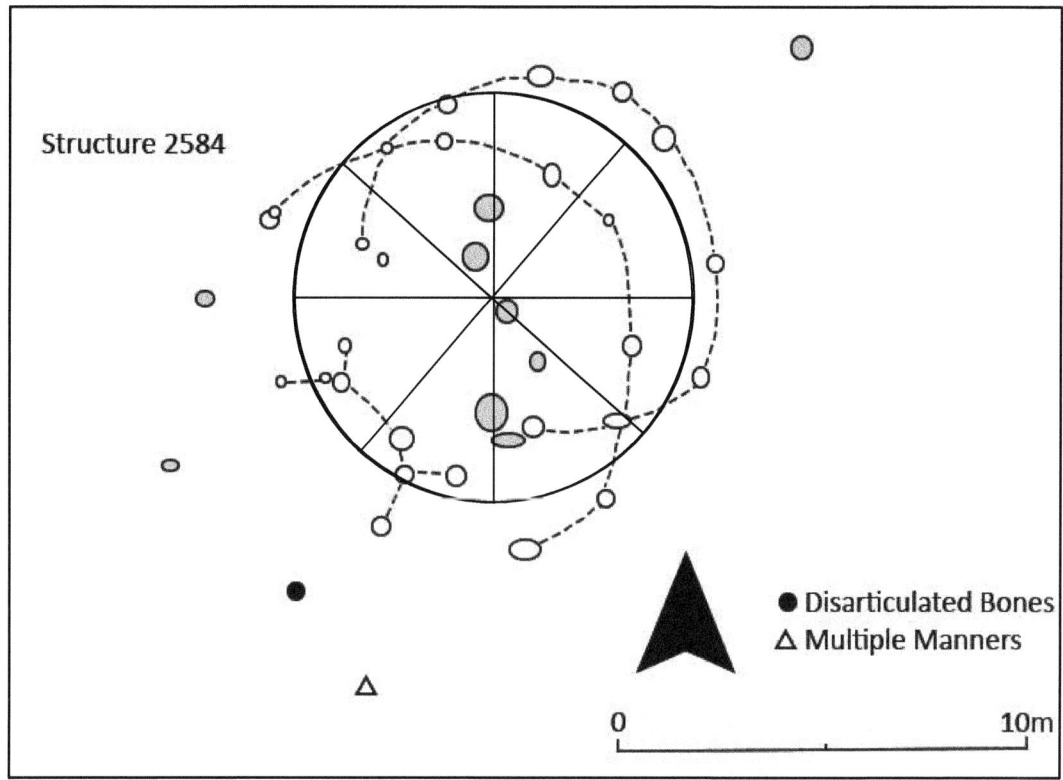

Figure 7. 125 Plan of Structure 2584 (with cardinal location) illustrating human remains deposits (after: Oxford Wessex Archaeology Joint Venture and HS 1 LTD, fig. 77; with permission)

Analysis of contexts (n=12)

All of the contexts with human remains occurrences are pits, with a greater proportion dating to the Early/Middle Iron Age (n=9, Late Bronze Age n=2, and Late Iron Age n=1). A greater frequency of the contexts contain only disarticulated bones (n=6, cremation n=4, inhumation n=1, and multiple manners n=1) and most have a single deposit (n=8, multiple deposits n=2). Ten contexts have depths averaging 0.57m. Two contexts have occurrences at depths averaging 0.36m. All twelve of the contexts' fills were backfills. Two of the contexts are associated with the structure discussed above. Both are pits and lie outside the structure within the south-to-southwest area.

Analysis of manner of disposal (n=21)

Inhumation (n=2)

The two inhumations from this site date to the Early/Middle Iron Age, and were found in pits. Each of the inhumations was crouched and one is a mature adult male orientated to the southeast, lying on his back with an unknown facial direction. The other is a sub-adult, of unknown sex, placed in a sitting or squatting position. Additionally, both the inhumations have signs of joint and dental disease. The only traumatic indicator is from the older inhumation that has an ante-mortem fracture. The sub-adult has a loomweight, plant remains, and ash/charcoal in association while the adult has two spindle whorls accompanying the burial. The sub-adult's

placement is near Structure 2548, on the exterior, in the south-to-southwest segment, near the entrance. The sub-adult is a single deposit but the pit in which it is interred also contains a disarticulated human bone in a layer separate to that containing the inhumation. The older inhumation is deposited just to the northwest of the sub-adult.

Disarticulated bones (n=15)

All of the disarticulated bones date to the Early/Middle Iron Age and are from pit contexts. The disarticulated bones are most often with other human remains (n=10, single deposits n=5). The element with the highest frequency is the skull (n=4; **Figure 7.126**) and sidedness of elements is shared between right (n=4) and left (n=3; **Table 7.10**). Demographically, a greater proportion of the disarticulated bones are adult (n=13, sub-adults n=2); seven bones could be sexed, of which all are male. Three occurrences have pathological indicators; one shows evidence of joint disease. Another disarticulated bone has signs of metabolic and neoplastic disease, while the third has evidence of dental and congenital disease. One of the disarticulated remains has a traumatic indicator that is a

Table 7. 10 Frequency of disarticulated bones' elements and sides

Element	Right	Left
Clavicle	1	0
Femur	0	1
Tibia	2	1
Fibula	1	1

peri-mortem cut mark on the bone. All of the disarticulated bones have associated material, eleven with multiple items. The highest occurring material is animal bone, which is present with all 15 disarticulated bones (**Figure 7.127**). Two disarticulated bones are associated with dog and deer bones, but the rest of the animal bones are from an unspecified species. Furthermore, two of the disarticulated bones are associated with the structure (Structure 2584) and lie outside the building in a pit near the entrance.

Cremations (n=5)

Many of the cremations date to the Late Bronze Age (n=3, Early/Middle Iron Age n=1 and Late Iron Age n=1) and all are from pit contexts. All five of the cremations are single deposits, and most are primary insertions (n=3; the other two may be primary burials or redeposited bone). The five cremations' weights average 471.2g and one was

in an urn. Most are adults (n=4, one older sub-adult), and only two are sexed, one being a male and the other a female. None of the cremations possesses pathological or traumatic indicators.

Summary

The burial evidence from White Horse shows different burial treatments throughout its occupational history. In addition, the burial evidence conforms to the change of practice seen across southern Britain in the Iron Age. At White Horse there are Late Bronze Age cremations followed by disarticulated bones and inhumations in the Early/Middle Iron Age then cremations again in the Late Iron Age. Unfortunately, the sample size is too small to allow further investigation or statistical analysis of this changing burial pattern.

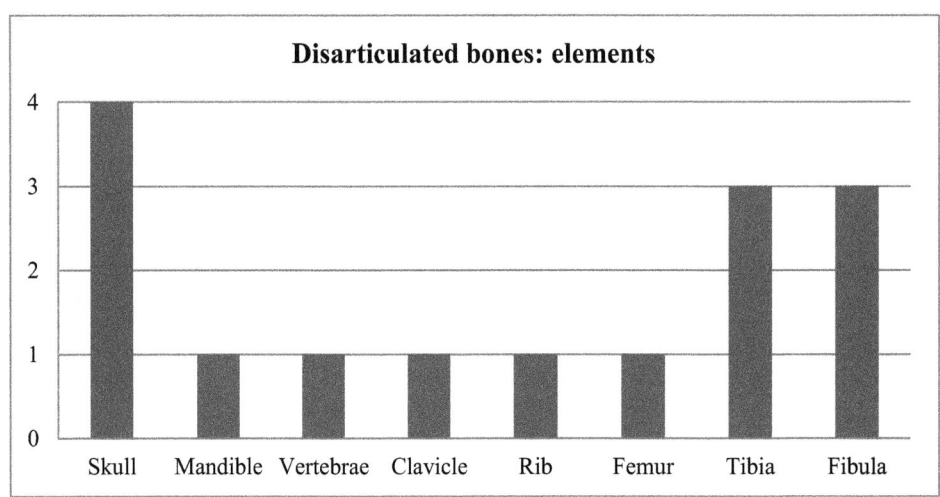

Figure 7. 126 Frequency of disarticulated bones' elements

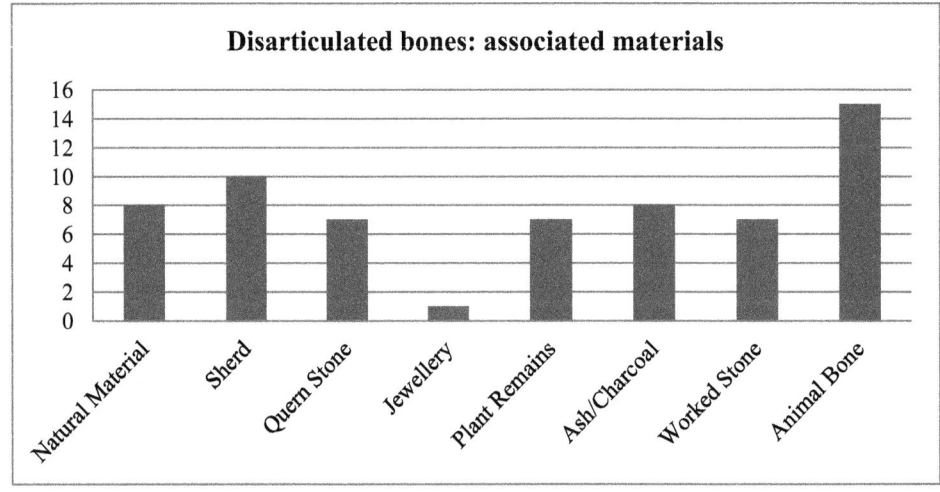

Figure 7. 127 Frequency of disarticulated bones' associated materials

Beechbrook Wood (TQ 9752 4660)

The multi-phase site of Beechbrook Wood near Hothfield (Kent) lies on the Folkestone Beds, Atherfield Clays and Lower Greensand (Brady 2006a, 1, **Figure 7. 128**). Oxford Archaeological Unit (2000-2001) and the Museum of London (1997-1998) carried out excavations and watching briefs that was part of a larger archaeological project in advance of the construction of the Channel Tunnel Rail Link (Brady. 2006a, 1). The investigations reveal activity at Beechbrook Wood dating from the Mesolithic to the Roman period (Brady 2006a). Evidence from the Late Bronze Age and Early Iron Age consists largely of field systems, thought to represent possibly agricultural intensification (Brady 2006a, 24; **Figure 7.129**). In the Middle Iron Age, a double-ditched

farmstead was constructed at the site and, by the Late Iron Age, a metalworking area was established to the north of the Middle Iron Age enclosure (Brady 2006a, 31; **Figures 5.131-32**). In addition, a small Late Iron Age cremation cemetery was placed just outside the Middle Iron Age enclosure and potentially '...is characteristic of a marking or closing deposit that may have marked the end of the original use of the enclosure (as a settlement/farmstead)' (Brady 2006a, 36; **Figure 7.130**). A total of 20 cremations, dating from the Late Bronze Age to the Late Iron Age, were recovered from 19 contexts (one of the contexts contains two cremation occurrences, each in a different layer from the other) and associated with four archaeological features. Annesofie Witkin (2006a) conducted the osteological analysis of the cremated remains[28].

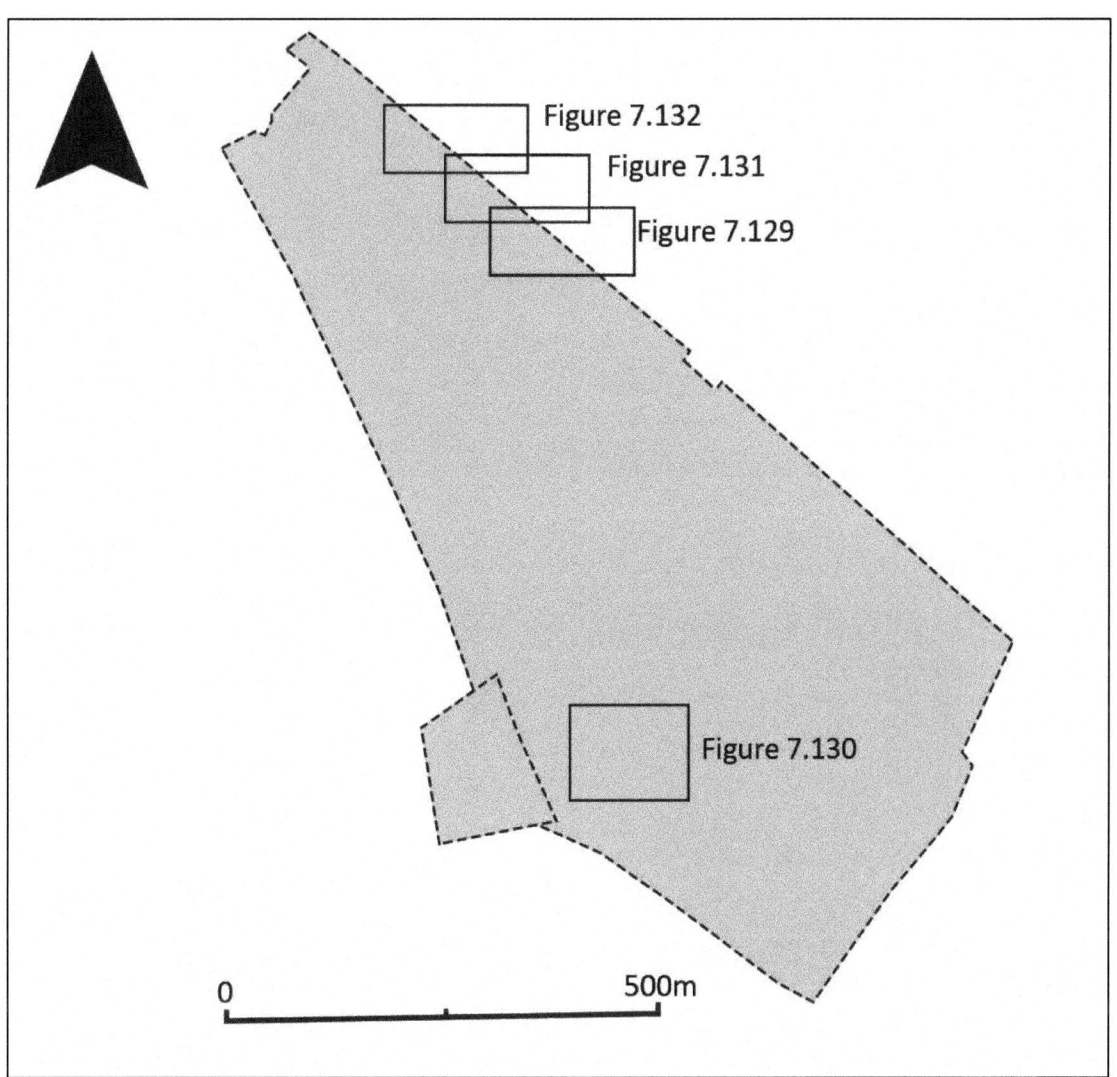

Figure 7. 128 General site plan of Beechbrook Wood (after: Oxford Wessex Archaeology Joint Venture and HS 1 LTD, fig. 4b; with permission)

---

[28] Locations of two human remains deposits are unknown.

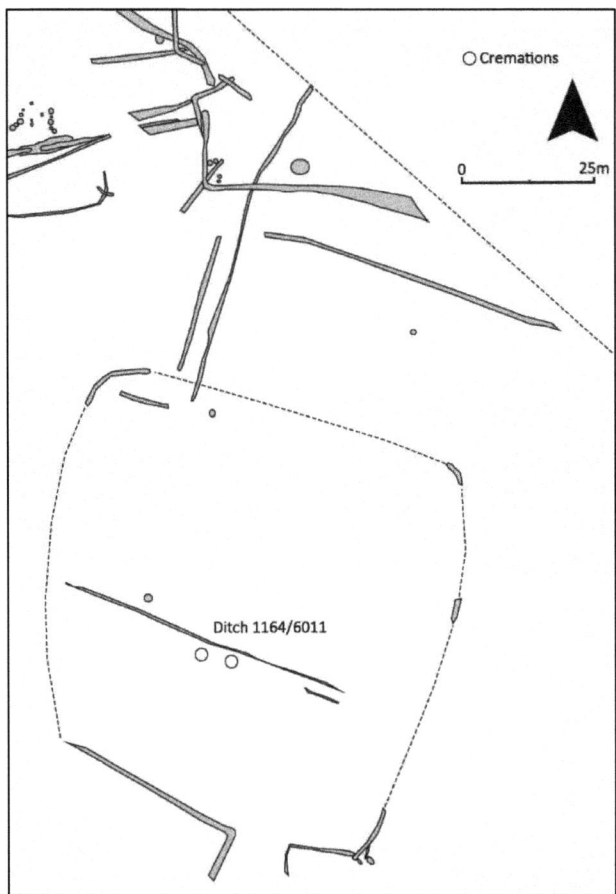

Figure 7. 129 Plan of Ditch 1164/6011 with Late Bronze Age human remains deposits (after: Oxford Wessex Archaeology Joint Venture and HS 1 LTD, fig. 7; with permission)

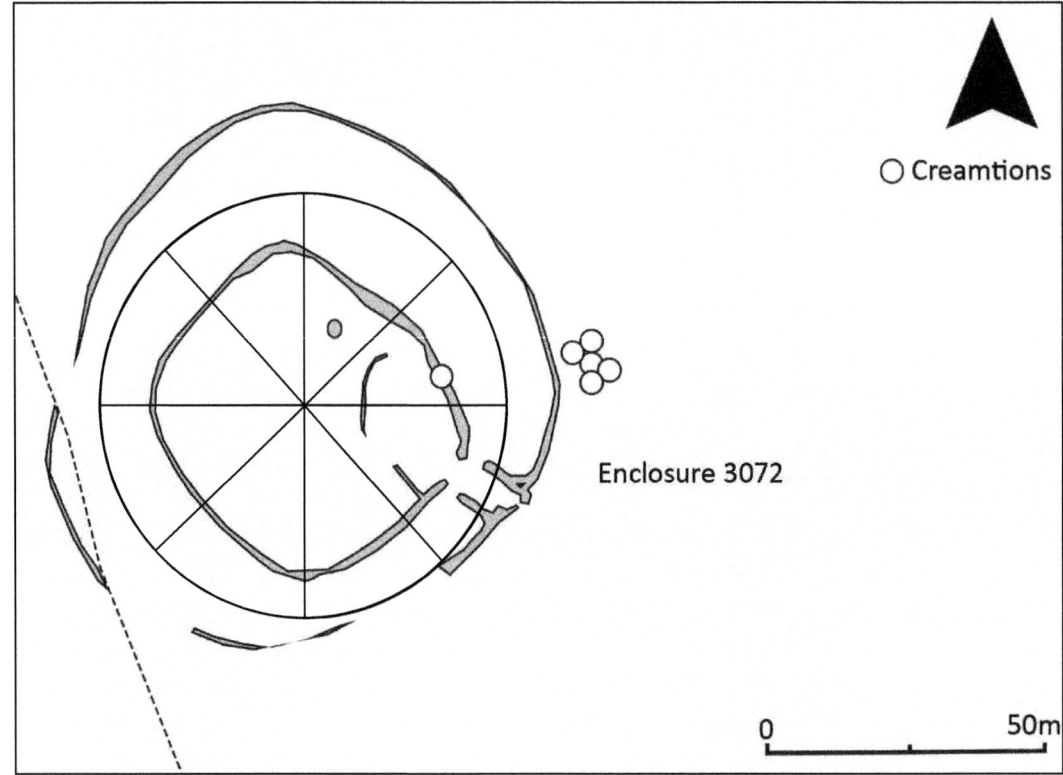

Figure 7. 130 Plan of Middle Iron Age Enclosure 3072 (with cardinal location) with associated human remains deposits (after: Oxford Wessex Archaeology Joint Venture and HS 1 LTD, fig. 11; with permission)

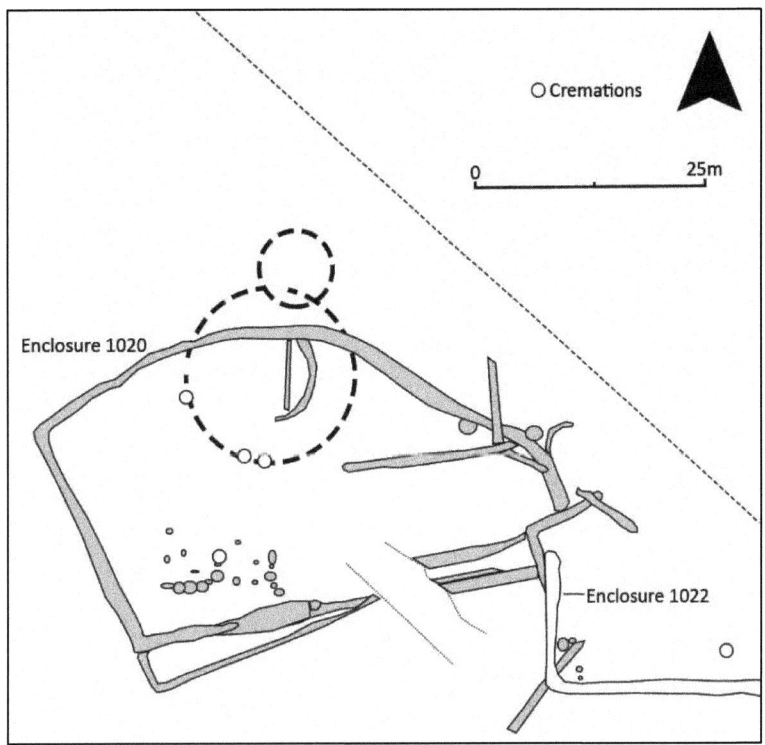

Figure 7. 131 Plan of Enclosure 1020 and 1022 indicating human remains deposits (human remains deposit was found in enclosure ditch 1022 but exact location is unknown) (after: Oxford Wessex Archaeology Joint Venture and HS 1 LTD, fig. 6; with permission)

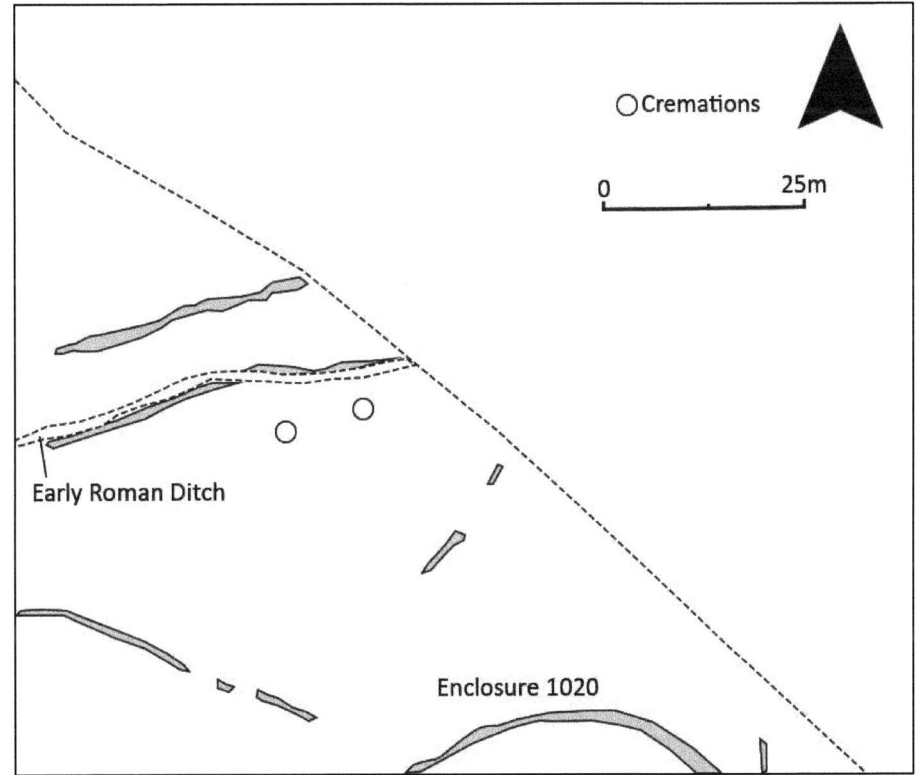

Figure 7. 132 Plan of archaeological features north of Enclosure 1020 indicating human remains deposits (after: Oxford Wessex Archaeology Joint Venture and HS 1 LTD, fig. 12; with permission)

The sample size from Beechbrook Wood allowed only limited analyses so this section will provide a synopsis of the burial characteristics. All cremations from Beechbrook Wood, except two, are associated with four archaeological features. One of the features is a ditch within a Late Bronze Age field system, with two cremation deposits along the side of the boundary (Brady 2006a, 24; Witkin 2006a, 4, 6). Two features are rectangular enclosures dating to the Late Iron Age and both were iron-working areas (Brady 2006a, 33-35). The last archaeological feature is also a rectangular enclosure that is the remains of a Middle Iron Age farmstead with its entrance opening to the east (Brady 2006a, 30). A small, Late Iron Age cremation cemetery lies just outside of the entrance of the Middle Iron Age enclosure and is thought to signify the end of the structure's use (Brady 2006a, 36), as discussed above.

All the contexts contain cremation occurrences, with many of the contexts dating to the Late Iron Age (n=16; **Figure 7.133**), and ditches are the most favoured contexts (n=7; **Figure 7.134**). Eighteen cremations have weights averaging 35.0g, and most are not in urns (n=15, urned n=5). None of the cremations could be sexed but five could be aged, all of them are adults. Pathological or traumatic indicators are not present on any of the

cremated bone. Thirteen cremations have associated material, six with multiple types of material; the most frequent is ash/charcoal from related pyre debris (n= 6; **Figure 7.135**). None of the statistical tests on the cremations returned significant results.

Although Beechbrook Wood provided no statistical results for burial characteristics, it is an example of cremation continuing through the Late Bronze Age to the Late Iron Age. In the Late Bronze Age there are two small cremation deposits (<1g and 52g) associated with a land division. In the Middle Iron Age, there is a cremation deposit within the inner ditch of the contemporary farmstead, possibly reinforcing the enclosure's boundary. Furthermore, there is a Late Iron Age cremation cemetery outside the farmstead's entrance possibly marking the abandonment of the building. The other cremation deposits are set near iron-working areas yet the contextual evidence suggests that these were not deliberate inclusions (Brady 2006a, 35). In all, most of the cremation deposits at Beechbrook Wood are associated with areas important to the community. Thus, it appears that the community at Beechbrook Wood used human remains to reinforce spatial boundaries and signify transitional moments and space.

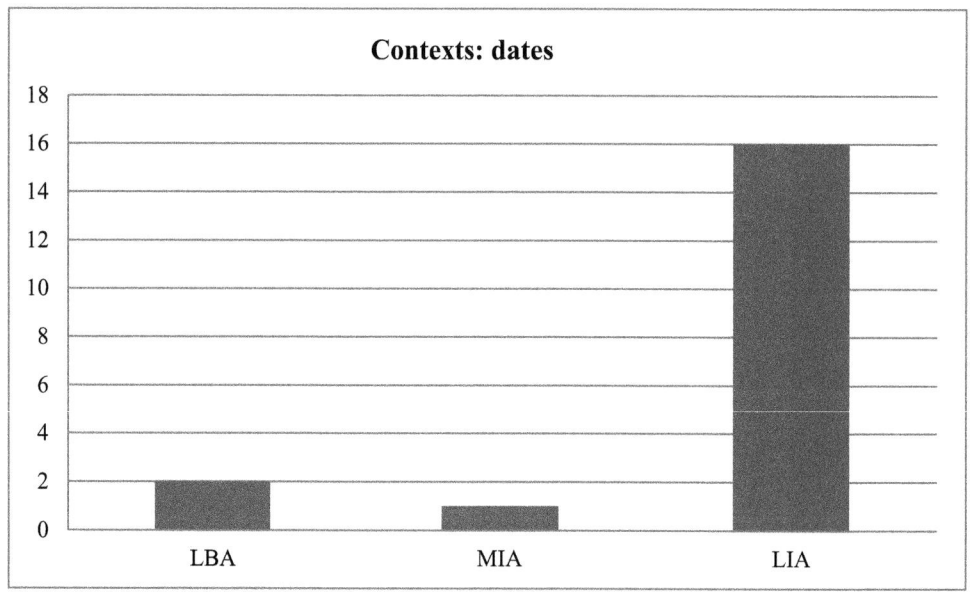

Figure 7. 133 Frequency of contexts' date

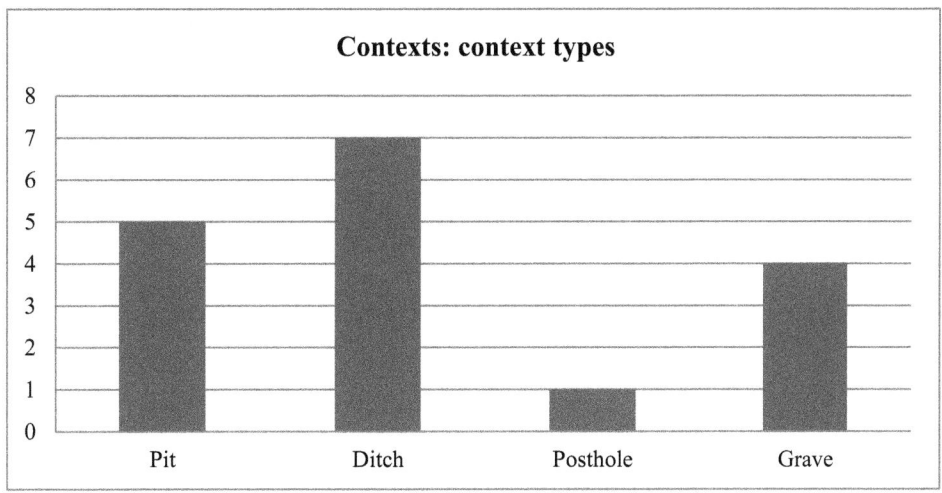

Figure 7. 134 Frequency of context types

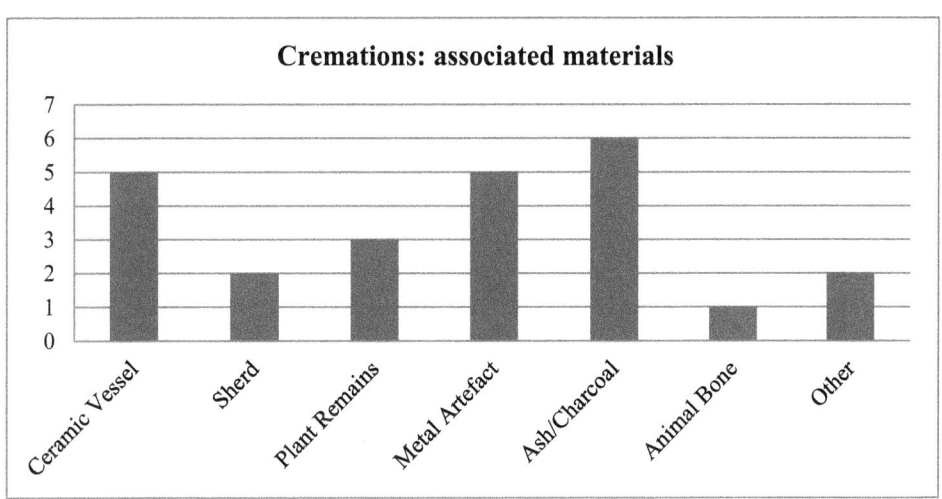

Figure 7. 135 Frequency of cremations' associated materials

Suddern Farm (SU 280 377)

Lying on a low spur of chalk in Middle Wallop (Hampshire) is the multi-enclosed settlement site of Suddern Farm (Cunliffe and Poole 2000e, 11, **Figure 7. 136-37**). The site's ditched enclosures encircle roughly 2.2 ha, with an entrance at the northwest end and another possible entry on the south side. Suddern Farm is also associated with a very complex system of prehistoric linear ditches (Cunliffe and Poole 2000e, 12). The site saw two phases of occupation, the first beginning in the Early Iron Age and lasting until the beginning of the Middle Iron Age then, after a brief hiatus, it was reoccupied in the Late Iron Age until the Roman period. Excavations were undertaken in 1991 and 1996 as part of the Danebury Environs Programme. The inhabitants of Suddern Farm, in both occupational phases, practiced a mixed-farming regime, consisting primarily of sheep rearing and cultivation of spelt-wheat and six-row barley

(Cunliffe and Poole 2000e, 12). A few disarticulated remains were uncovered within the interior of the settlement; however, on the outskirts of the site's boundaries, an Early/Middle Iron Age cemetery was discovered (Cunliffe and Poole 2000e, 143). Skeletal material from the cemetery represents about 60 individuals (31 adults, nine children, and 20 infants) and it is estimated that upwards of 500 individuals were interred at Suddern Farm (Cunliffe and Poole 2000e, 201). The cemetery lies within a prehistoric quarry complex (F429), where the burials cut into the pre-existing quarry holes (Book 59 A1996.65, 8 [archives]). One hundred and eighty-six human remains occurrences (42 inhumations, 138 disarticulated bones and six articulated limbs) were recovered from 24 contexts at Suddern Farm[29]. Bari Hooper (2000e) prepared the osteological report.

---

[29] Four human remains deposits could not be specifically located except to broadly within the southwest cemetery.

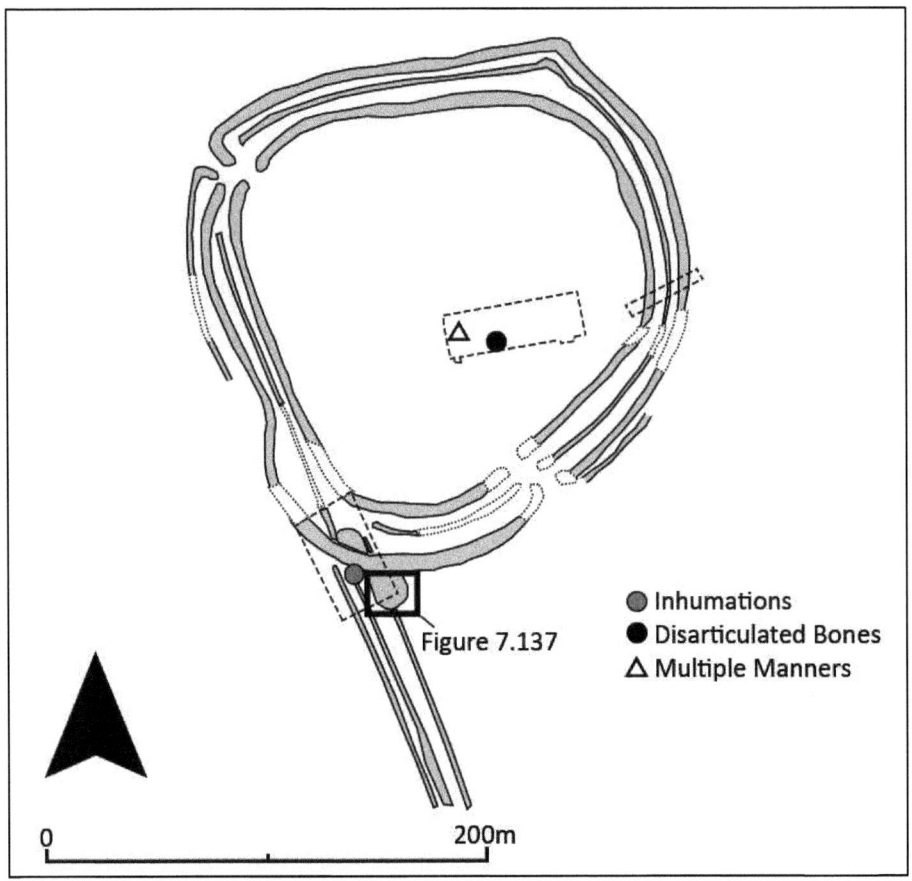

Figure 7. 136 Site plan of Suddern Farm indicating human remains deposits (after Cunliffe and Poole 2000e, 14); with permission

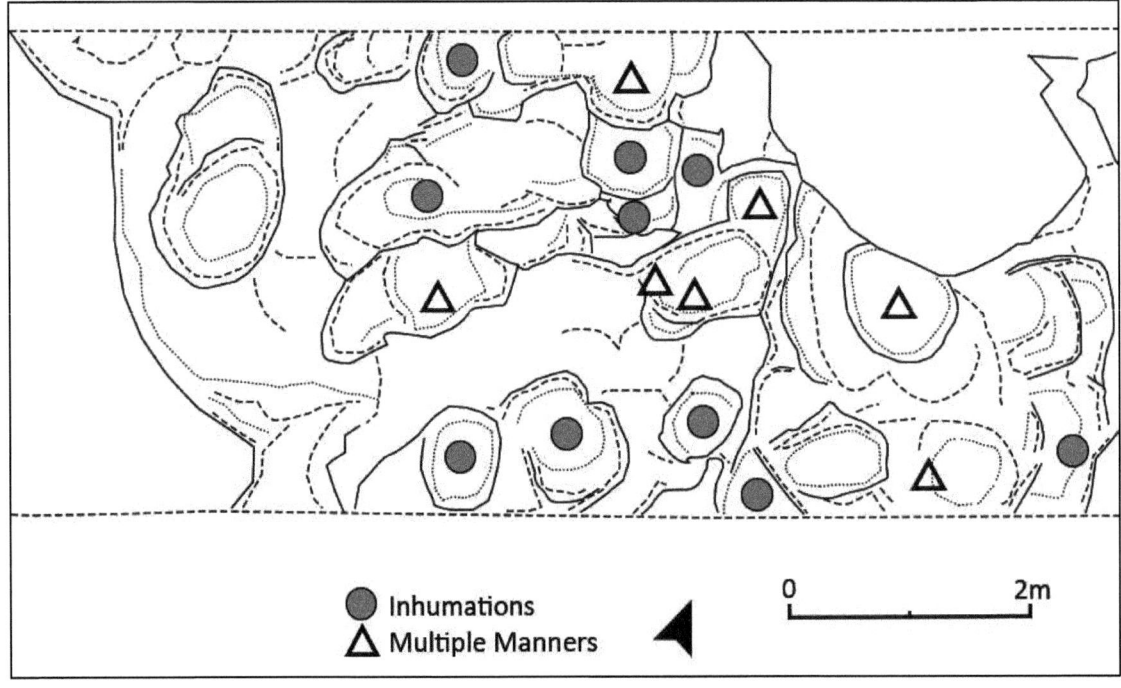

Figure 7. 137 Plan showing the cemetery, indicating human remains deposits (after Cunliffe and Poole 2000e, 152); with permission

Analysis of contexts (n=24)

The contexts most frequently date to the Early/Middle Iron Age (n=23, Late Iron Age n=1), and are graves (n=17, pits n=3, 'other' n=3, and one unknown). Many of the contexts contain only inhumations (n=13; **Figure 7.138**) or have multiple human remains with them (n=14, single deposits n=9 and one unknown). Twenty-two of the contexts are within the cemetery just outside the southwest area of the site and adjacent to the settlement boundary. The remaining two contexts are within the interior of the site (see **Figure 7.136**).

Analysis of manner of disposal (n=186)

A chi-square test for independence indicated a significant relationship between the manner of disposal and age (χ^2=4.017, p=0.045). By examining the breakdown between age groups and manner of disposal, it appears that there is a slight distinction between younger sub-adults and older sub-adult and adults (see **Figures 7.139-140**).

It is clear that the high count of adult disarticulated bone has influenced the significant results for all the statistical tests. However, the figures depict a potential age difference relating to types of disposal, with infants typically inhumed and adults deposited as disarticulated bones. The results, in particular the high number of infant inhumations over disarticulated infant bones, corresponds with the interpretation that, during the final use for the cemetery, only infants were being interred and thus did not suffer much disturbance from later use of the cemetery area (Cunliffe and Poole 2000e, 168). The implications of this observation will be discussed further in this site's summary.

Inhumations (n=42)

There are 42 inhumations from Suddern Farm, all of which date to the Early/Middle Iron Age except for one

that belongs to the Late Iron Age. Most inhumations are in graves (n=33, pit n=3 and 'other' n=6) and are found with other occurrences (n=32, single deposits n=10). Many inhumations are incomplete (n=26, complete n=16), mainly crouched (n=9; **Figure 7.141**) and resting on their left sides (n=12; **Table 7.11**). North is the most frequent direction for orientations (n=9; **Figure 7.142**).

Demographically, sub-adults are the most frequent (n=22, adult n=20; **Figure 7.143**), and males are most common (n=15, females n=5). Nineteen inhumations have pathological indicators, nine with multiple examples, and most frequent is joint disease (n=15, dental disease n=8 and haematological disease n=1). Eleven inhumations have traumatic indicators, three with multiple trauma, and the most common are fractures (n=5; **Figure 7.144**), with most trauma occurring pre-mortem.

A Fisher's Exact Probability test indicated a significant relationship between single/multiple deposition and 'condition of skeleton' variables (n=42, p=0.027). As **Figure 7.145** illustrates, more incomplete inhumations occur when they are associated with other occurrences (such as other inhumations and disarticulated bones), which may be result of continuous disturbance of inhumations. This continuous disturbance may be due to the community's reusing of graves and collecting of bones as argued by Sharples (2010, 277).

Articulated bones (n=6)

All the articulated bones date to the Early/Middle Iron Age and all are associated with other occurrences. Many of articulated bones are from lower limbs (n=4, upper limb n=1, and torso n=1), commonly from the right side of the body (a right upper and lower limb and one left lower limb). Each of the articulated bones is from the adult age group and is from the cemetery.

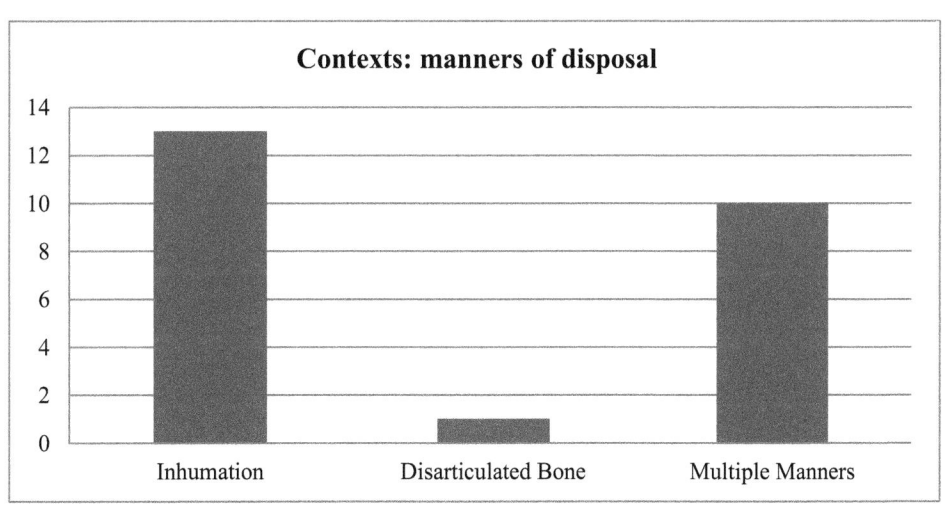

Figure 7. 138 Frequency of contexts according to manner of disposal

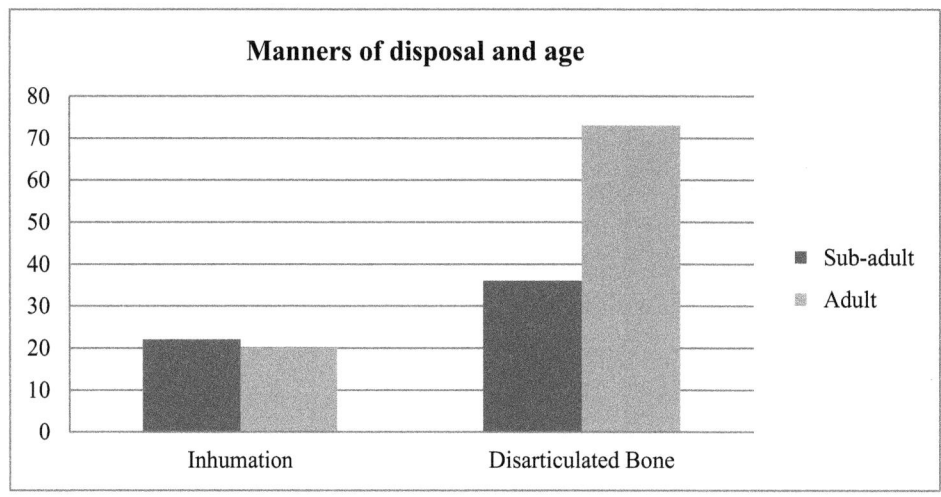

Figure 7. 139 Frequency of occurrences according to age and manner of disposal

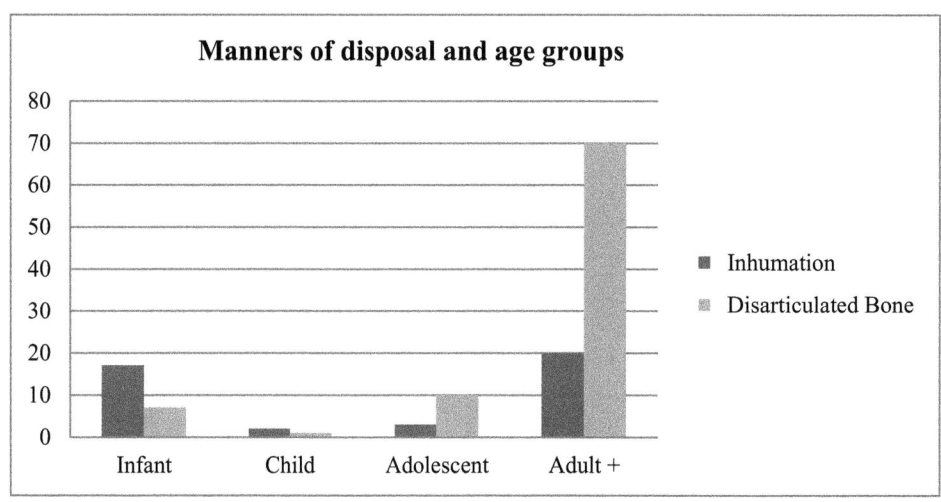

Figure 7. 140 Frequency of occurrences according to age and manner of disposal

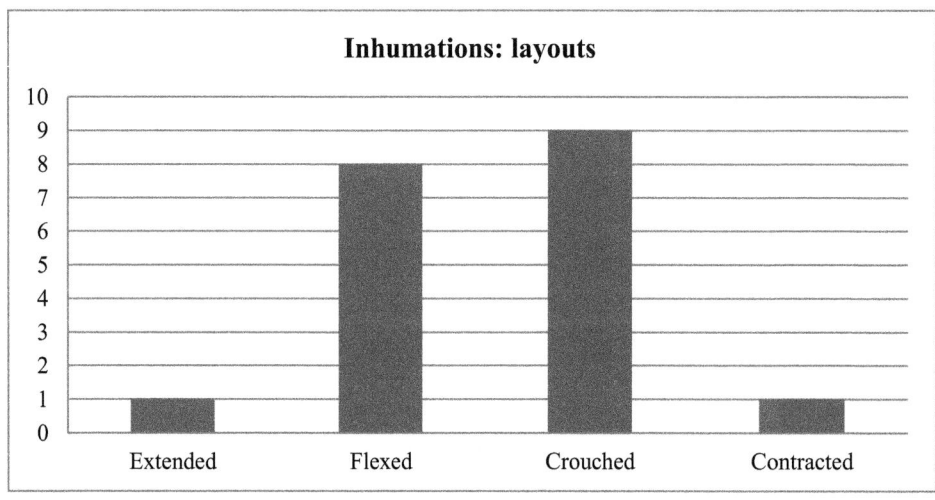

Figure 7. 141 Frequency of inhumations' layouts

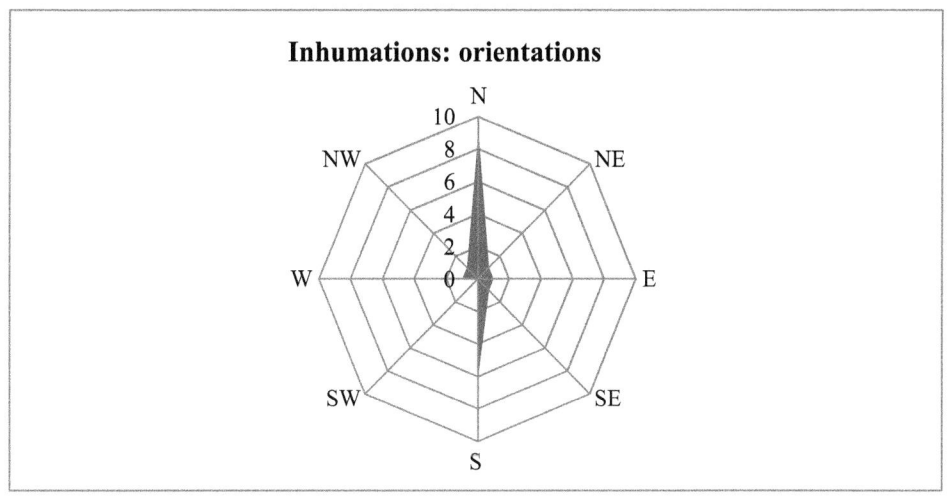

Figure 7. 142 Frequency of inhumations' orientations

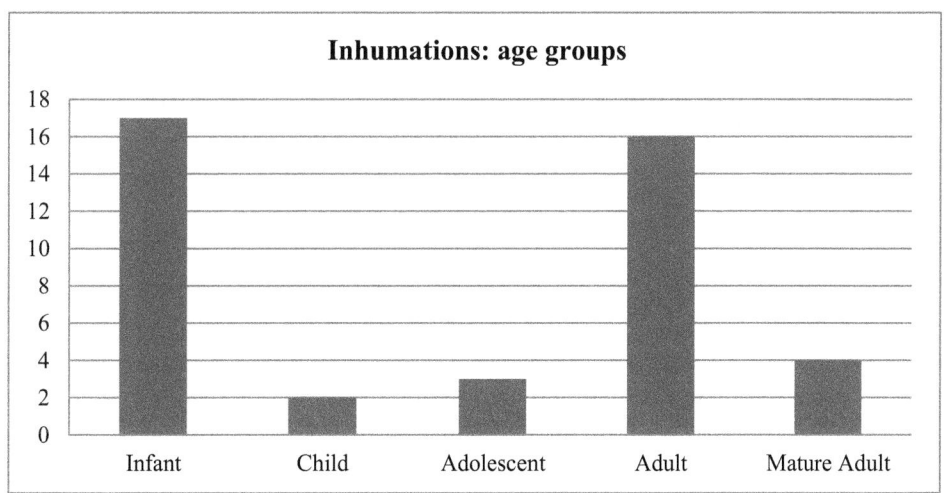

Figure 7. 143 Frequency of inhumations' age

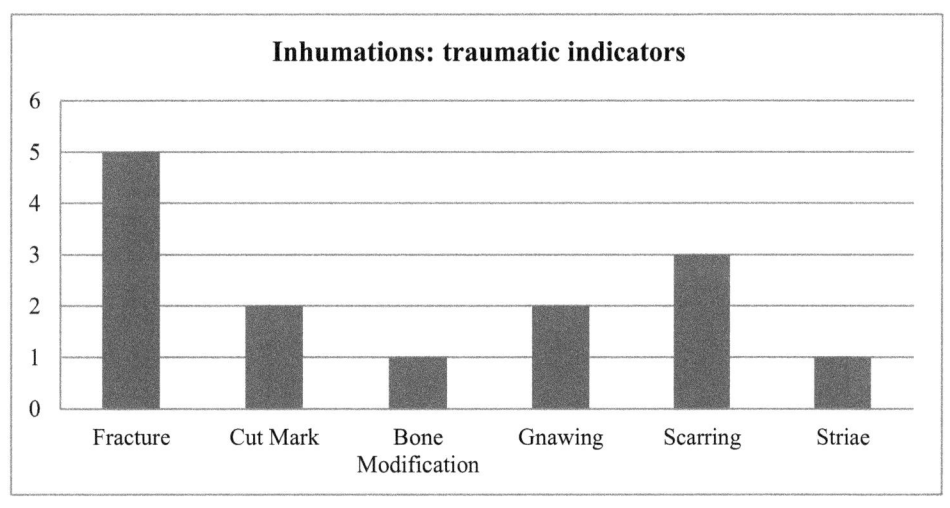

Figure 7. 144 Frequency of inhumations' trauma

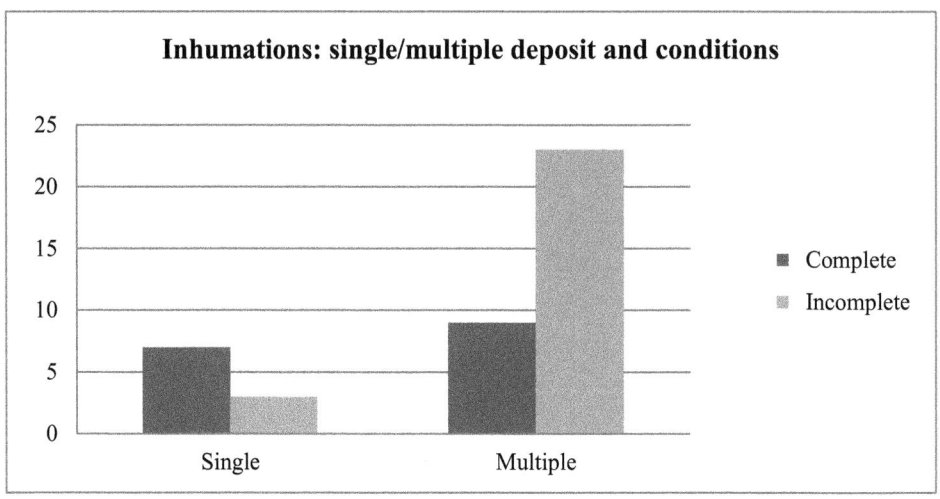

Figure 7. 145 Frequency of inhumations according to conditions and single/multiple deposits

Table 7. 11 Frequency of inhumations' positions

Left Side	12
Right Side	4
Supine	3
Prone	1

Disarticulated bones (n=138)

Almost all of the disarticulated bones from Suddern Farm date to the Early/Middle Iron Age (n=135, Late Iron Age n=3), and are commonly within graves and 'other' contexts (both n=64, pits n=6). A greater proportion are associated with other inhumations, articulated bones, and disarticulated remains (n=135, single deposits n=3). There is a relatively even representation of all the elements, although the most frequent are the femur and vertebrae (n=13; **Figure 7.146**). Each side of the body is evenly represented, though most of the elements are from the left side of the body (n=50, right n=47; **Figure 7.147**). Demographically, adults are the most commonly represented (n=73, sub-adult n=36) and, of the six disarticulated bones which could be sexed, most are male (n=4, female n=2). Nine disarticulated bones have pathological indicators, with the most frequent being joint disease (**Table 7.12**). Three have single traumatic indicators signifying a fracture, animal gnawing and 'other' (unknown cause of trauma). In addition, three disarticulated bones have multiple associated material, all being animal bone and quern stones. Most of the disarticulated bone is within the cemetery area (that is on the exterior of the settlement site in the south-to-southwest area adjacent to the settlement's boundary). None of the statistical test produced any valid significant results.

Table 7. 12 Frequency of disarticulated bones' pathologies

Dental Disease	1
Joint Disease	5
Infectious Disease	1
Haematological Disease	1
Other	1

Summary

An interesting aspect of the burial evidence from Suddern Farm is the cemetery area just outside the settlement's enclosure that is atypical for the Early and Middle Iron Age. Sharples (2010, 277) argues that the burial evidence from Suddern Farm is the result of grave reuse and the community's intentional reopening of graves to collect bones for later deposition. This activity would have symbolised the community's relationship and continuous interaction with their ancestors, and the burial evidence supports this claim. This study's analysis of Suddern Farm's human remains supports Sharples' argument. For example, there is equal representation of elements in the cemetery, suggesting that they are disturbed burials with no particular selection of bones. Additionally, the 'manner of disposal' analysis indicates that inhumations are typically infants and represent the final phase of the cemetery (Cunliffe and Poole 2000e, 168), which might symbolise closing off the community's access to its ancestors by interment of the lost generation.

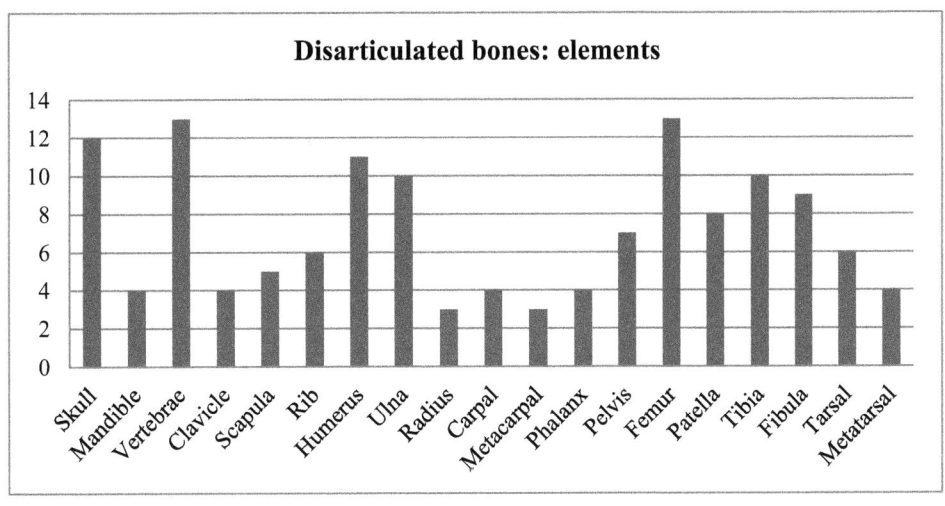

Figure 7. 146 Frequency of disarticulated bones' elements

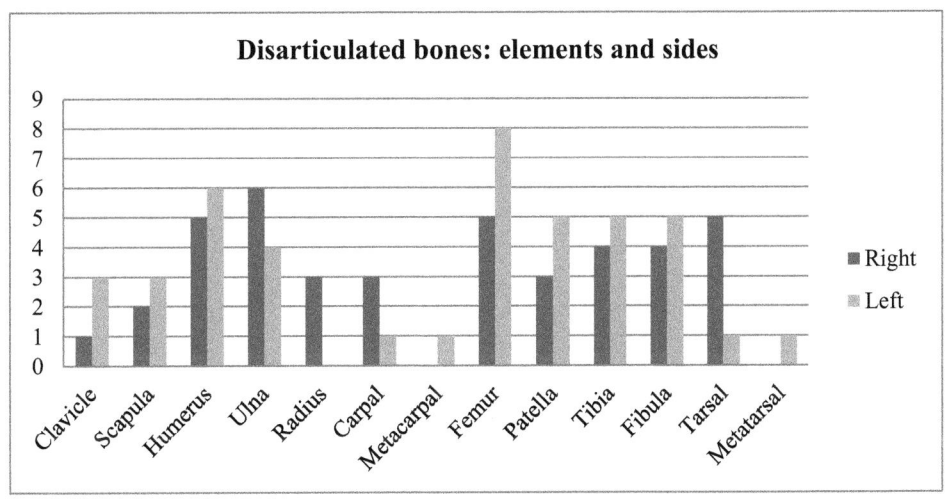

Figure 7. 147 Frequency of disarticulated bones' elements and sides

Maiden Castle (SY 66 88)

Maiden Castle is an Iron Age multivallate hillfort outside Dorchester (Dorset), underlain by Upper Chalk (Sharples 1991b, 12, **Figures 148-49**). Two major excavations have been carried out at the site. The first excavation was undertaken by R.E.M. Wheeler (1943), between 1934 and 1937, and the second under the supervision of Niall Sharples (1991b) for English Heritage. Maiden Castles saw multiple phases of construction throughout prehistory. In the Early Iron Age, the first single enclosure was constructed, with entrances to the west and east, and enclosed 6.47 hectares (Sharples 1991b, 57-58). Later, modifications to the enclosure with multiple ditches and

banks extended the settlement's boundaries to enclose 18.62 ha (Wheeler 1943, 36). Human remains were recovered from both Wheeler's and Sharples' excavations at Maiden Castle and most notable is the 'war cemetery' uncovered in the settlement's eastern entrance during Wheeler's investigation (Wheeler 1943, 46). From both Wheeler's (1943) and Sharples' (1991b; Archives) excavations, a total of 100 human remains occurrences, including 78 inhumations and 22 disarticulated bones, from 81 contexts were recovered from Maiden Castle. G.M. Morart and Christopher Goodman performed the osteological analysis for Wheeler's excavation, and Janet Henderson (1991) for Sharples' excavation. Rebecca Redfern (2008a; 2008b; 2009) conducted a reassessment of the skeletal material from Sharples' excavations.

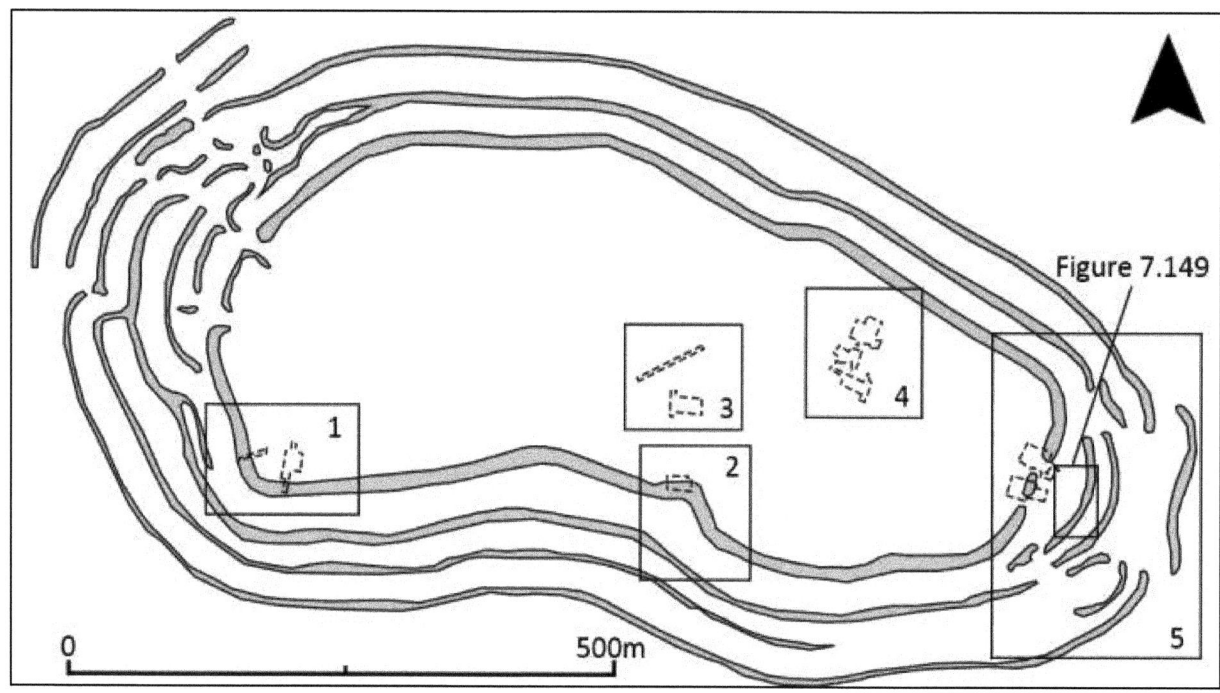

Figure 7. 148 Site plan of Maiden Castle indicating areas of human remains deposits (after Sharples 1991b, 54); ©Wessex Archaeology, with permission

Table 7. 13 List of areas and numbers of human remains deposits

Area number	Number of human remains deposits
1	3 Inhumations, 12 disarticulated bones, and 1 multiple manners
2	1 Inhumation and 1 disarticulated bone
3	3 Inhumations and 2 disarticulated bones
4	4 Inhumations and 2 disarticulated bones
5	51 Inhumations and 1 multiple manners

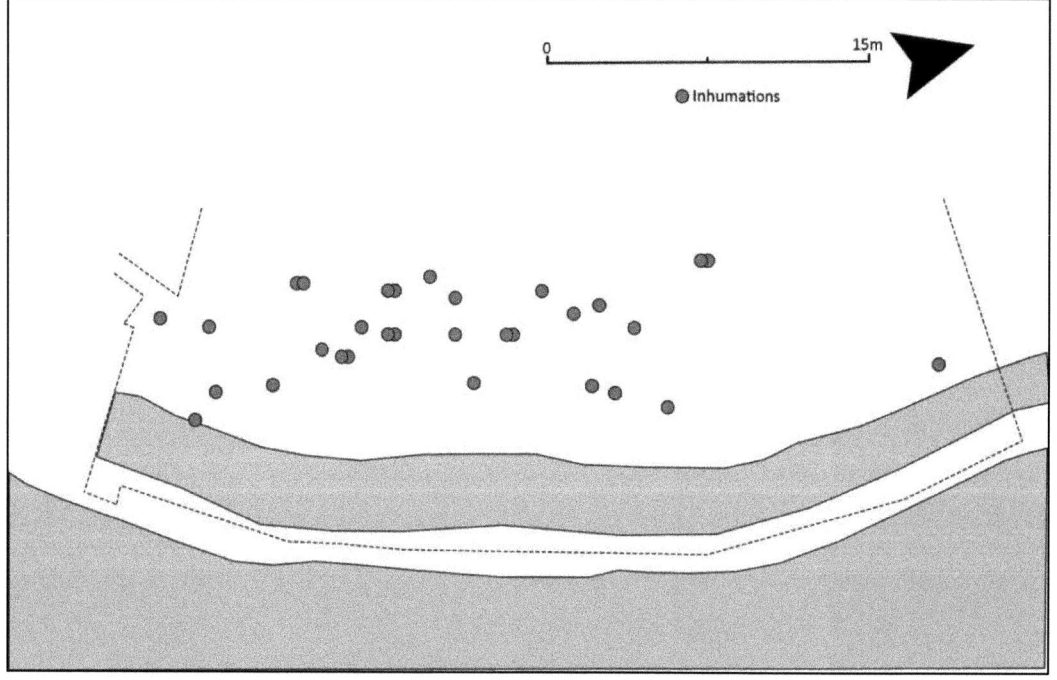

Figure 7. 149 Plan of the war cemetery, only depicting inhumations (after Wheeler 1943, Plate XVI); by the kind permission of the Society of Antiquaries of London

Analysis of contexts (n=81)

Half of the contexts with human remains occurrences date to the Late Iron Age (n=45; **Figure 7.150**), are graves (n=41; **Figure 7.151**), and contain mainly inhumations (n=62, disarticulated bones n=17, and multiple manners n=2). Single occurrences are the most frequent (n=64, multiple deposits n=12 and both single and multiple n=1). Many of the contexts with human remains are from the 'war cemetery'; thus, over half of the contexts lie along the perimeter of the site (n=54, interior n=27) and entrances are the most frequent architectural feature (n=50, boundary n=6).

Additionally, the war cemetery influenced strongly the statistical results from the context analysis. Three statistical test returned significant results. A chi-square test for independence indicated a significant relationship between context type and date (χ^2=49.822, p=0.000), context type and manner of disposal (χ^2=24.303, p=0.000) and manner of disposal and date (χ^2=29.544, p=0.000). The high count of Late Iron Age inhumations within graves, predominantly from the war cemetery by the eastern entrance, undoubtedly caused this significant outcome.

Inhumations (n=78)

Many of the inhumations are from the war cemetery and have similar burial characteristics discussed in the context analysis (see **Figures 7.152-3**). Over half of the inhumations are primary deposits (n=58, secondary deposits n=9) and are single occurrences (n=54, multiple

n=20). Many are complete (n=39, incomplete n=19), typically lying flexed (n=31; **Figure 7.154**) and resting on their right sides (n=28; **Figure 7.155**). Many are orientated towards the southeast (n=21; **Figure 7.156**). Demographically, over half of the inhumations are adults (n=54, sub-adult n=18), and most of these are males (n=33, females n=24). Five inhumations have a single pathological indicator, of these, three are of an unknown cause and the other two inhumations have signs of dental disease. Twenty-two inhumations have traumatic indicators,[30] five with multiple trauma, and the most common being cut marks (n=10; **Figure 7.157**). Most trauma occurred either peri- or post-mortem. Forty-four inhumations have associated materials, 17 with multiple materials, and most frequent are ceramic vessels (n=16; **Figure 7.158**).

Similar to the context analysis, the statistically significant results for inhumations is undoubtedly due to the high count of inhumations within the war cemetery. These include the following significant relationships:

- age and date (Fisher's Exact Probability test, n= 66, p=0.001)
- age and location (Fisher's Exact Probability Test, n=72, p=0.001)
- sex and date (Fisher's Exact Probability test, n=56, p=0.030)
- context type and date (Fisher Exact Probability test, n=63, p=0.000)
- context type and layout (Fisher's Exact Probability test, n=49, p=0.048)
- context type and age (Fisher Exact Probability test, n=66, p=0.000)

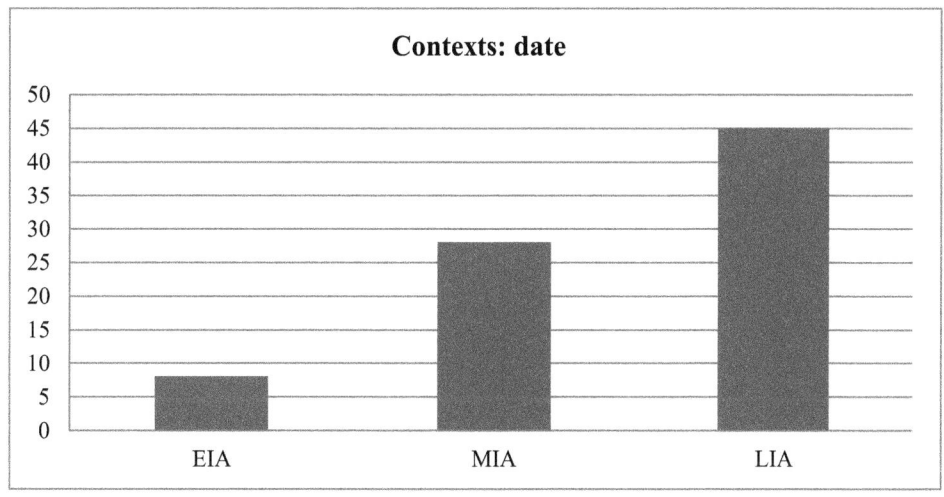

Figure 7. 150 Frequency of contexts according to date

---

[30] The 'other' category includes traumatic indicators of an unknown cause.

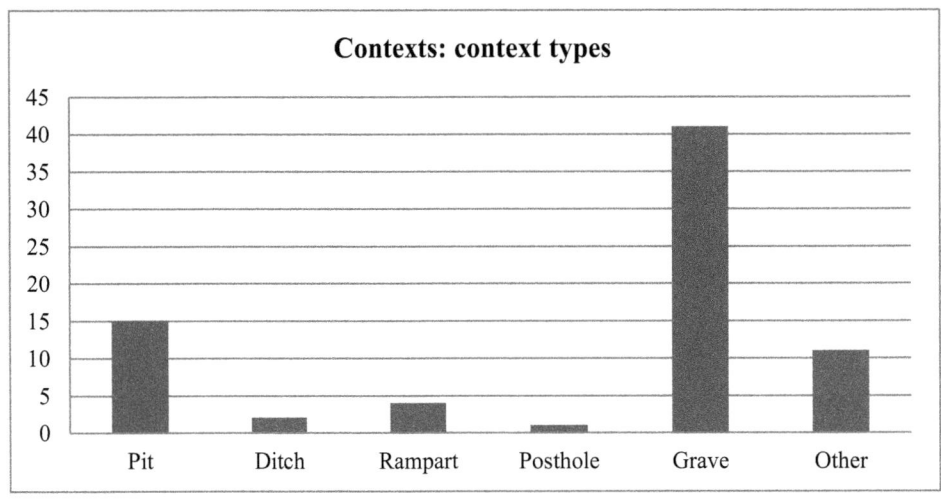

Figure 7. 151 Frequency of context types

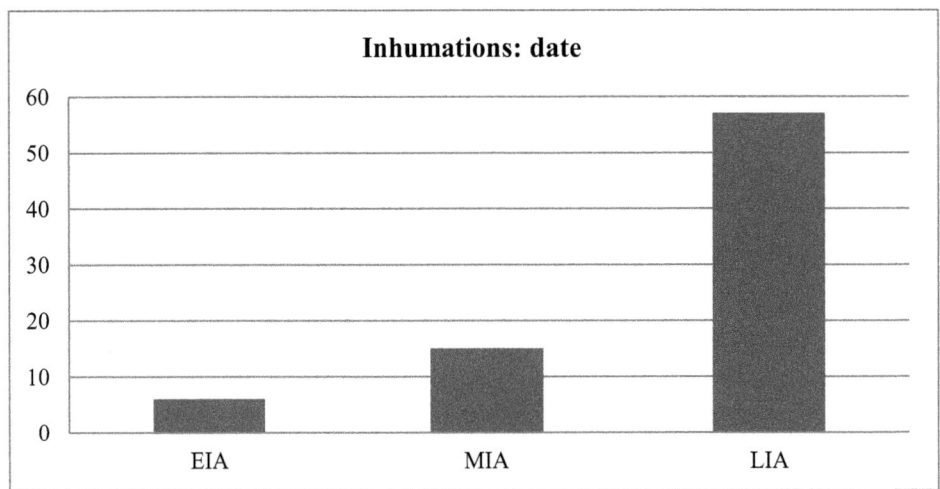

Figure 7. 152 Frequency of inhumations' date

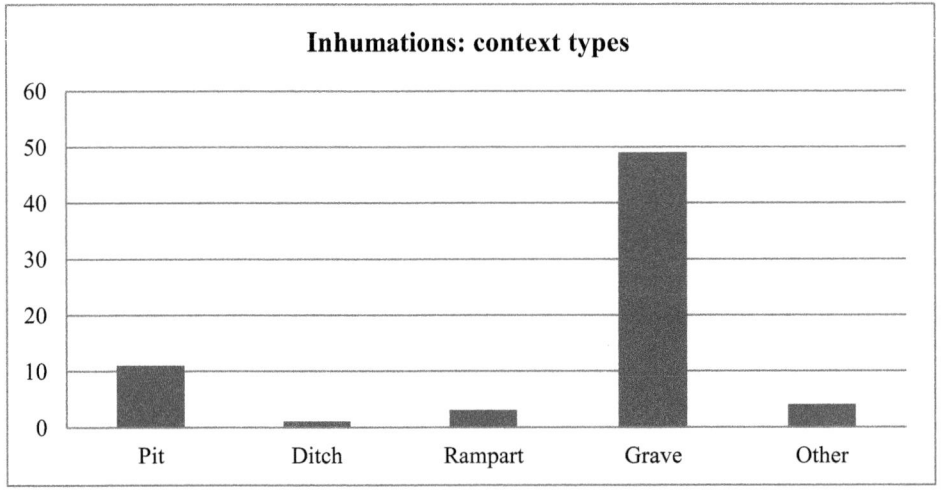

Figure 7. 153 Frequency of inhumations' context types

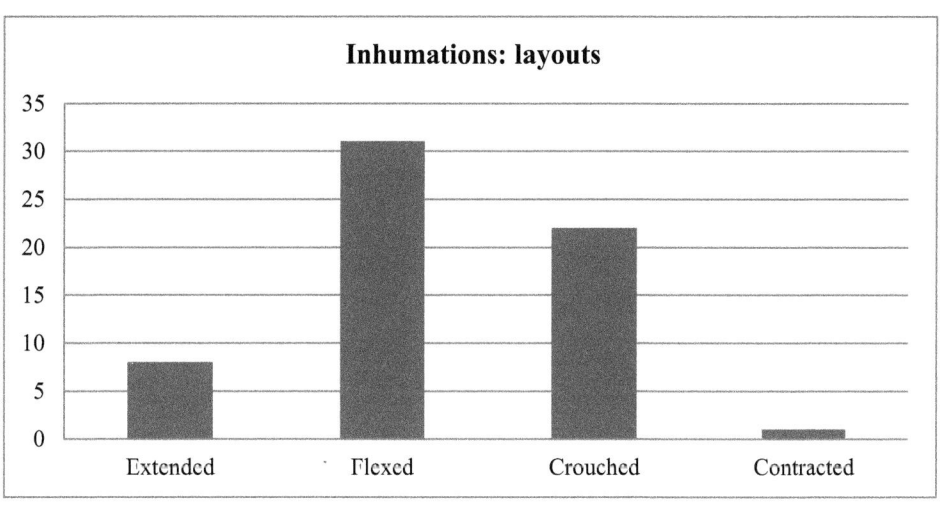

Figure 7. 154 Frequency of inhumations' layouts

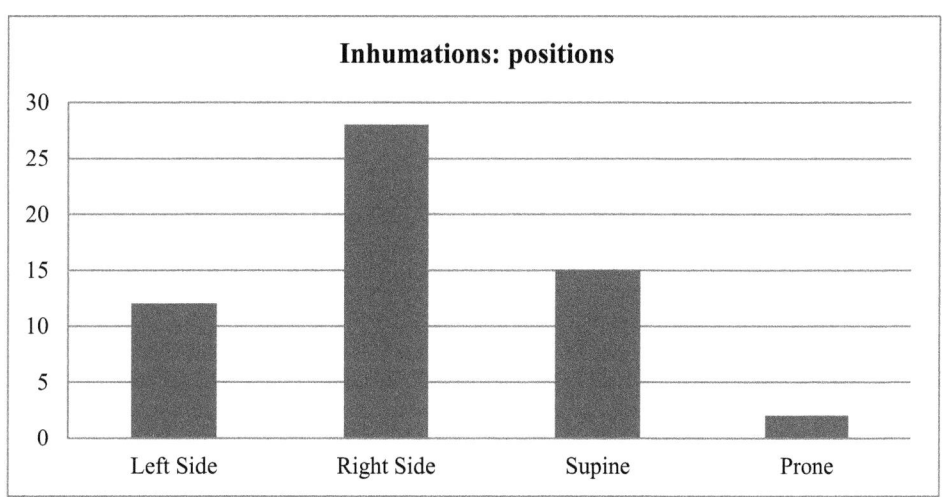

Figure 7. 155 Frequency of inhumations' positions

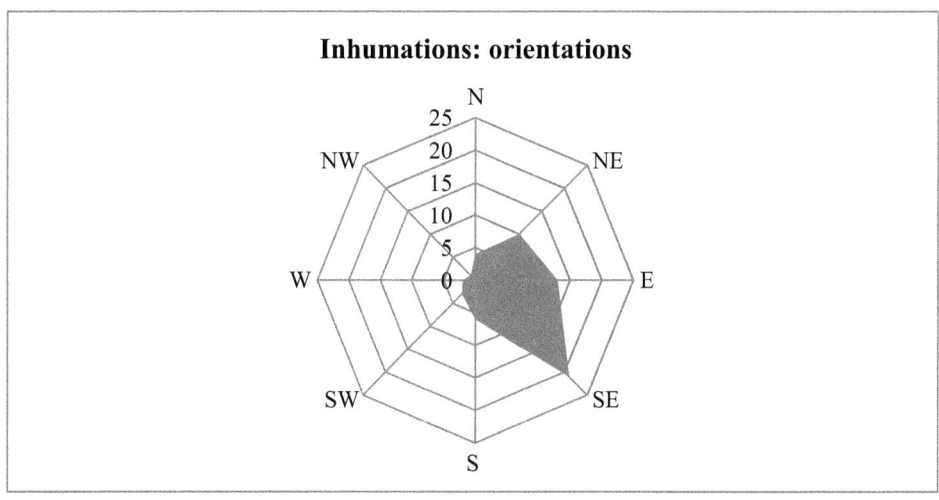

Figure 7. 156 Frequency of inhumations' orientations

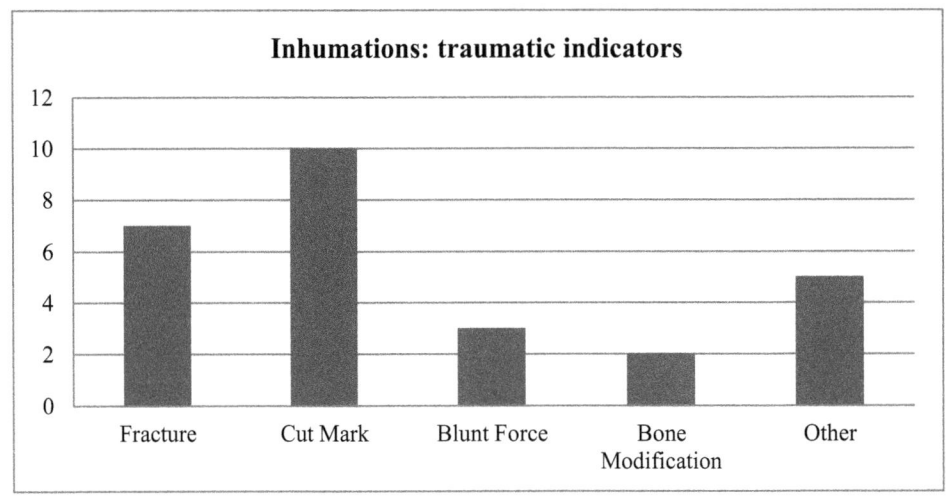

Figure 7. 157 Frequency of inhumations' trauma

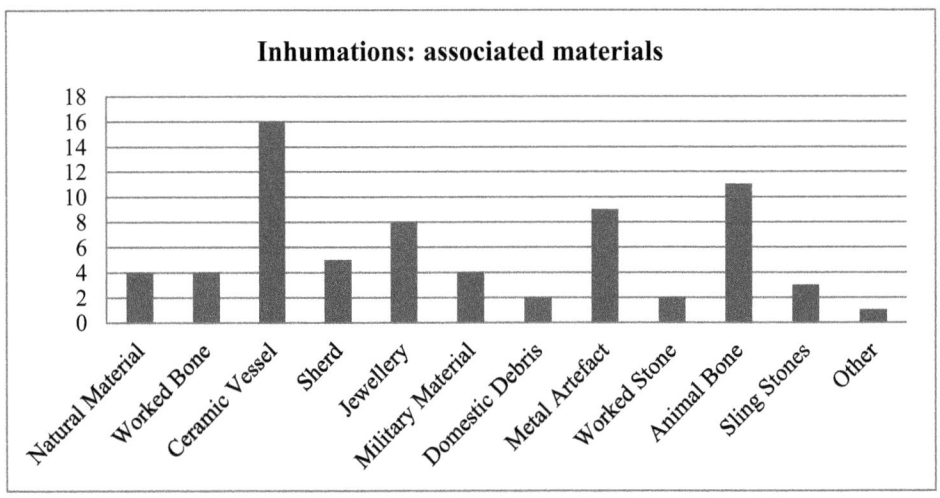

Figure 7. 158 Frequency of inhumations' associated materials

Disarticulated bones (n=22)

Many of the disarticulated bones date to the Middle Iron Age (n=20, Early Iron Age n=2), and are frequently in pits or 'other' contexts (both n=9; **Figure 7.159**). Half of the disarticulated bones have a known depth and are mostly within the bottom segment of their contexts (n=6, top n=3 and middle n=3). Additionally, half of the elements are cranial fragments (n=11; **Figure 7.160**) and many are from the right side of the body (n=4; **Table 7.14**). Adults are the most frequent (n=9, sub-adult n=5) and only three disarticulated bones are sexed, most of which are female (n=2, male n=1). No disarticulated bones had pathological indicators but one occurrence has a potential traumatic indicator, a depression of an unknown cause. A reassessment of the disarticulated bones from Sharples' excavations by Rebecca Redfern (2008a, 291-294) indicates that some bones have fine cut marks and dry

fractures, indicating secondary burial practices, which the original osteological report did not state. Fourteen have associated materials, five with multiple materials, and the most frequent are metal artefacts (n=9; **Figure 7.161**). Many of the disarticulated bone occurs within the interior of the site (n=20, perimeter n=2). Only four bones are associated with an architectural feature, most of them along its boundary (n=3, entrance n=1). None of the statistical tests returned significant results.

Table 7. 14 Frequency of disarticulated bones elements and sides

Element	Right	Left
Humerus	2	0
Radius	1	0
Femur	1	0
Tibia	0	1
Total	4	1

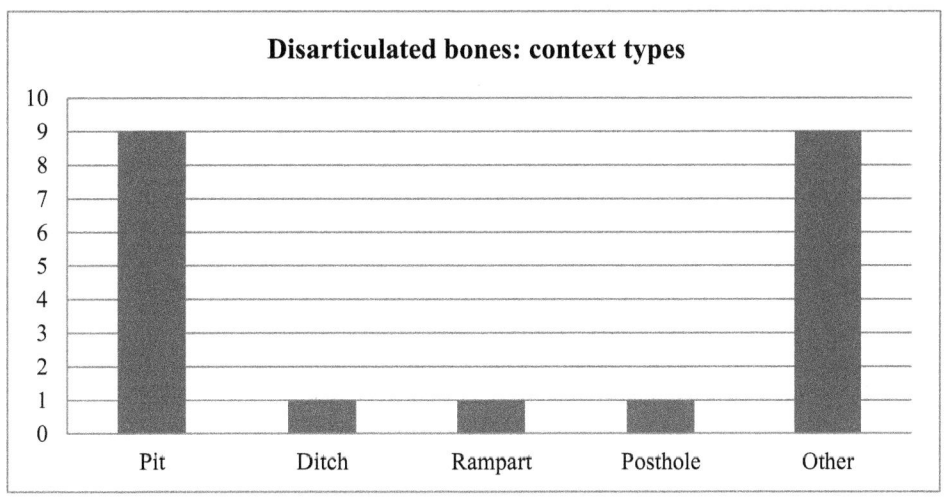

Figure 7. 159 Frequency of disarticulated bones' context types

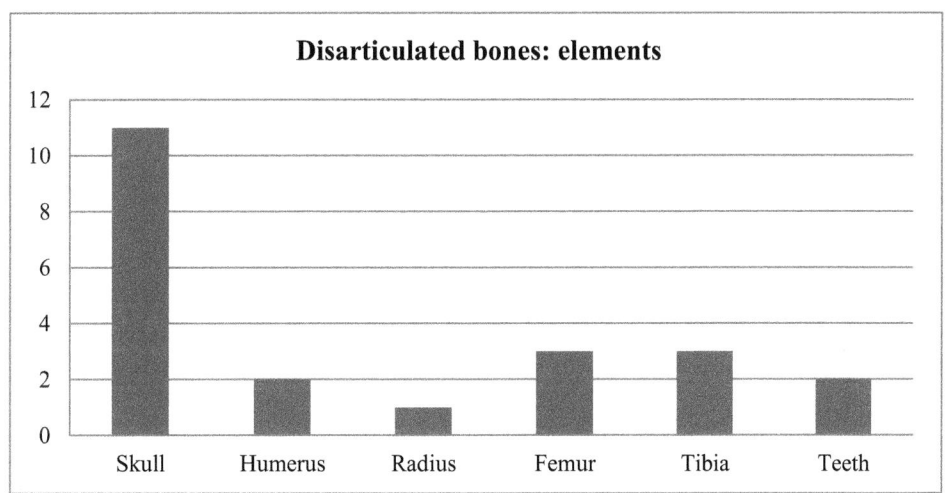

Figure 7. 160 Frequency of disarticulated bones' elements

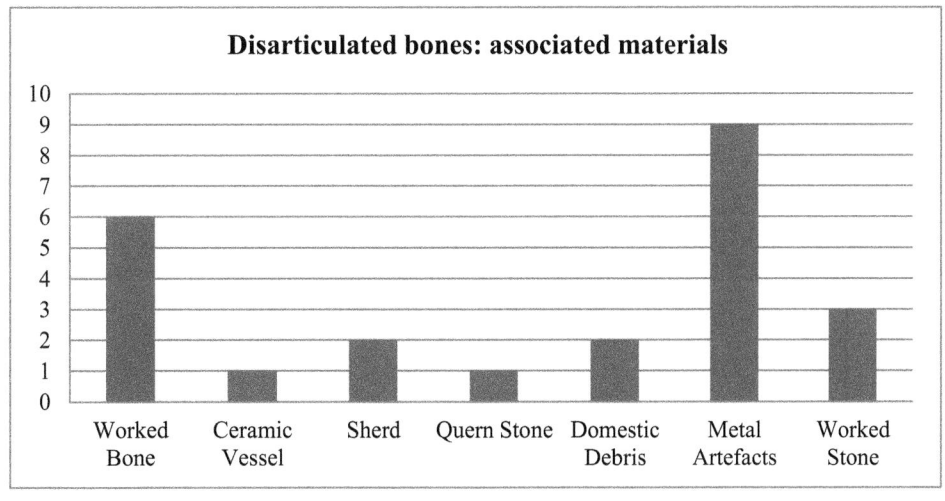

Figure 7. 161 Frequency of disarticulated bones' associated materials

Summary

Although the war cemetery hindered any meaningful, statistical results from this site, it does offer a probable example of an episode of violence in the Iron Age. The war cemetery along the perimeter of the site and adjacent to the entrance is similar to the cemetery found at Sutton Walls and both sites suggest that violence was a factor in Iron Age life. Maiden Castle also has an example of human remains signifying transition. In one of the hillfort's ramparts, there is a burial of an adult male that dates to the Early Iron Age and was deposited during the extension of the defences, possibly being a foundation burial (Wheeler 1943, 37, 122-123). Furthermore, Redfern (2008a) points out that some of the disarticulated bones suggest secondary burial rites. Evidence for the prolonged handling of bones is similar to that on other sites in the sample such as Potterne, Battlesbury Bowl, and Gussage All Saints.

Sutton Walls (SO 5256 4640)

Sutton Walls is an Iron Age hillfort in Herefordshire on a '...narrow mound of glacial gravel, rising steeply above the floodplain of the River Lugg' (Kenyon 1953, 2). Due to the site's location on gravel, it has fallen victim to quarrying and, in 1948, rescue excavations begun by the Ancient Monuments Department of the Ministry of Works (Kenyon 1953, 1). A single rampart and ditch, with entrances at the east and west ends, encircle Sutton Walls and enclose just under 11.74 ha (Kenyon 1953, 2, 4). The rescue excavations produced an enormous amount of animal remains and Kenyon interpreted Sutton Walls' former residents as being predominately herders, practicing some cultivation (Kenyon 1953, 8). Excavations within the northern rampart and the west entrance uncovered a significant number of skeletons. Many of the skeletons have traumatic indicators; a few had been decapitated, and all appear to have been deposited within a short period of time (Kenyon 1953, 8). Of the skeletons that could be sexed and aged, all were male with many in their prime of life. Kenyon interpreted the deposit as a violent event in Sutton Walls' history (Kenyon 1953, 9). Forty human remains occurrences, comprising 25 inhumations, 14 disarticulated bones and one articulated limb, were recovered from two contexts from Sutton Walls (**Figures 7. 162-63**). Ian W. Cornwall (1953) conducted and prepared the osteological assessment.

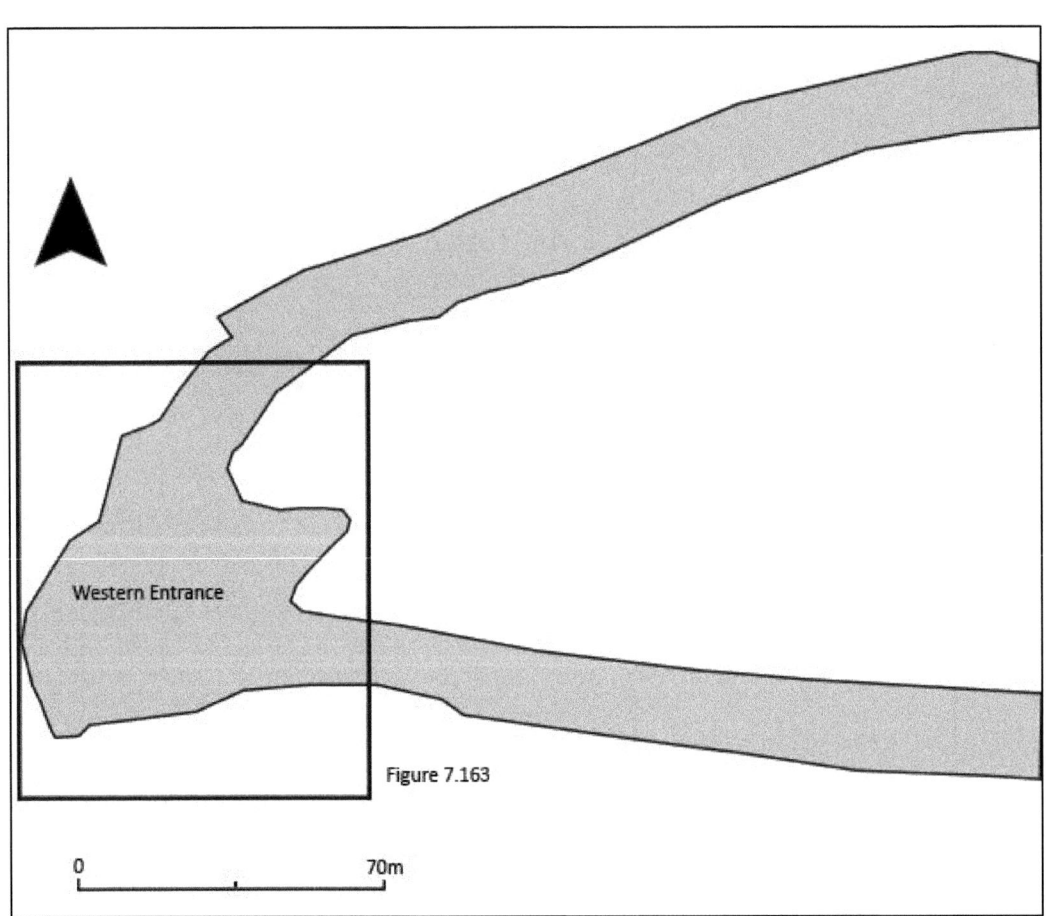

Figure 7. 162 Site plan of Sutton Walls (after Kenyon 1953, Plate I); by the kind permission of the Royal Archaeological Institute

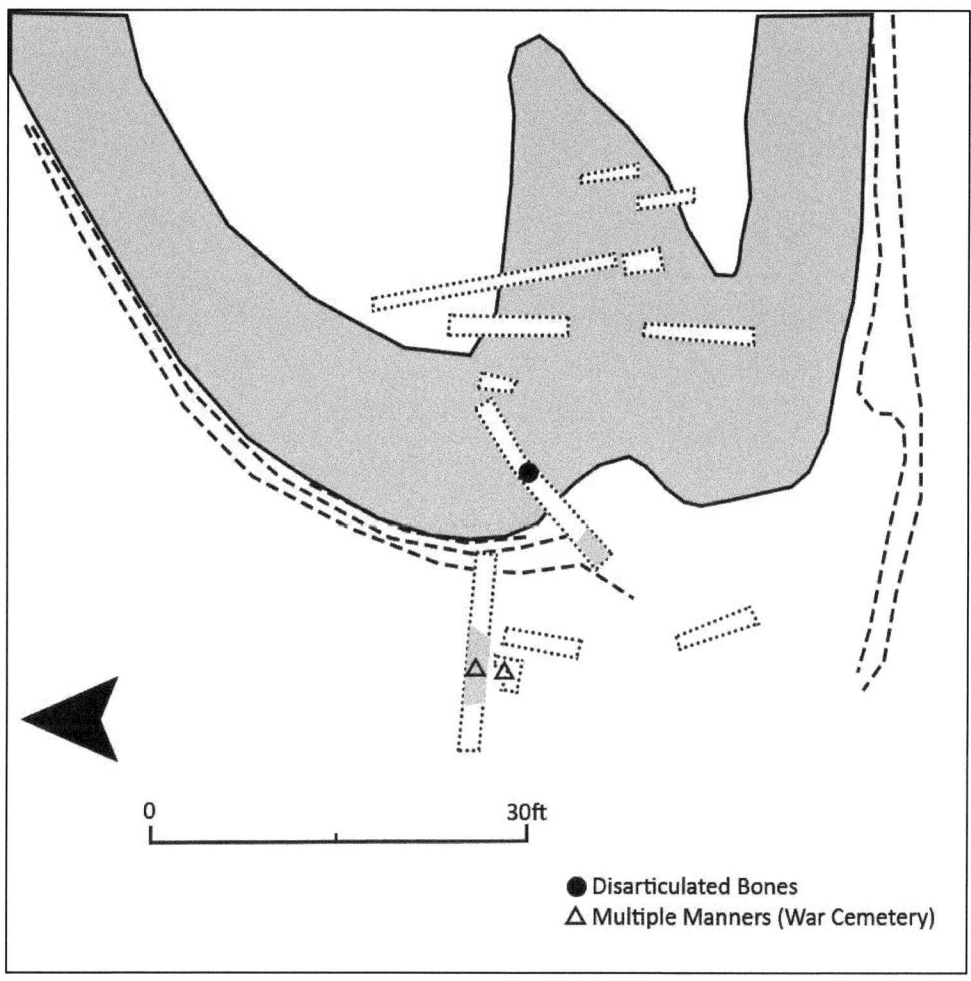

Figure 7. 163 Plan of west entrance of Sutton Walls indicating human remains deposits (after Kenyon 1953, 5); by the kind permission of the Royal Archaeological Institute

Analysis of contexts (n=2)

Two contexts[31] contained all the human remains occurrences for Sutton Walls. Both are Late Iron Age ditch contexts with primary and multiple deposits (all the occurrences interred in one episode). Each context contained both inhumations and disarticulated bones (one also has articulated bones), and the fills were a mix between backfill and natural silting. In addition, both contexts are on the perimeter of the site, in the southwest-to-west segment and near an entrance.

Analysis of manners of disposal (n=40)

Inhumations (n=25)

All 25 inhumations are thought to date to the Late Iron Age period and are primary and multiple deposits within two ditch contexts. Many of the inhumations were incomplete (n=11, complete n=10). Eleven inhumations have a known layout of which all are flexed. Orientation is most frequently to the northwest (n=7, west n=3 and

south n=1), and supine is the most common body position (n=9, left side n=1 and right side n=1). Only three facial directions could be determined, of which two were towards the northeast and the other to the east. Demographically, most inhumations are adults (n=16) followed by older adolescents (n=6) and there is a single child (about 12 yrs old) that has a cut wound to the neck. In addition, of the occurrences that were sexed, all are males (n=16). Seven occurrences possess only a single pathological indicator, the most frequent being dental disease (n=5, joint disease n=2). Thirteen occurrences possess traumatic indicators, two occurrences with multiple trauma, all occurring peri-mortem. The highest occurring traumatic indicator is dismemberment (n=6, the 'other' category refers to trauma of an unknown cause; **Figure 7.164**). None of the inhumations had associated material. Four of the inhumations did not have locational information, but the rest of the inhumations are from the mass burial near the western entrance. None of the statistical tests returned any meaningful results.

Articulated bones (n=1)

One occurrence of articulated bones was found within a ditch that dates to the Late Iron Age. It is a primary type of deposit, associated with other human remains. The

---

[31] **Figure 7.163** illustrates how two excavation trenches split the ditch that contains most of the human remains.

occurrence is an incomplete upper limb from an older sub-adult, and the side and sex are unknown. There is no presence of pathological or traumatic indicators, and no associated material and it was deposited in the mass burial by the western entrance.

Disarticulated bones (n=14)

All the disarticulated bones (n=14) placed within a rampart ditch date to the Late Iron Age. The skull is the most frequent element (n=5; **Figure 7.165**) and only two elements have a known side of the body: a right and left femora. Demographically, only seven are aged - all adults - and just two occurrences could be sexed, both of which are males. One disarticulated bone possesses a pathological indicator, which is dental disease. Two disarticulated bones possess multiple traumatic indicators. One disarticulated bone had a fracture and a cut mark; the

other had signs of dismemberment and perforation. Only twelve of the disarticulated bones had locational information, being near the western entrance.

Summary

Sutton Walls did not return any meaningful statistical results. However, it does provide a possible example of a violent episode in the Iron Age similar to the war cemetery at Maiden Castle. As explained above, many of the human bones have evidence of trauma and nearly all the remains are from adult males, which are the demographic group most likely to be victims of warfare. Furthermore, the contextual evidence suggests that the individuals were all interred within a short period, and this suggests that the individuals died at about the time.

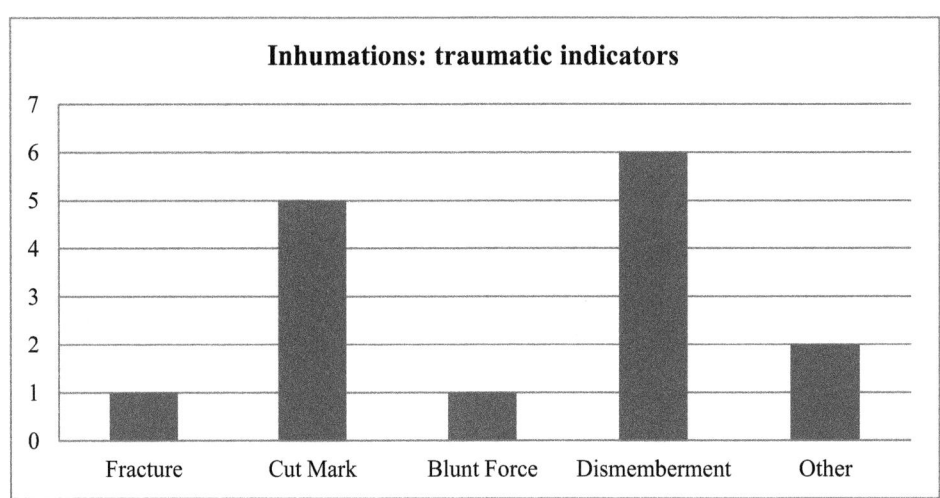

Figure 7. 164 Frequency of inhumations' trauma

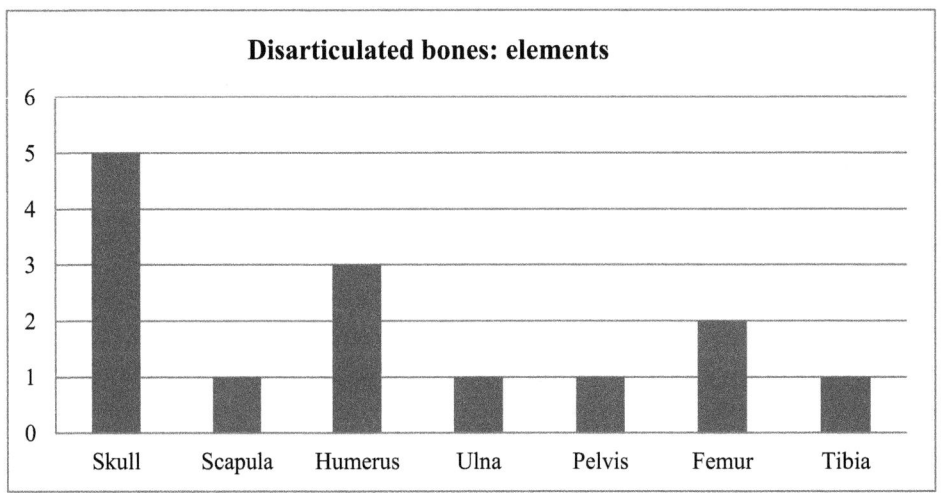

Figure 7. 165 Frequency of disarticulated bones' elements

Cemeteries

Mill Hill (TR 3631 5074)

The Iron Age cemetery of Mill Hill in Deal (Kent), lies on a ridge of Upper Chalk overlooking the sea (Parfitt 1995, 13). Due to advancing housing development in the area, the Dorset Archaeological Group began rescue excavations, lasting from 1984 to 1989, and investigated over 5,000m^2 (Parfitt 1995, 13, 15). The excavations revealed a multi-period funerary area, with activity lasting from the Neolithic into the Anglo-Saxon period (Parfitt 1995, 13). The cemetery complex comprises a central funerary area consisting of a large Bronze Age barrow with associated Iron Age and Anglo-Saxon inhumations

(**Figure 7. 166**). In addition, two other adjacent funerary areas are present, one to the southwest and the other to the southeast of the Bronze Age barrow (Parfitt 1995, 17). All three cemeteries contain Iron Age burials, totalling over 40 individuals. Mill Hill possesses evidence of minor occupation throughout the Iron Age, but never of any great intensity (Parfitt 1995, 15). In all, Mill Hill is a funerary/ritual site where the burial characteristics (flat, inhumed graves) may reflect continental influence penetrating the area, although this cannot be definitively stated (Parfitt 1995, 157). In total, 46 human remains occurrences, consisting of 41 inhumations and five cremations from 46 contexts, were recovered from Mill Hill. T. Anderson (1995) prepared the osteological report.

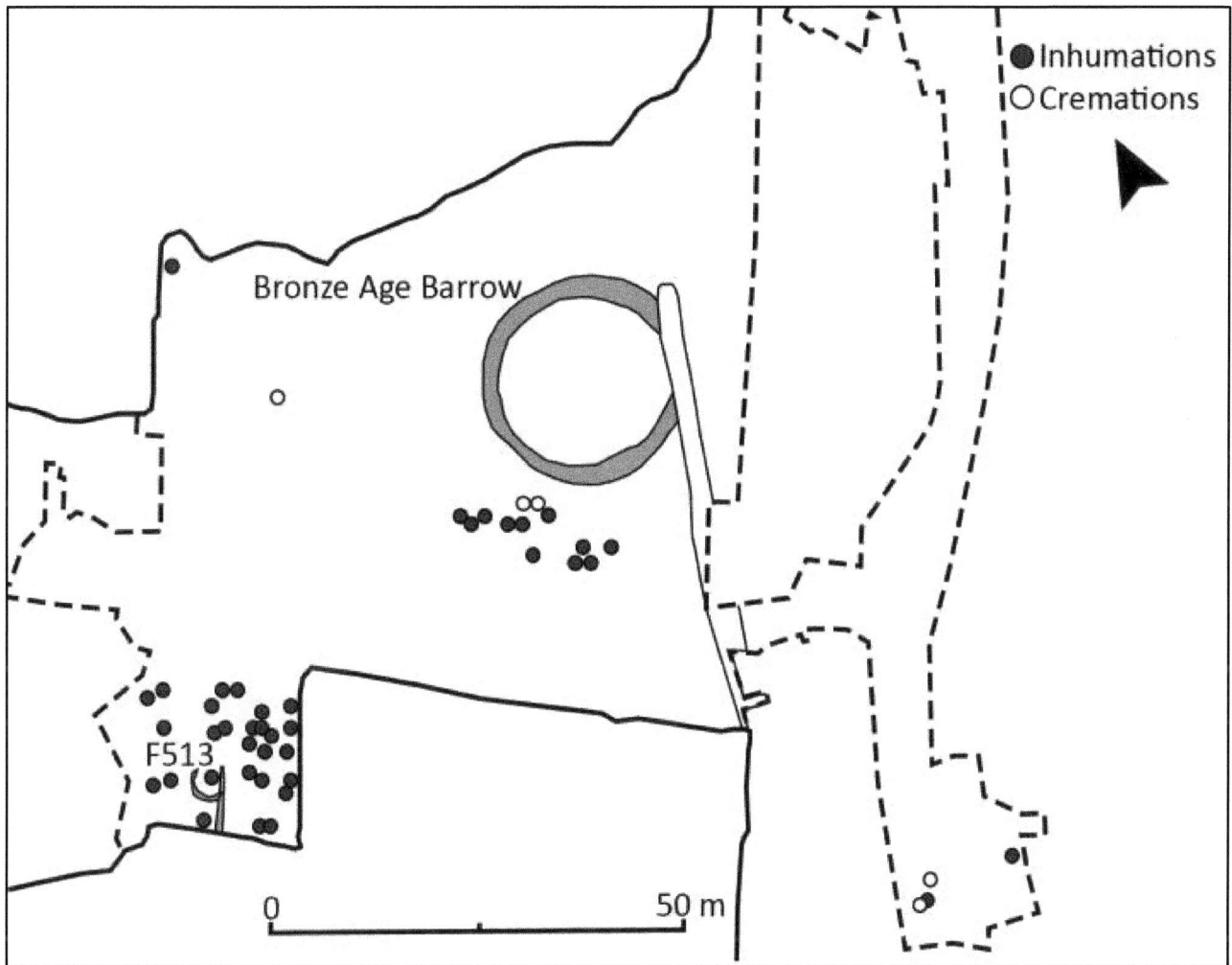

Figure 7. 166 Site plan of Mill Hill indicating human remains deposits (after Parfitt 2016, pers. comm.)

Analysis of archaeological features (n=2)

Two archaeological features have associated human remains occurrences. The first is a Bronze Age barrow (F200) and the second archaeological feature is a small ring-ditch (F513, possibly a small barrow) of Late Iron Age date that has a single inhumation at its centre.

Analysis of contexts (n=46)

Many of the contexts date to the Late Iron Age (n= 42, Middle Iron Age n=2, Early Iron Age n=1, unphased Iron Age n=1) and are graves (n=40, pits n=5, and one unknown). The highest occurring manner of disposal within contexts is inhumation (n=41, cremations n=5). All of the contexts contain single deposits (n=46) and are backfill (n=46). Many of the contexts' placements are outside the Bronze Age mound (n=45) in its southwest-to-west segment (n=33; **Table 7.15**). There is a single context within the Late Iron Age ring ditch discussed above. None of the statistical tests for contexts returned any meaningful results.

Analysis of manner of disposal

Inhumations (n=41)

A greater proportion of the inhumations date to the Late Iron Age (n=37, Middle Iron Age n=2, Early Iron Age n=1, and unphased Iron Age n=1) and are within grave contexts (n=40 and one unknown). All are within the bottom portions of their contexts and are primary deposits. Many of the skeletons were incomplete (n=22, complete n=19) and lay extended (n=25; **Figure 7.167**). Orientation favours the southwest (n=11; **Figure 7.168**) and it is noteworthy that inhumations are only orientated to northern and southern directions. Inhumations are frequently in a supine position (n=29; **Table 7.16**) and

north is the most frequent facial direction (n=5; **Figure 7.169**). Demographically, adults (n=25, sub-adult n=16) and females (n=16, male n=12) are the most frequent. Nineteen inhumations possess pathological indicators, eleven with multiple pathologies; the highest occurring is joint disease (n=16; **Figure 7.170**). Three possess single traumatic indicators, two with ante-mortem fractures (n=2) and another shows swelling of the vertebrae from a minor trauma (Anderson 1995, 159-161). Eighteen inhumations have associated materials, eleven with multiple materials, the most frequent item is jewellery (n=8; **Figure 7.171**).

The statistical analysis returned a single meaningful result that is a significant relationship between sex and facial direction (Fisher's Exact Probability Test, n=23, p=0.036). For statistical purposes, the facial directions were grouped into two categories: easterly or westerly. There are a small number of cases for this test but it does indicate a potential sex difference in the positioning of bodies within their graves. As **Figure 7.172** illustrates, most females face east while males generally face west. There is no other burial difference according to sex.

Cremations (n=5)

All five of the cremations are Late Iron Age in date, and are within pit contexts. Most are in bottom portions of contexts (n=4 and one unknown depth) and all cremations are single deposits. None of the cremations has a measurement for weight. Cremations are more frequently not in an urn (n=4, one urned cremation). Demographically, all cremations are adults, and two were sexed; both are males. None of the cremations has pathological or traumatic indicators. Four cremations have associated material, two with multiple materials, and the most common ceramic vessels (n=3; **Table 7.17**).

Table 7. 15 Frequency of contexts' cardinal directions

SE-S	4
S-SW	6
SW-W	33
W-NW	1
NW-N	1

Table 7. 16 Frequency of inhumations' positions

Left Side	3
Right Side	1
Supine	29
Prone	1

Table 7. 17 Frequency of cremations' associated materials

Ceramic Vessel	3
Sherd	1
Jewellery	1
Animal Bone	2
Other	2

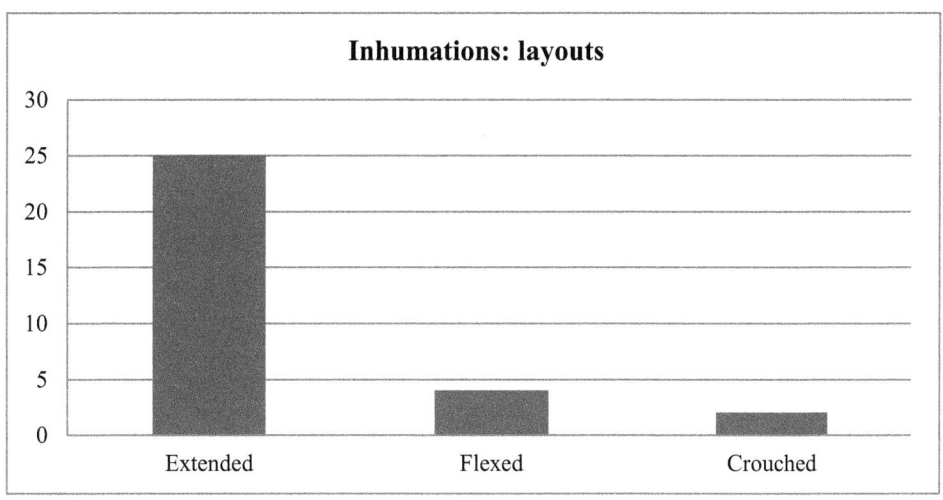

Figure 7. 167 Frequency of inhumations' layouts

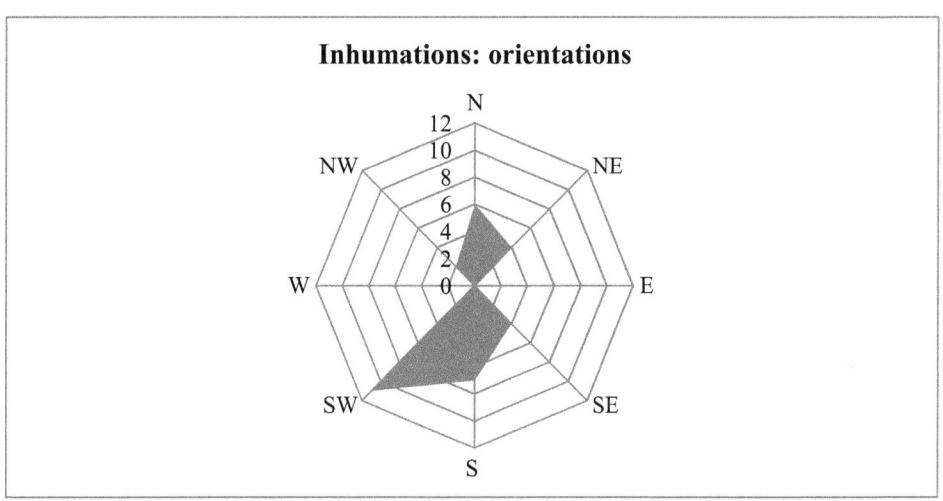

Figure 7. 168 Frequency of inhumations' orientations

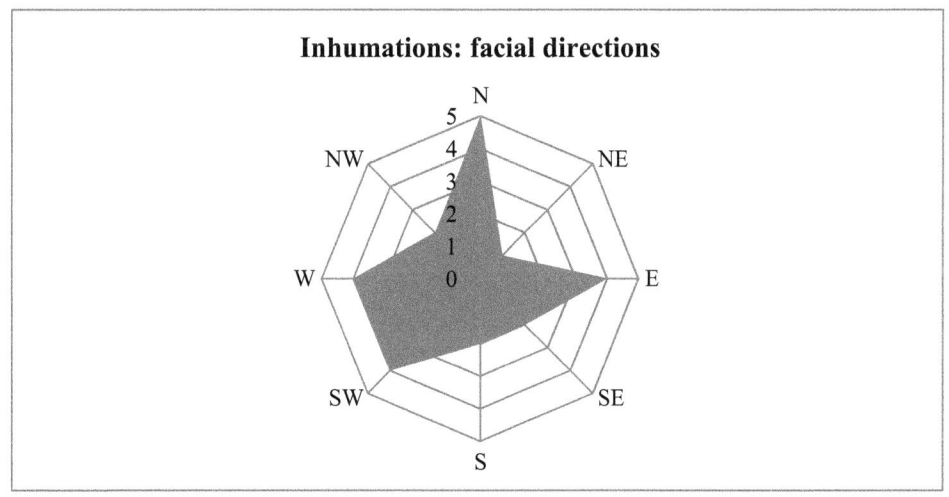

Figure 7. 169 Frequency of inhumations' facial directions

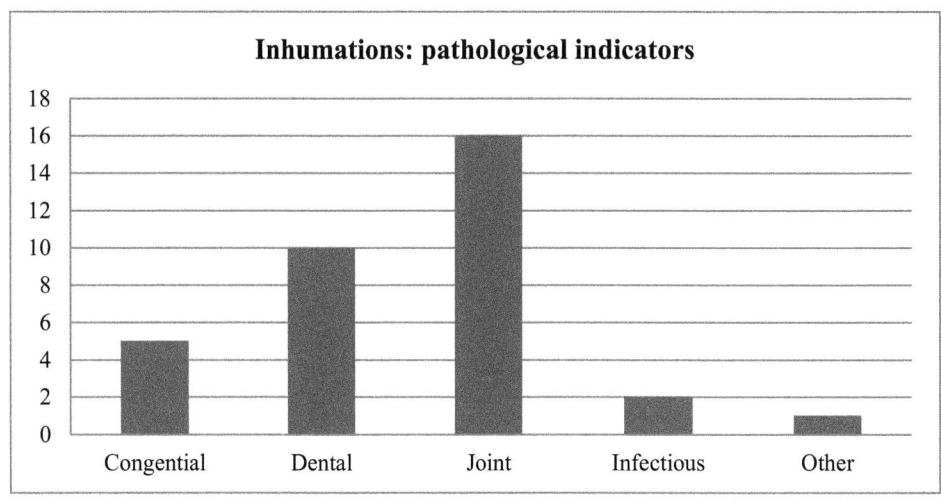

Figure 7. 170 Frequency of inhumations' pathologies

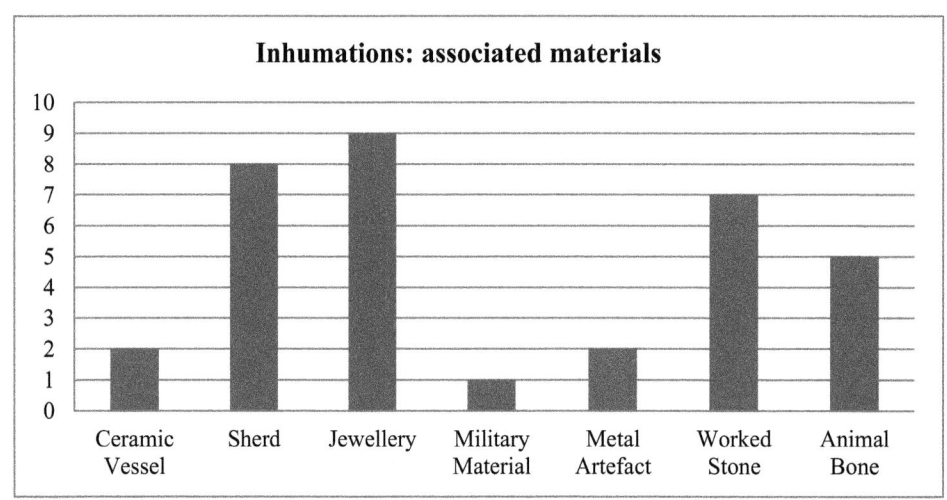

Figure 7. 171 Frequency of inhumations' associated materials

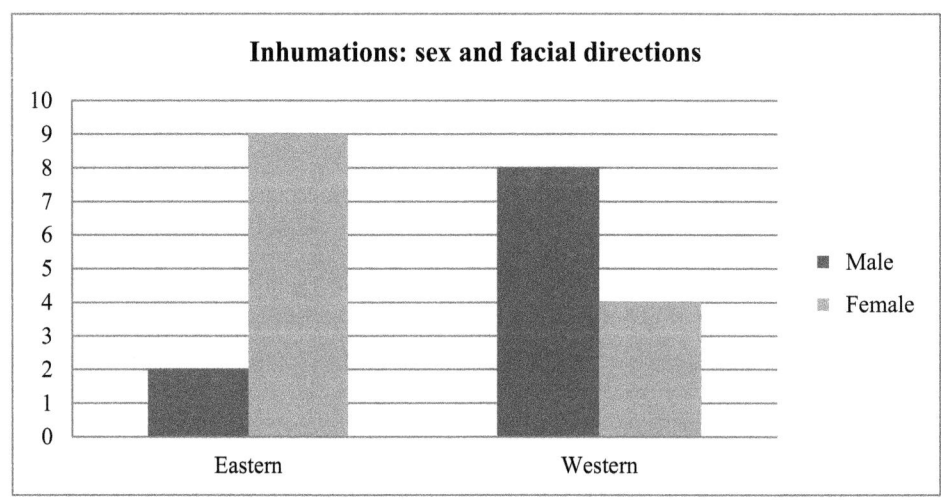

Figure 7. 172 Frequency of inhumations according to facial directions and sex

Summary

The analysis of the Mill Hill burial evidence indicated a possible sex difference in facial direction. This is interesting since most of the Iron Age burial evidence from southern Britain does not show any difference in treatment between males and females. That said, females are found more often as cremations than males, but the numbers involved are small and cannot be relied upon with such a limited sample. With respect to Mill Hill, the correlation between facial direction and sex also derives from a small sample, and Mill Hill is the only site with this characteristic. Furthermore, Mill Hill provides a prime example of a funerary area in use, to varying degrees, throughout the Iron Age. The Iron Age cemetery is set around a Bronze Age barrow and shows Iron Age communities incorporating prehistoric monuments into their burial rites.

A27 Westhampnett (SU 8930 0660)

Westhampnett lies near Chichester, in West Sussex, sitting on the Ipswichian Cliff on the coastal plain (Fitzpatrick 1997a, 3, **Figure 7. 173**). Wessex Archaeology undertook excavations in advance of the construction of the A27 Westhampnett Bypass (Fitzpatrick 1997a, 1). An area of 6,700m^2 was excavated revealing a Late Iron Age Aylesford-Swarling cremation cemetery (Fitzpatrick 1997a). In addition to the cremation cemetery, a number of funerary features were identified, such as pyre sites and mortuary structures (Fitzpatrick 1997a, 3). Adjacent to the cemetery laid a Bronze Age ring ditch (Fitzpatrick 1997a, 4). The site contained over two hundred graves dating from the Anglo-Saxon, Roman, and Late Iron Age periods; the latter yielding the largest number of graves (Fitzpatrick 1997a, 3). The spatial distribution of the cemetery suggests that the Late Iron Age cremation burials were placed in spatially distinct areas (Fitzpatrick 1997a, 13). The cremations outline a semi-circular space, with the interior mostly free of features, and with pyre-related features located towards the northeast of the graves (Fitzpatrick 1997a, 231). One hundred and ninety-two Late Iron Age cremations (MNI=121, with possible 14 other individuals) were recovered from 185 contexts (McKinley 1997, 63). Jacqueline McKinley (1997) conducted the osteological analysis of the cremations.

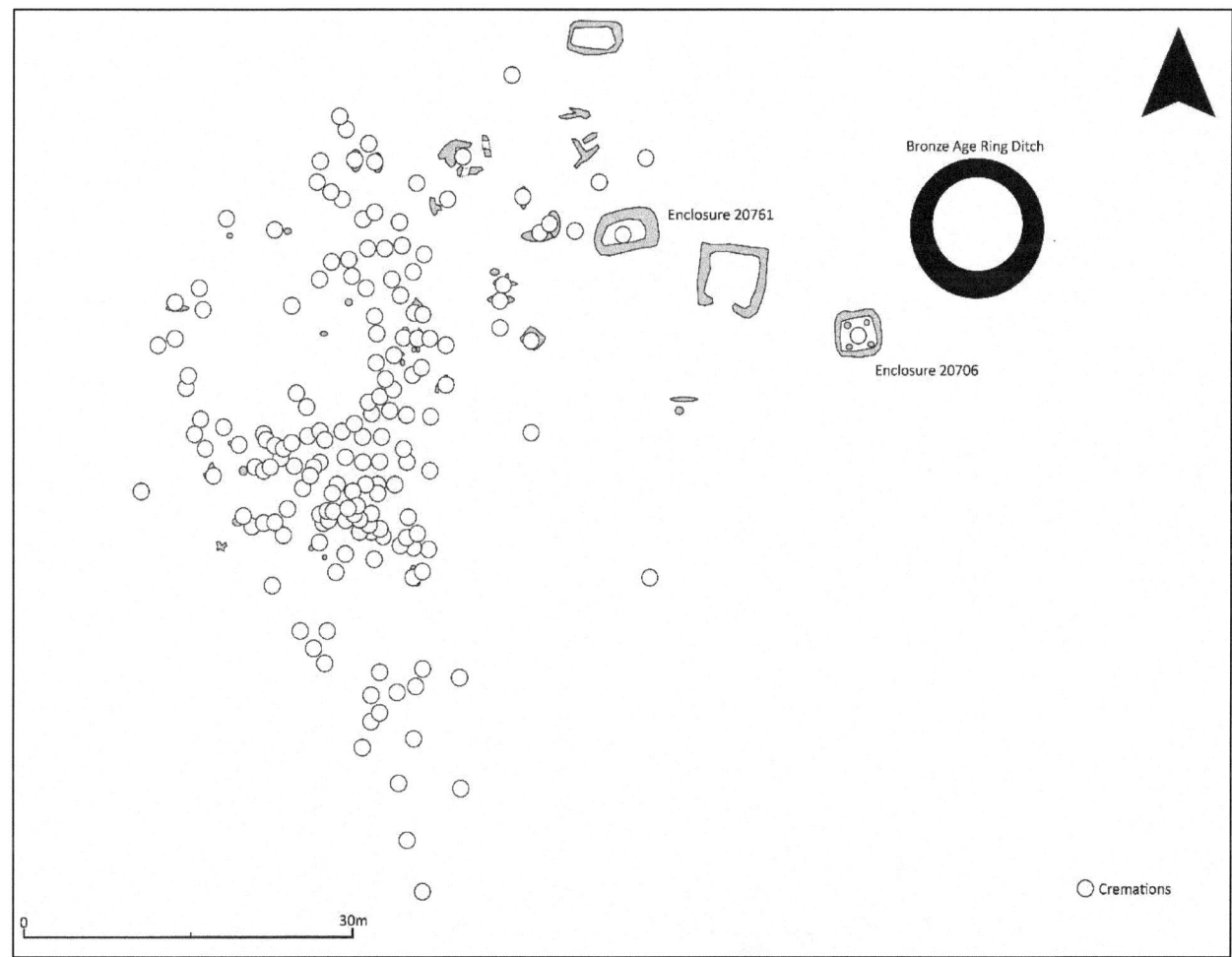

Figure 7. 173 Site plan of Westhampnett indicating human remains deposits (after Fitzpatrick 1997a, fig. 34-35); ©Wessex Archaeology

Analysis of archaeological features (n=2)

There are two archaeological structures (Enclosure 20706 and 20761), both rectangular enclosures of Late Iron Age date and thought to serve a ritual/funerary function. Enclosure 20706 is a rectangular structure with a four-post building within its interior and, in the centre of both of these, there is a cremation burial of an older sub-adult/adult (possible) female (Fitzpatrick 1997a, 13, 40; McKinley 1997, 161). This enclosure lies to the east of the burial ground and just southwest of the Bronze Age ring ditch. Enclosure 20761 is another rectangular enclosure that lies to the east of the cremation cemetery and has a cremation burial within a posthole at its centre (Fitzpatrick 1997a, 16). Both of these enclosures are interpreted as shrines (Fitzpatrick 1997a, 13).

Analyses of context (n=185)

Of the 185 contexts, all were Late Iron Age and the most frequently occurring contexts were graves (n=134; **Figure 7.174**). The next most frequent context type is the 'other' category, which refers to pyre-related features containing some cremated bone. Primary deposits are the most common type of deposit (n=131; secondary deposit n=2) and most of the contexts were single deposits (n=141; multiple deposit n=6). For the context fill, only 117 could be determined, all of which were backfill. The average context depth is 0.21m (n=132), which is the same average depth for cremation occurrences (n=102). Two cremation contexts were associated with an archaeological feature (Enclosures 20706 and 20761) previously described above.

Analysis of cremations (n=192)

The quantitative results for the cremation analysis are corresponds to those for context. The most frequent contexts for cremation occurrences are graves (n=141, 'other'=47, posthole n=1), most often in the bottom segment of the context (n=140, top n=2, middle n=3), and cremations are single deposits (n=145, multiple deposits n=12). A greater proportion of cremation burials lie to the southeast of the vacant, semi-circular space. One hundred and eighty-nine cremations have known weights, of which the average is 159.6g. Many of the cremations were interred without being set in an urn (n=152). Demographically, adults are the most common age group (n=125, sub-adult n=42), and females have the highest representation (n=28) as opposed to males (n=5). Twenty-six individuals possess pathological indicators, four of these having multiple indicators. Joint disease (n=13; **Figure 7.175**) is the most frequent pathology. The 'other' category for pathologies includes evidence on bone from a disease of an unknown or unidentifiable cause. Only one cremation has evidence of trauma, a fracture and it is not known whether the injury occurred ante-, peri-, or post-mortem. One hundred and seventy-eight cremation occurrences had associated material, 108 with more than one item. Ceramic vessels are present with the most cremation occurrences (n=132; **Figure 7.176**), the other category includes uncommon items such as textiles.

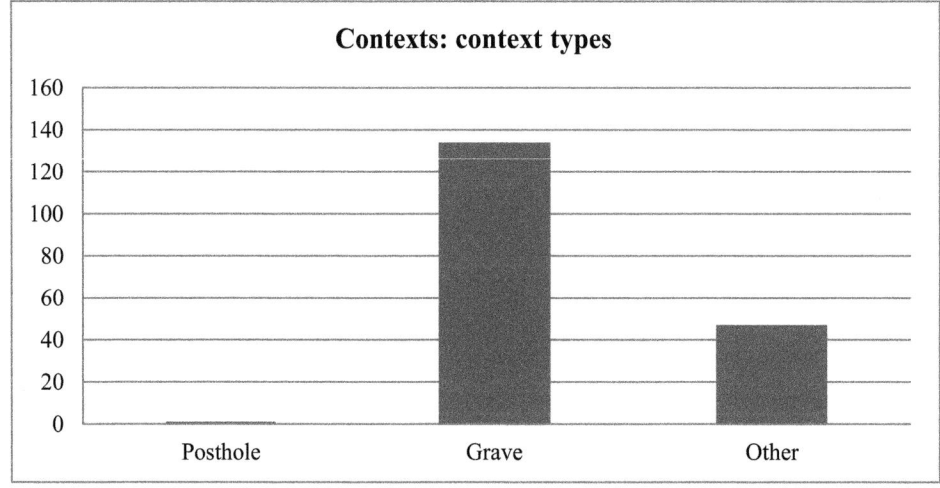

Figure 7. 174 Frequency of context types

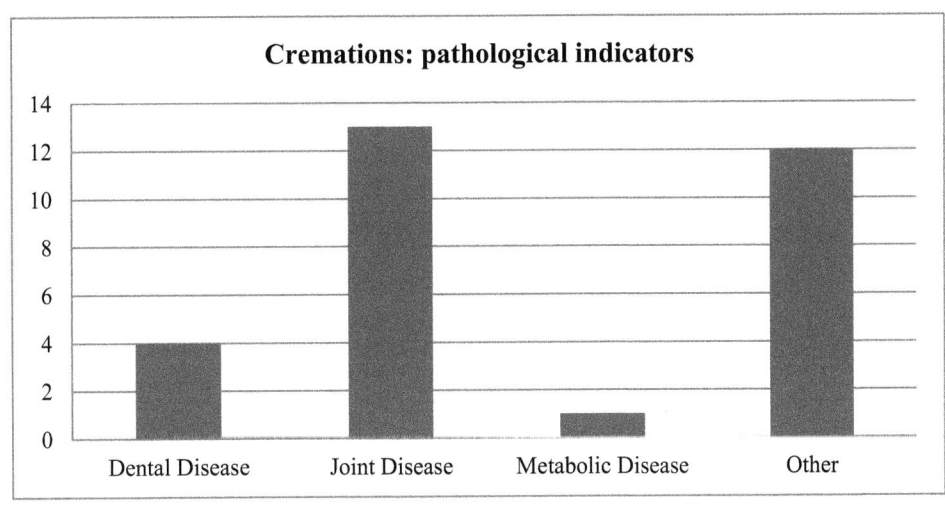

Figure 7. 175 Frequency of cremations' pathologies

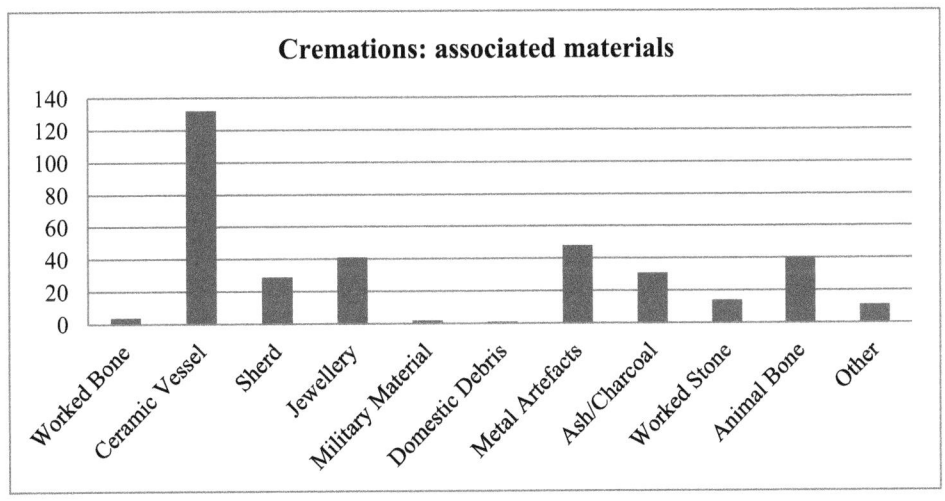

Figure 7. 176 Frequency of cremations' associated materials

Summary

Overall, the statistical and quantitative analyses did not reveal anything unknown about Westhampnett and supports the original conclusions about the site (Fitzpatrick 1997a). It may be one of the earliest examples of Aylesford-Swarling cremation rites in southeastern Britain (Fitzpatrick 1997a, 208). Westhampnett is also one of three sites (Broom [Area E] and Latton Lands being the other two) within this investigation's sample with evidence of pyre areas. Furthermore, an interesting aspect of the site is the spatial organisation of the burials and pyre-related features around a semi-circular space. Fitzpatrick (1997a, 42, 234) argues that the community established a spatial organisation at the start of the cemetery and adhered to it throughout its use, possibly through the employment of grave markers although none left any surviving evidence. Additionally, the cremation cemetery and an Iron Age shrine (Enclosure 20706) lie adjacent to a Bronze Age ring ditch. The vicinity of the Bronze Age ring ditch with the cemetery implies that the area had a spiritual significance for the Iron Age populations, thus making it a suitable space for burial (Fitzpatrick 1997a, 229). The location of the cemetery in relation to the Bronze Age feature suggests further engagement with a prehistoric monument, similar to the cemetery evidence from Mill Hill and other sites from this study.

Summary

In sum, the statistical analyses of sites with twenty or more human remains occurrences returned limited statistical results. This is largely due to the sample size for most tests, with the count of some variables being either too high or too low, thereby directly affecting the statistical outcome. What may be taken from these tests is that some results indicate temporal and demographic differences in the handling and placement of the dead.

The results from the 15 sites studied in this chapter correspond with patterns identified from the analysis of all 100 sites. All periods covered by this study (the Late Bronze Age, Early Iron Age, Middle Iron Age, and Late Iron Age) are represented by burial evidence from these 15 case studies. Generally, these illustrate changes in burial practices from the Late Bronze Age to the Late Iron Age that are evident in the overall study. In the Late Bronze Age, cremation sites (Beechbrook Wood and White Horse) are found towards the east in Kent and disarticulated bone sites to the west at Potterne and Battlesbury Bowl. Disarticulated bone and inhumation sites became more prominent in the Early Iron Age, evident at Battlesbury Bowl, Danebury, Potterne, Suddern Farm, and White Horse. This continued in the Middle Iron Age at the sites of Danebury, Gussage All Saints, Glastonbury Lake Village, Gravelly Guy, Maiden Castle, Winnall Down, Suddern Farm, and White Horse that typically have greater quantities of disarticulated bone and inhumation deposits. By the Late Iron Age there was a decrease in disarticulated bones while inhumations continued to increase, accompanied by a resurgence of cremations. Late Iron Age inhumations were present at Battlesbury Bowl, Gussage All Saints, Battlesbury Bowl, Glastonbury Lake Village, Sutton Walls, Maiden Castle and, particularly, at Mill Hill. In addition, the renewal of cremation burials is apparent at Beechbrook Wood, White Horse, and primarily at the cremation cemetery of Westhampnett.

Furthermore, one characteristic that is evident from a number of these case studies is the large proportion of infant remains. This point specifically refers to the sites of Gravelly Guy, Winnall Down, Glastonbury Lake Village, Gussage All Saints, Suddern Farm, and Micheldever Wood. Infants are not usually present in great numbers on Iron Age settlements but these sites are exceptions to this rule. It is uncertain why so many infant remains were buried at these sites. The analysis did not show any apparent difference in the treatment or disposal of infants between these communities.

Many of the larger sites show patterns of spatial organisation also evident from the wider study in chapter four. For example, there are two large cemeteries, Westhampnett and Mill Hill, demonstrating reuse of a prehistoric monument. These two sites are clear examples of how Iron Age communities incorporated such elements of their landscape/or physical world into their burial rite.

By associating their dead with these Bronze Age features, these communities symbolised their connection to the past while redefining the monuments for their own purposes. A similar connection to the past is also evident in the burial evidence from Suddern Farm where bones of the deceased were sought out as a means of signifying continued relationships with the community's ancestors (Sharples 2010, 277).

Additionally, there is evidence of human remains marking areas and times of significance. Both Maiden Castle and Beechbrook Wood have human remains deposits signifying either the renovation (Maiden Castle) or closing (Beechbrook Wood) of the site or structure. Furthermore, the burial evidence from Gravelly Guy illustrates human remains being incorporated into a specific spatial organisation of structures; those human remains associated with structures were usually deposited with respect to a right/left division with particular attention to the front/left of the buildings. The spatial patterning found at Gravelly Guy is analogous to results from the analysis of the larger sample of 100 sites.

Human remains from Battlesbury Bowl, Potterne, Gussage All Saints, and Maiden Castle show evidence for secondary burial rites as well as prolonged post-mortem handling. The community members of each of these sites manipulated the remains in different ways for different purposes. For example, at Potterne the remains were set within a midden area and had been continuously handled in a type of communal ritual (Waddington 2008). Another example is from Battlesbury Bowl where the skeletal evidence suggests that the community was conducting a prolonged process of breaking down the body and further post-mortem handling prior to deposition. These examples illustrate some of the different ways that communities used human remains in various social processes.

Chapter Eight

Regional patterning and burial trends

Introduction

The following chapter discusses the regional patterns of Iron Age burial practice. The results will be presented in two parts. The first part derives largely from the statistical results discussed in chapters four, five, and six. In this case, sites demonstrating significant relationships are geographically plotted, in order to identify any groupings in burial characteristics. The second part of the chapter discusses reoccurring trends in the burial practice. Evidence for repetition in burial trends was noticed during data collection, and their potential insights into Iron Age burial behaviour warrant further discussion (even though they may not be statistically testable).

Regional patterns

The first part of this chapter discusses potential regional patterns. The following sections investigate whether relationships between burial characteristics, outlined in chapters four through six, also demonstrate geographical relationships. In particular, this part focuses on the chronological relationship between the manner of disposal, context type, age at death, and sex. Additionally, the investigation will address the geographical distribution of structures with associated human remains.

Date and manner of disposal

As previously described, there is a significant relationship between the date and manner of disposal for both the larger and smaller sample.[32] The relationship between these two variables shows a steady increase in inhumations, beginning in the Late Bronze Age into the Late Iron Age. Cremations have a high count in the Late Bronze Age before nearly disappearing during the Early and Middle Iron Age, only to resurge again in the Late Iron Age. Disarticulated bones occur in high frequency during the Early and Middle Iron Age before dropping in the Late Iron Age, which coincides with the increase in cremation deposits. By plotting geographically the sites' manner of disposal and date variables, a potential regional pattern emerges.

To begin, **Figure 8.1** illustrates the distribution of sites with Late Bronze Age human remains deposits with manner of disposal.[33] Sites with Late Bronze Age

cremation deposits appear to cluster in southeast England, primarily in Kent, and to the north in the East Midlands. The westernmost site with a cremation deposit is at Broom (Area E) in Warwickshire, which is a pyre site (Palmer 1999, 36-38). The few sites with inhumation and disarticulated bone deposits occur mainly in the area of Wessex. However, Billingborough, in Lincolnshire, possesses the northernmost disarticulated bone deposit for this period.

Moving into the Early Iron Age (**Figure 8.2**), sites with cremation deposits are less frequent and more dispersed, although they are still primarily eastern. Sites with inhumation and disarticulated bone deposits are more frequent and seem to follow a similar distribution pattern. The sites with inhumations and disarticulated bones still cluster mainly in the Wessex area and extend northwards into the Midlands and into Norfolk. In southeast England (namely Kent and southern Essex), there is a series of sites with inhumation deposits along the coastal areas.

The distribution seen in the Early Iron Age becomes more visually distinct in the Middle Iron Age (**Figure 8.3**). Sites with inhumations and disarticulated bones share a similar distribution and concentrate in the Wessex area. Additionally, sites with inhumations and disarticulated bone deposits stretch northwards into the Midlands. Inhumation sites within southeast England still appear to favour coastal areas. Interestingly, in this studied sample, the northernmost site with an inhumation is Rushey Mead in Leicestershire. Here, a single adult male inhumation was uncovered within a pit (Pollard 2001). However, sites with disarticulated bone deposits continue further north into Lincolnshire and South Yorkshire. As for sites with cremation deposits, there are very few (n=6), half of them still within Kent. The lack of sites with cremation deposits correlates with statistical results that show their decline. Two sites with cremation deposits lie to the north, one in Leicestershire and the other in South Yorkshire. In Leicestershire, the site of Wanlip possesses a single cremation deposit set inside a post-built rectangular structure, with the cremation deposit's pit placed in the centre of the structure (Beamish 1998, 28). Sutton Common, in South Yorkshire, contains a cremation scatter near a mortuary ring, as well as series of disarticulated bone deposits (Van de Noort *et al.* 2007, 137, 151). Interestingly, in this sample there is a near absence of cremation sites within the Wessex area. The most westerly site with a cremation deposit is that of Easton Lane (Hampshire) where a small amount of probable cremated human bone was uncovered from a round structure's posthole (Fasham *et al.* 1989, 68).

---

[32] Not including articulated bone, due to low frequency.
[33] This map, as with the ones after, represents the presence of the particular variable, not the quantity.

Lastly, during the Late Iron Age there is a resurgence of sites with cremations in southeast England and further north in the East Midlands, as **Figure 8.4** illustrates. Broadly speaking, in most of Wessex there continues to be an absence of sites with cremation deposits. However, Latton Lands (in north Wiltshire), Gravelly Guy, and Barton Court Farm (both in Oxfordshire) are the westernmost occurrences for cremation deposits and are located along the northern edge of Wessex. Sites with inhumations and disarticulated bones are widely dispersed in the studied area, and continue to follow a distribution similar to that of the Middle Iron Age. Sites with inhumations and disarticulated bones still dominate the western areas of Wessex, and are present in the Midlands and southeast England. Towards the north into Lincolnshire, sites with disarticulated bones are more frequent than sites with inhumations, though these are few in number.

In sum, for the sites studied in this research, the relationship between the manner of disposal and date of deposit can be seen geographically. There appears to be a regional distinction between most of the Wessex area and the eastern part of England throughout the Iron Age, largely based on the presence and absence of sites with cremation deposits. Sites with cremation deposits appear to be regionally distinct. Late Bronze Age cremation sites have a distribution similar to that which we see in the Late Iron Age, with a high prevalence in southeast England and into the Midlands. The distributions of sites with inhumation and disarticulated bone are analogous to each other, typically favouring the Wessex area throughout the Iron Age and increasing in numbers within the Midlands during the Early and Middle Iron Age. However, sites with inhumations do not extend as far north in the studied area as sites with disarticulated bone. The similarity of the distributions of inhumations and disarticulated bones is what one would expect from communities practising excarnation. In general, the temporal change in the manner of disposal is also shown in regional distinction. Arguably, the change in this pattern relies heavily on the process of the near-complete breakdown of the corpse; the implications of such will be further explored in the following chapter.

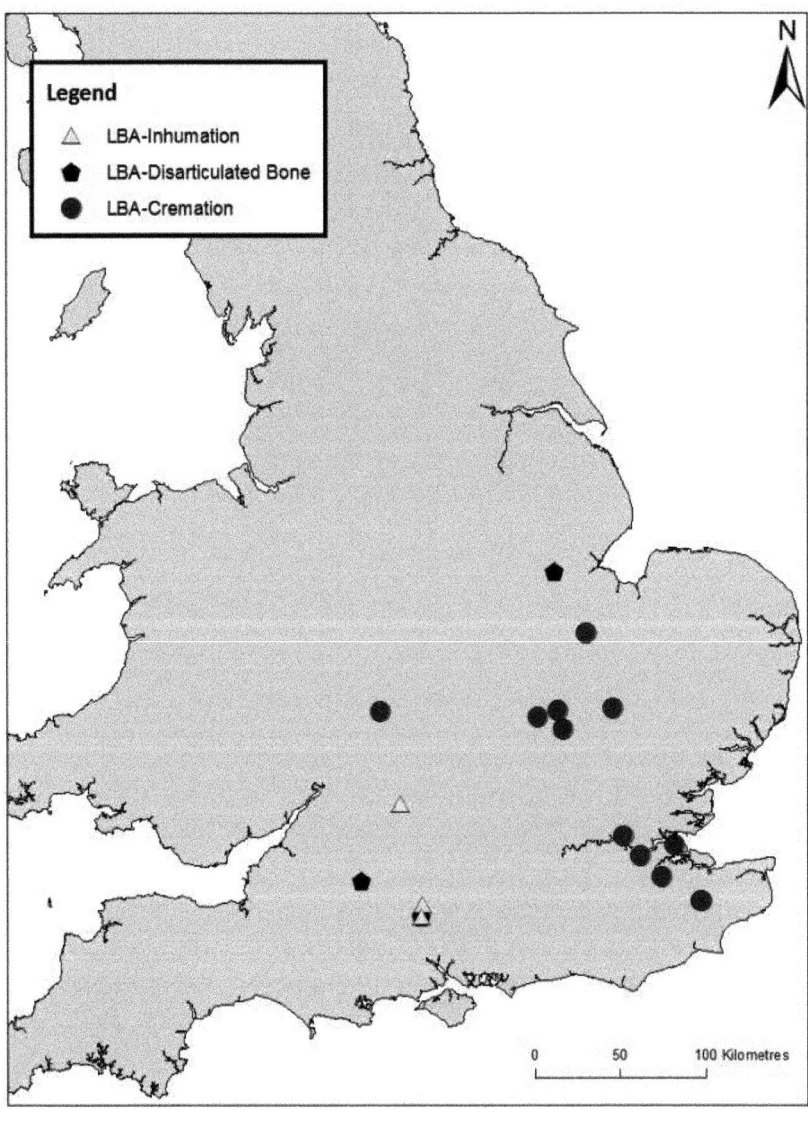

Figure 8. 1 Distribution of Late Bronze Age sites according to manner of disposal

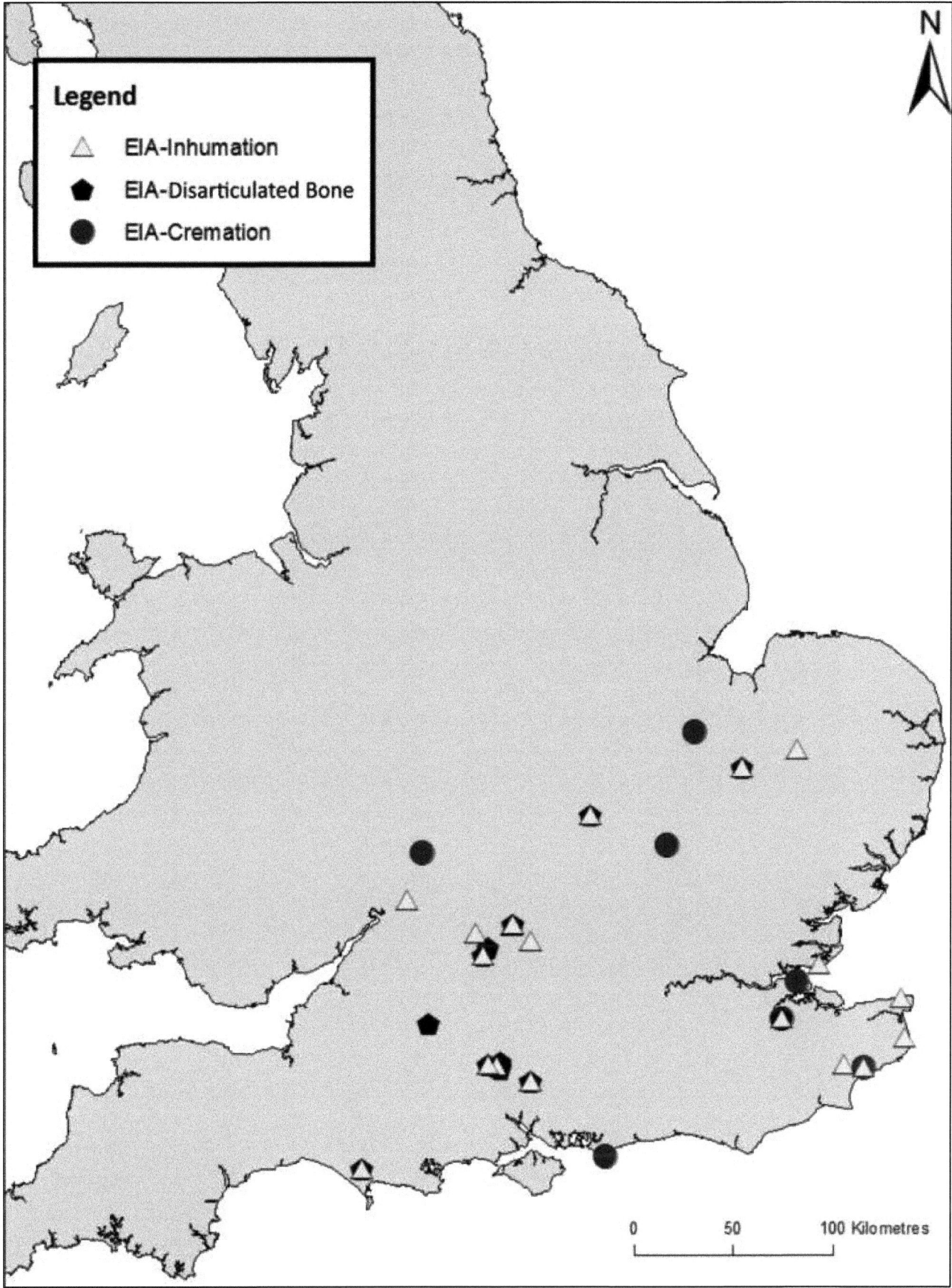

Figure 8. 2 Distribution of Early Iron Age sites according to manner of disposal

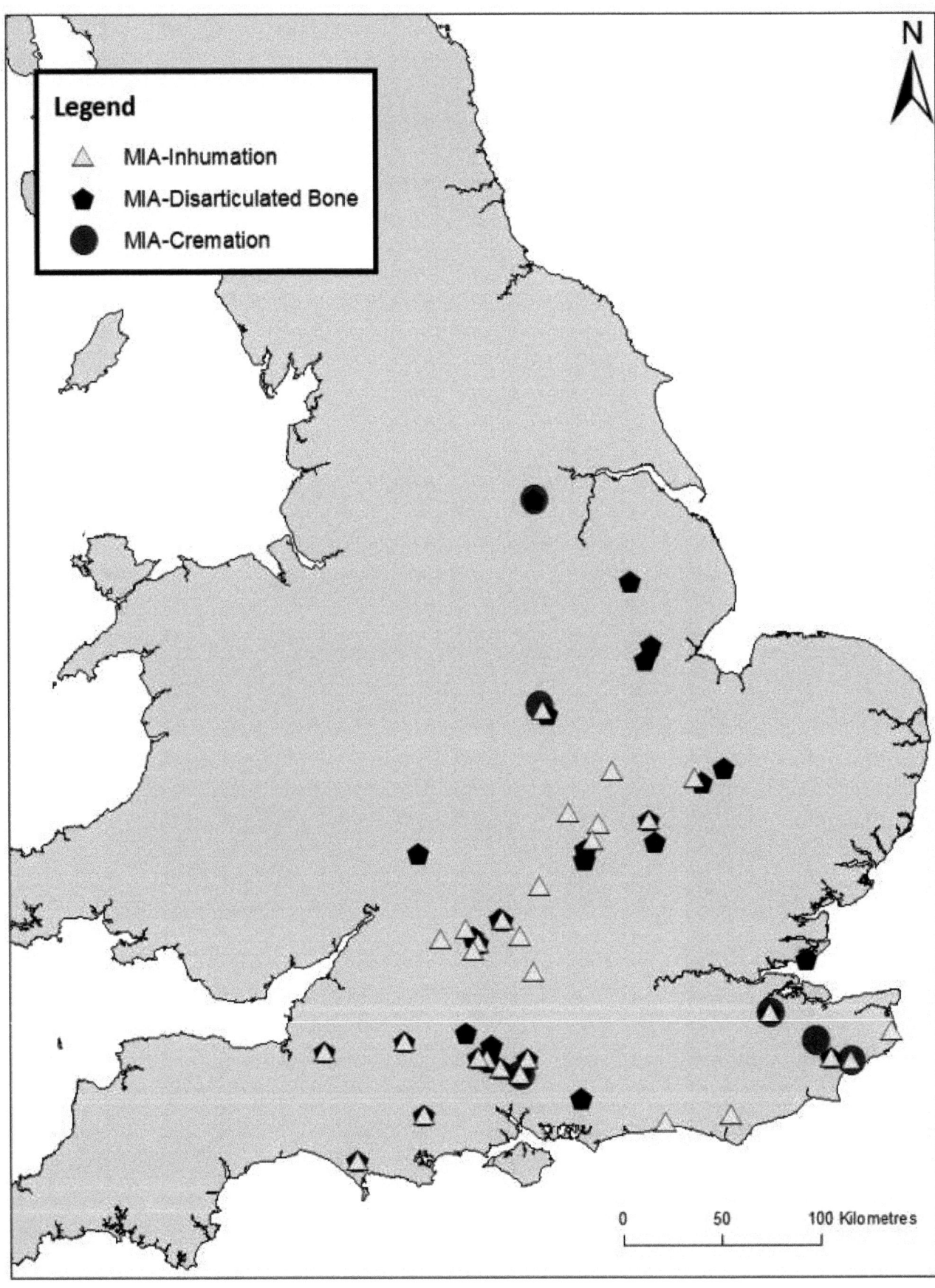

Figure 8. 3 Distribution of Middle Iron Age sites according to manner of disposal

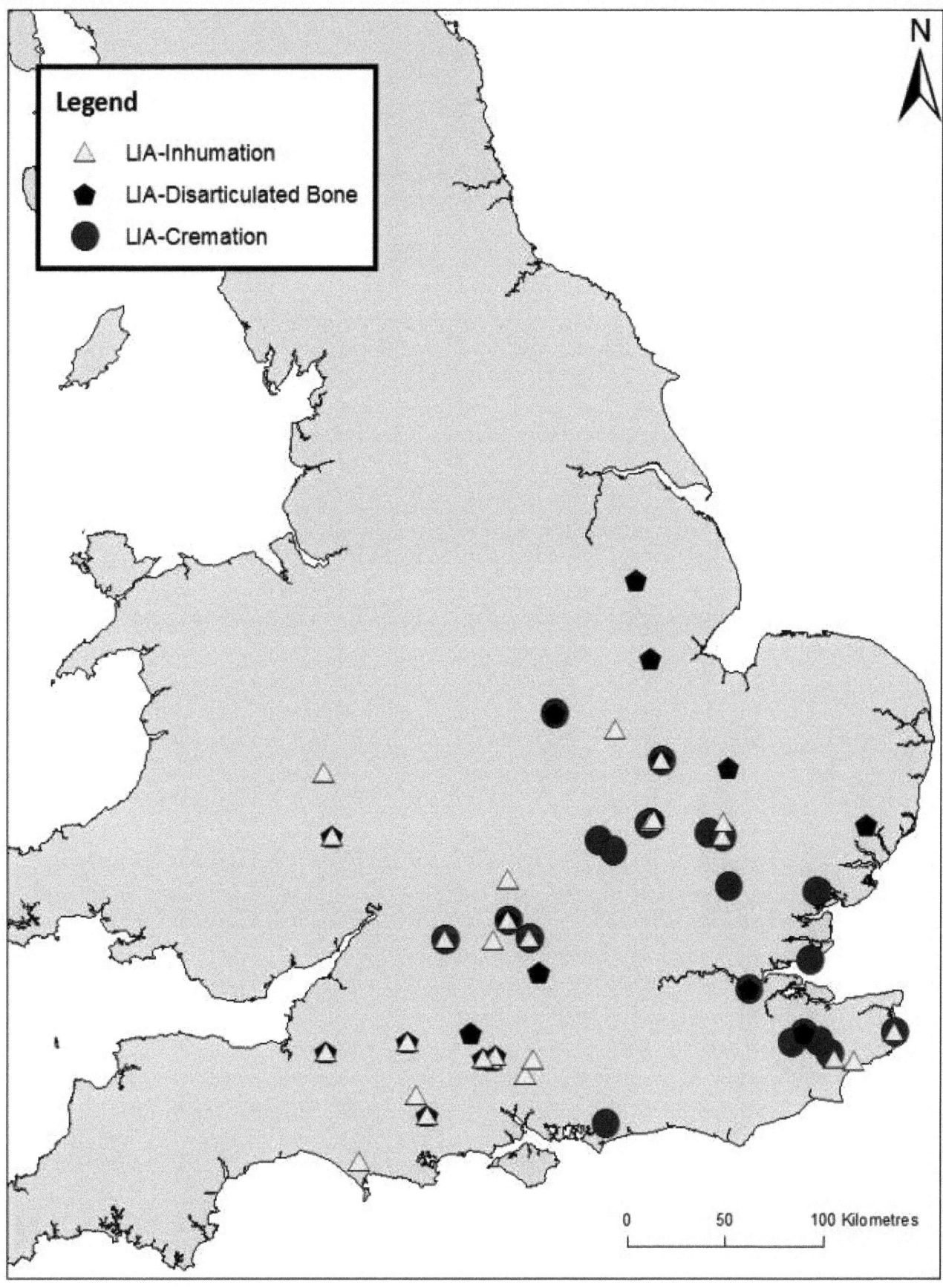

Figure 8. 4 Distribution of Late Iron Age sites according to manner of disposal

Date and context type

The following section discusses the geographical distribution of context types in accordance with date of deposition. As outlined above, human remains are most often placed in pits, graves or ditches; thus, this section will focus solely on these three types of context. Additionally, the statistical analysis for both the larger and smaller samples shows a temporal change in context type. The analysis reveals a change in context type occurring between the Early and Middle Iron Age (smaller sample), and the Middle and Late Iron Age (larger and smaller samples). However, this current section will also include the distribution by context for the Late Bronze Age to the Late Iron Age, in order to discern any regional groupings throughout these periods.

To begin, **Figures 8.5-8** illustrate the geographical distribution of context types by period. In the Late Bronze Age (**Figure 8.5**), there is a cluster of sites with pit contexts in southeast England, and slightly further north in the East Midlands. This clustering is not surprising, since it mirrors the spread of cremations during this period, of which the majority were set in pits. Another site that lies to the west, Roughground Farm (Gloucestershire), contains a single isolated burial within a pit (Allen *et al.*

1993, 28, 45). Two of the most northern sites in this sample are human remains within ditch contexts. One is Broom (Area E), a Late Bronze Age pyre site, and the other is the salt-working site of Billingborough. Moving into the Early Iron Age, it is apparent (**Figure 8.6**) that sites with human remains in pits become a bit more widely dispersed to the south. Additionally, sites with grave contexts emerge in Kent, Hampshire, Oxfordshire and Gloucestershire. Ditch contexts become slightly more frequent in the Early Iron Age and have a relatively similar distribution to pits, but in smaller numbers.

In general, there appears to be no clear regional grouping by context type in accordance with date of deposition. In the Late Bronze Age, there is a possible clustering of cremation deposits within pits in southeast England. However, during the rest of the Iron Age most areas show that a variety of context types were in use and differ only in their frequency. In the Middle Iron Age, the more northerly sites have deposits of human remains occurring only within ditch contexts. However, this point rests on only three sites, and the choice of deposition in a ditch may be the result of context availability. It may signify that such availability was a key factor in choosing contexts for deposition of human remains.

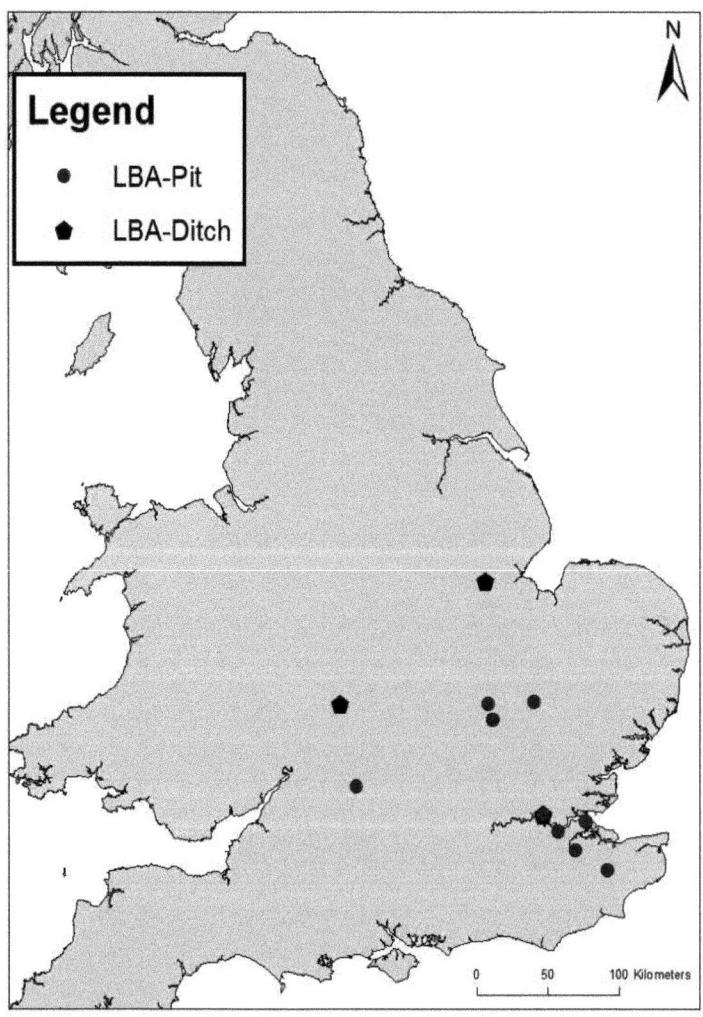

Figure 8. 5 Distribution of Late Bronze Age sites according to context type

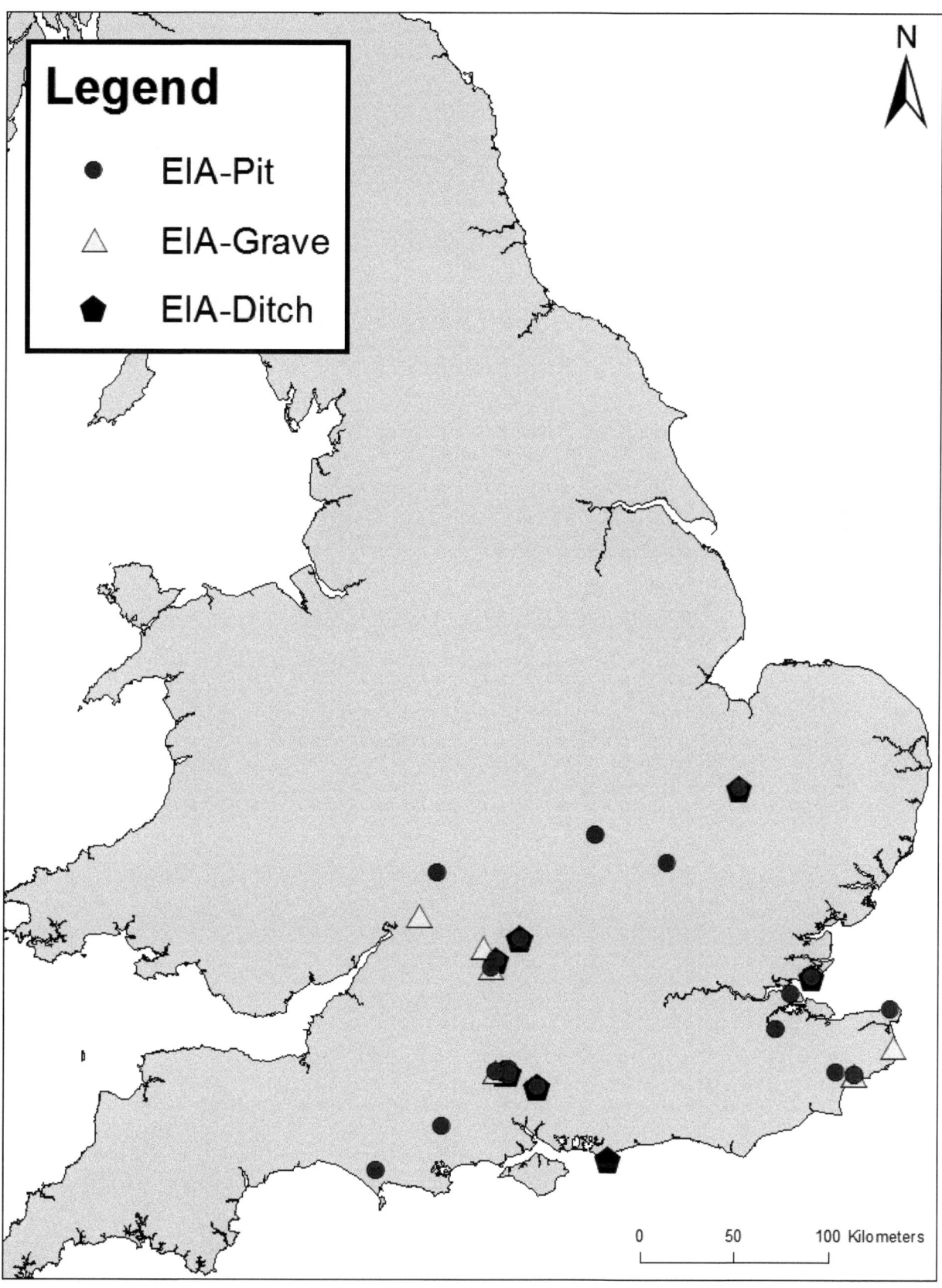

Figure 8. 6 Distribution of Early Iron Age sites according to context type

In the Middle Iron Age (**Figure 8.7**), there is a cluster of sites with pit contexts in Wessex, which coincides with the pit-burial tradition. Pits contexts also have a wider dispersal than in the Early Iron Age to that scattered across the Midlands and present in southeast England. Sites with ditch contexts are numerous in Wessex and, as before, follow a similar distribution to pits. However, ditch context sites are slightly more frequent than pit context sites in the East Midlands, and extend further north into Lincolnshire and South Yorkshire. The absence of sites with human remains in pit contexts may be the result of recovery bias. The majority of archaeological features, from sites in the northern area, consist largely of ditch, posthole, enclosure, and hearth contexts (Van de Noort *et al.* 2007 (Sutton Common); Healey 1999 (Helpringham Fen); Chowne *et al.* 2001 (Billingborough)). On the other hand, sites with grave contexts are also more frequent in the Middle Iron Age and have a wider distribution. Grave sites are present along southeast England's coast, are common within Wessex and extend further north with a lower frequency in the Midlands. Finally, in the Late Iron Age (**Figure 8.8**)

the distribution of sites with pit contexts is similar to that found in the Middle Iron Age. Pit contexts are frequent in southeast England, Wessex, and into the East Midlands. In addition, sites with grave contexts are widespread but, in the east of England, this context type does not appear further north than Cambridgeshire. As for sites with ditch contexts, they occur more frequently than other context types in the northern area of the East Midlands.

In general, there appears to be no clear regional grouping by context type in accordance with date of deposition. In the Late Bronze Age, there is a possible clustering of cremation deposits within pits in southeast England. However, during the rest of the Iron Age most areas show that a variety of context types were in use and differ only in their frequency. In the Middle Iron Age, the more northerly sites have deposits of human remains occurring only within ditch contexts. However, this point rests on only three sites, and the choice of deposition in a ditch may be the result of context availability. It may signify that such availability was a key factor in choosing contexts for deposition of human remains.

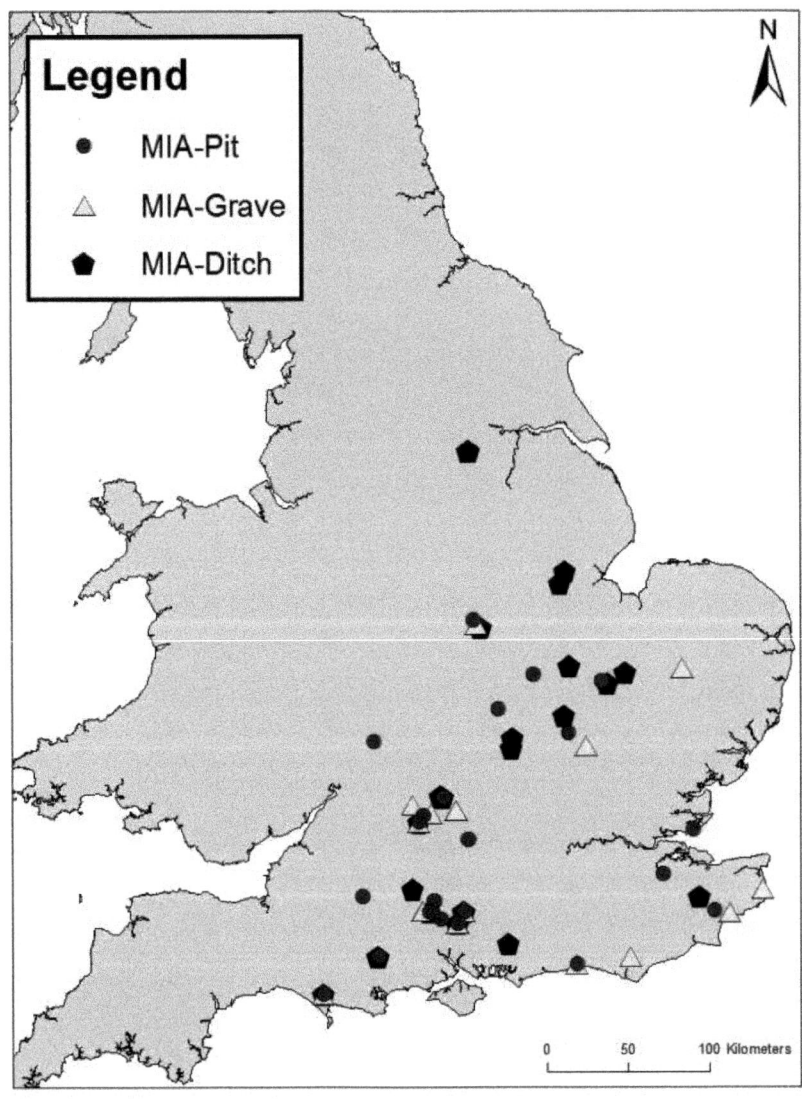

Figure 8. 7 Distribution of Middle Iron Age sites according to context type

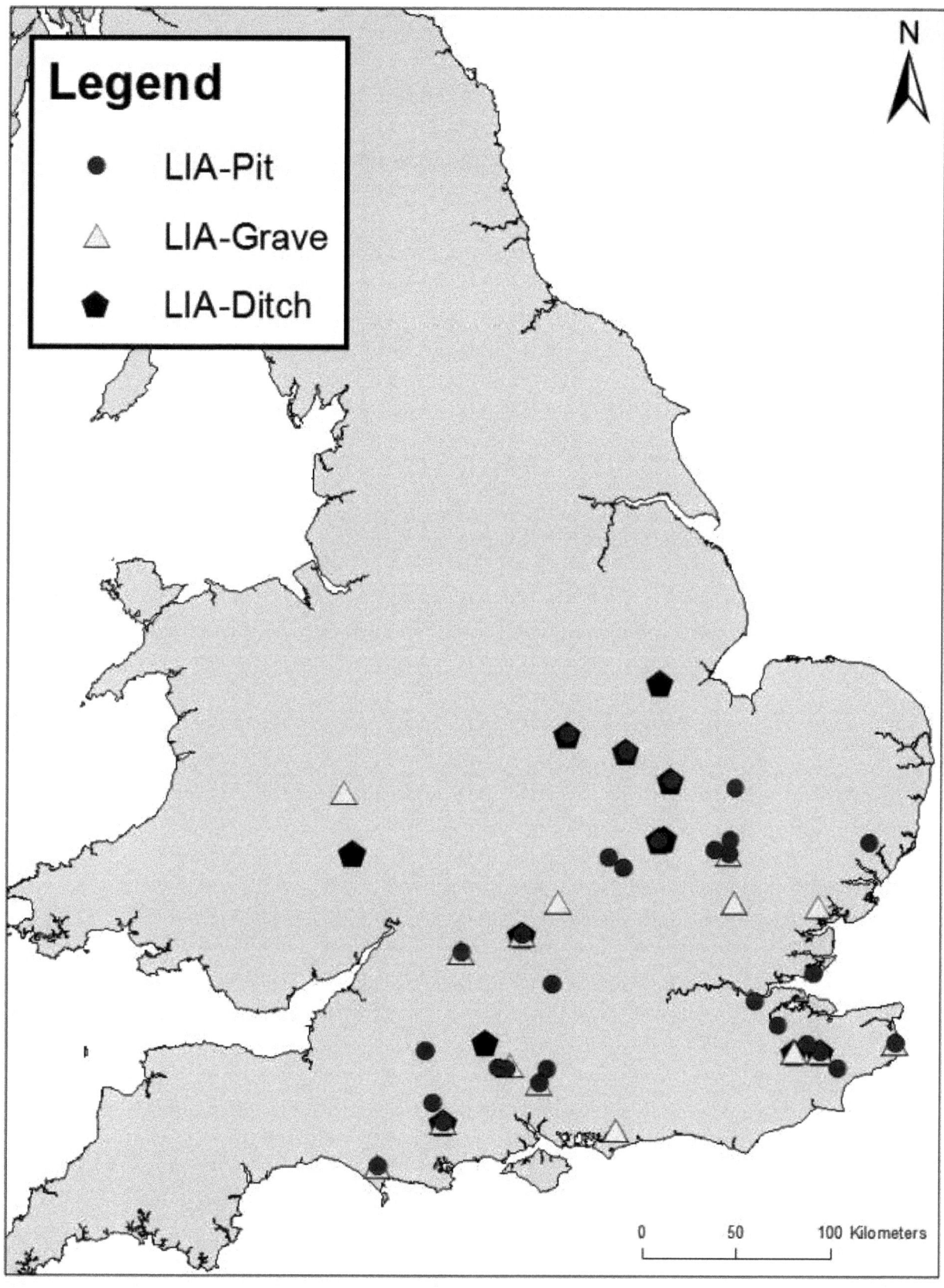

Figure 8. 8 Distribution of Late Iron Age sites according to context type

Date, manner of disposal, and age

This section addresses the geographical distribution of age groups (of human remains) in respect to the date of deposit. Furthermore, the discussion will also touch upon the manner of disposal to offer more insight into the possible relationship between age at death and date. Previously, the statistical analysis for the smaller sample showed the infant age group increasing in frequency from the Late Bronze Age into the Late Iron Age. Additionally, the increase in infants is predominantly seen in inhumations and disarticulated bones, and this group is nearly absent in cremations.

To begin, **Figures 8.9-12** illustrate the geographical distribution of age groups by date of deposit. As one can see (**Figure 8.9**), the majority of sites in the Late Bronze Age have only adult human remains, which also correlates with the distribution of cremation sites for this time period. Infant and child age groups are present only at two sites, both in Wessex. The distribution in the Early Iron Age shows slightly more variation; as **Figure 8.10** illustrates, many sites have multiple age groups present. The adult group is present at nearly every Early Iron Age site. In turn, infants are more frequent and appear more often on sites with adult skeletal material. In the Middle Iron Age (**Figure 8.11**), the majority of infant human

remains are found within Wessex, and this area has more of a mixture of age groups present on its sites. From southeast England, into the East Midlands and up into South Yorkshire, sites predominantly have adult and adolescent remains, largely from disarticulated bone and inhumation deposits. Lastly, in the Late Iron Age (**Figure 8.12**), the majority of sites have adult skeletal material, and infant deposits are slightly more frequent in the Midlands area. Overall, for the Late Iron Age the age categories have a relatively even distribution across the studied area.

Collectively, there does not appear to be a strong regional distinction between age at death and date of deposition. Most sites include the adult age group, while the second most frequently seen group is that of infants. As previously stated, infant cremations are rare; this most likely accounts for the lack of representation of this age group in eastern England until the Late Iron Age. Additionally, in eastern England, from the Late Bronze Age into the Middle Iron Age, most of the skeletal material is from older sub-adults and adults, possibly indicating a preference for older individuals in the community. However, in Wessex there is more variability among the age groups. Wessex contains the most sites with over twenty occurrences, and the quantities of human remains may account for the wider age variability in the selection of those interred.

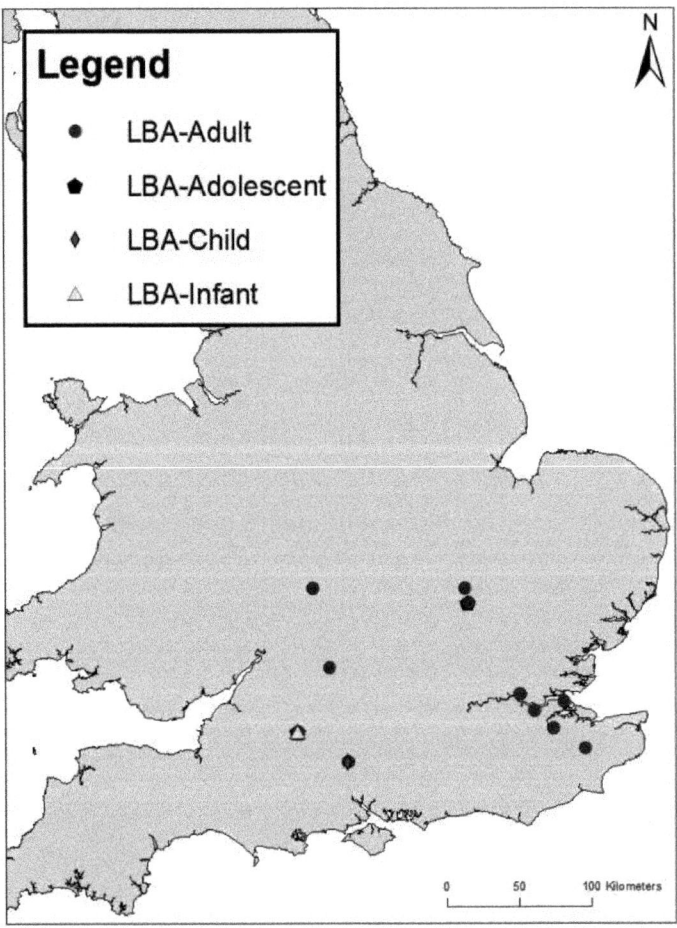

Figure 8. 9 Distribution of Late Bronze Age sites according to age

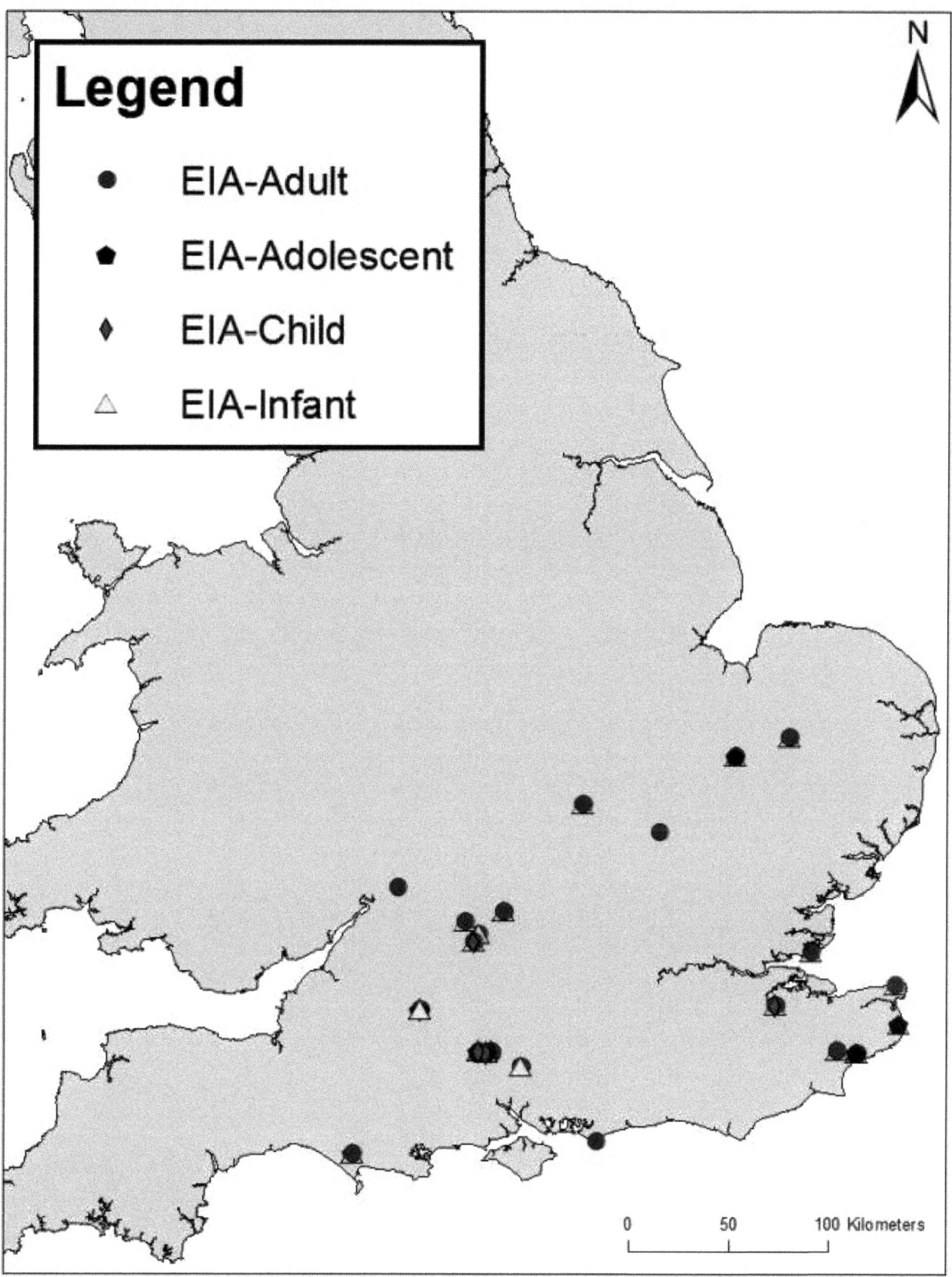

Figure 8. 10 Distribution of Early Iron Age sites according to age

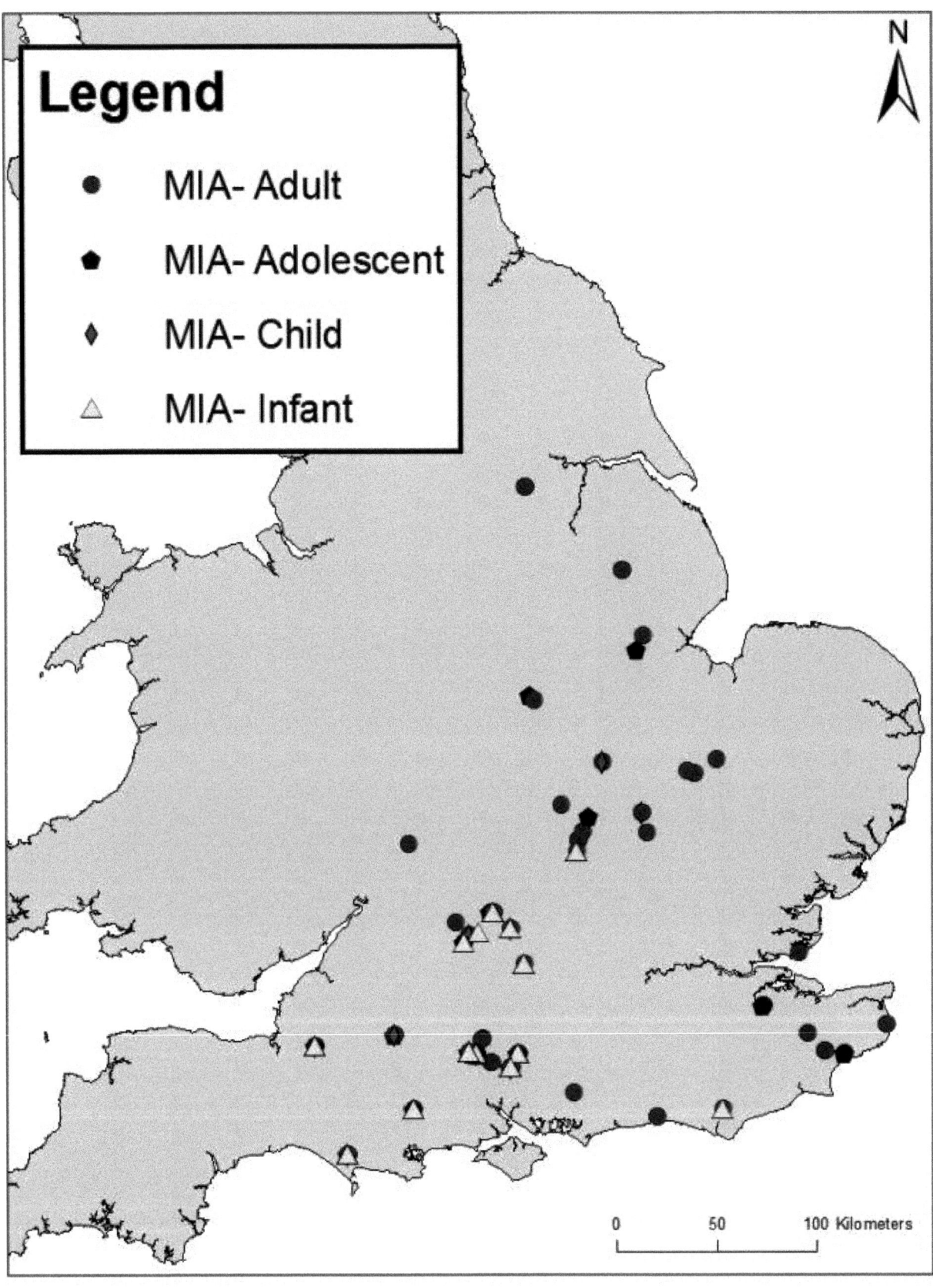

Figure 8. 11 Distribution of Middle Iron Age sites according to age

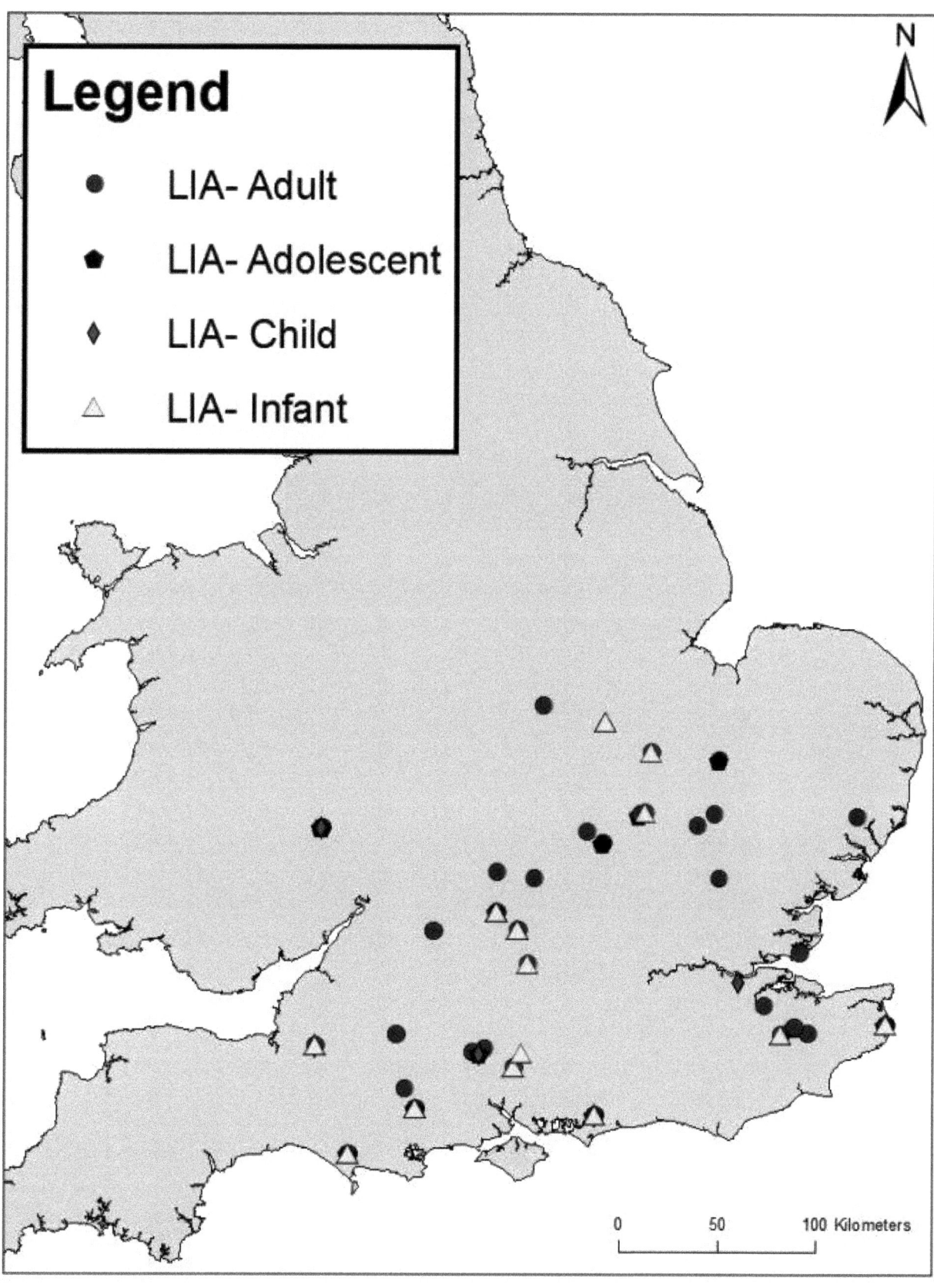

Figure 8. 12 Distribution of Late Iron Age sites according to age

Date, manner of disposal and sex

The statistical analysis reveals no significant relationship between the sex of the human remains and date of the deposit. However, there was a significant relationship between the manner of disposal and the sex of the individual. As previously described, males occur more frequently in inhumations and as disarticulated bones than females. In contrast, for cremations females have a higher count than males. This section explores whether there is a geographical preference for the biological sex and date of these deposits, in conjunction with their manner of disposal, focusing on cremation sites.

To begin, **Figures 8.13-6** depict the chronological distribution of sites showing whether males and/or females are present in the record. In the Late Bronze Age (**Figure 8.13**), the distribution sites with males and females are predominantly similar, and most have both sexes present. This trend follows through to the Early Iron Age (**Figure 8.14**), where the distribution of sites containing either male or female skeletal material is relatively comparable. For the Middle Iron Age, the distribution is once again similar to the previous periods; however, the sites north of Bedfordshire seem to consist solely of male deposits (see **Figure 8.15**). Finally, for the Late Iron Age (**Figure 8.16**) the distribution of sites with male or female deposits once again shows a similar spread across the studied area and does not suggest a regional bias.

For cremation sites, the distribution, in relation to the biological sex and date of deposit, does not show any particular geographical distinction. **Figures 8.17-9** show that there are a few sites with cremations that have a known sex. In general, there appears to be no sex preference in relation to either date or geographical distribution. Even though there is a significant relationship between the biological sex and manner of disposal of human remains, this relationship does not show any geographical pattern.

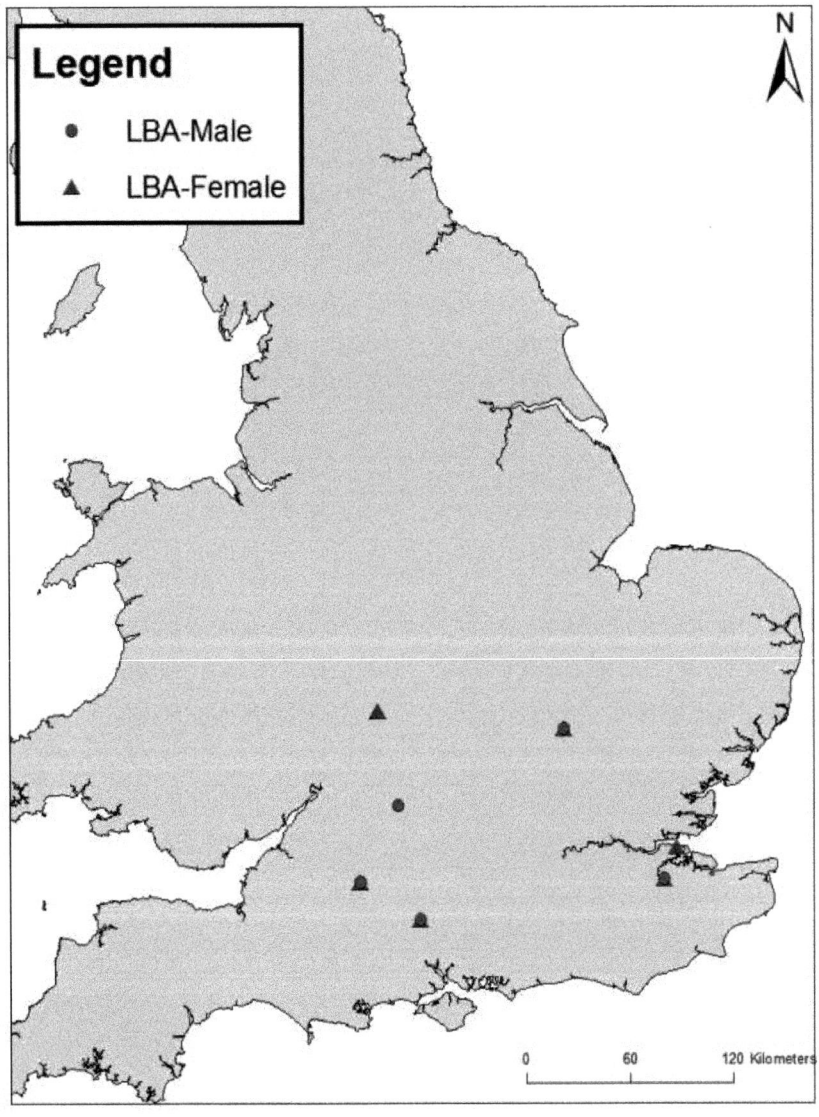

Figure 8. 13 Distribution of Late Bronze Age sites according to sex

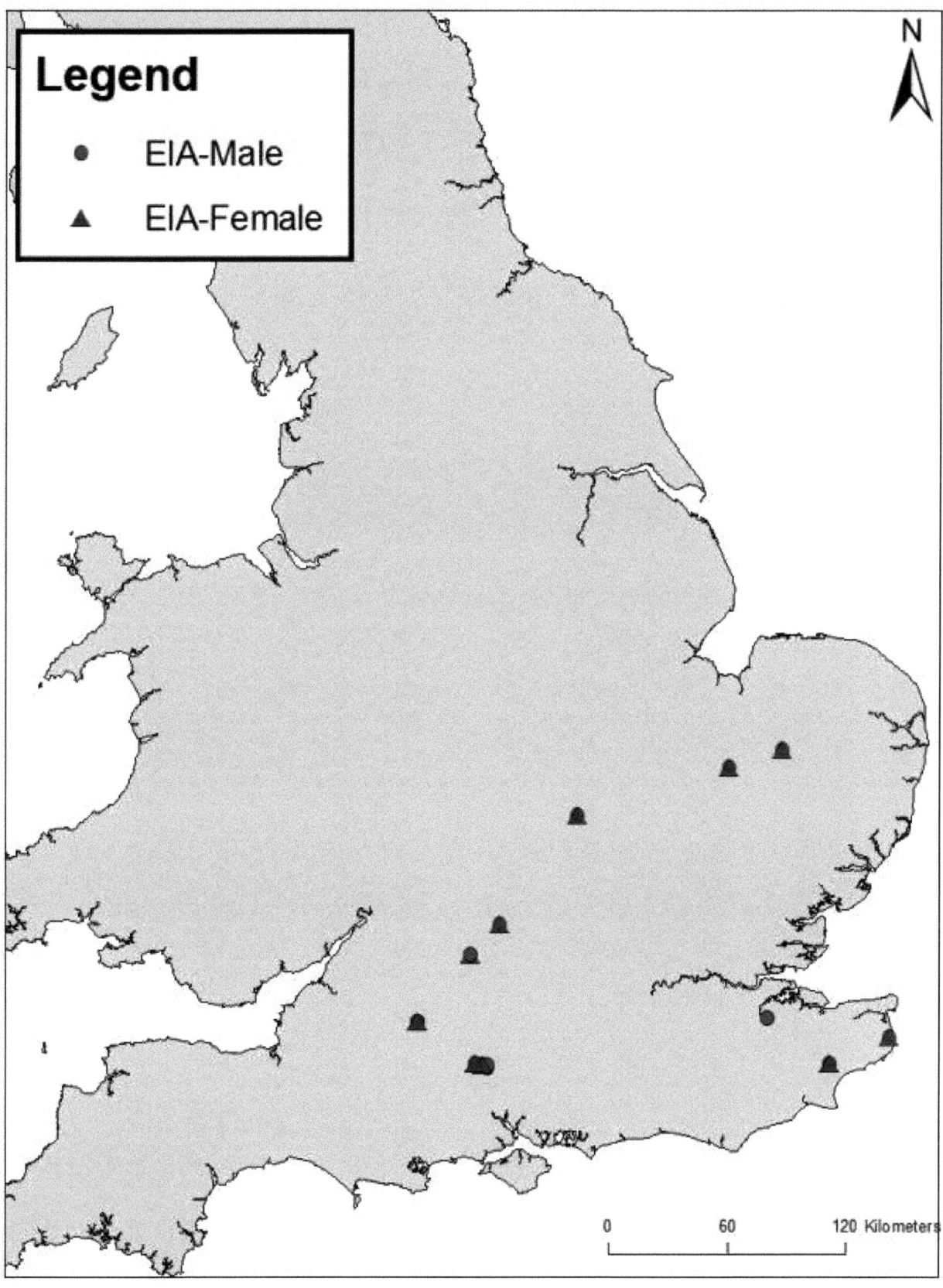

Figure 8. 14 Distribution of Early Iron Age sites according to sex

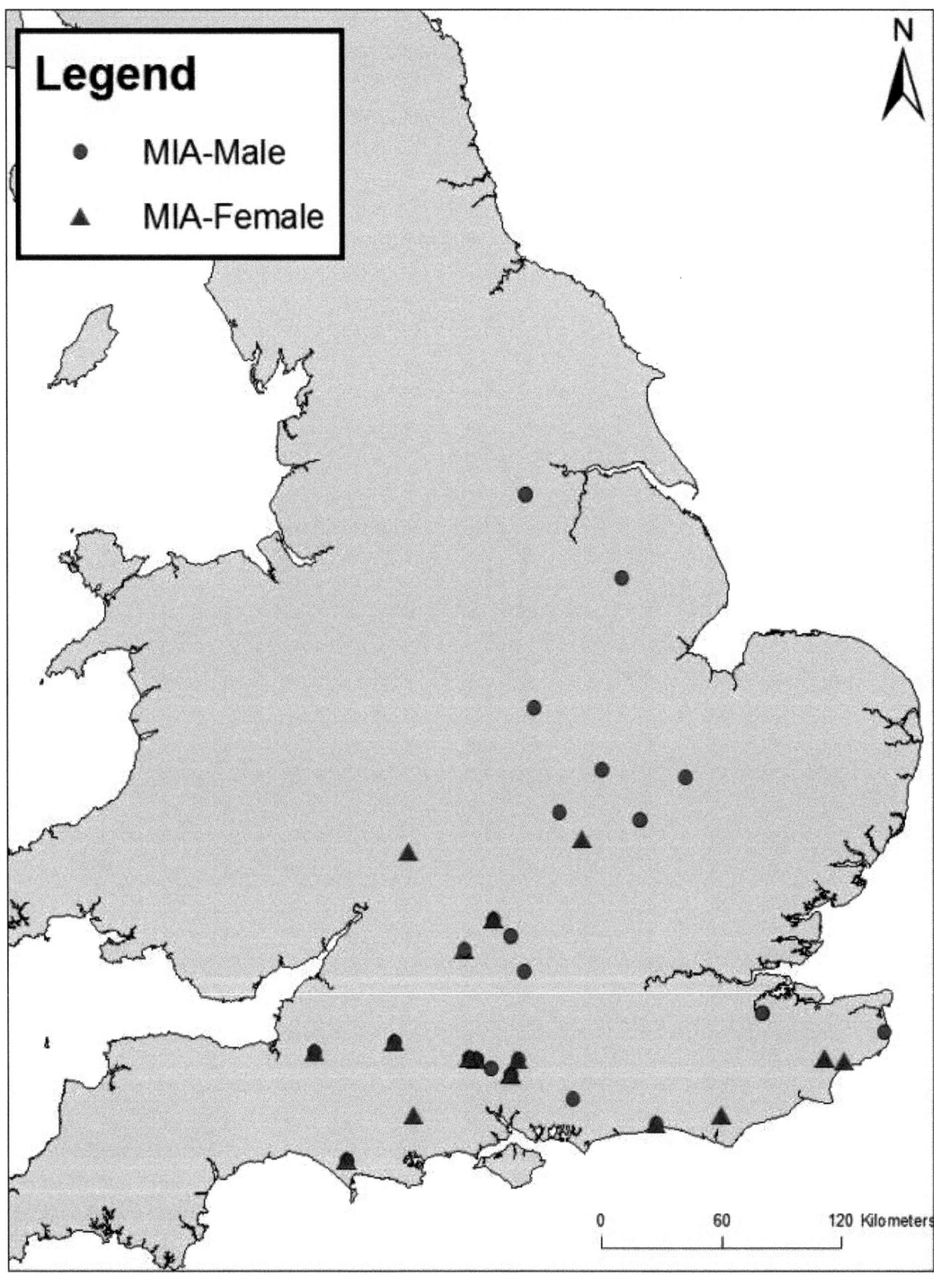

Figure 8. 15 Distribution of Middle Iron Age sites according to sex

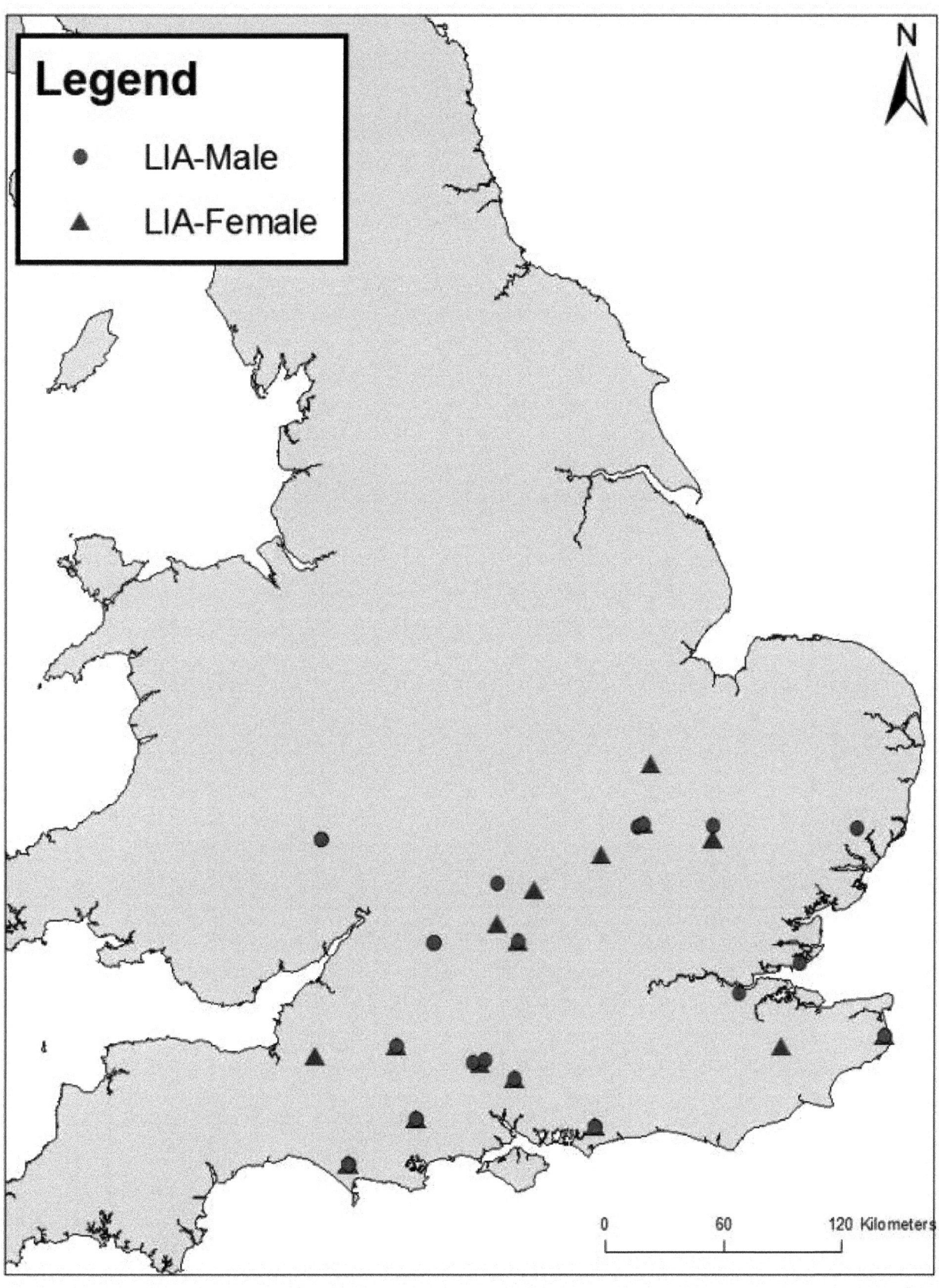

Figure 8. 16 Distribution of Late Iron Age sites according to sex

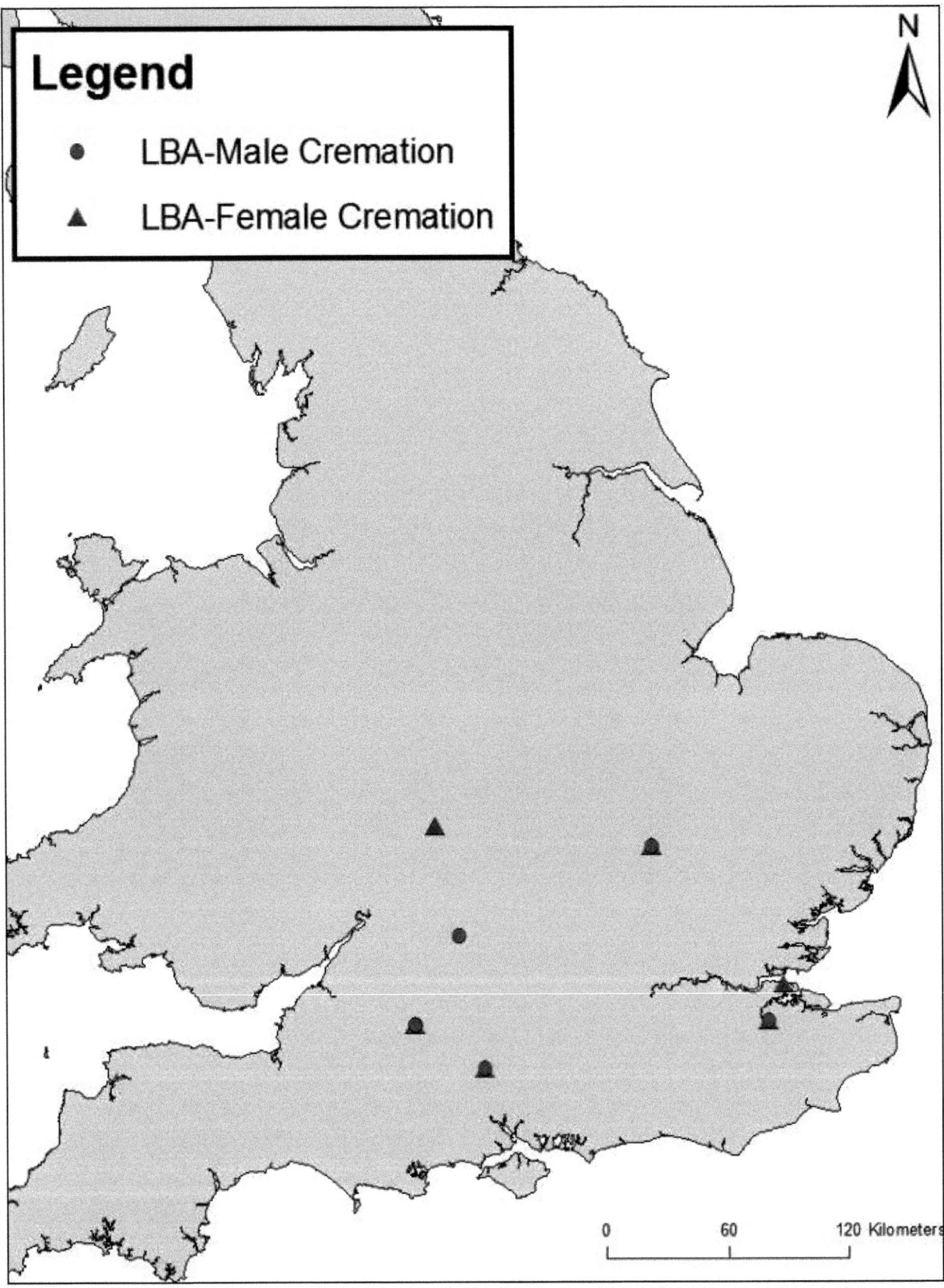

Figure 8. 17 Distribution of Late Bronze Age cremation sites according to sex

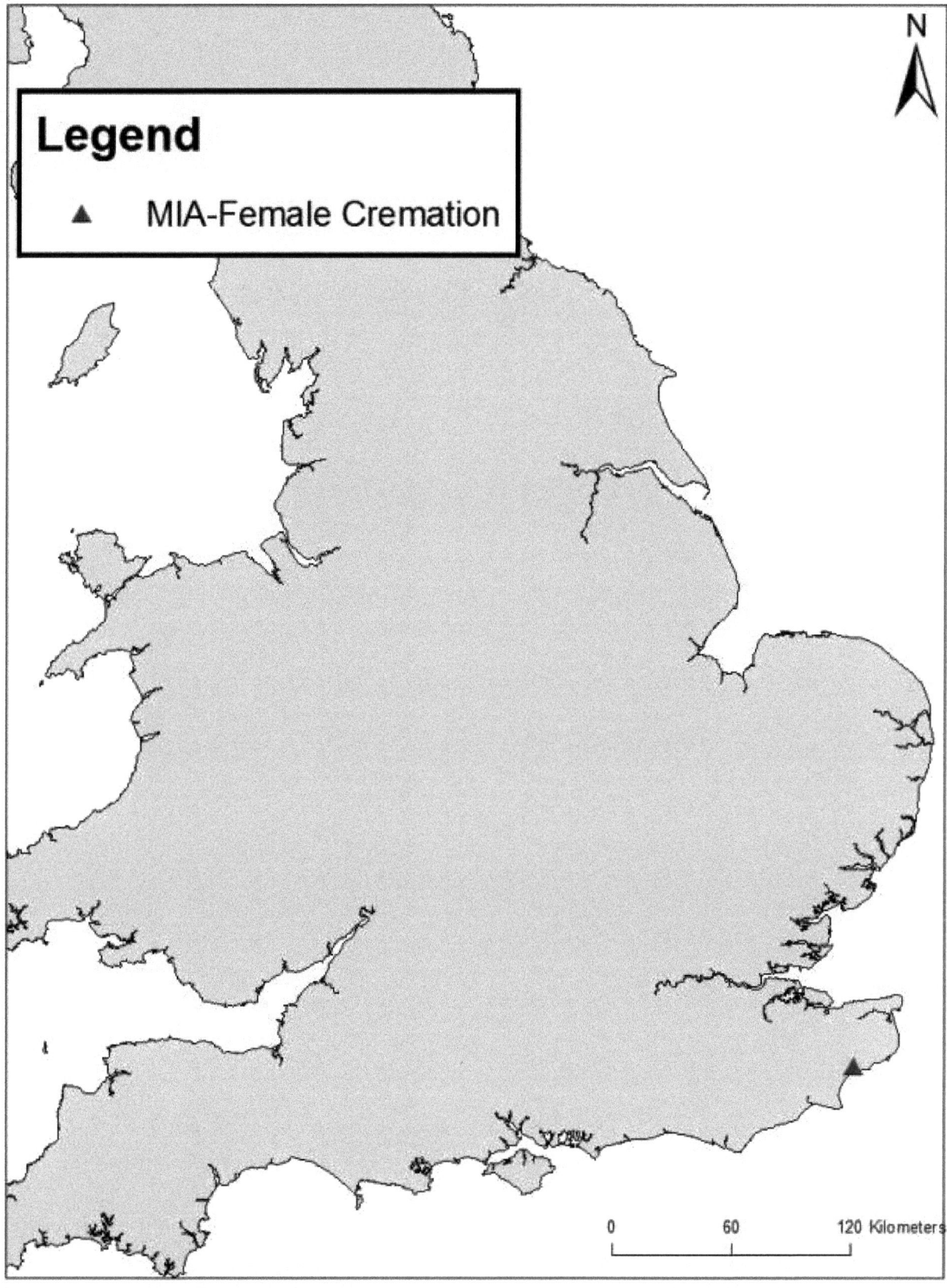

Figure 8. 18 Distribution of Middle Iron Age cremation site according to sex

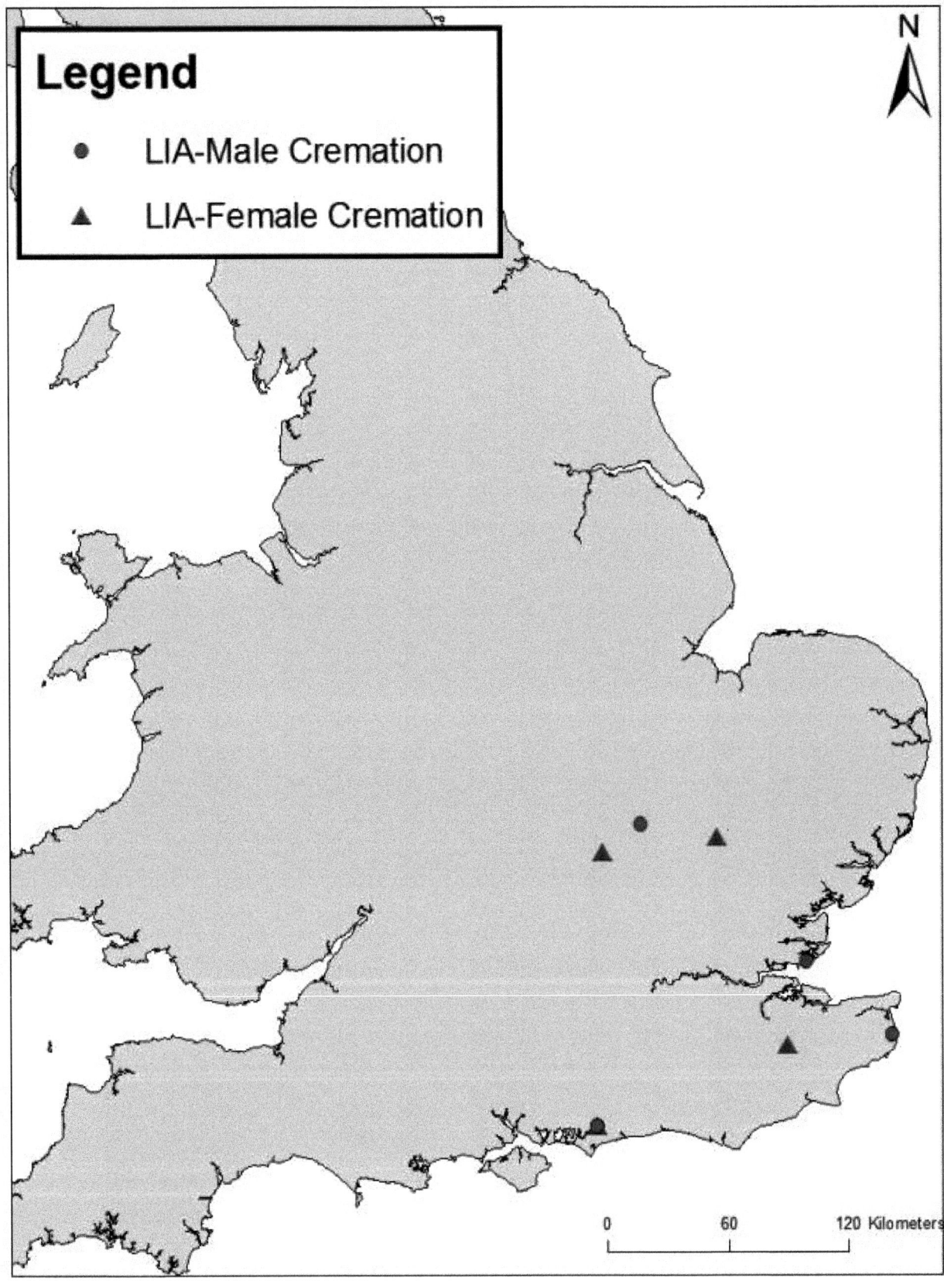

Figure 8. 19 Distribution of Late Iron Age cremation sites according to sex

Human remains associated with structures

There are a number of human remains occurrences associated with structures. Primarily these are round, rectangular, and irregular structures, and this section will focus on these three types. The quantitative analysis revealed a potential preference for placing human remains in and around these structures. In particular, remains tend to be placed in either the front or back, and the right or left segments of a building. The statistical analysis showed a distinct bias towards bones set within the right/interior and, notably, the left/perimeter of a structure.

We begin by looking at the overall distribution of round, rectangular and irregular structures with associated human remains occurrences. As **Figure 8.20** illustrates, the majority of sites have round structures with associated skeletal remains. However, the distribution of these three building types does not suggest geographical bias. Instead, there appears to be a relatively similar distribution of structure types within the studied area, differing only in their frequency.

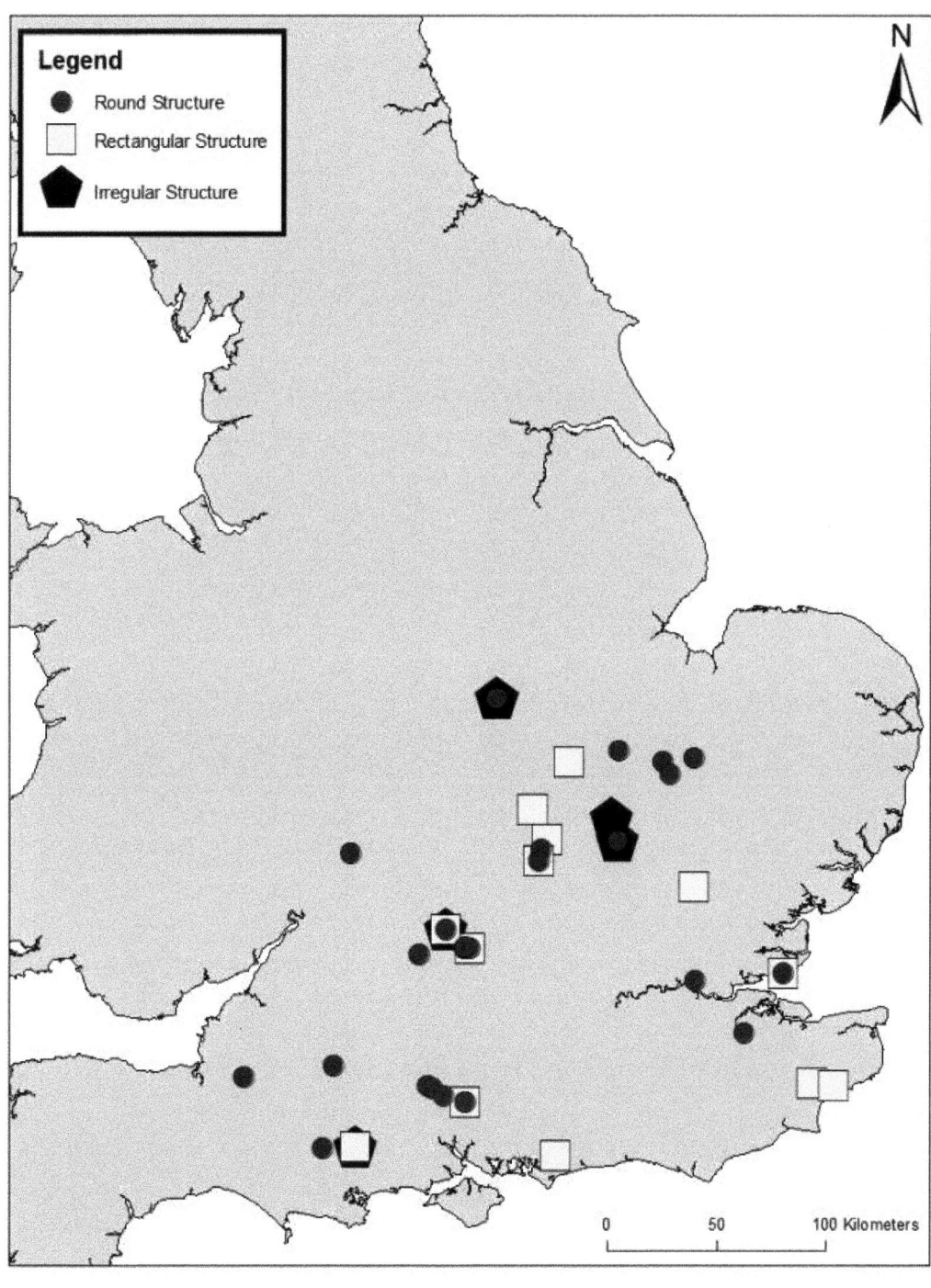

Figure 8. 20 Distribution of sites according to structure type

The following section focuses on the distribution of sites with human remains placed at either the front or back segments of a structure. **Figure 8.21** depicts this site distribution and, again there does not appear to be a particular geographical pattern for this characteristic. Instead, sites with remains set in the front areas of buildings have a distribution similar to those placed at the backs. This lack of regional difference is also found when focusing on sites whose occurrences are set on either the right/interior or left/perimeter of a building (see **Figure 8.22**).

In summary, there appear to be no distinct geographical groupings or distribution patterns based on the characteristics of structures associated with human remains. The lack of regional distinction may suggest that the communities practising this type of burial deposition did so in a similar fashion. If this is the case, it may imply strict spatial organisation for these three structure types for human remains deposits across a wider area. Further insights into this aspect will be discussed in the following chapter.

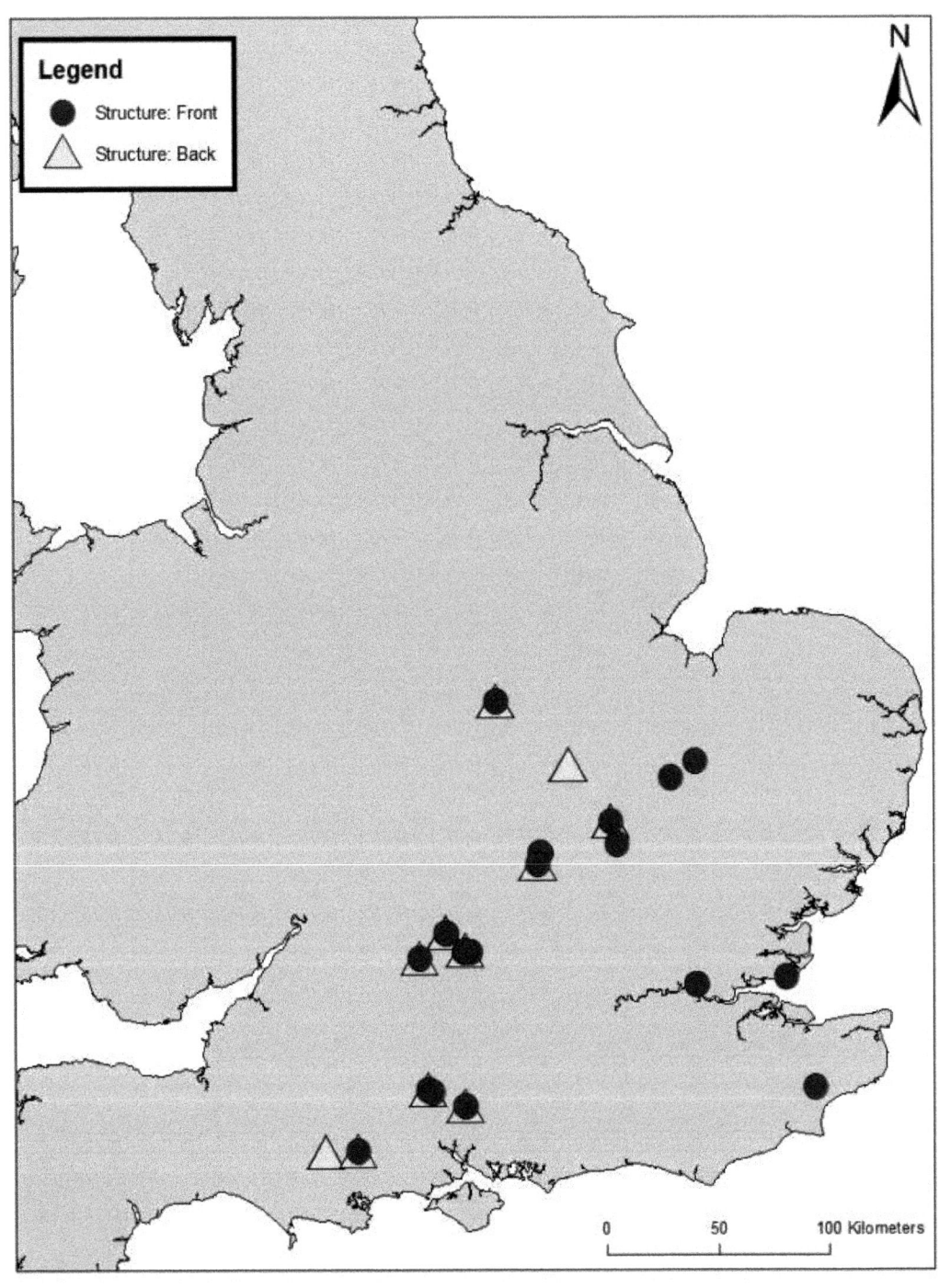

Figure 8. 21 Distribution of sites according to front/back placement

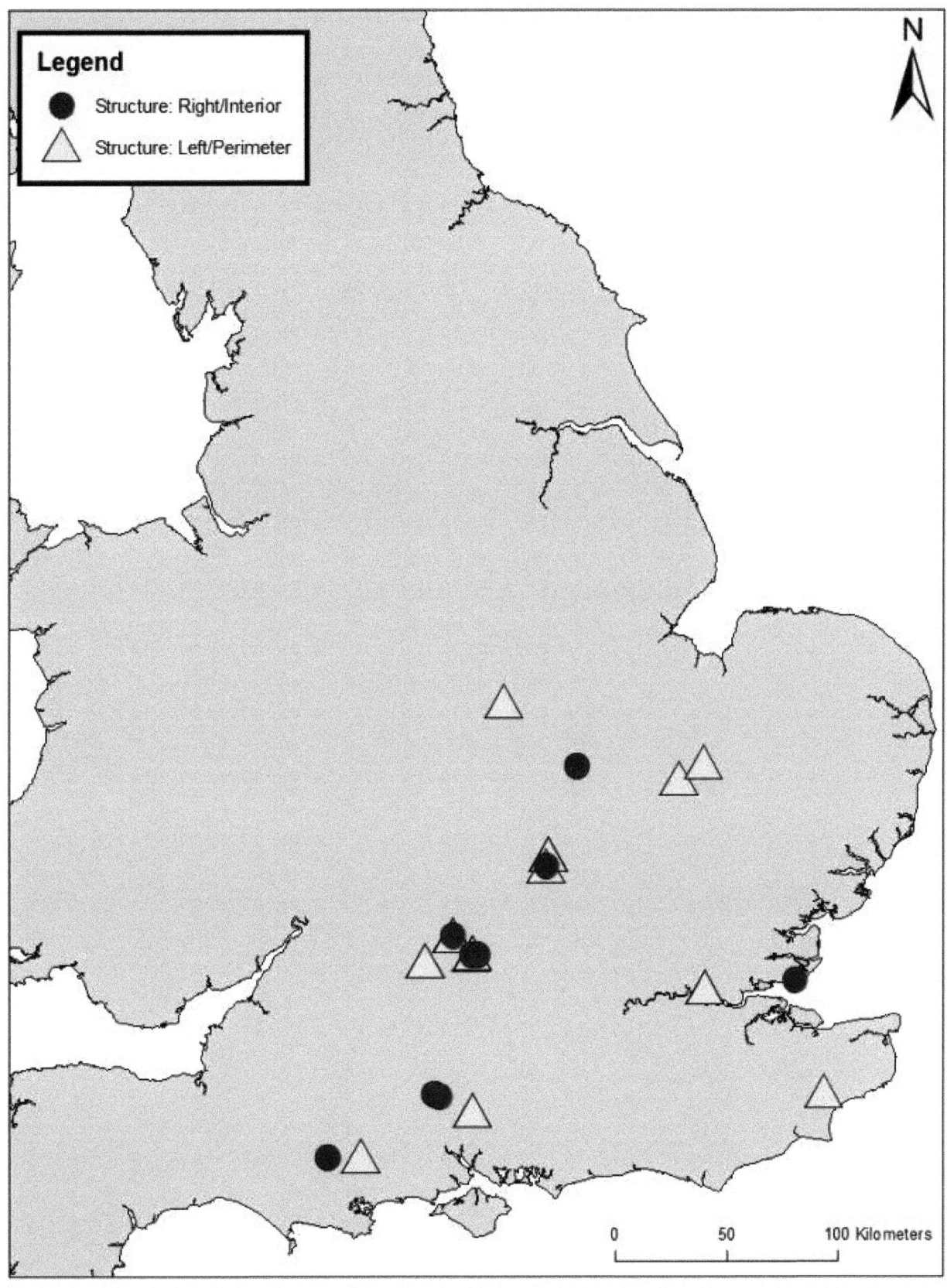

Figure 8. 22 Distribution of sites according to right/interior and left/perimeter placement

Burial trends

The second part of this chapter details burial trends for Iron Age human remains deposits. As stated above, these are recurring trends identified during data collection. The burial trends include the reuse of earlier monuments, human remains associated with places of economic significance, liminal markers, and complex treatments of the corpse. In general, the burial trends represent themes that may relate to how Iron Age cultures defined deposits of human remains.

Reuse of earlier monuments

To begin, the first trend under discussion is the reuse of earlier monuments, namely Late Neolithic/Early Bronze

Age barrows and ring ditches. **Figure 8.23** illustrates examples of sites with this trend. The reuse of these archaeological features is by no means universal; instead, just a handful of sites have this characteristic. However, the crucial point is that Iron Age people intentionally set human remains with regard to these landscape features. For example, from the archaeological site at Broom (Bedfordshire), four Late Bronze Age cremations were recovered from the eastern side of a Late Neolithic/ Early Bronze Age ring ditch (Cooper and Edmonds 2007, 64-65; 122-123). In addition, a poorly preserved Iron Age inhumation was set within the centre of the barrow mound (Dodwell 2007b, 275). The skeletal material and its location with the Bronze Age monument suggests that '...the old funerary monument not only provided the focus for this activity but was also thought to be the most appropriate place for depositing the material associated with it' (Cooper and Edmonds 2007, 124).

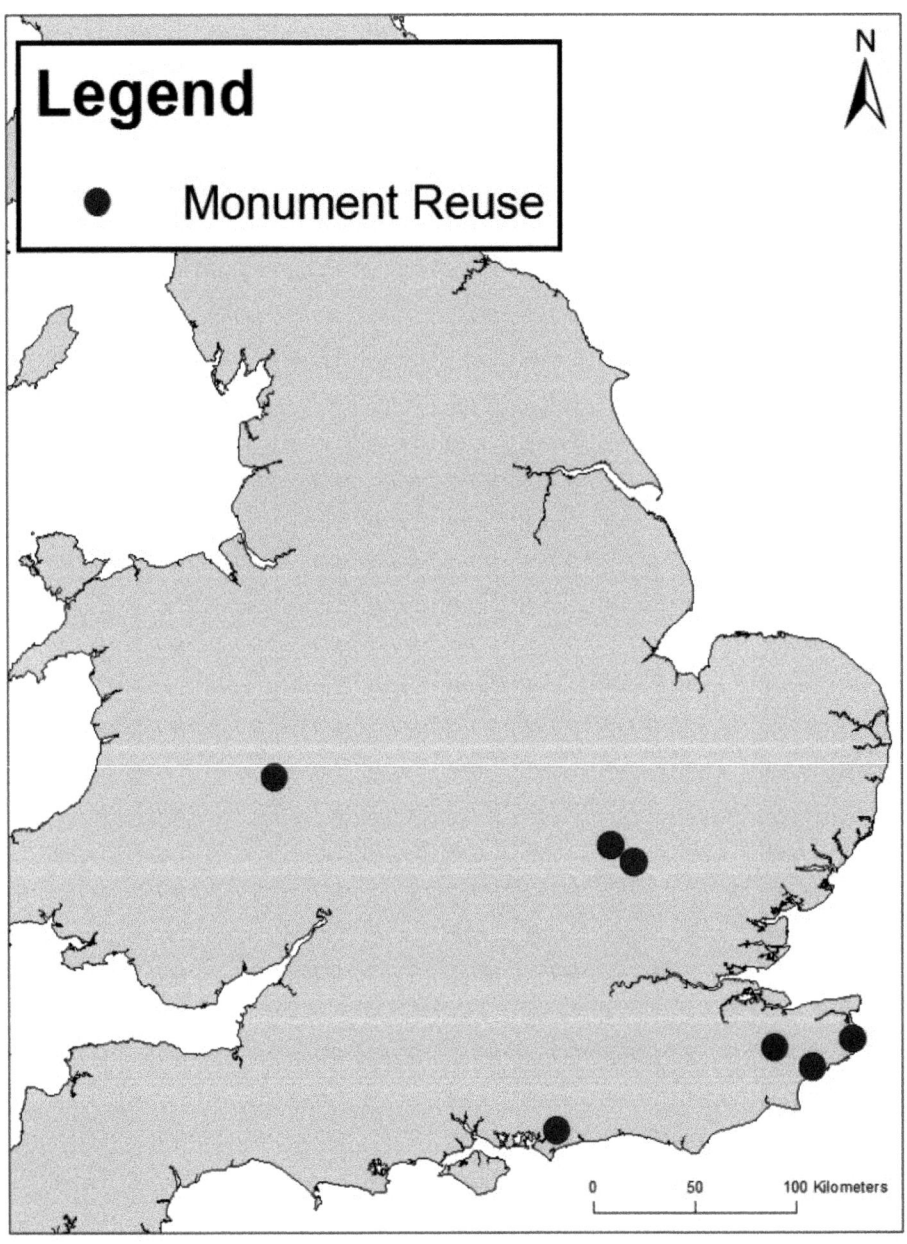

Figure 8. 23 Distribution of sites that have monument reuse

Similar to Broom, the archaeological site at Tutt Hill (Kent) contains four Late Neolithic/Early Bronze Age barrow ditches aligned along the River Stour and, later, a Late Bronze Age cremation deposit was set just to the south of one of the barrows (Brady 2006b, 18). In the Late Iron Age, another cremation deposit was set between two of the barrows, potentially signifying a revival in the ritual use of this area (Brady 2006b, 21). Also from Kent, Stone Farm Bridleway provides another example that demonstrates the reuse of earlier monuments. At Stone Farm Bridleway, there is an Early Bronze Age ring ditch where seven inhumations, dating to the Early/Middle Iron Age, lie just to the east of the Bronze Age monument (Crockett 2000, 2.2.9). Interestingly, a small amount of cremated bone was placed within a probable posthole, which is thought to be a possible grave marker for two of the inhumations that lie to the immediate south of the posthole (Crockett 2000, 2.2.9). Two additional inhumations are interred within the interior of the ring ditch (Crockett 2000, 2.2.10). Moreover, a small, sub-rectangular Iron Age enclosure lies directly to the east of the ring ditch as well. The interior of the rectangular enclosure lacks archaeological features, although five Early/Middle Iron Age cremation deposits were placed within the eastern arm of the structure (Crockett 2000, 2.2.10; see **Figure 8.24**).

In the Late Iron Age, the cremation cemetery at Westhampnett (Fitzpatrick 1997a) and the inhumation cemetery at Mill Hill (Parfitt 1995), each discussed in the previous chapter, were both set within the vicinity of Bronze Age barrows. Furthermore, at the A505 Baldock Bypass (Hertfordshire) there is a larger Bronze Age funerary complex containing numerous barrows (Thorpe *et al.* 2003). An unphased Iron Age inhumation deposit was set between two of the barrows within this funerary complex. Interestingly, the inhumation is of a young adult male who was decapitated with his head lying near his

arm. Later, a secondary cremation deposit was cut into the fill of the inhumation (Thorpe *et al.* 2003, 17). Lastly, the site at Bromfield (Shropshire) is a Bronze Age cremation cemetery consisting of barrows and ring ditches (Hughes *et al.* 1995). Within the centre of one of these Middle Bronze Age ring ditches are the scant remains of an unphased Iron Age inhumation (Hughes *et al.* 1995, 68).

Moreover, there are a couple of cases of Iron Age people reusing features from a more 'recent' past for burial. For example, excavations at the site of Aspreys, Olney, in Buckinghamshire, show a pit alignment that was constructed in the Early Iron Age (Webley 2007a). After the feature's construction, the pits were left to fill through natural processes, and have no evidence of re-cutting or modification (Webley 2007a, 68). However, in the Middle Iron Age an adolescent inhumation was placed within one of the silted-up though still visible pits with limestone slabs covering the body (Webley 2007a, 68, 73-74). In addition, at Salford (Bedfordshire) there was an Early Iron Age partially enclosed settlement that continued until the end of the Middle Iron Age (Dawson 2005, 169). Sometime after the settlement's abandonment in the Late Iron Age, four cremation burials were set between and aligned along the former double-ditched enclosure north of the settlement (Dawson 2005, 78).

The previous examples convey the impression that, for some Iron Age communities these earlier monuments were still a significant element within the landscape. In the Iron Age, these monuments were still a focal point for, in most cases, a select number of individuals to be buried. In addition, within the studied sample, all the sites with evidence of reuse tend to favour the eastern areas of England; none is seen within Wessex and areas to the north. However, there are only a handful of cases of human remains associated with earlier features. Thus, it is not an adequate sample to argue for any definite regional distinction.

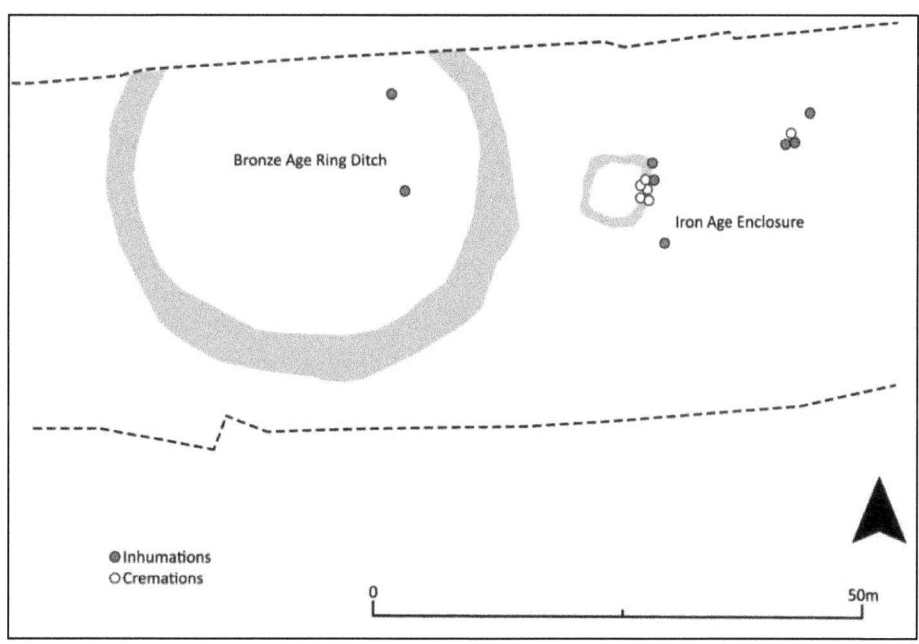

Figure 8. 24 Site plan of Stone Farm Bridleway (after Oxford Wessex Archaeology Joint Venture and HS 1 LTD, trench plan), with permission

Economic significance

The following examples discuss the possible cases of human remains deposits being used to mark an area of economic significance for the community (**Figure 8.25**). These areas of significance are thought to relate not just to agricultural activities, but also to other economic aspects that also had undoubted importance to Iron Age communities. For example, the univallate hillfort at Harting Beacon (West Sussex) lacks internal features, except for a ploughed-out round barrow and, due to the near-absence of grain storage pits and field systems nearby, it is theorised as possibly functioning as a seasonally used stock enclosure (Bedwin 1978, 227, 230; 1979, 25). A skull was set within a ditch adjacent to the western entrance of the hillfort, with three teeth in the entrance's two postholes. At Hartsdown Technology College, also in Kent, an early Iron Age inhumation lay within a ditch of one of the two enclosures at the site (Gardener and Gibson 2008, 6). The enclosure is thought to have functioned '...in the capacity of animal corrals, and associated with surrounding field systems' (Gardener and Gibson 2008, 19). At Little Stock Farm, an

inhumation may have been set at the entrance of a probable stock paddock before being exhumed and moved to the northern area of the site (Ritchie 2006, 9). Similarly, the Late Iron Age site at Wakerley (Northamptonshire) has nine infant burials set within the ditch of a large enclosure, which is presumably a stock compound (Jackson and Ambrose 1978, 122, 172). Moreover, at the Late Iron Age site of Jubilee Corner (Kent) there are six cremation burials all associated with a contemporary iron bloomery furnace (Aldridge 2005, 173; see **Figure 8.26**).

A possible explanation for human remains being associated with areas of economic significance is based on an elaboration of Cunliffe's fertility theory (1992; 1995; 2005). The difference here is that the interpretation does not assume that agriculture is the sole focus for economic benefit. Instead, Iron Age communities participated in a variety of practices for economic sustainability and gain, such as animal rearing and craftwork. Thus, it is just as probable that human remains may have been linked to these other economic activities, potentially reinforcing the significance of those spaces and their function for the wider community.

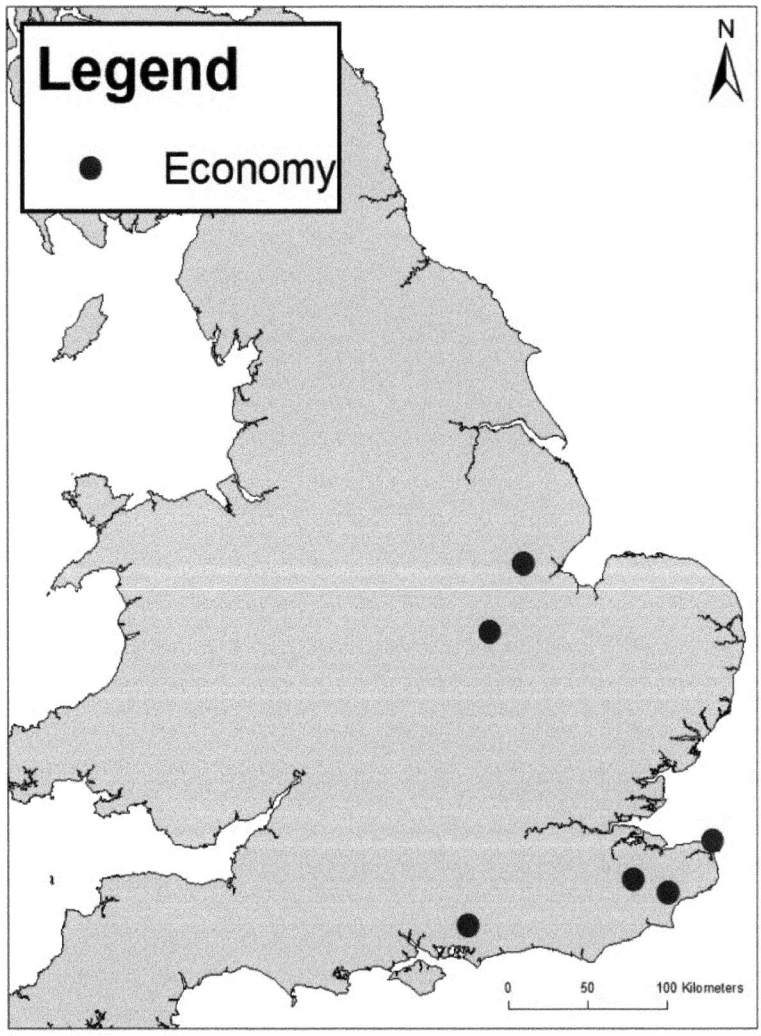

Figure 8. 25 Distribution of sites that have human remains in areas of economic significance

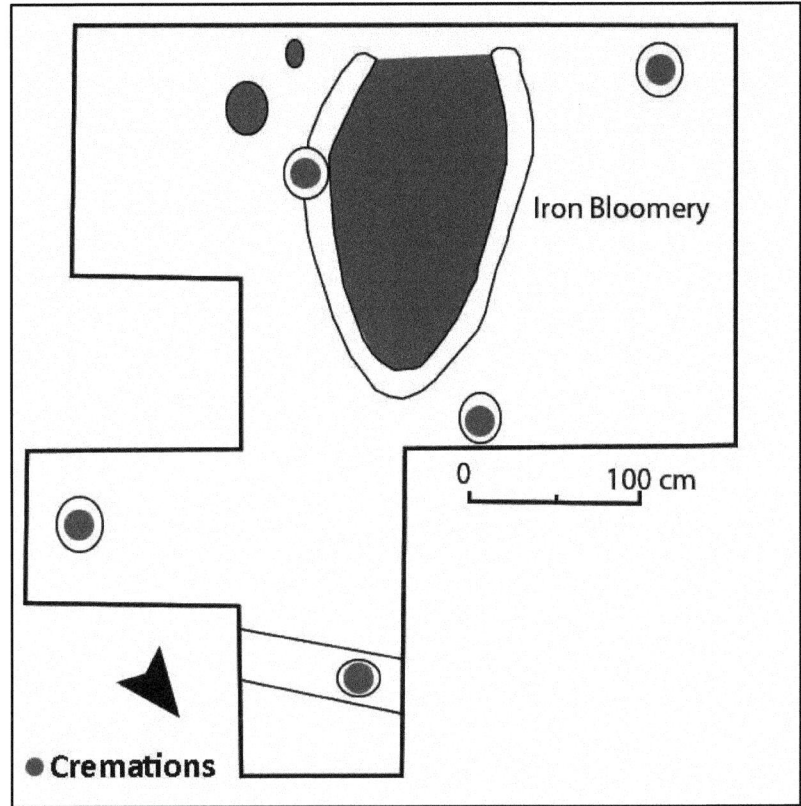

Iron Bloomery

0   100 cm

●Cremations

Figure 8. 26 Site plan of Jubilee Corner (after Aldridge 2005, 175); with the permission of the Kent Archaeological Society

Liminal markers

This section focuses on human remains deposited at transitional moments in the life of a site or structure. There is a wealth of research on the subject of liminal moments, and the recurrence of these types of deposits within the studied sample warrants further discussion (see Armit and Ginn 2007). In particular, there are three main times in the life (or use) of a structure or site, in which human remains may be used to signify or mark transitional moments. These periods include the beginning, renovation and abandonment of a site or structure. **Figure 8.27** illustrates the distribution of sites with this trend.

The discussion starts with four cases that demonstrate the use of human remains in marking the beginning of a site or building. The first case is from the open settlement site at Great Houghton in Northamptonshire (Chapman 2000-1). An Early Iron Age crouched inhumation of an adult woman was set within a pit that lies inside one of the domestic enclosures (Chapman 2000-1, 8-9). A radiocarbon date on the skeleton (405-370 cal BC) indicates that the deposit either pre-dates or is contemporary with the enclosure's early use (Chapman 2000-1, 8-9). At Maiden Castle, our second example, an Early Iron Age male inhumation deposit dates to the time of the extension of the hillfort's rampart, and the excavator suggests that the individual represents a foundation burial (Wheeler 1943, 37, 122-123). The third

example comes from North Shoebury (Essex) and is a deposit of an inverted skull within a pit near the gully of a roundhouse dating to the Middle Iron Age (Wymer and Brown 1995, 158). The function of the roundhouse is unknown (Wymer and Brown 1995, 34), although the authors theorise that the skull may have served as a foundation deposit for this building (Wymer and Brown 1995, 158). The final example is from the domestic site at Bluntisham in Cambridgeshire (Burrow and Mudd 2008) with the burial of an adult male inhumation dating to the Middle Iron Age, laid in a tight contracted position, possibly bound (Burrow and Mudd 2008, 9; Gerber 2008, 10-11). The radiocarbon date for the inhumation (200-110 cal BC) places the deposit just before the occupation or concurrent with the earliest part of it (Burrow and Mudd 2008, 9).

Human remains can also mark times of renovation of a site or building. The skeletal material may have signified a structure's transformation. There are two main examples that illustrate this point, and these are from Hod Hill (Dorset) and Spring Road (Oxfordshire). To begin, Hod Hill, an Iron Age hillfort, has an inhumation at Steepleton Gate, interred at the time of the entrance's rebuilding (Richmond 1968, 16). At Spring Road, four Middle Iron Age inhumations were set near a roundhouse, possibly signifying a small cemetery area (Allen 2008, 21). Originally, the roundhouse served a domestic function, and the inhumation burials date close to the time when the roundhouse went out of use (Allen 2008, 21). The later inhumations may signify the redefinition of the remaining building's space. In other words, the burials may have marked both the transfer of function of the building and the definition of its new use.

The last case from Spring Road leads into the final form of marking of liminal moments, which is when human remains signify the abandonment of a site or structure. Of all the liminal moments, abandonment deposits are the most common. The first example is from Broom (Toll House) in Bedfordshire (Cooper and Edmonds 2007). Here, a small amount of cremated bone (9g), dating to the Late Bronze Age, was inserted into the post-pipe of a roundhouse entrance's postholes (Cooper and Edmonds 2007, 107). The cremation deposit lay within the void made by the decaying posthole after the roundhouse fell into disuse (Cooper and Edmonds 2007, 107-108). Similarly, the last activity at the Late Bronze Age/Early Iron Age site of Kingsmead Park (Kent) was the deposition of three cremations (Greatorex 2005, 78-79). High Barns Road (Bedfordshire), a settlement site, has a complex deposit of an inhumation and three skull fragments along the western arm of one of the site's enclosures (Webley 2007b, 19). Interestingly, the skeletal remains were deposited in a single event, and one of the skull fragments returned a radiocarbon date earlier than the other bones, suggesting curation of this element (Webley 2007b, 19). Additionally, the skeletal deposit

marks the last activity for the enclosure (Webley 2007b, 19). Mingies Ditch (Oxfordshire), an occupation site, has a post-abandonment deposit of two Middle Iron Age disarticulated bones set in the northern half of the site (Allen and Robinson 1993, 141). In East Sussex, the domestic site of Norton has a double inhumation of a woman and infant in the midden area that signifies the last activity on the settlement (Thomas 2005, 99, 112; see **Figure 8.28**). The disarticulated bone deposit at Harting Beacon, previously discussed, dates to the time of dismantling of the hillfort's entrance and the bone deposit is one of the last pieces of evidence of activity on the site (Bedwin 1979, 25). Disarticulated bone deposits are set within the final fills of some of the enclosures at the Middle/Late Iron Age settlement site of Elms Farm (Leicestershire), representing the last period of use for these buildings (Charles *et al.* 2000, 197). The settlement site at Gayhurst Quarry has a Middle/Late Iron Age inhumation and Late Iron Age cremation deposit around the time of and just after the site's abandonment (Chapman 2007, 194, 203). Lastly, White Horse Stone (Kent) contains inhumation, disarticulated bone and cremation deposits dating to the Early/Middle Iron Age, which are contemporary with the settlement's abandonment (Hayden and Stafford 2006).

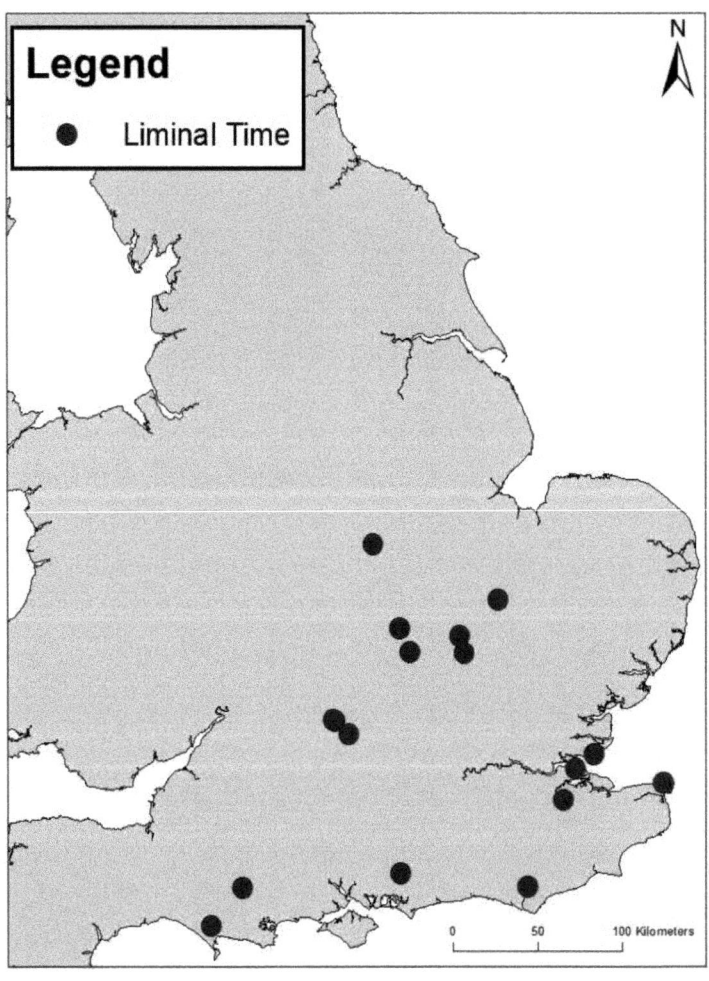

Figure 8. 27 Distribution of sites that have human remains as liminal markers

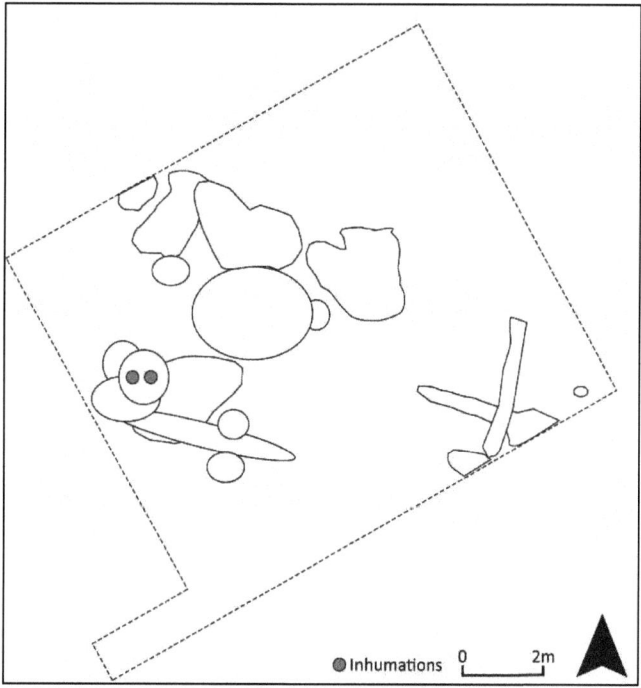

Figure 8. 28 Site plan of Norton (after Seager Thomas 2005, 84); reproduced from Susses Archaeological Collections 143 with kind permission of the Sussex Archaeological Society

Complex treatment

This last section discusses the complex treatment of human remains. Particular focus is given to sites that provide key examples illustrating the community's direct behaviour and activities in the treatment of the corpse. These examples have strong evidence for curation of bones, post-mortem modification and manipulation, and so forth. This section on complex treatment focuses first on the skull and is then followed by human remains in general. Fundamentally, the following examples are most insightful because they provide a direct link to the cultural processes performed on the dead.

Skulls

Disarticulated bones are the highest occurring manner of disposal and, amongst them; the skull is the most frequent element. **Figure 8.29** illustrates the distribution of sites with skull occurrences, and one can see that they are spread across the studied area. In addition, **Figure 8.30** depicts sites with skull occurrences that have evidence of some form of post-mortem manipulation and modification. Two prime examples of peri/post-mortem modification of the cranium come from Billingborough and Helpringham Fen, both in Lincolnshire. To begin, Billingborough began as mainly a Late Bronze Age/Early Iron Age salt-working area, and then later became a settlement during the Middle to Late Iron Age (Chowne *et al.* 2001). A number of skull fragments from ditch

contexts, dating to both the Late Bronze Age/Early Iron Age and Middle/Late Iron Age, possess evidence of post-

mortem modification (Bayley 2001, 73-74). The bone modifications include such indicators as weathering, possible head removal and, for some of the bones, '...the vaults were being cut or sawn from skulls and the rims perforated, presumably so they could be suspended and function as bowls' (Bayley 2001, 78). As for Helpringham Fen, also a salt-making industrial site, a single adult cranium fragment, dating to the Middle Iron Age, has evidence of weathering and of being 'sawn' off peri/post-mortem (Bayley 1999, 17).

In addition, from Oxfordshire, there are also two cases of probable skull modification, one from Watchfield and the other from Gravelly Guy. At the Early/Middle Iron Age settlement of Watchfield, within a pit and accompanied by a cow skull, there was a mature adult male skull fragment with a well-healed trepanation. In addition, the skull fragment had peri/post-mortem cut marks on the bone that are possibly evidence of scalping or defleshing (Birbeck 2001, 229; McKinley 2001, 267). At Gravelly Guy, a skull fragment, from an Early Iron Age pit, was fashioned into a disc with a central perforation and possesses evidence of wear (Wait 2004, 249). Similarly, at Glastonbury Lake Village (Somerset), an Iron Age skull fragment had been cut into a disc, also perforated in the centre, and may have functioned as an amulet or spindle whorl (Barber *et al.* 1995, 174). Lastly, at the settlement site of Houghton Down (Hampshire), within the basal layer of a pit, there was an Early Iron Age skull with blunt force trauma and possible evidence of intentional fragmentation of the skull (Hooper 2000b, 14:E4 [microfiche]).

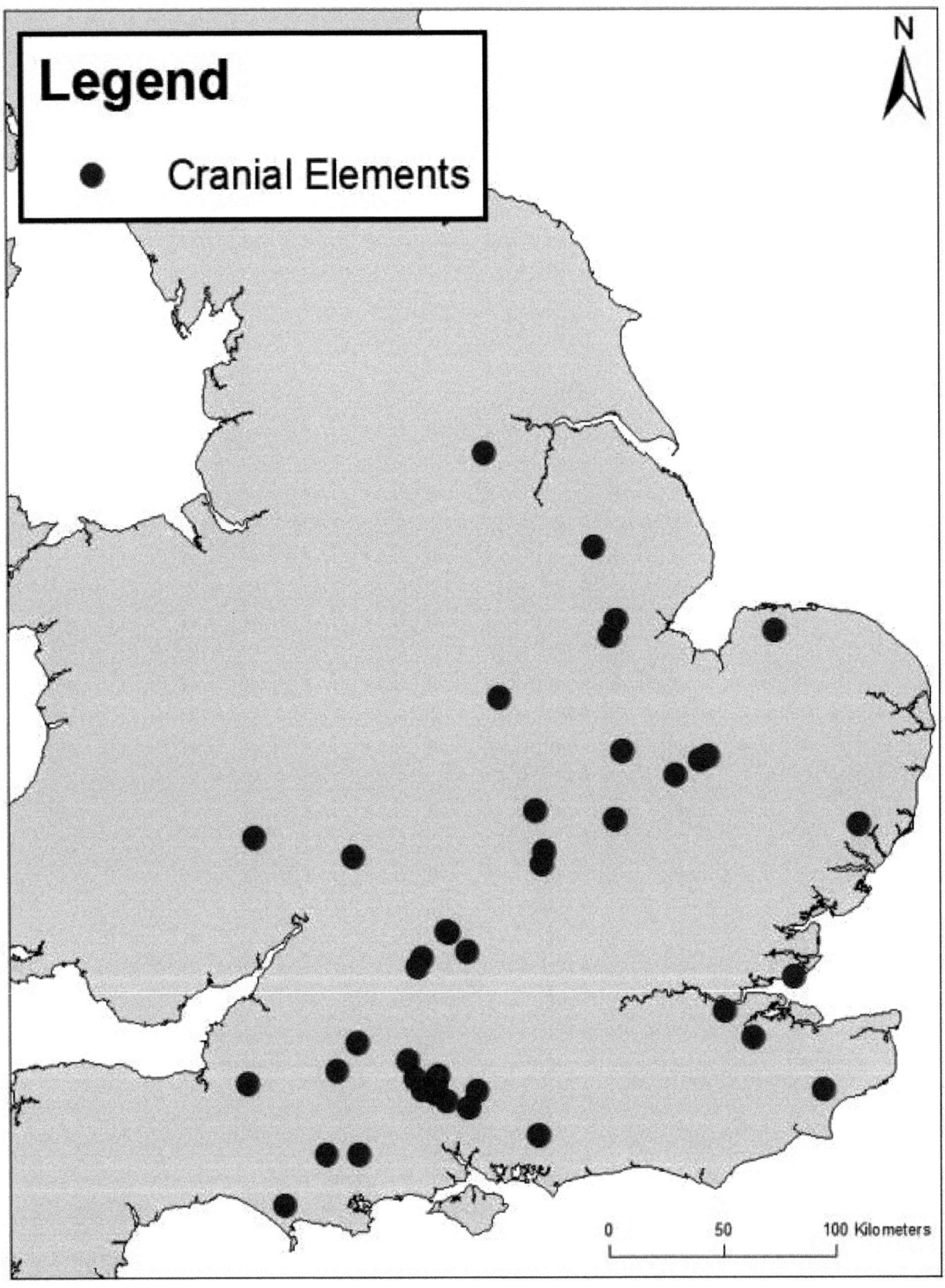

Figure 8. 29 Distribution of sites with cranial elements

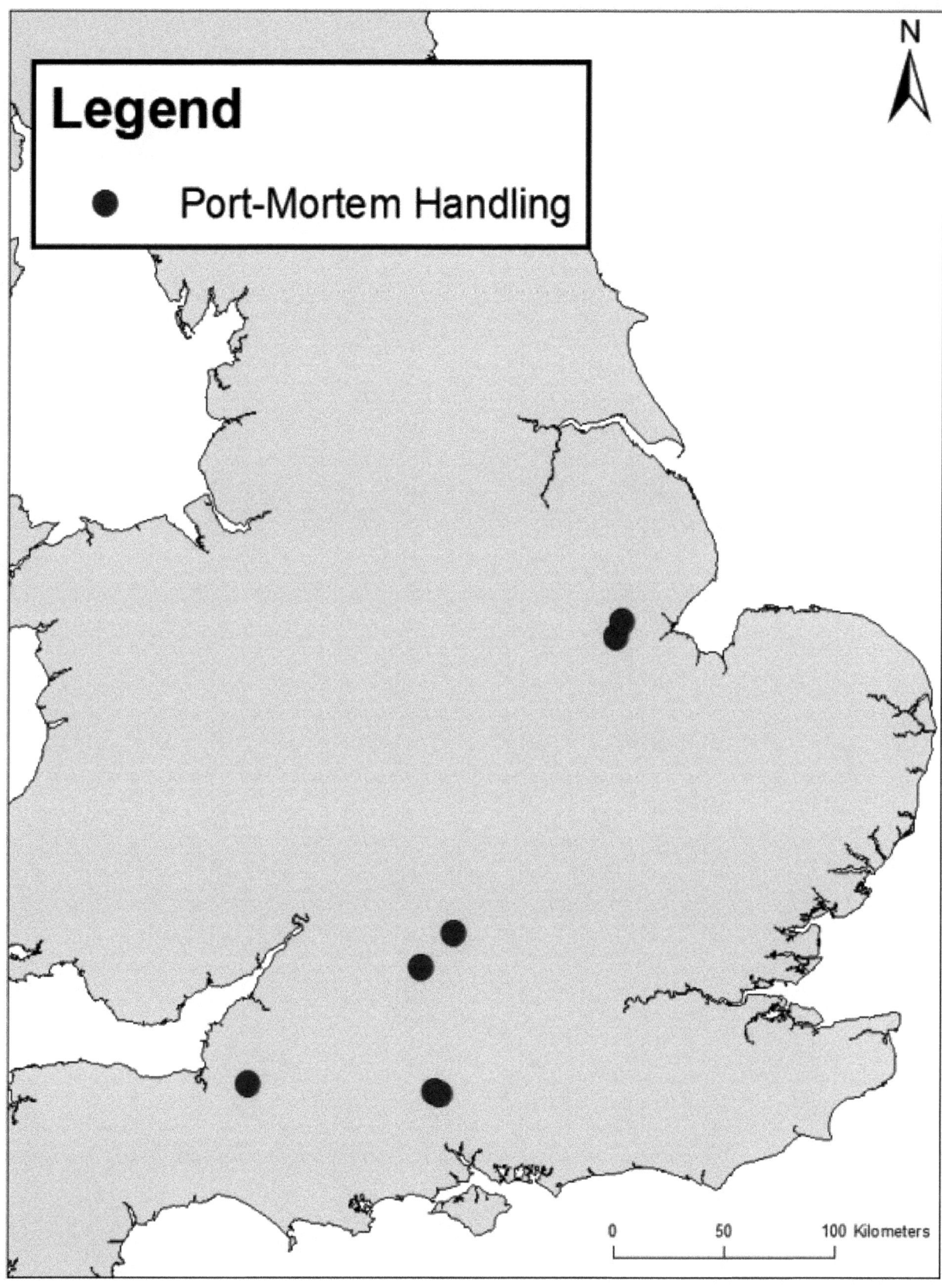

Figure 8. 30 Distribution of sites that have evidence of post-mortem handling of skulls

Complex treatment of human remains

Following on from examples of skull modification and post-mortem use, there is also a series of cases of a probably complex and long-lived burial rite. These examples (though not all), like the skull examples, have the most direct evidence of particular actions performed on the corpse, either directly following death or sometime after. The cases relate to the breakdown of the body and continued manipulation of the human remains. **Figure 8.31** indicates the sites with examples of complex treatment of human remains.

For example, at Battlesbury Bowl (Wiltshire), most of the disarticulated bone that dates to the Late Bronze Age to early Middle Iron Age has indicators of gnawing and weathering. 'The form and nature of the material is indicative of some level of exposure linked to deliberate

manipulation involving excarnation and possibly "curation"' (McKinley 2008, 81-82). Wandlebury Ringwork (Cambridgeshire) contains two cases of removing parts of the corpse while flesh was still attached (Hartley 1957). The first is a juvenile skeleton, the lower half of whose body was removed, and the upper part presumably wrapped in a shroud or sack, and then buried (Hartley 1957, 15). At the same site, an adult female possesses signs of dismemberment that include the skull being separated from the body, and the femoral heads still articulated with acetabulum yet broken off a few inches down from the joint (Hartley 1957, 15). A similar case of dismemberment is also evident at the farmstead site of Beard Mill in Oxfordshire (Williams 1951). Here, an Early/Middle Iron Age inhumation '...had been dismembered and heaped haphazard[ly] in the partly-filled pit; the foot-bones were found articulated but placed on top of a couple of rib bones; arm and leg bones lay above a badly damaged cranium' (Williams 1951, 14).

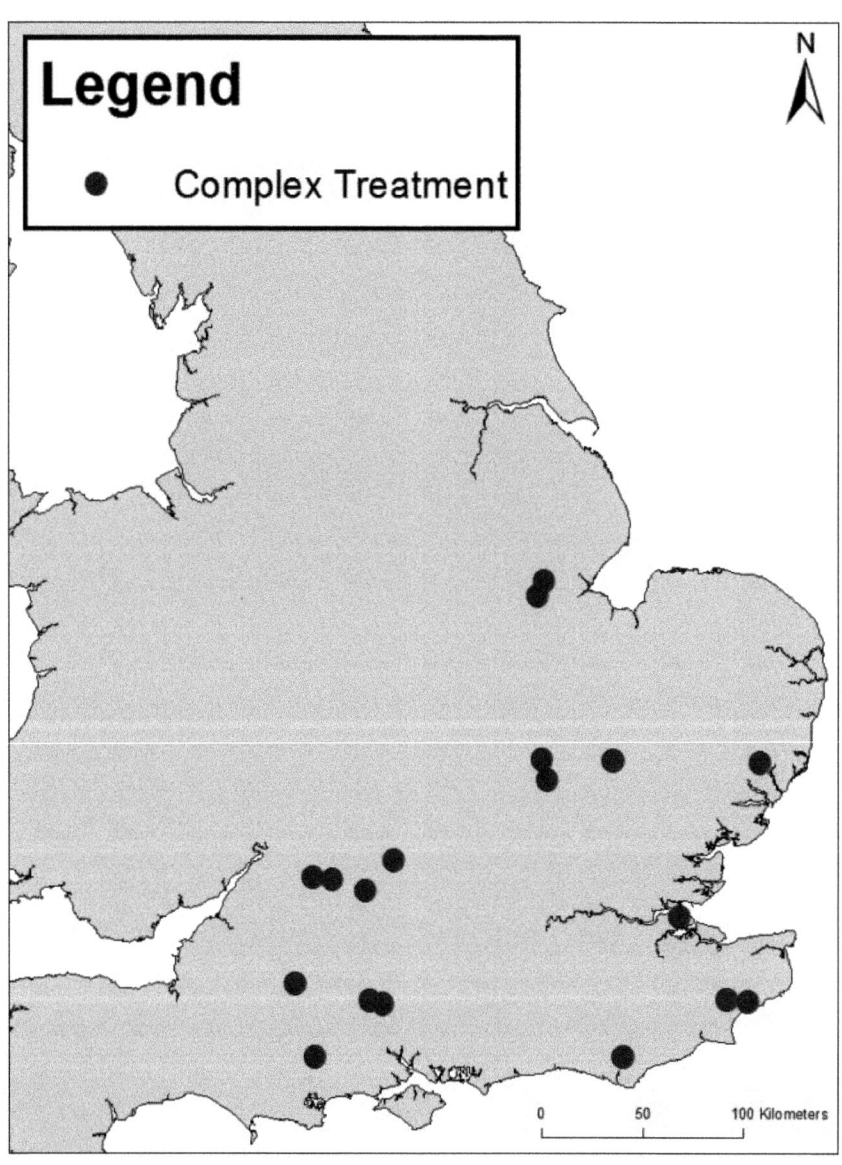

Figure 8. 31 Distribution of sites that have evidence of complex treatment to the human remains

An interesting case from Latton Lands (Wiltshire) shows a Middle/Late Iron Age adult male inhumation that may be the result of a failed *in situ* cremation (Powell *et al.* 2008, 45-46). The bones have evidence of burning and there was burnt timber and charcoal found above and below the remains within the grave (Gerber and Loe 2008, 122). As previously discussed, at the settlement at Little Stock Farm (Kent) an incomplete inhumation was found interred just north of the settlement area. Additionally, skull fragments were uncovered in a separate context that lies to the west of the settlement, at the entrance of a possible stock enclosure (Ritchie 2006, 9). It is possible that the skull fragments belong to the inhumation, suggesting that the skeleton was initially buried beside the stock enclosure before being exhumed and moved to the northern area of the site (McKinley 2006a, 69). The Little Stock Farm example suggests the possibility that even though the individual may be hidden (buried) from the community, it was still socially alive, to the point where sometime after its interment the community felt obliged to unearth the remains and then move them to a separate location. One possible explanation may be that the area of the first interment lost its significance or, alternatively, it may be evidence of a controlled practice of sub-terrain excarnation practice (see Madgwick 2008).

The preceding section has discussed only a handful of examples relating to complex treatment of the corpse. What the cases suggest is that there are varying elements and methods in processing the corpse, although a key factor that links them together is the ultimate goal of deconstructing the corpse. After these processes, the human remains either received their final deposition, or were further curated by the group.

Summary

In conclusion, this investigation into the regional patterns of Iron Age burial practice appears to show a geographical distinction in the manner of disposal with respect to date. The distribution by manner of disposal shows a difference between the eastern areas of England and the west, and the difference relates to varying methods in processing the dead. In addition, distribution by age at death for human remains suggests that areas to the east and towards the northern part of the studied area favoured deposition of older sub-adults and adults, especially during the Middle Iron Age. However, the distribution by biological sex, context type and structures does not seem to show any regional patterning.

Additionally, this chapter has also discussed trends in Iron Age burial practices. A common theme between the reuse of earlier monuments, areas of economic significance and liminal markers is the choice of spatial settings for deposits of human remains. More specifically, the meaning behind the deposits differs for each of these trends. Thus, it demonstrates the variety of purposes that human remains may have served for Iron Age communities, as well as the importance of the spatial setting of their deposits. Understanding the complex treatment of the dead is crucial because it offers a clear picture of the differing processes that the body underwent before deposition.

In general, from investigating regional patterns and burial trends, two main themes appear to emerge. One theme is the process of breaking down the body. This theme appears to be regionally distinct, and the varying processes performed on the body may relate to communities' differing perspectives on death and burial. The other theme is the spatial setting of human remains deposits. This includes the reuse of earlier monuments, areas of economic significance, liminal markers, and placement within structures; each of these demonstrates how the location of the deposit was a central component in defining the meaning of the skeletal material. The social implications for each of these themes will be explored further in the following chapter.

Chapter Nine

Discussion

Introduction

This chapter discusses the social implications for the analysis of Late Bronze Age and Iron Age burial practices. It begins by addressing taphonomic processes that possibly affected the Late Bronze Age and Iron Age burial record. After this, the chapter breaks into four main sections: the processing of the human remains, the spatial placement of the deposit, the identity of the skeletal material, and the overall implications of the burial rite based on the preceding sections. Each section addresses the related statistical and regional findings with respect to past interpretations of the evidence. Ultimately, the discussion outlines interconnected themes that are central to uncovering the social motivations behind Iron Age burial practices. Culture is a symbolic system in which human remains become a component of the network that communicates the ideological foundation of the group (Geertz 1973, 17). It is this study's stance that the processing, spatial context, and identity of the human remains acquired new, symbolic meanings through ritual activity and their interrelationship provides the framework towards approaching Late Bronze Age and Iron Age burial practices (Geertz 1973, 17, 91).

Taphonomic processes

This study's conclusions rely on human remains uncovered from Late Bronze Age and Iron Age sites. It is important to address the degree to which the patterns in the burial record are the result of Iron Age people or of taphonomic processes. There are a number of taphonomic processes that may affect the skeletal material and its presence or absence, such as excavation strategies and bone survival. The following section addresses taphonomic factors that may affect the skeletal material that influence the burial record for the Late Bronze Age and the Iron Age. Specifically, the discussion will centre on the soil conditions, recovery techniques, and excavation limitations.

Simon Mays (1992) demonstrated the effects of soil on bone survival that undoubtedly influences the burial record. In his study, Mays (1992, 54) investigated over 200 medieval burials in order to '...distinguish patterns of loss resulting from differential destruction of skeletal elements in the soil from those brought about by differential recovery during excavation'. Mays' (1992, 55) study demonstrated that bones such as the skull, mandible, and long bones preserve better in soil than more fragile bones, such as the hyoid and sternum. An extreme example from this study's sample that demonstrates the effects of soil in bone preservation is from Bromfield Gravel Quarry (Shropshire). This site has a possible Iron

Age inhumation inserted in the top of a Bronze Age ring ditch (Hughes *et al.* 1995). None of the skeleton survived due to soil conditions apart from an unusual soil stain. Later chemical analysis on the soil indicated a body was buried there (Hughes *et al.* 1995, 68). The only surviving material with the soil stain was an Iron Age brooch (Hughes *et al.* 1995, 68). Thus, this example illustrates the detrimental effects of soil on bone survival, which can contribute to the limited amount of skeletal material in the Iron Age burial record.

In order to address the soil preservation issue, this study recorded the total count of animal bone recovered from studied sites (where available) to compare to the amount of human remains (see chapter five). The purpose for this comparison was to offer a general measure to see if the low quantity of human bones present was due to factors of preservation or human intent. The comparison shows that human bones represent roughly 0.22 per cent of the animal bone assemblage. There are a number of implications from the human to animal bone ratios; for one, it further supports the idea that depositing human remains was a minority rite for communities in the first millennium BC. It implies, though not conclusively, that Iron Age communities may view human remains differently from animal bones, due to the different intensity levels of depositions. Additionally, this result suggests preservation is not the sole reason for the lack of human remains (since there is an abundance of animal bone that survived) but may be more the product of human intervention and intentional inclusion.

Recovery techniques during excavations can affect the state of human bones and the representation of particular elements. Machine trenching, hand troweling, and other excavation methods may result in the fracturing and breaking of skeletal remains (Stodder 2008, 76). This point in conjunction with the level of some field workers' ability to initially recognise and identify human bones, particularly smaller elements, undoubtedly influences the amount and specific bones present in an assemblage. This was the case initially at Potterne where, during the excavations, all the human bones were mistaken for animal remains, and it was not until post-excavation analyses that they were recognised (McKinley 2000). It is a reality when excavating skeletal remains that recovery technique can affect the quantity of human bone recovered. The data for this investigation's sample derives solely from literary sources, primarily site and osteological reports. Therefore, there is no control in preventing problems in recovery methods that influence the burial data. However, the majority of the sample's sites are from recent excavations that took place within the past thirty years. Recent archaeological investigations tend to be more cautious and thorough in their recovery techniques. Therefore, one can only assume that oversight in recovery methods is slight and will have little impact on the results from the burial analysis.

Furthermore, the elements represented in an assemblage and the quantity of human bone is dependent on the programme of excavation, such as how much of the site and its features are fully excavated (Stodder 2008, 76). Many of the sites in this study's sample were not been fully excavated due to either the excavation's research aim or the investigation being restricted to the areas affected by development. For example, the archaeological investigations at Etonbury Farm Bund (Bedfordshire), which took place in advance of road development, employed machine trenching that revealed a high number of Late Bronze Age to Roman features (Saunders 2003, 2). Considering the nature of the development and the density of the archaeological features, the investigators decided to leave the site *in situ* apart from three features, of which one was a disturbed Iron Age inhumation, the only human remains identified (Saunders 2003, 2). The method of investigation preserves the site, yet the single inhumation exhumed in the excavation may not accurately represent the quantity and/or state of the possible human remains from Etonbury Farm Bund. There are other examples from this research sample where excavations covered only a portion of the known site, such as Harting Beacon (Bedwin 1978, 1979), Suddern Farm (Cunliffe and Poole 2000e), and Sidbury Hillfort (Bradley *et al* 1994). It is not often for archaeological excavations to cover the entirety of a site; although, there are examples from the studied sample, such as Micheldever Wood (Fasham 1987), Winnall Down (Fasham 1987), and Glastonbury Lake Village (Coles and Minnit 1995), with each yielding a high number of human remains occurrences. In turn, the rescue excavations of the Iron Age, enclosed farmstead at Tollard Royal investigated the entire site, which recovered only a single inhumation from outside the settlement's boundary (Wainwright 1968).

The limits of an excavation may under-represent the quantity of human remains from a particular site. In terms of the current study at hand, it also affects the spatial analysis of human remains and its comparison between sites. If the excavation area for a site is largely within the interior, then any skeletal material will appear to favour that location. However, it is not entirely accurate to compare that spatial result with another site whose investigations largely focus on the settlement's perimeter. Such factors will impact the spatial results for both the site level and comparisons on the regional scale. Thus, we must acknowledge how this issue can skew the representation of human remains and its spatial analysis results, and one should consider this when discussing the conclusions.

Overall, taphonomic issues are a slight factor in the representation and state of human remains and one must consider its impacts on the data. In stating this, another issue to reassert briefly again is that the burial data from this investigation is a sample that represents about 25 per cent of known sites with human remains (as of 2009). The deposition of human remains is a minority rite in Iron Age society, and this study examined a portion of the evidence for this practice. In addition, not all areas within the studied geographical area are adequately depicted (e.g. London) for a number of reasons, such as source availability. Despite this, the studied sample covers a wide date range, incorporates recent information from commercial archaeology, and varying modes of disposing a corpse. The burial data provided from the sample presents, as the past chapters (chapters four through eight) show, an adequate picture into the nature and complexity of this funerary rite. Thus, the sample's data allows one to draw general conclusions of the social environment from which the burial evidence was derived.

Processing of the human remains

This section addresses the processing of human remains prior to deposition. It centres on how Late Bronze Age and Iron Age communities manipulated the corpse, and discusses the possible intent behind these activities. As we have previously discussed, much of the evidence from the Iron Age suggests a prolonged and complex transformation that the dead underwent before deposition, which extended beyond the practicality of corpse disposal. The discussion will centre on the excarnation and disinterment debate (as well as considering the practice of headhunting and bone selection), inhumation, cremation, and will end with a summary of the findings. It is the community's responsibility to dispose of their dead and, as a result, the various manners of disposal reflect the community's attitudes towards death and life (Parker Pearson 1999b, 45).

Excarnation and disinterment

The following discussion will focus on the possible processing methods that could account for the disarticulated bones, articulated bones, and partial inhumations. Past studies offer two general possibilities, which are excarnation and disinterment. The following section will examine these two methods by summarising the arguments for each technique as well as examine the validity of these assertions against the studied sample's results.

The practice of excarnation, or exposing the corpse to the point of disarticulation, is the long-standing accepted processing technique according in past works (Wilson 1981, 148-151; Wait 1985a, 249). Excarnation adequately accounts for the large amount of human remains in the state of disarticulated and partially articulated remains (Wilson 1981, 148-151; Wait 1985a, 249). Further support for this argument derives from some bone assemblages exhibiting taphonomic indicators that suggest a degree of exposure, such as weathering, animal gnawing, and bone breaking (Craig and Knüsel 1997; Redfern 2008a). Such osteological marks on the bones advocate this type processing technique, which, in some cases, is followed by later deposition of selected bones (Carr and Knüsel 1991; Redfern 2008a). Where the dead were placed to decompose is uncertain; it is probable that excarnation was conducted away from domestic areas, largely based on the near absence of concentrated bone scatters (Carr and Knüsel 1997, 168). However, it has been proposed that four-post structures, commonly found on settlements, worked as scaffolds for the dead (Ellison and Drewitt 1971; Carr and Knüsel 1997, 168). To account for the 'missing' population in the burial record, some argue that the majority of the dead were displaced naturally and only a handful of remains were later deposited (Carr and Knüsel 1997, 168). There are different ways of excarnating a corpse and Iron Age communities may have employed a variety of methods to achieve the removal of flesh, which may differ from site to site (Carr and Knüsel 1997, 171). There are two key points in this argument that this study will explore. The first is the taphonomic marks that are indicative of excarnation and, the second point, examining the possibility of four-post structures functioning as scaffolds.

Taphonomic indicators, such as weathering and animal gnawing, imply that the body underwent some degree of exposure. In this study, 8.3 per cent[34] of the entire sample of disarticulate bones, 21.0 per cent[35] for the smaller sample, exhibit the osteological markers for excarnation. These percentages only include skeletal marks that occur both peri- and post-mortem, which suggest the bones were subject to a period of handling or exposure prior to deposition. In addition, there are instances throughout the studied sample where bone assemblages show signs of excarnation. As previously discussed in chapter seven, the Late Bronze Age to early Middle Iron Age disarticulated bones from Battlesbury Bowl exhibit marks of animal gnawing and weathering that suggest the remains underwent a level of exposure and possible curation (McKinley 2008, 81-82). The Iron Age riverside farmstead at Haddenham (Site V, Cambridgeshire) yielded an adult frontal bone that was highly polished with possible cut marks (Evans and Hodder 2006, 246). Excavations at Wandlebury Ringwork (Cambridgeshire) recovered an Iron Age burial of a child, either wrapped in a shroud or contained in a sack, whose legs had been removed prior to deposition and before the flesh on the torso had fully decayed (Hartley 1957). The Iron Age farmstead at Beard Mill (Oxfordshire) contains a dismembered skeleton with some bones absent; although, it is uncertain if this is the result of excarnation or disturbance (Williams 1951, 14). At Watchfield (Oxfordshire), there is an Iron Age enclosed settlement where excavations recovered an adult femur that has evidence of animal gnawing (McKinley 2001, 267). The contextual evidence for this femur is not entirely clear, but it is possible the bone is the product of exposure followed by later reburial or scavenging dogs disturbing a shallow grave (McKinley 2001, 267). The Iron Age site at Woodcote Road (Oxfordshire) yielded three disarticulated bones and all these elements have old breaks that suggest they '...had clearly been lying around the settlement for some time prior to being deposited in the pits' (Timby *et al.* 2005, 284). Lastly, the Iron Age settlement at Elms Farm contains five, abraded skull fragments that implies these bones may have lain around the site for some time before their deposition in a ditch fill (Charles *et al.* 2000, 197). These preceding examples illustrate that there is evidence supporting a type of exposure, subsequent handling, and later reburial. In some cases, the archaeological record indicates that Iron Age people practiced this form of behavior on the dead.

The second element is the proposition that Iron Age communities used four-post structures to lay the dead upon for exposure (Craig *et al.* 2005, 167). To test the validity of this claim, this study investigated human remains and their contextual relationship with multi-post structures. This was done to see if the remains are the product of above ground exposure or intentional inclusion. The results showed only 29 human remains occurrences were associated with 17 multi-post structures. Four of these occurrences were cremations, which are not a direct product of excarnation. The remaining occurrences associated with multi-post structures come from five sites: Battlesbury Bowl (Wiltshire), Danebury (Hampshire), Gravelly Guy (Oxfordshire), New Buildings (Hampshire), and Oxley Park West (Buckinghamshire). At Battlesbury Bowl, two Early Iron Age cranial fragments were uncovered from a posthole fill of a multi-post structure thought to be a granary (Ellis and Powell 2008, 29; McKinley 2008, 72). At Danebury, nine structures have 14 occurrences, of which three are complete inhumations (Walker 1984b; Hooper 1991). Eleven of the occurrences are disarticulated bones, five of which were identified as cranial bones. In addition, the majority of the bones were from pit contexts, and only two postholes contained bone (Walker 1984b; Hooper 1991). The site of New Buildings (Hampshire) has a primary deposit of an incomplete skull, dating to the Late Bronze Age/Early Iron Age, in the top layer of a pit just outside a four-post structure, thought to have been used for storage (Cunliffe and Poole 2000d, 52, 8:D5 [microfiche], 7:A14 [microfiche]). At Gravelly Guy (Oxfordshire), there are two Early/Middle Iron Age four-post structures with five occurrences associated with them. One of the post structures (four-post a) has an associated pit that contains a single skull fragment worked into a disc-shape (Lambrick and Allen 2004, 145, 249). The other building (four-post b) has a pit lying to the northeast of the structure that contains an adult skull, an infant femur and tibia, and an incomplete infant inhumation (Lambrick and Allen 2004, 145, 249, 458). At Oxley Park West, there is a Middle Iron Age four-post structure that has an infant skull and vertebra within the southwest posthole of the structure (Webley 2009, 51, 65).

---

[34] This percentage indicates human bone occurrences with peri- or post-mortem traumatic indicators of probable excarnation (bone fractures (post-mortem), cut marks (post-mortem), gnawing, stria, weathering, and polishing).

[35] See above.

The sites with human remains associated with four-post structures are few, and none of the evidence suggests strongly that these structures were used for exposure. Many of the human remains were deposited intentionally in their contexts with multi-post structures and did not end up in their contexts by natural processes as one might expect from overhanging, exposed bodies. Furthermore, most of the bones are from skulls and long bones yet not from smaller elements, of which one might expect a higher presence in excarnation areas. This point, in conjunction with the preceding evidence suggests that processing the corpse by exposure was carried out away from domestic sites, and if multi-post structures were used, then the evidence for such is not present in this sample.

Alternatively, others (Sharples 2010; Madgwick 2008) suggest that, in some areas of Wessex, older graves were intentionally reopened in order to selectively retrieve bones of the deceased. After the collection, the bones were then redeposited in other contexts; thus, another plausible source of isolated bones (Sharples 2010, 277). This technique provides a type of controlled environment for the corpse's decomposition as well as lessening the effects of climatic agents and scavenging animals on the bones (Madgwick 2008, 108). The social implications of disinterment, Sharples (2010, 280) and Madgwick (2008, 111) surmise, is that the act denotes a collective, communal identity amongst its members with the individual not highly regarded.

In exploring this claim, we can consider the contextual evidence of intentional human disturbance of graves in an effort to retrieve bones. Sharples (2010) convincingly argues that Iron Age communities actively sought out older graves to collect remains of the deceased, based on the burial and contextual evidence at Suddern Farm, (see chapter seven) and Cockey Down (not included in this study, but see Lovell 1999). Furthermore, Madgwick (2008, 108) asserts that the disarticulated bones and partially articulated remains from Winnall Down and Danebury may be the result of '...decomposition in subterranean environments, followed by exhumation and re-deposition', due to the lack of modifications on the bones. As with the excarnation discussion, by combing through the burial evidence in the studied sample there are other potential examples of communities participating in a similar activity.

The univallate hillfort at Bloodgate Hill (Norfolk) yielded skull fragments of a young adult within a ditch fill (Penn 2004, 13). It is thought, though not certain, that the cranial fragments are from an earlier burial, either within the ditch's bank or further below the recovery location of these skull fragments (Penn 22004, 7). At Spring Road (Oxfordshire), there is an older sub-adult/young adult inhumation, dating to the Middle Iron Age, with its cranium missing (Hacking and Boyle 2008, 131). A possible posthole intruded into the burial context where the skull should have been and the contextual evidence is not clear as to whether the posthole was to accommodate or to remove the skull (Hacking and Boyle 2008, 131). Excavations at Little Stock Farm (Kent) revealed a complex burial journey one inhumation underwent before its final deposition (Ritchie 2006; McKinley 2006). Originally, the community interred an adult female at the entrance of an animal paddock. Later, the decaying body was exhumed, leaving behind a skull fragment in the original context, and redeposited nearly 200 metres away from its primary grave. After this, a second inhumation was set within the new burial's context, disturbing the female skeleton. In addition, the osteological evidence shows very little animal gnawing, which further supports that decomposition occurred underground and that the body was not exposed (McKinley 2006, 70).

In sum, the studied sample contains evidence of both excarnation and disinterment during the Iron Age. This implies that Iron Age communities employed different methods of defleshing a corpse, with a degree of variation within each technique. It is perfectly logical to suppose these groups utilised a variety of methods to achieve a similar goal, and to prefer one over the other would be misleading. For example, excavations at North Shoebury (Essex) recovered an Early Iron Age inhumation that may have been exposed for a period of time prior to burial (Wymer and Henderson 1995). In addition, the skull and mandible were missing from the burial; although, teeth from the upper and lower jaw were present, suggesting the possibility that there was removal of these elements after the teeth detached in the grave (Wymer and Henderson 1995, 129). This burial may be evidence of an Iron Age group that practiced both excarnation and disinterment.

There are also some similarities between these two processing techniques. One similarity is that this study's sample suggests both methods took place away from the settlement area. This assertion concurs with past research that argues exposure of the dead had been conducted away from the settlement area, with only a selected portion of skeletal material brought back for deposition (Wait 1985a, 249; Parker Pearson 1996, 123; Carr and Knüsel 1997, 168). As for disinterment, most of the burial evidence was outside the domestic areas, such as Suddern Farm whose cemetery was adjacent to the settlement's enclosure ditches. Furthermore, placing the corpse underground visually separates the living with the deceased. We may then argue that the evidence for excarnation and disinterment both visually and physically separated the living community from the dead during the transitional period of body to bones.

Another commonality between excarnation and disinterment is that each technique is a different method of defleshing the corpse that resulted in the fragmentation of the body. Following this manner of disposal, Iron Age communities strove for the near complete breakdown of the corpse into manageable pieces, yet achieved this similar goal through different methods. Deconstructing the body in this fashion is particularly evident during the

Early and Middle Iron Age, according to this sample. Presumably, the community wanted to break down the body to obtain desirable bones for further use in some form of social practices.

Headhunting and bone selection

Iron Age communities show a particular bias to the cranium, and the following section will address past studies on the skull and explanations for the Iron Age peoples' fixation on this element. The discussion will centre on headhunting and bone selection, which will include relevant, past Iron Age studies, and this studied sample's results in order to deduce the mechanisms at work in these activities.

Past research shows that disarticulated bones overwhelmingly make up the majority of human remains occurrences during the Early and Middle Iron Age, and that Iron Age communities strongly favoured cranial elements followed by long bones (Brück 1995, 256; Parker Pearson 1996, 123). Some postulate that Iron Age communities saw the skull as the area of the body that represented and housed the individual's soul and intellect (Megaw and Megaw 1989, 55; Sharples 2010, 290), which may explain why the skull was so highly regarded. Presumably, there are two activities that could result in the high numbers of skulls: headhunting for trophy skulls or selected retrieval from the dead. For trophy skulls, scholars argue that some of the heads represent fallen enemies (Wait 1985a, 120; Cunliffe 1995, 78; also see Collis 2003, 216). Additionally, it is suggested that some of the skulls on Iron Age sites are the result of the community's selected retrieval of heads from their own dead, which signifies a form of ancestral connection and veneration (Cunliffe 1995, 78; Sharples 2010, 289).

To explore the prevalence of headhunting during the Iron Age, the discussion will focus on the direct osteological evidence for this activity. This evidence would include inhumations with missing or intentionally displaced skulls and cut marks on the cervical vertebrae or at the base of the occipital (if the decapitator misses the neck). Cut marks on the cervical vertebrae would be more prevalent than on the occipital; unfortunately, cervical vertebrae are more affected by soil than cranial elements and less likely to survive in the burial record, which must be taken into account (Mays 1992, 55). Only 0.06 per cent[36] of the entire skeletal material from this investigation's sample contains direct evidence of traumatic episodes. However, there is some limited evidence of probable decapitation to obtain heads. The A505 Baldock Bypass site (Hertfordshire) contained a young adult inhumation with the head removed and placed under the left arm (Thorpe *et al.* 2003, 17). The site at Ford Place Nursing Home (Norfolk) has a Middle/Late Iron Age deposit containing the remaining articulated fragments of cervical vertebrae,

mandible and occipital (Emery 2005, 4-5, 18). The articulated bones belonged to an adult male (Emery 2005, 4-5, 18), and there is no mention of trauma to the remains, but the condition and context of the bones suggests that the head may have been intentionally removed and the body deposited elsewhere. In all, the preceding examples illustrate head removal, to some degree, occurred in the Iron Age, but not as a widespread phenomenon. This is not conclusive, however, since not all evidence of decapitation, such as cut marks on cervical vertebrae, may survive and prevents any strong assertions either way. The physical evidence present in this sample implies that most of cranial elements are the product of deliberate collection from decomposing bodies and grave reuse. Their selective retrieval may account for the high frequency of this skeletal element from Iron Age sites.

Bone selection (by various means) seems to be the most common cause for disarticulated bone on a site. This study shows that skulls and long bones are the most favoured elements, and this correlates with conclusions of past studies (Wait 1985a, 249; Parker Pearson 1996, 123; Carr and Knüsel 1997, 168). From the total sample of disarticulated bones, cranial elements (skull, mandible, and teeth) represent 38.3 per cent and long bones (humerus, ulna, radius, femur, tibia, and fibula) 37.6 per cent of the total sample. If we remove the sites with over 20 occurrences, the cranium makes up 56.6 per cent and the long bones 29.4 per cent of the sample.[37] In addition, smaller elements (phalanx, carpal, metacarpal, tarsal, and metatarsal) are a rare find on occupation sites, and these bones make up only 7.0 per cent of all the disarticulated bone in the sample.[38] Taphonomic issues are a factor and may account for the fact that skulls and long bones are highly represented, especially in comparison to the smaller elements. As discussed previously, skulls and long bones preserve better than smaller bones (e.g. ribs and vertebrae) and are easily identified during excavation and collecting after exhumation (Mays 1992; Stodder 2008). Cranial and long bone elements may be over-represented in the burial record due to fragmentation from both human and natural processes. To prevent this, the study recorded the amount of each bone present in the record yet variations in the site reports' descriptions made it impossible to resolve soundly the over-representation issue.

One means of addressing the over-representation of skulls and long bones is to focus on a site's formation processes of the human remains deposits in an effort to discern intentional deposition. The majority of the sites in this study have less than ten occurrences (n=76) and from these, the ones that have disarticulated bone deposits typically consist of intentionally placed cranial and/or long bones. For example, Conderton Camp in Worcestershire is a univallate hillfort with four occurrences that are all from the cranium (one skull and

---

[36] This percentage indicates human bone occurrences with ante- or peri-mortem traumatic indicators of probable violence (fractures, cut marks, blunt force trauma, and dismemberment)

[37] These percentages include the disarticulated bone from the Early Iron Age to the Late Iron Age.

[38] 4.7 per cent for the smaller sample

three teeth) that date between the Early and the Middle Iron Age (Musgrave 2005, 246). The excavations recovered the skull from the base of a pit, surrounded by a spread of large stones, intentionally deposited just prior to the natural filling of the context (Thomas 2005, 110). Haddenham (Site V, Cambridgeshire) has two disarticulated bone occurrences, both dating to the Middle Iron Age, of which one is an incomplete skull and the other is the shaft portion of a femur (Dodwell 2008, 246). Each of the bones recovered from Haddenham were set at either the entrance of the causeway or a building (Dodwell 2008, 246). Hurst Lane Reservoir (Cambridgeshire) contains four occurrences dating to the Middle/Late Iron Age, of which three were from the skull and the fourth, a phalanx (Dodwell 2007a, 66). One of the skulls from Hurst Lane has evidence of blunt force trauma as well as a cut mark and was deposited at the base of a pit, just outside a building, and set on top a large amount of pottery sherds (Evans *et al.* 2007, 51). Lastly, Burgh (Suffolk) contains a single human remain occurrence, which is a Late Iron Age skull that had a large stone covering the face (Derston 1988, 66). These preceding examples demonstrate that even if the high counts of cranial and long bones may be due to taphonomic issues, it does not negate their role in depositional practices and the selection bias towards these elements.

Inhumation

For the British Iron Age, disarticulated bones are presumably a product of excarnation or disinterment where the corpse had received ample time to decompose and consequently the bones became loose. This processing technique explains the high number of disarticulated bones, which accounts for over half (53.7 per cent) of the human remains occurrences from this investigation. Disarticulated bone is more frequent in the Early and Middle Iron Age and constitutes nearly three quarters of the total sample of human remains occurrences (Early Iron Age: 76.8 per cent[39], Middle Iron Age: 72.2 per cent[40]) before drastically reducing in the Late Iron Age (down to 15.6 per cent[41]). The decrease in the Late Iron Age may imply a lengthy time for decomposition going out of fashion and replaced by other processing techniques, such as cremation and interment before the beginning of decay. In other words, the study's results indicate a change in the processing techniques, which correlates with an increase in the occurrence of inhumations and cremations in the burial record shown in the archaeological record.

Iron Age human remains were reintegrated back into the community in various forms. Wait (1985a, 94, 255) points out that there was a significant increase in inhumations in the Middle and into the Late Iron Age, which he relates to a reduction in the exposure time for the dead. Individuals deposited as inhumations and as partially articulated

remains are evidence that there was, in most cases, little to no decomposition time. Undoubtedly, the completeness of their bodies suggests that there was limited time between death and burial. Some suggest that complete inhumations and partially articulated individuals are the result of an unclean or ritual death, or social exclusion (Cunliffe 1995, 78; Madgwick 2008, 111).

This study shows a change in burial practices, particularly in the Late Iron Age. The results illustrate an increase in the occurrence of inhumations in the burial record from the Early Iron Age to the Late Iron Age. In the Early Iron Age, inhumation deposits represent 19.8 per cent of occurrences and increase to 38.0 per cent in the Late Iron Age.[42] The results correlate with Wait's (1985a, 255) findings and it implies that there was a probable decrease in time given for the corpses to decompose. Additionally, there are instances where inhumations were exposed to the point where little flesh remained, which can account for tightly contracted inhumations, or were forcibly dismembered, such as the inhumation at Wandlebury Ringwork (see chapter eight, Hartley 1957, 15). The regional distribution of inhumations closely mirrors that of disarticulated bones, which would correlate with communities practicing excarnation or disinterment. The state of the human remains as inhumations, and as articulated, and disarticulated bones suggests degrees of variation in the duration over which the body was allowed to decompose. In some instances, after the allotted time, selections of the remains were returned to the settlement area to be deposited either immediately or later.

Cremation

Similar to excarnation and disinterment, cremation rites involve the breaking down of a corpse. However, cremation is much quicker and allows the living greater control over the process (Sharples 2010, 288). This investigation's results imply that the cremation process was also conducted away from occupation areas. From all the studied sites, only three contain pyre remains. The Late Bronze Age site at Broom (Area E) in Warwickshire has the remains of a collapsed pyre that was encircled by a ring ditch (Palmer 1999, 38). The pyre site at Broom is not associated directly with a settlement, and the area surrounding the site saw limited activity during this period (Palmer 1999, 218). There is also the failed, *in situ* burning of an inhumation at Latton Lands in Wiltshire (Powell *et al.* 2008, 45-46). The example from Latton Lands dates to the Middle/Late Iron Age and the burial occurred after the settlement's abandonment (Powell *et al.* 2008, 41-43). Lastly, the cremation cemetery at Westhampnett (West Sussex) has pyre areas set to the northeast of the burials (Fitzpatrick 1997). Overall, the community conducted the cremation process away from settlement areas and we may be able to view this as another method for 'breaking down the corpse'. Thus,

---

[39] Early Iron Age (smaller sample): 43.3 per cent
[40] Middle Iron Age (smaller sample): 61.0 per cent
[41] Late Iron Age (smaller sample): 40.0 per cent

[42] For the smaller sample, inhumations make up 13.5 per cent of occurrences in the Late Bronze Age and increase to 35.2 per cent representation in the Late Iron Age.

cremation, disinterment, and excarnation are different ways to process a corpse but have a similar result (fragmenting of the body) and it may suggest that similar principles motivating these acts.

The studied sample shows two main periods for cremation: the Late Bronze Age and again in the Late Iron Age. If we discount those sites with over 20 occurrences, cremation deposits make up 78.8 per cent of the Late Bronze Age human remains deposits and 46.3 per cent of the Late Iron Age. The cremation process destroys the corpse and produces fragments of the deceased of which, in most instances, only a portion is later deposited. Throughout the Late Bronze Age and the Iron Age, most cremation deposits contained less than 100g of bone (54.3 per cent for the larger sample, 58.6 per cent for the smaller sample). **Table 9.1** shows the percentage of cremation deposits that contains fewer than 100g according to date and it illustrates that the Late Iron Age cremation deposits include 'more' of the deceased individual. This is not a drastic difference, but generally, in comparing cremation deposits from the Late Bronze Age and the Late Iron Age more of the deceased is present in the record, which is roughly analogous to the increase of inhumations in the Late Iron Age when compared to disarticulated bones.

Table 9. 1 Percent of cremation weights under 100g

	Larger Sample	Smaller Sample
LBA	62.80 per cent	63.20 per cent
EIA	84.60 per cent	83.30 per cent
MIA	71.40 per cent	75.00 per cent
LIA	50.80 per cent	46.70 per cent

Cremation deposits were more frequent in the Late Bronze Age and, primarily, the Late Iron Age, which correlates with results from past studies (Wait 1985a, 249; Cunliffe 1995, 79; Sharples 2010, 283). The geographical distribution of cremation sites is mostly away from the concentration of sites with disarticulated bones and inhumations in Wessex, and suggests that these cremation-practicing areas were performing a different process in the destruction of the individual. Inhumations and disarticulated bones follow a similar distribution pattern in Wessex and towards the north, while cremations are prominent in the southeast of England, the East Midlands and towards the West Midlands. Generally, for the Iron Age, the study's results indicate different processing techniques for the corpse that are regionally and temporally distinct. The heterogeneous nature of the burial process is a common aspect of Iron Age mortuary ritual (Madgwick 2008, 94). Differences in processing the corpse are the basis for regional variation in Iron Age burial practices, producing either complete or fragmented bodies.

Summary

The preceding sections discussed the varying methods Iron Age communities employed in processing the dead. The reason behind areas practicing different processing techniques is not entirely clear. One way to look at this pattern is to consider how culture is complex and always changing. The awareness of other social groups influences the community's perception of itself (Boon 1982). Members of the same culture continuously define themselves by what they are not in contrast to *other* groups (Boon 1982, 232). Taking this view may imply that the varying burial rites were a means of expressing the group's communal identity by distinguishing themselves from others. As stated above, Iron Age communities worked to fragment the corpse and, in some instance, retain pieces of the dead. This was achieved through different means of excarnation, disinterment, and cremation. Generally speaking, we may argue this signifies a shared custom across southern Britain influenced by local traditions.

As with all cultures, the burial methods changed in the Iron Age moving from cremation to excarnation and/or disinterment then back to cremation as well as inhumations. The change in burial practices is most evident with the communities in the East Midlands (see chapter eight). Burial evidence in the East Midlands suggests the groups may be incorporating the trends of their surrounding areas and expressing it themselves. However, Boon's (1982) concept is not a satisfactory explanation for the burial customs that communities were performing in the Early and Middle Iron Age. In the studied area, cremation deposits largely disappeared in the east during the Early and Middle Iron Age, and are replaced by inhumation and disarticulated bone deposits, albeit not to the same extent as the sites in Wessex. This may signify that eastern communities adopted and redefined practices similar to their neighbours to the west while continuing to practice cremation.

The burial evidence from this study implies that there was a socially acceptable moment when the deceased (or fragments thereof) re-entered the visual and physical world of the living (Metcalf and Huntington 1991, 71). Generally, the time during decomposition may be seen as unclean, needing to be isolated from the living community. The transitional time of the corpse ends when the individual, in essence, becomes fragments of its former self. This process and period is when the deceased leaves the area of the living and passes on to the other world (Parker Pearson 1993, 204). Primarily, the Early and Middle Iron Age communities exposed the dead away from the living and, thus, hid the transitional period. The entire decomposition process was a method to physically separate the living from the dead and, presumably, symbolically transfer the deceased into an abstract realm. After which, the bones entered back into the living's sphere after the liminal transition time ended. We can speculate that the deceased's remains adopted a new meaning and formed new social relationships with the community (Fowler 2004, 59-60, 80; Sofaer 2006, 44). The bones now being fragments of the former individual, one may assert that they 'lost' their individuality. It is probable that the community, through their handling and manipulation, viewed the bones as symbolising a concept beyond that of the deceased individual.

The main points to emphasis at the close of the 'processing' section are that the methods for disposing the corpse were a means of breaking down the dead. Undoubtedly, the processing of the corpse was a transformation act for the deceased. Excarnation, disinterment, and cremation were carried out outside (either adjacent or far away from) the settlement, which implies a separation between the living and the dead during their transformation stage. After an allotted amount of time, the community integrated fragments of some of the deceased back into the social sphere for further manipulation or deposition. Thus, a central concept for these acts is that these processing techniques were transformative rites that allowed human remains to become symbolic elements, for later social activities.

Spatial placement of the human remains

This section discusses the various findings on spatial placement that have emerged from the analysis. These include the physical location of human remains deposits on and around the site, as well as those associated with archaeological features (with primary reference to structures), and their temporal placement. This research also suggests that human bones' association with areas of economic significance and with earlier prehistoric monuments were focal aspects of some burial rites. A central point to emphasise is the influence of spatial and contextual setting in defining the meaning driving human remains' deposition. The engagement with the physical environment through ritual activity allows the participants to perceive the area in a culturally specific way and thus guide their behaviour within that arena (Geertz 1973, 11; Ingold 1993, 152-153).

Location of the human remains

Both Wilson (1981, 141) and Wait (1985a, 116) suggest that human bone deposits favoured the perimeter areas of settlements during the Early Iron Age, and then became more frequent within the interior during the Middle and Late Iron Age. Human bones also supposedly favour boundaries as well as entrances of structures and, primarily, settlement enclosures (Hill 1995b, 79; Brück, 1995; Parker Pearson 1996, 126). Skeletal material set within boundaries reinforces their liminal qualities, emphasising these areas of transition from inside and out (Brück 1995; Parker Pearson 1996, 123). Similarly, human bone deposits have been used to mark the beginning, renovation of, and, particularly, the end of a building or site (Armit and Ginn 2007).

With all the studied Iron Age sites, there is no clear correlation between the date and the locations of contexts with human remains deposits on the site. The results from the research sample do not completely correspond with Wait (1985a, 116) and Wilson's (1981, 141) conclusion, although the majority of their studied sites are mainly from Wessex. If we focus just on sites in the sample from Wessex,[43] there is again no clear pattern in the placement, as **Figure 9.1** and **9.2**[44] illustrate. The Wessex sites show a clear preference for their interiors during the Middle Iron Age (70.8 per cent with Danebury, 56.5 per cent without Danebury); this trend does not carry through into the Late Iron Age when most of the contexts with human remains are found on perimeters (61.8 per cent, excluding Danebury).

This is in stark contrast to the sites outside of Wessex. Here we see the majority of contexts with human remains concentrated on exteriors of sites throughout most of the Iron Age, and perimeters of sites during the Middle Iron Age (see **Figure 9.3**). The communities in Wessex incorporated and deposited the remains of the deceased into their public living environment to some degree, while the groups outside of Wessex typically did not. Thus, we are left with the question of why this may be.

Communities from Wessex sites largely chose to place human remains in contexts within their settlements or along their boundaries for most of the Iron Age. This indicates that after the processing (transformation), generally, the remains of the deceased returned physically into the community. There was no more separation between the living and the dead. The act of bringing remains in to (or in to the vicinity of) the settlement and subsequent handling after was visually evident for the community's members. The proximity of remains implies that the community's members are aware of their presence and, thus, meaning. This is reinforced when bones are placed in public, accessible places, like a settlement's entrance or boundary. Within these contexts, activities resulting in bone deposition have the potential of being displayed to the public. All these components imply that the entire act was meant to be seen. It is possible that the bones were part of some type of public spectacle that focused the attention of the community for a specific cause. This type of event has many implications. Foremost is the reaffirmation communal identity. We may argue that activities at this level that involve human bones provided a platform for the participants to create and proclaim their sense of belonging to the group (Marshall 2002, 360, 365). This entire act implies that its intent lies on the communal level and, possibly, that the proximity of the dead allows the living to maintain 'an active association with the dead' (Cannon 2002, 192).

---

[43] Wessex sites include Balksbury Camp, Bury Hill, Danebury, Easton Lane, Gussage All Saints, Houghton Down, Little Somborne, Maiden Castle, Micheldever Woods, Nettlebank Copse, Suddern Farm, Tollard Royal and Winnall Down.
[44] Excluded Danebury to prevent bias

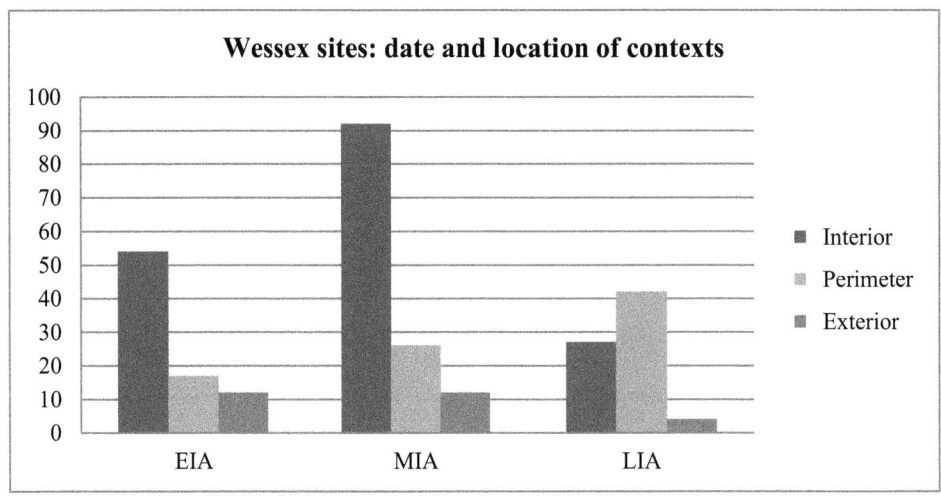

Figure 9. 1 Frequency of the location of contexts according to date

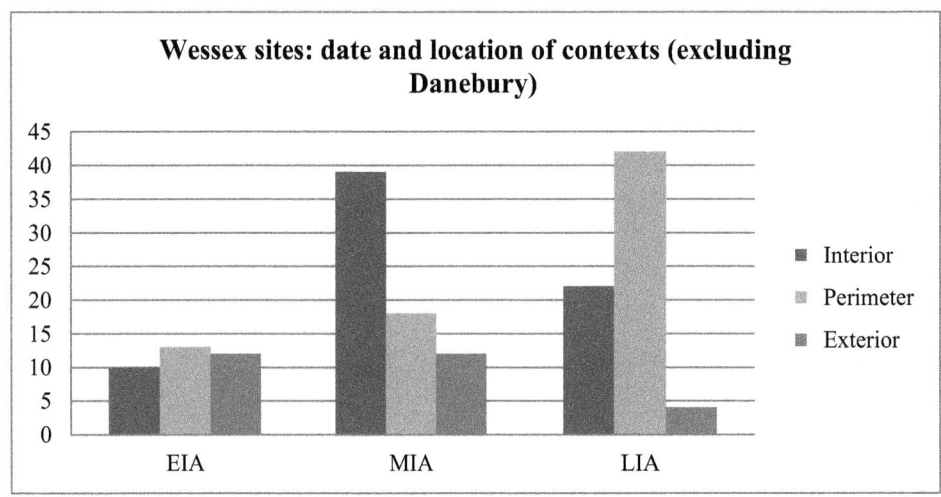

Figure 9. 2 Frequency of the location of contexts according to date, excluding Danebury

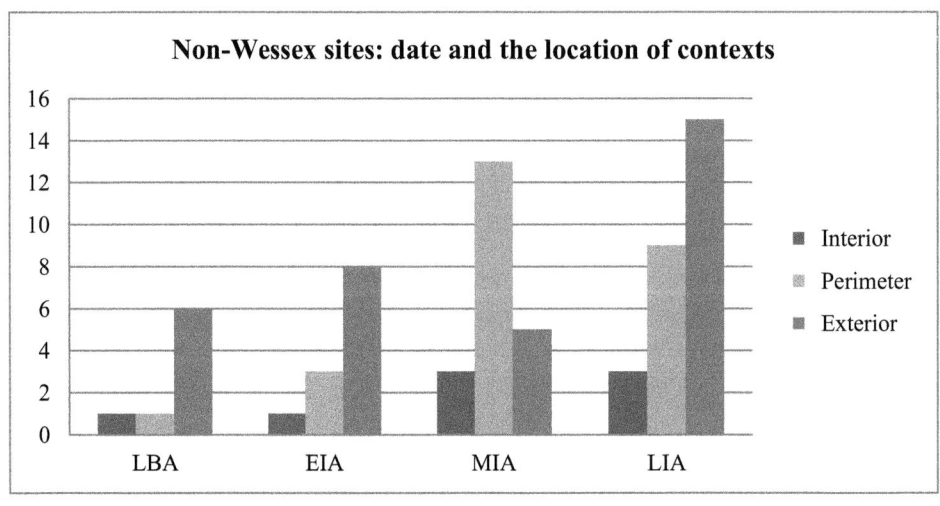

Figure 9. 3 Frequency of the location of contexts according to date

Alternatively, the communities outside of Wessex differ because from the Late Bronze Age to the Late Iron Age the majority of contexts chosen to deposit human remains were outside or on the perimeter of the settlement. The spatial location of the human remains implies that there continued to be a separation between the living and dead even after the transitional stage is over. It may be that activities involving human remains did not take place inside the domestic area, but rather outside of it. Equally as plausible, the community may have brought human remains into the settlement and manipulated them accordingly and then, after the use of human remains expires or the ritual ends, they deposited the skeletal material just outside the settlement. This may be the case at High Barns Road (Bedfordshire) where a skull fragment had been curated for a number of years before its final deposition with other human remains in the ditch of an enclosure that lies away from the domestic area (Webley 2007c, 63).

Ultimately, some human remains were brought into the settlement while others were left outside or along the edge of the site. Locations of skeletal material closely tie in with the purposes that human remains served in particular activities, and we must focus on the specific intent that incorporated human bones. For example, this research shows a high volume of skeletal material associated with boundaries and entrances of structures and settlement enclosures. In all, 33.1 per cent of human remains occurrences were associated with architectural features of a structure or settlement, with 71.3 per cent of these bones found near boundary areas. The skeletal material set along a settlement's boundaries serves to define the liminal space for the community's residents. In essence, ritual activities at the site level potentially have more involvement, and work to benefit most, if not all, members of the community. This point relates back to the discussion above where the deposition of human remains in these accessible areas create a public stage for communal involvement to benefit and reaffirm the collective identity of the group's members. The deposition of human remains in liminal areas is commonly practiced across the studied area with no regional distinction (see **Figure 9.4**).

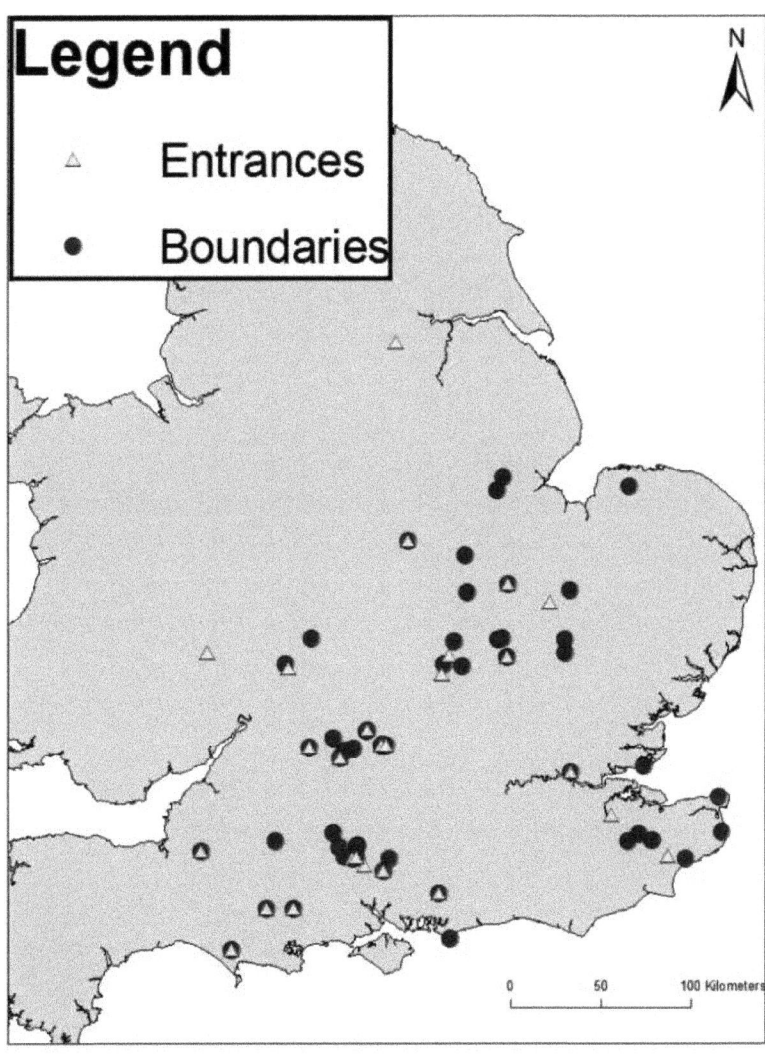

Figure 9. 4 Distribution of sites with human remains associated with architectural features

213

Similar to placing human remains at liminal places, there is evidence of depositing bones at key times in the lifecycle of a structure or site. The evidence from Iron Age southern Britain implies the importance of spatial and temporal settings in emphasising motivations for the deposition of human remains. For example, there is a Middle Iron Age foundation burial of a human skull with a roundhouse at North Shoebury (Essex, Wymer and Brown 1995, 158) and the cremation deposit marking the end of use of a roundhouse at Broom (Cooper and Edmonds 2007, 108). As these examples illustrate, the use of human bones for defining liminal areas and moments did not follow rigid rules. Instead, the variations in the manner of disposal suggest that human bone was just a medium in this depositional practice, and bone may have represented a meaning that extended beyond the identity of the deposited individual.

Archaeological features

The statistical and quantitative results from this study identified a regular spatial arrangement of human remains in association with round, rectangular and irregular structures, in terms of their deposition on the right or left side of a structure (as one enters the building). Specifically, bones within buildings tend to be placed within the right half of the interior, while remains on the perimeter are more common on the left side. This relationship is clearest for disarticulated bones and inhumations but also applies to cremations. **Figure 9.5** illustrates this deposition, which is statistically significant (see chapter four). The axial symmetry of domestic dwellings has been discussed in the literature in terms of emphasising the right side associated with death/night, and the left with living/day (Fitzpatrick 1994; 1997).

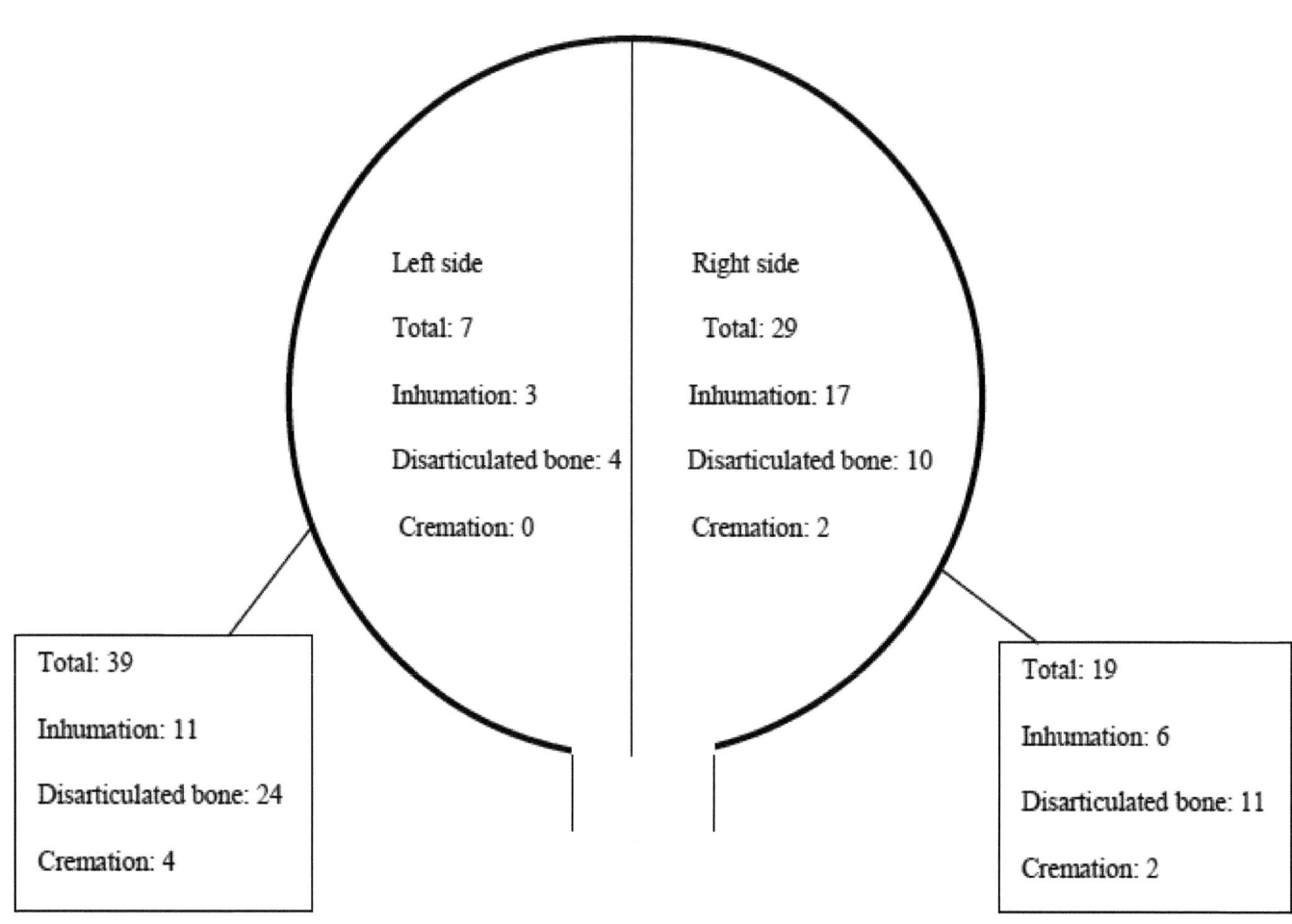

Figure 9. 5 Figure illustrating the frequency of human remains in and around structures

If we focus on the formation of these deposits, we can explore the validity of this spatial pattern. To begin, these human remains deposits within buildings were placed most often after their abandonment or during their occupation. For example, a roundhouse at Barton Court Farm in Oxfordshire has an inhumation inside it on the right side near the entrance (Miles 1986, 3:B14, 3:C4 [microfiche]). The inhumation is a primary deposit, accompanied by a piglet burial and deposited while the house was still in use (Miles 1986, 3:B14, 3:C4 [microfiche]). Bancroft in Buckinghamshire has four disarticulated bones and one articulated limb (probably a disturbed burial) along the perimeter of a round structure on its left side. The contextual relationship between the human remains deposits and the round structure suggests that the burial occurred around the time of the structure's abandonment (Williams and Zeepvat 1994b, 46). Broom in Bedfordshire (Toll House site) has a cremation deposit within the decaying posthole of a roundhouse (Cooper and Edmonds 2007, 108). The posthole formed part of the roundhouse's wall along the left side and the cremation deposit occurred shortly after the building's abandonment (Cooper and Edmonds 2007, 108). Similarly, a roundhouse at Easton Lane in Hampshire contained two human remains deposits (a disarticulated bone and a cremation) both in postholes along the structure's

perimeter, one posthole on the left side and the other on the right (Fasham *et al.* 1989). Spring Road in Oxfordshire has four inhumation burials along the left-side perimeter of a roundhouse, and the burials are contemporary with the structure's abandonment (Allen and Kamash 2008, 20). These examples are just a selection of the many human remains deposits that follow this spatial pattern, and demonstrate that the majority of these deposits were deliberate and not from random discard. Thus, these insights into formation processes support the claim that depositions following the right/left spatial pattern were intentional choices by the community at large.

Whilst, others have argued for a front/back division in the spatial organisation of houses (see Pope 2007), the results from this study indicate that human remains do not strongly follow this pattern. **Figure 9.6** illustrates the frequency of human remains in either the front or back halves of buildings, with reference to their location. However, the quantitative result for different quadrants within buildings (**Figure 9.7**) shows a preference for remains on the perimeter of the left/front segment of a building. Unfortunately, the number of human remains from this study's sample is too low to be statistically significant.

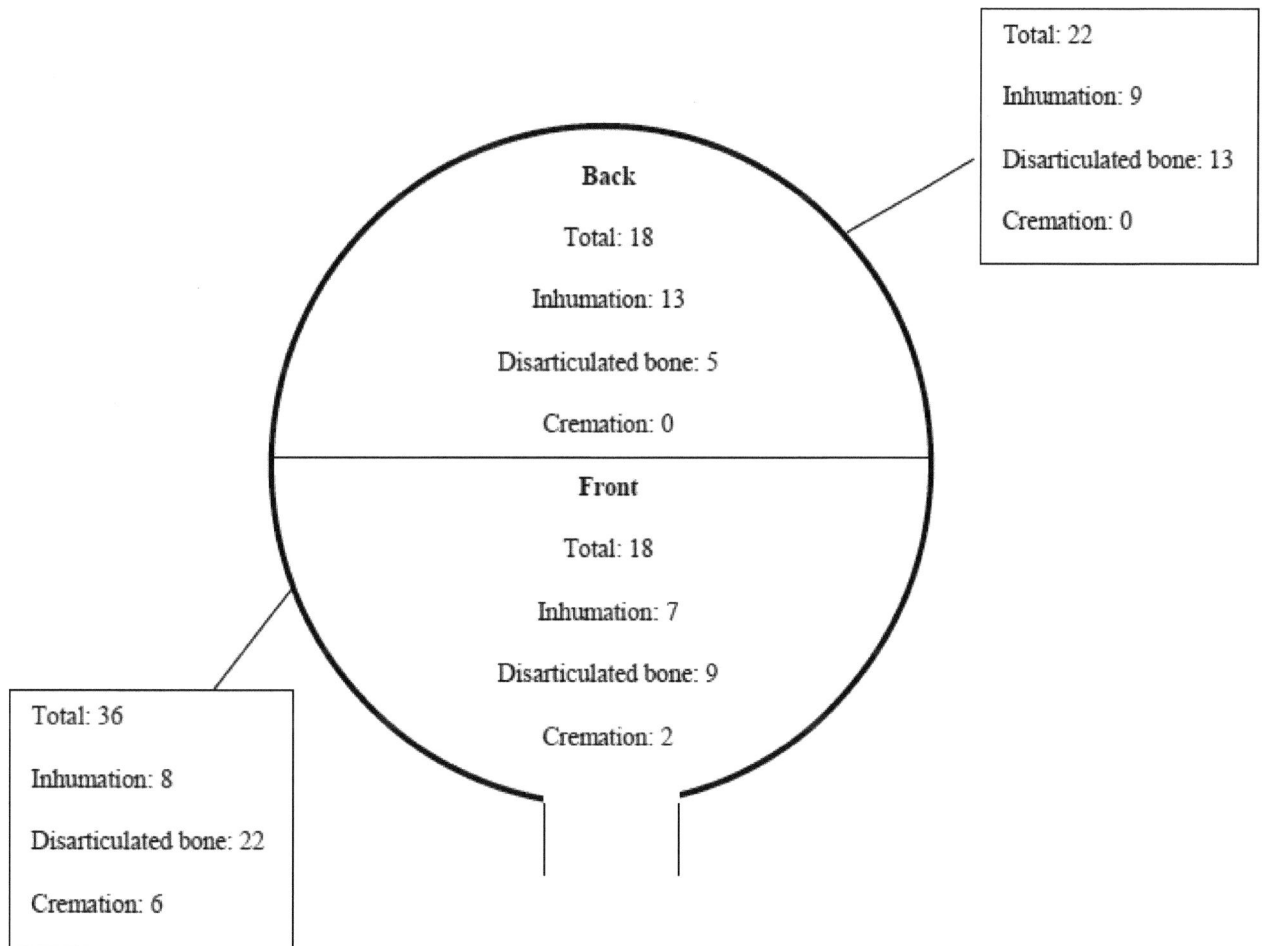

Figure 9. 6 Diagram illustrating the frequency of human remains in and around structures

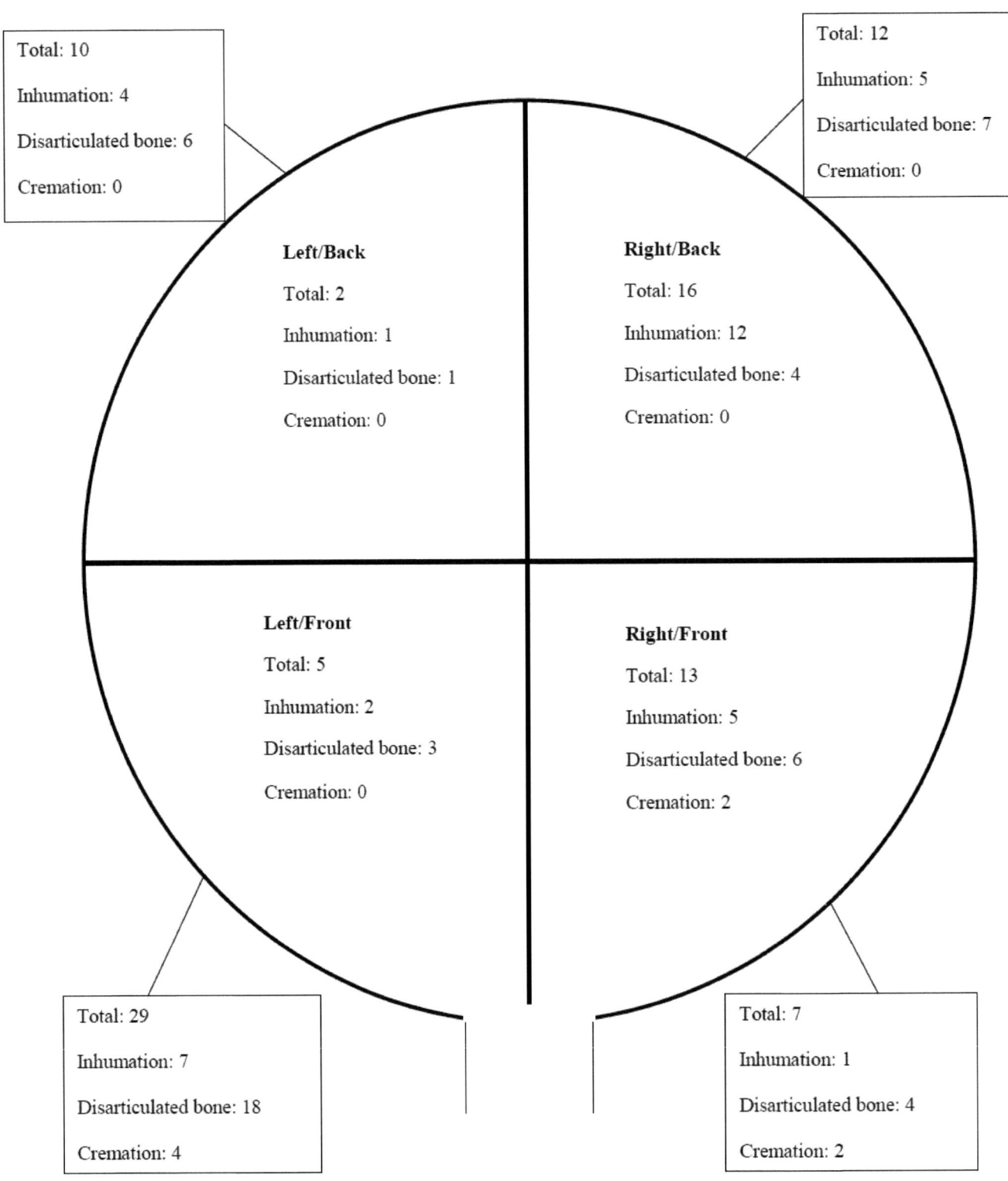

Figure 9. 7 Diagram illustrating the frequency of human remains in and around structures

Returning to the right/left spatial pattern, we now must ask what was the motivation behind these deposits. Human remains following the right/left spatial pattern support the argument that Iron Age houses were organised according to cosmological referents within a binary divide (living/sleeping) (Fitzpatrick 1994; 1997; Parker Pearson 1999a; Parker Pearson and Richards 1994b). However, the placing of human remains along the boundary on the left side of a structure such as Spring Road and Bancroft requires further explanation. This depositional trend is similar to that of human remains being buried within settlement boundaries as a means of symbolic reinforcing these boundaries. Bone, thus, emphasised the liminal space between the outside of the building and the living area within. The living (left) half of a structure (within the interior) rarely contains human remains. Instead, human remains deposits emphasised the boundary of the living area. Additionally, it is significant that deposits were often made along the structures' boundaries around the time or after their abandonment. It has been suggested (see Webley 2007d) that structured deposition at the time of the disuse of a building was part of rituals to mark the abandonment of the structure. This study's findings show that many of the human remains deposits associated with buildings occurred after they went out of use, supporting Webley's claim for post-abandonment rituals. It seems quite plausible that human remains would be integrated into such ritual activities, since there are similar instances of bone deposits at the time of a settlement's abandonment. An interesting point to emphasise is that human remains deposits continue to adhere to the right/left spatial organisation after a building went out use.

As discussed previously, human remains were used to mark liminal moments in a structures' life history as well as that of the larger settlement. Placing of remains within or near disused houses may have provided another public forum for communal activity. This may be evident at Spring Road with the establishment of a small cemetery adjacent to a disused roundhouse. However, human remains deposits made during the use of a building may signify ritual activity at the more *private* level. There are few definitive examples of deliberate deposition of human remains while a structure was still in use. Deposits of this nature, however, suggest that the building's inhabitants were actors in the depositions, utilising a space physically closed off from the rest of the community; possibly, this ritual activity was for their own personal benefit. In comparison, deposits within settlement enclosures and other public forums allowed accessibility and participation by all, while the deposits associated with structures during their use mainly served those living or working within. In sum, the spatial evidence for Iron Age burial practices indicates both public (primarily) and private (occasionally) levels for social practices involving human remains. Both public and private areas allowed the living to maintain a continued interaction with the remains and contributed to the space's social memory.

Economic significance

On a different note, in previous chapters the study has discussed the use of human remains for signifying areas of economic importance. The concept of places of economic significance is an expansion of Cunliffe's (1992; 2000) continued argument for the use of human remains in pits as propitiatory offerings to ensure agriculture fertility. The quantitative analysis for this study shows that pits are the most frequent context occurrences, which does correlate with this concept. However, human bones were employed not solely for ensuring agricultural fertility; Iron Age communities were engaged in numerous economic activities, such as stock rearing and crafts, which were important to the maintenance and sustainability of the group. Gwilt (1997, 160) suggests this idea in his assessment of Wakerley and argues the infant burials deposited in the ditch of a possible stock enclosure may relate to ensuring the sustainability of the herd and, thus, community. For this study, this point is illustrated by the human remains associated with stock-rearing areas at the sites of Harting Beacon (West Sussex; Bedwin 1978, 227, 230; 1979, 25), Little Stock Farm (Kent; Ritchie 2006, 9), and Hartsdown Technology College (Kent; Gardener and Gibson 2008, 6), as well as the iron bloomery site at Jubilee Corner (Kent; Aldridge 2005, 173). Human remains, thus, may have functioned to emphasise the importance and productivity of the particular trade. Again, it implies that the human bones in these contexts worked as objects to benefit the community. Similar to deposition of skeletal material along settlement boundaries, the intent behind deposition at economic areas was to benefit the community.

Reuse of prehistoric monuments

Another spatial characteristic of human remains deposits previously outlined by Whimster (1981a, 31-33) is the reuse of Bronze Age mounds for Iron Age burial. This research shows that only a small number of sites produced evidence for the reuse of earlier monuments. Iron Age human bones were set near Bronze Age monuments, and a few are associated with earlier, disused Iron Age features (see chapters four and eight). Finds of Iron Age human remains associated with earlier monuments imply that these features were still a significant element in the landscape. It is argued that prehistoric monuments represented a communal shared past for those Iron Age communities that utilised these features. The intent behind these deposits was either to form a connection to the ancestral past or mark a land claim. In essence, if a community marks their territorial claim by using earlier monuments for human remains deposits, it signifies that the group considers these monuments as their heritage. Therefore, both possibilities relate to an ancestral theme. It seems that a main objective for reusing earlier monuments was for the group to establish a connection to the past. Furthermore, Iron Age communities' activities with these landscape features contributed to the monuments' social narrative. Iron Age people redefined these prehistoric monuments according to their communal needs. Thus, the deposit may have represented an idea beyond that of the deceased individual, signifying the group that the dead derived from. 'Landscape is part of people's identity but is simultaneously part of the identity of the ancestral beings. Human identity thus is shared with something that has an existence independent of the person and which has the same origin: ancestral past' (Morphy 1995, 205).

Summary

In sum, it seems evident that the location of human remains deposits forms the foundation for reconstructing burial activity. Generally, the spatial setting created the arena for a particular activity that utilised human bone. The spatial setting served to create two broad types of forum for activity for Iron Age communities. The first is the public setting where there was an opportunity for group involvement to achieve a communal benefit. In most instances, the public setting was made manifest by deposits within settlement boundaries, areas of economic significance, earlier monuments, and by certain burials signifying liminal moments (such as marking the end of occupation). The second is the private setting; some deposits are associated with domestic structures that were still in use at the time of deposition. This suggests exclusivity and the fact that the deposition may have served to benefit only the residents of the building. Human remains in both the public and private arenas create a mechanism to define various concepts which contribute to the group's and individual's social agenda.

Identities of the human remains

This section addresses who, or what, the human remains represented to the community that deposited them. To achieve this, the discussion will draw upon the results focusing on the demographic profile of human remains outlined in the previous chapters. Furthermore, this section draws on past interpretations of the identity of the skeletal material, as victims of sacrifice or warfare/violence, elite or outcast individuals or ancestors, and evaluates the validity of these interpretations. Lastly, the section ends by theorising notions of personhood and identity from remains to their Iron Age communities.

Demographic profile of the studied sample

The skeletal material, according to past studies, shows a bias towards individuals in the adult age category (Wait 1985a, 116). For this study, all periods of the Iron Age have adults as the most represented age group, and they comprise of 59.6 per cent all occurrences. Infants are the second most represented age group and make up 24.4 per cent of the total human remains sample. The frequency of infants is particularly evident on some of the sites with 20 or more human remains occurrences, such as Gravelly Guy and Micheldever Wood. Interestingly, infant representation increases throughout the Iron Age and this

age group is more common in the Wessex area during the Early and Middle Iron Age. The depositional characteristic of infants from most sites suggests that their processing differed from adults. This implies that the social views and value of infants were not the same as adults and, thus, they received different burial treatments. For example, of the 20 human remains occurrences at Micheldever Wood, 17 are infants and two adults (with one being of an undetermined age). The two adult remains are disarticulated bones while 15 of the infant deposits were inhumations. The human remains from Wakerley in Northamptonshire are all infant inhumations and there is a complete absence of adult remains. Lastly, the cemetery that lies just outside Suddern Farm's enclosure contains many disarticulated remains from disturbed graves of older individuals yet the final use of the burial area was sealed by a number of infant inhumations (Cunliffe and Poole 2000e, 168).

Differential treatment of infants to older individuals is particularly evident in eastern England. During the Late Bronze Age and Late Iron Age, cremation deposits of older sub-adults and adults are common in eastern England. Most Iron Age infants are not afforded cremation rites with deposition following; this rite, according to the evidence, only appears to have been afforded to older individuals in the community. Since infant cremations are nearly absent from the entire cremation sample, this could explain their lack of representation in areas of eastern England. There are only three sites, all from southeast England, that have infant cremations. One of these sites is Stone Farm Bridleway (Kent) that has an Early Iron Age infant cremation (1.2g) in the eastern arm of a rectangular building that sits just to the east of a Bronze Age mound (Crockett 2000, 2.2.10). The second site is Jubilee Corner (Kent) that has two Late Iron Age infant cremations with one set in the fill of a bloomery, and the other placed to the northeast of the bloomery in a gully (Aldridge 2005, 176, 179). Lastly, the Late Iron Age cremation cemetery at Westhampnett contains at least four, definitive infant cremation burials (McKinley 1997, 63).

Previous research suggests that there is no preference by sex for the deposition of skeletal material (Wilson 1981, 145). The results from this study's analysis did not reveal any bias in biological sex between the varying burial characteristics. Instead, each sex is proportionally equal in its representation throughout the Iron Age within the study area. During the Late Iron Age, males and females are almost equally present in the burial record (males: 50.9 per cent, females: 49.1 per cent). However, males are more frequent than females in disarticulated deposits and inhumations and there are a higher number of females than males among the cremation burials. From the total amount of sexed cremations, females comprise of 77.6 per cent and males 22.4 per cent of the sample, which is a significant disparity. Little weight should be placed on this latter finding since only a fraction of all the cremations in the sample could be sexed. In all, the research did not reveal any strong preferential treatment by age or sex. Overall, apart from the different burial treatment to infants, there is no clear biological preference concerning who these remains represent within the community, and this would suggest that a separate cultural interpretation is necessary.

Victims of violence

One explanation might be that some of the individuals within Iron Age deposits are victims of sacrifice. Wait (1985a, 119) argues this to be an unlikely explanation because, though it may account for a small portion of the skeletal material, it does not explain the high presence of infants (which would be uncommon victims) and complete inhumations on farmsteads (which does not appear to be a likely social activity for small family units). However, Cunliffe (1995, 78) argues that complete inhumations from inside Danebury may have been the result of ritual deaths. Similarly, some argue that some Iron Age human remains are the products of violence or warfare (Carr *et al*. 2005; Redfern 2008a, 2009). Studies (Carr *et al*. 2005; Redfern 2008a, 2009) show traumatic indicators on some of the human bone from all periods of the Iron Age such as the inhumation at Maiden Castle with an arrowhead lodged in its spinal column (Wheeler 1943, 63). There are undoubtedly victims of violence within the burial record from this study's sample, such as the decapitated inhumation from the A505 Baldock Bypass (Hertfordshire, Thorpe *et al*. 2003) and the skull with a peri-mortem puncture wound from Houghton Down in Hampshire (Cunliffe and Poole 2000b, 129; 14:E4 [microfiche]). Thus, violence to some degree was a part of life for Iron Age communities.

In addition, Green (1998, 172, 178) suggests that, even though sacrifice was not the normative rite, there is no reason to think it did not happen: human remains with limestone slabs or flint nodules covering the bones could indicate sacrificial victim, with the stones acting to weigh down the individual. In addition, the examples of stones 'weighing' down the deceased have been argued to signify a sacrificial victim (see Green 1998, 172). This has been seen at Aspreys, Olney (Buckinghamshire), which had an inhumation with limestone slabs covering the burial (Webley 2007a). In a large pit, at the enclosed site of Burgh (Suffolk), there was a Late Iron Age skull that had a large stone covering the face of the individual (Martin 1988).

However, the evidence from this study's sample suggests that the majority of human remains were not the victims of violence, whether ritual or warfare. Those individuals subjected to violence account for only for a small fraction of the burial evidence. As previously stated in the section on processing, only 0.06 per cent[45] of the skeletal material contains direct evidence of traumatic episodes. There is

also the possibility that many other human remains derive from individuals who were victims of violence that left no marks on the skeleton, such as strangulation or wounds to the abdomen. Nonetheless, the direct osteological evidence does not support arguments that a large portion of the human remains are from individuals who were victims of some form of violence either ritual or warfare.

Social status

Another option is that Iron Age burial practices may signify the social standing of the deceased individuals, with particular reference to the manner of disposal. Those whose remains have survived may represent social elites, although Wait (1985a, 118) believes this to be unlikely. He argues that if the human remains were elites then their burials would have been more elaborate, in a special, restrictive place and '...members of an elite usually all receive the same basic rite', which does not explain the variation in burial practice (Wait 1985a, 118). In general, Iron Age societies appear to have been relatively egalitarian, and there are very few rich graves in the Late Bronze Age and Iron Age (Sharples 2010, 241, 245). The extent to which Iron Age society was stratified is not apparent from the southern British burial record. Unlike the burial evidence we see in East Yorkshire, which is littered with inhumation cemeteries, a number of which are accompanied by carts, brooches, and other prestigious material (Stead 1991, 179-184), the display of wealth in the burial rite is rare in southern Britain.

This investigation did not explore in detail the relationship between material goods and human remains apart from the frequency particular items are associated with bones. The quantitative results indicate most associated items are common materials recovered from Iron Age sites in great quantity, such as pottery and animal bones. Additionally, these items (in respect to depositional pattern) are often main elements in structured deposits of which human remains are part of as well (see Hill 1995b). For example, excavations at Burgh in Suffolk uncovered a massive pit (7.5 m long X 6.35 m wide X 3.2 m deep) that contained rapid deposits containing large amounts of pottery and animal bones as well as a human skull with a stone covering its face, and the excavators believe this to be a ritual pit (Martin 1988, 10-12). This example illustrates that material associated with human remains is not always a display or exhibition of the deceased's status but part of a broader ritual practice. In all, there are few examples from this study that shows the associated material is clearly indicative of the individual's standing. An example of an exception is from Mill Hill where an Iron Age inhumation, the 'warrior burial', was buried with a headdress, iron sword, brooch, scabbard, and a bronze shield (folded in half and placed over the body) (Parfitt 1995, 18-20). Overall, the high-standing status of an individual was not expressed commonly within the burial record.

---

[45] This percentage indicates human bone occurrences with ante- or peri-mortem traumatic indicators of probable violence (fractures, cut marks, blunt force trauma and dismemberment).

At the other end of the hierarchical spectrum, there is the possibility that some of the skeletal material represents outcasts from the community. Wait (1985a, 118-120) asserts that this is the most probable explanation for the Iron Age burial record. He reasons that outcasts or 'unclean' individuals generally did not receive the normal burial rite, but were given several different non-normative rites and this would have been an infrequent event- all of which could possibly explain the Iron Age burial evidence (Wait 1985a, 118-120). Cunliffe (1995) and Madgwick (2008) have argued that the articulated skeletal remains may be those of outsiders since they were not afforded the same liminal (exposure) time to fully break down to disarticulated bones (Cunliffe 1995, 78; Madgwick 2008, 111).

It is difficult to argue conclusively that Iron Age human remains are those of a lower social class. As discussed above, there generally appears to have been great emphasis on deconstruction of the corpse, especially in the Late Bronze Age and the Early and Middle Iron Age. If an incomplete body was the ultimate goal, than a fully or partially articulated individual might be seen as undesirable or insulting. It may be logical to argue that inhumations and articulated parts were social outcasts since these individuals never reached the full stage of deconstruction. However, this is not universal (as with most aspects of Iron Age burial practice), for this explanation does not account for the change in the burial record, primarily with the increase of inhumations in the Late Iron Age. The low-status explanation does not also adequately explain all inhumations in the Late Bronze Age, Early Iron Age and Middle Iron Age that are part of significant burial rites. For example, Little Stock Farm in Kent has an Early/Middle Iron Age inhumation that shows a prolonged and complex burial history. The contextual and osteological evidence for this inhumation indicates that burial was first within a pit marking the entrance of a possible stock enclosure, then later exhumed and reburied nearly 100 metres away from its original deposit (Ritchie 2006, 8; McKinley 2006a, 69). The inhumation at Little Stock Farm demonstrates the continued significance the community had for these remains, as evident by the depositional history - not the state or completeness of the body. In very general terms, it seems that the identity of the human remains was not emphasised in Iron Age deposits. The issue may not rest on who these people were but on what these deposits meant to the community.

Ancestors

This last point leads into the next interpretation concerning the possible identity of human bones as a form of ancestor representation and veneration. The remains of ancestors, in the form of disarticulated bones, are retrieved from the place of excarnation after the full liminal time and then deposited as possible offerings (Cunliffe 1995, 78). Sharples (2010, 289) argues that old burials were deliberately sought out to retrieve selected bones, thus allowing access to communal ancestors. He

suggests that complete individuals were separated from the group of ancestors (Sharples 2010, 290-291). Sharples' argument focuses on the site of Suddern Farm in Hampshire, where, if this is the case, the community's residents sought out communal graves to obtain bones and, thus, access to the ancestors. However, the final burials in the cemetery were infant inhumations. This may relate back to the previous discussion on the differential burial treatment for infants. The act of sealing off access to ancestors by infants may act as a metaphor of a lost generation closing the connection to the community's ancestors.

A number of disarticulated bones display evidence of post-mortem manipulation and some degree of continued handling prior to their deposition. This is apparent at the site of High Barns Road (Bedfordshire) where there is strong evidence that a skull fragment was curated for a number of years before its deposition (Webley 2007b, 19). Similar finds from both Gravelly Guy (Oxfordshire, Wait 2004, 249) and Glastonbury Lake Village (Somerset, Barber *et al.* 1995, 174), include a skull fragment fashioned into a disc with a central perforation, possibly for use as an amulet. The continued engagement with human bones in this fashion may be a form of ancestor veneration. In addition to curated remains, some Iron Age communities reused earlier monuments to reaffirm ancestral connections. Although there are a small number of sites demonstrating this characteristic, it illustrates a different interpretation and practice of the ancestor theme. Potentially, these communities may have viewed the monuments as visual manifestations of their ancestral past, which they incorporated into their burial rites. Generally, the human remains and spatial contexts acted as symbols for ancestor connection, and functioned to create and reaffirm the individual's place in the community by creating a sense of a shared heritage in which all members are connected. This point is evident at Mill Hill. The cemetery at Mill Hill consists of individual burials of the community's members around a Bronze Age mound. The spatial setting, in conjunction with the individual burials implies a communal effort represented by its individual members in proclaiming their connection to an ancestral past.

Summary

The inter-relationship between depositional properties and spatial organisation define how Iron Age communities ordered and manipulated skeletal remains. It also shows how the communities' burial practices '...associated with the dead may not be aimed at removing them [the deceased] from society...but at reintegrating them into society as different kinds of entities, different orders of person' (Fowler 2004, 81). It appears possible that Iron Age human remains could have had two different and broad identities. One was the corpse that retained some form of its individuality after death and still represented the person (similar to Mill Hill). The second is human remains which were objectified and lost their individuality and, through the community's handling, were redefined to represent something that was no longer the individual. In all, the symbolic meanings of the human remains and spatial context are not fixed; instead, they are ever changing according to social life, which accounts for the multiplicity of identities the dead take on (Robb 1998, 338).

Overall interpretation of the burial rite

This section presents an overall approach to the understanding of Iron Age burial practices and their implications. To begin, the burial record represents a minority rite, and there can be no simple universal explanation for these practices during the Iron Age (Wait 1985a, 116). The diverse nature of the burial evidence from this study supports this claim. However, this investigation also depicts variations of similar burial activities at play during the Iron Age. Each of these practices had a different purpose, with human bone being the common trait. Thus far, the discussion has considered separately the spatial context, identity, and processing of human remains. Now, it turns to explore these components together to illustrate their connection. Central to this are the living as active and conscious players in burial activities.

To begin with the spatial context, we may assert that the living viewed these areas as appropriate places to deposit the dead. As discussed, spatial placement was organised within two arenas: the public and private. Public disposal places are more commonly occurring than private. Deposits on settlement boundaries and as temporal markers, together with most instances of reuse of monuments and areas of economic significance are examples of burial activities performed in the public domain. Each of these locales held different meanings to the living as illustrated through the deposit. Even so, these areas were potentially accessible to all members of the community, meaning all could be involved. Besides accomplishing the deposition's main purpose (like marking liminal spaces), there is also another outcome. Activities involving the wider group would have created a sense of belonging for the group's members (Marshall 2002, 360, 363). Even if the community's members did not gather to witness the burial of human bones and other associated material, the mere presence of such in public places insinuates a shared knowledge that would still have the same outcome. Whether intended or not, human bones were part of public activities that created and defined the living's identity and affiliation within the collective group. In these contexts, we can see the bones operating on the communal level representing more than just a singular concept.

In contrast, burial practices in the private arena denote accessibility for a limited number of participants. Most deposits in domestic structures are a type of activity within the private sector. There may have been an element of public discourse, such as if the remains were publicly displayed outside the structure or post-abandonment rites. Depositional practices, however, while the structure was in use suggests exclusivity for the inhabitants. Incorporating the bones into the private sector allowed the occupants to create their own perception within the boundaries of the group ideology (Cohen 1994, 142). Ritual activities on this private level may have had a more domestic dimension, and possibly signified a sense of ownership of the bones or of belonging.

We can now see how the spatial context forms the basis for approaching Iron Age burial rites and now the discussion turns to who the bones were to the living. The results from this investigation did not show anything concrete in respect to the demographic profile, except differential treatment of infants. It is possible that the living viewed infants differently than other age groups, namely adults. Furthermore, it is not unreasonable to suppose that this may imply an age threshold. Infants may not have been seen as full members of the community; thus, not afforded the normative burial rite – whatever that may be. Moving to adults, after reviewing proposals of who the dead may represent, it appears that the bones representing ancestral concepts is the most plausible explanation for much of the burial material. This also correlates with the infant evidence, meaning that individuals who died before a certain age did not enter this "ancestor" category. But the ancestral explanation is just one layer to the multifaceted meaning bestowed on bones by the living. It may prove beneficial to view bone deposits not as representations of the deceased, but as a physical expression of an idea by the living.

Processing the dead is the time when human remains lose part or all of their original, living identity, and acquire a new meaning from the living members of the group (Parker Pearson 1993, 203-204; Fowler 2008, 80). It appears that deconstruction of the corpse was typically the ultimate goal for Iron Age people, particularly for the Late Bronze Age to the Middle Iron Age. Through this breakdown, the more fragmented remains may no longer have represented the deceased individual. In the earlier half of the first millennium BC, communities utilized different techniques to achieve this goal. Differences in the processing of the dead form distinct geographic and temporal patterns across southern Britain (the implications of which are discussed in the following chapter). This may be understood in two ways. First, the living practiced different methods to create the objects (bones) necessary for later social activities. Second, these varying techniques may be understood as local expressions of a shared custom. As the first millennium BC drew to a close, however, there is a change. During the Late Iron Age, we find more of the deceased present in the archaeological record (increase in inhumations and average cremation weight). It could be argued that the more "complete" burials retained part of their individuality. Generally, it appears that Iron Age populations moved from breaking down the body to keeping it whole.

In all, the evidence suggests that human remains deposits were not solely the by-products of disposing of the dead. Instead, they were active elements in a series of both public and private ritual activities that communicate society's perception of itself. It appears the cultural mechanisms motivating Iron Age burial rites may be best understood by Geertz's (1973, 17) view of culture, but summarized by Cohen (1994, 134):

'...culture is...a kaleidoscope, composed of a finite body of materials which can be arranged by their users into numerous different shapes and further modulated by being held at different angles to the light'

There were different ritual processes each with a different purpose, but using the same medium - human bone. The same objects (human remains) may have had different significance in different social contexts, and the same culture may have had different ways of using these objects for the same goal (Goldstein 1981, 53). Iron Age burial practices exemplify this concept, and this study illustrates those elements within the main themes (processing, spatial organization, and identity) that are essential to understand the social intent behind these practices.

Chapter Ten

Regionality and burial practices

Introduction

Understanding the Iron Age: an agenda for action devotes a section of its manifesto to the concept of regionality and its importance to future Iron Age studies (Haselgrove *et al.* 2001). In this work, it describes regionality as '...characteristics that have to be explained in other ways' than geographical and environmental factors (Haselgrove *et al.* 2001, 31). This stance suggests that regionality denotes variations in the patterns of social behaviour that is evident on a large geographical scale. In turn, the variability between areas '...points clearly to the construction and maintenance of distinct regional identities' (Haselgrove *et al.* 2001, 32). In keeping with this concept, this discussion will consist of a comparison between the results from this study and the established burial traditions present in the study area, specifically the Durotrigian inhumation tradition and the Aylesford-Swarling cremation rite. Here, the section re-examines the validity of these burial traditions while discussing the overall implications of regionality to Iron Age burial studies. Afterwards, the chapter broadens to a general discussion on regionality in burial practices and how this concept relates with other approaches, namely ceramics.

Past burial traditions

Durotrigian inhumation tradition

The Durotrigian inhumation tradition is one of the two, distinct, and established regional burial groups within this study sample. By the Late Iron Age, '[t]he Durotriges were a close-knit confederacy of smaller units centred upon modern Dorset' (Cunliffe 2005, 178). The area occupied by the Durotriges extends further north into Wiltshire and Somerset as well as to the west bordering Devon and eastward to the border of Hampshire (Hamilton 2007, 57). The material culture, such as the ceramics and coins, is distinct from groups outside this territory and there is evidence signifying long-distance trading, specifically with amphorae and glass (Cunliffe 2005, 179-180; Hamilton 2007, 57). The Durotrigian inhumation rite appeared during the first century BC and is characterised by flat, earthen inhumation graves in a formal burial ground, sometimes in stone-cists (Whimster 1981a, 37; Hamilton 2007, 63). Commonly the inhumations were laid in the crouched position on their right sides, orientated between the northeast to southeast, with a limited amount of associated materials, typically animal bone and Dorset black burnished vessels (Whimster 1981a, 43, 50). It is possible, Whimster

(1981a, 37) reasons, that the Durotrigian inhumation tradition derives from the pit-burial rite of the Middle Iron Age. Geographically, this inhumation tradition is only present in southern Dorset and is absent in the northern territory of the Durotriges (Whimster 1981a, 42).

A key site in this study sample is Maiden Castle (see chapter seven), which lies in southern Dorset and has a large inhumation cemetery outside its eastern gate, which is indicative of the Durotrigian tradition (Wheeler 1943; Sharples 1991). The burials from Maiden Castle are a distinct example of the Durotrigian inhumation tradition in the respect that their deposition characteristics differ from the normative rite, as Sharples (1991, 100) highlights. Most of the inhumations buried in the cemetery are supine, not crouched, favouring the southeast orientation and have a wealth of associated material culture (Sharples 1991, 101; also see chapter seven). Despite the divergence from the norm, the Maiden Castle sample illustrates key features of the Durotrigian inhumation tradition, such as a formal burial ground and inhuming the body. A nearby Durotrigian site in this study sample is Gussage All Saints (see chapter seven), but is not part of the Durotrigian inhumation tradition, and provides an interesting comparison to Maiden Castle. Gussage All Saints lies just to the northeast of Maiden Castle and it also contains a number of Late Iron Age inhumations (Wainwright 1979). The inhumations are mostly in pits (Wainwright 1979, 32-35); however, they are scattered throughout the settlement area with no clear prescribed area for burials. Maiden Castle has a separate burial area while the inhumations at Gussage All Saints are incorporated into the domestic sphere. The comparison of Maiden Castle and Gussage All Saints illustrate the difference in burial practice in terms of spatial placement even with geographically close communities. The evidence from this sample for the Durotrigian inhumation tradition corresponds with Whimster's original synopsis of the group. Particularly that this burial rite is distinct for Durotrigian communities in southern Dorset and not present in the northern territories.

In a similar vein, the regional distinction between the north and south in the Durotrigian inhumation rite exposes further implications in the broader approaches to burial practices in the Iron Age. The Durotrigian tribe is thought to occupy a wide area, as previously stated, which is evident by a distinct set of material culture. However, within this tribal group there is a sub-tradition in handling the dead within a restricted geographical area. This suggests a discrepancy between regional groups of material items and burial practices. In other words, the difference in burial practices between close social units does not entirely correspond in the material culture. Thus, there is variability in the burial rite within the regional group, which is a point that will be further examined in the following section.

Aylesford-Swarling cremation rite

To reiterate briefly, the Aylesford-Swarling rite is characterised by cremation burials, either urned or unurned, in flat graves that occur during the first century BC (Birchall 1964, 22; Fitzpatrick 1997, 208; Whimster 1981a, 148, 157). The burials are associated with a range of grave goods, such as ceramics, coinage, and metalwork (e.g. brooches) (Fitzpatrick 1997, 208; Whimster 1981a, 148). Pottery is the most common material and urned cremations were typically set in cinerary containers as well as tall pedestal urns, wide-mouthed bowls, Gallo-Belgic wares (e.g. King Harry Lane), and butt-beakers (Collis 1977, 5; Stead 1969, 49-50; Whimster 1981a, 157). There are instances of cremations placed in '...bronze or iron-bound wooden buckets and tankard-like vessels' (Whimster 1981a, 157). Aylesford-Swarling cremation burials appear as isolated deposits, small burial groups, and isolated cemeteries. Most cemeteries are small, but larger ones are known, such as King Harry Lane (Hertfordshire) and Westhampnett (West Sussex) (Stead 1969; Fitzpatrick 1997). In addition, the burial grounds are occasionally close to a settlement, but are more often isolated (Fitzpatrick 1997, 228). In groups of cremation burials, there is very little overlap, which may suggest some type of marker for the graves (Whimster 1981a, 155). Another spatial characteristic is that rich graves are encircled sometimes by lesser-furnished burials, and these clusters might represent family units or lineages (Collis 1977, 4; Stead 1969, 50; Whimster 1981a, 156-157). The distribution of Aylesford-Swarling cremation sites favour southeastern England; specifically Kent, Essex, Cambridgeshire as well as some instances further west into Dorset and Somerset (Whimster 1981a, 151). Particularly in areas assumed to be occupied by the tribal groups of the Catuvellauni/Trinovantes and Cantii (Cunliffe 2005, 149; Hamlin 2007, 62). Scholars agree that the Aylesford-Swarling tradition is a foreign element that infiltrated Britain and reintroduced cremation to the area (Whimster 1981a, 148; Haselgrove and Moore 2007, 1). The origins of this rite have been traced back to northern France, possibly Normandy, based on similarities in material culture and the practice of cremation (Haselgrove and Moore 2007, 1; Fitzpatrick 1997, 208-209; Birchall 1964, 21). It is argued that the archaeological remains of the Aylesford-Swarling tradition represents the waves of Belgic immigrants throughout the first century BC that colonised southeastern England, and who also brought their material cultural and funerary practice (Whimster 1981a, 165).

According to this investigation, communities in southeastern England practiced cremation continuously, though in varying degrees of intensity, from the Late Bronze Age into the Late Iron Age (see chapters six and eight). This does not entirely 'fit' into the assumption that the Aylesford-Swarling cremation rite as a foreign element. Instead, it begs the question of to what extent is this cremation rite a foreign phenomenon that transferred to Britain. Is there a comparable continuity in the cremation practice from the Late Bronze Age to the Late Iron Age in southeastern Britain? To answer these questions the discussion will detail the burial traits, associated material, spatial location, and geographical distribution of cremations from the Late Bronze Age to the Middle Iron Age, and then compare that to the Aylesford-Swarling cremations in the Late Iron Age.

Sites with Late Bronze Age cremation deposits concentrate in the southeast (see chapter eight and **Figure 8.1**), primarily in Kent (n=5 sites), and reach northwards into Bedfordshire, Cambridgeshire, and Essex. The most westerly cremation site in the sample is in Warwickshire. Besides the Late Iron Age, the Late Bronze Age has the highest instances of cremation deposits. The evidence from the Late Bronze Age cremation sites shows a range of varying burial deposits. There are instances of isolated cremation burials in the landscape a distance away from known habitation areas. For example, at Northumberland Bottom (Kent) excavations retrieved an urned cremation (50g) burial of an adult, and this was one of a few features indicating Late Bronze Age activity (Askew 2006, 16). This is similar to the Late Bronze Age burial evidence at High Barns Road (Bedfordshire) (Webley 2007b). At this site, only three features, all pits, date to the Late Bronze Age and within one of these pits was an unurned cremation burial of a mature adult (Webley 2007b, 11). At Broom (Area E, Warwickshire), in the Arrow Valley, there are the archaeological remains of a Late Bronze Age pyre site, with subsequent cremated bone scatter, yet there is little known settlement evidence within its vicinity (Palmer 1999, 6, 36, 218). Excavations at Beechbrook Wood (Kent, also see chapter seven) yielded two cremation burials (<1g; 52g), each in separate pits set along a ditch system (Brady 2006b, 7). Tutt Hill (Kent) also contains two cremation burials, one unurned (4g) and the other the remains of an adult male set within an urn (1288g), placed along a field system and to the south of a Bronze Age ring ditch (Brady 2006c). Although there is a settlement near Tutt Hill, the community deposited the cremations apart from the habitation area. Excavations at Highfields Farm (Cambridgeshire) recovered a couple of token, unurned cremation deposits, which were clustered in their own, separate burial grounds, away from the main occupation areas (Rothwell and Turner 2005, 25). The site at Bromham Road (Bedfordshire) contains six, Late Bronze Age/Early Iron Age cremations (10-530g), all unurned, placed near a land division with no direct settlement evidence in its vicinity (Turner 2005, 13).

The aforementioned examples illustrate how many Late Bronze Age cremation burials were set away or isolated from settlements. However, there are instances of cremated remains deposited within a settlement, such as the domestic site at Hutchinson in Cambridgeshire (Evans *et al.* 2008). Here, a single, unurned cremation (282g) was placed in a pit near what may be the densest area of domestic activity (Evans *et al.* 2008, 30). South Hornchurch (Essex) has 15 unurned cremations (1-180g) and many of these deposits are associated with roundhouses, multi-post structures, boundaries, and with a sheep run (Guttmann and Last 2006, 349-350, 356). The site at Broom (Bedfordshire) has two adjacent excavation areas, Hill Lane and Toll House, with both having cremation burials (Cooper and Edmonds 2007). The communities at Hill Lane buried their cremated dead outside the settlement area, with some associated with a nearby Bronze Age ring ditch (Cooper and Edmonds 2007, 124), while at Toll House, the cremation deposits were set within the domestic area (Cooper and Edmonds 2007, 114-115). Thus, Broom is an example of neighbouring communities practicing cremation that differ in their locations for burial.

In addition to the spatial characteristics, the cremation burials in this sample during the Late Bronze Age range in the quantity of deposited cremated bone, from less than 10g to over a 1000g. For example, investigations at Kingsmead Park (Kent) recovered two token cremations, one weighing 0.4g and the other 0.7g (McKinley 2005b, 77). One of the cremations at Beechbrook Wood weighs just under a gram (Witkins 2006, 4). Similarly, White Horse (Kent) contains a cremation deposit weighing just four grams (Hayden and Stafford 2006). As previously stated, there are also substantial deposits of cremated bone. Such is the case of the urned cremation burial at Tutt Hill with about 1288g of burnt bone (Brady 2006c), or the unurned cremation at White Horse that also weighs over 1000g (Hayden and Stafford 2006). Thus, there is a disparity in the quantity of collected bone. The range in weights may be the result of taphonomic processes, such as spongy bones being less likely to survive and will reduce the overall weight of a cremation (Mays 1992). The extent bone survival in the soil effects cremations within the studied sample is uncertain since not all the osteological reports were specific on the type of bone present in the deposit. In addition, later disturbance, most often by agricultural practices, can heavily influence the quantity of cremated bone. This may be the case at Kingsmead Park for the two cremations previously described were heavily truncated which may have resulted in bone loss (McKinley 2005b, 77). The low amount of cremated bone may be the result of both taphonomic issues (disturbance and bone survival) as well as human intent. McKinley (1997, 71-72) asserts that it is rare for all the cremated bone to be collected after burning. She suggests a community may collect just a small sample (token deposit) of the cremated deceased to represent death or for some ritual, although one must be cautious when using this term for it can be misleading and disregard taphonomic and extenuating circumstances.

Another aspect to consider with Late Bronze Age cremations is their frequency and assortment of associated materials. A range of material accompanied the majority (80.4 per cent) of cremation deposits. Pyre debris (ash and charcoal) are the most frequent with Late Bronze Age cremations as well as other items such as animal bones, pottery sherds, worked stones, plant remains, and metal artefacts. Overall, Late Bronze Age cremation sites concentrate in the southeast of England, and show isolated burials, small burial groups set away from domestic areas, as well as being incorporated within settlements. There is a disparity in cremation weights, possibly explained by token deposits and taphonomic factors as well as instances of 'more complete' burials. In addition, the vast majority of cremations are associated with a variety of items, all of which is similar, in varying degrees, to the Aylesford-Swarling tradition.

The frequency of sites with cremation deposits reduces in the Early Iron Age (n=7 sites, see **Figure 8.2**). Their geographical spread is dispersed, yet largely favours the eastern areas of England, such as Kent, Bedfordshire, and Cambridgeshire. Even though there is a reduction in frequency for cremation occurrences in this sample, there are similarities in their deposition with the Late Bronze Age. Cremations deposits are typically away from domestic areas. For example, the site at Stone Farm Bridleway (Kent) has four Early Iron Age cremations (all under 35g), as well as two additional ones dating to the Early/Middle Iron Age, with most inserted into the eastern arm of a rectangular structure, which is near a Bronze Age ring ditch (Crockett 2000). These features at Stone Farm Bridleway are located next to a field system and there is no mention of a settlement nearby (Crockett 2000). Similarly, at Chichester Road, close to Selsey in West Sussex, there are two cremation deposits (combined weight of 44.5g) in the same context, but in separate layers (Hammond and Preston 2000, 76, 81). The cremations are in a ditch fill that lies north of the settlement at this site (Hammond and Preston 2000, 81). At White Horse (Kent), there is an Early/Middle Iron Age cremation of a sub-adult (292g) deposited at the southern end of the site, slightly away from the main domestic activity area (Hayden and Stafford 2006, 10). The cremation from White Horse was associated with lots of pottery, a metal tool set that consists of an iron knife, blade, awls, copper alloy ring, head pin and may have been set originally in a ceramic bowl, but displaced by later disturbance (Hayden and Stafford 2006, 159).

By the Middle Iron Age, cremation occurrences are at its lowest for this studied sample. There are only six sites with cremations and many are still in Kent (n=3) and the others in South Yorkshire, Leicestershire, and Hampshire (see **Figure 8.3**). As with the depositional characteristics present during the Late Bronze Age and Early Iron Age, there are instances of cremation deposits segregated from settlement areas. For example, the marsh-fort at Sutton Common (South Yorkshire) contains no habitation evidence, but much in the way of storage facilities, evident by the high frequency of four-post structures (Van de Noort *et al.* 2007, 175-176). Here, there is a small amount of cremated bone (4g) inserted into a posthole (Van de Noort *et al.* 2007, 175-176). This is similar to the evidence found at Wanlip in Leicestershire (Beamish 1998). Excavations at Wanlip unearthed a possible small, domestic site that consists of a round structure and a large, separate enclosure, presumably for livestock (Beamish 1998). This site also contains a separate, multi-post structure with an unurned cremation burial of a young adult in its centre (Beamish 1998, 72). In contrast, Easton Lane yielded evidence of a cremation deposits within a posthole of a roundhouse (Fasham *et al.* 1989, 68).

Generally, the characteristics and geographical distribution of cremation deposits in the Late Bronze Age, Early Iron Age, and Middle Iron Age share common traits. Primarily, there is a similar regional distribution, which is evident by most cremation practising communities lying in the eastern areas of England. There are instances throughout the Late Bronze Age to the Middle Iron Age of isolated cremation burials and group burials placed away from domestic areas. This is not a universal, spatial characteristic, for there are examples of cremations integrated into the domestic sphere, as outlined above. Many cremations from the Late Bronze Age to the Middle Iron Age have associated materials, most of which is ash and charcoal, a by-product of the cremation process, as well as pottery. Overall, there is a degree of continuity in cremation practice from the Late Bronze Age to the Middle Iron Age that can be comparable to that of the Late Iron Age, Aylesford-Swarling cremation tradition.

The Late Iron Age witnessed a resurgence of cremation burials. From this sample, sites with cremation deposits concentrate in the southeast, namely in Kent and stretch out towards the East Midlands and to the west in Oxfordshire (see **Figure 8.4**). The geographical distribution compliments with what is known of the Aylesford-Swarling spread. Furthermore, the sample contains instances of small burial groups and cemeteries, another characteristic of the Aylesford-Swarling tradition. Such is the case of the cremation cemetery at Westhampnett previously discussed in chapter seven. The site at Salford (Bedfordshire) has a small cremation cemetery aligned along an old Early/Middle Iron Age settlement boundary (Dawson 2005). Hinxton Quarry (Cambridgeshire) contains a small cremation cemetery, with five cremation burials encircled by ring ditches and also includes three inhumations (Hill *et al.* 1999). In addition, at North Shoebury (Essex) there is a small cremation cemetery placed on the eastern boundary of the settlement site (Wymer and Brown 1995). The separation of cremation burials and settlement, common in the Late Iron Age, is similar to the evidence from the Late Bronze Age to the Middle Iron Age. However, there are examples of Late Iron Age cremation deposits within the domestic sphere. A prime example of such is a cremation burial from Gravelly Guy (Oxfordshire) placed within the main settlement area and is associated with loose infant bones (Lambrick and Allen 2004, 250, 461). Furthermore, the site at Gayhurst Quarry (Buckinghamshire) contains an

urned cremation buried in a pit, just outside a domestic structure (Chapman 2007, 203).

The Late Iron Age cremations within this studied sample are associated with a wealth of materials. Of the 264 cremations, 90.2 per cent have associated material. At Hinxton Quarry, an abundant amount of items was buried with the cremations, such as pottery, (e.g. pedestal urn and Tazzae bowls), iron fibula, nail cleaner, and brooches (Hill *et al.* 1999, 252). The cremations at Duckend Car Park (Essex) contained brooches, a copper ring, ceramic vessels, and metal artefacts (Havis and Brook 2005). The range and frequency of associated items is a common trait of the Aylesford-Swarling rite, and the type of material and intensity differs slightly from the cremation evidence described during the Late Bronze Age to the Middle Iron Age.

The burial evidence of the Late Iron Age cremations in this sample is parallel to that of the Aylesford-Swarling tradition. There are separate burial areas, a wealth of associated material, and the regional distribution favours the southeast and eastern areas of England. However, we return to the question that opened this section, which is to what extent is the Aylesford-Swarling cremation rite a foreign import that includes the reintroduction of cremation? As the evidence from this sample shows, this is not entirely the case. The implications from this study sample are that the Aylesford-Swarling tradition did not 'reintroduce' cremation to England. Instead, there is continuity in the act of cremating the body with later deposition since the Late Bronze Age in the eastern areas of England. In addition, there is a commonality in the spatial setting of cremation burials throughout the periods with the deposits often placed away from domestic areas. There are, of course, differences in the practice throughout the Late Bronze Age and the Late Iron Age. The frequency of cremation deposits varies in intensity from the Late Bronze Age to the Late Iron Age as well as a specific material culture accompanying them. The material culture from the Late Iron Age, specifically the pottery and metal works, reflect the continental influence in England, which this is not disputed. However, this author argues for Iron Age studies to reconsider the assumption of the Aylesford-Swarling tradition as a purely foreign import. Instead, the evidence from this sample implies a foreign influence on a long-established, British burial rite.

Wider approaches to regionality

The regional distribution of the Aylesford-Swarling cremation rite brings the discussion back to an issue previously raised. As discussed earlier, the Durotrigian inhumation tradition is present only in the southern area of the Durotrigian confederacy. In contrast, the Aylesford-Swarling rite covers a large area that includes the territories of the Catuvellauni/Trinovantes, Atrebates and Cantii tribes (Cunliffe 2005, 149; Hamilton 2007, 62). It is argued that the aforementioned tribal units share commonalities in ceramics, economics, and burial; yet are distinguished by their coinage (Cunliffe 2005, 149). This distribution of both burial traditions show the Aylesford-Swarling cremation rite crossed tribal boundaries, while the Durotrigian inhumation rite was restricted to a select number of communities within a single territory.

In very general terms, the preceding points on the Durotrigian inhumation rite and the Aylesford-Swarling cremation tradition show that there is disconnection between different modes of defining regionality. The lack of cohesion in distributions between various materials, burial, and assumed tribal boundaries (particularly in the Middle and the Late Iron Age) exposes the difficulty in comparing regional studies for different aspects of Iron Age societies. By comparing the distributions between burial patterns indicated in this study and ceramic style zones advocated by Cunliffe (1982; 2005, 103, 588) with the subsequent implications this point is further heightened. The reason for focusing on this one type of material is that pottery production occurred on a massive scale during the Iron Age and is the most abundant item recovered from excavations (Collis 1977c, 29). The quantity and sensitivity to chronological change allowed scholars to construct style zones that correlate with defined geographical regions (Cunliffe 2005, 83, 87).

As stated in chapter one, Cunliffe (2005, 87-120) provides a chronological break down of ceramic styles and their geographical areas where they were commonly used. In respect to the ceramic distribution in the Middle and the Late Iron Age, Cunliffe (1982; 2005, 103, 588) asserts that these ceramic-style zones in central and southern Britain are indicative of tribal groups. However, it is notable that the methods of processing the dead do not strongly adhere to tight geographic boundaries, let alone strict ceramic, and subsequently tribal, areas. By following Cunliffe's (1982; 2005, 103, 588) argument, however, the ceramic evidence is indicative of the ethnic groups showing strong borders, while the geographical patterns in handling the dead are blurry and have no specific boundaries.

Most aspects of Iron Age society, such as pottery and burial customs, may allow one to construct visual representations of regional groups. This alludes to a level of group homogeneity. Returning to the aforementioned definition of regionality from the *Understanding the Iron Age: an agenda for action* (Haselgrove *et al.* 2001), this concept refers to discernible patterns of social behaviour within different geographical areas that relate to the construction and preservation of identity. Ceramics, as well as other material items, is a form of identity expression. People define the objects and material they handle, and this manipulation reflects back on their perception of themselves. Yet, the extent this material denotes larger, social entities are still debateable (see Collis 1977a; 1977e). As for burial practices, this study shows how Iron Age communities expressed different forms of their identity through various handling and placement of the human remains. Furthermore, the

analysis showed the methods and process of disposing the dead varies chronologically and is broadly, geographically sensitive. Although, the regional patterns of behaviour towards the dead does not allow one to simply draw a line separating one group from the other. Creating such arbitrary boundaries on the burial evidence would be misleading. Instead, the burial evidence appears to suggest that there are shared, ideological principles amongst Iron Age communities, such as veneration of ancestors and constructing and renewing both communal and individual identities, but varies in the mode of expressing such ideas, and these methods of expression are not fixed.

This illustrates a broader point with the concept of regionality and its use in Iron Age studies. The burial patterns for Late Bronze Age and Iron Age communities show that there is not a unified burial rite, but common principles expressed differently amongst these communities. The burial patterns do not strongly correlate with other types of evidence, namely ceramics. It may be reasoned that identity, both communal and individual, resides in social groups not geographical territories. This point needs to be considered when examining the burial evidence of a site and incorporating this into the larger, regional interpretations. Ultimately, one cannot mould evidence from an individual site to fit into prescribed and agreed upon ideas. Instead, we need to advocate the differences in expressing the similar concepts within communities and focus on why this might be. This approach needs to be applied for all elements in Iron Age societies. Furthermore, we must be cautious in comparing the conclusions drawn from different lines of evidence.

Summary

This chapter has addressed the concept of regionality in respect to the burial evidence and within the broader field of Iron Age studies. In respect to regional traditions in burial practices, the study puts forward the argument that the practice of cremation was continuously in use in eastern England before the infiltration of the Aylesford-Swarling cremation rite. It is the stance of this research that there is a need to reconsider the extent of the Aylesford-Swarling tradition being a foreign implant; instead, this study argues that it is an influence on a British burial tradition. In addition, the study is in agreement with Whimster (1981a, 42) that the Durotrigian inhumation rite is a sub-tradition within a larger confederacy. This point reverberates to the broader approach of regionality. Iron Age studies have different methods of creating regional groups, particularly with material culture. However, in respect to the regional patterns in burial practices, these geographical groups do not always adhere. Regional studies are beneficial to Iron Age studies for it widens our perception of this period and provides the social context for interpretation. Yet, our interpretations should work from the site-level up into the regional level, and not try to manipulate evidence from a site into preconceived notions of Iron Age societies.

Chapter Eleven

Conclusion and recommendations for future research

Introduction

This chapter summarises the findings from this study and offers recommendations for future research. The chapter divides into two sections; the first discusses how the burial evidence from a selection of well-studied sites, not included in this study, compliment and adhere to this investigation's findings. The intent for this is to demonstrate that even though this study was unable to incorporate all the thoroughly examined burial evidence into the research, the conclusions are applicable to sites not within the studied sample. The final part of the chapter outlines recommendations for future research based on the conclusions of this thesis.

To clarify, this study's evidence implies most Iron Age communities strove towards the destruction, or near to, of the corpse. Excarnation, disinterment, and cremation are the main corpse-processing techniques evident from this sample. Furthermore, the manner of disposal of the dead is regionally and chronologically distinct. Cremation rites are favoured in the eastern area of England, primarily in the Late Bronze Age and the Late Iron Age, while excarnation and disinterment practices are frequent in Wessex mainly in the Early Iron Age to the Late Iron Age. The regional distribution of cremation-practising communities indicates that this processing method was in use from the Late Bronze Age to the Late Iron Age in eastern areas of England. Thus, the evidence calls into question the assumption that cremation was reintroduced from the continent in the Late Iron Age. The burial record from the East Midlands is interesting because it depicts dramatic changes in burial rite, with cremations present in the Late Bronze Age, followed by a high number of inhumations and disarticulated bones in the Early and Middle Iron Age and then a mixture of all three in the Late Iron Age. The processing of the dead was a period of symbolic transformation at the end of which the remaining human bone represented an entity typically beyond that of the deceased individual. The new symbolic meaning behind the human remains was also dependent on their associated spatial context.

This study argues that the spatial context of the human remains provides the foundation for understanding these ritual practices. For the Iron Age, there are two forums, public and private, which created the stage on which human remains acted in and influenced their meaning. The public arena allowed for large group involvement and, subsequently, reaffirmed a sense of belonging for the community's members. Examples of these activities on the public arena include deposits around the occupation area, liminal moments, reuse of prehistoric monuments,

and bones associated with areas of economic significance. The liminal theme is also evident with human remains associated with structures, particularly roundhouses. The analysis indicated that skeletal materials adhere to the right/left spatial organisation with specific reference to the living area's boundary. Most of the deposits of human bones associated with structures occurred near or just after the building's abandonment, which implies that the spatial organisation continued after the end of the structure's use and the bones were elements in its post-abandonment ritual. The private forum was restricted to a limited number of participants and primarily related to social activities in domestic structures where human remains are found.

Both the processing and the spatial context work to define the identity of the human remains to the community. The evidence from this study implies that human remains might receive two different forms of identity. In one form, is the human bones still represented their former, living self, and this appears evident in Late Iron Age burials with the increase in inhumations and the higher quantity of cremated bone. In the second form, the human remains lost all trace of their former self and represented a more abstract concept, such as that of ancestors. In all, this study argues that there was a series of ritual activities each with a different purpose, of which human bone was the common medium; understanding this concept is central to interpreting Iron Age funerary practices.

Comparison to sites outside the study

The sites studied in this sample constitute only a portion of known Iron Age sites in southern Britain that contain human remains. As outlined in chapter three, the study has aimed to include a balance of well-studied sites, more recently excavated sites, and those with unpublished reports. With respect to some of the better-known sites, not all were included due to various reasons such as source availability and time constraints, even though these well-studied sites have helped to create our understanding of the Iron Age as it is today. This investigation aimed to include many of these better-known sites, such as Danebury and Maiden Castle, but was unable to include sites such as Cadbury Castle, Owslebury, Poundbury, and Yarnton. However, much is known about these sites' character and their burial evidence allows comparison with the overall patterns noted in this study's conclusions. A brief examination of these excluded sites can show how their findings fit within the wider schemes identified from this sample.

To begin, Cadbury Castle is a multivallate hillfort in Somerset that was investigated by Leslie Alcock (1972), but the results were later published by John Barrett and others (2000). Cadbury Castle yielded a number of human remains of which the majority are from a 'massacre' deposit by the southwest entrance of the hillfort (Alcock 1972). This massacre deposit contained numerous iron pikes and javelins as well as the fragmented remains of nearly 30 men, women, and children. Thus, Alcock believed the deposit to be the remains of a battle between native Britons and Romans in which, after the battle, the dead were left unburied and pulled apart by scavenging animals (Alcock 1972, 105-106, 159). Years later, Barrett's team revisited the evidence of the massacre deposit by conducting a revaluation of the skeletal material and its formation processes to create a clearer picture of the events leading to its deposition (Woodward and Hill 2000). The conclusions from the reanalysis indicated that only nine of the human remains displayed evidence of trauma. In addition, some showed evidence of animal gnawing while other bones had signs of burning (Woodward and Hill 20000, 110-111). The formation processes including the remains by the southwest gate, Woodward and Hill (2000, 111) argue, show at least two or more patterns of distribution. Woodward and Hill (2000, 111) explain that some of the remains with evidence of different degrees of burning were the product of partial cremations that took place near the entrance. Additionally, the entrance's passageway yielded most of the skulls recovered from Cadbury Castle, which may indicate that heads were on display only to later filter down into the battle area's context (Woodward and Hill 2000, 111). In the wider scheme, the human remains deposit by the southwest entrance at Cadbury Castle is quite similar to the burial evidence from Maiden Castle (Wheeler 1943) and Sutton Walls (Kenyon 1953). All three of these sites have mass deposits of human remains, in various states that were interpreted originally as evidence for conflict near the hillforts' entrances. However, the reanalysis of Cadbury Castle demonstrates that the warfare scenario may not be a straightforward interpretation of the skeletal material (e.g. display of skulls and an area for partial cremations). Instead, they may represent a series of events that led to their deposition. The deposit by the southwest gate, as suggested by Woodward and Hill (2000), may have signified the community's engagement in multiple practices. This created a burial record with elements that are similar to other examples from this study's sample. The fixations on the head and its display, as well as methods of processing the dead to break up and fragment the body, are well known at other sites. Similarly, Cadbury Castle has a foundation burial in the form of an inhumation that was interred prior to construction of one of the hillfort's ramparts (Alcock 1972, 103). This is analogous to Maiden Castle and other sites, and it adds to the growing evidence that human remains marked liminal times and places in the Iron Age.

Another well-studied site that contains human remains is the settlement of Owslebury in Hampshire (Collis 1968; 1970). Excavations by John Collis (1968; 1970) uncovered a Late Iron Age cemetery associated with the settlement, with most of the burials lying within two rectangular enclosures. The cemetery includes both inhumations and cremations (Collis 1968, 23-28), which is particularly interesting because this study's sample does not include a single site with Late Iron Age cremations in Hampshire. The cemetery at Owslebury demonstrates that by the late Middle Iron Age the cremation rite had filtered further into Wessex than this study's sample has shown. Additionally, the burial evidence from Owslebury confirms this study's findings that the two main burial rites (cremations and inhumations) were practiced together during the Late Iron Age, along with the deposition of many infant burials.

Poundbury is a hillfort in Dorset with occupation evidence spanning throughout the Iron Age (Farwell and Mollesen 1993). During the Late Iron Age, the occupants of Poundbury established an inhumation cemetery (a 'Durotrigian' cemetery) in three separate areas within the site (Farwell and Molleson 1993, 6-7, 216). At one of these, the placement of the inhumations aligned with a disused Early Iron Age ditch (Farwell and Molleson 1993, 6). This may be indicative of the community continuing to engage and incorporate this earlier feature through their burial rite, perhaps comparable to the burial evidence from sites within this research's sample, such as Salford (see chapter eight and Appendix). In addition, Poundbury's cemetery consisted of 28 adults and 31 children; of the 31 children, 22 are under a year old (Farwell and Molleson 1993, 6-7). The age representation among Poundbury's inhumations provides another example of a site with a high count of infant remains comparable to Micheldever Wood and Gravelly Guy. Yet infants appear to have been treated in a manner similar to adults, perhaps signifying that the community did not treat the infants differently from other age groups in the Late Iron Age. Overall, the evidence from the inhumation cemetery at Poundbury compares well to that from the studied sites within the region by demonstrating how the burial of complete individuals increasingly became the norm towards the end of the Iron Age.

A more recently excavated site with an interesting burial record is Yarnton in Oxfordshire, a Middle Iron Age open settlement with two separate cemeteries just outside the occupation area (Hey *et al.* 1999). Cemetery areas are adjacent to the settlement, and in general, are rare in the Middle Iron Age (Hey *et al.* 1999, 551, 553), though a similar example is known from Suddern Farm. The location of Yarnton's cemeteries in relation to the settlement implies that the community did not incorporate the dead into the living sphere but kept them on its periphery. This spatial context for the dead correlates with most communities in the Middle Iron Age who were burying human remains along the periphery or just outside the settlement area. Furthermore, the cemeteries at

Yarnton contain both inhumations and cremation deposits, demonstrating this community practiced both processing techniques simultaneously. However, the sample from this study does not show a mixing of corpse-processing techniques in Oxfordshire until the Late Iron Age, whilst, cremations in the Middle Iron Age are only evident from a few sites in southeast England, South Yorkshire and Leicestershire. Thus, the burial evidence from Yarnton may indicate the early appearance of an archaeologically visible cremation rite in this area.

In sum, these represent just a small selection of Iron Age sites with human remains that were not included in this study's sample for various reasons. Each demonstrates burial themes similar to those indicated by this study. These themes include multiple processing to fragment the corpse, a preference for use of the skull, spatial segregation of the dead, selective burial of infants, and the use of human remains to mark liminal times and places. Moreover, the examples from Cadbury Castle, Owslebury, Poundbury and Yarnton illustrate how Iron Age communities incorporated human remains into various ritual practices along similar lines to those of other communities yet differing in their precise means of expressing these ideas. Overall, the picture from these omitted sites conform closely to this study's findings and enhance the theoretic framework identified for understanding the use and deposition of human remains more widely within the southern Britain iron Age.

Recommendations for future research

The initial objective for this study was to recognise regional patterns and review the cultural explanations for Iron Age burial practices. The findings imply that the majority of human remains occurrences were the product of intentional processing and depositional schemes. Grounds for this argument rely on the repeated and similar aspects of the spatial, processing, and contextual nature of the human bones. The Iron Age burial record suggests that most of the human remains deposits are the product of three objectives. One scheme is the disposal of the deceased; the second is the bones were elements in a wider social practice and, three, is a mixture of the two. The patterns in the burial record that relate to three interconnected themes - processing, spatial context, and identity - that are central to understanding the cultural mechanisms behind Iron Age funerary practices.

The findings presented are still far from creating a complete narrative of Iron Age burial practices. Much of the evidence from the studied sites is fragmented and it leaves open questions into the specific nature of the burial record. However, this study identified a number of themes and patterns in Iron Age burial practices, which justifies further study. One avenue is to incorporate more Iron Age sites with human remains into the existing research. This will create a more complete and clear depiction of burial patterns in the British Iron Age. It will also be useful with new information coming from recent excavations. For example, excavations in 2009 at an Iron Age site near Bilham in South Yorkshire uncovered a Middle Iron Age inhumation buried just outside an enclosure (Colin Merrony pers. comm.). Adding more evidence such as this to existing research will test the consistency of this study's findings and possibly identify new patterns within the burial practices.

Studies in Iron Age burial practices would also benefit from a comprehensive study that expands to include Wales, the southwest peninsula, northern England, and Scotland. A study that includes all of Iron Age Britain will undoubtedly create a cohesive picture of burial trends for this period. The research area for this investigation focused on a restricted part of England, set within arbitrary boundaries. By expanding the research area to other parts of Britain, other regional variations in burial rites would presumably become evident. Additionally, it would be interesting to see how diverse the burial traditions are across Britain and how this relates to other regional divisions apparent in pottery styles, settlement patterns, and other forms of material culture.

Iron Age studies would also benefit from more studies into burial rites within focused areas, such as the East Midlands, East Anglia, and West Midlands. This study illustrated a number of areas, outside Wessex, where there is a concentration of neighbouring sites with burial evidence, such as within Oxfordshire, Cambridgeshire, and Kent. Focused studies in areas like these would allow the variation in burial traditions between sites to become clearer. Ultimately, it will provide a detailed perspective in site relationships that will not be as evident in large regional studies.

Another recommendation is for a comprehensive investigation into the similarities and differences in the treatment of skeletal material between site types. For example, are there different ways of treating the dead on hillforts as opposed to a single-family farmstead; if so then why? This research did not explore this issue in depth, but it would be advantageous to see if the difference in processing and handling of the corpse related to the social structure implied by the site's layout. This type of study may allow better understanding of the inhabitants' social dynamics on particular sites.

Iron Age burial studies would also benefit from further research into the nature of human remains associated with areas of economic importance. It is already evident that human remains were used to signify places of economic importance other than arable agriculture, such as animal paddocks. Further study into this area in respect to the variations of burial practices may provide insights into the varying values of different Iron Age economy strategies. Additionally, if different treatments of the dead varied according to economic activity, this might show how valuable non-agricultural activities were perceived to be.

Future research into Iron Age burial practices would benefit from a broader investigation into the reuse of prehistoric monuments in the later prehistory and early historical periods. This study illustrates how Iron Age communities placed human remains deposits in relation to earlier monuments in various ways and how this related to social organisation. Further investigation of this topic may highlight ways in which Iron Age people commemorated their heritage. In particular, comparing the different methods by which Iron Age groups used human remains for purposes of ancestor veneration, such as prolonged handling of disarticulated bone or burials near prehistoric monuments, would be particularly enlightening. In such cases, it appears that both practices functioned to satisfy a similar goal, through different methods.

Another recommendation for future Iron Age research is a study into the material associated with human remains. This study focused only on identifying the types and quantity of associated material and not the specific relationships between that and the skeletal remains. Additionally, it would be insightful to investigate more closely the ceramic associated with human remains.

In closing, this investigation has illustrated the potential for the study into Iron Age burial practices and its contributions to a wider understanding of the period. In many instances, the human remains represented a concept beyond that of the deceased individual. Human bone symbolised ancestral connections, created liminal times and places, signified areas of economic importance, and framed elements of public and private ritual activities. Human remains in Iron Age funerary practices were mediums in a variety of activities, each with their own purpose. Thus, human remains had a multifaceted meaning, and this was dependent on the activities in which they served. The next step for Iron Age burial studies is for others to add to the academic debate by testing and challenging this study's findings to further progress this field of study.

Bibliography

ABERCROMBY, J., 1912. *A Study of the Bronze Age Pottery of Great Britain and Ireland and its associated Grave-goods.* Oxford: The Clarendon Press.

ABRAMS, J., and GREGSON, R., 2005. *Home Farm, Cranfield, Bedfordshire: archaeological field evaluation* [online]. Bedford: Albion Archaeology. Available at: <http://archaeologydataservice.ac.uk/archives/view/greylit/details.cfm?id=2350&CFID=906&CFTOKEN=2AD8A524-9A87-4A4F-B3955C5EFE4445DF> [Accessed: 24 January 2010].

ALBARELLA, U., 2007. The end of the sheep age: people and animals in the Late Iron Age. *In:* C. HASELGROVE and T. MOORE, eds. *The Later Iron Age in Britain and Beyond.* Oxford: Oxbow Books, 2007, pp. 389-402.

ALCOCK, L., 1972. *'By South Cadbury is that Camelot...': the excavations of Cadbury Castle 1966-1970.* Aylesbury: Thames and Hudson.

ALDRIDGE, N., 2005. A Belgic cremation cemetery and iron bloomery furnace at Jubilee Corner, Ulcombe. *Archaeologia Cantiana,* 125, 173-182.

ALEXANDER, M., and HILL, J.D., 1996. Excavation of a Late Iron Age Cemetery at Hinxton, Cambridgeshire [unpublished]. Cambridge Archaeological Unit Report 159.

ALLEN, D.F., 1961. The origins of coinage in Britain: a reappraisal. *In*: S.S. Frere, ed. *Problems of the Iron Age in Southern Britain.* London: University of London Institute of Archaeology, 1961, pp. 97-308.

ALLEN, T.G., 2008. Iron Age. *In*: T.G. ALLEN and Z. KAMASH, eds. *Saved from the Grave: Neolithic to Saxon discoveries at Spring Road Municipal Cemetery, full research volume.* Thames Valley Landscapes Monograph No. 28. Oxford: Oxford Archaeological Unit, 2008, pp. 18-24.

ALLEN, T.G., and KAMASH, Z., eds., 2008. *Saved from the Grave: Neolithic to Saxon discoveries at Spring Road Municipal Cemetery, full research volume.* Thames Valley Landscapes Monograph No. 28. Oxford: Oxford Archaeological Unit.

ALLEN, T.G., and ROBINSON, M.A., 1993. *The Prehistoric Landscape and Iron Age Enclosed Settlement at Mingies Ditch, Hardwick-with-Yelford, Oxon.* Thames Valley Landscapes: the Windrush Valley, Vol. 2. Oxford: Oxford Archaeological Unit.

ALLEN, T.G., *et al.*, 1993. *Excavations at Roughground Farm, Lechlade, Gloucestershire: a prehistoric and Roman landscape.* Thames Valley Landscapes: the Cotswold Water Park, Volume 1. Oxford: Oxford University Committee for Archaeology.

ANDERSON, T., 1995. The human skeletons. *In*: K. PARFITT, ed. *Iron Age Burials from Mill Hill Deal.* London: British Museum Press, 1995, pp. 114-144.

ANDERSON, T., 2000-1. The human skeletons. *In*: A. CHAPMAN, ed. Excavations of an Iron Age settlement and a Middle Saxon cemetery at Great Houghton, Northampton, 1996. *Northamptonshire Archaeology*, 29, 1-41, 2000-1, pp. 28-31.

ANDERSON, T., 2003. Human bone. *In*: R. ATKINS and A. MUDD, eds. An Iron Age and Romano-British settlement at Prickwillow Road, Ely, Cambridgeshire: excavations 1999-2000. *Proceedings of the Cambridge Antiquarian Society*, 92, 5-55, 2003, pp. 36-40.

ARMIT, I., 2006. Inside Kurtz's compound: headhunting and the human body in prehistoric Europe. *In*: M. BONOGOFSKY, ed. *Skull Collection, Modification and Decoration.* British Archaeological Report S1539. Oxford: Archaeopress.

ARMIT, I., 2007. Hillforts at war: Maiden Castle to Taniwaha Pā. *Proceedings of the Prehistoric Society*, 73, 25-37.

ARMIT, I., and GINN, V., 2007. Beyond the Grave: human remains from domestic contexts in Iron Age Atlantic Scotland. *Proceedings of the Prehistoric Society,* 73, 113-134.

ASKEW, P., 2006. *The Prehistoric, Roman and Medieval Landscape at Northumberland Bottom, Gravesend, Kent* [online]. London: London and Continental Railways. Available at: < http://archaeologydataservice.ac.uk/archives/view/ctrl/wnbisr/downloads.cfm?CFID=906&CFTOKEN=2AD8A524-9A87-4A4F-B3955C5EFE4445DF> [Accessed 15 June 2010].

ATKINS, R., and MUDD, A., 2003. An Iron Age and Romano-British settlement at Prickwillow Road, Ely, Cambridgeshire: excavations 1999-2000. *Proceedings of the Cambridge Antiquarian Society*, 92, 5-55.

AUFDERHEIDE, A. C., and RODRÍGUEZ-MARTIN, C., 1998. *The Cambridge Encyclopaedia of Human Paleopathology*. Cambridge: Cambridge University Press.

BARBER, G., WIGGINS, R., and ROGERS, J., 1995. Human Remains. *In:* J. COLES and S. MINNITT, eds. *Industrious and Fairly Civilized: the Glastonbury Lake Village*. Exeter: Somerset Levels Project and Somerset County Museums Service, 1995, pp. 170-174.

BARRETT, J.C., 1980. The pottery of the later Bronze Age in lowland England. *Proceedings of the Prehistoric Society*, 46, 297-319.

BARRETT, J.C., 1989. Food, Gender, and Metal: questions of social reproduction. *In*: M. L. SØRENSEN and R. THOMAS, ed. *The Bronze Age-Iron Age Transition in Europe*, Oxford: B.A.R. British Series 483(iii), 1989, pp. 304-320.

BARRETT, J.C., 1994. *Fragments of Antiquity: an archaeology of social life in Britain, 2900- 1200 BC*. Oxford: Blackwell.

BARRETT, J.C., FREEMAN, P.W.N., and WOODWARD, A., eds., 2000. *Cadbury Castle Somerset: the later prehistoric and early historic archaeology*. English Heritage Archaeological Report No. 20. London: English Heritage.

BARTII, Г., 1987. *Cosmologies in the Making*. Cambridge: Cambridge University Press.

BAYLEY, J., 1978. The human bones. *In:* D. A. JACKSON and T. M. AMBROSE, eds. Excavations at Wakerley, Northants, 1972-1975. *Britannia*, 9, 115-242, 1978, pp. 234-235.

BAXTER, M., 2003. *Statistics in Archaeology*. London: Hodder Arnold.

BAYLEY, J., 1980. Human bones. *In*: D. S. NEAL, ed. Bronze Age, Iron Age and Roman settlement at Little Somborne and Ashley, Hampshire. *Proceedings of the Hampshire Field Club and Archaeological Society*, 36, 91-143, 1980, pp. 121-122.

BAYLEY, J., 1999. Human skull fragment. *In*: A. BELL, D. GURNEY and H. HEALEY, eds. *Lincolnshire Salterns: excavations at Helpringham, Holbeach St Johns and Bicker Haven*. Heckington: Heritage of Lincolnshire, 1999, pp. 17.

BAYLEY, J., 2001. Human skeletal material. *In*: P. CHOWNE *et al.*, eds. *Excavations at Billingborough, Lincolnshire, 1975-8: a Bronze-Iron Age settlement and salt-working site*. East Anglian Archaeology Report No. 94. Salisbury: The Trust for Wessex Archaeology Ltd, 2001, pp. 73-78.

BAYLEY, J., FASHAM, P.J., and POWELL, F.V.H., 1985. The human skeletal remains. *In*: P.J. FASHAM, ed. *The Prehistoric Settlement at Winnall Down, Winchester*. Hampshire Field Club Monograph 2. Winchester: Hampshire Field Club and Archaeological Society, 1985, pp. 119-122.

BAXTER, I., 2004. Faunal remains. *In*: A. HATTON, ed. *Prehistoric, Medieval and Post-Medieval features on land to the south of High Street, Foxton*. Report No. 1999. Fulborn: Archaeological Field Unit Cambridgeshire County Council, 2004, pp. 42-43.

BAXTER, I., 2008. Animal bone. *In*: R. GARDNER and C. GIBSON, eds. *An Iron Age Site at Hartsdown Technology College, Margate, Kent* [online]. Hertford: Archaeological Solutions Ltd. Available at: <http://www.kentarchaeology.ac/archrep/archrep.html> [Accessed 26 February 2010], 2008, n.p.

BEAMISH, M., 1998. A Middle Iron Age Site at Wanlip, Leicestershire. *Transactions of the Leicestershire Archaeological and Historical Society*, 72, 1-91.

BEDWIN, O., 1978. Excavations inside Harting Beacon Hill-Fort, West Sussex, 1976. *Sussex Archaeological Collections*, 116, 225-240.

BEDWIN, O., 1979. Excavations at Harting Beacon, West Sussex; second season 1977. *Sussex Archaeological Collections*, 117, 21-36.

BELL, C., 1992. *Ritual Theory, Ritual Practice*. Oxford: Oxford University Press.

BELL, M., 1982. Pedogenesis during the later prehistoric period in Britain. *In*: A. HARDING, ed. *Climatic Change in Later Prehistory*. Edinburgh: Edinburgh University Press, 1982, pp. 114-126.

BELL, M., 1996. Environment in the first millennium BC. *In:* T.C. CHAMPION and J.R. COLLIS, eds. *The Iron Age in Britain and Ireland: recent trends*. Sheffield: J. R. Collis Publications, 1996, pp. 5-16.

BELL, A., GURNEY, D., and HEALEY, H., eds., 1999. *Lincolnshire Salterns: excavations at Helpringham, Holbeach St Johns and Bicker Haven*. Heckington: Heritage of Lincolnshire.

BEVAN, B., 1999. The landscape context of the Iron Age square-barrow burials, East Yorkshire. *In:* J. DOWNES and T. POLLARD, eds. *The Loved Body's Corruption: archaeological contributions to the study of human mortality*, Glasgow: Cruithne Press, 1999, pp. 69-93.

BINFORD, L. R., 1962. Archaeology as anthropology. *American Antiquity*, 28(2), 217-225.

BIRBECK, V., 2001. Excavations at Watchfield, Shrivenham, Oxfordshire, 1998. *Oxoniensia*, 66, 221-288.

BIRCHALL, A., 1964. The Belgic pottery: Aylesford revisited. *The British Museum Quarterly*, 28(1), 21-29.

BIRD, P.F., 1968. Appendix III: animal bones from Tollard Royal. *In:* G..J. WAINWRIGHT, ed. The excavation of a Durotrigian farmstead near Tollard Royal in Cranbourne Chase, southern England. *Proceedings of the Prehistoric Society*, 34, 102-147, 1968, pp. 146-147.

BLOM, D.E., and JANUSEK, J.W., 2004. Making place: humans as dedications in Tiwanaku. *World Archaeology*, 36(1), 123-41.

BOON, J. A., 1982. *Other Tribes, Other Societies: symbolic anthropology in the comparative study of cultures, histories, religions, and texts*. Cambridge: Cambridge University Press.

BOOTH, P., and SIMMONDS, A., 2004. An Iron Age and Early Romano-British site at Hatford Quarry, Sandy Lane, Hatford. *Oxoniensia*, 69, 319-354.

BOURDIEU, P., 2003. The Berber House. *In:* S.M. LOW and D. LAWRENCE-ZÚÑIGA, eds. *The Anthropology of Space and Place: locating culture*. Oxford: Blackwell Publishers Ltd, 2003a, pp. 131-141.

BOWDEN, M., and McOMISH, D., 1989. Little boxes: more about hillforts. *Scottish Archaeological Review*, 6, 12-16.

BOYLE, A., 1999. The human bone. *In:* A. M. CROMARTY, S. FOREMAN, S., and P. MURRAY, eds. The excavations of a Late Iron Age enclosed settlement at Bicester Fields Farm, Bicester, Oxon. *Oxoniensia*, 64, 153-233, 1999, pp. 201.

BOYLE, A., 2000a. Assessment of human remains. *In:* C. HAYDEN, ed. *Chapel Mill, Lenham, Kent, ARC CML 99* [online]. London: London and Continental Railways. Available at: < http://archaeologydataservice.ac.uk/archives/view/ctrl/cmlisr/downloads.cfm?CFID=906&CFTOKEN=2AD8A524-9A87-4A4F-B3955C5EFE4445DF> [Accessed 1 August 2010], 2000, pp. 28-30.

BOYLE, A., 2000b. The human remains. *In:* B. M. CHARLES, A. PARKINSON AND S. FOREMAN, eds. A Bronze Age ditch and Iron Age settlement at Elms Farm, Humberstone, Leicester. *Transactions of the Leicestershire Archaeological and Historical Society*, 74, 113-220, 2000, pp. 196-197.

BRADLEY, R., 1994. The selection of a study area. *In:* R. BRADLEY, R. ENTWISTLE, and F. RAYMOND, eds. *Prehistoric Land Divisions on the Salisbury Plain: work of the Wessex Linear Ditches Project*. London: English Heritage Archaeological Report 2, 1994, pp. 17-25.

BRADLEY, R., 1998. *The Passage of Arms: an archaeological analysis of prehistoric hoards and votive deposits*. Oxford: Oxbow Books.

BRADLEY, R., ENTWISTLE, R., and RAYMOND, F., eds., 1994. *Prehistoric Land Divisions on the Salisbury Plain: the work of the Wessex Linear Ditches Project*. London: English Heritage Archaeological Report 2.

BRADLEY, R., and GORDON, K., 1988. Human skulls from the River Thames, their dating and significance. *Antiquity*, 62, 503-509.

BRADY, K., 2006a. *The Prehistoric and Roman Landscape at Beechbrook Wood, Westwell, Kent* [online]. London: London and Continental Railways. Available at: < http://archaeologydataservice.ac.uk/archives/view/ctrl/bbwisr/downloads.cfm?CFID=906&CFTOKEN=2AD8A524-9A87-4A4F-B3955C5EFE4445DF> [Accessed 13 May 2010].

BRADY, K., 2006b. *The Prehistoric Landscape at Tutt Hill, Westwell, Kent* [online]. London: London and Continental Railways. Available at: < http://archaeologydataservice.ac.uk/archives/view/ctrl/tutisr/downloads.cfm?CFID=906&CFTOKEN=2AD8A524-9A87-4A4F-B3955C5EFE4445DF> [Accessed 24 July 2010].

BROWN, L., STANSBIE, D., and WEBLEY, L., 2009. An Iron Age settlement and post-Medieval farmstead at Oxley Park West, Milton Keynes. *Records of Buckinghamshire*, 49, 43-72.

BROWNE, D.M., SILVERMAN, H., and GARCIA, R., 1993. A cache of 48 Nasca trophy heads from Cerro Carapo, Peru. *Latin American Antiquity*, 4(3), 274-94.

BRUNDENELL, M., 2008. Reclaiming the Early Iron Age in eastern England. *In:* O. DAVIS, N. SHARPLES, and K. WADDINGTON, eds. *Changing Perspectives on the First Millennium B.C.*. Oxford: Oxbow Books, 2008, pp. 185-198.

BRÜCK, J., 1995. A place for the dead: the role of human remains in Late Bronze Age Britain. *Proceedings of the Prehistoric Society*, 61, 245-277.

BRÜCK, J., 1999. House, lifecycles and deposition on Middle Bronze Age settlements in Southern England. *Proceedings of the Prehistoric Society*, 65, 145-166.

BRYANT, S., 1997. Iron Age. *In:* J. GLAZEBROOK, ed. *Research and Archaeology: a Framework for the Eastern Counties, 1. Research Assessment.* Norwich: Scole Archaeological Committee, 1997, pp. 23-34.

BUIKSTRA, J.E., and UBELAKER, D.H., 1994. *Standards for Data Collection from Human Skeletal Remains.* Fayetteville: Arkansas Archaeological Survey Research Series No. 44.

BUNTING, G., and VERITY, D., 1968. Report on human and animal bones from pits 15b and 15c, and on the human skeleton from the Steepleton Gate. *In:* I. Richmond, ed. *Hod Hill, Volume two: excavations carried out between 1951 and 1958 for the Trustees of the British Museum.* London: The Trustees of the British Museum, 1968, pp. 123-126.

BURROW, A., and MUDD, A., 2008. *An Early Bronze Age pit, and Iron Age burial and late Iron Age/early Roman settlement at Bluntisham, Cambridgeshire: excavations 2005* [online]. Northampton: Northamptonshire Archaeology. Available at: <http://archaeologydataservice.ac.uk/archives/view/greylit/details.cfm?id=4206&CFID=906&CFTOKEN=2AD8A524-9A87-4A4F-B3955C5EFE4445DF> [Accessed: 16 December 2009].

BUSHE-FOX, J.P., 1925. *Excavations of the Late-Celtic Urn-field at Swarling, Kent.* Society of Antiquaries Research Committee Report No. 5. London: Society of Antiquaries.

CAESAR. *The Conquest of Gaul. Tr:* S. A. Handford. Hanmondsworth: Penguin Books, 1982.

CANNON, A., 2002. Spatial narratives of death, memory, and transcendence. *Archaeological Papers of the American Anthropological Association*, 11(1), 191-99.

CARR, G., 2007. Excarnation or cremation: continuity or change? *In:* C. HASELGROVE and T. MOORE, eds. *The Later Iron Age in Britain and Beyond.* Oxford: Oxbow Books, 2007, pp. 444-453.

CARR, G. and KNÜSEL, C., 1997. The ritual framework of excarnation by exposure as the mortuary practice of the early and middle Iron Age of central southern Britain. *In:* A. GWILT and C. HASELGROVE, eds. *Reconstructing Iron Age Societies.* Oxford: Oxbow Monograph 71, 1997, pp. 73-86.

CERUTI, C., 2004. Human bodies as objects of dedication at Incan mountain shrines (north-western Argentina). *World Archaeology*, 36(1), 103-22.

CHAMBERLAIN, A.T., 2003a. The human bone. *In:* N. FIELDS and M. PARKER PEARSON, eds. *Fiskerton: an Iron Age timber causeway with Iron Age and Roman votive offerings.* Oxford: Oxbow Books, 2003, pp. 125-126.

CHAMBERLAIN, A.T., 2003b. Lunar eclipses, sanos cycle and the construction of the causeway. *In:* N. FIELDS and M. PARKER PEARSON, eds. *Fiskerton: an Iron Age timber causeway with Iron Age and Roman votive offerings.* Oxford: Oxbow Books, 2003, pp. 136-143.

CHAPMAN, J., 1994. The living, the dead and the ancestors: time, lifecycles and the mortuary domain in later European prehistory. *In:* J. DAVIES, ed. *Ritual and Remembrance: responses in human societies.* Sheffield: Sheffield Academic press, 1994, pp. 40-85.

CHAPMAN, A., 2000-1. Excavations of an Iron Age settlement and a Middle Saxon cemetery at Great Houghton, Northampton, 1996. *Northamptonshire Archaeology*, 29, 1-41.

CHAPMAN, A., 2007. A Bronze Age barrow cemetery and land boundaries, pit alignments and enclosures at Gayhurst Quarry, Newport Pagnell, Buckinghamshire. *Records of Buckinghamshire*, 47(Part 2 of 2), 81-211.

CHAPMAN, C., KINNES, I., and K. RANDSBORG, 1981. *The Archaeology of Death.* Cambridge: Cambridge University Press.

CHAMPION, S., 2001. The human remains. *In:* R. POLLARD, ed. An Iron Age inhumation from Rushey Mead, Leicester. *Transactions of the Leicestershire Archaeological and Historical Society*, 75, 20-35, 2001, pp. 28-29.

CHARLES, B., 1999. The animal bone. *In:* A. M. CROMARTY, S. FOREMAN, S., and P. MURRAY, eds. The excavations of a Late Iron Age enclosed settlement at Bicester Fields Farm, Bicester, Oxon. *Oxoniensia*, 64, 153-233, 1999, pp. 201-222.

CHARLES, B., 2000a. Animal bone report. *In*: B. M. CHARLES, A. PARKINSON and S. FOREMAN, eds. A Bronze Age ditch and Iron Age settlement at Elms Farm, Humberstone, Leicester. *Transactions of the Leicestershire Archaeological and Historical Society*, 74, 113-220, 2000, pp. 197-206.

CHARLES, B., 2000b. Assessment of animal bone. *In*: C. HAYDEN, ed. *Chapel Mill, Lenham, Kent, ARC CML 99* [online]. London: London and Continental Railways. Available at: < http://archaeologydataservice.ac.uk/archives/view/ctrl/cmlisr/downloads.cfm?CFID=906&CFTOKEN=2AD8A524-9A87-4A4F-B3955C5EFE4445DF> [Accessed 1 August 2010], 2000, pp. 31.

CHARLES, B., 2000c. Assessment of the animal bone. *In*: C. HAYDEN, ed. *Boys Hall Balancing Pond, Sevington, Kent, ARC BHB 98* [online]. London: London and Continental Railways. Available at: <http://archaeologydataservice.ac.uk/archives/view/ctrl/bhbisr/downloads.cfm?CFID=906&CFTOKEN=2AD8A524-9A87-4A4F-B3955C5EFE4445DF> [Accessed 16 March 2010], 2000, pp. 27.

CHARLES, B., 2004. Animal bone. *In*: J. COOK., E. B. A. GUTTMAN, and A. MUDD, eds. Excavations of an Iron Age site at Coxwell Road, Faringdon. *Oxoniensia*, 69, 181-285, 2004, pp. 257-266.

CHARLES, B., 2008. Animal bones. *In*: T. G. ALLEN and Z. KAMASH, eds. *Saved from the Grave: Neolithic to Saxon discoveries at Spring Road Municipal Cemetery, full research volume.* Thames Valley Landscapes Monograph No. 28. Oxford: Oxford Archaeological Unit Ltd, 2008, pp. 132-136.

CHARLES, B.M., PARKINSON, A., AND FOREMAN, S., 2000. A Bronze Age ditch and Iron Age settlement at Elms Farm, Humberstone, Leicester. *Transactions of the Leicestershire Archaeological and Historical Society*, 74, 113-220.

CHILD, A. M., 1995. Microbial taphonomy of archaeological bone. *Studies in Conservation*, 40(1), 19-30.

CHOWNE, P., *et al.*, eds., 2001. *Excavations at Billingborough, Lincolnshire, 1975-8: a Bronze-Iron Age settlement and salt-working site.* East Anglian Archaeology Report No. 94. Salisbury: The Trust for Wessex Archaeology Ltd.

CLARKE, G., 1966. The invasion hypothesis in British archaeology. *Antiquity*, 40, 172-189.

CLOUGH, S., 2007. Human remains. *In:* L. WEBLEY, ed. An Iron Age pit alignment and burial at Aspreys, Olney. *Records of Buckinghamshire*, 47(1), 63-80, 2007, pp. 73-74.

COHEN, J., 1990. Structuration theory and social order: five issues in brief. *In:* J. CLARK, C. MODGIL, and S. MODGIL, eds. *Anthony Giddens: consensus and controversy*, London: The Falmer Press, 1990, pp. 33-45.

COLES, J., and MINNITT, S., 1995. *'Industrious and Fairly Civilized': the Glastonbury Lake Village.* Somerset: Somerset Levels Project and Somerset County Council Museum Services.

COLLIS, J. R., 1968. Excavations at Owslebury, Hants.: an interim report. *Antiquaries Journal*, 48(1), 18-31.

COLLIS, J.R., 1970. Excavations at Owslebury, Hants. *Antiquaries Journal*, 50, 246-261.

COLLIS, J.R., 1973. Burials with weapons in Iron Age Britain. *Germania*, 51, 121-133.

COLLIS, J.R., 1977a. An approach to the Iron Age. *In*: J.R. COLLIS, ed. *The Iron Age in Britain: a review.* Sheffield: Department of Prehistory and Archaeology, University of Sheffield, 1977b, pp. 1-7.

COLLIS, J.R., 1977b. *The Iron Age in Britain: a review.* Sheffield: Department of Prehistory and Archaeology, University of Sheffield.

COLLIS, J.R., 1977c. Pre-Roman burial rites in north-western Europe. *In*: R. REECE, ed. *Burial in the Roman World.* CBA Research Report No. 22, London: The Council for British Archaeology, 1977, pp. 1-12.

COLLIS, J.R., 1977d. Owslebury (Hants.) and the problem of burials on rural settlements. *In*: R. REECE, ed. *Burial in the Roman World.* CBA Research Report No. 22, London: The Council for British Archaeology, 1977, pp. 26-34.

COLLIS, J. R., 1977e. The proper study of mankind is pots. *In*: J. R. COLLIS, ed. *The Iron Age in Britain: a review.* Sheffield: Department of Prehistory and Archaeology, University of Sheffield, 1977b, pp. 29-31.

COLLIS, J. R., 1996. Hill-forts, enclosures and boundaries. *In:* T.C. CHAMPION and J.R. COLLIS, eds. *The Iron Age in Britain and Ireland: recent trends.* Sheffield: J.R. Collis Publications, 1996, pp. 87-94.

COOK, J., GUTTMAN, E.B.A., and MUDD, A., eds., 2004. Excavations of an Iron Age site at Coxwell Road, Faringdon. *Oxoniensia*, 69, 181-285.

COOPER, A., and EDMONDS, M., 2007. *Past and Present: excavations at Broom, Bedfordshire 1996-2000*. Cambridge: Cambridge Archaeological Unit.

CORNEY, M., 2005. An analytical earthwork survey of Conderton Camp and an assessment of its environs. *In*: N. THOMAS, ed. *Conderton Camp, Worcestershire: a small Middle Iron Age hillfort on Bredon Hill*. CBA Research Report 143. York: Council for British Archaeology, 2005, pp. 1-9.

CORNWALL, I.W., 1953. The human remains from Sutton Walls. *In*: K.M. KENYON, ed. Excavations at Sutton Walls, Herefordshire, 1948-1951. *Archaeological Journal*, 110, 1-87, 1953, pp. 66-79

CORNWALL, I.W., 1968. Human remains from beneath the outer rampart, Steepleton section. *In*: I. RICHMOND, ed. *Hod Hill, Volume two: excavations carried out between 1951 and 1958 for the Trustees of the British Museum*. London: The Trustees of the British Museum, 1968, pp. 126.

COY, J.P., 1987. Animal bones. *In*: P. J. FASHAM, ed. *A Banjo Enclosure at Micheldever Wood, Hampshire*. Hampshire Field Club Monograph No. 5. Winchester: Hampshire Field Club and Archaeological Society, 1987, pp. 45-53.

CRAIG, C.R., KNÜSEL, C., CARR, G., 2005. Fragmentation, mutilation and dismemberment: an interpretation of human remains on Iron Age sites. *In*: M. PARKER PEARSON & I.J.N.THORPE, eds. *Warfare, Violence and Slavery in Prehistory: proceedings of a prehistoric conference at Sheffield University*. Oxford: British Archaeological Report Series 1374, 2005, pp. 165-180.

CRAWFORD, O.G.S., 1925. A prehistoric invasion of England. *Antiquaries Journal*, 2(1), 27-35.

CROCKETT, A., 2000. *Channel Tunnel Rail Link: archaeological excavations at Stone Farm Bridleway* [online].*Wessex Archaeology Report No. 45999b* [online]. London and Continental Railway. Available at: <http://archaeologydataservice.ac.uk/archives/view/ctrl/sfb99/sfb99_interim_rep.cfm?CFID=906&CFTOKEN=2AD8A524-9A87-4A4F-B3955C5EFE4445DF> [Accessed 15 September 2009].

CROMARTY, A.M., FOREMAN, S., and MURRAY, P., 1999. The excavations of a Late Iron Age enclosed settlement at Bicester Fields Farm, Bicester, Oxon. *Oxoniensia*, 64, 153-233.

CUNLIFFE, B., 1982. Settlement hierarchy and social change in southern Britain. *In*: C.C. Bakels, *et al.*, eds. *Prehistoric Settlement Patterns around the Southern North Sea*. Analecta Praehistorica Leidensia XV. Leiden: University of Leiden, 1982, pp. 161-181.

CUNLIFFE, B., 1983. *Danebury: anatomy of an Iron Age hillfort*. London: Batsford.

CUNLIFFE, B., 1984a. *Danebury: an Iron Age hillfort in Hampshire, Volume 1: the excavations, 1969-1978: the site*. CBA Research Report No. 52. London: Council for British Archaeology.

CUNLIFFE, B., 1984b. *Danebury: an Iron Age hillfort in Hampshire, Volume 2: the excavations, 1969-1978: the finds*. CBA Research Report No. 52. London: Council for British Archaeology.

CUNLIFFE, B., 1991. The deposition of human remains. *In*: B. CUNLIFFE and C. POOLE, eds. *Danebury: an Iron Age hillfort in Hampshire, Volume 5: the excavations, 1979-1988: the finds*. CBA Research Report No. 73. London: Council for British Archaeology, 1991b, pp. 418-425.

CUNLIFFE, B., 1992. Pits, preconception and propitiation in the British Iron Age. *Oxford Journal of Archaeology*, 11(1), 69-83.

CUNLIFFE, B., 1995. *Danebury: an Iron Age hillfort in Hampshire, Volume 6: a hillfort community in perspective*. CBA Research report No. 102. London: Council for British Archaeology.

CUNLIFFE, B., 2000. *The Danebury Environs Programme: the prehistory of a Wessex landscape. Volume 1, introduction*. Monograph No. 48. Oxford: English Heritage and Oxford University Committee for Archaeology.

CUNLIFFE, B., 2005. *Iron Age Communities in Britain: an account of England, Scotland and Wales from the seventh century BC to the Roman conquest*. 4th ed. London: Routledge.

CUNLIFFE, B., and HOOPER, B., 1991. Gazetteer of human remains. *In*: B. CUNLIFFE and C. POOLE, eds. *Danebury: an Iron Age hillfort in Hampshire, Volume 5: the excavations, 1979-1988: the finds*. CBA Research Report No. 73. London: Council for British Archaeology, 1991b, pp. 31:B5-31:F9[microfiche].

CUNLIFFE, B., and POOLE, C., 1991a. *Danebury: an Iron Age hillfort in Hampshire, Volume 4: the excavations, 1979-1988: the site*. CBA Research Report No. 73. London: Council for British Archaeology.

CUNLIFFE, B., and POOLE, C., 1991b. *Danebury: an Iron Age hillfort in Hampshire, Volume 5: the excavations, 1979-1988: the finds*. CBA Research Report No. 73. London: Council for British Archaeology.

CUNLIFFE, B., and POOLE, C., 2000a. *The Danebury Environs Programme: the prehistory of a Wessex landscape, Volume 2- Part 2, Bury Hill, Upper Clatford, Hants, 1990.* Oxford: English Heritage and Oxford University Committee for Archaeology Monograph 49.

CUNLIFFE, B., and POOLE, C., eds., 2000b. *The Danebury Environs Programme : the prehistory of a Wessex landscape. Volume 2- Part 6, Houghton Down, Stockbridge, Hants, 1994.* Oxford: English Heritage and Oxford University Committee for Archaeology Monograph 49.

CUNLIFFE, B., and POOLE, C., eds., 2000c. *The Danebury Environs Programme: the prehistory of a Wessex Landscape, Volume 2- Part 5, Nettlebank Copse, Wherwell, Hants, 1993.* Oxford: English Heritage and Oxford University Committee for Archaeology Monograph 49.

CUNLIFFE, B., and POOLE, C., 2000d. *The Danebury Environs Programme : the prehistory of a Wessex landscape. Volume 2- Part 4, New Buildings, Longstock, Hants, 1992 & Fiveways, Longstock, Hants, 1996.* Oxford: English Heritage and Oxford University Committee for Archaeology Monograph 49.

CUNLIFFE, B., and POOLE, C., eds., 2000e. *The Danebury Environs Programme : the prehistory of a Wessex landscape. Volume 2- Part 3, Suddern Farm, Middle Wallop, Hants, 1991 and 1996.* Oxford: English Heritage and Oxford University Committee for Archaeology Monograph No. 49.

CUNLIFFE, B., and POOLE, C., eds. 2000f. *The Danebury Environs Programme : the prehistory of a Wessex landscape. Volume 2- Part 7, Windy Dido, Cholderton, Hants, 1995.* Oxford: English Heritage and Oxford University Committee for Archaeology Monograph 49.

CUNNINGTON, M.E., 1932. Was there a second Belgic invasion (represented by bead-rim pottery)? *Antiquaires Journal*, 12, 27-34.

DARVILL, T.C., 2010. *Prehistoric Britain: 2nd edition.* London: Routledge.

DAVIS, O., 2008. Twin freaks? Paired enclosures in the Early Iron Age of Wessex. *In:* O. DAVIS, N. SHARPLES, and K. WADDINGTON, eds. *Changing Perspectives on the First Millennium B.C.*, Oxford: Oxbow Books, 2008, pp. 31-42.

DAVIS, O., SHARPLES, N. and WADDINGTON, K., eds., 2008. *Changing Perspectives on the First Millennium B.C.* Oxford: Oxbow Books.

DAWSON, M., 2005. *An Iron Age Settlement at Salford, Bedfordshire.* Bedfordshire Archaeological Monograph No. 6. Bedford: Bedfordshire County Council and Bedfordshire Archaeological Council (Albion Archaeology).

DEIGHTON, K., 2000-1. The animal bone. *In*: A. CHAPMAN, ed. Excavations of an Iron Age settlement and a Middle Saxon cemetery at Great Houghton, Northampton, 1996. *Northamptonshire Archaeology*, 29, 1-41, 2000-1, pp. 26-28.

DEIGHTON, K., 2003. Animal bone. *In*: R. ATKINS and A. MUDD, eds. An Iron Age and Romano-British settlement at Prickwillow Road, Ely, Cambridgeshire: excavations 1999-2000. *Proceedings of the Cambridge Antiquarian Society*, 92, 5-55, 2003, pp. 40-44.

DEIGHTON, K., 2007. The Iron Age animal bone. *In:* A. CHAPMAN, ed. A Bronze Age barrow cemetery and land boundaries, pit alignments and enclosures at Gayhurst Quarry, Newport Pagnell, Buckinghamshire. *Records of Buckinghamshire*, 47(Part 2 of 2), 81-211, 2007, pp. 202-203.

DENSTON, C. B., 1988. The human bones. *In*: E. MARTIN, ed. *Burgh: the Iron Age and Roman enclosure.* East Anglian Archaeological Report No. 40. Suffolk: Suffolk County Council, 1988, pp. 66.

DEROCHE, C. D., 1997. Studying Iron Age production. *In:* A. GWILT and C. HASELGROVE, eds. *Reconstructing Iron Age societies: new approaches to the British Iron Age.* Oxbow Monograph 71. Oxford: Oxbow Books, 1997, pp. 19-25.

DOBNEY, K., and ERVYNCK, A., 2007. To fish or not to fish? Evidence for the possible avoidance of fish consumption during the Iron Age around the North Sea. *In:* C. HASELGROVE and T. MOORE, eds. *The Later Iron Age in Britain and Beyond.* Oxford: Oxbow Books, 2007, pp. 403-418.

DODWELL, N., 2004. Human remains. *In:* R. REGAN, C. EVANS and L. WEBLEY, eds. *The Camp Ground excavations: Colne Fen, Earith, Volume I.* Cambridge: University of Cambridge and Cambridge Archaeological Unit, 2004, pp. 27-35.

DODWELL, N., 2004-5. The human skeleton in pit F229. *In:* C. FRENCH, ed. Evaluation survey and excavation at Wandlebury Ringwork, Cambridgeshire, 1994-7. *Proceedings of the Cambridge Antiquarian Society*, 93, 15-66, 2004-5, pp. 57-59.

DODWELL, N., 2007a. Human remains. *In:* C. EVANS, M. KNIGHT, and L. WEBLEY, eds. Iron Age settlement and Romanisation on the Isle of Ely: the Hurst Lane Reservoir site. *Proceedings of the Cambridge Antiquarian Society*, 96, 41-78, 2007, pp. 66.

DODWELL, N., 2007b. Human skeletal remains (cremations and inhumations). *In*: A. COOPER and M. EDMONDS, eds. *Past and Present: excavations at Broom, Bedfordshire 1996-2000.* Cambridge: Cambridge Archaeological Unit, 2007, pp. 273-281.

DUNIG, C., 2004. Human remains. *In*: A. HATTON, ed. *Prehistoric, Medieval and Post-Medieval features on land to the south of High Street, Foxton*. Report No. 1999. Fulborn: Archaeological Field Unit Cambridgeshire County Council, 2004, pp. 40-41.

EDEN, C., 1999. Human remains. *In*: J.D. HILL, C. EVANS, and M. ALEXANDER, eds. The Hinxton Rings- a Late Iron Age cemetery at Hinxton, Cambridgeshire with a reconsideration of Northern Aylesford-Swarling distributions. *Proceedings of the Prehistoric Society*, 65, 1999, pp. 252-253.

EDMONDS, M., and SEABORNE, T., 2001. *Prehistory in the Peak*. Stroud: Tempus.

EDWARDS, E., 1978. The human remains. *In*: M. PARRINGTON, ed. *The Excavations of an Iron Age Settlement, Bronze Age Ring Ditch and Roman Features at Ashville Trading Estate, Abingdon (Oxfordshire) 1974-76*. London: Oxford Archaeological Unit and Council for British Archaeology, pp. 90-92.

ELDON, S. M., 1992. East Midlands Scored Ware. *Transactions of the Leicestershire Archaeological and Historical Society*, 66, 83-91.

ELLIS, C., and POWELL, A. B., eds., 2008. *An Iron Age Settlement Outside Battlesbury Hillfort, Warminster and Sites along the Southern Range Road*. Wessex Archaeology Report No. 22. Salisbury: Wessex Archaeology Ltd.

ELLISON, A., and DREWITT, P., 1971. Pits and post-holes in the British Early Iron Age: some alternative explanations. *Proceedings of the Prehistoric Society*, 37, 183-194.

EMERY, G., 2005. *Assessment report and updated project design for an archaeological excavation at Ford Place Nursing Home, Thetford* [online]. Norfolk Archaeological Unit Report No. 1005. Norfolk: Norfolk Archaeological Unit. Available at: <http://archaeologydataservice.ac.uk/archives/view/greylit/details.cfm?id=2042&CFID=1927&CFTOKEN=E6E04465-FF0B-4BDA-8471B5D30B0817F3> [Accessed: 3 March 2010].

ENTWISTLE, R., 1994. The development and application of the field methodology. *In*: R. BRADLEY, R. ENTWISTLE, and F. RAYMOND, eds. *Prehistoric Land Divisions on the Salisbury Plain: work the Wessex Linear Ditches Project*. London: English Heritage Archaeological Report 2, 1994, pp. 26-68.

EVANS, A.J., 1890. On a Late-Celtic urn-field at Aylesford, Kent, and on the Gaulish, Illyro-Italic, and classical connexions of the forms of pottery and bronze-work there discovered. *Archaeologia*, 52(2), 318-388.

EVANS, E-J., 2004. Animal bone. *In:* P. BOOTH and A. SIMMONDS, eds. An Iron Age and Early Romano-British site at Hatford Quarry, Sandy Lane, Hatford. *Oxoniensia*, 69, 319-354, 2004, pp. 346-347.

EVANS, E-J., 2005. Animal bone. *In*: J. TIMBY, *et al.*, eds. Excavations along the Newbury Reinforcement Pipeline: Iron Age-Roman activity and Neolithic pit group. *Oxoniensia*, 70, 203-307, 2005, pp. 284-290.

EVANS, C., and HODDER, I., 2006. *Marshland Communities and Cultural Landscapes from the Bronze Age to Present Day: the Haddenham Project Volume 2*. Cambridge: McDonald Institute for Archaeological Research.

EVANS, C., KNIGHT, M., and WEBLEY, L., 2007. Iron Age settlement and Romanisation on the Isle of Ely: the Hurst Lane Reservoir site. *Proceedings of the Cambridge Antiquarian Society*, 96, 41-78.

EVANS, C., MACKAY, D., and WEBLEY, L., 2008. *Borderlands: the archaeology of the Addenbrooke's Environs, south Cambridge*. Cambridge: Cambridge Archaeological Unit.

FASHAM, P.J., ed., 1985. *The Prehistoric Settlement at Winnall Down, Winchester*. Hampshire Field Club Monograph 2. Winchester: Hampshire Field Club and Archaeological Society.

FASHAM, P.J., ed., 1987. *A Banjo Enclosure at Micheldever Wood, Hampshire*. Hampshire Field Club Monograph No. 5. Winchester: Hampshire Field Club and Archaeological Society.

FASHAM, P.J., FARWELL, D.E., and WHINNEY, R.J.B., eds., 1989. *The Archaeological Site at Easton Lane, Winchester*. Hampshire Field Club Monograph 6. Winchester: Hampshire Field and Archaeological Society.

FARWELL, D.E., and MOLLESON, T.I., 1993. *Excavations at Poundbury 1966-80. Volume 2, the cemeteries*. Dorset Natural History and Archaeological Society Monograph Series No. 11. Dorset: Dorset Natural and Historical and Archaeological Society.

FIELD, D., 2008. The development of an agricultural countryside. *In:* J. Pollard, ed. *Prehistoric Britain*. Oxford: Blackwell Publishing, 2008, pp. 202-224.

FIELDS, N., 2003. Topography and setting. *In:* N. FIELDS and M. PARKER PEARSON, eds. *Fiskerton: an Iron Age timber causeway with Iron Age and Roman votive offerings*. Oxford: Oxbow Books, 2003, pp. 1-2.

FIELDS, N., PALMER-BROW, C., and PARKER PEARSON, M., 2003. The excavation. *In:* N. FIELDS and M. PARKER PEARSON, eds. *Fiskerton: an Iron Age timber causeway with Iron Age and Roman votive offerings.* Oxford: Oxbow Books, 2003, pp. 2-16.

FIELDS, N., and PARKER PEARSON, M., eds., 2003 *Fiskerton: an Iron Age timber causeway with Iron Age and Roman votive offerings.* Oxford: Oxbow Books.

FITZPATRICK, A.P., 1994. Outside in: the structure of an Early Iron Age house at Dunston Park, Thatcham, Berkshire. *In:* A.P. FITZPATRICK and E.L. MORRIS, eds. *The Iron Age in Wessex: recent work.* Salisbury: Trust for Wessex Archaeology, 1994, pp. 68-72.

FITZPATRICK, A. P., 1997a. *Archaeological Excavations on the Route of the A27 Westhampnett Bypass, West Sussex, 1992, Volume 2: the cemeteries.* Wessex Archaeological Report No. 12. Salisbury: Wessex Archaeology Ltd.

FITZPATRICK, A.P., 1997b. Everyday life in Iron Age Wessex. *In:* A. GWILT and C. HASELGROVE, eds. *Reconstructing Iron Age Societies.* Oxford: Oxbow Monograph 71, 1997, pp. 73-86.

FITZPATRICK, A.P., and MORRIS, E.L., eds. 1994. *The Iron Age in Wessex: recent work.* Salisbury: Trust for Wessex Archaeology.

FLEMING, A., 1987. Coaxial field systems: some questions of time and space. *Antiquity,* 61, 188-202.

FOWLER, C., 2004. *The Archaeology of Personhood: an anthropological approach.* London: Routledge.

FRENCH, C., 2004-5. Evaluation survey and excavation at Wandlebury Ringwork, Cambridgeshire, 1994-7. *Proceedings of the Cambridge Antiquarian Society,* 93, 15-66.

FRERE, S.S., ed., 1961. *Problems of the Iron Age in southern Britain.* London: University of London Institute of Archaeology.

GANDY, H., 1999. Animal bones. *In:* A. BELL, D. GURNEY and H. HEALEY, eds. *Lincolnshire Salterns: excavations at Helpringham, Holbeach St Johns and Bicker Haven.* Heckington: Heritage of Lincolnshire, 1999, pp. 17.

GARDNER, R., and GIBSON, C., 2008. *An Iron Age Site at Hartsdown Technology College, Margate, Kent* [online]. Hertford: Archaeological Solutions Ltd. Available at: <http://www.kentarchaeology.ac/archrep/archrep.html> [Accessed 26 February 2010].

GARLAND, N., 2004. Cremated human remains. *In:* R. HAVIS and H. BROOKS, eds. *Excavations at Stansted Airport, 1986-91, Volume 1: prehistoric and Romano-British.* East Anglian Archaeology Report No. 107. Essex: Essex County Council, 2004, pp. 247-254.

GEBER, J., 2008. The human bone. *In:* A. BURROW and A. MUDD, eds. *An Early Bronze Age Pit, and Iron Age Burial and Late Iron Age/early Roman Settlement at Bluntisham, Cambridgeshire: excavations 2005* [online]. Northampton: Northamptonshire Archaeology. Available at: <http://archaeologydataservice.ac.uk/archives/view/greylit/details.cfm?id=4206&CFID=906&CFTOKEN=2AD8A524-9A87-4A4F-B3955C5EFE4445DF> [Accessed: 16 December 2009], 2008, pp. 10-11.

GEBER, J., and LOE, L., 2008. Human remains. *In:* K. POWELL, G. LAWS and L. BROWN, eds. *A Late Neolithic/Early Bronze Age Enclosure and Iron Age and Romano-British Settlement at Latton Lands, Wiltshire* [online]. Oxford: Oxford Archaeological Unit. Available at: <http://archaeologydataservice.ac.uk/archives/view/greylit/details.cfm?id=4138&CFID=906&CFTOKEN=2AD8A524-9A87-4A4F-B3955C5EFE4445DF>[Accessed: 30 May 2010], 2008, pp. 114-133.

GEERTZ, C., 1973. *The Interpretations of Cultures.* New York: Basic Books, Inc.

GENT, H., 1983. Centralized storage in later prehistoric Britain. *Proceedings of the Prehistoric Society.* 49, 243-267.

GIDDENS, A., 1984. *The Constitution of Society: outline of the theory of structuration.* Cambridge: Polity Press.

GIBSON, A., 2002. *Prehistoric Pottery in Britain and Ireland.* Stroud: Tempus.

GIBSON, A., ed., 2003. *Prehistoric Pottery: people, pattern and purpose.* BAR 1156, Oxford: Archaeopress.

GOLDHAHN, J., 2008. From monuments in landscape to landscapes in monuments: monuments, death and landscapes in Early Bronze Age Scandinavia. *In:* A. JONES, ed. *Prehistoric Europe: theory and practice.* Chichester: Wiley- Blackwell, 2008, pp. 56-85.

GOLDSTEIN, L., 1981. One-dimensional archaeology and multi-dimensional people: spatial organisation and mortuary analysis. *In:* C. CHAPMAN, I. KINNES and K. RANDSBORG, eds. *The Archaeology of Death.* Cambridge: Cambridge University Press, 1981, pp. 53-69.

GOODMAN, C.N., and MORANT, G M., 1940. The human remains of the Iron Age and other periods from Maiden Castle, Dorset. *Biometrika*, 31(3-4), 295-312.

GOSDEN, C., 1994. *Social Being and Time*. Oxford: Blackwell.

GOSS, R.E., and KLASS, D., 1997. Tibetan Buddhism and the resolution of grief: the *Bardo-Thodol* for the dying and the grieving. *Death Studies*, 21(4), 377-95.

GRANT, A., 1984. Animal husbandry. *In*: B. CUNLIFFE, ed. *Danebury: an Iron Age hillfort in Hampshire, Volume 2: the excavations, 1969-1978: the finds*. CBA Research Report No. 52. London: Council for British Archaeology, 1984b, pp. 496-548.

GRANT, A., 1991. Animal husbandry. *In*: B. CUNLIFFE and C. POOLE, eds. *Danebury: an Iron Age hillfort in Hampshire, Volume 5: the excavations, 1979-1988: the finds*. CBA Research Report No. 73. London: Council for British Archaeology, 1991b, pp. 447-487.

GREATOREX, C., 2005. Later prehistoric settlement on the Hov Peninsula: excavations at Kingsmead Park, Allhallows. *Archaeologia Cantiana*, 125, 67-81.

GREEN, M., 1998. Humans as ritual victims in the later prehistory of western Europe. *Oxford Journal of Archaeology*, 17(2), 169-89.

GRIFFIN, S., MANN, A., and WESTERN G., 2002. *Excavations at Old Yew Hill Wood, Church Lench, Worcestershire* [online]. Worcestershire: Archaeological Service, Worcestershire County Council. Available at: <www.p:\projects\worcestershire\p1797_church_lench_burial\p1797rep.doc> [Accessed: 24 May 2009].

GUTTMANN, E.B.A., and LAST, J., 2000. A Late Bronze Age landscape at South Hornchurch. *Proceedings of the Prehistoric Society*, 66, 319-359.

GWILT, A., 1997. Popular practices from material cultures: a case study of the Iron Age settlement at Wakerley. *In:* A. GWILT and C. HASELGROVE, eds. *Reconstructing Iron Age Societies*. Oxbow Monograph No. 71. Oxford: Oxbow Books, 1997, pp. 153-166.

GWILT, A., and HASELGROVE, C., 1997. *Reconstructing Iron Age Societies*. Oxbow Monograph No. 71. Oxford: Oxbow Books.

HACKING, P., and BOYLE, A., 2008. Human skeletal assemblage. *In*: T.G. ALLEN and Z. KAMASH, eds. *Saved from the Grave: Neolithic to Saxon discoveries at Spring Road Municipal Cemetery, full research volume*. Thames Valley Landscapes Monograph No. 28. Oxford: Oxford Archaeological Unit Ltd, 2008, pp. 123-132.

HALEY, S., 1999. Death and after death. *In:* J. DOWNES and T. POLLARD, eds. *The Loved Body's Corruption: archaeological contributions to the study of human mortality*. Glasgow: Cruithne Press, 1999, pp. 1-8.

HAMBLETON, E., 1999. *Animal Husbandry Regimes in Iron Age Britain: a comparative study of faunal assemblages from British Iron Age sites*. BAR 282, Oxford: Archaeopress.

HAMBLETON, E., and MALTBY, M., 2008. Faunal remains. *In*: C. ELLIS and A. B. POWELL, eds. *An Iron Age Settlement outside Battlesbury Hillfort, Warminster and Sites along the Southern Range Road*. Wessex Archaeology Report No. 22. Salisbury: Wessex Archaeology Ltd, 2008, pp. 84-93.

HAMILTON, J., 2000a. Animal bones. *In:* B. CUNLIFFE, and C. POOLE, eds. *The Danebury Environs Programme: the prehistory of a Wessex landscape, Volume 2- Part 2, Bury Hill, Upper Clatford, Hants, 1990*. Oxford: English Heritage and Oxford University Committee for Archaeology Monograph 49, 2000a, pp. 67-73.

HAMILTON, J., 2000b. Animal bones. *In:* B. CUNLIFFE and C. POOLE, eds. *The Danebury Environs Programme: the prehistory of a Wessex landscape. Volume 2- Part 6, Houghton Down, Stockbridge, Hants, 1994*. Oxford: English Heritage and Oxford University Committee for Archaeology Monograph 49, 2000b, pp. 131-146.

HAMILTON, J., 2000c. Animal bones. *In:* B. CUNLIFFE, and C. POOLE, eds. *The Danebury Environs Programme: the prehistory of a Wessex landscape, 2- Part 5, Nettlebank Copse, Wherwell, Hants, 1993*. Oxford: Institute of Archaeology, 2000c, English Heritage and Oxford University Committee for Archaeology Monograph No. 49, 2000c, pp. 101-116.

HAMILTON-DYER, S., 2001. Animal bone. *In*: V. BIRBECK, ed. Excavations at Watchfield, Shrivenham, Oxfordshire, 1998. *Oxoniensia*, 66, 221-288, 2001, pp. 274-280.

HAMILTON-DYER, S., 2004. Animal Bone. *In*: S. D. G. WEAVER and S. FORD, eds. An Early Iron Age occupation site, a Roman shrine and other prehistoric activity at Coxwell Road, Faringdon. *Oxoniensia*, 69, 119-180, 2004, pp. 160-172.

HAMLIN, C., 2007. *The Material Expression of Social Change: the mortuary correlates of gender and age in late pre-Roman Iron Age and Roman Dorset. Volume I*. Ph.D. dissertation, the University of Wisconsin-Milwaukee.

HAMMOND, S., and PRESTON, S., 2005. Bronze Age and Iron Age occupation at Chichester Road, Selsey, West Sussex. *Sussex Archaeological Collections*, 143, 71-82.

HARCOURT, R. A., 1975. The animal bones. *In:* D.A. JACKSON, ed. An Iron Age site at Twywell, Northamptonshire. *Northamptonshire Archaeology*, 10, 31-93, 1975, pp. 88-89.

HARCOURT, R., 1979. The animal bone. *In:* G.J. WAINWRIGHT, ed. *Gussage All Saints: an Iron Age settlement in Dorset*. Department of Environment Archaeological Reports No. 10. London: Her Majesty's Stationery Office, 1979, pp. 150-160.

HARMAN, M., 2004. The human remains. *In:* G. LAMBRICK and T. ALLEN, eds. *Gravelly Guy, Stanton Harcourt Oxfordshire: the development of a prehistoric and Romano-British community*. Thames Valley Landscape Monograph No. 21. Oxford: Oxford Archaeological Unit, 2004, pp. 457-462.

HARMAN, M., and MILES, D., 1986. The human burials. *In:* D. MILES, ed. *Archaeology at Barton Court Farm Abingdon, Oxon.: an investigation of late Neolithic, Iron Age, Romano-British, and Saxon Settlements*. CBA Research Report No. 50 (Oxford Archaeological Unit Report No. 3). Oxford: Oxford Archaeological Unit, 1986, pp. 4:C1-4:D14 [microfiche].

HARRISON, R. J., 1968. Appendix I: skeletal remains from Tollard Royal. *In:* G. J. WAINWRIGHT, ed. The excavation of a Durotrigian farmstead near Tollard Royal in Cranbourne Chase, southern England. *Proceedings of the Prehistoric Society*, 34, 102-147, 1968, pp. 143-145.

HARTLEY, B. R., 1957. The Wandlebury Iron Age hill-fort, excavations of 1955-6. *Proceedings of the Cambridge Antiquarian Society*, 50, 1-27.

HARTRIDGE, R., 1978. Excavations at the prehistoric site and Romano-British site on Slonk Hill, Shoreham, Sussex. *Sussex Archaeological Collections*, 116, 69-142.

HASELGROVE, C., 1999. The Iron Age. *In:* R. HUNTER and I. RALSTON, eds. *The Archaeology of Britain: an introduction from the Upper Palaeolithic to the Industrial Revolution*. London: Routledge, 1999, pp. 113-134.

HASELGROVE, C., *et al.*, 2001. *Understanding the British Iron Age: an agenda for action*. Salisbury: Trust for Wessex Archaeology.

HASELGROVE, C., and MOORE, T., 2007. *The Later Iron Age in Britain and Beyond*. Oxford: Oxbow Books.

HASELGROVE, C., and POPE, R., eds., 2007. *The Earlier Iron Age in Britain and the Near Continent*. Oxford: Oxbow Books.

HATT, B., 1969. Cremating in Aboriginal Australia. *Mankind*, 7(2), 104-19.

HATTON, A., 2004. *Prehistoric, Medieval and Post-Medieval features on land to the south of High Street, Foxton*. Report No. 1999. Fulborn: Archaeological Field Unit Cambridgeshire County Council.

HAVIS, R., and BROWN, H., 2004. *Excavations at Stansted Airport, 1986-91, Volume 1: prehistoric and Romano-British*. East Anglian Archaeology Report No. 107. Essex: Essex County Council.

HAWKES, C., 1931. Hill-forts. *Antiquity*, 5(17), 60-97.

HAWKES, C., 1959. The ABC of the British Iron Age. *Antiquity*, 33, 170-182.

HAYDEN, C., 2000a. *Boys Hall Balancing Pond, Sevington, Kent, ARC BHB 98* [online]. London: London and Continental Railways. Available at: <http://archaeologydataservice.ac.uk/archives/view/ctrl/bhbisr/downloads.cfm?CFID=906&CFTOKEN=2AD8A524-9A87-4A4F-B3955C5EFE4445DF> [Accessed 16 March 2010].

HAYDEN, C., 2000b. *Chapel Mill, Lenham, Kent, ARC CML 99* [online]. London: London and Continental Railways. Available at: < http://archaeologydataservice.ac.uk/archives/view/ctrl/cmlisr/downloads.cfm?CFID=906&CFTOKEN=2AD8A524-9A87-4A4F-B3955C5EFE4445DF> [Accessed 1 August 2010].

HAYDEN, C., and STAFFORD, E., 2006. *The Prehistoric Landscape at White Horse Stone, Aylesford, Kent* [online]. London: London and Continental Railways. Available at: <http://archaeologydataservice.ac.uk/archives/view/ctrl/whsisr/downloads.cfm?CFID=906&CFTOKEN=2AD8A524-9A87-4A4F-B3955C5EFE4445DF> [Accessed: 26 July 2010].

HEALEY, H., 1999. Chapter 1: an Iron Age salt-making site at Helpringham Fen, Lincolnshire: excavations by the Car Dyke Research Group 1972-7. *In:* A. BELL, D. GURNEY and H. HEALEY, eds. *Lincolnshire Salterns: excavations at Helpringham, Holbeach St Johns and Bicker Haven*. Heckington: Heritage of Lincolnshire, 1999, pp. 1-19.

HENDERSON, J. D., 1995. Report on human remains. *In:* J. J. WYMER and N. R. BROWN, eds. *Excavations at North Shoebury: economy in south-east Essex 1500 BC-AD 1500.* East Anglian Archaeology Report No. 75. Chelmsford: Essex County Council Archaeology Section, 1995, pp. 129-130.

HENDERSON, J., BAYLEY, J., and GARWOOD, S., 1995. Human remains. *In:* G. J. WAINWRIGHT and S. M. DAVIES, eds. *Balksbury Camp Hampshire: excavations 1973 and 1981.* London: English Heritage Archaeological Report 4, 1995, pp. 82-83.

HENDERSON, J.D., and CAERON, A., 1989. The human bones. *In:* P. J. FASHAM, D. E. FARWELL, and R. J.B. WHINNEY, eds. *The Archaeological Site at Easton Lane, Winchester.* Hampshire Field Club Monograph 6. Winchester: Hampshire Field and Archaeological Society, 1989, pp. 120-121.

HENDON, J. A., 2000. Having and holding: storage, memory, knowledge, and social relations. *American Anthropologists,* 102(1), 42-53.

HEY, G., 2007. Unravelling the Iron Age landscape of the Upper Thames Valley. *In:* C. HASELGROVE and T. MOORE, eds. *The Later Iron Age in Britain and Beyond.* Oxford: Oxbow Books, 2007, pp. 156-172.

HEY, G., BAYLISS, A., BOYLE, A., 1999. Iron Age inhumation burials at Yarnton, Oxfordshire. *Antiquity,* 73, 551-562.

HIGBEE, L., and CLARKE, A., 2007. Animal bone. *In:* C. EVANS, M. KNIGHT, and L. WEBLEY, eds. Iron Age settlement and Romanisation on the Isle of Ely: the Hurst Lane Reservoir site. *Proceedings of the Cambridge Antiquarian Society,* 96, 41-78, 2007, pp. 62-65.

HILL, J.D., 1994. Why we should not take the data from Iron Age settlements for granted: recent studies of intra-settlement patterning. *In:* A.P. FITZPATRICK and E.L. MORRIS, ed. *The Iron Age in Wessex: recent work.* Salisbury: Trust for Wessex Archaeology, 1994, pp. 4-8.

HILL, J.D., 1995a. The Pre-Roman Iron Age in Britain and Ireland: an overview. *Journal of World Prehistory,* 9(1), 47-98.

HILL, J.D., 1995b. *Ritual and rubbish in the Iron Age of Wessex: a study on the formation of a specific archaeological record.* BAR 242, Oxford: Archaeopress.

HILL, J.D., 1996. Hill-forts and the Iron Age of Wessex. *In:* T.C. CHAMPION and J.R. COLLIS, eds. *The Iron Age in Britain and Ireland: recent trends.* Sheffield: J. R. Collis Publications, 1996, pp.95-116.

HILL, J.D., 2007. The dynamics of social change in later Iron Age eastern and south-eastern England. *In:* C. HASELGROVE and T. MOORE, eds. *The later Iron Age in Britain and beyond.* Oxford: Oxbow Books, 2007, pp. 16-40.

HILL, J.D., EVANS, C., and ALEXANDER, M., 1999. The Hinxton Rings- a Late Iron Age cemetery at Hinxton, Cambridgeshire with a reconsideration of Northern Aylesford-Swarling distributions. *Proceedings of the Prehistoric Society,* 65, 243-273.

HILLAM, J., 2003. Tree-ring analysis of the causeway timbers. *In:* N. FIELDS and M. PARKER PEARSON, eds. *Fiskerton: an Iron Age timber causeway with Iron Age and Roman votive offerings.* Oxford: Oxbow Books, 2003, pp. 25-37.

HINGLEY, R., 1990a. Iron Age 'currency bars': the archaeological and social context. *Archaeological Journal,* 147, 91-117.

HINGLEY, R., 1990b. Domestic organisation and gender relations in Iron Age and Romano-British households. *In:* R. SAMSON, ed. *The Archaeology of Houses.* Edinburgh: Edinburgh University Press, 1990, pp. 125-147.

HINGLEY, R., 1996. Ancestors and identity in the later prehistory of Atlantic Scotland: the reuse and reinvention of Neolithic monuments and material culture. *World Archaeology,* 28(2), 231-243.

HINGLEY, R., 1997. Iron, iron working and regeneration: a study of the symbolic meaning of metalworking in Iron Age Britain. *In:* A. GWILT and C. HASELGROVE, eds. *Reconstructing Iron Age societies: new approaches to the British Iron Age.* Oxbow Monograph 71, Oxford: Oxbow Books, 1997, pp. 9-18.

HINGLEY, R., 2006. The deposition of iron objects in Britain during the later prehistoric and Roman periods: contextual analysis and the significance of iron. *Britannia,* 37, 213-257.

HODSON, F.R., 1960. Reflections on 'The ABC of the British Iron Age'. *Antiquity,* 34, 138-140.

HODSON, F.R., 1962. Some pottery from Eastbourne, the 'Marnians' and the pre-Roman Iron Age in southern England. *Proceedings of the Prehistoric Society,* 28, 140-155.

HODSON, F.R., 1964. Cultural groupings within the British pre-Roman Iron Age. *Proceedings of the Prehistoric Society,* 30, 99-110.

HOLMES, J., and RIELLY, K., 1994. Animal bone from the mausoleum. *In*: R. J. WILLIAMS and R. J. ZEEPVAT, eds. *Bancroft: a Late Bronze Age/Iron Age Settlement, Roman Villa and Temple-Mausoleum, Volume 2: finds and environmental evidence.* Buckinghamshire Archaeological Society Monograph Series No. 7. Aylesbury: Buckinghamshire Archaeological Society, 1994b, pp. 515-536.

HOOPER, B., 1984. Anatomical considerations. *In*: B. CUNLIFFE, ed. *Danebury: an Iron Age hillfort in Hampshire, Volume 2: the excavations, 1969-1978: the finds.* CBA Research Report No. 52. London: Council for British Archaeology, 1984b, pp. 463-474.

HOOPER, B., 1991. Anatomical considerations. *In*: B. CUNLIFFE and C. POOLE, eds. *Danebury: an Iron Age hillfort in Hampshire, Volume 5: the excavations, 1979-1988: the finds.* CBA Research Report No. 73. London: Council for British Archaeology, 1991b, pp. 425-431.

HOOPER, B., 2000a. The human remains. *In*: B. CUNLIFFE, and C. POOLE, eds. *The Danebury Environs Programme: the prehistory of a Wessex landscape, Volume 2- Part 2, Bury Hill, Upper Clatford, Hants, 1990.* Oxford: English Heritage and Oxford University Committee for Archaeology Monograph 49, 2000a, pp. 65.

HOOPER, B., 2000b. The human remains. *In*: B. CUNLIFFE and C. POOLE, eds. *The Danebury Environs Programme : the prehistory of a Wessex landscape. Volume 2- Part 6, Houghton Down, Stockbridge, Hants, 1994.* Oxford: English Heritage and Oxford University Committee for Archaeology Monograph 49, 2000b, pp. 14:E1-E14 [microfiche].

HOOPER, B., 2000c. The human remains. *In*: B. CUNLIFFE, and C. POOLE, eds. *The Danebury Environs Programme: the prehistory of a Wessex landscape, 2- Part 5, Nettlebank Copse, Wherwell, Hants, 1993.* Oxford: English Heritage and Oxford University Committee for Archaeology Monograph 49, 2000c, pp. 10: D7-9 [microfiche].

HOOPER, B., 2000d. The human remains. *In*: B. CUNLIFFE and C. POOLE, eds. *The Danebury Environs Programme : the prehistory of a Wessex landscape. Volume 2- Part 4, New Buildings, Longstock, Hants, 1992 & Fiveways, Longstock, Hants, 1996.* Oxford: English Heritage and Oxford University Committee for Archaeology Monograph 49, 2000d, pp. 8:D1-5 [microfiche].

HOOPER, B., 2000e. The human remains. *In*: B. CUNLIFFE and C. POOLE, eds. *The Danebury Environs Programme : the prehistory of a Wessex landscape. Volume 2- Part 3, Suddern Farm, Middle Wallop, Hants, 1991 and 1996.* Oxford: English Heritage and Oxford University Committee for Archaeology Monograph No. 49, 2000e, 6: C3-6:E4 [microfiche].

HOOPER, B., 2000f. The human remains. *In*: B. CUNLIFFE and C. POOLE, eds. *The Danebury Environs Programme : the prehistory of a Wessex landscape. Volume 2- Part 7, Windy Dido, Cholderton, Hants, 1995.* Oxford: English Heritage and Oxford University Committee for Archaeology Monograph 49, 2000f, pp. 35.

HOSKINS, J., 1996. *Headhunting and the Social Imagination in Southeast Asia.* Stanford: Stanford University Press.

HUGHES, E. G., 1994. An Iron Age barrow burial at Bromfield Shropshire. *Proceedings of the Prehistoric Society*, 60, 395-402.

HUGHES, G., 1995. Ring ditch. *In:* G. HUGHES, P. LEACH, and S.C. STANFORD, eds. Excavations at Bromfield, Shropshire 1981-1991. *Shropshire History and Archaeology Transactions of the Shropshire Archaeological and Historical Society*, 70, 23-94, 1995, pp. 64-69.

HUGHES, G., LEACH, P., and STANFORD, S.C., eds., 1995. Excavations at Bromfield, Shropshire 1981-1991. *Shropshire History and Archaeology Transactions of the Shropshire Archaeological and Historical Society*, 70, 23-94.

HUTCHESON, N., 2007. An archaeological investigation of later Iron Age Norfolk: analysing hoarding patterns across the landscape. *In:* C. HASELGROVE and T. MOORE, eds. *The Later Iron Age in Britain and Beyond.* Oxford: Oxbow Books, 2007, pp. 358-370.

HUTTON, R., 2004. Animal bone. *In*: R. HAVIS and H. BROOKS, eds. *Excavations at Stansted Airport, 1986-91, Volume 1: prehistoric and Romano-British.* East Anglian Archaeology Report No. 107. Essex: Essex County Council, 2004, pp. 316-327.

ILES, M., 2001. Animal bone. *In*: P. CHOWNE *et al.*, eds. *Excavations at Billingborough, Lincolnshire, 1975-8: a Bronze-Iron Age settlement and salt-working site.* East Anglian Archaeology Report No. 94. Salisbury: The Trust for Wessex Archaeology Ltd, 2001, pp. 79-86.

INGOLD, T., 1993. The temporality of the landscape. *World Archaeology*, 25(2), 152-174.

JACKMAN, T., WELLS, T., and VINER, L., 1996. The human burials. *In:* R. KING, A. BARBER and J. TIMBY, eds. Excavations at West Lane, Kemble: an Iron-Age, Roman and Saxon burial site and a medieval building. *Transactions of the Bristol and Gloucestershire Archaeological Society*, 114, 15-54, 1996, pp. 19-23.

JACKSON, D. A., 1975. An Iron Age site at Twywell, Northamptonshire. *Northamptonshire Archaeology*, 10, 31-93.

JACKSON, D.A., 1988-9. An Iron Age enclosure at Wootton Hill Farm, Northampton. *Northamptonshire Archaeology*, 22, 3-21.

JACKSON, D.A., and AMBROSE, T.M., eds., 1978. Excavations at Wakerley, Northants, 1972-1975. *Britannia*, 9, 115-242.

JACKSON, T. A., 2005. Human bone. *In*: M. DAWSON, ed. *An Iron Age Settlement at Salford, Bedfordshire*. Bedfordshire Archaeological Monograph No. 6. Bedford: Bedfordshire County Council and Bedfordshire Archaeological Council (Albion Archaeology), 2005, pp. 145-146.

JAMES, S., 2007. A bloodless past: the pacification of Early Iron Age Britain. *In*: C. HASELGROVE and R. POPE, eds. *The Earlier Iron Age in Britain and the Near Continent*. Oxford: Oxbow Books, 2007, pp. 160-173.

JAY, M., 2008. The diet at Glastonbury Lake Village: the isotopic evidence for aquatic resource consumption. *Oxford Journal of Archaeology*, 272(2), 201-216.

JAY, M., and RICHARDS, M. P., 2007. British Iron Age diets: stable isotopes and other evidence. *Proceedings of the Prehistoric Society*, 73, 169-190.

JONES, A. M., 2008. Houses for the dead and cairns for the living: a reconsideration of the Early to Middle Bronze Age in south-west England. *Oxford Journal of Archaeology*, 27(2), 153-174.

JONES, M., 1996. Plant exploitation. *In:* T.C. CHAMPION AND J.R. COLLIS, eds. *The Iron Age in Britain and Ireland: recent trends*. Sheffield: J. R. Collis Publications, 1996, pp. 29-40.

JONES, R., 1978. The animal bones. *In:* D.A. JACKSON and T.M. AMBROSE, eds. Excavations at Wakerley, Northants, 1972-1975. *Britannia*, 9, 115-242, 1978, pp. 235-241.

JONES, R.T., *et al.*, 1988. Animal bones. *In*: E. MARTIN, ed. *Burgh: the Iron Age and Roman enclosure*. East Anglian Archaeological Report No. 40. Suffolk: Suffolk County Council, 1988, pp. 66-67.

KATZENBERG, M.A., and SAUNDERS, S.R., 2008. *Biological Anthropology of the Human Skeleton, Second Edition*. Hoboken: John Wiley and Sons, Inc.

KEEPAX, C.A., 1979. The human bone. *In*: G. J. WAINWRIGHT, ed. *Gussage All Saints: an Iron Age settlement in Dorset*. Department of Environment Archaeological Reports No. 10. London: Her Majesty's Stationery Office, 1979, pp. 161-171.

KELLY, J. D., and KAPLAN, M., 1990. History, structure and ritual. *Annual Review of Anthropology*, 19, 119-150.

KENWARD, R.P., 1981. Human Skeletal Material. *In*: R.J. MERCER, ed. *Grimes Graves, Norfolk: excavations 1971-72: Volume I*. Department of the Environment Archaeological Reports No. 11. London: Her Majesty's Stationary Office, 1981, pp. 76-78.

KENYON, K.M., 1953. Excavations at Sutton Walls, Herefordshire, 1948-1951. *Archaeological Journal*, 110, 1-87.

KING, R., BARBER, A., and TIMBY, J., 1996. Excavations at West Lane, Kemble: an Iron-Age, Roman and Saxon burial site and a medieval building. *Transactions of the Bristol and Gloucestershire Archaeological Society*, 114, 15-54.

KIRK, G.J.D., BELLAMY, P.H., LARK, R.M., 2010. Changes in soil pH across England and Wales in response to decreased acid deposition [online]. *Global Change Biology*: Blackwell Publishing Ltd. Available at: http://www3.interscience.wiley.com/journal/122688612/abstract [Accessed 25 January 2010].

KITCH, J., 2006. *Animal bone from White Horse Stone, Aylesford, Kent* [online]. London: London and Continental Railways. Available at: <http://archaeologydataservice.ac.uk/archives/view/ctrl/envspr/downloads.cfm?volume=fauna&CFID=906&CFTOKEN=2AD8A524-9A87-4A4F-B3955C5EFE4445DF> [Accessed 26 July 2010].

KNIGHT, D., MARSDER, P., and CARNEY, J., 2003. Local or non-local? Prehistoric granodiorite-tempered pottery in the East Midlands. *In:* A. GIBSON, ed. *Prehistoric Pottery: people, pattern and purpose*. BAR 1156, Oxford: Archaeopress, 2003, pp. 111-125.

LALLY, M., 2008. Bodies of difference in Iron Age southern England. *In:* O. DAVIS, N. SHARPLES, and K. WADDINGTON, eds. *Changing Perspectives on the First Millennium B.C.*, Oxford: Oxbow Books, 2008, pp. 119-138.

LAMBRICK, G., 2004. Early and Middle Iron Age occupation. *In*: G. LAMBRICK and T. ALLEN, eds. *Gravelly Guy, Stanton Harcourt Oxfordshire: the development of a prehistoric and Romano-British community*. Thames Valley Landscape Monograph No. 21. Oxford: Oxford Archaeological Unit, 2004, pp. 103-159.

LAMBRICK, G., and ALLEN, T., eds., 2004. *Gravelly Guy, Stanton Harcourt Oxfordshire: the development of a prehistoric and Romano-British community*. Thames Valley Landscape Monograph No. 21. Oxford: Oxford Archaeological Unit.

LAWSON, A.J., ed., 2000. *Potterne 1982-5: animal husbandry in later prehistoric Wiltshire*. Wessex Archaeology Report No. 17. Salisbury: Trust for Wessex Archaeology Ltd.

LOCKER, A., 1980. Animal bones. *In:* D.S. NEAL, ed. Bronze Age, Iron Age and Roman settlement at Little Somborne and Ashley, Hampshire. *Proceedings of the Hampshire Field Club and Archaeological Society*, 36, 91-143, 1980, pp. 122-124.

LOCKER, A., 2000. Animal bone. *In:* A.J. LAWSON, ed. *Potterne 182-5: animal husbandry in later prehistoric Wiltshire*. Wessex Archaeology Report No. 17. Salisbury: Trust for Wessex Archaeology Ltd, 2000, pp. 101-119.

LOVELL, J., 1999. Further investigation of an Iron Age and Romano-British farmstead on Cockey Down, near Salisbury. *Wiltshire Archaeological and Natural History Magazine*, 92, 33-38.

LOW, S. M., and LAWRENCE-ZÚÑIGA, D., eds., 2003a. *The Anthropology of Space and Place: locating culture*. Oxford: Blackwell Publishers Ltd.

LOW, S. M., and LAWRENCE-ZÚÑIGA, D., 2003b. Locating culture. *In:* S.M. LOW and D. LAWRENCE-ZÚÑIGA, eds. *The Anthropology of Space and Place: locating culture*, Oxford: Blackwell Publishers Ltd, 2003, pp. 1-48.

MADGWICK, R., 2008. Patterns in the modification of animal and human bones in Iron Age Wessex: revisiting the excarnation debate. *In:* O. DAVIS, N. SHARPLES, and K. WADDINGTON, eds. *Changing Perspectives on the First Millennium BC*, Oxford: Oxbow Books, 2008, pp. 99-118.

MALTBY, J.M., 1985. The animal bones. *In:* P. J. FASHAM, ed. *The Prehistoric Settlement at Winnall Down, Winchester*. Hampshire Field Club Monograph 2. Winchester: Hampshire Field Club and Archaeological Society, 1985, pp. 97-112.

MALTBY, J.M., 1989. The animal bones. *In:* P. J. FASHAM, D. E. FARWELL, and R. J. B. WHINNEY, eds. *The Archaeological Site at Easton Lane, Winchester*. Hampshire Field Club Monograph 6. Winchester: Hampshire Field and Archaeological Society, 1989, pp. 122-131.

MALTBY, J.M., 1995. Animal bone. *In:* G. J. WAINWRIGHT and S. M. DAVIES, eds. *Balksbury Camp Hampshire: excavations 1973 and 1981*. London: English Heritage Archaeological Report 4, 1995, pp. 83-87.

MALTBY, J.M., 1996. The exploitation of animals in the Iron Age: the archaeo-zoological evidence. *In:* T.C. CHAMPION AND J.R. COLLIS, eds. *The Iron Age in Britain and Ireland: recent trends*. Sheffield: J. R. Collis Publications, 1996, pp. 17-27.

MARLOW, C.A., 1992. Human bone. *In:* C. SCULL, ed. Excavation and survey at Watchfield, Oxfordshire, 1983-92. *Archaeological Journal*, 149, 124-281, 1992, pp. 155.

MARSHALL, D.A., 2002. Behaviour, belonging, and belief: a theory of ritual practice. *Sociological Theory*, 20(3), 360-380.

MARSHALL, P., 2003. The radiocarbon for the human bone. *In:* N. FIELDS and M. PARKER PEARSON, eds. *Fiskerton: an Iron Age timber causeway with Iron Age and Roman votive offerings*. Oxford: Oxbow Books, 2003, pp. 127.

MÁRQUEZ-GRANT, N., 2006. *Human Remains from Boys Hall Balancing Pond* [online]. London: London and Continental Railways. Available at: < http://archaeologydataservice.ac.uk/archives/view/ctrl/humspr/downloads.cfm?CFID=906&CFTOKEN=2AD8A524-9A87-4A4F-B3955C5EFE4445DF > [Accessed 16 March 2010].

MARTIN, E., ed., 1988. *Burgh: the Iron Age and Roman enclosure*. East Anglian Archaeological Report No. 40. Suffolk: Suffolk County Council.

MAYS, S., 1992. Taphonomic factors in a human skeletal assemblage. *Circaea*, 9(2), 54-58.

McKINLEY, J., 1997. The cremated human bone from burial and cremation-related contexts. *In:* A.P. FITZPATRICK, ed. *Archaeological Excavations on the Route of the A27 Westhampnett Bypass, West Sussex, 1992, Volume 2: the cemeteries*. Wessex Archaeological Report No. 12. Salisbury: Wessex Archaeology Ltd, 1997, pp. 55-73.

McKINLEY, J., 1999. Cremated bone. *In:* S.C. PALMER, ed. Archaeological excavations in the Arrow Valley, Warwickshire. *Transactions of the Birmingham and Warwickshire Archaeological Society*, 103, 1-231, 1999, pp. 50-52.

McKINLEY, J., 2000. Human bone. *In:* A.J. LAWSON, ed. *Potterne 182-5: animal husbandry in later prehistoric Wiltshire*. Wessex Archaeology Report No. 17. Salisbury: Trust for Wessex Archaeology Ltd, 2000, pp. 95-101.

McKINLEY, J., 2001. Human bone. *In:* V. BIRBECK, ed. Excavations at Watchfield, Shrivenham, Oxfordshire, 1998. *Oxoniensia*, 66, 221-288, 2001, pp. 266-274.

McKINLEY, J., 2005a. Human bone. *In*: S. HAMMOND and S. PRESTON, eds. Bronze Age and Iron Age occupation at Chichester Road, Selsey, West Sussex. *Sussex Archaeological Collections*, 143, 71-82, 2005, pp. 81.

McKINLEY, J., 2005b. The cremated bone. *In*: C. GREATOREX, ed. Later prehistoric settlement on the Hov Peninsula: excavations at Kingsmead Park, Allhallows. *Archaeologia Cantiana*, 125, 67-81, 2005, pp. 77-78.

McKINLEY, J., 2006a. Assessment of human bone. *In*: K. RITCHIE, ed. *The Prehistoric Settlement at Little Stock Farm, Mersham, Kent* [online]. London: London and Continental Railways. Available at: < http://archaeologydataservice.ac.uk/archives/view/ctrl/lsfisr/downloads.cfm?CFID=906&CFTOKEN=2AD8A524-9A87-4A4F-B3955C5EFE4445DF> [Accessed 3 March 2010], 2006, pp. 69-71.

McKINLEY, J., 2006b. *Human Remains from Saltwood Tunnel, Saltwood, Kent* [online]. CTRL Specialist Report Series: London and Continental Railways. Available at: <http://archaeologydataservice.ac.uk/archives/view/ctrl/humspr/downloads.cfm?CFID=906&CFTOKEN=2AD8A524-9A87-4A4F-B3955C5EFE4445DF> [Accessed 26 August 2010].

McKINLEY, J., 2007. The human bone. *In*: R. VAN de NOORT, H.A. CHAPMAN and J.R. COLLIS, eds. *Sutton Common: the excavation of an Iron Age 'marsh-fort'*. CBA Research report 154. York: Council for British Archaeology, 2007, pp. 156-157.

McKINLEY, J., 2008. Human remains. *In*: C. ELLIS and A. B. POWELL, eds. *An Iron Age Settlement Outside Battlesbury Hillfort, Warminster and Sites along the Southern Range Road*. Wessex Archaeology Report No. 22. Salisbury: Wessex Archaeology Ltd, 2008, pp. 71-83.

McKINLEY, J., SMITH, P., and FITZPATRICK, A. P., 1997. Animal bone from burials and other cremation-related contexts. *In*: A. P. FITZPATRICK, ed. *Archaeological Excavations on the Route of the A27 Westhampnett By pass, West Sussex, 1992, Volume 2: the cemeteries*. Wessex Archaeological Report No. 12. Salisbury: Wessex Archaeology Ltd, 1997a, pp. 73-77.

McOMISH, D., 1996. East Chisenbury: ritual and rubbish at the British Bronze Age-Iron Age transition. *Antiquity*, 70, 68-76.

MERCER, R. J., ed., 1981. *Grimes Graves, Norfolk: excavations 1971-72: Volume I*. Department of the Environment Archaeological Reports No. 11. London: Her Majesty's Stationary Office.

MEGAW, R. and MEGAW, V., 1989. *Celtic Art: from its beginnings to the book of Kells*. London: Thames and Hudson.

METCALF, P., and HUNTINGTON, R., 1991. *Celebrations of Death: the anthropology of mortuary ritual. 2nd edition*. Cambridge: Cambridge University Press.

MICOZZI, M. S., 1991. *Postmortem change in human and animal bone: a systematic approach*. Springfield: Charles C. Thomas Publisher.

MILES, D., ed., 1986. *Archaeology at Barton Court Farm Abingdon, Oxon.: an investigation of late Neolithic, Iron Age, Romano-British, and Saxon Settlements*. CBA Research Report No. 50 (Oxford Archaeological Unit Report No. 3). Oxford: Oxford Archaeological Unit.

MIRACLE, P., CORRADO, A., and HANKS, B., 2004-5. The faunal remains. *In:* C. FRENCH, ed. Evaluation survey and excavation at Wandlebury Ringwork, Cambridgeshire, 1994-7. *Proceedings of the Cambridge Antiquarian Society*, 93, 15-66, 2004-5, pp. 43-47.

MOORE, T., 2007. Lie on the edge? Exchange, community, and identity in the later Iron Age of Severn-Cotswolds. *In:* C. HASELGROVE and T. MOORE, eds. *The Later Iron Age in Britain and Beyond*. Oxford: Oxbow Books, 2007, pp. 41-61.

MORPHY, H., 1995. Landscape and the reproduction of the ancestral past. *In*: E. HIRSCH and O. HARTON, eds. *The Anthropology of Landscape: perspectives on place and space,* Oxford: Clarendon, 1995, pp. 184-209.

MORRIS, E.L., 1994. Production and distribution of pottery and salt in Iron Age Britain: a review. *Proceedings of the Prehistoric Society*, 60, 371-393.

MORRIS, E.L., 2007. Making magic: later prehistoric and early Roman salt production on Lincolnshire fenland. *In:* C. HASELGROVE and T. MOORE, eds. *The Later Iron Age in Britain and Beyond*. Oxford: Oxbow Books, 2007, pp. 430-443.

MULVILLE, J., and LEVITAN, B., 2004. The animal bone. *In*: G. LAMBRICK and T. ALLEN, eds. *Gravelly Guy, Stanton Harcourt Oxfordshire: the development of a prehistoric and Romano-British community*. Thames Valley Landscape Monograph No. 21. Oxford: Oxford Archaeological Unit, 2004, pp. 463-478.

MUSGRAVE, J., 2005. Miscellaneous human skeletal remains. *In*: N. THOMAS, ed. *Conderton Camp, Worcestershire: a small middle Iron Age hillfort on Bredon Hill*. CBA Research Report 143. York: Council for British Archaeology, 2005, pp. 246.

NEAL, D.S., 1980. Bronze Age, Iron Age and Roman settlement at Little Somborne and Ashley, Hampshire. *Proceedings of the Hampshire Field Club and Archaeological Society*, 36, 91-143.

NEEDHAM, S., 2007. 800 BC, the great divide. *In:* C. HASELGROVE and R. POPE, eds. *The Earlier Iron Age in Britain and the Near Continent.* Oxford: Oxbow Books, 2007, pp. 39-63.

NELSON, B.A., DARLING, J.A., and KICE, D.A., 1992. Mortuary practices and the social order at La Quemada, Zacatecas, Mexico. *Latin American Antiquity*, 3(4), 298-315.

NEWTON, A.A.S., DAVIES, C., and GEORGE, C., eds., 2008. *Land at Black Horse Farm, Old Great North Road, Sawtry, Cambridgeshire* [online]. AS Report No. 2999. Hertford: Archaeological Solutions Ltd. Available at: <http://archaeologydataservice.ac.uk/archives/view/greylit/details.cfm?id=4991&CFID=906&CFTOKEN=2AD8A524-9A87-4A4F-B3955C5EFE4445DF> [Accessed: 18 February 2010].

NORTHOVER, P., 1984. Iron Age bronze metallurgy in central southern England. *In*: B. CUNLIFFE and D. MILES, eds. *Aspects of the Iron Age in Central Southern Britain.* Oxford: Oxford University Committee for Archaeology Monograph No. 2, 1984, pp. 136-145.

OGIVILE, M.D., and HILTON, C.E., 2000. Ritualized violence in the prehistoric American Southwest. *International Journal of Osteoarchaeology*, 10, 27-48.

ORTNER, S.B., 2001. Theory in anthropology since the sixties. *In*: P. ERICKSON and L. D. MURPHY, eds. *Readings for a History of Anthropological Theory*, New York: Broadview Press, 2001, pp. 642-687.

OUTRAM, A., 2007. Animal bone. *In*: R. VAN de NOORT, H.A. CHAPMAN and J.R. COLLIS, eds. *Sutton Common: the excavation of an Iron Age 'marsh-fort'.* CBA Research Report No. 154. York: Council for British Archaeology, 2007, pp. 139-142.

PADER, E-J., 1982. *Symbolism, Social Relations and the Interpretation of Mortuary Remains.* Oxford: B.A.R. British Series 130.

PALLANT, J., 2007. *SPSS Survival Manual: a step by step guide to data analysis using SPSS for Windows third edition.* Maidenhead: Open University Press.

PALMER, S.C., 1999. Archaeological excavations in the Arrow Valley, Warwickshire. *Transactions of the Birmingham and Warwickshire Archaeological Society*, 103, 1-231.

PARFITT, K., 1995. *Iron Age Burials from Mill Hill Deal.* London: British Museum Press.

PARKER PEARSON, M., 1993. The powerful dead: archaeological relationships between the living and the dead. *Cambridge Archaeological Journal*, 3(2), 203-229.

PARKER PEARSON, M., 1996. Food, fertility and front doors in the first millennium BC. *In:* T.C. CHAMPION and J.R. COLLIS, eds. *The Iron Age in Britain and Ireland: recent trends.* Sheffield: J. R. Collis Publications, pp. 117-132.

PARKER PEARSON, M., 1999a. Food, sex and death: cosmologies in the British Iron Age with particular reference to east Yorkshire. *Cambridge Archaeological Journal,* 9(1), 43-69.

PARKER PEARSON, M., 1999b. *The Archaeology of Death and Burial.* Stroud: Sutton Publishing.

PARKER PEARSON, M., 2003. Environmental overview. *In:* N. FIELDS and M. PARKER PEARSON, eds. *Fiskerton: an Iron Age timber causeway with Iron Age and Roman votive offerings.* Oxford: Oxbow Books, 2003, pp. 23-24.

PARKER PEARSON, M., and RICHARDS, C., 1994a. Ordering the world: perceptions of architecture, space and time. *In:* M. PARKER PEARSON and C. RICHARDS, eds. *Architecture and Order: approaches to social space*, London: Routledge, 1994, pp. 1-37.

PARKER PEARSON, M. and RICHARDS, C., 1994b. Architecture and order: spatial representation and archaeology. *In:* M. PARKER PEARSON and C. RICHARDS, eds. *Architecture and Order: approaches to social space*, London: Routledge, 1994, pp. 38-72.

PARKER PEARSON, M., and BRADLEY, R., eds., 1994c. *Architecture and Order: approaches to social space.* London: Routledge.

PARRINGTON, M., 1978. *The Excavations of an Iron Age Settlement, Bronze Age Ring Ditch and Roman Features at Ashville Trading Estate, Abingdon (Oxfordshire) 1974-76.* London: Oxford Archaeological Unit and Council for British Archaeology.

PEACOCK, D.P.S., 1968. A petrological study of certain Iron Age pottery from western England. *Proceedings of the Prehistoric Society*, 13, 414-429.

PEACOCK, D.P.S. 1970. The scientific analysis of ancient ceramics: a review. *World Archaeology*, 1(3), 375-389.

PENN, K., 2004. *An archaeological evaluation at Bloodgate Hill, South Creake, Norfolk* [online]. Norfolk Archaeological Unit Report No. 913. Norfolk: Norfolk Archaeological Unit. Available at: <http://archaeologydataservice.ac.uk/archives/view/greylit/details.cfm?id=1972&CFID=1927&CFTOKEN=E6E04465-FF0B-4BDA-8471B5D30B0817F3> [Accessed: 3 May 2010]

PEREGRINE, P.N., 2001. Cross-cultural comparative approaches in archaeology. *Annual Review of Anthropology*, 30, 1-18.

PEREGRINE, P.N., 2004. Cross-cultural approaches in archaeology: comparative ethnology, comparative archaeology, and archaeoethnology. *Journal of Archaeological Research*, 12(3), 281-308.

PHILLIPS, C., 2008a. Animal bone. *In*: A.A.S. NEWTON, C. DAVIES and C. GEORGE, eds. *Land at Black Horse Farm, Old Great North Road, Sawtry, Cambridgeshire* [online]. AS Report No. 2999. Hertford: Archaeological Solutions Ltd. Available at: <http://archaeologydataservice.ac.uk/archives/view/greylit/details.cfm?id=4991&CFID=906&CFTOKEN=2AD8A524-9A87-4A4F-B3955C5EFE4445DF> [Accessed: 18 February 2010], 2008, pp. 70-88.

PHILLIPS, C., 2008b. Human bone. *In*: A.A.S. NEWTON, C. DAVIES and C. GEORGE, eds. *Land at Black Horse Farm, Old Great North Road, Sawtry, Cambridgeshire* [online]. AS Report No. 2999. Hertford: Archaeological Solutions Ltd. Available at: <http://archaeologydataservice.ac.uk/archives/view/greylit/details.cfm?id=4991&CFID=906&CFTOKEN=2AD8A524-9A87-4A4F-B3955C5EFE4445DF> [Accessed: 18 February 2010], 2008, pp. 88-90.

POLLARD, R., 2001. An Iron Age inhumation from Rushey Mead, Leicester. *Transactions of the Leicestershire Archaeological and Historical Society*, 75, 20-35.

POLLARD, J., ed., 2008. *Prehistoric Britain*. Oxford: Blackwell Publishing.

POOLE, C., 2000. Behaviour and beliefs. *In:* B. CUNLIFFE and C. POOLE, eds. *The Danebury Environs Programme : the prehistory of a Wessex landscape. Volume 2- Part 6, Houghton Down, Stockbridge, Hants, 1994*. Oxford: English Heritage and Oxford University Committee for Archaeology Monograph 49, 2000b, pp. 123-129.

POOLE, K., 2007. Faunal remains. *In:* L. WEBLEY, ed. An Iron Age pit alignment and burial at Aspreys, Olney. *Records of Buckinghamshire*, 47(1), 63-80, 2007, pp. 74-75.

POOLE, K., 2008. Animal remains. *In*: K. POWELL, G. LAWS and L. BROWN, eds. *A Late Neolithic/Early Bronze Age Enclosure and Iron Age and Romano-British Settlement at Latton Lands, Wiltshire* [online]. Oxford: Oxford Archaeological Unit. Available at: <http://archaeologydataservice.ac.uk/archives/view/greylit/details.cfm?id=4138&CFID=906&CFTOKEN=2AD8A524-9A87-4A4F-B3955C5EFE4445DF>[Accessed: 30 May 2010], 2008, pp. 133-150.

POPE, R., 2007. Ritual and roundhouse: a critique of recent ideas on the use of domestic space in later British prehistory. *In:* C. HASELGROVE and R. POPE, eds. *The Earlier Iron Age in Britain and the Near Continent*. Oxford: Oxbow Books, 2007, pp. 204-228.

POWELL, F. V. H., 1987. The human bone. *In*: P.J. FASHAM, ed. *A Banjo Enclosure at Micheldever Wood, Hampshire*. Hampshire Field Club Monograph No. 5. Winchester: Hampshire Field Club and Archaeological Society, 1987, pp. 53-54.

POWELL, K., LAWS, G., and BROWN, L., 2008. *A Late Neolithic/Early Bronze Age Enclosure and Iron Age and Romano-British Settlement at Latton Lands, Wiltshire* [online]. Oxford: Oxford Archaeological Unit. Available at: <http://archaeologydataservice.ac.uk/archives/view/greylit/details.cfm?id=4138&CFID=906&CFTOKEN=2AD8A524-9A87-4A4F-B3955C5EFE4445DF>[Accessed: 30 May 2010].

POWERS, R., and CULLEN, R., 1975. The human skeletal material. *In:* D.A. JACKSON, ed. An Iron Age site at Twywell, Northamptonshire. *Northamptonshire Archaeology*, 10, 31-93, 1975, pp. 87-88.

PRED, A., 1986. *Place, Practice and Structure: social and spatial transformation in Southern Sweden: 1750-1850*. Totowa: Barnes and Noble Books.

PRYOR, F., ed., 2001. *The Flag Fen Basin: archaeological and environment of a Fenland landscape*. Swindon: English Heritage.

RAPP JR., G., and HILL, C.L., 1998. *Geoarchaeology: the Earth-Science approach to archaeological interpretation*. New Haven: Yale University Press.

RAPPAPORT, R. A., 1999. *Ritual and Religion in the Making of Humanity*. Cambridge: Cambridge University Press.

REDFERN, R., 2008a. New evidence for Iron Age secondary burial practice and bone modification from Gussage All Saints and Maiden Castle (Dorset England). *Oxford Journal of Archaeology*, 27(3), 281-301.

REDFERN, R., 2008b. A bioarchaeological analysis of violence in Iron Age females: a perspective from Dorset, England (fourth century BC to the first century AD). *In:* O. DAVIS, N. SHARPLES, and K. WADDINGTON, eds. *Changing Perspectives on the First Millennium B.C.*, Oxford: Oxbow Books, 2008, pp. 139-160.

REDFERN, R., 2009. Does cranial trauma provide evidence for projectile weaponry in Late Iron Age Dorset? *Oxford Journal of Archaeology*, 28(4), 399-424.

REED, M., 1990. *The Landscape of Britain: from the beginnings to 1914.* London: Routledge.

REES, G., 2008. Enclosure boundaries and settlement individuality in the Iron Age. *In:* O. DAVIS, N. SHARPLES, and K. WADDINGTON, eds. *Changing Perspectives on the First Millennium B.C.*, Oxford: Oxbow Books, 2008, pp. 61-82.

REESE, R., ed., 1977. *Burials in the Roman World.* CBA Research report No. 22. London: The Council for British Archaeology.

REGAN, R., EVANS, C., and WEBLEY, L., eds., 2004. *The Camp Ground Excavations: Colne Fen, Earith, Volume I.* Cambridge: University of Cambridge and Cambridge Archaeological Unit.

REYNOLDS, P.J., 1974. Experimental Iron Age storage pits: an interim report. *Proceedings of the Prehistoric Society*, 40, 118-131.

RICHMOND, I., ed., 1968. *Hod Hill, Volume two: excavations carried out between 1951 and 1958 for the Trustees of the British Museum.* London: The Trustees of the British Museum.

RIDDLER, I., McKINLEY, J., and SKITTRELL, S., eds., 2006. *The Prehistoric, Roman and Anglo-Saxon Funerary Landscape at Saltwood Tunnel, Kent: the grave catalogue* [online]. London: London and Continental Railways. Available at: <http://archaeologydataservice.ac.uk/archives/view/ctrl/sltisr/downloads.cfm?CFID=906&CFTOKEN=2AD8A524-9A87-4A4F-B3955C5EFE4445DF> [Accessed 26 August 2010].

RITCHIE, K., 2006. *The Prehistoric Settlement at Little Stock Farm, Mersham, Kent* [online]. London: London and Continental Railways. Available at: <http://archaeologydataservice.ac.uk/archives/view/ctrl/lsfisr/downloads.cfm?CFID=906&CFTOKEN=2AD8A524-9A87-4A4F-B3955C5EFE4445DF> [Accessed 3 March 2010].

ROBB, J.E., 1998. The Archaeology of symbols. *Annual Review of Anthropology*, 27, 329-346.

ROBERTS, A.F., 2005. Animal bone. *In:* M. DAWSON, ed. *An Iron Age Settlement at Salford, Bedfordshire.* Bedfordshire Archaeological Monograph No. 6. Bedford: Bedfordshire County Council and Bedfordshire Archaeological Council (Albion Archaeology), 2005, pp. 146-149.

ROBERTS, C., and COX, M., 2003. *Health and Disease in Britain: from prehistory to the present day.* Stroud: Sutton Publishing.

ROBERTSON, A., 2005. *Land Adjacent to Water Treatment Works Layer-de-la-Haye, Colchester, Essex* [online]. Chelmsford: Field Archaeology Unit, Essex County Council. Available at: http://archaeologydataservice.ac.uk/archives/view/greylit/details.cfm?id=4559&CFID=1927&CFTOKEN=E6E04465-FF0B-4BDA-8471B5D30B0817F3 [Accessed: 12 February 2010].

ROBINSON, M., 1984. Landscape and environment of central southern Britain in the Iron Age. *In:* B. CUNLIFFE and D. MILES, eds. *Aspects of the Iron Age in Central Southern Britain.* Oxford: Oxford University Committee for Archaeology Monograph No. 2, 1984, pp. 1-11.

ROSALDO, M.Z., 1980. *Knowledge and Passion: Ilongot notions of self and social life.* Cambridge: Cambridge University Press.

ROTHWELL, A., and TURNER, C., 2005. *Highfields Farm, Coates, Whittlesey, Cambs. Archaeological evaluation* [online]. Letchworth: The heritage Network Ltd. Available at: http://archaeologydataservice.ac.uk/archives/view/greylit/details.cfm?id=2448&CFID=906&CFTOKEN=2AD8A524-9A87-4A4F-B3955C5EFE4445DF [Accessed: 13 March 2010].

ROWNTREE, D., 1981. *Statistics without Tears: a primer for non-mathematicians.* Harmondsworth: Penguin Books Ltd.

SALTON, C., and EHRENRICH, R., 1984. Iron Age iron metallurgy in central southern England. *In:* B. CUNLIFFE and D. MILES, eds. *Aspects of the Iron Age in Central Southern Britain.* Oxford: Oxford University Committee for Archaeology Monograph No. 2, 1984, pp. 146-161.

SAUNDERS, G., 2003. *Etonbury Farm Bund Stotfold Road, Arlesey, Beds.. HN 362. Archaeological assessment report* [online]. Report No. 179. Baldock, Hertfordshire: The Heritage Network Ltd. Available at: <http://archaeologydataservice.ac.uk/archives/view/greylit/details.cfm?id=2442&CFID=906&CFTOKEN=2AD8A524-9A87-4A4F-B3955C5EFE4445DF> [Accessed: 1 June 2010].

SCULL, C., 1992. Excavation and survey at Watchfield, Oxfordshire, 1983-92. *Archaeological Journal*, 149, 124-281.

SEAGER THOMAS, M., 2005. Understanding Iron Age Norton. *Sussex Archaeological Collections*, 143, 83-115.

SEEMAN, M. F., 1988. Ohio Hopewell trophy-skull artifacts as evidence for competition in Middle Woodland societies circa 50B.C.-A.D. 350. *American Antiquity*, 53(3), 565-577.

SHARPLES, N.M., 1991a. *English Heritage Book of Maiden Castle*. London: Batsford/ English Heritage.

SHARPLES, N.M., ed., 1991b. *Maiden Castle: excavations and field survey 1985-6*. English Heritage Archaeological Report No. 19. London: Historic Buildings and Monuments Commission for England.

SHARPLES, N.M., 2007. Building communities and creating identities in the first millennium BC. *In:* C. HASELGROVE and R. POPE, eds. *The Earlier Iron Age in Britain and the Near Continent*. Oxford: Oxbow Books, 2007, pp. 174-184.

SHARPLES, N.M., 2010. *Social Relations in Later Prehistory: Wessex in the first millennium BC*. Oxford: Oxford University Press.

SHEPPARD, P., 1978a. Animal remains. *In*: R. HARTRIDGE, ed. Excavations at the prehistoric site and Romano-British site on Slonk Hill, Shoreham, Sussex. *Sussex Archaeological Collections*, 116, 69-142, 1978, 133-140.

SHEPPARD, P., 1978b. The human remains. *In*: R. HARTRIDGE, ed. Excavations at the prehistoric site and Romano-British site on Slonk Hill, Shoreham, Sussex. *Sussex Archaeological Collections*, 116, 69-142, 1978, 140-141.

SIEVEKING, D. de G., LONGWORTH, I.H., WILSON, K.E., eds. 1976. *Problems in Economic and Social Archaeology*. London: Gerald Duckworth and Co., Ltd.

SMITH, A., 2004. Human bone. *In*: S.D.G. WEAVER and S. FORD, eds. An Early Iron Age occupation site, a Roman shrine and other prehistoric activity at Coxwell Road, Faringdon. *Oxoniensia*, 69, 119-180, 2004, pp. 172.

SOFAER, J. R., 2006. *The Body as Material Culture*. Cambridge: Cambridge University Press.

SOMERVILLE, E. M., 2005. Animal bones. *In*: M. SEAGER THOMAS, ed. Understanding Iron Age Norton. *Sussex Archaeological Collections*, 143, 83-115, 2005, pp. 111.

SPERBER, D., trans. MORTON, A.L. 1974. *Rethinking Symbolism*. Cambridge: Cambridge University Press.

STALLIBRASS, S., 1992. Animal bone. *In*: C. SCULL, ed. Excavation and survey at Watchfield, Oxfordshire, 1983-92. *Archaeological Journal*, 149, 124-281, 1992, pp. 154.

STANSBIE, D., 2009. Archaeological sequence. *In*: L. BROWN, D. STANSBIE and L. WEBLEY, eds. An Iron Age settlement and post-Medieval farmstead at Oxley Park West, Milton Keynes. *Records of Buckinghamshire*, 49, 43-72, 2009, pp. 46-53.

STEAD, I.M., 1969. Verulamium, 1966-8. *Antiquity*, 43, 45-52.

STEAD, I.M., 1976. The earliest burials of the Aylesford culture. *In*: G. de G. SIEVEKING, I.H. LONGWORTH and K.E. WILSON, eds. *Problems in Economic and Social Archaeology*. London: Gerald Duckworth and Co., Ltd, 1976, pp. 401-416.

STEAD, I.M. 1991. *Iron Age Cemeteries in East Yorkshire*. London: English Heritage.

STEAD, I.M., BOURKE, J.B., and BROTHWELL, D., 1986. *Lindow Man: the body in the bog*. London: Trustees of the British museum Publications.

STICKLE, T., 2003. The animal bone. *In* A. THOMAS, N. HOLBROOK and C. BATEMAN, eds. *Later Prehistoric and Romano-British Burial and Settlement at Hucclecote, Gloucestershire*. Bristol and Gloucestershire Archaeological Reports No. 2. Cirencester: Cotswold Archaeological Trust, 2003, pp. 57-61.

STIRLAND, A., and DENSTON, C. B., 1994. Human bone. *In*: R. J. WILLIAMS and R. J. ZEEPVAT, eds. *Bancroft: a Late Bronze Age/Iron Age settlement, Roman Villa and Temple-Mausoleum, Volume 2: finds and environmental evidence*. Buckinghamshire Archaeological Society Monograph Series No. 7. Aylesbury: Buckinghamshire Archaeological Society, 1994b, pp. 550-562.

STODDER, A. L. W., 2008. Taphonomy and the nature of archaeological assemblages. *In:* M.A. KATZENBERG and S.R. SAUNDERS, eds. *Biological Anthropology of the Human Skeleton, Second Edition*. Hoboken: John Wiley and Sons, Inc., 2008, pp. 71-114.

SWAYSLAND, C., 2004. Animal bone. *In:* R. REGAN, C. EVANS and L. WEBLEY, eds. *The Camp Ground Excavations: Colne Fen, Earith, Volume I*. Cambridge: University of Cambridge and Cambridge Archaeological Unit, 2004, pp. 48-52

SWAYSLAND, C., 2008. Faunal remains. *In*: C. EVANS, D. MACKAY, and L. WEBLEY, eds. *Borderlands: the archaeology of the Addenbrooke's Environs, south Cambridge.* Cambridge: Cambridge Archaeological Unit, 2008, pp. 106-110.

TIERNEY, J. J., 1960. The Celtic ethnography of Posidonius. *Proceedings of the Royal Irish Academy*, 60, 189-275.

TIMBY, J., *et al.*, 2005. Excavations along the Newbury Reinforcement Pipeline: Iron Age-Roman activity and Neolithic pit group. *Oxoniensia*, 70, 203-307.

TIMBY, J., 2007. Chapter 1: introduction. *In:* J. TIMBY *et al.*, eds. *Settlement on the Bedfordshire Claylands: archaeology along the A421 Great Barford Bypass.* Bedfordshire Archaeology Monograph No. 8. Oxfordshire: Bedfordshire County Council and Oxford Archaeological Unit, 2007, pp. 1-10.

TIMBY, J., *et al.*, eds., 2007. *Settlement on the Bedfordshire Claylands: archaeology along the A421 Great Barford Bypass.* Bedfordshire Archaeology Monograph No. 8. Oxfordshire: Bedfordshire County Council and Oxford Archaeological Unit.

THOMAS, N., ed., 2005. *Conderton Camp, Worcestershire: a small middle Iron Age hillfort on Bredon Hill.* CBA Research report 143. York: Council for British Archaeology.

THOMAS, A., HOLBROOK, N., and BATEMAN, C., eds., 2003. *Later Prehistoric and Romano-British Burial and Settlement at Hucclecote, Gloucestershire.* Bristol and Gloucestershire Archaeological Reports No. 2. Cirencester: Cotswold Archaeological Trust.

THOMAS, T., SHEPPARD, P., and WAITER, R., 2001. Landscape, violence and social bodies: ritualized architecture in a Solomon Islands society. *The Journal of the Royal Anthropological Institute*, 7(3), 545-72.

THORPE, R., *et al.*, eds., 2003. *A505 Baldock Bypass archaeological field evaluation* [online]. Bedford: Albion Archaeology. Available at: <http://archaeologydataservice.ac.uk/archives/view/greylit/details.cfm?id=4605&CFID=1927&CFTOKEN=E6E04465-FF0B-4BDA-8471B5D30B0817F3> [Accessed: 5 April 2010].

TOASE, S., 2008. The pairing of hillforts: Conflict, complementary, coincidence or complex. *In:* O. DAVIS, N. SHARPLES, and K. WADDINGTON, eds. *Changing Perspectives on the First Millennium B.C.*, Oxford: Oxbow Books, 2008, pp. 21-42.

TRUEMAN, C., and MARTILL, D. M., 2002. The long-term survival of bone: the role of bioerosion. *Archaeometry*, 44(3), 371-382.

TULLETT, A., 2008. Black earth, bone and bits of old pot: the Pewsey Middens. Recent work by the University of Sheffield. *In:* O. DAVIS, N. SHARPLES, and K. WADDINGTON, eds. *Changing Perspectives on the First Millennium B.C.*, Oxford: Oxbow Books, 2008, pp. 11-20.

TURNER, C., 2005. *Land off Bromham Road Biddenham, Beds. HN 475, stage 2: excavation and watching brief, archaeological assessment report* [online]. Letchworth, Hertfordshire: The Heritage Network Ltd. Available at: <http://archaeologydataservice.ac.uk/archives/view/greylit/details.cfm?id=4780&CFID=906&CFTOKEN=2AD8A524-9A87-4A4F-B3955C5EFE4445DF> [Accessed: 21 March 2010].

TURNER, V., 1969. *The Ritual Process: structure and anti-structure.* New York: Cornell University Press.

UCKO, P.J., 1969. Ethnography and archaeological interpretation of funerary remains. *World Archaeology*, 1(2), 262-280.

VAN de NOORT, R., CHAPMAN, H.A., and COLLIS, J.R., eds., 2007. *Sutton Common: the excavation of an Iron Age 'marsh-fort'.* CBA Research report 154. York: Council for British Archaeology.

VAN der VEEN, M., 1992. *Crop Husbandry Regimes: an archaeobotanical study of farming in northern England 1000 BC-AD 500.* Sheffield Monographs 3. Sheffield: J. R. Collis Publications.

WADDINGTON, K., 2008. Topographies of accumulation at Late Bronze Age Potterne. *In:* O. DAVIS, N. SHARPLES, and K. WADDINGTON, eds. *Changing Perspectives on the First Millennium B.C.*, Oxford: Oxbow Books, 2008, pp. 161-184.

WAGNER, R., 1981. *The Invention of Culture: revised and expanded edition.* Chicago: The University of Chicago Press.

WAINWRIGHT, G.J., 1968. The excavation of a Durotrigian farmstead near Tollard Royal in Cranbourne Chase, southern England. *Proceedings of the Prehistoric Society*, 34, 102-147.

WAINWRIGHT, G. J., 1969. The excavations of Balksbury Camp, Andover, Hants. *Proceedings of the Hampshire Field Club and Archaeological Society*, 26, 21-55.

WAINWRIGHT, G.J., 1979. *Gussage All Saints: an Iron Age settlement in Dorset.* Department of Environment Archaeological Reports No. 10. London: Her Majesty's Stationery Office.

WAINWRIGHT, G. J., and DAVIES, S. M., eds., 1995. *Balksbury Camp Hampshire: excavations 1973 and 1981*. London: English Heritage Archaeological Report 4.

WAIT, G.A., 1985a. *Ritual and Religion in Iron Age Britain*. Oxford: B.A.R. British Series 149(i).

WAIT, G.A., 1985b. *Ritual and Religion in Iron Age Britain*. Oxford: B.A.R. British Series 149(ii).

WAIT, G. A., 2004. Human and animal burials. *In*: G. LAMBRICK and T. ALLEN, eds. *Gravelly Guy, Stanton Harcourt Oxfordshire: the development of a prehistoric and Romano-British community*. Thames Valley Landscape Monograph No. 21. Oxford: Oxford Archaeological Unit, 2004, pp. 221-257.

WALDRON, T., 2000. Human remains. *In:* E.B.A. GUTTMANN and J. LAST, eds. A Late Bronze Age landscape at South Hornchurch. *Proceedings of the Prehistoric Society*, 66, 319-359, 2000, pp. 346.

WALDRON, T., 2003. The human remains. *In* A. THOMAS, N. HOLBROOK and C. BATEMAN, eds. *Later Prehistoric and Romano-British Burial and Settlement at Hucclecote, Gloucestershire*. Bristol and Gloucestershire Archaeological Reports No. 2. Cirencester: Cotswold Archaeological Trust, 2003, pp. 56-57.

WALDRON, T., 2008. Human remains. *In*: R. GARDNER and C. GIBSON, eds. *An Iron Age Site at Hartsdown Technology College, Margate, Kent* [online]. Hertford: Archaeological Solutions Ltd. Available at: <http://www.kentarchaeology.ac/archrep/archrep.html> [Accessed 26 February 2010], 2008, n.p.

WALKER, L., 1984a. The deposition of human remains. *In*: B. CUNLIFFE, ed. *Danebury: an Iron Age hillfort in Hampshire, Volume 2: the excavations, 1969-1978: the finds*. CBA Research Report No. 52. London: Council for British Archaeology, 1984b, pp. 442-463.

WALKER, L., 1984b. Population and behaviour. *In*: B. CUNLIFFE, ed. *Danebury: an Iron Age hillfort in Hampshire, Volume 2: the excavations, 1969-1978: the finds*. CBA Research Report No. 52. London: Council for British Archaeology, 1984b, pp. 14:A2-15:A10 [microfiche].

WEAVER, S.D.G., and FORD, S., eds., 2004. An Early Iron Age occupation site, a Roman shrine and other prehistoric activity at Coxwell Road, Faringdon. *Oxoniensia*, 69, 119-180.

WEBLEY, L., 2007a. An Iron Age pit alignment and burial at Aspreys, Olney. *Records of Buckinghamshire*, 47(1), 63-80.

WEBLEY, L., 2007b. Chapter 2: prehistoric sites: archaeological descriptions. *In*: J. TIMBY *et al.*, eds. *Settlement on the Bedfordshire Claylands: archaeology along the A421 Great Barford Bypass*. Bedfordshire Archaeology Monograph No. 8. Oxfordshire: Bedfordshire County Council and Oxford Archaeological Unit, 2007, pp. 11-49.

WEBLEY, L., 2007c. Chapter 3: the first settlers: overview of the prehistoric evidence. *In*: J. TIMBY *et al.*, eds. *Settlement on the Bedfordshire Claylands: archaeology along the A421 Great Barford Bypass*. Bedfordshire Archaeology Monograph No. 8. Oxfordshire: Bedfordshire County Council and Oxford Archaeological Unit, 2007, pp. 51-65.

WEBLEY, L., 2007d. Using and abandoning roundhouses: a reinterpretation of the evidence from the Late Bronze Age-Early Iron Age southern England. *Oxford Journal of Archaeology*, 26(2), 127-144.

WEBLEY, L., 2009. Discussion: a Middle Iron Age community. *In*: L. BROWN, D. STANSBIE and L. WEBLEY, eds. An Iron Age settlement and post-Medieval farmstead at Oxley Park West, Milton Keynes. *Records of Buckinghamshire*, 49, 43-72, 2009, pp. 60-65.

WHEELER, R.E.M., 1943. *Maiden Castle, Dorset*. Reports of the Research Committee of the Society of Antiquaries of London No. 12. Oxford: University Press.

WHIMSTER, R., 1981a. *Burial Practices in Iron Age Britain: a discussion and gazetteer of the evidence c. 700 B.C- A.D. 43*. Oxford: B.A.R. British Series 90 (i).

WHIMSTER, R., 1981b. *Burial Practices in Iron Age Britain: a discussion and gazetteer of the evidence c. 700 B.C- A.D. 43*. Oxford: B.A.R. British Series 90 (ii).

WHITE, B., 2006. *Human remains from Northumberland Bottom, Southfleet, Kent* [online]. London: London and Continental Railways. Available at: < http://archaeologydataservice.ac.uk/archives/view/ctrl/humspr/downloads.cfm?CFID=906&CFTOKEN=2AD8A524-9A87-4A4F-B3955C5EFE4445DF> [Accessed 15 June 2010].

WHITEMAN, C., and MACPHAIL, R., 2003. The soils. *In:* N. FIELDS and M. PARKER PEARSON, eds. *Fiskerton: an Iron Age timber causeway with Iron Age and Roman votive offerings*. Oxford: Oxbow Books, 2003, pp. 17-18.

WILLIAMS, A., 1951. Excavations at Beard Mill, Stanton Harcourt, Oxon., 1944. *Oxoniensia*, 16, 5-22.

WILLIAMS, M., 2003. Growing Metaphors: the agricultural cycles as metaphors in the later prehistoric period of Britain and north-west Europe. *Journal of Social Archaeology*, 3, 223-255.

WILLIAMS, R.J., and ZEEPVAT, R.J., eds., 1994a. *Bancroft: a Late Bronze Age/Iron Age settlement, Roman Villa and Temple-Mausoleum, Volume 1: building and materials*. Buckinghamshire Archaeological Society Monograph Series No. 7. Aylesbury: Buckinghamshire Archaeological Society.

WILLIAMS, R.J., and ZEEPVAT, R.J., eds., 1994b. *Bancroft: a Late Bronze Age/Iron Age settlement, Roman Villa and Temple-Mausoleum, Volume 2: finds and environmental evidence*. Buckinghamshire Archaeological Society Monograph Series No. 7. Aylesbury: Buckinghamshire Archaeological Society.

WILSON, B., 1986. Faunal remains: animal bones and marine shells. *In*: D. MILES, ed. *Archaeology at Barton Court Farm Abingdon, Oxon.: an investigation of late Neolithic, Iron Age, Romano-British, and Saxon Settlements*. CBA Research Report No. 50 (Oxford Archaeological Unit Report No. 3). Oxford: Oxford Archaeological Unit, 1986, pp. 8:A1-A2 [microfiche].

WILSON, B., 1993. Reports on the bones and oyster shells. *In:* T. G. ALLEN and M. A. ROBINSON, eds. *The Prehistoric Landscape and Iron Agee Enclosed Settlement at Mingies Ditch, Hardwick-with-Yelford, Oxon.* Thames Valley Landscapes: the Windrush Valley, Vol. 2. Oxford: Oxford Archaeological Unit, 1993, pp. 123-139.

WILSON, B., *et al.*, 1978. The animal bones. *In*: M. PARRINGTON, ed. *The Excavations of an Iron Age Settlement, Bronze Age Ring Ditch and Roman Features at Ashville Trading Estate, Abingdon (Oxfordshire) 1974-76*. London: Oxford Archaeological Unit and Council for British Archaeology, pp. 110-139.

WILSON, C. E., 1981. Burials within settlements in southern Britain during the Pre-Roman Iron Age. *University of London Institute of Archaeology Bulletin*, 18, 127-169.

WITKIN, A., 2004a. Human bone. *In:* P. BOOTH and A. SIMMONDS, eds. An Iron Age and Early Romano-British site at Hatford Quarry, Sandy Lane, Hatford. *Oxoniensia*, 69, 319-354, 2004, pp. 345-346.

WITKIN, A., 2004b. The human skeletal remains. *In*: J. COOK., E. B. A. GUTTMAN, and A. MUDD, eds. Excavations of an Iron Age site at Coxwell Road, Faringdon. *Oxoniensia*, 69, 181-285, 2004, pp. 254-257.

WITKIN, A., 2005. Human skeletal remains. *In*: J. TiIMBY, *et al.*, eds. Excavations along the Newbury Reinforcement Pipeline: Iron Age-Roman activity and Neolithic pit group. *Oxoniensia*, 70, 203-307, 2005, pp. 279-284.

WITKIN, A., 2006a. Human remains from Beechbrook Wood, Westwell, Kent [online]. London: London and Continental Railways. Available at: < http://archaeologydataservice.ac.uk/archives/view/ctrl/humspr/downloads.cfm?CFID=906&CFTOKEN=2AD8A524-9A87-4A4F-B3955C5EFE4445DF> [Accessed 13 May 2010].

WITKIN, A., 2006b. *Human Remains from Tutt Hill, Westwell, Kent, CTRL Specialist Report Series* [online]. London: London and Continental Railways. Available at: < http://archaeologydataservice.ac.uk/archives/view/ctrl/humspr/downloads.cfm?CFID=906&CFTOKEN=2AD8A524-9A87-4A4F-B3955C5EFE4445DF> [Accessed 24 July 2010].

WITKIN, A., 2006c. *The human remains from White Horse Stone, Aylesford, Kent* [online]. London: London and Continental Railways. Available at: <http://archaeologydataservice.ac.uk/archives/view/ctrl/humspr/downloads.cfm?CFID=906&CFTOKEN=2AD8A524-9A87-4A4F-B3955C5EFE4445DF> [Accessed 26 July 2010].

WOODWARD, A., 1997. Size and style: an alternative study of some Iron Age pottery in southern England. *In:* A. GWILT and C. HASELGROVE, eds. *Reconstructing Iron Age Societies*. Oxford: Oxbow Monograph 71, 1997, pp. 26-35.

WOODWARD, A., HILL, J.D., 2000. The human bodies. *In:* J.C. BARRETT, P.W.N. FREEMAN, and A. WOODWARD, eds. *Cadbury Castle Somerset: the later prehistoric and early historic archaeology*. English Heritage Archaeological Report No. 20. London: English Heritage, 2000, pp. 109-115.

WYMER, J.J., and BROWN, N.R., eds., 1995. *Excavations at North Shoebury: economy in south-east Essex 1500 BC-AD 1500*. East Anglian Archaeology Report No. 75. Chelmsford: Essex County Council Archaeology Section.

YATES, D.T., 1999. Bronze Age field systems in the Thames Valley. *Oxford Journal of Archaeology*, 18(2), 157-170.

Guide to the appendix

The following is a brief explanation of the organisation of the digital appendix that accompanies this study. The information included and its design is intended to be used in conjunction with the respective excavation report. Furthermore, the data is coded (as discussed in chapter three) and a key to the coding system follows this guide.

Each site has its own individual folder that includes a brief summary (Microsoft Word document) and the archaeological feature, context and human remains data sheets (Microsoft Excel document). The summary is a concise introduction to the studied site that describes the site type, its location, the excavators, underlying geology, the duration of occupation and the amount of recovered human remains. In addition to the summary are two Excel files; one containing the coded data on the archaeological features and contexts, and the other with information on

the human remains (organised by 'manner of disposal'). Chapter three details the data included in these Excel files.

It should be noted that in some instances the osteological and/or excavation report did not reference the skeletal number of human remains occurrences. In such cases, in order to differentiate between bones the occurrences were labelled X (1, 2, 3, and so forth). The number assigned to the occurrence corresponds with their order as presented within the report. This method of labelling the human remains also applies to skeletal deposits that contain more than once occurrence yet given a single skeleton number. For instance, skeletal deposit 1289 contains both a femur and a skull. On the record sheets, the femur would be labelled 1289(1) and the skull 1289(2). Furthermore, if a context is not assigned a number then it is identified on the context sheets in a similar fashion as the human remains, except labelled C (1, 2, 3 and so forth).

Key to coding (each heading on a separate page)

Dates

1. Unknown
2. LBA
3. EIA
4. MIA
  5. LIA

Location Information

Location with respect to feature/site

1. Unknown
2. Interior
3. Perimeter
4. Exterior

Cardinal direction to feature

1. Unknown
2. N-NE
3. NE-E
4. E-SE
5. SE-S
6. S-SW
7. SW-W
8. W-NW
9. NW-N

Associated architectural feature

1. Unknown
2. Entrance
3. Wall
4. Posthole-entrance
5. Posthole-wall
6. Boundary
Feature type
1. Unknown
2. Round Structure
3. Rectangular Structure
4. Irregular Structure
5. 2-Post Structure
6. Multi-Post Structure
7. Settlement Enclosure
8. Field System Boundary
9. Other

Function/activity of feature

1. Unknown
2. Domestic/occupation
3. Processing
4. Storage
5. Midden/refuse
6. Enclosure/boundary
7. Funeral/ritual
8. Other

Location of feature in respect to site/feature (structure)

1. Unknown
2. Interior
3. Perimeter
4. Exterior

Orientation of feature (1 and 2)

1. Unknown
2. N
3. NE
4. E
5. SE
6. S
7. SW
8. W
9. NW

Context/deposit

Context

1. Unknown
2. Pit
3. Ditch/gully
4. Rampart/bank
5. Posthole
6. Grave
7. Other

Depth of disposal

1. Unknown
2. Top
3. Middle
4. Bottom

Manner of disposal

1. Other
2. Inhumation
3. Disarticulated bones
4. Cremation
5. Articulated bones

Context type of deposit

1. Unknown
2. Primary
3. Primary intrusive
4. Natural

Single/multiple deposit

1. Unknown
2. Single
3. Multiple

Context fill

1. Unknown
2. Silting
3. Backfill
4. Building

Inhumation

Condition

1. Unknown
2. Complete
3. Incomplete (partial)

Layout

1. Unknown/not specified
2. Extended
3. Flexed
4. Crouched
5. Contracted (possible bound)

Orientation

1. Unknown
2. North
3. Northeast
4. East
5. Southeast
6. South
7. Southwest
8. West
9. Northwest

Position

1. Unknown
2. Left side
3. Left side supine
4. Right side
5. Right side supine
6. Prone
7. Head to ground
8. Upright
9. Supine
10. Right side, prone
11. Left side, prone

Position (2)

1. Unknown
2. Left side
3. Right side
4. Supine
5. Prone
6. Other

Face

1. Unknown
2. North
3. Northeast

4. East
5. Southeast
6. South
7. Southwest
8. West
9. Northwest

Disarticulated bone

Element

1. Unknown
2. Skull (including maxilla; with or without mandible)
3. Mandible
4. Vertebrae
5. Clavicle
6. Scapula
7. Ribs
8. Sternum
9. Humerus
10. Ulna
11. Radius
12. Carpal
13. Metacarpal
14. Phalanx
15. Pelvis
16. Femur
17. Patella
18. Tibia
19. Fibula
20. Tarsal
21. Metatarsal
22. Teeth

Element (2)

1. Unknown
2. Crania
3. Axial/torso
4. Upper limb
5. Lower limb
6. Phalange

Portion

1. Unknown
2. Proximal
3. Shaft
4. Distal
5. Complete
6. Fragment/fragmentary
7. Incomplete

Side

1. Unknown
2. Right
3. Right (?)
4. Left
5. Left (?)
6. Both
7. None

Side (2)

1. Unknown
2. Right
3. Left
4. Both
5. None

Cremation

Evidence for Fragmentation

    1. Unknown
    2. Yes
    3. No

Evidence of Urn

    1. Unknown
    2. Urn
    3. Unurned

Articulated bone

Condition

1. Unknown
2. Complete
3. Incomplete

Portion Present

1. Unknown
2. Upper limb
3. Lower limb
4. Torso/axial
5. Crania

Portion

1. Unknown
2. Proximal
2. Shaft
3. Distal
4. None

Side

1. Unknown
2. Right
3. Right (?)
4. Left
5. Left (?)
6. Both
7. None

Side (2)

1. Unknown
2. Right
3. Left
4. Both
5. None

Demography

Age

1. Unknown
2. Infant (0-3)
3. Child (4-12)
4. Adolescent (13-20)
5. Adult (21-35)
6. Mature adult (35+)

Age (2)

1. Unknown
2. Sub-adult (0-20)
3. Adult (21+)

Sex

1. Unsexed
2. Male
3. Male (?)
4. Female
5. Female (?)

Sex (2)

1. Unknown
2. Male
3. Female

Pathological indicators

1. Unknown
2. Congenital disease
3. Dental disease
4. Joint disease
5. Infectious disease
6. Metabolic disease
7. Neoplastic condition
8. Haematological disease
9. Other

Traumatic indicators

1. Unknown
2. Fracture
3. Cut Mark
4. Blunt Force Trauma
5. Dismemberment
6. Burning
7. Bone Modification (holes, punctures)
8. Gnawing
9. 'Scarring' on Bone
10. Stria ('scratches')
11. Weathering

12. Polishing
13. Other

Trauma in respect to death

1. Unknown
2. Pre-mortem
3. Peri-mortem
4. Post-mortem

Associated material

Associated artefacts

    1. Unknown
    2. Natural material/layer
    3. Worked bone
    4. Complete ceramic vessel
    5. Ceramic vessel intentionally broken at time of deposit
    6. Pottery sherd
    7. Quern stone
    8. Jewellery
    9. Military material
    10. Domestic debris
    11. Plant remains
    12. Metal tools/artefacts
    13. Ash, charcoal and charcoal wood
    14. Worked stone
    15. Other
    16. Animal bone
    17. Sling stones

Associated animal species

    1. Unknown
    2. Cow
    3. Sheep
    4. Pig
    5. Dog
    6. Horse
    7. Other

Manner of disposal (animal)

    1. Unknown
    2. Complete/incomplete inhumation
    3. Partial inhumation
    4. Disarticulated bones
    5. Articulated bones
    6. Skull
    7. Cremated